Spike Lee

Recent Titles in
Modern Filmmakers
Vincent LoBrutto, Series Editor

SPIKE LEE
Finding the Story and Forcing the Issue

JASON P. VEST

Modern Filmmakers
Vincent LoBrutto, Series Editor

 PRAEGER

AN IMPRINT OF ABC-CLIO, LLC
Santa Barbara, California • Denver, Colorado • Oxford, England

Library of Congress Cataloging-in-Publication Data

Vest, Jason P., 1972–
    Spike Lee : finding the story and forcing the issue / Jason P. Vest.
        pages cm. — (Modern filmmakers)
    Includes bibliographical references and index.
    ISBN 978-0-313-39226-9 (hard copy : alk. paper) — ISBN 978-0-313-39227-6
(ebook) 1. Lee, Spike—Criticism and interpretation. I. Title.
    PN1998.3.L44V47 2014
    791.4302'33092—dc23   2014019180

ISBN: 978-0-313-39226-9
EISBN: 978-0-313-39227-6

18 17 16 15 14   1 2 3 4 5

This book is also available on the World Wide Web as an eBook.
Visit www.abc-clio.com for details.

Praeger
An Imprint of ABC-CLIO, LLC

ABC-CLIO, LLC
130 Cremona Drive, P.O. Box 1911
Santa Barbara, California 93116-1911

This book is printed on acid-free paper ∞

Manufactured in the United States of America

For Patricia Thomas

Contents

Series Foreword

The Modern Filmmakers series focuses on a diverse group of motion picture directors who collectively demonstrate how the filmmaking process has become the definitive art and craft of the twentieth century. As we advance into the twenty-first century, we begin to examine the impact these artists have had on this influential medium.

What is a modern filmmaker? The phrase connotes a motion picture maker who is au courant—they make movies currently. The choices in this series are also varied to reflect the enormous potential of the cinema. Some of the directors make action movies, some entertain, some are on the cutting edge, others are political, some make us think, some are fantasists. The motion picture directors in this collection will range from highly commercial, mega-budget blockbuster directors to those who toil in the independent, low-budget field.

Gus Van Sant, Tim Burton, Charlie Kaufman, and Terry Gilliam are here, and so are Clint Eastwood and Steven Spielberg—all for many and for various reasons, but primarily because their directing skills have transitioned from the twentieth century to the first decade of the twenty-first century. Eastwood and Spielberg worked during the 1960s and 1970s and have grown and matured as the medium transitioned from mechanical to digital. The younger directors here may not have experienced all of those cinematic epochs themselves, but nonetheless they remained concerned with the limits of filmmaking: Charlie Kaufman disintegrates personal and narrative boundaries in the course of his scripts, for example, while Tim Burton probes the limits of technology to find the most successful way of bringing his intensely visual fantasies and nightmares to life.

The Modern Filmmakers series will celebrate modernity and postmodernism through each creator's vision, style of storytelling, and character presentation. The directors' personal beliefs and worldviews will be revealed through in-depth examinations of the art they have created, but brief biographies will also be provided where they appear especially relevant. These books are intended to open up new ways of thinking about some of our favorite and most important artists and entertainers.

Vincent LoBrutto
Series Editor
Modern Filmmakers

Acknowledgments

This book would not exist without the tireless efforts of my research assistant, Leiana Naholowa'a. Her insight, wit, and friendship immeasurably enriched this study.

This project also profited from the enthusiasm and acumen of its two editors: Daniel Harmon helped launch this book, while James Sherman saw it to completion. Their expertise, professionalism, and patience were invaluable.

Rebecca Matheson's, Sasikala Rajesh's, and Sivakumar Vijayaraghavan's meticulous attention to all matters—factual, grammatical, mechanical, and stylistic—has improved this project at every turn. Their diligence, patience, and good cheer were instrumental to this book's success.

Special thanks go to the University of Guam's College of Liberal Arts and Social Sciences, which awarded several research grants and a year-long sabbatical that vastly aided this project's completion. The support of CLASS's Academic Affairs Committee, Dean James Sellmann, and Associate Dean Troy McVey is greatly appreciated.

My colleagues, as always, provided welcome encouragement and collegial advice during this book's composition. Dr. Evelyn Flores, Dr. David Gugin, Dr. Andrea Sant-Hartig, and Dr. Christopher Schreiner of the University of Guam's Division of English and Applied Linguistics, Dr. Richard Colfax of the University of Guam's School of Business and Public Administration, and Dr. Douglas Farrer of the University of Guam's Anthropology Program were especially helpful during this study's long gestation.

My family and friends offered incomparable inspiration and, when necessary, a kick in the pants to ensure that this book was finished on time.

Malcolm X concludes his remarkable *Autobiography of Malcolm X* by stating that, no matter how meager or substantial his accomplishments may be, "only the mistakes have been mine." That sentiment provides a fitting inscription for this study.

Thank you all.

Introduction
"Still a Motherfucker"–Spike Lee in the Twenty-First Century

CINEMATIC CONNOISSEUR, CULTURAL PROVOCATEUR

In 2002, during two weeks of mandatory rehearsals for *25th Hour*'s cast, Spike Lee screened several movies every evening at 8 P.M. Lee, one of America's most prolific filmmakers, does so for every project he directs to give his actors information, ideas, and insights about the production they will soon undertake. Edward Norton, who plays *25th Hour* protagonist Montgomery Brogan, takes up the story in Lee's cheekily titled, as-told-to autobiography, *That's My Story and I'm Sticking to It,* written by Kaleem Aftab. Lee and his actors watched William Wyler's *Dead End* (1937)—the first film starring the group of young actors now known as the Dead End Kids—because their New York experience bonds them, Elia Kazan's *On the Waterfront* (1954) because Lee admires the moral upheaval that protagonist Terry Malloy (Marlon Brando) undergoes, and John Schlesinger's *Midnight Cowboy* (1969) because this film's story, according to Norton, almost floats through the New York night to capture the city's textures as well as any other movie he and Lee know.[1] Norton found Lee's zeal for film to be infectious, telling Aftab, "It is inspiring to see someone who is that passionate about movies. . . . When he screened *Midnight Cowboy*, I don't think a lot of us had seen the movie on screen for a long time, and when the lights came up at the end, Spike stood up and screeched, 'Still a motherfucker.' It was so funny."[2]

This anecdote speaks to Lee's cinematic enthusiasm, acumen, and connoisseurship. His extensive knowledge of movies does not dim Lee's fervor for the art form that he has devoted his adult life to furthering, while Lee's appreciation of film's potential to shape its viewer's perception of people and places reflects his firm command of cinema's vocabulary, grammar, and syntax. Norton reveals how Lee understands the moving picture's visual, thematic, and intellectual potential in a tidbit that also communicates the director's frankness, brio, and sense of humor. This behind-the-scenes snippet, in other words, reflects Lee's love of movies as capably as any story that has been told about him since he first achieved public notoriety with his 1986 debut feature film, *She's Gotta Have It.*

Spike Lee is a cinematic artist who refuses to comfort his audience, to soft-pedal his opinions, or to remain complacent in the face of criticism. That he is best known by the nickname bestowed upon him by his mother, Jacquelyn Shelton Lee, while still an infant attests to the uncompromising stances for which Lee is now famous or, depending upon one's perspective, infamous. Born Shelton Jackson Lee in Atlanta, Georgia, on March 20, 1957, Lee was called Spike, according to *That's My Story and I'm Sticking to It,* due to his "petulant and fiery nature, one that his four younger siblings"—Chris, David, Joie, and Cinque Lee—"found considerably irksome"[3] and, moreover, one that has troubled many film viewers in the years since *She's Gotta Have It* first appeared on movie screens. Lee tells Nelson George, in the November 21, 1986, interview printed in *She's Gotta Have It*'s companion publication, *Spike Lee's Gotta Have It: Inside Guerrilla Filmmaking,* that his mother, finding him to be a difficult baby, dubbed him "Spike" when he was three or four months old,[4] marking Lee's path as a disputatious rabble-rouser from the earliest moments of his life.

This anecdote also discloses Lee's talent for self-promotion, since the origin of his nickname allows Lee to construct a legend that has served his career well. The possibility that Lee was tough, difficult, and irksome from the beginning helps explain to admirers and detractors Lee's penchant for public commentary, controversy, and contention. Even casual observers of American cinema are aware of Lee's provocative persona, whether through his plentiful comments about film, politics, and history in media interviews; his avid support of the New York Knicks professional basketball team during grandstanding appearances at Madison Square Garden; or his insistent examination of difficult American social issues—including race, religion, and socioeconomic class—in the feature films, documentaries, Broadway shows, and television projects (whether cable films, miniseries, episodes, or commercials) that he has directed during more than twenty-five years as a creative presence in American popular culture. Lee, as of this study's writing, released (in November 2013) his nineteenth feature film, *Oldboy*—an American version of the second movie in South Korean director Park Chan-wook's Vengeance Trilogy, 2003's *Oldeuboi* (itself a loose adaptation of the Japanese manga series *Orūdo Bōi* written by Garon Tsuchiya, illustrated by Nobuaki Minegishi, and published in installments between 1996 and 1998)—and has completed principal photography on his twentieth feature, a movie tentatively titled *Da Sweet Blood of Jesus*[5] that Lee financed by raising more than $1.4 million[6] on the crowd-funding website Kickstarter in a campaign that drew criticism from media observers who accused Lee, a cinematic professional with sufficient resources to bankroll 2012's *Red Hook Summer* (at the cost of $1 million), of drawing money away from emerging independent moviemakers hoping to fund their projects' budgets.

Lee's fiery response to these charges, documented in two July 31, 2013, appearances on CNBC television's business-roundtable program *Squawk on the Street* and Bloomberg TV's business-affairs series *Street Smart,* demonstrate not only his vigorous personality but also, in the case of *Street Smart,* his willingness to confront what he perceives as unfair treatment by journalists, interviewers, and commentators.[7] A visibly upset Lee chastises *Street Smart* host Trish Regan for assuming facts about the relationship of his personal wealth to funding low-budget (but nonetheless expensive) projects such as *Da Sweet Blood of Jesus.* Hollywood studios, Lee implies, lavish more money on tent-pole films such as *The Hunger Games* (2012) and *Man of Steel* (2013), upon which they can build franchises with wide audience appeal that earn blockbuster profits, rather than small-scale movies about minority characters. These studios, in other words, choose not to finance independent films like Lee's because, in the profit-maximizing mentality that pervades early twenty-first-century Hollywood moviemaking, the margins are too low. Lee tells *Squawk on the Street* panelist Simon Hobbs "you're not my accountant"[8] during his chat with the program's four hosts to make a similar point about his difficulties in financing lower budgeted, more intimate films, even reminding Hobbs that he (Lee) has been unable to get a sequel to his largest commercial hit, the 2006 heist thriller *Inside Man,* into production despite this movie grossing nearly $185 million against its $45-million budget.[9]

Lee, as such, remains unafraid to dispel misperceptions about his films, his finances, and himself when discussing his career in public fora. This forthrightness has gained Lee the reputation of a man who speaks his mind, who does not suffer fools, and who enjoys challenging conventional wisdom. The stereotypical view of Lee's public persona constructs him as a fearsome provocateur who strikes observers unacquainted with his impish sense of humor (as revealed in Lee's autobiography, longer interviews, and DVD audio commentaries) as unreasonable, so much so that Lee comes to embody one of the oldest, most prevalent stereotypes circulating throughout American culture: the angry black man. This tendency reached its zenith in *Esquire* magazine's October 1992 issue, which, despite promoting Lee's soon-to-be-released epic film biography *Malcolm X* with a cover image of Lee's arms crossed in an "X" pose, included a profile of the movie's contentious production infamously titled "Spike Lee Hates Your Cracker Ass."[10] Although *Esquire*'s editors rather than author Barbara Grizzuti Harrison may have selected this heading, the title mistakenly confirms misbegotten ideas about Lee's racial politics that the article itself alternately embraces and disclaims, with Harrison writing, "[Lee] is convinced that the word *nigger* plays its awful music in every white person's head" just after saying "Birds in separate cages and we can't get out"[11] to convey the difficult, distant, and diffident relationship between herself and Lee that obsesses Harrison throughout the article.

She takes Lee's standoffishness as proof that his racial obsessions trap them in a cycle of recrimination that they cannot escape, although Lee seems less resentful of Harrison's racial assumptions (mentioned in the story but never verbalized to Lee) than simply bored by the interview. This article, according to Kaleem Aftab, made Lee miserable for days,[12] while Lee tells James Verniere in "Doing the Job," a February 1993 interview with *Sight and Sound* magazine, that Harrison "turned me off from the first minute of the interview because I guess she felt she had to tell me all about her black boyfriend and how they went to see Billie Holiday" before asking, "Do you have any white friends, Spike?"[13] This question illustrates the false social constructions to which media commentators subject Lee and other African American artists by holding them to standards that their Caucasian counterparts evade. Few, if any, white American film directors have ever been (or ever will be) asked whether they have black, brown, or other minority friends, so Lee's disdain for Harrison becomes understandable, if still rude, in light of her insensitivity. For all its faults, however, "Spike Lee Hates Your Cracker Ass" demonstrates a long-standing truth about Lee, whose divisive public persona, as much as his filmography, is responsible for his survival on the American cultural scene. As character assassination, Harrison's article is little more than a curated tour of her racial anxieties and white guilt. As evidence of Lee's cultural prominence, however, it remains a potent example of his relevance to American cinema then and now.

Lee, indeed, is neither the angry black man that stereotype suggests nor the spokesman for all African American filmmakers, artists, and people that cultural observers like Harrison assert. Lee, indeed, takes pains to puncture both claims in many interviews he has given during his decades-long career, saying in "Outside Man: Spike Lee's Unending Struggle," John Colapinto's revealing September 2008 *New Yorker* profile, "People think I'm this angry black man walking around in a constant state of rage," a complaint that Colapinto contextualizes by writing, "His annoyance at this perception is understandable; he can be funny and warm, and even his angriest movies are leavened with humor. Yet the persona he projects, imperious and impatient, can be intimidating," as when, while listening to jazz musician, film composer, and frequent Lee collaborator Terence Blanchard's small band playing in a New York City jazz club, Lee "gave me a stern glance when I tried to initiate conversation between numbers" and, "afterward, when some of Lee's fans gathered to ask for autographs, Lee responded to the smiling face of a white woman from Cincinnati with a glare so unwelcoming that she quickly retreated."[14] This final observation might seem to confirm Lee's dislike of white people, but the full article, like *That's My Story and I'm Sticking to It*, indicates how Lee's prickly demeanor affects everyone he knows. As Ernest Dickerson, the cinematographer who attended New York University (NYU) film school with Lee and shot the man's first six feature films (up to *Malcolm X*), says, "He's never suffered fools. You've got to bring your best game to him. He looks at everybody with 'O.K., what're you doing?' On *Mo' Better Blues* [Lee's fourth feature film and his first to star Denzel Washington], I had to fire most of my camera crew because mistakes were being made. And there's nothing worse than sitting next to Spike in dailies when the dailies have problems."[15]

Lee's fabled brusqueness, however, has become an integral aspect of his persona that works to his advantage by motivating collaborators to do good work (despite the discomfort that Lee inflicts upon them when they do not meet his expectations) and to his disadvantage by confirming to casual observers the short-tempered reputation that Lee cultivates or repudiates depending upon circumstances. One challenge of this book, like any study devoted to Lee's career (or, for that matter, to the career of any well-known public figure), is sorting the various personae that Lee adopts without falling prey to the entrenched and enforced narratives about his forceful personality that, while evidence of Lee's talent for self-promotion, must not obscure a critical examination of the merits and liabilities of his intriguing, provocative, and untidy movies.

A related challenge is not to nominate Lee as a spokesperson for all African American filmmakers or to legitimize the perception that he alone represents this diverse group of artists simply by being the most outspoken black director working in American cinema. Lee's movies possess a unique outlook, style, and approach to filmmaking that diverges from the work of earlier black directors like Oscar Micheaux, Michael Schultz, Melvin Van Peebles, and Spencer Williams as much as it does from Lee's contemporaries Camille Billops, Charles Burnett, Lee Daniels, Julie Dash, Kasi Lemons, Tyler Perry, and John Singleton. Lee, like these creative professionals and many earlier generations of black novelists, poets, painters, and playwrights, must walk the gauntlet of being both an African American and American artist whose body of work exists in a racially stratified society that has historically consigned black artists to subordinate positions, not only within the commercial marketplace but also within America's cultural landscape, where they are expected to concern themselves with their nation's shameful history of racial suppression, segregation, and exclusion that, no matter how powerful, comes nowhere close to describing the full measure of any black American's life. Lee's films examine the complexities of African American experiences and perspectives, yet refuse to restrict themselves to black characters, to stories of woe and regret, or to hand-wringing appraisals of America's fractious racial politics. Lee's career, instead, covers a vast expanse of African American themes that are also unmistakably American themes.

Lee, therefore, dislikes being assigned the role of spokesperson for all black filmmakers or, even worse, for all African Americans, telling Nelson George during their 1986 *Spike Lee's Gotta Have It* interview, "I'm determined not to let people turn me into a savior" because he does not wish "to right everything that's been wrong as far as film and black people are concerned for the last hundred years";[16] telling David Breskin in their lengthy July 1991 *Rolling Stone* interview (reprinted in Breskin's invaluable 1997 book *Inner Views: Filmmakers in Conversation*), after Breskin reads the preceding quotation to Lee, "That just happens when any black person is successful in any field— there's so few of us that when we do break through, the weight of the whole race is thrust upon our shoulders. And it can't be done by one person";[17] and telling Elvis Mitchell in their July 1991 *Playboy* magazine interview, "I think that this is what happens when the media appoints their so-called spokesperson for black people. This is something I have never wanted to achieve. It's not something I've chased after."[18] Many similar comments litter Lee's media appearances, university lectures, and press statements over the years, indicating that, while he may speak only for himself, Lee refuses to shy away from offering opinions and insights for public consumption. Doing so permits Lee to discuss issues that he considers significant while raising his media profile, thereby promoting his creative pursuits in a shrewd cycle that has kept Lee in the public eye for most of his adult life.

Lee's cinematic artistry is in some sense inseparable from his marketing savvy. Lee's fierce intelligence, creative drive, and profound knowledge of film history combine with his promotional talents to make him an uncommon specimen: the film connoisseur who is also an unrepentant cultural provocateur. This final label, moreover, is not pejorative, but becomes an emblem of Lee's commitment to forcing his viewers to think and feel about his movies more deeply than they might engage other, more conventional Hollywood productions. Lee's ability to secure studio financing and distribution for smaller pictures that repudiate the easy treatments of race, gender, and class preferred by Hollywood studios marks him as an even rarer specimen: the independent filmmaker who participates in Hollywood's industrial production, distribution, and marketing systems while mostly maintaining his creative independence. Lee may not always succeed in this mission, but, as this book establishes, his efforts bear fruit more often than they fail.

INSIDE OUT

This book demonstrates that Spike Lee is a major American filmmaker whose work remains fascinating three decades after it first appeared on movie screens, is significant despite its variable quality, and proves worthwhile due to the diverse genres, themes, and styles that it adopts. Lee's ability to write, direct, and produce so many feature films, documentaries, and television projects for so long a period is unusual for a black American moviemaker. Oscar Micheaux is Lee's most important forerunner in this regard, directing as many as forty-two, mostly self-financed films during his thirty-year career (Micheaux's first movie, *The Homesteader,* appeared in 1919, while his last, *The Betrayal,* arrived in 1948) to help pioneer independent African American cinema as a viable artistic pursuit. As John R. Howard writes in *Faces in the*

Mirror: Oscar Micheaux and Spike Lee, Howard's dual biography of both men's careers, "Despite differences in aspects of their racial philosophy the similarities outweigh the differences. For both, the insanely difficult business of making commercial films was made more difficult by race," only to expand this comparison by noting, "Oscar Micheaux toiled in one kind of environment relative to wealth and power, Lee toils in another. The relative fortunes of each reflect changes in the larger society attending black access to power and wealth and the opportunity to shape the dreams that float across the nation's screens."[19] This analysis demonstrates how Lee participates in a lineage stretching back to commercial American cinema's earliest days, one that bucks Hollywood trends by producing assertive movies that dramatize African American lives, culture, and history from an insider's perspective.

Lee's closest contemporary in terms of prolificacy is Tyler Perry, who has written, directed, and produced at least eighteen feature films, fifteen stage plays, and five television series since 1992. Even so, Perry's debut as a feature-film writer came only with 2005's *Diary of a Mad Black Woman* and, as a feature-film director, with 2006's *Madea's Family Reunion,* while his first television series, *House of Payne,* began in 2006, making Perry's track record not yet as proven—and his influence not yet as durable—as Lee's. Perry's commercial success, however, outstrips Lee's, whose movies sometimes fail to make back their production budgets (1996's *Girl 6,* 2004's *She Hate Me,* and 2008's *Miracle at St. Anna,* are notorious examples) and who, apart from directing two episodes of the miniseries *Miracle's Boys* (2005) and the pilot episode of Ian Biederman's legal drama *Shark* (2006–2008), has seen two other attempts at producing weekly television series fail (with his 2004 television movie *Sucker Free City* originally serving as the pilot for a program that premium-cable network Showtime refused to approve for weekly production and the pilot of boxing drama *Da Brick*—directed by Lee in 2011— failing to receive Home Box Office's approval as a continuing series). Lee's box-office and small-screen woes, as such, may distinguish him from Perry, but Lee's filmography remains thematically richer and stylistically more mature. Pondering Lee's cinematic antecedents, influences, and development, therefore, becomes necessary to understanding his career.

Lee's desire to work as a filmmaker came relatively late, while he was attending Morehouse College as an undergraduate communications major in the late 1970s. His father Bill Lee, a jazz bassist and composer searching for work as a musician in the late 1950s, moved the family from Atlanta, Georgia, to Chicago, Illinois, soon after Spike's 1957 birth, then to Brooklyn, New York's Crown Heights and Cobble Hill neighborhoods (in 1960 and 1962, respectively) before purchasing a Fort Greene brownstone in 1969, where Spike's love of the borough and the city became deeply entrenched. Lee, thanks to his father's profession and his schoolteacher mother's determination to expose her children to New York's diverse cultural offerings, developed an affinity for the arts that did not immediately translate into a committed pursuit of cinema. Lee, in fact, tells Elvis Mitchell in their 1991 *Playboy* interview, "I didn't grow up thinking I wanted to make movies, be a director. Everybody in my neighborhood saw a lot of movies. There was nothing special about going to the movies. I didn't know what I wanted to do"[20] before disclosing that he never saw a film so rousing that he suddenly aspired to become a moviemaker: "I never had a moment like that. It was never, 'I saw *Lawrence of Arabia* when I was two and suddenly I was hit by the magic power of film.' That's bullshit. Like I told you, I just went to the movies. Nobody thought about being a director, not me or anybody else."[21] Majoring in communications at Morehouse, however, piqued Lee's interest in the mechanics of filmmaking, causing Lee to tell Kaleem Aftab in *That's My Story and I'm Sticking to It* that he chose to become a director between his second and third years at Morehouse.[22] During the summer break of 1977, Lee shot footage of New York City with a Super-8 camera he had received as a gift the previous Christmas, so that, when he returned to college in August 1977, a shift in Lee's outlook occurred. Declaring his major in mass communications, Lee tells Aftab that his instructor, Dr. Herb Eichelberger, not only took an interest in him but also pushed to Lee to excel, which prompted his decision to pursue a career in moviemaking.[23]

Eichelberger's influence proved decisive. Encouraging Lee to transform his summer 1977 New York material into a movie, Eichelberger saw Lee edit the raw film (including footage of the famous blackout that afflicted the city on July 13 and 14, 1977) into a forty-minute film titled *Last Hustle in Brooklyn*. The success of this experience not only set Lee's path but also fired his cinematic passion, for, as Lee writes in his introduction to *Spike Lee's Gotta Have It,* "I truly believe I was put here to make films, it's as simple as that. I'm doin' what I'm 'posed to be doin.'"[24] Lee's dedication to film, as well as his sense of humor, is evident in this short passage, which violates formal English grammar as playfully as Lee's movies violate classical Hollywood filmmaking style.

After graduating from Morehouse, Lee enrolled in NYU's Tisch School of Arts graduate-filmmaking program, where Ernest Dickerson, Ang Lee, and Jim Jarmusch were classmates. Lee wrote and directed three short movies while here: *The Answer* (1980), a twenty-minute narrative about an African American filmmaker given $50 million to remake D. W. Griffith's notorious 1915 *The Birth of a Nation* that indicts the earlier movie's racism; *Sarah* (1981), a film dramatizing a disastrous Thanksgiving Day dinner that Lee made for his maternal grandmother, Zimmie Shelton; and *Joe's Bed-Stuy Barbershop: We Cut Heads* (1983), his one-hour thesis film about Brooklyn barbershop owner Zachariah Homer's (Monty Ross) attempts to extricate himself from a numbers racket that gangster Nicholas Lovejoy (Tommy Redmond Hicks) runs out of the shop that Homer inherits from his murdered business partner, Joe Ballard (Horace Long).[25] Ernest Dickerson served as cinematographer, Ang Lee as first-assistant director, and Bill Lee as composer for *Joe's Bed-Stuy Barbershop,* which won one of two 1983 Dramatic Merit Awards from the Academy of Motion Picture Arts and Sciences (better known as the Student Academy Awards). This coup, along with his admiration for Jarmusch's breakthrough feature *Stranger than Paradise* (1984), launched Lee into his professional career. He next wrote a partially autobiographical screenplay titled *The Messenger* about an African American bikeriding deliveryman whose father marries a white woman after his mother's death (paralleling Lee's dismay when his mother, Jacquelyn, died of liver cancer in 1977 and his father, Bill, began dating a woman named Susan Kaplan whom the elder Lee later married). Spike cast future collaborators Giancarlo Esposito and Laurence Fishburne in this film, scouted locations, and had begun rehearsing the actors when he realized that the movie's budget (nearly $20,000 of which was provided by his grandmother, Zimmie, who had also financed *Joe's Bed-Stuy Barbershop*'s $10,000 budget) would not cover the necessary costs, forcing him to cancel production. Depressed by this failure, Lee eventually began putting together the screenplay for *She's Gotta Have It,* which he shot in twelve days for $175,000 that he cobbled together from family, friends, film-foundation grants, and his work as a film-print cleaner at First Run Features (a small New York City distributor of independent films run by Lee's future editor, Barry Alexander Brown).[26]

She's Gotta Have It, as Elvis Mitchell notes in the introduction to his 1991 *Playboy* interview with Lee, "made $8,000,000 and turned Lee into an overnight sensation"[27] upon its 1986 release. Lee, not content to be a one-hit wonder, began mounting a new film almost every year, directing *School Daze* (1988), *Do the Right Thing* (1989), *Mo' Better Blues* (1990), *Jungle Fever* (1991), *Malcolm X* (1992), *Crooklyn* (1994), *Clockers* (1995), *Girl 6* (1996), *Get on the Bus* (1996), *4 Little Girls* (1997), *He Got Game* (1998), and *Summer of Sam* (1999) over the next decade, amassing a body of work that remains notable for its energy, audacity, and diversity. Lee, beginning with *School Daze,* partnered with major Hollywood studios (in this case, Columbia Pictures) to help finance and distribute many (but not all) of his films while retaining creative control, particularly the right of final cut, in a moviemaking model that combines (or tries to combine) independent cinema's unconventional approaches to narrative, subject, and style with Hollywood's financial clout and wide reach.

Paula J. Massood, indeed, calls Lee "the quintessential inside/outside man, often working with the industry, but just as often looking elsewhere for financing"[28] in her introduction to *The Spike Lee Reader,* the invaluable scholarly anthology about Lee's films that Massood edited for Temple University Press in 2008. The title of Massood's piece, "We've Gotta Have It—Spike Lee, African American Film, and Cinema Studies," indicates just how important she considers Lee's output to the revival (and survival) of black American cinema, as well as his salutary effect upon independent cinema and, inevitably, film scholarship. This study shares all three perspectives, while agreeing with Massood that "Lee's production and advertising companies (the latter in particular) provide the financial foundations that enable him to make films that otherwise would not be made."[29] Lee's significance as a dissident voice in American movies arises from his willingness to dispute conventional ideas about African American lives, experiences, and attitudes, as well as subvert the classical, supposedly invisible filmmaking style that Hollywood films have for decades reinforced. By accepting studio money to fund and distribute his productions, however, Lee calls into question both his independence from Hollywood's industrial moviemaking approach and his commitment to alternative ways of telling cinematic stories. Although Massood writes that Lee's business enterprises "have also guaranteed that [he] retains the right of final cut over his films, a form of directorial control that remains rare in the industry and provides us with, perhaps, one of the strongest cases of a director fully in charge of his work,"[30] Lee's elephantine knowledge of American film ensures a familiarity with Hollywood techniques that risks co-opting his artistic choices even as Lee struggles to bring stories to the screen that, without his intervention, would almost certainly never see the light of day.

Despite Hollywood's brief forays into supporting films with predominantly African American casts during the blaxploitation movement of the 1970s and the so-called black film renaissance of the early 1990s (which saw the release of several movies written and directed by African American filmmakers that Lee's success partially inspired), the industry prefers to greenlight films that, if they deal with African American characters and themes at all, cover issues and genres that studio executives consider most salient to black audiences' lives (and most profitable for the studios' bottom lines), namely quasi-tragedies that address racism, economic struggle, social oppression, and drug use (often set in underprivileged neighborhoods rife with crime and violence) or light comedies that chronicle the relentless yet adorable relationship problems of black men and women who, despite not understanding one another, somehow manage to enjoy athletic sex when not engaged in banter that advertises how hip, cool, and urban they are. Lee's work presents far more nuanced settings, storylines, and textures about African American life than these films, refusing the dichotomy just outlined, to retain his status as an independent moviemaker who resists, with varying degrees of success, Hollywood's straitened sensibilities. Massood, for instance, writes of Lee's career, "Starting as an independent filmmaker at a time when American independents were gaining global status, Lee helped usher in a new cinematic look and vocabulary in American filmmaking" before pointing out that he "gained visibility at a moment when African American film was at a nadir [following] the industry's shift into blockbuster filmmaking in the mid-1970s."[31] Massood relates how "the studios abandoned blaxploitation film, their sole investment in African American cinema during the decade (and only marginally associated with African American filmmaking, since the majority of personnel associated with the genre were not black)"[32] to demonstrate how the commercial strictures of blaxploitation movies—and the subsequent impoverishment of black cinema—pushed Lee to write, direct, and produce films that resist industry standards even while adopting some of Hollywood's narrative, thematic, and generic conventions. Lee, therefore, is an inside/outside man like Dalton Russell (Clive Owen), the antiheroic protagonist (and heroic antagonist) of Lee's 2006 revisionist heist thriller *Inside Man,* because Lee has a similar talent for inhabiting and manipulating institutional structures—in this case, the Hollywood conventions that determine a movie's story and style—that he then subverts in ways both fresh and recognizable to audiences accustomed to the commercial, narrative, and stylistic tidiness of standard Hollywood films.

SOCIAL CLASS, STREETWISE STYLE

This book explores the complications of Lee's position as a significant African American filmmaker who, by not restricting himself to studio-approved notions of what constitutes authentic black cinema, becomes an innovative American artist whose movies appear messy, inelegant, and even incoherent to viewers expecting the sleek, pristine, and glossy films that Hollywood studios regularly release. This study does not share assumptions that Lee's middle-class background, formal education at elite institutions, and career success condemn him to being, in Amiri Baraka's words, "a recognizable type and trend in American society. He is the quintessential buppie, almost the spirit of the young, upwardly mobile, Black, petit bourgeois professional."[33] Baraka, one of Lee's harshest critics, makes this claim in his provocative, yet problematic essay "Spike Lee at the Movies," which was published in Manthia Diawara's excellent 1993 academic collection *Black American Cinema* after Lee declined to include it in *Five for Five: The Films of Spike Lee,* the 1991 book of essays, still photographs, and behind-the-scenes information that Lee commissioned to commemorate the release of his fifth feature film, *Jungle Fever. Five for Five* includes writing by prominent African American intellectuals (Terry McMillan, Toni Cade Bambara, Nelson George, Charles Johnson, and Henry Louis Gates, Jr.) who analyze each Lee movie in turn and, despite the vanity-project aura attending this book, offer intelligent, fair-minded, and occasionally hard-hitting essays that refuse to celebrate uncritically Lee's success. *Five for Five's* contributors instead note each film's aesthetic, narrative, and political shortcomings without ignoring their virtues. Baraka's vituperative analysis, by contrast, raises certain intriguing points about Lee's cinematic inadequacies from a resolutely antibourgeois perspective that culminates in the accusation "the irony is that often the middle class who most directly benefited from the militant sixties, as far as the ending of legal American apartheid and the increased access to middle-management resources are concerned, not only take it for granted because they have not struggled for this advance, but believe it is Black people's fault that we have not made more progress."[34] This intemperate judgment excoriates Lee and other so-called buppies for turning their backs on the economic, political, and social struggles of less-privileged African Americans, but naïvely assumes that socioeconomic status so determines a person's outlook, to say nothing of an artist's output, that class position creates a pervasive ideological blindness that inevitably weakens art.

Lee, who not only dated but also collaborated with Baraka's daughter Lisa Jones on three books (the companion volumes to *School Daze, Do the Right Thing,* and *Mo' Better Blues*), defends himself against Baraka's charge that his films, especially *Malcolm X,* offer too few institutional criticisms of black America's history (favoring instead, according to Baraka, an ethos of individual striving that supports capitalism's worst tendencies) by telling Aftab in *That's My Story and I'm Sticking to It* how hypocritical he finds Baraka's implication that Lee's middle-class upbringing compromises his films' quality (particularly *Malcolm X*): "I don't know what is more middle class than being a college professor. And I think that my first five films cover a lot of aspects of African American society."[35] Lee's perspective here is far from comprehensive or detailed, while many Lee movies, especially *Do the Right Thing,* reinforce Reagan-era bromides (about the moral benefits of hard work and the personal satisfactions of wage labor) as much as they contest them. Lee, however, underscores Baraka's ostensible hypocrisy about bourgeois livelihoods to suggest that class position and political outlook, while they may affect a filmmaker's work, do not preclude critical or even radical ideas from finding expression in it. Lee's *oeuvre,* indeed, offers a running commentary about socioeconomic class, race relations, and social justice that stakes no single position on these issues, but that permits an array of attitudes, outlooks, and viewpoints to exist in movies that sometimes foreground these ideas, but that just as often consign them to narrative subtext.

Baraka's analysis also misses how routinely Lee's visual style undermines Hollywood conventions and expectations. Lee's films, even upon first viewing, call attention to their visual construction by including numerous jump cuts, direct-to-camera addresses, canted angles, and, beginning with *Mo' Better Blues,* what Lee (alongside many film reviewers and scholars) calls his signature shot: a character floats forward, toward the viewer, seemingly disconnected from the on-screen world that she inhabited moments before and that she now traverses in an unrealistic manner. As Jerold J. Abrams observes in his fine essay "Transcendence and Sublimity in Spike Lee's Signature Shot," this technique's effect "is mildly shocking to the viewer and sufficient to suspend for a moment the viewer's immersion in a continuous cinematic narrative. In this way, Lee injects a moment of phenomenological complexity into the film, recasting the view of the film as a whole because this moment throws into relief the relation between the viewer and the film viewed."[36] The signature shot, Lee's other interventions in the seamless camerawork and editing of standard Hollywood cinema, and his propensity to disregard the tidy three-act structure (with clearly defined actions, characters, and resolutions) of most Hollywood movies disrupt the easy viewing that decades of studio filmmaking have inculcated in American audiences. Lee compels viewers to regard his movies from different, more critical perspectives not only by "breaking the fourth wall" with techniques like the signature shot but also by using bold primary colors, non-diegetic sound, eccentric angles, chiaroscuro lighting, and other practices that recall influences and innovations from American film noir, French New Wave cinema, Italian Neorealism, and Japanese postwar movies that oblige his audiences to encounter, experience, and absorb his films actively, from conscious perspectives that classical Hollywood style underplays or suppresses.

Lee's films, indeed, manifest little interest in classical Hollywood style, or the presumed invisibility that a film's cinematography, musical score, set and costume design, blocking, editing, and acting (or what film theorists such as André Bazin refer to as mise-en-scène) help create. John Belton, in *American Cinema/American Culture* (first published as a textbook supplement to PBS's 1995 ten-part documentary series *American Cinema: One Hundred Years of Filmmaking*), succinctly defines "classical Hollywood cinema" as:

A mode of production associated with American cinema that involves certain narrative and stylistic practices. Narratives are structured around characters who have specific, clearly defined goals and deal with their triumph over various obstacles that stand in the way of attainment of those goals. These narratives are presented in a manner that is both as efficient and as (stylistically) invisible as possible.[37]

Lee's movies, beginning with *She's Gotta Have It,* so frequently and so freely violate these precepts—particularly stylistic invisibility—that viewers might infer his disdain for classical Hollywood cinema despite Lee's admiration for several films in this tradition, including Billy Wilder's *Sunset Boulevard* (1950) and Elia Kazan's *A Face in the Crowd* (1957).

An important precursor to Belton's definition and discussion of classical Hollywood style is David Bordwell, Janet Staiger, and Kristin Thompson's 1985 book *The Classical Hollywood Cinema: Film Style & Mode of Production to 1960.* This text's inaugural section ("The Classical Hollywood Style, 1917–1960"), written by Bordwell, titles its first chapter "An Excessively Obvious Cinema" to underscore Bordwell's theoretically rigorous analysis of how Hollywood films produced between 1917 and 1960, despite their individual variations, demonstrate "a distinct and homogenous style . . . whose principles remain quite constant across decades, genres, studios, and personnel."[38] Bordwell notes that, in 1939, Bazin declared, "Hollywood filmmaking had acquired 'all the characteristics of a classical art,'"[39] making it sensible "to retain the term in English, since the principles which Hollywood claims as its own rely on notions of decorum, proportion, formal harmony, respect for tradition, mimesis, self-effacing craftsmanship, and cool control of the perceiver's response—canons which critics in any medium usually call 'classical.'"[40] Classical Hollywood cinema's mimetic aspirations, Bordwell suggests, seek to obscure the many visual, editorial, and musical techniques employed to fashion any film's narrative effects, thereby rendering these practices imperceptible to the movie's spectator.

Belton, in *American Cinema/American Culture*, goes even further by identifying the fundamental paradox of classical Hollywood style: "Beneath the apparent artlessness of the surface lies a solid foundation of highly crafted narrative techniques that . . . function to deliver the story as powerfully as possible without interrupting its flow with intrusive marks or signs that might betray the fact that the story is itself a product of careful construction."[41] Lee's films repudiate these classical principles so frequently that their style becomes visible in ways that conventional Hollywood movies elide. Lee's films, in other words, intrude upon the viewer's attention not only to betray their status as filmic constructions but also to provoke the audience's critical intelligence, rousing viewers from the passivity—indeed, the near somnolence—that Belton and Bordwell assume characterizes standard Hollywood audiences. The surface of Lee's work, rarely as artless as Belton defines this term, is instead artful—full of color, vibrancy, and life—to propel viewers into a different, more dynamic relationship with the cinematic story unfolding before them.

Provoking audiences in this fashion accounts for the didacticism or soap boxing that viewers, critics, and scholars sometimes reproach Lee for indulging. The sense that certain Lee films, or at least certain Lee characters, lecture their audiences about race, economics, and politics has become so prevalent that the "Message Boards" section of Lee's Internet Movie Database (IMDb) entry[42] is rife with discussion threads admonishing Lee for preaching social messages directly at his viewers. Audiences, critics, and scholars also disagree about Lee's tendency to refuse clear, trim, and definitive resolutions for his films, especially the open-ended (or, to less charitably minded viewers, dissatisfying) conclusions of *School Daze, Do the Right Thing, Jungle Fever, Malcolm X, She Hate Me,* and, especially, *Miracle at St. Anna.* Lee believes that he should not spoon-feed audiences insights into his films, or even certify their messages, saying as much to Nelson George in their 1986 *Spike Lee's Gotta Have It* interview[43] and telling Kaleem Aftab in *That's My Story and I'm Sticking to It,* regarding his films' resolutions, "More often than not, I let the audience do some work."[44] Nelson George elaborates this perspective in *That's My Story* by noting the ambiguity that typifies Lee's narrative structures (not simply their denouements). George writes that, when people feel that Lee's movies (especially their endings) are problematic from the perspective of classical Hollywood style, Lee's statement, "I don't believe in Hollywood script structure"[45] becomes significant. This idea serves as a near-manifesto for Lee's movies, whose unusual storylines, inconsistent pacing, variegated tones, and shifting genres (often within the same picture) do not simply challenge, but seem regularly to demolish classical Hollywood style. Viewers accustomed to more traditional film structure will find Lee's work messy, incoherent, and upsetting by comparison.

George, demonstrating why he is an incisive cultural critic of American film, music, and art, identifies how Lee's films, by refusing to resolve all conflicts, differ from movies that embody the classical Hollywood style that Belton and Bordwell anatomize: "Spike consistently goes against that: he defies expectation, he has multiple endings, he does not always pick up threads, some threads are just essays in the middle of the film."[46] This analysis not only encompasses Lee's overall cinematic effect but also explains why his movies so passionately divide audiences. Lee, to his credit, does not aim to please all viewers, but trusts them enough to undermine their preconceptions about race, religion, politics, economics, gender, and cinema itself. This filmmaking method virtually guarantees that Lee will discomfit, dissatisfy, disappoint, or alienate some audiences, which testifies to his assertive (even combative) determination to upend commercial cinema's pedestrian pieties, conventional forms, and conservative aesthetics.

Lee has written, produced, and directed such a diversity of movies that he has dabbled in nearly every existing film genre (with the notable exceptions of science fiction and slave epic). He has so far avoided narratives set in the distant past or distant future, preferring contemporary settings for his stories about America's fractious politics, race relations, and cultural crossings, although *Malcolm X, Crooklyn, 4 Little Girls,* and *Miracle at St. Anna* all take place in (or heavily refer to) past decades and events. Lee, as this book demonstrates, possesses a restless creative spirit that impels him to experiment with form, structure, genre, mood, tone, and narrative to achieve a singular style that, being immediately recognizable as his own, causes Nelson George, Roger Ebert, and Michael Eric Dyson—among other commentators, critics, and scholars—to proclaim Lee a cinematic auteur. This designation, while appropriate, should not suggest that Lee makes his movies alone or that he disregards the creative contributions of his collaborators. Lee, indeed, offers generous and sometimes fulsome praise for his casts and crews in interviews, behind-the-scenes documentaries, and audio commentaries that help clarify, if not demystify, the various processes that filmmaking entails. Lee's collaborative nature, however, cannot obscure the insistent, compelling, and complex style that characterizes Spike Lee joints. His movies sometimes shift ideas, tones, storylines, and genres within a single scene to offer the viewer an ever-changing cinematic experience that remains memorable long after the film finishes. This always-in-motion technique, indeed, explains the fascination and frustration that Lee's movies regularly evoke.

RIDING HIGH

David Breskin introduces his *Inner Views* interview with Lee by writing, "Marketeer, provocateur, propagandist, genius, racist, humorist, writer, actor, director, producer, pitchman, chauvinist, homophobe, hoop fan, hype artist, egotist, entrepreneur, caricaturist, visionary, radical, reactionary: Spike Lee has been called all these things. What he wants you to know, though, is that he is a Strong Black Man. You can call him anything you like."[47] The many labels that attach themselves to Lee indicate just how complicated an American artist he is, as well as how successful he has been at maintaining his public persona for more than twenty-five years. Lee's career has inevitably experienced peaks and valleys, with the 1990s films following *Malcolm X* receiving less acclaim than his earlier pictures despite several fine efforts (*Clockers, He Got Game,* and *Summer of Sam,* for instance, are as good as any movie that Lee has directed). *Bamboozled* appeared in 2000 to prove to audiences that Lee could still produce thoughtful, scabrous, and provocative entertainment in a brutal satire of American media that has never been surpassed, while *25th Hour* (2002) and *Inside Man* (2006) were critical triumphs for Lee, with *Inside Man* being his most profitable film to date.

Another measure of Lee's influence is the extensive scholarship about his career that regularly achieves publication. This book, indeed, engages the academic conversation about Lee's films to unveil just how intricate his movies are, to credit his achievements, and to examine his failings. It also cites pertinent mainstream (or popular-press) sources, including movie reviews, to contextualize the reception of Lee's films in their historical moment. If journalism is the first draft of history, reviews offer the inaugural drafts of cinematic scholarship. Lee, as a controversial artist, has provoked unusually rich popular-press writing about his films, with influential critics like Roger Ebert penning smart articles and essays about Lee's cultural productions that demand a hearing in any book that hopes to chronicle the changing reputation of Lee's films. As scholars examine and re-examine Lee's career, considering popular responses to his work helps readers understand Lee's relationship with the reporters, commentators, and critics who frequently set the preliminary terms of debate about his movies. Lee's willingness to discuss his projects, his opinions of American and African American cinema, and his political sentiments in mainstream media outlets makes him, as Breskin indicates, a talented promoter who excels at hype.

The sheer amount of research about Lee's life, work, and art is daunting for anyone wishing to grasp his contribution to American cinema, testifying both to Lee's longevity and relevance. The work of certain scholars has become so important to academic conversations about Lee's movies that this study cites them many times, with Dan Flory, Ed Guerrero, bell hooks (pen name for Gloria Jean Watkins), Paula J. Massood, and S. Craig Watkins achieving special significance as careful, incisive, and necessary observers of Lee's career. This book offers a roughly chronological appraisal of Lee's feature films, as well as his notable documentaries and valuable television projects, by mixing chapters that profile a single movie with chapters that discuss as many as four different productions. This study, due to Lee's prolificacy, is not comprehensive despite offering an overview of his cinematic career. Lee, indeed, has written, directed, produced, and performed in too many films, television programs, and commercials for any single volume to analyze them all.

Even so, certain principles are important to codify. Although methodological pronouncements in scholarly studies can be as tedious as a movie's end credits, this book combines film scholarship, critical-race studies, feminist analyses, formalist readings, genre studies, historical contexts (often gleaned from mainstream press clippings), and (auto)biographical research into its examination of Lee's long and varied career. This study pays close attention to Lee's movies, discussing their intertextual connections with other artists and artworks as necessary, but does not provide a comparative analysis like John R. Howard's *Faces in the Mirror.* Readers interested in such assessments should consult three indispensable academic collections devoted to Lee's work—Paula J. Massood's previously mentioned *The Spike Lee Reader,* Janice D. Hamlet and Robin R. Means Coleman's *Fight the Power!: The Spike Lee Reader,* and Mark T. Conard's *The Philosophy of Spike Lee*—for fascinating discussions of Lee's debts to moviemakers as diverse as Julie Dash, Howard Hawks, Martin Scorsese, Melvin Van Peebles, and Billy Wilder; playwrights Amiri Baraka, Berthold Brecht, Eugene O'Neill, and August Wilson; novelists James Baldwin, Ralph Ellison, Zora Neale Hurston, Toni Morrison, and Richard Wright; and composers Aaron Copland, Duke Ellington, and Scott Joplin.

The most common charge made against Lee is that he traffics not only in rampant homophobia but also in a pernicious sexism that approaches misogyny, topics that several chapters examine in detail. The writing of bell hooks, Wahneema Lubiano, and Michele Wallace (among others) bring focus to analyses of *She's Gotta Have It, School Daze, Do the Right Thing, Jungle Fever, Malcolm X, Girl 6, Bamboozled,* and *She Hate Me* in particular, although Lee's entire cinematic corpus is a goldmine for feminist scholars and queer theorists. Lee's depiction of women becomes more complex and mature in later films, but he remains possessed of a patriarchal mind-set that condemns his female characters to less-accomplished roles than his men. The same statement applies to the heterosexist preferences that make Lee's gay and lesbian characters much less successful than his straight ones, to the point that *She Hate Me*'s lesbian characters verge into caricature. These observations, indeed, are perhaps the only persistent conclusions to be made about Lee's cinema, which otherwise mutates from genre to genre, from tragedy to comedy, and from adventurous fun to grim sententiousness and back in a filmography whose multiplicity is commendable.

Lee considers the mixture of tones, plots, and genres that typifies his films to be integral to their effect. Lee's 1991 interview with David Breskin underscores the importance he (Lee) places upon breaking Hollywood conventions, for when Breskin claims that Lee's movies (unlike many mainstream American films) include conflicting styles, Lee objects to this characterization, preferring the term juxtaposition to describe what Breskin then calls the tendency of Lee's movies to switch between "a presentational style and a dramatic style, between a documentary style and a realistic style, or even between a kind of romantic tone and a satirical, edgy tone."[48] Lee tells Breskin, in one of their conversation's most edifying exchanges, "It doesn't bother me to mix stuff like that up, because I don't think I make genre films. I don't think I make films that can be classified in one specific cubbyhole."[49] While Lee certainly makes genre films as far as Hollywood studios and their marketing departments are concerned (namely, independent films about African American characters and themes, or, in short, black cinema), Lee's filmography reveals that his work cannot be pigeonholed into simple categories. Lee says to Breskin, "I think the better question might be: do you think you've been successful with the juxtaposition? I really couldn't do a film that's one thing all the way through. That wouldn't be very interesting to me."[50] Lee's question becomes an animating concern of this book, for determining how effectively his films juxtapose different plots, themes, characters, symbols, tones, and genres is one of this study's primary goals. Lee's evaluation of his movies up to 1991 also applies to the films that follow because he has never directed a picture that remains tonally, thematically, and narratively consistent, with *Inside Man* being the closest example, but even this movie changes gears, moods, and genres when its heist-film architecture gives way to searching subtextual commentaries about global capitalism's corrupt foundations.

Lee's juxtaposed style, as such, will appear jumbled, incoherent, and inartistic to audiences schooled in classical Hollywood filmmaking. Lee makes no apologies for this effect, responding to Breskin's assertion that mixing styles can upset some viewers by saying, "Most of the movies that people are used to suck anyway! They're the same old tried and true formula, and at the end of the movie everything is wrapped up in a nice little bow. And very rarely do those movies ever make you think"[51] to declare his opposition to Hollywood storytelling norms and aesthetic standards, even repudiating preferences for tidy conclusions by saying, "I just don't think everything has to be resolved."[52] Such intentions more closely align with the narrative and stylistic rhythms of independent black cinema, French New Wave Cinema, and Italian Neorealism, yet Lee's movies bear sufficient traces of classical Hollywood style to become compelling hybrids that merge these disparate influences into an uncommon body of work.

The most specious charge against Lee is that he and his work are racist. Lee's determination to spotlight African American characters, stories, and themes inevitably provokes claims that his concerns about how American cinema depicts black people and black culture are themselves expressions of racist anger, bitterness, and hatred. This rhetorical trope is a customary method of diverting attention from, or entirely ignoring, the abysmal history of white supremacy that undergirds not only Hollywood's attitudes toward minority characters but also America's shameful history of racial oppression. The easiest way to dismiss any black artist's attempts to examine American racial dynamics is to accuse that artist of reverse discrimination, which Lee recognizes as an all-too-common ploy that denies a more complex truth about how racism operates within American society and, consequently, Hollywood film culture. Lee, echoing comments in his introduction to *Spike Lee's Gotta Have It,* tells Breskin, "You got to have a two-part program. On one hand, you have to say you cannot deny the injustices that have been against you as a people. On the other hand, you cannot use as an excuse, 'Well, I really would have liked to have done that, but Mr. Charlie was blocking me every single time.' I think that's the more complete statement."[53] This pronouncement affirms Lee's conviction that, while racism is an undeniable obstacle for black artists in particular and black people in general, they must struggle against (and attempt to surmount) it by openly, committedly, and directly confronting the unfairness they face.

Lee then explains why his understanding of racism's institutional character precludes African Americans from being racist. "For me," Lee says, "there's a difference between racism and prejudice. Black people can be prejudiced. But to me, racism is the *institution*. Black people have never enacted laws saying that white folks cannot own property, white folks can't intermarry, white folks can't vote. You got to have power to do that. That's what racism is, an institution."[54] This ideology, heavily influenced by Malcolm X's analysis of American racial dynamics (as well as the black-nationalist philosophy espoused by Marcus Garvey in the early twentieth century and the Nation of Islam in midcentury), distinguishes institutional domination from individual bigotry to identify how white supremacy enmeshes all Americans in a political, economic, and social system that separates them based on skin color, cultural inheritance, and historical circumstance. From Lee's perspective, accusing black Americans of racism falsely equates their experiences as the victims of institutional oppression with the individual prejudice that they face. Lee expresses similar sentiments to Elvis Mitchell in their 1991 *Playboy* interview and to Henry Louis Gates, Jr. in "Final Cut," their 1991 interview for the scholarly journal *Transition,* telling Gates, "Well, people might say I'm prejudiced, people might say I'm racist," but once again differentiates between racism and prejudice by saying, "The reason why I say black people can't be racist is because black people have never been in a position in the United States of America where we could say that white people can't vote, that white people can't own property, that white people can't marry a black person. That stuff is institutional, where you have to be in control, of the police, government, and so on."[55] Although Lee quickly adds, "Black people have never been in a position to do that," he then observes, "And that's not to say that we're not prejudiced. I think everybody's prejudiced. I think that for me prejudice comes down to name-calling. Anybody can call anybody a nigger or a white motherfucker; but, I mean, sticks and stones. . . . But when they set the law saying, you can't vote, that's totally different. That's totally different."[56]

These perspectives, offered five years after *She's Gotta Have It*'s debut and sixteen months before *Malcolm X*'s theatrical premiere, show how Lee's approach to racism is more consistent throughout his films than critics such as Stanley Crouch, David Denby, and Armond White admit. Lee does not absolve African Americans of prejudice, but instead outlines the broader formal foundations of American racism to offer a thoughtful analysis (grounded in his reading of *The Autobiography of Malcolm X*, James Baldwin, Zora Neale Hurston, and Richard Wright) that, similar to Frantz Fanon's writing about the psychopathology of colonization (especially in *Black Skin, White Masks*), notes how the all-encompassing institution of racism fosters feelings of inadequacy in African Americans that they nevertheless cannot accept as an excuse for tolerating their difficult position within American society. Lee's filmography, indeed, represents a long-term engagement with multiple, divergent, and dueling notions about the origins and effects of anti-black racism, as well as the most effective responses to it. Yet Lee does not confine himself to stories about racial oppression or black characters even as he spotlights African American people, ideas, and themes in much of his work.

Lee, therefore, is more than an intriguing filmmaker or a notable cultural figure, but becomes a complex American artist who elicits heated responses about his nation's historical traumas, social values, and human diversity. Lee's work defies the easy summaries and casual assumptions sometimes made about it, while his reputation as a cultural provocateur sometimes clouds the quality of his contributions to American cinema, television, and the other performing arts. Lee is also a master entertainer whose movies are engaging, funny, unsettling, and uncompromising in equal measure, demonstrating that, for him, entertainment is far more than mindless diversion or crass commercialism. This study's central challenge is gauging the aesthetic successes, failures, and effects of Lee's artistry, while its central assumption is that Lee's work constitutes artistry of sufficient profundity to merit sustained attention. This book, therefore, maintains respect for Lee's accomplishments even when it disagrees with his creative choices, a position borne out of the conviction that a filmmaker so passionately committed to expanding his artistic prowess, to furthering his nation's understanding of its own contested history, and to forcing his viewers into critical considerations of cinema's potential deserves the scholarly recognition that this study, by adding its voice to the ongoing conversation about Lee's career, now offers.

1

Men at Work

EARLY DAYS

Spike Lee's inaugural efforts as a feature-film director—1986's *She's Gotta Have It* and 1988's *School Daze*—synthesize his cinematic ambition, talent, and myopia. Both movies weave provocative topics, contrasting styles, and multiple genres into surprising narratives that, at key moments, appear unpolished by classic Hollywood standards. Lee's willingness to challenge American cinematic conventions in these early films has generated substantial mainstream and scholarly debate about his untraditional approaches to visual storytelling, to narrative pacing, and, most tellingly, to character development. Interested writers—whether magazine profilers, movie reviewers, or academic analysts—cannot agree about these films' overall quality beyond noting that neither *She's Gotta Have It* nor *School Daze* copies any movie that preceded it.

This accomplishment, particularly in Hollywood's culturally conservative cinematic marketplace, might seem a victory in its own right. Lee's fresh, bracing, and no-holds-barred approach—what he terms "guerrilla filmmaking"[1]—disrupts the easy spectatorship that film scholars John Belton, David Bordwell, Janet Staiger, and Kristin Thompson associate with classical Hollywood style.[2] *She's Gotta Have It* and *School Daze,* as even perfunctory screenings reveal, make demands on their audiences' assumed patience, presumed passivity, and political sympathies. Both films cater to active viewers who desire unconventional narratives, stylized visuals, generic *bricolage,* and political engagement, thereby refusing simple assessments and easy analyses.

Each movie, despite its original sensibility, remains indebted to earlier films, filmmakers, and film styles. *She's Gotta Have It*'s fractured narrative, for instance, recalls Akira Kurosawa's *Rashomon* (1950), Anthony Asquith's *The Woman in Question* (1950), and Sundaram Balachander's *Andha Naal* (1954) by presenting divergent accounts of Nola Darling's (Tracy Camilla Johns) relationships with three male lovers. The story's major participants—Nola, Mars Blackmon (Spike Lee), Greer Childs (John Canada Terrell), and

Jamie Overstreet (Tommy Redmond Hicks)—directly address the camera to offer contrasting perspectives about Nola's sexually liberated behavior, which alternately perplexes, frustrates, and angers her lovers, but that Nola defends by saying, "I consider myself normal, whatever that means."[3]

She's Gotta Have It's multiple viewpoints remind its audience not only of *Rashomon*'s influential storytelling approach but also of documentary films in which subjects discuss their thoughts, feelings, and attitudes with an unseen interlocutor, conveying the impression that they converse with the viewer. This cinematic intimacy helps propel *She's Gotta Have It*'s narrative even while shattering the stylistic invisibility that, according to David Bordwell, characterizes classical Hollywood cinema. The film, indeed, disrupts its narrative from the opening moments: still photographs of Nola Darling's Brooklyn neighborhood construct the character's cinematic world from diverse images and tones before the camera finds Nola under the covers of her "loving bed."[4] She sits up, then declares, "I want you to know the only reason I'm consenting to this is because I wish to clear my name. Not that I care what people think, but enough is enough." Emphasizing *She's Gotta Have It*'s confessional nature aligns Lee's movie with documentary films, with direct cinema, and with *cinema vérité* to spotlight how *She's Gotta Have It*'s fragmented story seeks to capture reality even while distorting it. Lee, indeed, speaks openly of mixing cinematic modes in his production journal (included in the film's invaluable companion publication, *Spike Lee's Gotta Have It: Inside Guerrilla Filmmaking*). In the entry dated October 11, 1984, Lee writes, "No way will this be a straight, linear, cut-and-dry narrative film. I want to break on the narration, flashbacks, talking directly into the camera, people asking the audience questions. A lot of camera movement, experimental stuff."[5] One week later, in the October 18, 1984, entry, Lee notes that the movie will combine narrative and documentary styles.[6] Even at these early dates (*She's Gotta Have It* would not begin shooting until July 5, 1985), Lee repudiates classical Hollywood cinema's supposedly unseen design as implicitly inflexible, distinguishing it from his more improvisational approach.

School Daze may not include direct-to-camera confessions, but this film extends its predecessor's formal inventiveness by evoking one of Lee's favorite genres, the Hollywood musical, only to revise this mode's apolitical parameters by exploring the racial and economic tensions besetting fictional Mission College's all-black student body. The film's musical performances not only interrupt its storyline but also comment upon the themes set in motion by the opening credits, which assemble still diagrams and photos (of a slave ship's interior, of notable black Americans, and of significant twentieth-century historical events) to condense the African American experience into a three-minute, thirty-second sequence. The musical numbers' imaginative choreography, particularly "Good and Bad Hair," may recall Busby Berkeley's *Gold Diggers of 1935* (1935), Stanley Donen and Gene Kelly's *Singin' in the Rain* (1952), and Robert Wise and Jerome Robbins's *West Side Story*

(1962), but Lee deploys their lyrics to acknowledge issues of colorism, sexual propriety, and American academia's complicity in South African apartheid. Lee does not consign *School Daze* to light entertainment, or what Todd Gitlin (while analyzing American network television's worst tendencies in *Inside Prime Time*) calls "mind candy,"[7] but instead alters the Hollywood movie musical's happy, inoffensive, middle-of-the-road template to explore political themes that may discomfit *School Daze*'s audience. The film, despite its influences and forerunners, does not affectionately reproduce the movie musicals that Lee enjoyed as a child, but instead rewrites their conventions to serve its director's satirical ends.

School Daze is also considerably more complicated than the college movies that Desson Howe's February 12, 1988, *Washington Post* review invokes: "*School Daze* is something like a black *Animal House* or *Revenge of the Nerds,* in which various student factions are engaged in a mindless intramural struggle while the women exhibit vanity, the men lust and the faculty gapes."[8] These campus films lack *School Daze*'s political dimension despite their superficial similarities of genre, but such problematic comparisons do not stop Rita Kempley, also writing in the *Washington Post*'s February 12, 1988, edition, from mocking *School Daze* as a "didactic collegiate farce—*Animal House* with pan-African politics."[9] John Landis's 1978 movie, however, has few connections to Lee's second film beyond their academic setting. *School Daze*'s political concerns not only undergird its story but also distinguish it from campus comedies like *Animal House, Revenge of the Nerds* (1984), and *Back to School* (1986). Kempley finds this perspective unpersuasive, scorning Lee's artistic overreach by noting that the writer-director's "eagerly awaited musical comedy began as a standard collegiate farce—geeks versus Greeks—but Lee wanted more depth, he wanted issues," thereby producing a movie with a "pompous patchwork plot" that becomes "an arrogant, humorless, sexist mess."[10] Kempley's assessment expresses relevant concerns about *School Daze*'s antifeminism, but portraying the movie as Lee's attempt to rewrite *Animal House* from an African American perspective unwisely privileges Landis's film as a cinematic model that *School Daze* weakly cribs. Neither Kempley nor Howe examines *School Daze* in detail (providing, as short newspaper reviews must, facile analyses), but these articles demonstrate the precarious position that Lee occupies within the American cinematic tradition, fulfilling as he does the double role of American and African American filmmaker. This dual status recalls W.E.B. Du Bois's famous formulation of double-consciousness—"this sense of always looking at one's self through the eyes of others, of measuring one's soul by the tape of a world that looks on in amused contempt and pity. One ever feels his two-ness,—an American, a Negro; two souls, two thoughts, two unreconciled strivings; two warring ideals in one dark body"[11]—to complicate the viewer's response to Lee's eccentric movie narratives.

Lee's first two films, indeed, consciously subvert classical Hollywood style even while reproducing its broadest parameters. Neither *She's Gotta Have It* nor *School Daze*, after all, is a fully experimental film that renounces narrative continuity in favor of indecipherable impressionism. Both movies prefer to disrupt, rather than to demolish, the aesthetic invisibility that Belton and Bordwell identify as Hollywood cinema's most salient trait, which opens each film to charges of poor craftsmanship. *School Daze*, as Kempley's evaluation indicates, was occasionally condemned as an inept mishmash of conflicting techniques,[12] while *She's Gotta Have It*, by contrast, was celebrated as a fresh and invigorating (although unpolished) example of independent American moviemaking that, much to its credit, so disregarded Hollywood conventions that it won the *Prix de la Jeunesse* (Youth Award) at the 1986 Cannes International Film Festival.[13]

Both movies' generic, stylistic, and narrative ambiguities—even indeterminacies—signal Lee's fascination with cultural intertextuality. This concept offers a useful method for analyzing Lee's cinematic oeuvre. Gladstone L. Yearwood, in *Black Film as a Signifying Practice: Cinema, Narration and the African American Aesthetic Tradition*, stresses the importance of intertexuality to black American cinema: "In the development of black film, filmmakers have been striving to make film do what its intertextual supports such as forms of black oratory and African American classical music do. This is why it is an error and a severe devaluation to evaluate black film as a poor imitation of Hollywood cinema."[14] Yearwood, in this passage, corrects the (perhaps unconscious) errors that Howe and Kempley make in their *School Daze* reviews before noting, "the most successful films in the African American tradition are those that go beyond dominant approaches to film and use black cultural expression to transform the cinematic medium."[15] Such transformations, however, do not wholly reject Hollywood tropes: "This helps explain the importance of Spike Lee as a filmmaker within the African American tradition. Although Lee borrows freely from the language of Hollywood films, he grounds black film within the intertexual space of the black experience. Like African American classical music, the black cultural tradition is . . . open to change and welcomes new ideas."[16] Lee's movies, in other words, are not closed texts, but rather flexible productions that defy rigid classification. *She's Gotta Have It* and *School Daze*, as such, inaugurate a tradition that continues throughout Lee's cinematic career. Absent the generic, thematic, and narrative elasticity pioneered by Lee's first two films, *Do the Right Thing* (1989), *Jungle Fever* (1991), *Malcolm X* (1992), *Crooklyn* (1994), *Get on the Bus* (1996), *Bamboozled* (2000), *25th Hour* (2002), *Inside Man* (2006), and *Miracle at St. Anna* (2008) would not be as distinctive as they are.

MALE GAZES

The foregoing plaudits, however, should not suggest that Lee's work is unproblematic. The most persistent criticism of his films involves their reputed sexism and homophobia. *She's Gotta Have It* and *School Daze*, in the quarter century since their release, have received sustained scholarly attention that disputes their unreconstructed portraits of heterosexual women, lesbians, and gay men. *She's Gotta Have It,* in particular, is both celebrated as advancing an exciting, even revolutionary, image of liberated black female sexuality and vilified as indulging pernicious stereotypes about uncontrolled black female desire that culminate in Nola Darling's rape by Jamie Overstreet. These contradictory assessments speak not only to the film's laudable complexities but also to its troubling repercussions.

The most influential academic analysis of *She's Gotta Have It*'s gender politics is bell hooks's "'Whose Pussy Is This?': A Feminist Comment," an article (first published in 1989) that generously praises Lee's debut film despite serious misgivings about its regressive treatment of Nola Darling's character. "A passionate viewer of films, especially the work of independent filmmakers," hooks writes, "I found much to appreciate in the technique, style, and overall production of *She's Gotta Have It*. It was especially refreshing to see images of black people on-screen that were not grotesque caricatures, images that were familiar, images that imaginatively captured the essence, dignity, and spirit of that elusive quality known as 'soul.'"[17] Yet, hooks quickly notes, "Thinking about the film from a feminist perspective, considering its political implications, I find it much more problematic,"[18] objecting that "Nola Darling's sexual desire is not depicted as an autonomous gesture, as an independent longing for sexual expression, satisfaction, and fulfillment. Instead her assertive sexuality is most often portrayed as though her body, her sexually aroused being, is a reward or gift she bestows on the deserving male."[19]

The essay, as these comments demonstrate, is no broadside attack against *She's Gotta Have It* or its writer-director. Conceding Lee's achievements in producing the film, hooks states that Nola embodies a superficially perfect vision of "woman as desiring subject—a representation that does challenge sexist notions of female sexual passivity," before reminding her reader, "from slavery on, black women have been portrayed in white racist thought as sexually assertive, although this view contrasts sharply with the emphasis on chastity, monogamy, and the male right to initiate sexual contact in black culture, a view held especially among the middle classes."[20] This argument's force results from its nuanced appreciation not only of *She's Gotta Have It*'s underlying themes but also of the historical, cultural, socioeconomic, and political tensions that Lee's film confronts. No matter how groundbreaking *She's Gotta Have It* may seem, hooks does not consider the movie a bold step forward because "it is a patriarchal tale—one in which woman does not emerge triumphant, fulfilled. While we can applaud Nola's feeble attempt to tell a new story at the end of the film, it is not compelling, not enough—it is not satisfying."[21]

This perspective has so influenced the movie's scholarly reputation that many discussions of *She's Gotta Have It*'s putative sexism operate within the parameters that hooks's article establishes. Despite her multilayered evaluation of the film's strengths and weaknesses, later observers sometimes forget hooks's opening proviso that Lee's movie soulfully dramatizes the dignity of its African American characters' daily lives. *She's Gotta Have It*'s sexism, therefore, is frequently assumed rather than examined, consigning its gendered representation of female desire to a critical dustbin that condemns the film's patriarchal approach as reproducing the scopophilia, voyeurism, and narcissism so famously analyzed by Laura Mulvey's "Visual Pleasure and Narrative Cinema." *She's Gotta Have It,* indeed, may strike the reader of Mulvey's psychoanalytic article as tailor-made for her argument that, "in a world ordered by sexual imbalance, pleasure in looking has been split between active/male and passive/female. The determining male gaze projects its phantasy on the female figure which is styled accordingly. In their traditional exhibitionist role women are simultaneously looked at and displayed, with their appearance coded for strong visual and erotic impact."[22] Nola's nudity, for instance, always occurs during sexual congress with Mars, Greer, or Jamie, coding her as an erotic object both for her male partners' and the audience's pleasure. Lee, as writer and director, arranges Nola's naked body to fulfill the erotic implications of his film's title: the "it" that Nola must have, in this reading, is nothing more than passionate coitus. Her desire may provoke anxiety by threatening to overwhelm her lovers (Mars calls her "freaky-deaky" during his first direct-to-camera confession and later tells Jamie, "The sister was bogus 24, 7, 365"), but, taking up hooks's and Mulvey's concerns, the movie's prurient fascination with Nola's lovemaking fulfills the audience's need for erogenous visual stimulation. *She's Gotta Have It,* therefore, projects a fantasy fixed by the film's insistent male gaze.

Yet this approach cannot fully account for novelist Terry McMillan's response, recounted in "Thoughts on *She's Gotta Have It,*" first published as the lead essay in 1991's *Five for Five: The Films of Spike Lee,* the retrospective volume that accompanied the release of Lee's fifth film, *Jungle Fever.* McMillan, like hooks, mentions the word-of-mouth buzz that *She's Gotta Have It* generated, but remains skeptical until seeing the movie. Standing in line with other, mostly African American viewers at Manhattan's Cinema Studio, located at 66th Street and Broadway Avenue, on a hot 1986 day causes the crowd to be excited by the prospect of enjoying a new filmic representation of black American life. This collective reaction, McMillan notes, became fixed in the audience's mind as the novelty of Nola asserting herself throughout the film took hold. McMillan considers Nola less a pliant sexual object bent on gratifying her partners than a woman defying social tradition to pursue her desires. "At first," McMillan writes, "I just thought she was an attractive sister, but by the time she finished telling me the deal, she was sexy and sensuous and became beautiful because she seemed to know exactly who she was,"[23] even if, during the movie's celebrated Thanksgiving scene (Nola invites Mars, Greer, and Jamie to dinner, only to see them compete for her attention by criticizing one another), "somehow we know they've met before and it's a territorial thing they're dealing with, and *Nola* is the territory."[24] McMillan cannot discount the objectifying tendencies of Nola's suitors, yet concludes that *She's Gotta Have It*'s "story was about power: exercising power over your own body and mind. In this case, it was a black woman. . . . So what Spike Lee has done is give viewers not only a female version of male sexual mores but a main character who is still very much a woman."[25]

McMillan's essay never mentions hooks's "'Whose Pussy Is This?,'" but implicitly rejects the earlier article's criticism of Nola as an unfulfilled, unsatisfied, and unsatisfying female character. McMillan finds Nola's sexual passions (and, consequently, Lee's film) liberating because Nola's lovemaking combines physical, cultural, and spiritual elements, nowhere better expressed than in McMillan's "most favorite scene of all . . . when Mars finally got a shot at it."[26] McMillan's assessment is worth quoting at length:

> Spike Lee put the lens on Nola's breasts, and we see how beautifully and tenderly Mars kisses and (well, you know) them. Spike Lee should cut this part of the film and send it to all the men who don't know what to do with a woman's breasts, because the noise made in that theater when we saw this happening was not just envy. We were grateful that her body was shown in such a beautiful, sensuous manner and appreciated by a black man who knew what to do with it.[27]

Nola's nudity, in McMillan's estimation, neither demeans nor disempowers her character, but instead celebrates Nola's unfettered physicality. The animalistic stereotypes (of uncontrollable sexual desire, unthinking assertiveness, and unrepentant whoring) that white racist thought attributes to black women fall away as Nola and Mars share intimacies of body and mind that signal their mutual admiration. Equally notable is McMillan invoking the term *we* to confirm that her fellow female viewers appreciated *She's Gotta Have It*'s depiction of black sexuality. Nola's lovemaking, at least for McMillan, is satisfying, if not triumphant, to demonstrate the conflicting responses that Lee's film evokes.

Such disagreements may typify Lee's cinematic corpus, but they do little to resolve the question of *She's Gotta Have It*'s sexism. The film's production journal, on this score, does the director few favors. The story of *She's Gotta Have It*'s uncertain genesis—thanks to mainstream articles, academic analyses, and Lee's shrewd marketing efforts (the companion volume, which includes Nelson George's extensive interview, Lee's production diary, and the film's third-draft script, is perhaps the best example)—is now famous in independent-film circles: shot in twelve days on a budget of $175,000 that its writer-director cobbled together from family, friends, and foundations, *She's Gotta Have It*'s completion was so tenuous that Lee, who cast himself as Mars Blackmon to save money and edited the film himself on a

rented, six-plate Steenbeck machine located in his small Brooklyn apartment,[28] found the movie's negative held hostage when New York's DuArt
Laboratories demanded that Lee pay overdue bills (for transferring the film
from Super-16-mm to Super-35-mm film stock) or the movie's negative
would be auctioned to the highest bidder.[29] These financial pressures lead
Lee to make questionable comments about feminism in *Spike Lee's Gotta
Have It*. Entries from January 1985 reveal Lee's frustration about applying
for a grant from the Film Fund, whose director, Lillian Jimenez, tells Lee
on January 9, 1985, "that the screening panel will be suspicious of a male
doing a sensitive piece about a woman."[30] One week later, on January 17,
1985, Lee writes, after receiving a phone call from Jimenez in which she
expresses concern over *She's Gotta Have It*'s potential sexism, "Spike, let's
be honest. There are feminists running that place so my chances are slim and
none."[31] Lee associates feminism with unbending essentialism, saying later
in this entry that, even if the Film Fund denies him money, "I won't compromise my script. The film will not be sexist. It will be anything but sexist.
Their problem is that a MALE is doing a film like this."[32] These comments
illustrate Lee's fierce creative independence, yet also suggest his superficial
understanding of feminism as a movement populated by women who cannot tolerate men artistically representing female characters and concerns.
This notion endorses persistent stereotypes about feminists (that they are all
women, that they see men as incapable of understanding female experience,
that they automatically condemn men's artistic depictions of women) without critically examining Lee's own position. Saying that *She's Gotta Have
It* "will be anything but sexist," after all, does not prove this point, but
merely asserts it. Blaming the Film Fund's directors in advance indicates
that Jimenez's friendly advice to Lee (about the screening panel's understandable suspicions concerning his film) was well founded. Rather than
considering his story's troubling aspects (as he does in other entries, struggling with the authenticity of Nola's characterization), Lee uses feminism as
a convenient scapegoat.

Lee's innuendo in a later entry (dated January 20, 1985) is, in this context, disturbing: "This week I'm gonna start working on my application to
the Film Fund even though those feminists will probably try to jerk me."[33]
Lee presumes that he will not receive a fair evaluation by feminists who enjoy jerking him around (or, extending the sexual metaphor that this entry
implies, jerking him off), thereby refusing to consider legitimate questions
about *She's Gotta Have It*'s treatment of Nola Darling. He presumes that all
members of the Film Fund's screening panel identify themselves as feminists
rather than crediting Jimenez for alerting him to difficulties about *She's Gotta
Have It*'s potential sexism that have hounded the film ever since its 1986
release.

Lee ignores similar concerns in a much-later journal entry when, on
October 17, 1985, while screening the movie's opening reels at a playwriting

course taught by his friend Dave Davidson at the City College of New York, one female student comments that *She's Gotta Have It* only portrays Nola as a sexual object with little life outside her romantic pursuits. Lee confesses, "That's true. But SEX is the most important thing in her life, or at least it's at the top of the list."[34] He, in this passage, certifies bell hooks's criticism that Nola's sexual obsession reproduces racist and sexist stereotypes about black women. Even more surprising, Lee's refusal to present aspects of Nola's life outside her sexual relationships with Mars, Greer, and Jamie contradicts his stated goal of creating a fully realized woman. More than one year earlier, in one of the production journal's first entries (dated October 9, 1984), Lee makes his strongest statement about Nola's character: "Nola Darling is my heroine. I love and respect her, and I must show that love and respect in my treatment of her in the script."[35] Eight days later, Lee writes in the October 17, 1984, entry, "It's important that I not exploit women in this film. I have enough enemies already"[36] before cautioning, "One thing I've gotta watch for is, I don't want Nola to be stupid, the audience can't be laughing at her. With her is fine, but not at her, that's out."[37] Lee's concern about presenting Nola's humanity rather than exploiting her sexual passion demonstrates not only his empathy for *She's Gotta Have It*'s protagonist ("I love and respect her") but also his concern about the consequences of tackling a controversial subject ("I have enough enemies already").

Lee also reveals in the October 9, 1984, entry that he decides to conduct extensive research about female sexuality and sexual behavior by speaking with female friends and acquaintances: "I have to assure them that I will value their privacy and I'm just doing this background information to give my heroine, Nola Darling, depth."[38] This plan reflects well on Lee's intentions for Nola, leading him, with the help of friends Barbara Russell and Tracey Willard, to compose a forty-question survey that, he hopes, other women will agree to answer on videotape. His October 12, 1984, journal entry observes that, since some queries are quite intimate, personal, and private, he will be surprised if any respondent answers them all.[39] Lee does not ignore his request's sensitive nature, but wishes to seek information directly from women about their own experiences. Going to this trouble illustrates Lee's respect for his film, his protagonist, and his audience. Rather than writing *She's Gotta Have It*'s screenplay from his limited knowledge, Lee chooses to compile firsthand accounts of female attitudes toward sex, intimacy, and love to add complexity to Nola Darling's character so that, as his October 9th entry announces, "It's important that audiences have sympathy with Nola. She can't be a FREAK."[40]

The survey includes queries such as, "Do your morals or scruples sometimes conflict with desire/need?," "Were you raised in a strict home?," and "What do you feel when you have to have it? Tense? Evil? Explain."[41] The moralistic tone of these questions implies that Lee reproduces bourgeois patriarchal attitudes toward female sexuality, although such queries also acknowledge the unfair position that American women occupy in their nation's sexual economy. Lee's first production-journal entry, written on October 4, 1984, declares this imbalance to be *She's Gotta Have It*'s fundamental premise: "[Men] are encouraged to have and enjoy sex, while it's not so for women. If they do what men do they're labeled whore, prostitute, nympho, etc. Why this double standard?"[42] Lee, therefore, does not unthinkingly recapitulate restrictive patriarchal judgments, but intends to examine them in entertaining fashion. His successes and failures on this score have driven critical responses to the film since its initial release.

She's Gotta Have It, because it parodies its era's sexual mores rather than overturning their unfair basis, cannot satisfy viewers (like bell hooks) yearning for the counter-hegemonic cinematic narrative of an African American woman who rejects the middle-class values of chastity, monogamy, and male sexual assertiveness that perpetuate patriarchy's oppressive influence. The film, indeed, marginalizes Nola in several scenes to develop Mars's, Greer's, and Jamie's personalities. Lee deliberately constructed the screenplay this way, commenting in his production journal's initial entry (dated October 4, 1984) that "this film has to be really more about men, and the crazy things they do and why they do'em."[43] This structure shortchanges *She's Gotta Have It*'s female protagonist, extending the male gaze that, Mulvey might argue, undergirds many American films (even those productions that challenge, oppose, or renounce classical Hollywood style). It also illustrates the uncomfortable interactions between men and women that Lee takes as his film's thematic spine. A later journal entry (written on October 9, 1984) reads, "What I'm trying to do is show there is a lot of miscommunication, no understanding between the sexes, hence 'that's why people do what they do'"[44] to suggest that *She's Gotta Have It* evokes believable sexual relationships despite satirically exaggerating these associations to humorous proportions. The Thanksgiving scene, for instance, improbably finds Nola cooking dinner for her three suitors, yet their competition for Nola's attention (and, as McMillan notes, the sexual territory that she represents) speaks truthfully to the absurd and chauvinistic lengths to which men will go to impress and possess women. Nola's exasperated response and sarcastic comments, well played by Tracy Camilla Johns, demonstrate her regret at having convened this meeting in the first place.

She's Gotta Have It's ambivalent approach fuses comedy, melodrama, farce, and realism into a story that permits conflicting critical positions about its gender politics, sexism, and, especially, Nola's character. Richard A. Blake, in *Street Smart: The New York of Lumet, Allen, Scorsese, and Lee*, declares, "Lee's script offers no criticism of [Nola's] promiscuous behavior, however. She merely plays her natural role in a sexually charged atmosphere."[45] By contrast, Heather E. Harris and Kimberly R. Moffitt, in "A Critical Exploration of African American Women through the 'Spiked Lens,'" recall bell hooks's judgment that Hollywood cinema traditionally portrays African American love relationships "as a dichotomy of 'fucking or fighting,'" before stating, "Although given ample opportunities to showcase images counter to this dichotomy, Lee has chosen instead to conform to recycled stereotypes that shed only a negative and limited light on African American relationships."[46] Ed Guerrero, in *Framing Blackness: The African American Image in Film,* counters this criticism by noting that *She's Gotta Have It*'s "power and value derive from the rich complexity and comedy of a narrative that depicts a range of black male and female characters with diverse social interests and philosophical outlooks, pursuing their desires within the space of the black world."[47] Michele Wallace, in "Spike Lee and Black Women," synthesizes these three perspectives by cautioning against celebratory assessments of the movie's groundbreaking portrayal of black American sexuality, noting that "*She's Gotta Have It,* the showpiece of the new black aesthetic, was about a black woman who couldn't get enough of the old phallus and who therefore had to be raped" before observing, "Nola, her male lovers, and her female friends all address the camera to supply competing versions of who she really is. The structure of the film thus subverts whatever masculine authority Lee, as director, writer, and producer, intermittently imposes."[48] These diverse scholarly perceptions indicate that no final judgment about *She's Gotta Have It*'s sexism is possible because the movie's shifting attitudes toward Nola Darling prohibit definitive conclusions. Lee's debut film poses numerous contradictions about Nola's character—she is central and marginal, assertive and mute, liberated and restricted, unconventional and traditional—that it refuses to (and perhaps cannot) resolve.[49]

As disappointing as this outlook may seem, it alerts critical viewers to *She's Gotta Have It*'s underlying plausibility. Nola Darling cannot wholly transgress or fully transform her society's structural sexism, thereby failing to liberate herself from all patriarchal restrictions. Harris and Moffitt harshly criticize a pattern afflicting Lee's cinematic corpus that Nola's failure embodies: "His lack of character development, especially as it pertains to women, results in contradictory emancipatory messages within a patriarchal frame. The outcome, though probably not intended, is mostly recycled stereotypical images and fantasies of black women, through the gaze of black men—a sexist bamboozling of sorts."[50] While focusing *She's Gotta Have It* on its male characters calls one detail of Harris and Moffit's comment into question (Lee, his production diary makes clear, intended this outcome), it nonetheless substantiates their larger point. Yet neither *She's Gotta Have It* nor its creator claims to destroy patriarchy. The movie instead reverses traditional gender roles (Lee, in his *School Daze* DVD audio commentary, calls this process "flipping the script"[51]) to explore—sometimes seriously, sometimes lightheartedly—the sexual double standards that infect mid-1980s America. Even so, and much as the film's admirers might wish to dismiss hooks's, Harris's, and Moffitt's criticisms as the oversensitive tirades of aggrieved feminists, such viewpoints accrue renewed legitimacy when considering *She's Gotta Have It*'s most objectionable act: Jamie Overstreet's rape of Nola Darling.

FORCING THE ISSUE

Nola, despite pursuing the sexual freedom that causes Mars Blackmon to brand her a freak, decides to end her relationships with Mars and Greer Childs to commit to Jamie. This decision is unsurprising since *She's Gotta Have It* portrays Jamie not only as Nola's most dependable, sincere, and stable partner but also as her best lover. After their first sex session, Jamie asks Nola, "What can I do for you?," then, at her request, massages Nola's neck, shoulders, and back. This moment so surprised Terry McMillan upon first viewing that, in "Thoughts on *She's Gotta Have It*," the novelist confesses, "I was almost in shock. I elbowed my girlfriend. 'When was the last time some man asked you that afterwards?' She just shook her head and said, 'Girl, I can't remember, ever,'" causing McMillan to reappraise her judgment of Jamie: "So Jamie wasn't a selfish lay. He cared about old Nola, and when she told him that most men she's dealt with don't know a thing about a woman's body, the whole theater said aloud, 'Amen,' and 'I wanna thank you!'"[52] Lee's production journal adds weight to McMillan's view by revealing, in its January 30, 1985, entry, that Nola only experiences orgasm with Jamie,[53] even if this notion is less clear in the film itself. Nola's sexual congress with Mars is certainly sensual and satisfying, but, in the end, she chooses Jamie. He, however, upset by Nola's serial sexual escapades with Mars and Greer, has begun dating another woman (significantly, Ava [Cheryl Burr], the female dancer who, in an earlier scene, performs at Nola's birthday picnic, an event that Jamie organizes).[54] Jamie tells Nola that he cannot abide sharing her with other men, yet grows angry when Nola, after breaking up with Mars and Greer, pleads with Jamie to visit her apartment. When he arrives, Jamie refuses to make love with Nola as he did earlier, instead forcefully taking her from behind. In the scene's (and the film's) most shocking moment, Jamie demands, "Whose pussy is this? Whose is it?!" Nola, upset but powerless to stop the assault, eventually answers, "It's yours."

This incident has received more discussion, censure, and condemnation than any other scene in Lee's filmography. Appropriating Jamie's question as the title of her scholarly assessment of *She's Gotta Have It*, bell hooks writes, "In this instance, rape as an act of black male violence against a black woman was portrayed as though it was just another enjoyable sexual encounter, just another fuck,"[55] reporting that, although the scene disturbed some female viewers (especially herself), "sexist male viewers feeling vilified cheered, expressing their satisfaction that the uppity black woman had been put in her place—that male domination and patriarchal order were restored."[56] Even more distressing to hooks is the fact that both male and female viewers doubted whether or not Jamie's act qualifies as rape, "stress[ing] in conversation with me, she called him—she wanted to be sexual—she wanted it. Embedded in such thinking is the sexist assumption that woman as desiring subject, as active initiator, as sexual seducer is responsible for the quality, nature, and content of male response."[57] Michele Wallace, in "Spike Lee and Black Women," correctly summarizes the uncertainty that Lee's production journal expresses about this scene: "[Lee] doesn't know how Nola should react to Jamie's rape. Should she enjoy it? He settles for having Jamie reluctantly admit that he enjoyed it. Perhaps most important, Lee never calls it a rape."[58] Heather E. Harris and Kimberly R. Moffitt, in "A Critical Exploration of African American Women through the 'Spiked Lens,'" note that Jamie's rape makes sense within *She's Gotta Have It*'s patriarchal narrative: "While Nola's goal is mutual sexual satisfaction, the goal of the men is the transformation of Nola from a 'jezebel' to a nice girl; an unrefined to refined woman; or a whore to what Mars referred to as a 'righteous' woman. Her lifestyle is perceived as deviant by both men and women. And in the end, she is punished for the sin of living the joy of sex."[59]

Such evaluations correctly identify flaws in the rape's presentation, although, contrary to hooks's judgment, the scene is far from enjoyable. Nola is hesitant before allowing Jamie to unzip his pants and enter her, but his aggressive copulation makes her visibly uncomfortable to the point that she tells him, "You're hurting me!" Nola, bent over her bed and facing away from Jamie, cannot physically push him off or escape, thereby demonstrating that his action is, indeed, rape. When Nola answers "yours" to Jamie's brazenly sexist question "Whose pussy is this?," Tracy Camilla Johns delivers the line feebly, adopting a pinched facial expression that indicates Nola's distress, embarrassment, and shame. Nola also flinches when Jamie abruptly finishes, distinguishing this sexual act from their sensual, mutual, and pleasurable lovemaking earlier in the film.

Lee, as Wallace observes, never calls Jamie's action rape in his production diary, while the third-draft screenplay (dated March 1985) demonstrates Lee's ambivalence. After Jamie unzips his pants and forcibly penetrates Nola, the script reads, "He's frustrated and he's treating her rough. While Jamie is doing this he's yelling all kinds of stuff at her. He's trying his best to hurt her feelings, he's demeaning her."[60] This passage suggests that Jamie assaults Nola, confirming his intention to degrade her, yet minimizes Jamie's behavior by emphasizing his emotions over Nola's. The script marginalizes its victimized protagonist by dismissing her bodily and psychological violation as a simple case of Jamie attempting to injure her feelings.

Nola herself refuses to label this assault rape, referring to it only as a "near rape" when she sees Jamie at a local park the next day, neither expressing much visible anger nor forcefully rejecting him. Nola, refusing to have Jamie arrested, appears to accept some blame for the previous night's event. Although Nola soon leaves Jamie sitting alone, concluding the film by again addressing the camera from her bed to reveal that returning to him was a "momentary weakness," their final interaction implies that Nola may be too traumatized to admit to herself that Jamie has sexually abused her. Nola's concluding monologue elides this truth by claiming her own territory, distinct from all her lovers: "[Jamie] wanted a wife, that mythic old-fashioned girl next door. But it's more than that. It's about control: my body, my mind. Who was gonna own it? Them? Or me?" Although this speech might seem to vindicate audiences who celebrate Nola's liberated sexuality, it strikes the attentive viewer as not entirely believable, suggesting that she has not fully come to terms with Jamie's assault. Furthermore, asserting her own agency by posing rhetorical questions rather than making declarative statements contradicts the strong façade that Nola adopts. The film ends on this ambiguous note to deny Nola full triumph over the patriarchal attitudes that define and confine her identity.

Lee, reflecting upon *She's Gotta Have It* in his 2006 autobiography, *That's My Story and I'm Sticking to It* (written in collaboration with Kaleem Aftab), agrees that the scholarly condemnations about Jamie's assault are accurate, saying that the rape scene, by not truly portraying the act as a violation, is the single aspect of his movies that he would change: "It was ill thought out and ill conceived—all the ills that you can get. It just made light of rape, and it really comes down to immaturity on my part."[61] This confession expresses Lee's regret at overlooking the rape's consequences; criticizes his naïveté about sexual assault (Lee was twenty-eight years old while writing *She's Gotta Have It*'s screenplay and twenty-nine on the film's opening day); and upholds the criticisms forwarded by hooks, Wallace, Harris, and Moffitt. That this scene is the only aspect of Lee's extensive filmography that he would alter indicates its prominence.

Lee's immaturity, however, mirrors the cultural, social, and legal understanding of rape that characterized the United States in 1985 and 1986. Rape-shield laws, for instance, had been adopted by many American jurisdictions in the late 1970s and early 1980s, but their enforcement wavered. Their presence did not banish sexist presumptions that a rape victim's appearance, dress, and previous sexual behavior might mitigate the perpetrator's culpability, as bell hooks notes when mentioning that some *She's Gotta Have It* viewers fail to consider Jamie's assault to be rape. Lee was less sensitive to victims of sexual assault during the 1980s than later observers might prefer, but he is able, thanks to the perspective afforded by twenty years of growth as a person and as an artist, to recognize that his handling of Nola's rape is *She's Gotta Have It*'s greatest failing.

Yet even this viewpoint is open to challenge. Ed Guerrero, in *Framing Blackness*, defends *She's Gotta Have It*'s rape scene as more mature than Lee or his critics realize. Calling Jamie's assault "frank and brutal," Guerrero nonetheless cautions that it "cannot be read literally, solely, as a crude celebration of black male chauvinism."[62] Guerrero credits the scene as challenging the

socioeconomic assumptions about sex, desire, and violence that characterize classical Hollywood style: "The scene works against the staid Hollywood
convention of depicting rape à la *Straw Dogs* (1971) as officially bad and
simultaneously a titillating spectacle for male enjoyment. Opposed to the
dominant 'look,' the scene comes off as dialectically shocking, discomfort-
ing because of the issues it raises for the entire audience."[63] This judgment
correctly assesses the scene as shot. Nola does not experience pleasure during
Jamie's assault, so, far from being either sexy or titillating, the scene permits
contradictory responses, ranging from disgust to approval, in the movie's
viewers. Guerrero also persuasively discusses the rape's class implications as
destroying patriarchy's power over Nola (and, implicitly, *She's Gotta Have It*'s
audience): "Moreover, it works . . . to discredit Jamie and his black bourgeois
patriarchal values by revealing his inability to accept Nola as an independent
woman, free of his masculine projections and class expectations. Thus the
rape scene shatters the illusory spell of middle-class patriarchy at the center
of the narrative."[64] Guerrero shrewdly perceives how Jamie's bourgeois attitudes, particularly his dismay at Nola's rejection of monogamy, define her as
a stereotypical male fantasy, one that covets uninhibited female sexual desire,
yet abhors the power to resist, reduce, and renounce male dominance that
such desire grants women. The need to affirm patriarchal control of female
sexuality requires Nola's diminishment, even debasement, if she is to become
an acceptable long-term partner. Her rape, considered in this light, enacts the
class concerns that Guerrero discusses.

Nola's assault also provides somber counterpoint to *She's Gotta Have It*'s
earlier, achingly funny "dog sequence," which Guerrero believes has sociopolitical resonances: "The film jump-cuts to a long montage of black men
framed in frontal medium shots, mugging for the camera and delivering lines
as predictable and stale as they are hilarious: 'Baby I'd drink a tub of your
bathwater.' The political point is clear, as a kind of reflex, one-dimensional
black male chauvinism is ridiculed."[65] Guerrero fails to mention the most
outrageous pick-up lines uttered by "the dogs," as Lee's screenplay dubs
them (played by, among others, *She's Gotta Have It*'s producer Monty Ross,
cinematographer Ernest Dickerson, and *House Party* director Reginald Hudlin), including "Congress has just approved me to give you my heat- and
moisture-seeking MX missile" and "Girl, I got plenty of what you need:
ten throbbing inches of USDA, government-inspected, prime-cut Grade
A tubesteak!" These comments objectify women as either empty targets or
hungry carnivores searching, per Michele Wallace, for "the old phallus."
Nola rejects these weak come-ons in favor of Jamie's more authentic approach when, after following her down a Brooklyn street, he says, "Nola, I
don't want to chance not seeing you again. Whatever you wanna do, I'll do.
Wherever you wanna go, I'll take you. Will you see me?" Jamie does not seem
solely interested in sex, which suggests that Nola is not, either, despite her
liberated sensibility.

Nola's rejection of Jamie after he rapes her, therefore, demonstrates that she is not the vacuous character that Stanley Crouch, Donald Bogle, and other observers suggest.[66] She disdains Jamie's middle-class need for the "girl next door" as traditional patriarchy's most common fantasy, seeking to trap her in unequal monogamy. Nola's question-filled final monologue may tenuously sever her ties to Jamie, but she articulates (uncertainly and imprecisely, to be sure) that control over her body and mind is primary. Nola, refusing to become Jamie's prize, never truly deals with his sexual assault despite claiming her own power. The viewer, as a result, watches Nola, in *She's Gotta Have It*'s waning moments, strive to define her identity beyond "living the joy of sex" (in Harris and Moffitt's evocative phrase) to encompass a nascent feminism that includes, but does not restrict itself to, sexual passion. This project remains unresolved, refusing the transcendent victory that bell hooks craves, but the movie's story of a young woman struggling with her own agency is more believable for it.

Lee, who once considered making Nola Darling a resident of *Do the Right Thing*'s Bedford-Stuyvesant block, briefly returns to the character in *Red Hook Summer* (2012) to show Nola, twenty-six years after her cinematic debut, as a fervent Jehovah's Witness who preaches her faith in the Red Hook housing project that she now calls home. No mention of Nola's previous career or lovers is heard, but the film's protagonist, Bishop Enoch Rouse (Clarke Peters) of the Lil' Peace of Heaven Baptist Church, tells his grandson, Silas "Flik" Royale (Jules Brown), that Nola, now known as Mother Darling, saw her son die of AIDS. This tragedy, Rouse implies, spurred Nola's religious conversion and a visible somberness that she conceals with warmth and affection when talking to her neighbors. Nola even demonstrates a hint of her former playfulness when, in a scene that recalls her interactions with Mars in *She's Gotta Have It,* she takes Flik's face in her hands and comments how handsome he is. Nola does not mention her previous life, or even if she ever married, but Tracy Camilla Johns plays the character as a person dedicated to her faith in the same way she once pursued a life of free-spirited pleasure. *Red Hook Summer* suggests that Nola was not as ambivalent as her final *She's Gotta Have It* confession implies, demonstrating that Lee's first movie empathizes with her even if *Red Hook Summer* illustrates that the younger Nola was a confused woman who allowed the men in her life to define her as much as she defined herself.

She's Gotta Have It, therefore, deserves more credit than it sometimes receives. Terry McMillan, discussing the "dog sequence," writes, "Spike Lee was working this from the inside, and I appreciated that."[67] This judgment aptly describes the film's satirical exploration of American patriarchy's absurdist fears about female sexual independence, but does not apply to Nola's sometimes marginalized and underdeveloped character. Her words may frame *She's Gotta Have It*'s narrative, but her male lovers speak in the loudest voices. Nola's psychological depth is, finally, secondary to the film constructed around her. This drawback marks *She's Gotta Have It* as a fascinating, funny, and flawed exploration of mid-1980s American sexuality that Lee continues in his more technically ambitious second feature, *School Daze.*

CAMPUS POLITICS

Lee began thinking about *School Daze* even before beginning production on *She's Gotta Have It.* The October 9, 1984, entry of Lee's *She's Gotta Have It* production diary lists rewriting and tightening the in-progress script for *It's Homecoming* (the film's original title) as one of Lee's tasks to accomplish during the winter months.[68] He refers to *Homecoming* again, two days later (October 11, 1984), as an ongoing project,[69] while the December 21, 1984, entry states that, while attending a taping of *The Cosby Show* with his friend (and future editor) Barry Brown, he saw actress (and former Miss America) Vanessa Williams, who, Lee feels, could capably assume the role of Jane Touissant, the character played by Tisha Campbell in the final film.[70] Bill Lee, the writer-director's father (and the composer of *She's Gotta Have It, School Daze, Do the Right Thing,* and *Mo' Better Blues*), notes in *Uplift the Race: The Construction of "School Daze"* (the movie's companion publication) that the idea for Lee's second film predated *She's Gotta Have It:* "Spike and I weren't aware of it at the time, but we were simultaneously writing about our experiences at Morehouse College. I was starting my eighth opera, *Colored College,* at the same time that Spike was writing *Homecoming,* the script that later became *School Daze.*"[71]

Lee's original screenplay was much different from the produced film, with *That's My Story and I'm Sticking to It* revealing that the original plot, of Mission College trying to prevent "being absorbed into the large majority-white state university," became a story "looking at how students at Mission were politically divided along interracial lines over the school's investments in apartheid South Africa."[72] Giancarlo Esposito, who plays Julian "Big Brother Almighty" Eaves (imperious leader of the Gamma Phi Gamma fraternity) in *School Daze,* confirms that Lee heavily revised the script, saying that the movie, unlike John Landis's "silly" *Animal House,* dealt with more difficult issues in a story that was not at first a musical, but rather "a film with music in it. Spike kept working on the piece over six or seven months, streamlining it from the original 175-page script."[73] Esposito not only rejects the easy comparisons with *Animal House* that Desson Howe and Rita Kempley make in their *School Daze* reviews but also notes that the film's debt to movie musicals evolved over time. Esposito also correctly judges *School Daze* as more intellectually and politically ambitious than *Animal House.* The final screenplay, according to Esposito, examines "the relationship between African American males and females, and friendships and moral values that are hazy in the African American community."[74]

Esposito's intelligent assessment, however, overlooks *School Daze*'s difficult gender politics and regrettable homophobia. Set at Mission College during homecoming weekend, Lee's second film deserves tremendous credit for criticizing American academia's—and particularly historically black colleges'—history of supporting South Africa's apartheid regime through investments in that nation's corporations and government, as well as for courageously dramatizing the colorism that divides Mission College's campus. The film's female characters, indeed, fall into two groups: the "Wannabees," lighter-skinned African American women who straighten their hair and wear contact lenses in the belief that such changes, by conforming to European standards of beauty, make them more attractive, and the "Jigaboos," who feel that their darker skin tones, brown eyes, and curly hair are more natural and, therefore, authentically attractive. *School Daze,* by rewriting the Hollywood movie musical's sedate conventions to satirize color, class, and economic divisions within Mission College's all-black student body, also becomes a prime example of Lee's cinematic intertexuality and stylistic complexity. The movie makes little effort to smooth its sometimes jarring generic mixtures, in which solemn discussions of campus politics worthy of serious drama, silly confrontations among the male students reminiscent of adolescent campus comedies, and musical set pieces tangentially related to the dominant storyline that recall MGM musicals of the 1940s and 1950s pile atop one another in what Rita Kempley calls a "patchwork plot." Even more noticeable is *School Daze*'s abrupt editing, which cuts to the next scene or musical number before what seems the prior scene's (or sequence's) appropriate end. The film's stylized cinematography and set design range from realistically rendered dorm rooms lit in naturalistic fashion to exaggerated sets like Madame Re-Re's beauty salon, which cinematographer Ernest Dickerson lights in rich primary colors (particularly deep reds and oranges) during the film's cheekily titled musical number "Good and Bad Hair" (originally titled, as *Uplift the Race* reveals, "Straight and Nappy"). These apparent contradictions, far from being evidence of *School Daze*'s shoddy production values, reject classical Hollywood style's seamless fluidity to notify the viewer that Lee pursues an overt political project that earlier campus comedies, movie musicals, and college dramas rarely achieve.

The film's changing registers, tones, genres, and modes frustrate audiences expecting a single, coherent storyline with smooth transitions, invisible editing, and unified themes. Donald Bogle summarizes *School Daze*'s initial critical reaction well in *Toms, Coons, Mulattoes, Mammies, & Bucks: An Interpretive History of Blacks in American Films* by contrasting his own assessment with mainstream reactions to Lee's second movie:

Despite the flaws—its canvas was so broad that it failed to cover any of its subjects with enough detail and as many women pointed out, its female characters were vapid, dimensionless sisters caught up mainly in men—*School Daze* nonetheless remained an uncompromising black film. It refused to make concessions to please a white audience. Indeed white critics seemed bewildered by it.[75]

Bogle's evaluation of *School Daze* is intelligent, even if his final comment overlooks Roger Ebert's laudatory review in the *Chicago Sun-Times'* February 12, 1988, edition. Ebert begins by writing that *School Daze* "is the first movie in a long time where the black characters seem to be relating to one another, instead of to a hypothetical white audience," noting that the film's structural deficiencies cannot alter the fact that "there was never a moment when it didn't absorb me, because I felt as if I was watching the characters talk to one another, instead of to me."[76] Observing that *School Daze* "confronts a lot of issues that aren't talked about in the movies these days: not only issues of skin color and hair, but also the emergence of a black class, the purpose of all-black universities in an integrated society, and the sometimes sexist treatment of black women by black men," Ebert praises Lee for "just sort of assum[ing] a completely black orientation for his film" that includes "no self-conscious references to blackness. The result is an entertaining comedy, but also much more than that. There is no doubt in my mind that *School Daze*, in its own way, is one of the most honest and revealing movies I've ever seen about modern middle-class black life in America."[77]

Ebert recognizes *School Daze*'s crucial qualities, pinpointing issues of color and class as integral to the film's effect. Lee's third-draft script—dated January 1, 1987, and included in *Uplift the Race*—includes a note (dated September 14, 1986) certifying this perspective: "The student body is divided into two factions: the Haves and the Have-Nots. This division is based upon class and color. . . . It's the WANNABEES VS. THE JIGS!!! Wanna Be White and Jigaboos. Remember, it's about class and color."[78] Ebert also underscores how unusual *School Daze* is for raising such issues, leading some critics and viewers to dislike the film for, as Lee says in *That's My Story and I'm Sticking to It*, "airing dirty laundry"[79] about African American life. Lee reveals in *Uplift the Race* that, just before filming was to commence at his alma mater, Atlanta, Georgia's Morehouse College (the clear inspiration for Mission College), the school's administration (led by its president, Dr. Hugh Gloster), refused permission to shoot there because "they feared that *School Daze* would portray a negative (shit, that word again) image of Black colleges, and more importantly of Black people as a whole."[80] As Ronald Jemal Stephens recalls in "The Aesthetics of *Nommo* in the Films of Spike Lee," even "Bryant Gumbel of NBC expressed disapproval of *School Daze* because it was a case of Spike airing 'Black folks' dirty laundry.'"[81] Lee's weariness at fending off charges of negative portrayals leads him, in *Uplift the Race*, to indict the "'negative image' trap that's set for Black artists. Yes, Black people have been dogged in the media from day one. We're extrasensitive and we have every right to be. But we overreact when we think that every image of us has to be 100 percent angelic—Christ-like even."[82] *School Daze*, per Lee's intentions, declines to sanitize intraracial tensions about skin color, apartheid, and socioeconomic class despite its comic touches.

Ebert's perspective, unlike many scholars and reviewers, credits *School Daze* with commendable nuance to demonstrate that not everyone objects to what Michele Wallace, in "Spike Lee and Black Women," calls "the film's animated pastiche of classic homecoming-football-game movies; slapstick humor and sight gags; Motown and Busby Berkeley production numbers; jazz, R&B, and funk performance; black English, style, and dance."[83] Wallace also connects *School Daze* to its literary forbears by noticing that Lee's movie "takes on a scene that is already familiar to readers of the canon of Afro-American literature. It's the black college campus of Booker T. Washington's *Up from Slavery*, W.E.B. Du Bois's *The Souls of Black Folk*, Jean Toomer's *Cane*, Ralph Ellison's *Invisible Man*, Amiri Baraka's *Tales*,"[84] but recognizes that these allusions cannot compete with the film's energetic cinematic effects. *School Daze*'s filmic and literary allusiveness, however, stresses its native intertexuality to illustrate Lee's affection for earlier movies and books that echo his film's predominant concerns.

MEN AT PLAY

Any acclaim that *School Daze* receives, however, pales in comparison to the charges of sexism and homophobia made against the movie since its original release. Wallace finds the political project that so concerns protagonist Dap Dunlap (Laurence Fishburne, credited as Larry Fishburne)—forcing Mission College to stop funding apartheid South Africa's government and corporations—to be a MacGuffin that masks Lee's true focus: "While the film halfheartedly focuses on a conflict between students and administration over whether black Mission College should divest from South Africa, its obsession is with gender and sexuality," leading the audience "to witness entirely distinct male and female versions of a contest between light-skinned, affluent Wannabees and dark-skinned, nappy-haired, lower-class Jigaboos."[85] Dap, indeed, stops preaching against apartheid as more personal concerns—his relationship with girlfriend Rachel (Kyme) and his cousin Half Pint's (Spike Lee) desire to join Julian Eaves's Gamma Phi Gamma fraternity—overtake him. As Richard A. Blake pronounces in *Street Smart*, "Dap proves to be a half-hearted revolutionary"[86] whose friends, collectively known as Da Fellas, refuse to jeopardize their education and future careers by pursuing overtly political projects, preferring to joke about women when not pursuing them. "Under Dap's leadership," Blake writes, "they are willing to fight for their cause, but not at the risk of their personal security."[87]

The color, class, and gender divisions that Wallace identifies as *School Daze*'s major subject lead Wahneema Lubiano, in one of the most significant articles ever published about Lee's filmography, "But Compared to

What?: Reading Realism, Representation, and Essentialism in *School Daze*, *Do the Right Thing*, and the Spike Lee Discourse," to declare, "Although *Do the Right Thing* received far more positive press than *School Daze*, perhaps because its working-class subjects seemed more 'authentic' to critics than the middle-class subjects of *School Daze*, I contend that *School Daze* is the more complicated movie" even though Lee's second feature is "masculinist," as well as "explicitly and viciously homophobic."[88] Lubiano contests the uncritical tendency of film reviewers and scholars to praise Lee's movies for their realistic portrayals of black characters because "realism as the bedrock of narrative is inherently problematic. Realism poses a fundamental, longstanding challenge for counter-hegemonic discourses, since realism, as a narrative form, enforces an authoritarian perspective."[89] Lubiano disputes the claims to unbiased truth that literary and cinematic realism make because "realism establishes a claim to truth, but it also presents the ground for its own deconstruction—somebody else's truth. . . . 'Reality' is promiscuous, at the very least."[90] Lubiano's complicated argument about realism, based on work by Raymond Williams, Suzette Elgin, Kobena Mercer, and Coco Fusco,[91] attends to larger theoretical issues at play in Lee's movies, but helps viewers understand how *School Daze* develops a seemingly authentic portrait of black campus life—by creating African American characters who (to adopt Ebert's view) make no concessions to white audiences—while its narrative, generic, and stylistic deformations disrupt the realistic effects that classical Hollywood cinema pursues.

School Daze, considered in this vein, is not a realistic film, as the intrusion of "Good and Bad Hair" (occurring after the Wannabees and Jigaboos argue in a dormitory common room) makes clear. The abrupt transition from the dorm's quotidian appearance to Madame Re-Re's beauty salon, with the women continuing their competition by singing and dancing while dressed in athletic jerseys, parodies the pettiness of their disagreement even while celebrating the movie's willingness to dramatize conflicts among black characters that rarely make it to American movie screens. Yet, as Lubiano argues, the film, "unfortunately and myopically, presents aesthetics as formal matters of physical appearance in which women only participate."[92] *School Daze*, in other words, relegates its female characters to being satellites of men like Dap. Rachel seems to break this marginalization when she comments that Dap dates her as much for her dark complexion as her personality, but cannot sustain this criticism until the end of the scene, instead revealing that she wishes to join the Gamma Ray sorority led by Jane Touissant, so-called queen of the Wannabees. Rachel, moreover, never articulates a reason for joining the Gamma Rays beyond desiring the false community that Dap identifies as the collegiate Greek system's largest lie. Rather than repudiating Dap's perspective, Rachel weakly states that the Gamma Rays do good work in the neighborhood surrounding Mission College (never, however, specifying what this work is) before accusing him of perpetuating the same colorism that his arguments about unifying the student body around South African divestment criticize. Rachel's subplot (or mini-plot, since it occupies only this scene) is forgotten as *School Daze*'s episodic narrative moves to another vignette. She soon forgives Dunlap, taking him to bed, to illustrate how the film relentlessly endorses male privilege.

Toni Cade Bambara, in "Programming with *School Daze*" (an essay first published in *Five for Five*), compliments the film as "a good-looking, ambitiously mounted, imaginatively designed production characterized by a bold mix of both dance and musical idioms and performatory and acting styles"[93] telling disparate stories that "make useful points about intracommunity contradictions."[94] The film nevertheless disappoints Bambara because its "agenda to make a wake-up call is undermined by its misogynistic and gay-hating sensibility."[95] Bambara's final point has merit since *School Daze*'s homophobia appears in numerous places, including Julian Eaves's repeated exhortation that "only a Gamma man is a real man,"[96] his constant hectoring of Half Pint as a "pussy" and a "loser," and his assertions that Half Pint's sexual inexperience reflects homosexual desire. The most disturbing display of antigay discourse, however, comes during the homecoming rally's step show, wherein Gamma Phi's members and pledges perform a complicated, human-chain dance only to see Da Fellas, led by Dap Dunlap, overtake them with a call-and-response routine whose refrain is, "When I say Gamma, you say fag! Gamma, fag! Gamma, fag! When I say Gamma, you say fag! Gamma, Gamma, Gamma, Gamma! Fag, fag, fag, fag!" This impromptu production number's immaturity demonstrates that Dunlap's political commitment does not encompass gay rights, allowing Lee, in his DVD audio commentary, to note that such homophobia was unfortunately prevalent during his time at Morehouse College. Lee claims that the antigay attitudes exhibited by *School Daze*'s male characters realistically depict the unfortunate behavior of mid-1980s college students, stressing at many points that they reflect neither his nor the movie's overarching political beliefs. The sheer joy that Da Fellas take in demeaning the Gamma Phi Gamma men as "fags," however, to say nothing of the crowd's enthusiastic response, praises this homophobic chant. Lee's defense, in this context, is little more than the warmed-over cliché that "boys will be boys," thereby ignoring how the step routine's prominence within *School Daze* authorizes (perhaps unconsciously) the homophobic slurs that Da Fellas hurl at their rivals.

Disturbing as the movie's homophobia may be, its sexism is even more pronounced. S. Craig Watkins addresses *School Daze*'s chauvinistic attitude in *Representing: Hip Hop Culture and the Production of Black Cinema* by writing, "the spheres of conflict and scenarios that dramatize the dynamic struggles and divisions within the African American community are imaginatively figured, by Lee, as the dominion of men. Lee's cinematic portrayal of the black American social world elides the voices of black women."[97] Watkins, who argues that *School Daze*'s characters should "not be read as realistic figures but rather as animated constructs that mobilize and put on display certain values (individualism) as well as certain ideological discourses (patriarchy),"[98] nonetheless finds that Lee offers "a sharper critique of the class differences *within* the African American community that operate as a constant source of conflict prohibiting a monolithic experience based simply on race."[99] The female characters, except for "Good and Bad Hair," peripherally dramatize the clash of values and ideologies that Watkins finds in *School Daze*, while their class differences, as Toni Cade Bambara notes, are visually coded (by eye color, skin color, hair style, and dress) rather than discussed in political protests and dormitory bull sessions.

School Daze's women, for instance, have no parallel sequence to the confrontation between Da Fellas and several working-class black men at a local Kentucky Fried Chicken franchise that explores issues of class as honestly as any scene in the movie. The men, dubbed "Local Yokels" in Lee's screenplay and the closing credits, angrily accuse Dap and his college friends of looking down at them despite the fact that the Yokels have lived in the neighborhood all their lives. The lead Yokel, appropriately named Leeds (Samuel L. Jackson, credited as Sam Jackson), offers this accusation: "I'll bet you niggers do think y'all white. College don't mean shit. Y'all niggers, and you gonna be niggers forever, just like us!" Dap, saddened by this perspective, says, "You're not niggers" before backing away to defuse the tension. This powerful scene links education to race and class, revealing how socioeconomic fissures within black America fuel anger, resentment, and self-hatred. It also reprises the movie's antigay discourse when Leeds addresses Da Fellas in a high-pitched, stereotypically gay voice, asking "Is it true what they say about Mission men?," only to see Jordan (Branford Marsalis), one of Dap's friends, later comment that the shower cap that Leeds wears over his Jheri curls makes him look "like a fuckin' bitch." The primary way to diminish another man in *School Daze*, this scene confirms, is to link him to the perceived weakness of women and gay men by accusing him of effeminacy.

School Daze's sexism does not surprise Watkins, who observes, "In reality, the cinema is a male-dominated sphere of cultural production. Traditionally, women have been relegated to the role of sexualized object, although more women are challenging the gender hierarchies that structure film production."[100] The movie's women, however, rarely confront their college campus's sexist presumptions, leading to two competing scenes that illustrate just how ambiguous Lee's gender politics are. Both involve Half Pint, but they move in opposite directions.

The first scene is Lee's witty reversal of *She's Gotta Have It*'s dog sequence, in which Half Pint searches for a homecoming date. He does so at the insistence of Julian Eaves, who, in typically belligerent fashion, commands Half Pint to prove his manhood: "You better get a freak over here tonight. . . . I don't care if she's blind, fat, no teeth, one leg in a kickstand. I ain't pledging no virgins." This misogynistic outburst causes Half Pint to visit Flemister Hall to ask Perry, Muriel, Carla, and Roz (played, respectively, by Kasi Lemons, Toni Ann Johnson, Paula Birth, and Tracy Robinson) to accompany him for the evening. Each woman directly faces the camera while speaking, but the scene jump cuts through their increasingly hostile reactions, which culminate with Carla saying, "All you guys are dogs" and Roz telling Half Pint, "And you're so small, I'd probably break you in two." Lee structures Half Pint's humiliation as a response to the sexist one liners of *She's Gotta Have It*'s dog sequence, allowing *School Daze*'s women, unlike Nola Darling, to answer these pick-up lines. This intertextual nod to Lee's earlier film is just as funny as the dog sequence not only because each actress delivers her character's lines with sharp-tongued precision but also because all four deride a character played by Spike Lee. This choice suggests that Lee, aware of *She's Gotta Have It*'s cool reception among some feminist viewers, allows his second film's female characters to criticize him in the most direct fashion possible: to his face. This choice supports Watkins's observation that, although Lee "has not been as sensitive to the ways in which the commercial film industry also frames gender and sexuality," Lee, "unlike other filmmakers . . . has not been detached from this criticism. The filmmaker's loose affiliation with the world of scholarly and cultural criticism has compelled him, for example, to reconsider his representation of gender."[101]

The shaming of Half Pint by four women demonstrates that Lee accepted certain objections to his gender politics between making *She's Gotta Have It* and *School Daze*. The director, indeed, admits to *Rolling Stone* writer David Breskin, in their extensive interview reprinted in *Inner Views: Filmmakers in Conversation*, "I think the best criticism I've read has been about my female characters. You know, that was on the mark."[102] Yet *School Daze* owes another debt to its predecessor by including a scene as disturbing as Nola's assault in *She's Gotta Have It*. Julian Eaves manipulates Jane Toussaint into sleeping with Half Pint (as the final stage of Half Pint's fraternity initiation) by stressing that doing so will prove her devotion to Julian and to the Gamma Phi Gamma fraternity. When Jane reluctantly complies, Half Pint, who has been instructed by Julian to "wear her out like a natural Gamma man," tells the crying Jane that she need not have sex with him. Jane's response is terse: "Shut up and get undressed." Tisha Campbell plays this moment as one of simultaneous sadness, betrayal, and anger to reflect how lost her character feels.

The worst experience, however, happens after Jane and Half Pint leave what Lee's screenplay names the "Bone Room."[103] The Gamma Phi members, who have stood watch outside the bedroom, surround Half Pint to congratulate him about his conquest, but Julian soon accuses Jane of cheating on him with a fraternity brother. This reversal so distresses Jane that, hurt and confused, she can only ask, "Why are you doing this to me? Why are you doing this to me?" Jane's grief is so palpable and so well performed by Tisha Campbell that Roger Ebert, in his review, accurately observes, "although the scene was so painful it was difficult to watch, I later reflected that Lee played it for the pain, not the kind of smutty comedy we might expect in a movie about undergraduates."[104] *School Daze* may not endorse Julian's misogynistic behavior, but Jane receives no additional screen time to resolve, to process, or even to discuss her torn feelings. She is left crying, only to reappear briefly in the film's final scene, when Dap Dunlap runs across campus exhorting every person to "Waaake Upppp!" The film, in other words, depicts appalling sexist behavior by its male characters, but diminishes its female protagonist in a way that *She's Gotta Have It* does not. Lee's earlier movie gives Nola Darling the last word, helping to repudiate the misogyny of Jamie Overstreet's rape even if Nola's comments only tentatively establish her personal agency. *School Daze,* by contrast, removes all power from Jane Toussaint by leaving her mute.

Toni Cade Bambara is therefore correct to note, "Gender issues receive no better treatment in *Daze* than in usual commercial fare. But the possibility, and perhaps the intent, were present."[105] Even so, Bambara observes that the frat brothers' "presence outside the door and their readiness to go in and 'check out how Half-Pint's doing' are suggestive enough of gang rape."[106] Lee's film, in the end, fails to liberate its male characters from their sexist mind-sets or its female characters from public, private, and institutional patriarchy. Although Dap Dunlap rejects Half Pint when the latter proudly tells him about sleeping with Jane, in the process rejecting Julian as this sordid event's instigator, Dap still "welcomes Julian into the inner circle of the final wake-up call in the film"[107] to overlook, in Bambara's opinion, Julian's dreadful behavior. *School Daze,* as such, dramatizes sexist behavior rather than interrogating it. Lee's film, while undoubtedly a more serious treatment of campus patriarchy than *Animal House,* adopts an ambivalent outlook that evades, rather than explores, the difficulties raised by its sexist stance.

WAKE-UP CALLS

The conflicting reception of *She's Gotta Have It* and *School Daze* might suggest that Spike Lee's first two feature films are intriguing precursors to his later, more mature work that cannot match the power of *Do the Right Thing, Malcolm X, Bamboozled, 25th Hour,* and *Inside Man.* This judgment, however, ignores their narrative, generic, and aesthetic inventiveness. Lee, from the beginning of his cinematic career, tells stylized stories about African American characters that neither rely upon nor cater to white expectations. As such, each movie handles political discourse differently: *She's Gotta Have It*'s subdued approach privileges Nola Darling's sexual exploits over her political sympathies (which are indicated by the mural/collage she paints in her loft apartment dedicated to Malcolm X and the victims of New York Police Department brutality such as Eleanor Bumpers and Edmund Perry), while *School Daze* directly tackles colorism, socioeconomic class, and South

African divestment without resolving these issues. Lee seeks to portray African American characters from the inside (so to speak) to demonstrate their diverse, rich, and multivalent lives.

Lee succeeds more often than he fails in *She's Gotta Have It* and *School Daze*, although the scholarly conversation about these movies examines recurring problems with his portrayal of straight women, lesbians, and gay men. Lee's preference for ambivalent conclusions also diminishes his cinematic credibility to proponents of classical Hollywood style, who prefer definitive resolutions. Yet, as Gladstone L. Yearwood suggests, evaluating the movies of black filmmakers against this restrictive standard not only misunderstands their goals but also subjects them to unfair charges of narrative, visual, and technical incompetence. Lee demonstrates with *She's Gotta Have It* and *School Daze* that his keen knowledge of Hollywood moviemaking cannot prevent his films from violating the principles of classical Hollywood cinema when he deems it necessary.

Lee aims in both movies to accomplish what Dap Dunlap attempts in *School Daze*'s closing sequence: to wake up viewers to the different textures of middle-class African American life while not remaining complacent about the challenges that black Americans face. Dap himself voices this final point when confronted by Mission College's president McPherson (Joe Seneca) and Cedar Cloud (Art Evans), chairman of its Board of Trustees, about his tactics in organizing campus protest rallies. Dap is unimpressed by McPherson's and Cloud's personal roles in the Civil Rights Movement: "So what? You marched with King in the sixties. Big deal. That was over twenty years ago. Black people still catching hell all over the world, you know." When McPherson points out that progress has occurred, Dap responds by asking, "Says who?" This short interaction's intergenerational conflict embodies the project of Lee's first two films: melding the personal, political, and historical concerns of African American characters into entertaining portraits that refuse to depict black Americans as monolithic. Lee pursues this goal by mixing generic conventions, visual styles, and narrative strategies to produce movies that make no attempt to tie up loose ends: Nola Darling, in *She's Gotta Have It*, claims her own agency, but isolates herself from the outside world to do so, while Dap Dunlap, having awakened Mission College's entire administration and student body the morning after homecoming, looks into the camera and urges the viewer to "Please wake up" as an alarm clock rings.

These open-ended finales reject happy Hollywood conclusions in favor of more difficult, less satisfying portraits of black America. Lee's critics fault him for inconsistency, particularly in terms of each film's political message, while his refusal to reject Hollywood cinema's patriarchal assumptions permits troublingly sexist and homophobic messages to circulate in both movies. Lee, indeed, has pronounced *She's Gotta Have It* to be the one film that he can no longer watch, due not only to its immature handling of Nola Darling's rape but also to poor acting. In "Five for Five," his introduction to *Five for Five: The Films of Spike Lee,* the director states that *She's Gotta Have It* "is the one I don't, can't, and refuse to watch. Why, you ask? It's because of the filmmaking and the performances," then expands this criticism by writing, "You have to understand that when you see poor performances in a film, it's always the director's fault, for at least one of two reasons: Number one: He or she wasn't directing, so the actors were left to fend for themselves; actors need direction. Number two: The actors were miscast."[108] Lee does not say which option explains his distaste for *She's Gotta Have It,* but his later diplomatic statement, "I feel the director has to take the blame, and on *She's Gotta,* I was obviously still learning how to work with actors"[109] implies that he paid less attention to the film's cast members than they deserved. Lee's perspective here, although understandable for a moviemaker retrospectively evaluating his inaugural film, is unfair. *She's Gotta Have It* features good work from its major cast members, especially Tracy Camilla Johns, who cleverly sketches Nola Darling's nuances in a naturalistic and (considering the amount of on-screen nudity) fearless performance. Nola's reactions during Thanksgiving dinner, along with her opening and closing monologues, are adeptly played by Johns, while Tommy Redmond Hicks's alternately sweet, stern, and abusive performance as Jamie Overstreet testifies to the movie's good acting. The film is so full of humor, warmth, and wit (thanks in part to Lee's funny turn as Mars Blackmon) that the director's judgment, on this score, is skewed.

These last points indicate that *She's Gotta Have It* and *School Daze* are valuable films in their own right, not simple forerunners of Lee's later, better known, and more accomplished movies. They remain fascinating, provocative, and problematic films, which does not forgive their sexist and homophobic impulses. Lee's earliest movies, as such, mark narrative, visual, and political pathways that his later films will follow, for good and for ill, making *She's Gotta Have It* and *School Daze* rewarding, if imperfect, maiden efforts. Their drawbacks are as intriguing as their advantages, demonstrating that Spike Lee, from his earliest movies, challenges rather than comforts his audiences in a pattern that characterizes his professional life.

2

The Right Stuff

CRITICAL CONDITIONS

Do the Right Thing, in the quarter century since its 1989 theatrical release, has become Spike Lee's best-known, best-remembered, and best-regarded feature film. So much mainstream and scholarly commentary about Lee's third movie exists that confronting this extensive material exposes the reader to an onslaught of differing opinions, responses, and analyses that testify to *Do the Right Thing*'s now-central status, both within Lee's filmography and within American cinema. The American Film Institute, for instance, includes *Do the Right Thing* in its "100 Years . . . 100 Movies" list of the best American films produced during the twentieth century,[1] the British Film Institute's *Sight and Sound* Critics' Poll places *Do the Right Thing* as the 127th-best movie out of 250 international films (tied in this ranking with sixteen other movies, including François Truffaut's *Jules et Jim* and Quentin Tarantino's *Pulp Fiction*),[2] the National Society of Film Critics cites *Do the Right Thing* on its unranked "100 Essential Films" list,[3] the *New York Times* considers *Do the Right Thing* one of the "Best 1,000 Movies Ever Made,"[4] and, in a 1999 decision that secures *Do the Right Thing*'s status as a significant American artwork, the National Film Preservation Board placed it in the United States National Film Registry.[5] The movie's numerous academic citations, to take another measure, indicate *Do the Right Thing*'s importance to film, media, and literary scholars. These honors form a general consensus, particularly advanced by popular-press observers, that *Do the Right Thing* is Lee's earliest (and perhaps only) masterpiece.

The mixed reviews that attended the film's opening, therefore, may surprise viewers accustomed to hearing *Do the Right Thing* praised not merely as Lee's best movie, but as perhaps the greatest feature film ever made about American race relations. W.J.T. Mitchell, in his perceptive essay "The Violence of Public Art: *Do the Right Thing*," comments upon the curious effect that the film's ascent to classic status produces in Lee's moviemaking career: "One of the interesting developments in the later reception of *DRT* has been its rapid canonization as Spike Lee's 'masterpiece.' Critics who trashed the film in 1989 now use it as an example of his best, most authentic work in order to trash his later films (most notably *Malcolm X*)."[6] This outcome, among many crucial observations in Mitchell's article, indicates just how contested *Do the Right Thing* was upon its release. Lee's movie, indeed, became a lightning rod for criticism not only of its filmmaker's supposed political opportunism but also of the difficult state of race relations in New York City (and, by extension, the United States). Mitchell may be among *Do the Right Thing*'s finest academic analysts, but the initial mainstream response to Lee's movie illuminates the racial animus that afflicted even educated (and supposedly enlightened) popular-press critics.

David Denby, for instance, concludes "He's Gotta Have It," his June 26, 1989, *New York Magazine* review of *Do the Right Thing*, by stating, "If an artist has made his choices and settled on a coherent point of view, he shouldn't be held responsible, I believe, if parts of his audience misunderstand him. He should be free to be 'dangerous.' But Lee hasn't worked coherently. The end of this movie is a shambles, and if some audiences go wild, he's partly responsible."[7] Privileging narrative coherence, however, is a serious misreading of Lee's stylized, ever-changing film. The writer-director structures *Do the Right Thing* as a series of genial vignettes about the downtrodden residents of a single Bedford-Stuyvesant block who, on the hottest day of the summer, see their polyglot lives descend into racial conflagration. Moreover, Denby's suggestion that certain audiences might "go wild" is, as Lee himself points out in numerous articles and interviews,[8] racially coded language that presumes younger black viewers will become violent after watching the movie's conclusion, in which New York City Police Department officers murder a young African American man named Radio Raheem (Bill Nunn). This callous action provokes the destruction of the movie's principal location, Sal's Famous Pizzeria, by the block's furious African American and Latino residents. Denby's incoherent perspective identifies *Do the Right Thing* as an unrealistic story whose messy, violent ending is nonetheless so authentic that "some audiences" (read: black teenagers) may recapitulate its rage.

Denby's review, despite these problems, cannot fully dismiss *Do the Right Thing*. It admires the film's well-crafted visuals by commending Ernest Dickerson's cinematography and applauds the story's comic touches by declaring, "the first three quarters of the movie has the jumping vitality and buoyant, light touch of a good musical."[9] Denby finds *Do the Right Thing* to be significantly better than *School Daze*, but still condemns *Do the Right Thing*'s urban naïveté: "Lee's version of a poor neighborhood is considerably sanitized, without rampaging teenagers, muggers, or crack addicts."[10] Denby speciously assumes that most poor New York City neighborhoods are crime-infested dystopias beset by out-of-control young people, meaning that accurate fictional representations of these places require Lee to include elements that *Do the Right Thing* omits. Denby, under the guise of correcting Lee's skewed vision, perpetuates racial stereotypes about economically depressed communities of color that not only pervaded late-1980s New York City but also reveal his unthinking (or uncaring) prejudices.

New York Magazine's political reporter, Joe Klein, goes even further in "Spiked?," an article published in the same June 26, 1989, issue as Denby's review, by linking David Dinkins's mayoral prospects to *Do the Right Thing*, which Klein calls, "Spike Lee's reckless new movie about a summer race riot in Brooklyn . . . which opens June 30 (in not too many theaters near you, one hopes)."[11] Klein fears the reaction of African American viewers: "If Lee does hook large black audiences, there's a good chance the message they take from the film will increase racial tensions in the city. If they react violently—which can't be ruled out—the candidate with the most to lose will be David Dinkins"[12] (the Manhattan Borough president who successfully opposed Ed Koch and Rudy Giuliani to become New York City's first—and, so far, only—African American mayor on November 7, 1989). This claim's unapologetic bigotry leads Klein to note that, despite the "almost Dickensian quality to [Lee's] sense of slum life" and the "wonderful characters who are at once simple and complicated—poignant and ridiculous, dangerous and funny," Lee is "a classic art-school dilettante when it comes to politics" whose film reflects "the latest riffs in hip black separatism rather than taking an intellectually honest look at the problems he's nibbling around."[13] Even more damning for Klein is that, "Like Stokeley Carmichael, [Lee] is a middle-class intellectual trying to prove his solidarity with 'the people' by demonstrating his outrage over white oppression."[14] *Do the Right Thing*, in Klein's estimation, boils down to two messages for black viewers: "*The police are your enemy*" and "*White people are your enemy,* even if they appear to be sympathetic."[15]

Klein's analysis features so many misunderstandings of *Do the Right Thing* that the critical viewer scarcely knows where to begin. Lee, however, rebukes Klein and Denby's backward view of African American audiences (in a letter published under the title "Say It Ain't So, Joe" in *New York Magazine*'s July 17, 1989, issue) by noting, "Klein and Denby were so busy accusing me of inciting the black masses to riot, they didn't stop to take stock of their own inferences."[16] Lee defends *Do the Right Thing* as telling "the story of race relations in this city from the point of view of black New Yorkers" and as being "very accurate in its portrayal of the attitude that black and Hispanic New Yorkers have toward the police."[17] Invoking accuracy does not deny *Do the Right Thing*'s insistent stylization, but Lee's assertion of his film's attitudinal realism forces the viewer to consider just how true to life *Do the Right Thing* is, a topic that has fascinated mainstream and scholarly commentators ever since.

Stanley Crouch, not to be outdone by Denby and Klein, derides *Do the Right Thing*'s portrait of American bigotry in his June 20, 1989, *Village Voice* article (provocatively titled "Do the Race Thing: Spike Lee's Afro-Fascist Chic") by pronouncing Lee's film the "sort of rancid fairy tale one expects from a racist."[18] Amiri Baraka, in his essay "Spike Lee at the Movies," dismisses *Do the Right Thing* as the work of "the quintessential buppie, almost the spirit of the young, upwardly mobile, Black, petit bourgeois professional" who, as part of "the middle class [that] most directly benefited from the militant sixties, as far as the ending of legal American apartheid and the increased access to middle-management resources are concerned, not only take it for granted because they have not struggled for this advance, but believe it is Black people's fault that we have not made more progress."[19] Terrence Rafferty's long, intriguing, and misguided *New Yorker* review (titled "Open and Shut") claims that *Do the Right Thing*, despite its visual inventiveness, "winds up bullying the audience—shouting at us rather than speaking to us. It is, both at its best and at its worst, very much a movie of these times."[20] Murray Kempton's "The Pizza Is Burning!," his September 28, 1989, *New York Review of Books* article about *Do the Right Thing*, claims, "American artists from Mark Twain to Spike Lee have confronted the conflict between white and black for more than a century, and it would not be easy to recall many scenarios that so heavily and pitilessly loaded the dice against the better side" before proclaiming Mookie (Spike Lee), the pizza deliveryman who functions as one of the film's many down-on-his-luck protagonists, to be "not just an inferior specimen of a great race but beneath the decent minimum for humankind itself."[21]

Kempton's caustic appraisal of *Do the Right Thing*'s central character leads W.J.T. Mitchell to call his (Kempton's) essay "perhaps the most hysterically abusive of the hostile reviews"[22] to illustrate the movie's contested reception. Some observers found fault with *Do the Right Thing*, particularly the film's refusal to examine the structural causes of American racism and Lee's unwillingness to develop his female characters. Notable scholarly analyses offer similar criticisms, thereby agreeing that *Do the Right Thing* is not as good as its reputation suggests.

The movie, indeed, provokes such divergent responses that it risks falling into a critical netherworld of political, cultural, and ideological mystification from which it cannot hope to emerge. Toni Cade Bambara, in "Programming with *School Daze*," identifies this characteristic not only as integral to Lee's cinematic approach but also as evidence of his talent. The diversity of viewers who "champion Spike Lee films"—sexists, homophobes, progressives, reactionaries, and independent thinkers—do so "not because the texts are so malleable that they can be maneuvered into any given ideological space, but because many extratextual elements figure into the response. . . . That the range of spectators is wide speaks to the power of the films and the brilliance of the filmmaker."[23] Such praise notwithstanding, David Denby, Stanley Crouch, and Murray Kempton (among others) remain unimpressed by *Do the Right Thing*, raising the possibility that the film's critical rehabilitation is a sham. *Do the Right Thing*'s admirers, however, note that Lee's superbly crafted slice-of-life drama tackles uncomfortable truths about race and racism. Their best representative is Roger Ebert, who, in his original June 30, 1989, review (published in the *Chicago Sun-Times*), declares, "Lee's writing and direction are masterful throughout the movie; he knows exactly where he is taking us, and how to get there, but he holds his cards close to his heart, and so the movie is hard to predict, hard to anticipate. After we get to the end, however, we understand how, and why, everything has happened."[24] Ebert implicitly disputes David Denby's judgment that *Do the Right Thing*'s conclusion is a poorly conceived shambles to argue that the movie's structure perfectly serves Lee's politically charged narrative.

Ebert's esteem only grows with time. He begins his May 27, 2001, retrospective review (for his "Great Movies" series) this way: "I have been given only a few filmgoing experiences in my life equal to the first time I saw *Do the Right Thing*. Most movies remain up there on the screen. Only a few penetrate your soul. In May of 1989 I walked out of the screening at the Cannes Film Festival with tears in my eyes. Spike Lee had done an almost impossible thing," which, in Ebert's estimation, is making "a movie about race in America that empathized with all the participants."[25] This response credits *Do the Right Thing* as a full-throated work of art to contradict Murray Kempton's hyperbolic dismissal, implying that Lee's controversial third film provokes, even cajoles, viewers into debating its fundamental themes. The resulting popular-press disagreements, indeed, have spurred cinema and media specialists to transform *Do the Right Thing* from a cultural cause célèbre into a touchstone of contemporary film scholarship.

ACADEMIC ADVENTURES

The numerous scholarly articles devoted to Lee's third movie prompt Norman K. Denzin, in his fine essay "Spike's Place," to comment, "Little new can be written about *DRT*."[26] This conviction, however, should neither obscure *Do the Right Thing*'s significance nor overlook the film's flaws. Denzin finds the movie's representation of African American communities and characters problematic because "Lee reduces the film's conflict to a dispute between personalities, to personal and group bigotry, not to the larger structures of institutional racism,"[27] thereby adopting a position influenced by three major, early contributions to *Do the Right Thing* scholarship: bell hooks's 1989 essay "Counter-Hegemonic Art: *Do the Right Thing*," Wahneema Lubiano's 1991 article "But Compared to What?: Reading Realism, Representation, and Essentialism in *School Daze, Do the Right Thing*, and the Spike Lee Discourse," and Ed Guerrero's 1993 book *Framing Blackness: The African American Image in Film*.[28] All three texts take *Do the Right Thing* to task for its simplistic approach to American racism's political, sociological, and economic causes. Their authors challenge the movie's august reputation by concluding that *Do the Right Thing* is a conservative cinematic portrait of social bigotry that focuses on individuals rather than institutions.

Hooks repeatedly makes this point in "Counter-Hegemonic Art," stating in a particularly hard-hitting passage, "*Do the Right Thing* does not evoke a visceral response. That any observer seeing this film could have thought it might incite black violence seems ludicrous," because, hooks writes, "it is highly unlikely that black people in this society who have been subjected to colonizing brainwashing designed to keep us in our place and to teach us how to submit to all manner of racist assault and injustice would see a film that merely hints at the intensity and pain of this experience and feel compelled to respond with rage."[29] Lee's dramatic approach, in hooks's view, founders on its inability to explore how systemic racism imperceptibly perpetuates itself, preferring instead to focus on characters who, by struggling to maintain dignity within their unfair society, cannot criticize (or even comprehend) the structural forces that restrict their lives: "The film does not challenge conventional understandings of racism; it reiterates old notions. Racism is not simply prejudice. It does not always take the form of overt discrimination. Often subtle and covert forms of racist domination determine the contemporary lot of black people."[30] This final charge identifies Lee's greatest failing in *Do the Right Thing* as his refusal to question the economic order that privileges white ownership in the film's Bedford-Stuyvesant setting, which restricts *Do the Right Thing*'s portrait of racial animus to parochial rather than institutional concerns. Even worse, hooks implies that Lee softpedals the sting (if not agony) of racism to blame his working-class black characters for their diminished political, economic, and social opportunities.

Lee's *Do the Right Thing* production journal—written in collaboration with Lisa Jones and published in the movie's companion volume, *Do the Right Thing: A Spike Lee Joint*—disputes this last criticism by stating, in its inaugural entry (dated December 25, 1987), "In this script I want to show the Black working class. Contrary to popular belief, we work. No welfare rolls here, pal, just hardworking people trying to make a decent living."[31] Lee, rather than judging, berating, or belittling the working-class African Americans and Latinos who populate his film's fictional Bed-Stuy block, defends them by challenging the largest stigma affecting their daily lives: that they use welfare programs to avoid earning money at good, socially approved occupations. This stereotype had gained tremendous resonance in American political discourse by *Do the Right Thing*'s 1989 release thanks to the racial rhetoric of President Ronald Reagan's repeated invocations of welfare queens, along with his many other coded references to poor, mostly African American people. This discourse cemented in the minds of the wider American electorate the spurious idea that inner-city people are all lazy, good-for-nothing freeloaders who, to support their families, prefer taking government handouts to holding regular jobs. This notion became so fixed in American politics that its specious factual basis had little effect on its currency, even though Chicago resident Linda Taylor, the "Cadillac-driving welfare queen" that Reagan first mentioned in his failed 1976 presidential campaign (and continued to cite throughout his successful 1980 White House bid), was a contested case of welfare fraud that Reagan and his handlers frequently mentioned during Reagan's race-baiting campaign.[32] Similar ideas promulgated during Reagan's presidency became pervasive facts of American civic life even when demonstrably false.

Herman Gray, in the second chapter of his superlative *Watching Race: Television and the Struggle for Blackness,* evaluates the rhetorical bigotry that underlies these politically influential concepts: "Although unmarked, Reagan's references to this Chicago 'welfare queen' and to 'you' play against historic and racialized discourses about welfare at the same time they join law-abiding taxpayers to an unmarked but normative and idealized racial and class subject—hardworking whites."[33] Gray's analysis notes how "the new right effectively appealed to popular notions of whiteness in opposition to blackness, which was conflated with and came to stand for 'other.' . . . As a sign of this otherness, blackness was constructed along a continuum ranging from menace on one end to immorality on the other, with irresponsibility located somewhere in the middle."[34] These notions grew into stigmas, then stereotypes, and, finally, into cultural commonplaces. Gray's study identifies the origin of many biases against African American working-class people prevalent in 1980s American culture, biases that *Do the Right Thing* takes as its subject, that Lee's production journal questions, and that bell hooks wishes Lee's third film would resolutely contest. Lee's desire to break from regressive portrayals of poor and working-class black people remains evident throughout his journal, nowhere more clearly than in its February 14, 1988, entry: "If I'm dealing with the Black lower class, I have to acknowledge that the number one thing on folks' minds is getting paid. It's on everyone's mind, lower class or not, but the issue has more consequences when you're poor, flat broke, busted."[35] Lee, at least while conceptualizing *Do the Right Thing,* remembers the challenges facing his film's disadvantaged characters, thereby rejecting the most piercing elements of hooks's criticism. Lee's sympathy, nonetheless, revolves around the primacy of individuals earning money rather than the structural unfairness of American capitalism.

Wahneema Lubiano, on this score, feels that *Do the Right Thing*'s relentless focus on money inhibits the institutional appraisal necessary to any honest examination (fictional or otherwise) of American racism. Lubiano, in "But Compared to What?," writes that Lee "produces representations that suggest particular Euro-American hegemonic politics. His *Do the Right Thing* is imbued with the Protestant work ethic: There is more language about work, responsibility, and ownership in it than in any five Euro-American Hollywood productions."[36] This hegemony, for Lubiano, simplifies inherently complicated economic realities: "The film insists that, if African Americans just work like the Koreans, like the Italians, like the Euro-American brownstone owner [the character Clifton, played by John Savage], these problems could be averted; or, if you own the property, then you can put on the walls whatever icons you want; or, if you consume at (materially support) a locale, then you can have whatever icons you want on the walls."[37] Lubiano, therefore, finds *Do the Right Thing*'s dramatic premise unpersuasive: the film's conflict begins when Buggin' Out (Giancarlo Esposito), a self-styled neighborhood revolutionary (and budding black nationalist), asks Salvatore "Sal" Fragione (Danny Aiello), owner and proprietor of Sal's Famous Pizzeria, why he (Sal) does not include photos of black celebrities on the pizzeria's Wall of Fame, which includes framed shots of Italian American stars such as Joe DiMaggio, Rocky Marciano, Frank Sinatra, Robert De Niro, Al Pacino, and Liza Minnelli. Sal's response is a paen to the rights of private-property owners: "You want brothers on the wall? Get your own place. You can do what you wanna do. You can put your brothers and uncles and nieces and nephews, your stepfather, stepmother, whoever you want. See? But this is *my* pizzeria. American-Italians on the wall only."[38]

Lubiano finds the movie so imbued with talk of work, property, and money that it defines manhood purely in economic terms: "And its masculinist focus could be distilled into the slogan that screams at us throughout the film: 'Real men work and support their families.' These representations compared to what? Within the representations of *Do the Right Thing,* what are the ideologies being engaged here, or critiqued here, or, more to the point, not critiqued here?"[39] Lubiano comments that such narrow definitions (of manhood, of property, and of work) refuse to examine, much less indict, the Protestant work ethic that both Sal and Mookie embody. Even Buggin' Out barely questions the assumptions that undergird the neighborhood's shaky economy, responding to Sal's declaration by conceding the man's ownership rights: "Yeah, that might be fine, Sal, but you own this. Rarely do I see any American-Italians eating in here. All I see is black folks. So since we spend much money here, we do have some say." Buggin' Out begins the economic analysis that Lubiano recommends, even going so far as to stage an attempted boycott of the pizzeria after Sal, who, rather than addressing Buggin' Out's point about the responsibility that he (Sal) owes his customers, responds by asking, "You looking for trouble? Are you a troublemaker? Is that what you are?" Sal brandishes a baseball bat when Buggin' Out demands that Sal put photos of Malcolm X, Nelson Mandela, and Michael Jordan on the Wall of Fame. No matter how correct Buggin' Out's point may be or how provocative Sal's response is, the younger man fails to note the institutional barriers that prevent his fellow African Americans from receiving the same access to capital that Sal enjoys. Buggin' Out, therefore, remains a feeble revolutionary who, much like Dap Dunlap in *School Daze,* seems unwilling to expend the effort necessary to building and maintaining a successful protest movement.

Lubiano finds such discussions misguided and, finally, tedious: "Against, I suppose, the long-held racist charge that African Americans neither work nor want to work, this film spends much of its running time assuring its audience that African Americans in Bed-Stuy certainly do value work! (By its end, I am so overwhelmed by its omnipresent wage-labor ethos that I find myself exhausted)."[40] Lubiano rightly perceives Lee's desire to alter the stereotypical images of shiftless black people that characterized Reagan-era America, but she finds that, by doing so, *Do the Right Thing* reinforces the same unfair economic policies and conditions that help create those images in the first place: "I am not anti-labor; however, this film makes no critique of the conditions under which labor is drawn from some members of the community, nor are kinds of labor/work differentiated. Instead, without any specific contextualization, work is presented as its own absolute good."[41] This problem becomes worse when Lubiano considers the failed promise of the Corner Men, three black friends named Sweet Dick Willie (Robin Harris), Coconut Sid (Frankie Faison), and M.L. (Paul Benjamin) who sit on a street corner across from the block's Korean-owned fruit market while drinking beer and discussing the day's events. "Early on," Lubiano writes, "the film promises a class critique of sorts in the discussion of Sweet Dick Willie and his buddies on the corner. M.L. begins a complaint that the Koreans, like so many other immigrant groups, move into the neighborhood and seem immediately to 'make it,' only to lose the focus of his critique"[42] because he does not (or cannot) criticize the systemic roadblocks that retard African American progress: "The men make no mention of differential capital bases or accesses to bank loans—and there is no reason to think that vernacular language could not handle that analysis."[43] Lubiano, in this passage, interrogates *Do the Right Thing*'s (and Lee's) failure to mention America's long history of racial exclusion, particularly the unfair lending, housing, and employment practices that restricted African American economic advancement during the nineteenth and twentieth centuries. *Do the Right Thing*'s man-on-the-street perspective, to Lubiano, repudiates institutional analysis in favor of individual portraits that prevent the film from achieving the political ends that its director, in both his production journal and public appearances, desired. Lubiano, although admiring *Do the Right Thing*'s style and energy, considers it a politically contradictory narrative: "For a filmmaker who claims the mantle of transgression, cultural opposition, political righteousness, and truth-telling, the political ambitions of this film are diffuse and, by its end, defuse into nothingness."[44]

Lee's journal demonstrates his willingness to upset typical depictions of American racism, but never suggests the institutional appraisal that Lubiano recommends. Lee's January 1, 1988, entry connects his early wish to cast Robert De Niro as Sal with *Do the Right Thing*'s treatment of American racism. Lee reveals that he met De Niro one year prior, "the night after the Howard Beach incident. We discussed racism and how the animosity between Blacks and Italians has escalated. I think we can make an important film about the subject."[45] The Howard Beach incident refers to the tragic event that first inspired Lee to create *Do the Right Thing*: just before midnight on

December 19, 1986, the automobile of four African American men driving through the predominantly Italian American neighborhood in Howard Beach, Queens, stalled on Cross Bay Boulevard. Three passengers—Michael Griffith, 23; Cedric Sandiford, 36; and Timothy Grimes, 20—tried to locate a pay phone on foot. When confronted by a group of white pedestrians yelling racial epithets, these men entered the New Park Pizzeria. Lee's autobiography, *That's My Story and I'm Sticking to It,* collates many different accounts to describe what happened next, saying that all three men entered the pizzeria, but, when told they could not use the phone to call for assistance, decided to eat. Two police officers arrived not long after, having been notified that "three suspicious black males" were inside the establishment, but departed when they determined that Griffith, Sandiford, and Grimes had done nothing wrong, which escalated the trouble when white patrons "chased the black youths out of the pizzeria toward a gang of accomplices waiting with baseball bats."[46] Grimes, pulling a knife, escaped, but Sandiford was beaten unconscious. The severely injured Griffith, trying "to stagger away from his pursuers," instead "wandered onto the busy Belt Parkway, where he was hit and killed by a passing automobile. New York erupted, witnessing the largest black protest rallies since the civil-rights movement."[47]

Lee, as this description makes clear, includes so many references to Howard Beach in *Do the Right Thing* that audiences at the time of the film's 1989 release, particularly in New York City, could not miss them: the main action occurs in an Italian American pizzeria, Sal wields his Louisville Slugger baseball bat to assert dominance, and his son Pino (John Turturro) utters racial epithets at nearly every turn.

Lee, however, reverses Howard Beach's primary setting to comment upon the changing urban demographics that the United States had witnessed during the previous thirty years. Rather than tell the story of African Americans stranded in a mostly Caucasian neighborhood, Lee isolates his three Italian characters—Sal, Pino, and Sal's younger son Vito (Richard Edson)—in black and Latino Bedford-Stuyvesant. Sal, in other words, has not fully participated in the "white flight" of the 1950s, 1960s, and 1970s that saw Caucasian residents and business owners abandon American cities for more suburban areas as African Americans, Latinos, and Asians moved into previously all-white enclaves. Sal proudly plies his trade in Bed-Stuy, although he and his family now live in Bensonhurst, driving to work each morning to spend their days amongst the Bed-Stuy block's minority residents. *Do the Right Thing,* therefore, offers an African American perspective, aesthetic, and approach to its narrative that strikes many viewers as authentic. Lee, indeed, strives for authenticity, as his January 1, 1988, production-journal entry states: "Truth is more important than an evenhanded treatment of the subject. No matter what, the story has to be told from a Black perspective."[48] Even so, *Do the Right Thing* avoids addressing the systemic racism noted in bell hooks's and Wahneema Lubiano's essays, preferring a granular approach that depicts the lives of individual human beings trying to survive the racial, social, and economic circumstances they have inherited.

Critical viewers, however, should recognize that neither *Do the Right Thing* nor its writer-director claims to deliver a neutral account of urban racism. The movie, despite all talk of its realism, naturalism, and authenticity, is a highly stylized representation of American race relations, as well as an effective response to the Howard Beach incident (among other tragic confrontations between black New Yorkers and the New York Police Department in the years immediately preceding the movie's release[49]), not a cinematic documentary offering objective viewpoints. Although hooks and Lubiano criticize *Do the Right Thing*'s inability to diagnose racism's institutional foundations, Lee's production journal demonstrates his awareness of the socioeconomic issues in play. The January 4, 1988, entry, in fact, equates social class with educational achievement: "Both Pino and Vito only made it through high school. They will work in their father's pizzeria probably for the rest of their lives and are ill-equipped to do otherwise. They're lower-middle class and basically uneducated."[50]

Pino's toxic racism, as the character's dialogue and John Turturro's fine performance confirm, has many causes, but he expresses disdain for customers he calls "niggers" (even telling Sal, "I don't like being around them. They're animals") due to the rage that he feels knowing that his life is no better than theirs. Pino's economic opportunities are scarcely broader than the African American residents he serves every day, yet detests. Even Pino's claims that he works harder than everyone on the block (except Sal) ring hollow because Pino has no appreciable skills beyond taking orders, making change, cleaning the shop, and occasionally helping his father cook pizza (although Sal lords over this task as much as all others). *Do the Right Thing*, indeed, compares Pino to the person he most loathes, Mookie, by paralleling their circumscribed choices. This thematic twinning increases the tension between both men as the film unfolds, for *Do the Right Thing* exposes Pino's hatred of Mookie as a pernicious form of self-hatred. Lee's January 4th journal entry makes this point, as well: "Pino, Vito, and Mookie have many similarities. All three are high school graduates and are stuck in dead-end jobs. They are trapped. They would never discuss it amongst themselves."[51]

Pino and Mookie, therefore, have no class consciousness (and indeed never directly discuss socioeconomic issues), but the scene just before the altercation among Sal, Buggin' Out, and Radio Raheem that precipitates the pizzeria's destruction captures the subtext of Lee's January 4th entry. Sal, happy that the shop has done good business during the day, praises Pino, Vito, and Mookie as a family working together. He says that the shop should be renamed Sal and Sons Famous Pizzeria, even telling Mookie, "there's always gonna be a place for you here, right here at Sal's—Sal's Famous Pizzeria—because you've always been like a son to me." The shocked, disbelieving, and silent expressions on Pino's, Vito's, and Mookie's faces are testaments to

Turturro's, Edson's, and Lee's acting talents, for they perfectly capture the stage directions specified by *Do the Right Thing*'s screenplay: "The horror is on their faces, with the prospect of working, slaving in Sal's and Sons Famous Pizzeria, trapped for the rest of their lives. Is this their future? It's a frightening thought."[52] The reference to "slaving" is deliberate, drawing out the scene's most troubling implication as written, performed, and edited: Pino, Vito, and Mookie are condemned to a life of wage slavery as long as they work for Sal, who, despite his effusive demeanor, is little more than a benevolent tyrant who controls their future earnings. Lee even revisits this notion in *Red Hook Summer* (2012) by showing Mr. Mookie (as this film's end credits identify him) still delivering pies for Sal's Famous Pizzeria in Brooklyn's Red Hook district. Mookie never mentions Pino or Vito by name in *Red Hook Summer,* but the fact that he remains a pizza deliveryman twenty-three years after *Do the Right Thing*'s events implies that they, too, still work at Sal's.

Do the Right Thing, therefore, is as symbolic as realistic by presenting the economic hierarchy of Sal's Famous Pizzeria as a microcosm of late-1980s American capitalism. Sal does not see himself as an oppressor, but rather as a man who offers opportunity to everyone: his family, his customers, and his sole African American employee. This hidden, subtextual discourse counters some of hooks's and Lubiano's criticisms about the movie's inadequacies, yet fails to convince Ed Guerrero that *Do the Right Thing* is a groundbreaking work of American cinema even if it "explores the great unspeakable, repressed topic of American cultural life: race and racism."[53] Guerrero states that Lee's mastery of the techniques of Hollywood studio filmmaking leads him into "a contained, mainstream sensibility" that finds the director "diligently struggling to learn the conventions and clichés of market cinema language, instead of struggling to change the dominant system by creating a visionary language of his own."[54] Guerrero finds "the glossy, wide-screen, poster-bright colors, sanitized streets, overworked theatrical settings, and up-to-the-moment fashions that constitute so much" of *Do the Right Thing*'s visual style deficient because, "in contrasting irony, it is the film's alleged sense of 'authenticity' and 'realness' that some critics have praised. But the film's slick, color-saturated look has the effect of idealizing or making nostalgic the present, rather than dramatizing any deep sense of social or political urgency."[55]

Do the Right Thing's signature look—the bold primary colors in which Lee and cinematographer Ernest Dickerson bathe nearly every scene, combined with canted camera angles that make everyday conversations and confrontations unsettling—becomes, in Guerrero's analysis, evidence of political naïveté, particularly the narrative's apparent dismissal of collective political action. The movie, Guerrero writes, makes its two proto-revolutionaries, Buggin' Out and Radio Raheem, "supercilious and unreasonable characters advocating the most effective social action instrument of the civil rights movement, the economic boycott," but, in the end, *Do the Right Thing*'s audience sees "the possibility of social action dismissed by the neighborhood youth for the temporary pleasures of a good slice of pizza," meaning that "the film trivializes any understanding of contemporary black political struggle, as well as the recent history of social movements in this country."[56] Guerrero, like hooks and Lubiano, charges Lee with adopting an individualist stance that ignores, when not actively repudiating, organized political protest as an effective response to institutional racism: "Thus, Lee inadvertently gives way to dominant cinema's reflex strategy of containment, that of depicting complex social conflicts as disputes between individuals, where deliberated collective action is either impossible or unnecessary."[57] Lee's heart, in other words, may be in the right place, just as his intentions may be for the best, but *Do the Right Thing* is neither a guerrilla film nor a call to arms. For Guerrero, the movie fails to address the true origins and outcomes of American racism.

The important objections raised by hooks, Lubiano, and Guerrero dispute *Do the Right Thing*'s classic status and extend criticisms registered in the unappreciative reviews that greeted the film's 1989 release, but without the bigotry evident in Joe Klein's and David Denby's articles. The nuanced arguments that hooks, Lubiano, and Guerrero construct pose sophisticated challenges for later assessments of *Do the Right Thing*. One conclusion seems clear: *Do the Right Thing* cannot fulfill the diverse expectations of its many viewers, critics, and scholars (as, indeed, no film could). This truth should not suggest that *Do the Right Thing* is so indeterminate that it means whatever particular audiences wish it to mean. The movie, as Toni Cade Bambara suggests, is not so malleable that it fits into innumerable ideological boxes, even if *Do the Right Thing* permits multivalent reactions. Despite the prognostications of Klein, Denby, and Denzin, the film reveals different facets with each viewing.

SATURDAY NIGHT (AND DAY) FEVER

The scholarly articles that defend *Do the Right Thing,* in whole or in part, are as numerous as those sources that condemn it. Important texts in this regard include Nelson George's "*Do the Right Thing:* Film and Fury" (first published in *Five for Five: The Films of Spike Lee,* the retrospective 1991 volume that celebrated the release of *Jungle Fever*), Mark A. Reid's edited 1997 essay anthology *Spike Lee's "Do the Right Thing"* (particularly Douglas S. Kellner's "Aesthetics, Ethics, and Politics in the Films of Spike Lee" and W.J.T. Mitchell's aforementioned "The Violence of Public Art: *Do the Right Thing*"), S. Craig Watkins's 1998 book *Representing: Hip Hop Culture and the Production of Black Cinema,* Paula J. Massood's 2003 book *Black City Cinema: African American Urban Experiences in Film,* and, especially, Dan Flory's 2006 article "Spike Lee and the Sympathetic Racist." Each writer considers Lee's third movie a complicated cinematic probing of American race and social class. Massood, indeed, argues that *Do the Right Thing* succeeds precisely where bell hooks, Wahneema Lubiano, and Ed Guerrero think it fails: "Rather than exploring the macrocosm of causes and effects leading to the conditions on this particular block, Lee lets the block, its residents, and the day's events reveal the conditions and pressures of the inner city."[58] Noting that the movie uses "many of the techniques introduced by the Italian Neorealists, the French New Wave, and Soviet filmmaking from the 1920s," Massood cites literary theorist Mikhail Bakhtin's concept of heteroglossia before arguing that *Do the Right Thing* "bears the influence of the French New Wave, especially in the use of the Brechtian concepts of alienation and distanciation and their related formal and narrative techniques."[59] The film, therefore, cinematically addresses "racism, its many causes and effects, and how it all plays out in this small urbanscape. Its single-block setting embodies multiple signifiers of the extradiegetic conditions affecting the neighborhood."[60] Massood, unlike hooks, finds *Do the Right Thing*'s granular approach (emphasizing individual over institutional concerns) to resemble Bakhtinian and Brechtian modernism by underscoring the ceaseless play of signifiers (music, costumes, colors, angles, and editing) that influence, without fully determining, the lives of the movie's characters.

Douglas S. Kellner also discusses Berthold Brecht's German modernist theater as an important forerunner of Lee's American cinema. "Both Brecht and Lee," Kellner writes, "produce a sort of 'epic drama' that paints a wide tableau of typical social characters, shows examples of social and asocial behavior, and delivers didactic messages to the audience. Both Brecht and Lee utilize music, comedy, drama, vignettes of typical behavior, and figures who present the messages the author wishes to convey."[61] This final point rehabilitates a common criticism of *Do the Right Thing* and Lee's other films: that their characters function as little more than mouthpieces for their director's social, cultural, and political beliefs, along with his pet peeves and hobbyhorses. In Brecht's plays and Lee's films, such characters (who are perhaps better described as animated, ambulatory characteristics rather than psychologically realistic people) allow both playwright and filmmaker, in Kellner's words, to "present didactic learning plays, which strive to teach people to discover and then do 'the right thing,' while criticizing improper and antisocial behavior. Brecht's plays (as well as his prose, his film *Kuhle Wampe,* and his radio plays) depict character types in situations that force one to observe the consequences of typical behavior,"[62] a modernist trait that Brecht's writing shares with *Do the Right Thing*. Kellner also argues that Lee's third movie "is arguably modernist in that it leaves unanswered the question of the politically 'right thing' to do. By 'modernist,' I refer, first, to aesthetic strategies of producing texts that are open and polyvocal, that disseminate a wealth of meanings rather than a central univocal meaning or message, and that require an active reader to produce the meanings."[63] *Do the Right Thing* fulfills all these criteria, generating so many divergent responses that, from Kellner's perspective, scholars like hooks, Lubiano, and Guerrero mistake the film for a realistic account of the block's warmest day when it instead resembles a symbolist play. Even so, Kellner points out how the movie celebrates mass-market consumerism to confirm one fundamental conclusion propounded by *Do the Right Thing*'s critics: "Lee excels in presenting small-group dynamics but has not been successful in articulating the larger structures—and structural context of black oppression—that affect communities, social groups, and individual lives. Thus, he does not really articulate the dynamics of class and racial oppression in U.S. society."[64] Kellner regards Lee's personal rather than systemic focus as evidence of *Do the Right Thing*'s modernist, Brechtian aesthetic more than a regrettable failure, although, for Kellner, "Lee's politics, by contrast [with Brecht's avowed Marxism], appear more vague and indeterminate"[65] in their expression, thereby promoting an ambivalence that some viewers (particularly Amiri Baraka) read as bourgeois conservatism.

Lee's film, despite its powerful effect on viewers, is not the epic drama that Kellner claims, or at least not epic in the sense of covering vast historical and geographical territory. Following its characters throughout a single twenty-four-hour period restricts *Do the Right Thing*'s narrative to the more modest scope of slice-of-life fiction, causing Kellner to criticize the effect of Lee's "tendency to use Brechtian 'typical' characters to depict 'typical' scenes. The 'typical,' however, is a breath away from the stereotypical, archetypal, conventional, representative, average, and so on, and lends itself to caricature and distortion."[66] *Do the Right Thing* fulfills this dictum through the characters who receive designations rather than names, the most prominent being Buggin' Out; Radio Raheem; Da Mayor (Ossie Davis), a shambling alcoholic who functions as the neighborhood's de facto mediator; and Mother Sister (Ruby Dee), a griot who watches the block's events from her dilapidated brownstone's front window while dispensing advice to Mookie and his sister, Jade (Joie Lee). Their stereotypical traces—or their stock roles (frustrated revolutionary, fearsome block boy, town drunk, and old maid)—may work against *Do the Right Thing*'s putative realism, but these characters push critical viewers to recognize, along with S. Craig Watkins, that Lee's movie "operated more at the level of allegory and symbolism"[67] than quotidian fidelity.

For Watkins, this development liberates the movie's story from the shackles of strict realism while paradoxically invoking real-world issues: "Thus, if we view Sal and the black youths in the film as vehicles for expressing some of the shifting racial moods and sensibilities of the late twentieth century, then the politics of the film become much more dynamic and discernible: the intensification of racial tension between black youth, downwardly mobile whites, and institutions of social control."[68] *Do the Right Thing*, in this reading, does not ignore social or institutional concerns, but instead mixes closely observed, traditionally realistic characters (Sal, Mookie, Pino) with broader types (Buggin' Out, Da Mayor, Mother Sister) to question the economic influences and impacts, but not the origins, of American racism. Watkins, like Massood, notes that *Do the Right Thing*'s multivalent storyline—replete with unresolved themes, characters, and plots—reproduces heteroglossia, as well as the Bakhtinian concept of polyphony, to challenge classical Hollywood style's preference for tidy and reassuring resolutions. Lee, in this film (and several others), "privileges multiple story-plots over the single-story-plot formula" in a structure that "fractures the primary story-plot. Consequently, his film narratives tend to develop acute fissures. So instead of constructing a single homogenous world, Lee opts for creating a filmic world in which a polyphony of issues, conflicts, and enigmas seem to proliferate unabashedly."[69] *Do the Right Thing* leaves its audience to ponder difficult events that the film makes no effort to reconcile. Its ambivalent conclusion sees Radio Raheem dead, Sal's Famous Pizzeria destroyed, and Mookie determined to receive his wages despite throwing a trash can through Sal's front window. This ending subverts classical Hollywood's preference for, in Watkins's words, "easy resolution and narrative closure,"[70] or "the happy-ending cliché" that "reaffirms dominant ideological values like individualism and patriarchy and further suggests that heroic, often male, deeds are the solution to social problems."[71] *Do the Right Thing,* by partially rejecting these values and deeds, criticizes racism's social, economic, and institutional foundations to become, if not the counter-hegemonic cinema that bell hooks favors, at least a film that interrogates its era's dominant racial ideologies.

Yet no matter how intelligently the film's mainstream and scholarly observers present their arguments, they rarely acknowledge the second, crucial aspect of *Do the Right Thing*'s setting. Every newspaper review, magazine article, and scholarly essay discusses the movie's primary locale, sometimes criticizing this neighborhood block as too clean and too drug-free to be an authentic representation of Bedford-Stuyvesant, but rarely mentions that *Do the Right Thing* takes place on Saturday. This significant detail is easy to miss, but, in one of the film's earliest scenes, Mookie's sister Jade lies sleeping in bed when he playfully touches her lips and face, then tells her, recalling Dap Dunlap's final plea in *School Daze,* to "Wake up!" Jade, complaining about Mookie's interference, says, "Saturday's the only day I get to sleep late." Jade's dialogue also rebukes the energetic words of Mister Señor Love Daddy (Samuel L. Jackson, credited as Sam Jackson), disc jockey for neighborhood radio station WE LOVE 108FM, who, in *Do the Right Thing*'s opening scene, tells his listeners, "Waaaaake up! Wake up! Wake up! Wake up! Up ya wake! Up ya wake! Up ya wake! Up ya wake!" Lee's decision to cast Jackson as Love Daddy connects *Do the Right Thing* even more closely to *School Daze,* suggesting that *Do the Right Thing* not only picks up where its predecessor ends but also promises to fulfill Dap Dunlap's fervent dream of African American characters who finally comprehend the political conditions that restrict their daily lives. Jade's comment, as such, ironically suggests that she prefers pursuing individual interests to the communal action that *School Daze* states is necessary for black Americans to collectively advance. Jade's perspective gains credence when she refuses to join Buggin' Out's boycott of Sal's Famous Pizzeria, asking him, "What good is that gonna do, huh? You know, if you really tried hard, Buggin' Out, you could direct your energies in a more useful way, you know?" This response illustrates the point made by hooks, Lubiano, and Guerrero that *Do the Right Thing* underplays (or dismisses) the benefits of organized protest to the detriment of its African American characters.

Jade, indeed, relentlessly preaches what Lubiano calls the movie's exhausting wage-labor ethos, voicing this work ethic even more frequently than Sal and Pino. Jade badgers Mookie throughout *Do the Right Thing* to fulfill his responsibilities at work and home, equating his ability to earn enough money to support his young son, Hector (Travell Lee Tolson), and Hector's mother, Tina (Rosie Perez), with Mookie's full identity. That Mookie works on Saturday, the traditional American weekend, escapes her notice as much as *Do the Right Thing*'s critics. The block's residents fill the streets to seek relief from the day's oppressive heat because, contrary to careless assumptions that they are idle welfare recipients, they wish to enjoy time away from their jobs. The rage that they unleash against Sal's Pizzeria after Radio Raheem's murder, in this context, transcends its immediate cause to represent communal anger at the economic inequalities that allow Sal to prosper while everyone else struggles in economically uncertain conditions. This reading also explains why Mother Sister (who, along with Da Mayor, represents the older generation of black Americans who endured Jim Crow segregation) screams, "Burn it down! Burn it down!" after the police haul Raheem's corpse away from the pizzeria. The stage directions in Lee's screenplay offer a fascinating gloss on her anger: "One might have thought that the elders—who through the years have been broken down, whipped, their spirits crushed, beaten into submission—would be docile, strictly onlookers. That's not true except for Da Mayor. The rest of the elders are right up in it with the young people."[72] The block's hottest day unveils the long-simmering dismay that working-class African Americans feel when confronting the truth that they are unimportant to the institutions that regulate their lives. The police and Sal seem to prize property over life throughout the movie, leaving the distraught onlookers to express their helplessness at Raheem's murder by attacking the pizzeria as the only symbol of social oppression available to them.

Do the Right Thing, moreover, subtly controls its mise-en-scène to demonstrate that the block's inhabitants are not universally poor: Jade wears colorful clothing and hats when visiting Sal's; Love Daddy wears similarly distinct clothing while working his day-long shift at the radio station; Mother Sister implies that her ex-husband's poor business sense caused her to accept tenants in her brownstone; Buggin' Out observes that his fellow black patrons spend "much money" on Sal's pizza and wears new Nike shoes (thereby falling prey to the crass commercialism that Douglas S. Kellner criticizes); and Mookie's introduction finds him counting money (not food stamps or welfare checks) in his bedroom. These characters exemplify Lee's production-journal reference to hardworking people earning their keep. Saturday, for most residents, becomes a respite from their occupational challenges and tensions, meaning that *Do the Right Thing* is not the simple celebration of bourgeois conventionality that Amiri Baraka claims.

The movie's Saturday setting, therefore, helps sketch its character's polyvalent lives, while acknowledging the existence of people who buck the film's insistence on the necessity and dignity of labor: Mother Sister tells Mookie not to work too hard in the day's intense heat, Da Mayor sweeps the sidewalk in front of Sal's pizzeria just long enough to accumulate the spare change that supports his alcoholism, Radio Raheem walks the block listening to Public Enemy's anthem "Fight the Power" rather than pursuing the difficult political action that would fulfill the song's title, and the Corner Men pontificate about the block's problems rather than trying to solve them. Lee's screenplay, indeed, describes the Corner Men as having "no steady employment, nothing they can speak of; they do, however, have the gift of gab. These men can talk, talk, and mo' talk, and when a bottle is going round and they're feeling 'nice,' they get philosophical. These men become the great thinkers of the world, with solutions to all its ills."[73] Their job in *Do the Right Thing*'s narrative is to observe, to comment, and to advise (much like a traditional Greek chorus), not to seek financial reward. Da Mayor likewise watches, engages, and advises his neighbors (telling Mookie, in the movie's titular line, "Doctor, always do the right thing"), but pursues no career ambitions beyond scrounging enough money for his next drink. Mother Sister demonstrates no interest in leaving her home, but remains content to offer wisdom to whomever will listen. Saturday, for these characters, is just another day rather than a reprieve from the working world's pressures, yet *Do the Right Thing* does not exclude or overlook their voices even if the Corner Men, Da Mayor, and Mother Sister reject socially approved forms of industrial labor.

Lee's third film, considered in this light, develops a discourse about the value of capitalism that may not directly challenge the wage-labor ethos that Lubiano finds pervasive, but that nonetheless undermines easy faith in earning profit to support one's family. Mookie, after all, resists Sal's, Pino's, and Jade's imprecations to be a diligent worker by taking longer to deliver pizzas than he should, even visiting Tina in an erotic sequence that finds Mookie rubbing ice cubes along her lips, thighs, and breasts. Pino and Vito argue about finishing the tasks assigned by their father, who, early in the film, presciently says, "I'm gonna kill somebody today." Sal, for his part, ignores his employees and his customers when Jade enters the pizzeria to make her a special meal. Money, therefore, is not the sole motivator for the movie's characters even if it underscores their major actions. *Do the Right Thing*, indeed, cannot examine the long-term influences of institutional capitalism on American racism in the same manner as David Simon's superb, sixty-episode HBO television series *The Wire*, but neither does the movie avoid making such points. Lee eschews polemics in favor of vignettes that illustrate the block's economically restrictive conditions from a ground-floor perspective.

Do the Right Thing's Saturday setting, consequently, is central to its portrayal of working- and lower-class people who cannot (or will not) defy the economic and racial restrictions they face until Radio Raheem's murder provides the impetus to act. Their destruction of Sal's pizzeria is not as thoughtless an undertaking as critics like Denby suggest, but builds upon key sequences that foreshadow the oncoming violence.

SONS, SLURS, AND SAL

Three sequences illustrate *Do the Right Thing*'s complex rendering of race, class, and bigotry in late-1980s America. The first occurs when Pino, upset that Mookie uses the pizzeria's phone for personal calls, asks, "How come niggers are so stupid?" Mookie replies, "If you see a nigger, kick his ass" before asking Pino about the man's favorite celebrities. Pino admires Magic Johnson, Eddie Murphy, and Prince, but sees no conflict with his racist viewpoints. "Magic, Eddie, and Prince are not niggers," Pino says. "I mean they're black, but they're not really black. They're more than black. It's different." This short dialogue displays Lee's genius for compression, encapsulating in a few words the contradictions of American racist thought, or, as Nelson George observes in "*Do the Right Thing:* Film and Fury," "one of the ironies of the post civil-rights era is that the wide acceptance of black stardom hasn't really changed ground-level racism—something King had hoped for, but Malcolm X had anticipated."[74] Pino speaks for white ethnic men who regard themselves as hardworking, fair-minded Americans happy to credit individual black men as outstanding contributors to society. Yet Pino and his friends demonstrate little understanding of the historical, political, and economic barriers that restrict many African Americans from achieving the success that Johnson, Murphy, and Prince enjoy. Pino implicitly takes each man's wealth and notoriety as evidence that America has overcome its racist past, but disregards the patterns of marginalization, discrimination, and exclusion that black Americans at large must overcome. Pino's notion that his African American heroes are "more than black" recalls the racist stereotypes—enhanced by Ronald Reagan's neoconservative rhetoric—that hardworking Americans are white, that lazy freeloaders are black (or, if not, members of minority groups), and that black Americans who succeed in their nation's economic free-for-all transcend their racial background to become culturally white (in much the same way that ethnic Europeans from Ireland, Italy, Greece, and Poland who migrated to the United States in the late nineteenth and early twentieth centuries came to consider themselves white as they assimilated into the dominant culture to fulfill the metaphor of America as an ethnic, racial, and cultural melting pot).[75] Pino alludes to the political complications of race by mocking Louis Farrakhan, even telling Mookie to "get the fuck out of here" when the latter says that Pino wishes he were black.

Lee then cuts to perhaps *Do the Right Thing*'s most famous sequence (apart from its concluding violence), which his screenplay dubs the "Racial Slur Montage."[76] Five characters (Mookie; Pino; Stevie, a Latino man played by Luis Ramos; Officer Long, a white police officer played by Rick Aiello; and Sonny, the Korean co-owner of the block's fruit-and-vegetable market played by Steve Park), without embarrassment or hesitation, hurl racial insults directly at the viewer as the image abruptly jumps from one to the next. Mookie attacks Italian Americans as "You dago, wop, guinea, garlic-breath, pizza-slinging, spaghetti-bending, Vic Damone, Perry Como, Luciano Pavarotti, *Sole Mio,* non-singing motherfucker"; Pino abuses African Americans as "You gold-teeth, gold-chain-wearing, fried-chicken-and-biscuit-eatin', monkey, ape, baboon, big-thigh, fast-running, high-jumping, spear-chucking, three-hundred-and-sixty-degree-basketball-dunking *titsun,* spade, Moulan Yan"; and Officer Long demeans Latinos as "Goya-bean-eating, fifteen-in-a-car, thirty-in-an-apartment, pointed-shoes, red-wearing, Menudo, *miramira,* Puerto Rican cocksucker." This invective assaults the audience by placing each viewer in a firing line of crude stereotypes that does not relent until the screen cuts to Mister Señor Love Daddy screaming, "You need to cool that shit out!" Lee's inventive visual composition underscores the sequence's simultaneous horror and comedy: the camera zooms from a medium shot toward each character's face as he utters vile, racist words until reversing this movement when Love Daddy appears. The camera, in fact, remains stationary as Love Daddy rolls toward the radio station's microphone in an office chair, ending in a medium close-up of his face as he rebukes the foregoing tirades. Lee, by forcing *Do the Right Thing*'s audience to endure racist vilification, reproduces the powerlessness that victims of racial stereotyping experience. The viewer's inability to respond mimics the incapacity of racism's victims to prevent their abuse in a brilliant cinematic strategy that interrupts the film's ongoing narrative, but that, like similar episodes in Italian Neorealism, French New Wave film, and Brechtian drama, distills the story's themes into a disturbing, darkly humorous, and unforgettable sequence.

The Racial Slur montage also continues a tradition that Lee establishes in his first two movies—*She's Gotta Have It*'s dog sequence and Half Pint searching for female companionship in *School Daze*—to illustrate how freely Lee dilutes classical Hollywood filmmaking to achieve stylistically clever sequences that function as micro-narratives within the movie's overall story. The slur montage, indeed, transcends commentary to make *Do the Right Thing*'s audience complicit in the bigotry that its characters indulge. Lee also carefully positions these epithets immediately after Pino and Mookie discuss the former's racist attitudes not only to illustrate how prejudice cuts across different racial and ethnic (yet not gender) lines but also to suggest that Pino's racism has communal roots that implicate his father. Sal, who proudly tells Pino that "they [the block's black and Hispanic residents] grew up on my food," seems perplexed by Pino's vitriolic racism, yet, rather than telling his son that such beliefs are morally reprehensible, Sal instead appeals in roundabout fashion to the melting-pot metaphor that elides racial and ethnic differences: "I never had no trouble with these people. I sat in this window. I watched the little kids get old. And I seen the old people get older. Yeah, sure, some of them don't like us, but most of them do." Sal's response, along with his repeated references to "these people" and "you people," suggests that Pino learned his bigotry, at least in part, from his father. Sal unthinkingly endorses white supremacy despite treating individual black people—particularly Da Mayor and Jade—with fondness, even confessing to Pino that economic reasons explain his decision not move the business to his family's home neighborhood of Bensonhurst ("there's too many pizzerias already there") more than his commitment to the block's black and Latino customers.

Sal's patronizing attitude may not be as vicious as Pino's noxious racism, but it helps explain why Pino behaves as he does. Lee addresses this possibility in several venues, including "Spike Lee's Bed-Stuy BBQ," his 1989 *Film Comment* interview with Marlaine Glicksman, by saying, "Pino didn't pick up that stuff out of the air. Some of it had to have been taught him by his father, Sal."[77] This notion echoes Lee's most mature statement about Sal's bigotry, in his production journal's January 3, 1988, entry: "This is the tricky thing. Like many people who have racist views, these views are so ingrained, they aren't aware of them. We should see that in Sal. Basically he's a good person, but he feels Black people are inferior."[78] Lee understands that American anti-black prejudice is pervasive, invisible, and natural for its adherents. Identifying Sal as a genial, yet bigoted person offers a key insight into *Do the Right Thing*'s effectiveness. Neither the movie nor Lee portrays Sal as a reprehensible racist, but instead as a pleasant man who suppresses his bigotry to the point that he no longer recognizes it. This all-too-common outcome causes Nelson George to see Sal as "represent[ing] every paternalistic member of an old-line New York ethnic group who has a kind but condescending view of his customers. That he feels they are childlike and irresponsible is apparent in his dealings with Da Mayor and Mookie, and in his refusal to include African Americans on his Wall of Fame."[79] George's analysis insightfully summarizes both Sal's behavior and Danny Aiello's terrific performance in the role. Aiello plays Sal as simultaneously kind, gruff, generous, condescending, good humored, and overbearing to draw out the man's paternalism.

Aiello finds so many nuances in Sal's character that Sal becomes what Dan Flory calls a sympathetic racist. Flory's splendid essay "Spike Lee and the Sympathetic Racist" notes that Lee creates such characters because "seeing matters of race from a nonwhite perspective is typically a standpoint unfamiliar to white viewers," causing Lee to offer these audience members "depictions of characters . . . with whom mainstream audiences readily ally themselves but who embrace racist beliefs and commit racist acts."[80] These sympathetic racists, "by introducing a critical distance between viewers and what it means to be white," permit Lee to make "a Brechtian move with respect to race," namely offering white viewers a way "of experiencing what they have been culturally trained to take as typical or normative—being white—and see it depicted from a different perspective, namely, that of being black in America, which in turn removes white viewers from their own experience and provides a detailed access to that of others."[81] This perspectival shift is crucial to Lee's African American aesthetic. Caucasian viewers, according to Flory's complex argument, "have trouble imagining what it is like to be African American 'from the inside'—engaging black points of view empathetically—because they often do not understand black experience from a detailed or intimate perspective. It is frequently too far from their own experience of the world."[82] Flory, following Thomas E. Hill, Jr. and Bernard Boxill's scholarship about American racial formation, writes, "this limitation in imagining other life possibilities may interfere with whites knowing the moral thing to do because they may be easily deceived by their own social advantages into thinking that such accrue to all, and thus will be unable to perceive many cases of racial injustice."[83] *Do the Right Thing,* indeed, presents Sal so approvingly that his racist behaviors—scorning Buggin' Out's use of the word *brother* when the latter requests black celebrities on the Wall of Fame; threatening Buggin' Out with a baseball bat to recall the Howard Beach incident; employing the phrases "these people" and "you people" to construct his customers as foreign others; and, most objectionably, heaping a torrent of racial abuse ("Turn that jungle music off! We ain't in Africa!"; "black cocksucker"; "nigger motherfucker") on Radio Raheem and Buggin' Out when they, near the film's conclusion, loudly play "Fight the Power" to demand that Sal address their grievances—may not appear as bigoted as they are.

Danny Aiello, like some *Do the Right Thing* viewers, refuses to see Sal as racist, as his comments in St. Claire Bourne's documentary *Making "Do the Right Thing"* reveal. During a table reading of the script, Aiello says, "I thought he's not a racist. He's a nice guy. He sees people as equal." Later, Aiello elaborates his feelings about Sal: "Is he a racist? I don't think so. But he's heard those words so fucking often, he reached down. If it was me and I said it, I'm capable of saying those words, I'm capable, and I have said 'em, but I'm not a racist."[84] Aiello believes that Sal makes the mistake of reaching into himself to find the most offensive words possible to use against Radio Raheem and Buggin' Out rather than seeing this response as evidence of Sal's suppressed racism. Flory argues that Aiello's reaction embodies a specific type of racial allegiance that certain white viewers (and, in Aiello's case, white performers) develop with characters like Sal:

> The explanation for why many white viewers—and Aiello himself—resist seeing Sal as a racist might be formulated the following way. A white audience member's understanding of a white character's actions often accrues from a firm but implicit grasp of white racial experience, which presupposes the many ways in which the long histories of world white

supremacy, economic, social, and cultural advantage, and being at the top of what was supposedly a scientifically proven racial hierarchy, underlay and remain influential in white people's lives.[85]

Do the Right Thing, Flory persuasively argues, forces white viewers to consider their whiteness from the outside by critically examining their privileged position within American society (and, in a further move, their privileged viewing position as the primary consumers of American cinema). Lee's movie seeds bigoted statements and behaviors from Sal throughout its narrative to discomfit audience members who nonetheless identify and bond with him. White viewers, in Flory's view, "resist the possibility of race being an issue and overlook crucial pieces of information that would require them to revise their typical ways of thinking about race because their previous experience has prepared them cognitively neither for the possibility of changing their standard ways of thinking nor for properly incorporating such information."[86] Flory's analysis, based on the work of such scholars as Linda Martin Alcoff, Richard Dyer, Emmanuel C. Eze, Frantz Fanon, Charles W. Mills, and Lewis R. Gordon, powerfully explains how Lee positions Sal as a good-hearted, generous, and affable person who nonetheless espouses bigoted ideas that neither he nor the audience members who enjoy his character recognize as racist.

Do the Right Thing, however, makes its viewer participate in Sal's racism even if, as Flory notes, "some empathy for Sal, of course, must be attributed to nonracial factors. To present a nuanced sympathetic racist character for whom viewers might initially establish a solid favorable outlook, Lee makes him narratively central and treats him compassionately much of the time."[87] Lee's strategy seems risky to Flory because the film's audience might so empathize with Sal that it overlooks his bigotry, but this danger does not prevent critical viewers from noticing the movie's cues (sometimes subtle, sometimes explicit) that the man carries deep-seated prejudices against his African American and Latino customers. The riot that concludes the film, therefore, is not the explosion of purposeless violence that reviewers such as David Denby and Stanley Crouch believe, but becomes an understandable response to the persistent prejudice that the block's residents face (but not do not consistently challenge). Radio Raheem's murder at the hands of police officers who break up the fight among Raheem, Buggin' Out, Sal, Pino, and Vito (after Sal destroys Raheem's stereo) may be this bigotry's most tragic expression, but *Do the Right Thing* carefully prepares its audience for what Lee's January 12, 1988, production-journal entry calls "the riot scene—or here's a better term, uprising."[88] Lee, by choosing this word, reframes the destruction of Sal's property as an act of civil disobedience that protests (and feebly avenges) the loss of Raheem's life. Paula J. Massood claims that *Do the Right Thing*'s "riot touches upon the fear of racial violence repressed at the core of American culture throughout the twentieth century,"[89] but her conclusion underplays just how skillfully the sequence depicts the effects of pent-up rage on communities whose inhabitants, feeling powerless to change their economic and political circumstances, claim agency in what seems an otherwise hopeless situation. Sal, in Lee's first-draft screenplay (a handwritten reproduction of which, dated March 16, 1988, appears in *Spike Lee: Do the Right Thing*, the 2010 retrospective book about the movie's production written by Lee and Jason Matloff), even feels that destroying his pizzeria represents a kind of progress, telling Mookie, "I think you Blacks might be wising up. . . . Twenty years ago you Blacks would have burned down your own buildings."[90]

Lee wisely omits this moralistic declaration, along with Mookie's reply ("Maybe we are a little smarter"[91]), from the final film, preferring an unresolved conclusion that appears in no publicly available draft of *Do the Right Thing*'s script. The morning after the violence, Sal becomes enraged when Mookie interrupts his (Sal's) inspection of the pizzeria's damages to demand that Sal pay his (Mookie's) weekly wages. Sal throws five $100 bills at Mookie's chest, yelling "You're wealthy, Mookie! You're a real fucking Rockefeller!" in a scene so rife with recrimination that the viewer half expects Sal to strike Mookie, or vice versa, after Mookie defiantly observes that Sal's insurance policy will compensate his property loss, but that Radio Raheem's death cannot be reversed. Sal, so overcome by emotion he cannot acknowledge that Raheem's life means more than any piece of property, screams, "I built this fucking place with my bare fucking hands!" Mookie weathers Sal's outburst, telling him, "Sal, I gotta go see my son if it's all right with you" before picking up the money that lies on the ground. This interaction not only mirrors the previous night's events (fury burns itself out to leave few resolutions and fewer solutions to the systemic problems that the movie's characters face) but also suggests, as Michael Silberstein notes in "The Dialectic of King and X in *Do the Right Thing*," that their tension arises from the unequal distribution of wealth in the neighborhood (and, by implication, within America).[92] *Do the Right Thing* here elliptically criticizes the economic inequality of American racism that bell hooks, Wahneema Lubiano, and Ed Guerrero note, although the film does so symbolically (by having Mookie and Sal represent their nation) rather than directly indicting American capitalism's racial iniquities.

Mookie then walks away from the pizzeria as Mister Señor Love Daddy, expressing his incredulity ("My people, my people: What can I say? Say what I can. I saw it, but I didn't believe it. I didn't believe it, what I saw. Are we gonna live together? Together are we gonna live?"), tells his listeners that a mayoral commission will investigate the incident (because property damage cannot be tolerated), and encourages everyone to vote in the forthcoming election (clearly referencing the Democratic primary contest between incumbent New York City mayor Ed Koch and challenger David Dinkins that Dinkins won on September 12, 1989). Love Daddy then dedicates the next song to Radio Raheem: "We love you, brother." The film concludes with two quotations, the first from Dr. Martin Luther King, Jr., and the second from Malcolm X, about the place of violence in the civil-rights struggle, before fading to the only known photo of both men smiling and shaking hands, an image (snapped on March 26, 1964) that the character Smiley (Roger Guenveur Smith) unsuccessfully attempts to sell to the block's residents throughout the movie.

This ambiguous conclusion has provoked many interpretations since *Do the Right Thing*'s release, to the point that the final words from King and Malcolm X are considered contradictory ideas, dueling quotations, or false oppositions. King's quote, adapted from "The Quest for Peace and Justice," the Nobel Lecture that he delivered on December 11, 1964, after accepting that year's Nobel Peace Prize, states, in part, "Violence as a way of achieving racial justice is both impractical and immoral. It is impractical because it is a descending spiral ending in destruction for all. The old law of an eye for an eye leaves everybody blind. It is immoral because it seeks to humiliate the opponent rather than win his understanding; it seeks to annihilate rather than to convert."[93] Malcolm X's quote reads:

> I think there are plenty of good people in America, but there are also plenty of bad people in America and the bad ones are the ones who seem to have all the power and be in these positions to block things that you and I need. Because this is the situation, you and I have to preserve the right to do what is necessary to bring an end to that situation, and it doesn't mean that I advocate violence, but at the same time I am not against using violence in self-defense. I don't even call it violence when it's self-defense, I call it intelligence.[94]

These quotations, as any close reading reveals, neither oppose nor contradict one another. King denounces violence as a method of achieving racial justice, a stance that Malcolm X endorses by stating that he does not advocate violence. Malcolm X, however, redefines violence as an intelligent strategy of self-defense for African Americans suffering racist oppression, thereby questioning the wisdom of passively accepting the violence perpetrated by authority figures hoping to maintain the nation's racially inequitable power relations. Lee, in much the same manner, redefines *Do the Right Thing*'s concluding violence as an uprising rather than a riot to challenge the existing power structure that Mookie, Sal, and the block's inhabitants must endure. The movie, by citing King and Malcolm X at its conclusion, acknowledges that each man was approaching the other's outlook toward the end of his life, making much the same point that James H. Cone's book *Martin and Malcolm and America: A Dream or a Nightmare* does: "Martin's and Malcolm's movement toward each other is a clue that neither one can be fully understood or appreciated without serious attention to the other. They complemented and corrected each other; each spoke a truth about America that cannot be fully comprehended without the insights of the other."[95]

Do the Right Thing also speaks truths about America by making its final image the photograph of Martin and Malcolm smiling, shaking hands, and demonstrating respect for one another. This choice illustrates Lee's repeated statement that the film uses King's and Malcolm X's quotations to support their outlooks, tactics, and strategies about achieving political, economic, and social equality. Lee's response to the charge that *Do the Right Thing* creates a false opposition between the two leaders, given to David Breskin during their long *Rolling Stone* interview (reprinted in *Inner Views: Filmmakers in Conversation*), eloquently makes this point: "The most important thing for me about Martin Luther King and Malcom [*sic*] X is that they both wanted the same thing for black people; it's just that they chose very different routes to arrive there. This has always been a choice that black people have had to make: which way to go to achieve our freedom? It doesn't have to be either/or; it can be a synthesis."[96] *Do the Right Thing* offers little synthesis beyond the tenuous truce that Mookie and Sal achieve before the final credits roll. A more uplifting conclusion would falsify the state of late-1980s American race relations, yet Lee's third film offers hope as well as despair by mixing cinematic realism, naturalism, symbolism, and surrealism into a movie that, in Roger Ebert's words, empathizes with all its participants. The film, by doing so, signals Lee's growing maturity as an artist, social critic, and cinematic storyteller. Despite *Do the Right Thing*'s drawbacks as a diagnosis of American racism's institutional foundations, the film earns its reputation as a masterpiece of late-twentieth-century cinema by provoking serious arguments about race in a way that few other American movies ever have. The film's status as entertainment and as art, therefore, is secure, making *Do the Right Thing* a watershed entry in the American cinematic canon.

3

Dancing with Denzel

TAKE THE A-TRAIN

For film reviewers, Hollywood observers, and even the director himself, Spike Lee's four collaborations with Denzel Washington—*Mo' Better Blues* (1990), *Malcolm X* (1992), *He Got Game* (1998), and *Inside Man* (2006)—are milestones in their careers. Although these projects tend to confirm each man's artistic gifts, mainstream discussions surrounding *Malcolm X* so widely judge this film a landmark accomplishment for American (and African American) cinema that the movie now stands as a masterpiece of early 1990s' American popular art. The Library of Congress endorsed this perspective in 2010 by selecting *Malcolm X* for preservation in its National Film Registry, offering the imprimatur of the organization created by the U.S. Congress to maintain, according to its website, "a list of films deemed 'culturally, historically or aesthetically significant' that are earmarked for preservation by the Library of Congress. These films are not selected as the 'best' American films of all time, but rather as works of enduring importance to American culture. They reflect who we are as a people and as a nation."[1]

The fact that a movie devoted to dramatizing the life of the black revolutionary once so reviled by the American government that the Federal Bureau of Investigation's (FBI's) official surveillance file of Malcolm X runs to more than 5,000 pages[2] entered the nation's official film archive less than twenty years after its theatrical release speaks not only to Lee and Washington's passion in pursuing *Malcolm X*'s production but also to Malcolm X's changing reputation, from frightening critic of American racism, capitalism, and militarism to socially acceptable icon of American dissent, protest, and progress. Lee's cinematic treatment of Malcolm's life, at least according to the Registry's mission statement, exhibits such momentous concerns about American history, culture, and politics that *Malcolm X* tells its viewers fundamental truths about the national experience. The U.S. Postal Service subsequently affirmed Malcolm's importance by issuing a postage stamp bearing his likeness in January 1999, only six years and two months after *Malcolm X*'s

November 1992 theatrical release. This event caused actor, activist, and long-time Lee collaborator Ossie Davis—the man whose moving eulogy of Malcolm closes Lee's film—to comment at the stamp's unveiling ceremony, "We in this community look upon this commemorative stamp finally as America's stamp of approval"[3] and Attallah Shabazz, Malcolm's oldest daughter, to write in her foreword to the 1999 edition of *The Autobiography of Malcolm X,* "This national commemoration, three decades after his lifetime, pays tribute to his immeasurable contributions on behalf of one's innate right to self-preservation and human dignity."[4]

Lee's film did not directly inspire the stamp's issuance, but the movie participated in a cultural movement to renew and reclaim Malcolm's historical significance that began shortly after his assassination on February 21, 1965, that gained traction during the 1970s, and that became a noticeable aspect of African American youth culture throughout the 1980s. As S. Craig Watkins notes in *Representing: Hip Hop Culture and the Production of Black Cinema*'s astute discussion of *Malcolm X*'s production, "And perhaps most important, black youth had created a popular culture based on Malcolm X as a symbol of race pride and cultural resistance. By the early 1990s, the renewed interest in Malcolm X sparked a proliferation of rap songs, caps, T-shirts, books, and posters that saturated the popular cultural world of black youth."[5] Lee, indeed, designed a Malcolm X baseball cap to promote his film long before principal photography began, as he recounts in *By Any Means Necessary: The Trials and Tribulations of the Making of "Malcolm X" (While Ten Million Motherfuckers Are Fucking with You!),* the movie's cheekily titled companion publication: "While we were shooting *Jungle Fever* in late 1990, I made up an initial design for the 'X' cap. I'd already decided I had to do *Malcolm X,* and marketing is an integral part of my filmmaking. So the X was planned all the way out. I came up with a simple design—silver X on black baseball cap."[6] These hats began appearing alongside the T-shirts, posters, books, and songs devoted to Malcolm X that African Americans of all ages, but particularly young people, had embraced in the preceding years, meaning that Lee's public-relations savvy helped build enthusiasm not only for Malcolm himself but also (and just as importantly) for the film *Malcolm X.* "The colors could be changed later on as the campaign advanced," Lee says in *By Any Means Necessary,* revealing just how deliberately he pursued this marketing strategy: "It looked good. I started wearing it, and we began selling it in our store, Spike's Joint, and in other places. I gave them away strategically. I asked Michael Jordan to wear it, and he has. Then I asked some other stars to wear it and, what can I say, it just caught on. Then the knock-offs started appearing."[7] Jordan's assistance was invaluable, particularly when he wore an "X" cap during his televised interview after the National Basketball Association's 1991 All-Star Game in Charlotte, North Carolina, bringing wide exposure to *Malcolm X* in an endorsement that, according to Lee's autobiography, *That's My Story and I'm Sticking to It,* made the caps "the must-have accessory of the year."[8]

This testament to Lee's promotional prowess, however, raises the troubling possibility that he crassly commercializes Malcolm's memory rather than capturing this complex man's revolutionary life, political philosophy, and social impact on-screen. Watkins, indeed, forthrightly addresses this point by writing, "It was the popularization of Malcolm X and his attractiveness to black youth that both Warner Brothers and Lee sought to exploit"[9] in bringing the long-delayed biopic of Malcolm's life to cinema screens in 1992, although Lee's commitment to the film throughout its troubled production demonstrates that making *Malcolm X* was not simply a vanity project designed to generate cash for himself, his collaborators, and his production company. Yet this concern—expressed before, during, and after *Malcolm X*'s release by scholars as varied as Amiri Baraka, Clayborne Carson, and Manning Marable[10]—indicates deeper flaws in *Malcolm X*, which, while an accomplished film, exemplifies Lee's problematic representations of black radicalism, black militancy, and black women. These challenges do not detract from the scale of *Malcolm X*'s achievement, especially Denzel Washington's astonishing performance in the title role, Lee's assured direction, Ernest Dickerson's admirable cinematography, and Terence Blanchard's engaging score, but they indicate how straitened Lee's outlook can be when dealing with historically, politically, and culturally charged material.

These drawbacks to an otherwise masterful movie, however, find precursors in Lee and Washington's first collaboration, *Mo' Better Blues,* the story of jazz trumpeter Bleek Gilliam's professional and personal woes. This movie's considerable pleasures cannot hide its sometimes distressingly regressive approach to African American women, making it almost a trial run for *Malcolm X*'s flawed magnificence. Both films are intricate cinematic narratives that evince skillful, dedicated, and passionate craft on the part of their makers, but neither movie can escape the limitations that typify Lee's early work. Their blemishes, indeed, are nearly as instructive as their triumphs to demonstrate how Lee's cinematic vision, like important aspects of Malcolm's political ideology, is simultaneously revolutionary and traditional. Both *Mo' Better Blues* and *Malcolm X* are fascinating productions that advance troubling representations of women (particularly African American women) to unite them in a sexist narrative that underscores Lee's virtues and shortcomings as a filmmaker of provocative subject matter.

BLUE NOTES

Mo' Better Blues is not merely *Malcolm X*'s forerunner, but a complicated work of art in its own right. Lee, the son of noted jazz bassist and composer Bill Lee, wrote the film not only to dramatize his appreciation for this music but also in response to three prior films: Bertrand Tavernier's '*Round Midnight* (1986), Clint Eastwood's *Bird* (1988), and his own *Do the Right Thing* (1989). Lee confesses in his production notes (compiled in *Mo' Better*

Blues: A Spike Lee Joint, the film's companion publication written in collaboration with Lisa Jones), "Not to negate love and relationships, but I don't think *Mo' Better Blues* is as important a film as *Do the Right Thing*. This doesn't mean that I like it less—it was the right film for me to do at the time. However, the issue of racism is one I want to explore again on film."[11] Lee's major interest in creating *Mo' Better Blues*, however, involves his marrow-deep love of jazz, perhaps best exemplified by the companion volume's opening paragraph: "I always knew I would do a movie about the music. When I say the music, I'm talking about jazz, the music I grew up with. Jazz isn't the only type of music that I listen to, but it's the music I feel closest to."[12]

Although Lee wished to honor his father Bill Lee's life and career by making a movie about jazz musicians, Tavernier's and Eastwood's films inspired him to fashion *Mo' Better Blues* as an insider's view of contemporary jazz artists that avoided the problems he saw in '*Round Midnight* and *Bird*. "Both were narrow depictions of the lives of Black musicians, as seen through the eyes of White screenwriters and White directors,"[13] Lee writes in the companion volume, while telling Kaleem Aftab in *That's My Story* that, despite the fact that both Tavernier and Eastwood might love jazz as much as (and probably know more about it than) he does, the problem with both films is that they offer little warmth, preferring to forward images of tormented musicians who "never laughed, they never had joy in their life, they're all tragic and torn and twisted."[14] Lee points out that the jazz performers of his generation are not one-dimensional artists condemned to lives of self-destruction by citing Branford and Wynton Marsalis, Terence Blanchard, and Donald Harrison as examples of jazz artists who "weren't rich, but they were making good money. . . . [T]hey had family, they had girlfriends, had a good time going out, living—they're not simply moping around lamenting the misery of their lives."[15] Lee, therefore, sees *Mo' Better Blues* as a way to correct the cinematic record by offering a broader portrait of African American jazz and blues musicians than Hollywood typically allows, not just in Tavernier's and Eastwood's films, but stretching back to Allen Reisner's *St. Louis Blues* (1958), Martin Ritt's *Paris Blues* (1961), Leo Penn's *A Man Called Adam* (1966), and Sidney J. Furie's *Lady Sings the Blues* (1972). Lee's desire to dramatize the wider experiences of late-twentieth-century jazz artists leads *Mo' Better Blues* to repudiate the film cliché of the tragic jazz performer battling his inner demons, especially feelings of artistic inadequacy and commercial failure that lead to drug addiction, by making Bleek Gilliam (Denzel Washington) a disciplined musician and composer involved with two women—aspiring singer Clarke Betancourt (Cynda Williams) and elementary-school teacher Indigo Downes (Joie Lee)—who places his creative life ahead of these (and, truth be told, all other) relationships.

Herein lies the movie's major problem, for despite this premise's dramatic potential and the rich terrain that *Mo' Better Blues* covers in its best moments, the film does not pay sufficient attention either to Clarke or Indigo as individuals or develop them into autonomous personalities. As satellites to Bleek's sexual needs who remain subservient to his artistic pursuits, they are two in a long line of Lee's hollow female characters. Indigo—despite working as a professional educator (like Lee's mother, Jacquelyn Shelton Lee) and being well played by his sister, Joie Lee—telegraphs her forgiving nature during her first appearance, when Indigo tells Bleek, after a night of lovemaking, that she should have followed her mother's advice by not getting romantically involved with a musician, who will bring "grief and pain and tears and heartbreak to my doorstep." Bleek is "a good brother . . . but you still don't know what you want" and "a dog . . . a nice dog, but you're a dog nonetheless."[16] Bleek does not protest these descriptions, but instead utters the film's most famous (and infamous) line when he tells Indigo, "I'm not gonna argue the point. You know how I am. With men, it's a dick thing." This bald, unreconstructed, and bracing declaration of Bleek's ingrained sexism indicates his adolescent view of romantic relationships. Sex, for Bleek, is merely an anatomical pursuit that reduces both partners to pleasure-seeking fleshpots. He justifies this outlook to his father, Big Stop (Dick Anthony Williams), by telling the older man, simply, "I like women" to explain his refusal to commit to Indigo. This paradox reveals how Bleek regards Indigo and Clarke less as human beings than as physical bodies that offer sexual stimulation, gratification, and relief, but who retain the potential to disrupt Bleek's life with emotional considerations that restrict his career ambitions. Bleek, in other words, is a classic sexist who thinks that women, while worthy of physical intimacy, should not intrude into his highly regulated life.

Bleek's first interaction with Clarke reinforces this point when he chastises her for interrupting his practice session, saying that they might as well make love because she has disturbed his tightly organized schedule. Bleek, indeed, dubs their sexual escapades "the mo' better" as a comfortable euphemism for coitus that avoids all suggestion of emotional entanglement. Clarke, no stranger to their relationship's limitations, accepts her status as Bleek's casual lover by saying, "We don't make love because you don't love me. But in the meantime, I'll settle for some of that mo' better." This capitulation to Bleek's desire praises his sexual prowess while fortifying Bleek's view of their relationship as little more than physical release. Clarke is not upset by this state of affairs, but instead jokes with Bleek about his emotional deficiencies in a scene that, from the perspective of Hollywood's long history of sexually passive female characters, shows Clarke to be more independent than usual. She is, after all, a woman who pursues physical intimacy with Bleek because it pleases her, not because it ties her to him in more complicated ways.

Lee, indeed, sketches these scenes with good dialogue, while the performances are uniformly excellent. Denzel Washington and Joie Lee are particularly effective, but more intriguing is how first-time actress Cynda Williams infuses Clarke with the subdued eroticism of *She's Gotta Have It*'s Nola Darling (Tracy Camilla Johns). Clarke and Indigo, however, are far less interesting than Nola, for however progressive their open sensuality may seem, their willingness to subordinate themselves to Bleek rather than pursuing multiple amorous affairs (like Nola) reveals an ultimately regressive view of women that, despite Lee's stated commitment to expanding his female characters' horizons, fails in *Mo' Better Blues*. Clarke may seem to fulfill Lee's goal when she leaves Bleek for his quintet's saxophone player, Shadow Henderson (Wesley Snipes), after Shadow offers her the opportunity to sing with the new jazz combo he forms near the film's conclusion, but, despite Shadow's charm and Snipes's good performance in the role, Clarke merely substitutes one domineering man for another.

Bleek, however, loses the ability to play music after his violent encounter with two enforcers, Madlock (Samuel L. Jackson) and Rod (Leonard Thomas). While beating Bleek's manager, Giant (Spike Lee), for not paying his gambling debts to their boss, the bookie and loan shark Petey (Rubén Blades), Madlock and Rod damage Bleek's lip by smacking him in the mouth with his own trumpet. Shadow, having chafed against Bleek's overbearing control of the Bleek Gilliam Quintet earlier in the movie, takes this opportunity not only to form his own band but also to encourage Clarke's talent in ways that Bleek (who refuses to let Clarke sing with his combo because she does not have sufficient vocal training) never does. Yet even this beneficence is a sexual scam insofar as the smooth-talking Shadow uses his appreciation of Clarke's talent as his primary seduction strategy, getting her into bed before giving her the job. Clarke, true to Bleek's evaluation, is a passable (but far from terrific) singer who still headlines Shadow's band, thereby developing greater confidence in her own talent. Indigo, by contrast, becomes less interesting by *Mo' Better Blues*'s conclusion. She exercises her own agency by rejecting Bleek when, one night during sex, he mistakenly calls her Clarke, but then mysteriously takes him back when, one year after his injury, the despondent Bleek pleads with Indigo to marry him so that they may start a family. This development suggests that the attractive and intelligent Indigo has had no romantic prospects for the entire year of Bleek's recovery. She submits to his request because, having no better possibilities, Indigo settles for the now-reformed Bleek, who, no longer pursuing music as either his occupation or avocation, prepares himself for commitment. The film's unlikely conclusion sees Bleek and Indigo marry, have a son named Miles (Zakee Howze), and live as a reasonably happy middle-class family in the same brownstone that served as Bleek's childhood home. This denouement demonstrates *Mo' Better Blues*'s essential sexism, for Indigo surrenders to marriage and motherhood with scant motivation. Indeed, only her physical attraction to Bleek explains Indigo's willingness to accept his questionable confession of love, which, in truth, is merely his plea for Indigo to fulfill him because music no longer can.

Treating the film's female characters so cavalierly weakens Lee's approach to *Mo' Better Blues* despite the movie's other merits, setting a path that *Malcolm X* follows. As bell hooks notes in "Male Heroes and Female Sex

Objects: Sexism in Spike Lee's *Malcolm X*," her caustic review of the latter film, "it is *Mo' Better Blues* that sets paradigms for black gender relations. Black females are neatly divided into two categories—ho' or mammy/madonna. The ho' is out for what she can get, using her pussy to seduce, conquer, and exploit the male. The mammy/madonna nurtures, forgives, provides unconditional love."[17] Creating such stereotypical women strands Lee's male protagonists in an untenable situation that, for hooks, reinforces the director's worst propensities: "Black men, mired in sexism and misogyny, tolerate the strong, 'bitchified,' tell-it-like-it-is black woman but also seek to escape her. In *Mo' Better Blues,* the black woman who gets her man in the end does so by surrendering her will to challenge and confront. She simply understands and accepts. It's a bleak picture. In the final analysis, mo' better is mo' bitter."[18] This evaluation perceptively identifies *Mo' Better Blues'* major flaw, which *Malcolm X* both extends and revises by including female characters—especially Malcolm's wife, Betty Shabazz (Angela Bassett)—who, despite their intelligence and dignity, remain satellites to the protagonist's quest for political and personal liberation. Although hooks sees both movies as victims of Lee's cinematic chauvinism, this underlying truth misses the political, cultural, and sexual complexities that make *Mo' Better Blues* and *Malcolm X* worthwhile films to watch. Both movies are revolutionary and traditional, progressive and regressive, liberatory and restrictive texts that cannot be reduced to simple failures of vision because they chronicle, with occasional insight, the problematic African American masculinities so typical of Lee's most provocative productions.

REEL WOMEN

Lee's difficulties with female characterization help explain why *Malcolm X* is such a patriarchal film, a reality with precedent in *The Autobiography of Malcolm X* that Lee's movie accentuates by sidelining or omitting significant women in Malcolm's life. Malcolm's mother Louise Norton Little (Lonette McKee), like his father Earl Little (Tommy Hollis), appears only in flashbacks, where, in her first appearance, the pregnant Louise attempts to protect her children (including the unborn Malcolm) from Ku Klux Klansmen who break all the windows of their Omaha, Nebraska house when the Klansmen realize that Earl, an itinerant preacher and supporter of Marcus Garvey whom they blame for inciting local African Americans to become "uppity,"[19] is not at home. Louise's subsequent appearances become shorter and more disturbing, until, after moving with Earl to Lansing, Michigan, she endures the indignities that follow his violent death (Earl is run down by a trolley car after being attacked by men belonging to the Black Riders, a local racist militia). Louise fights the life-insurance company that refuses to honor Earl's policy after judging his death a suicide, protests the visits of social worker Miss Dunne (Karen Allen) as intrusive and racially insensitive, loses control of her family, sees her children become wards of the state, and, finally, sits prostrate and unmoving in the Kalamazoo mental hospital to which she is forcibly committed.

These vignettes follow the *Autobiography*'s narrative sequence, bringing Louise to vivid life (McKee is excellent in the role), but devote less attention to her than Malcolm's book, even allowing for the narrative compression necessary to adapt the *Autobiography* into a three-hour, twenty-two-minute movie. *Malcolm X*, in a serious omission, fails to dramatize the domestic violence that Louise suffered at Earl's hands, violence that Malcolm describes in resolutely sexist terms. The *Autobiography*'s first chapter, for instance, notes that Malcolm's parents "seemed to be nearly always at odds. Sometimes my father would beat her. It might have had something to do with the fact that my mother had a pretty good education. Where she got it I don't know. But an educated woman, I suppose," Malcolm writes in a passage revealing his patriarchal beliefs, "can't resist the temptation to correct an uneducated man. Every now and then, when she would put those smooth words on him, he would grab her."[20] This statement, one of many in the *Autobiography* to expose Malcolm's entrenched sexism, prepares the reader for his eventual recognition of women's importance to the black freedom struggle, both in America and in Africa's newly independent nations. Lee's exclusion of this material, however, deprives *Malcolm X* of a key flashback that would help contextualize Louise's mental breakdown not simply as the product of racial discrimination, but as the culmination of long-term racial and gender inequality that, when coupled with the stress of raising seven children alone, provokes the depression and despair that Malcolm's *Autobiography* forlornly documents. Scrubbing Earl's violence against his wife from the film may seem to offer Louise more agency than the *Autobiography* permits, but this decision restricts her character to a common stereotype: the wild-eyed black mother incapable of caring for her children.

Malcolm's cinematic voiceover, taken from the *Autobiography*, notes that, "if ever a state agency destroyed a family, it destroyed ours" in Lee's effort to capture the sexist-yet-sympathetic portrait of Louise Little that the *Autobiography*'s first chapter conveys. Observations (in the book) such as "Nothing that I can imagine could have moved me as deeply as seeing her pitiful state"[21] are particularly poignant. Lee visually suggests this comment by having the adult Malcolm sit in a corner of Louise's hospital room with his face (in one of Denzel Washington's finest moments) covered by appalled regret, but Lee still chooses not to dispute the *Autobiography*'s patriarchal treatment of Louise. Jeffrey B. Leak, in his cogent essay "Malcolm X and Black Masculinity in Process," agrees with Hilton Als's assessment (propounded in Als's article about the *Autobiography*'s treatment of Louise Little, "Philosopher or Dog?") that Louise "only serves two purposes for Malcolm: to give birth to him and to symbolize the stain of white blood on the Negro race"[22] because, as a light-skinned black woman, she offers visual proof of the historical crime of white masters raping their female slaves. Leak points out that, in the *Autobiography*, "Malcolm objectifies her, rendering her as nothing more than an extension of white supremacy and colonialism. He is able to explain why his father would strike her, but he fails to explain or consider the notion that his mother had a right to offer an opinion (and even a criticism) when necessary."[23] Failing to challenge more forcefully, this sexist depiction of Louise in *Malcolm X* demonstrates that Lee, at least in this instance, remains more concerned about faithfully rendering the *Autobiography*'s chauvinistic view of women than offering a broader portrait of Louise. Lee's interest in her, like Clarke and Indigo in *Mo' Better Blues*, remains more symbolic than realistic. Louise, indeed, becomes the first woman to disappoint Malcolm and, consequently, the model upon which he bases his future opinions of women, making him receptive, once he becomes a member of the Nation of Islam (NOI), to the Nation's strict ideology that the sexes should inhabit separate spheres; that women are, in the words of the memorably troubling NOI rally banners that *Malcolm X* reproduces in two different scenes, black America's "most valuable property"; and, most famously, that women should confine themselves to submissive, nurturing roles that revolve around husbands and children rather than independent lives, ambitions, and careers.

Leak's analysis shows that Malcolm's attitudes toward women were not static despite the patriarchal affirmation they received once he joined NOI. Any detailed reading of the *Autobiography* exposes the considerable understatement Leak indulges when writing, "Malcolm certainly began his ruminations about his life with, at best, a deep indifference toward women,"[24] yet Leak correctly observes that Malcolm's relationship with his half-sister and eventual guardian, Ella Little-Collins, "depicts Malcolm's struggle with patriarchy and his willingness to reveal his rather narrow-minded views about women, perspectives that by the end of the *Autobiography* are in the process of reformulation but far from complete revisions."[25] Ella takes Malcolm into her home when he relocates to Boston's all-black Roxbury neighborhood; offers him guidance about life as a young African American man; succeeds in transferring him from the Charlestown State Prison to the Norfolk Prison Colony (described by the *Autobiography* as "an experimental rehabilitation jail"[26]) after Malcolm is arrested for burglarizing Boston homes and sentenced to ten years imprisonment; finances his 1964 trip to Mecca, during which he undergoes spiritual transformation while on *hajj*; and, after his death, helps preserve Malcolm's legacy by running the Organization of Afro-American Unity that Malcolm founded less than one year before his assassination. Malcolm explains Ella's immense effect on him by commenting in the *Autobiography* that, during their first meeting, Ella visits his family in Lansing, where he notices that "she was the first really proud black woman I had ever seen in my life. She was plainly proud of her very dark skin. This was unheard of among Negroes in those days, especially in Lansing."[27] Ella's dignified bearing, however, cannot overcome Malcolm's sexist appraisal of her when he arrives in Boston to find that Ella has prepared a room in her Roxbury home for him. The *Autobiography,* in a pattern that typifies Malcolm's depiction of Ella and other independent women, mingles praise with skepticism about unconventional female lives. "Ella still seemed to be as big, black, outspoken and impressive a woman as she had been in Mason and Lansing," Malcolm says, but then reveals, "Only about two weeks before I arrived, she had split up with her second husband . . . but she was taking it right in stride. I could see, though I didn't say, how any average man would find it almost impossible to live for very long with a woman whose every instinct was to run everything and everybody she had anything to do with— including me."[28] Malcolm, by indicating that only extraordinary men can tolerate strong-willed women like his half-sister, repeats the sexist canard that proper female behavior defers to men rather than challenges male authority. Average men, the *Autobiography* implies, find Ella (and women like her) so intimidating that the emasculating potential such women represent strikes fear in them. Malcolm, in the passage's most significant subtext, feels just as threatened as Ella's husband despite admiring her race pride. He refuses to contemplate how Ella's strong will enhances her compassion for him, which, rather than dominating Malcolm into submission, instead protects him for several years from the vicissitudes of growing up as a ne'er-do-well young black man in Boston. Ella becomes Malcolm's surrogate mother, who, as bell hooks notes, "helped educate him for critical consciousness,"[29] but also ensured that Malcolm would rebel against her influence. Ella's significance as a symbol of assertive black femininity appears at key junctures throughout the *Autobiography* to illustrate, just as Jeffrey B. Leak argues, that, despite the book's persistent chauvinism, Malcolm's patriarchal view of women is not so ironclad that it resists all modification.

Malcolm X, however, eliminates Ella from its cinematic narrative. This elision prevents the film from demonstrating how crucial she was to Malcolm's development, particularly how his time as a hustler, as a sexually promiscuous criminal who parades his white girlfriend Sophia (Kate Vernon) throughout Harlem and Roxbury, and as an NOI minister preaching sexism under the guise of Muslim propriety contradicts Ella's example and approbation. Her presence is a vital component of Malcolm's life that Lee's movie avoids to maintain its resolutely patriarchal character. This aesthetic decision, in hooks's estimation, allows Lee "to create a film that does not break with Hollywood conventions and stereotypes," which, true to form, remain invested in portraying "the super-masculine hero . . . as a loner, an outlaw, a cultural orphan estranged from family and society."[30] Erasing Malcolm's relationship with Ella and marginalizing his relationship with Louise transform *Malcolm X* into a masculine fantasy that hooks finds not merely regrettable, but fully objectionable. "To have shown the bonds between Ella and Malcolm which were sustained throughout his life," hooks writes, "Lee would have needed both to break with Hollywood representations of the male hero as well as provide an image of black womanhood never before imagined on the Hollywood screen. The character of Ella would have been a powerful, politically conscious black woman who could not be portrayed as a sex object."[31] This damning assessment recognizes how thoroughly Lee rewrites Malcolm's life to emphasize the masculine stereotypes that align *Malcolm X* with the Hollywood biographical pictures (biopics) that Lee both emulates and revises. Choosing Malcolm as the subject of such a film expands the biopic's traditional boundaries, since no previous studio-backed movie of *Malcolm X*'s scale had tackled the life of an African American revolutionary leader (cinematic portrayals of Nat Turner, Frederick Douglass, Martin Luther King, Jr., Medgar Evers, and Huey P. Newton restricted them to supporting roles in theatrical films or to the subjects of television movies and miniseries), yet respects the genre's conventions by making the protagonist a dominant male who interacts with women on his own terms and as he pleases. Reducing Louise Little's presence and eliminating Ella Little-Collin's role in *Malcolm X* not only extend the problematic representation of women in Lee's earlier films but also repeat *Mo' Better Blues*'s depiction of women as either irritants or accessories to the protagonist's unquestioned masculinity.

BIOPICS, BITCHERY, AND BETTY

Malcolm X's debt to the biopic, however, helps account for its patriarchal attitude. Thomas Doherty's insightful essay "Malcolm X: In Print, On Screen" carefully analyzes the links between Lee's film and the genre that proves so influential to his narrative choices. "Just as *The Autobiography of Malcolm X* was read by the light of classic American literature," Doherty writes, "*Malcolm X* unspooled in the shadow of one of Hollywood's most durable motion picture genres: the biopic. During the classical studio era, the biopic thrived by celebrating the great (white) men of science, politics, and the arts, and the loyal women who stood behind them."[32] This final clause well describes *Malcolm X*'s depiction of Betty Shabazz, Malcolm's charming and intelligent wife, as a woman who occasionally prods him to be a better provider for his growing family and who, in a powerful scene, forces Malcolm to question the moral rectitude of NOI leader Elijah Muhammad (Al Freeman, Jr.) when reports of Muhammad's infidelities with NOI secretaries surface. Angela Bassett so beautifully plays Betty that the woman's status as a doting spouse might escape the viewer's notice when first watching the film, but Bassett-as-Betty contradicts the image that bell hooks advocates in "Male Heroes and Female Sex Objects" of a woman who "seduces and traps" Malcolm into marriage and who "'reads' her man in the bitchified manner that is Lee's trademark representation of heterosexual black coupling."[33] Betty neither appears in enough scenes to justify the charge of seduction nor pursues Malcolm in the open, sensual, and aggressive manner of Sophia, who, early in *Malcolm X*, offers herself to him at Boston's Roseland Ballroom after the frenetic and exceptionally well-choreographed Lindy Hop dance number that becomes the film's first show-stopping set piece. Despite hooks's generally acute assessment of *Malcolm X*'s sexism, she misreads Betty's character as a temptress when neither Lee's direction nor Bassett's acting substantiate this conclusion, especially considering that Betty's earnest interest in Malcolm's welfare (visible during their first meeting at one of Malcolm's public speeches, during their later meal at a Muslim cafeteria where Malcolm lectures Betty about women's deceitful ways, during a subsequent trip to New York's American Museum of Natural History, and during their visit to a diner where they share ice-cream sundaes) remains so chaste that Betty barely registers as a sexual presence, to say nothing of Malcolm's marriage proposal, which he makes from a Detroit phone booth in what may be the least romantic scene of a man asking a woman to join him in matrimony ever depicted in an American studio film. Betty instead so perfectly fulfills the biopic's stock role of faithful spouse to a man destined for greatness that only her race and Bassett's terrific performance distinguish Betty from the trustworthy wives who appear in dozens of earlier Hollywood biopics.

Malcolm X, in other words, captures the *Autobiography*'s conservative view of women, especially black women, with Betty standing as a symbol of strength, dignity, and submission in both book and film. Sheila Radford-Hill addresses the realities of Betty's life in her important essay "Womanizing Malcolm X" by noting, "Betty Shabazz was a well-educated black woman who was willing to conform to the Black Muslim feminine ideal," being "one of the many Muslim women who did not outwardly defy their husbands as their behavior was intimately connected to their religious conviction."[34] Betty, however, was no wilting flower, as her friend Myrlie Evers-Williams (widow of Medgar Evers) writes in her foreword to Russell J. Rickford's biography *Betty Shabazz, Surviving Malcolm X,* describing Betty as a "highly unusual woman of strength and courage"[35] who learned "how to survive heartache, self-doubt, anger, bitterness, and personal growth";[36] who once told Evers-Williams, "My children think my persona is me, when actually it is their father's";[37] and "who was complex and yet simple in her wisdom."[38] These comments and Rickford's well-researched book demonstrate that Betty was a complicated person who, despite her intellectual independence, accepted NOI's teachings about women out of religious faith. Radford-Hill explains this seemingly contradictory outlook by writing, "Women like Betty Shabazz respected the Nation's masculine ideal as it offered provision, protection, honor, and respect for black women who had an important, though subordinate, role in building the black nation."[39] Betty's religious commitment to Islam, indeed, began as dedication to NOI, but underwent a similar transformation to Malcolm's when she left the Nation with him in 1964, made pilgrimage to Mecca in 1965 (after Malcolm's assassination), embraced Sunni Islam, and returned to the United States to earn master's and doctoral degrees while raising six daughters. Lee's movie depicts some of this strength, as well as Betty's understated sense of humor, when, during Malcolm's lecture about women's wicked ways, Angela Bassett's fine acting comes to the fore. Betty smiles skeptically, knowingly, and sweetly in the same moment before commenting, "I think you've made your points, Brother Minister Malcolm. You haven't any time for marriage," causing the rueful Malcolm to laugh. Denzel Washington and Bassett play this scene not only with the tentative affection appropriate to a couple just learning about one another but also with the warmth that characterizes their companionable marriage later in the film. Most notable, however, is Bassett's talent at communicating Betty's inner strength and determination by subtly challenging, rather than directly contradicting, Malcolm's (and Elijah Muhammad's) overbearing sexism.

Lee's film, in this and other scenes, follows the *Autobiography*'s lead by depicting Betty as "a good Muslim woman and wife"[40] about whom Malcolm, in one of the book's most revealing passages, writes, "I guess by now I will say I love Betty. She's the only woman I ever even thought about loving. And she's one of the very few—four women—whom I have ever trusted."[41] This hesitant declaration ("I guess by now I will say I love Betty," not "I love Betty") comes after Malcolm mentions their four daughters by name to suggest that Betty's status as mother of his children, not her other qualities, convinces him to love and trust her. Malcolm immediately expands this portrait by noting that what he calls the "Western 'love' concept . . . really is lust. But love transcends just the physical. Love is disposition, behavior, attitude, thoughts, likes, dislikes—these things make a beautiful woman, a beautiful wife. This is the beauty that never fades," meaning that actual love appreciates deeper merits in a woman and should not wait until her "physical beauty fails"[42] to declare itself. Malcolm's fascinating but troubling perspective here recommends a spiritual connection between husband and wife that sees beyond a woman's surface appearance in what resembles a laudable attempt to appreciate women in general—and Betty in particular—for their strength of character, but that nonetheless privileges masculine control. Malcolm, after all, neither enumerates the qualities that make a beautiful (or handsome) husband appealing to his partner nor considers how a man's failing appearance might make him less attractive to his wife. Malcolm's most egalitarian statement about such relationships comes via religious explanation: "But Islam teaches us to look into the woman, and teaches her to look into us."[43] Yet this declaration also takes for granted a man's privilege in evaluating a woman's life, character, and potential, raising him to an unchallenged position by employing the plural term *us* to implicate Malcolm, his amanuensis Alex Haley, and his reader in a narrative that constructs its audience as male to help Malcolm relate his (and NOI's) conviction about women's subordination. By citing Betty as a specific example of a woman who fulfills the roles of good wife and mother for the benefit of all African Americans, Malcolm's effort to reframe his sexist assumptions merely helps reinforce them.

Seeing into a person is one of the *Autobiography*'s central metaphors for developing a secure understanding of another human being's beliefs and attitudes. It also cements NOI's foundational sexism. Malcolm later states that, because Betty looks into him as Islam teaches, "so she understands me. I would even say I don't imagine many other women might put up with the way I am. Awakening this brainwashed black man and telling this arrogant, devilish white man the truth about himself, Betty understands, is a full-time job."[44] Betty's forbearance and patience are prime values for black women to adopt if they wish to support their husbands in liberating African Americans from the political, economic, and social bonds that restrict them. These virtues demand, as Radford-Hill recognizes, "submissiveness and single-minded attention to the care and nurture of black children, the fruit of the black nation"[45] that defines NOI's feminine ideal, a mindset that Malcolm wholeheartedly adopts during his time as the Nation's most visible spokesperson, both in the *Autobiography* and in *Malcolm X*.

This patriarchal view so typified black-nationalist pronouncements about the freedom struggle during the 1950s and 1960s that Radford-Hill analyzes the sociopolitical context in which Malcolm made similar statements, not to excuse his sexist (and occasionally misogynistic) opinions, but to understand how they developed within the larger systems of thought, behavior, and culture that affected Malcolm's political stance. Writing that "black feminist and womanist scholars have long recognized that black nationalism promoted a pernicious machismo,"[46] Radford-Hill reminds her reader that research into the factors surrounding NOI's conservative sexual roles permits readers of the *Autobiography* (and viewers of *Malcolm X*) to understand the loyalty of NOI women to Elijah Muhammad's doctrine of female submission, for, in perhaps Radford-Hill's most important insight, "feminists and womanists have also exposed how patriarchal dominance manipulates female expectations of men to enforce gender codes favorable to male interests."[47] Malcolm X and Betty Shabazz were as captive to these codes as anyone else, while the passages in Malcolm's *Autobiography* about Betty's exemplary behavior become, in this light, interventions in their era's gender discourse that fortify patriarchal understandings of women's proper roles relative to masculine authority. Critical readers may even say that Malcolm manipulates theses gender codes to reinforce his reputation as a fearless truth-teller and to enhance his image as the strong male who keeps his wife in line, but Radford-Hill notes this image's nuances by writing, "another aspect of gender research involves how black manhood is constructed and performed. The short history of Malcolm's manhood suggests that his family provided examples of determined black women and that as he developed politically, he remade his masculine subjectivity in ways that allowed him to see women as agents of social change."[48] This judgment becomes clear to anyone who studies Malcolm's final year when, after two 1964 trips to Africa, he becomes impressed by how forcefully women play roles in the decolonization movements that, beginning in the 1950s, swept the continent, with seventeen African nations achieving independence from European colonial powers and becoming United Nations member states in 1960 alone.[49]

Malcolm, indeed, says during a 1964 interview conducted in Paris, France, after his second African visit, "One thing that I became aware of in my traveling recently through Africa and the Middle East, in every country you go to, usually the degree of progress can never be separated from the woman. If you're in a country that's progressive, the woman is progressive."[50] He elaborates this theme, saying, "If you're in a country that reflects the consciousness toward the importance of education, it's because the woman is aware of the importance of education," enabling him to repudiate the *Autobiography*'s and NOI's pervasive sexism by concluding, "So one of the things I became thoroughly convinced of in my recent travels is the importance of giving freedom to the woman, giving her education, and giving her the incentive to get out there and put that same spirit and understanding in her children," even going so far as observing, "And I frankly am proud of the contributions that our women have made in the struggle for freedom and I'm one person who's for giving them all the leeway possible because they've made a greater contribution than many of us men."[51] These words demolish many of Malcolm's earlier regressive statements about women, including declarations laced throughout the *Autobiography*. This single interview response, of course, cannot undo the damage inflicted by years of preaching NOI's sexist ideology, but Radford-Hill recognizes that, although "Malcolm X internalized masculine regimes or attitudes, values, and beliefs about manhood based on cultural norms, race consciousness, religious identity, and the social norms of the urban working class,"[52] he also worked with many forthright, assertive, and independent women—including Maya Angelou, Ruby Dee, Shirley Graham Du Bois (widow of legendary black intellectual and activist W.E.B. Du Bois), Fannie Lou Hamer, Coretta Scott King, and his half-sister Ella Little-Collins—after leaving NOI. He also "recruit[ed] such women as Lynne Shifflett, Muriel Feelings, and Alice Mitchell to play key roles in the early development of the Organization of Afro-American Unity."[53] These professional relationships demonstrate Malcolm's evolving perspective about the place, potential, and role of black women in the freedom struggle, an outlook that was by no means complete at the time of his death, but that indicates the growing distance between the sexism of Malcolm's NOI years and his enlightenment about issues of gender, sexism, and feminism that began transforming Malcolm's views during his final months of life.

Malcolm X, however, does not dramatize this shift in Malcolm's attitudes, but instead portrays his sincerely held conviction that Elijah Muhammad's infidelities illustrate the older man's personal failings more than the systemic sexism propagated by NOI's severe (and, in Muhammad's case, hypocritical) gender ideology. This failure fortifies the patriarchal attitudes that Malcolm displays throughout the film, causing bell hooks to write that Lee's choice to underplay Malcolm's changing views of women "creates a version of black political struggle where the actions of dedicated, powerful, black female activists are systematically devalued and erased. By writing Ella out of Malcolm's history, Spike Lee continues Hollywood's devaluation of black womanhood."[54] This assessment suggests that *Malcolm X*'s fealty to the *Autobiography*'s provincial regard for women demonstrates Lee's commitment to rendering faithfully Malcolm's influential text for moviegoers who may never have read the book (or never have finished it). Abolishing Ella from *Malcolm X*'s narrative is, therefore, a curious oversight given Lee's repeated public pronouncements about wanting to get Malcolm right, although Lee, during his long interview with Henry Louis Gates, Jr., about the movie's production titled "Generation X," defends this choice by saying, "Our intention is not to tear down Malcolm; for us this is an act of love. And in those cases where we had to change names, change events, or make three or four characters into one, well, I don't think that's distorting the Malcolm X story. You have to realize we're not making a documentary, we're making a drama,"[55] which, in Lee's mind, justifies significant omissions: "Ella Collins is not in this film; Farrakhan is not in this film; you don't have Reginald [Malcolm's brother] introducing him to Islam in this film. So you've got the same problem as a filmmaker adapting a vast novel to the screen. You can't include everything; some things you switch or turn around."[56] Lee also neglects including Alex Haley and Malcolm's adult siblings as characters, thereby giving the impression that Malcolm not only worked in isolation from meaningful human contact but also endured the political and personal setbacks depicted throughout *Malcolm X* alone.

This portrayal conforms to the traditional biopic's fascination with active, assertive, and aggressive men who require few emotional connections to achieve their destiny, extending the American fascination with rugged individualism into cinematic myth. Lee's proclamation that the temporal limitations of even this epic film govern aesthetic choices that he makes out of love, however, ignores the antifeminist implications of deleting so many important women from *Malcolm X*. The confluence of Lee's patriarchal depiction of Malcolm's life and the biopic's preference for lone-wolf heroes (who affirm their masculinity by secluding themselves as much as possible from female influence) reduces the movie's effectiveness despite its excellent performances, direction, set design, musical score, and cinematography. Angela Bassett's admirable turn as Betty Shabazz and Kate Vernon's effective performance as Sophia cannot overcome *Malcolm X*'s backward attitude toward women, which was far from inevitable given the project's disputatious production history and James Baldwin's early work as its screenwriter. The film's difficulties with female characters in some measure mirror its political hesitance about presenting Malcolm's most radical ideas, especially after his break with NOI, but these problems do not condemn *Malcolm X* to irrelevance. While remaining a praiseworthy accomplishment for Lee and his collaborators, the film's political inhibitions, no less than its feminist implications, prevent *Malcolm X* from becoming the groundbreaking production that its most fervid admirers believe, but also far from the outright failure that scholars such as bell hooks and Amiri Baraka proclaim.

RAGE, REVOLUTION, AND REDEMPTION

No single film devoted to Malcolm X could dramatize every important individual, incident, and intention documented in the *Autobiography*, to say nothing of Malcolm's entire life. Doing so would require a long-running television series staffed by writers willing to reconcile the *Autobiography*'s claims with the vast scholarship about Malcolm that has developed since his 1965 assassination (including two controversial biographies, Bruce Perry's *Malcolm: The Life of the Man Who Changed Black America* and Manning Marable's *Malcolm X: A Life of Reinvention*), the many memoirs published by people who knew or were influenced by Malcolm (including his third daughter Ilyasah Shabazz's *Growing Up X: A Memoir by the Daughter of Malcolm X* and his nephew Rodnell P. Collins's *Seventh Child: A Family Memoir of Malcolm X*), and the massive government surveillance files of Malcolm available at the FBI's official website (and in Clayborne Carson's book *Malcolm X: The FBI File*, with an introduction written by Spike Lee). The scope of this imaginary project increases any critical viewer's appreciation for Lee's achievement in making *Malcolm X* a quarter century after producer Marvin Worth first optioned the rights to *The Autobiography of Malcolm X* in, depending upon which source one consults, 1967 or 1968.[57]

That Lee was only ten (or eleven) years old when Columbia Pictures first considered bringing Malcolm X to cinematic life illuminates how Malcolm's contested reputation, controversial image, and revolutionary politics made him not only a difficult subject to capture on film but also a risky commercial gamble for any Hollywood studio hoping to attract substantial crossover audiences and box-office profits. The fact that such studios backed movies that lost more money than *Malcolm X*'s eventual $33-million budget, including Anthony Mann's *The Fall of the Roman Empire* (1964), Michael Cimino's *Heaven's Gate* (1980), Elaine May's *Ishtar* (1987), and Brian De Palma's *The Bonfire of the Vanities* (1990), indicates that the studios' concern with money (Warner Brothers eventually took over the film from Columbia) was not the only, or even primary, reason for taking so long to get *Malcolm X* into theaters. Malcolm's contentious politics—particularly his insistence that anti-black racism was the province (and product) of a pernicious white supremacy that America could not easily, if ever, overcome and that African Americans were morally obligated to defend themselves against the violence that they suffered at the hands of white people by, if necessary, taking up arms (as guaranteed by the U.S. Constitution)—frightened casual observers schooled in media reports like

Mike Wallace and Louis Lomax's 1959 television documentary *The Hate That Hate Produced*, as well as numerous mainstream newspaper, magazine, and journal articles that erroneously portrayed Malcolm as a vehement reverse racist advocating preemptive violence against white Americans. The reluctance of Hollywood corporations to produce a feature-film adaptation of *The Autobiography of Malcolm X*, therefore, had as much to do with Malcolm's bracing, yet incisive analysis of how centuries of white supremacy had inculcated self-hatred in black Americans as it did with the possibility of the movie not recovering its costs. Many films, after all, lose money at the box office, although fears that Malcolm's stridency would put off viewers (particularly white viewers) affected studio thinking about *Malcolm X*'s financial viability.

The difficulties that Lee encountered while directing *Malcolm X* were well documented at the time because Lee, ever the canny promoter, freely discussed them in press interviews, eventually referring to Warner Brothers as "the Plantation"[58] for its refusal to fund the project's $33-million budget or agree to its epic, three-hour-and-twenty-two-minute length despite offering at least $50 million for Oliver Stone's three-hour *JFK* (1991) and, in a decision that Lee rightly protested as an example of the studio's double standard about funding films by black directors, $45 million for actor-comedian Dan Aykroyd's directorial debut, the instantly forgettable *Nothing But Trouble* (1991). Lee's companion volume, *By Any Means Necessary*, adopts Malcolm X's most famous phrase as its title to recount, through the recollections of key production personnel, the challenges that the film presented its makers. These issues included Lee's public skepticism that a white director, whether Sidney Lumet or Norman Jewison (who were both attached to the project at various points), could direct the movie with the necessary political sensitivity or inside knowledge of African American culture; his choice to revise a screenplay originally written by James Baldwin and Arnold Perl rather than use the later screenplays penned by David Bradley, Charles Fuller, David Mamet, and Calder Willingham; and his insistence on travelling to Egypt and Saudi Arabia to shoot Malcolm's 1964 Mecca trip, as well as to South Africa to film Nelson Mandela for the movie's final sequence. Lee also publicly courted African American celebrities Tracy Chapman, Peggy Cooper-Cafritz, Bill Cosby, Janet Jackson, Magic Johnson, Michael Jordan, Prince, and Oprah Winfrey to donate cash to help him complete *Malcolm X* when the film's completion-bond company, named Century City California (hired by Warner Brothers to guarantee the film's budget and to pay all excess costs should the movie go over the $28-million budget cobbled together from Warner Brothers' $20-million investment and the $8 million paid by Largo Entertainment for *Malcolm X*'s foreign-distribution rights), halted postproduction while editor Barry Alexander Brown was cutting the film's extensive footage into a rough assembly because, true to Lee's predictions, *Malcolm X* overran its allotted budget (ultimately costing $33 million, the figure that

Lee and line producer Jon Kilik had calculated would be necessary to make the film as scripted when first negotiating its budget with Warner Brothers in 1991).[59]

Lee, indeed, contributed $2 million of his $3-million fee to continue the editing process, then shamed Warner Brothers into rectifying this situation by holding a press conference at the New York Public Library's Schomburg Center for Research in Black Culture on what would have been Malcolm's sixty-seventh birthday—May 19, 1992—to applaud these celebrity donations as prime examples of Malcolm's repeated recommendation that African Americans come together to support one another's creative and commercial ventures. Lee tells Kaleem Aftab in *That's My Story and I'm Sticking to It* that this event had the desired effect, becoming such a negative public-relations spectacle that Warner Brothers began funding the movie the following day.[60] Lee's strategy of openly discussing *Malcolm X*'s production difficulties generated substantial press coverage that raised the film's profile before its November 1992 theatrical release, thereby compensating for what Lee considered Warner Brothers' weak promotional campaign while at the same time maintaining his own notoriety as the most-famous black director working in American film.

These problems, which threatened to overwhelm the movie itself, constituted only the final leg of *Malcolm X*'s long production odyssey. Decades-long script difficulties preceded them, as Marvin Worth details in *By Any Means Necessary* (among other venues), to illustrate the challenges of cinematically adapting not only the *Autobiography* but also Malcolm's vituperative attacks on white supremacy, American racism, and the "white devils" that he criticized during NOI rallies. This ideology, considered radical as well as racist in its day, conflicts with Hollywood's preference for conservative, comforting, and conformist filmic narratives invested in racial reconciliation rather than honest, complex, and difficult examinations of the economic, political, social, and religious factors that perpetuate, even as they modify, America's racial animosities. The possibility of making a transformative film about Malcolm's life, one that respected his revolutionary vision, was enticing enough that James Baldwin (a friend and mutual admirer of Malcolm X) agreed in 1968 to adapt the *Autobiography* for Columbia Pictures, working on drafts that culminated in a 250-page screenplay rejected by studio executives because, according to David Leeming's *James Baldwin: A Biography*, it "read more like a novel than a screenplay."[61] Brian Norman offers the best scholarly analyses of Baldwin's aborted attempts at dramatizing Malcolm's life for the silver screen in the indispensable essays "Reading a 'Closet Screenplay': Hollywood, James Baldwin's Malcolms and the Threat of Historical Irrelevance" and "Bringing Malcolm X to Hollywood," noting in the former that, after the studio "disliked the effect of Baldwin's early drafts and forced upon him Arnold Perl as a 'technical assistant,'" Baldwin began to fear "that his script would be technically cut down to easily digested action scenes. In fact, Baldwin's former secretary, David Leeming, notes [in the Baldwin biography] that familiar actor-heroes were considered for the role of Malcolm X, even Charlton Heston—'darkened up a bit.'"[62] Baldwin, no stranger to Hollywood's aesthetic seductions and cultural cachet, which he trenchantly analyzes in the books *No Name in the Street* (1972) and, especially, *The Devil Finds Work* (1976), rightly saw these suggestions as presaging a terrible future for *Malcolm X*. "Anticipating the inevitable," Norman writes in "Reading a 'Closet Screenplay,'" Baldwin "hastily published his original version of the script in 1972 as *One Day, When I Was Lost,* and split town,"[63] leaving behind the unproduced "closet screenplay" (subtitled "A Scenario Based on Alex Haley's *The Autobiography of Malcolm X*") that Norman defines as "a print version of a film never realized in the visual medium."[64]

The disagreements that prompted Baldwin to leave the project, while familiar (even common) to Hollywood's committee-driven brand of moviemaking, raise questions about the capacity of any studio film to do justice to Malcolm X's life and legacy. The most fundamental query, according to Norman, is "Does a blockbuster film inherently fall short of Malcolm's radical vision?"[65] The temptation to answer affirmatively acknowledges the restrictions imposed upon such movies by the commercial aspirations of studio paymasters who, desiring profit over artistic integrity, historical accuracy, and biographical fidelity, remain less interested in the evolving revolutionary activism that Malcolm embraced after leaving NOI—itself a remarkably complex social philosophy that would prove difficult (but not impossible) to dramatize on-screen—than in the story of Malcolm's personal transformation from street hustler to national leader (and, after his death, internationally respected icon). These constraints are not as problematic as they seem if filmmakers and viewers consider Malcolm's investiture in radical politics as one (albeit complicated) aspect of his life, although underscoring his individual journey from prison to prominence diverts attention from the institutional, structural, and foundational causes of American racism that Malcolm analyzed (and regularly thrashed) in his public speeches, media appearances, and *Autobiography*.

Expecting *Malcolm X* to accomplish so many goals is a fool's errand, at least as far as Jacquie Jones is concerned in "Spike Lee Presents *Malcolm X:* The New Black Nationalism," a contrarian *Cineaste* essay that discusses the trend of criticizing *Malcolm X* for not presenting a sufficiently radical portrait of its subject's life, work, and beliefs (Amiri Baraka, Gerald Horne, William Lyne, and Nell Irvin Painter, among others, all published scholarly pieces around this theme in the twelve months surrounding the movie's production[66]). Jones then states what seems a simple truth about the American movie business: "The charge of Hollywood has never been to produce functional political documents."[67] Jones argues that, while *Malcolm X* deserves criticism, it is neither a thesis film nor a political treatise. For Jones, commentators like Baraka, Horne, Lyne, and Painter "are suffering from an elemental delusion with regards to Hollywood and its capabilities and some pretty off-base assumptions about contemporary African American popular culture, in which the cinema is the most coveted vehicle," meaning that, had Lee tried to "capture faithfully the meaning and the resilient spirit of Malcolm in a manner that would satisfy the needs of every person of African descent in the United States, it would have remained as unmade as it has been for the past two decades."[68] Jones defends Lee's version of *Malcolm X* as realizing a goal—getting the picture into theaters—that no one else had achieved. She praises the film for accomplishing "something that is rarely done well, and even then most often in fictions like Richard Wright's *Native Son* and Toni Morrison's *Beloved:* it details the tragic and profound effects of racism on the construction of the African American self-image, and the equally unfortunate repercussions the resulting absence of self-esteem can have on society as a whole."[69] This judgment correctly describes the film's overall effect, particularly its middle section, when Malcolm endures harsh treatment in prison, where he is quickly nicknamed Satan for his violent and antireligious behavior, only to experience misery while locked in solitary confinement and enlightenment when, after returning to the general population, he encounters a prisoner named Baines (Albert Hall) who converts Malcolm to Islam (and NOI) by stressing the importance of education, self-respect, and discipline. The prison conversations between Malcolm and Baines develop substance thanks not only to Denzel Washington and Albert Hall's excellent acting but also to Lee's narrative patience. Scenes of Malcolm reading in his prison cell long into the night follow scenes of him reading in the prison library until kicked out by guards, while Malcolm's newfound intellectual discipline finds visual expression in his physical appearance, with Washington transforming the loose-limbed swagger he exhibits during the movie's first act—set during Malcolm's days as a Harlem and Roxbury hustler that Lee and cinematographer Ernest Dickerson shoot with the romantic lighting and sweeping camera movements of MGM musicals of the 1940s and 1950s—into a straighter posture and less flamboyant gait that, when combined with the earnest studiousness on Malcolm's face and his noticeably improved grooming, reflect the inner transformation that he experiences as a result of Baines's tutelage.

The most effective scene comes when Baines encourages Malcolm, who will eventually copy every word from *Webster's Collegiate Dictionary* (beginning with *aardvark*) into a notebook to improve his penmanship and increase his vocabulary, to compare the definitions of the words *black* and *white*. As Baines and Malcolm read these entries aloud, Lee and editor Barry Alexander Brown cut to close-up and panning shots of the words on the page to reinforce their differing registers: *black* refers to unfavorable concepts such as "enveloped in darkness, hence utterly dismal or gloomy; soiled with dirt; foul; sullen; hostile; forbidding; foully or outrageously wicked; indicating disgrace, dishonor, or culpability" while *white* refers to progressive ideas such as "free from spot or blemish; innocent; pure; without evil intent; harmless; honest; square-dealing; honorable" and, tellingly, "the opposite of black." These images, intercut with Malcolm's changing facial expression and vocal tone as he realizes just how biased such definitions are, provoke the realization that Baines intends when Malcolm asks him, "This was written by white folks, though, right? This is a white folks' book?" Malcolm then locates an illustration of Noah Webster in the dictionary's opening pages to confirm his suspicion. This scene illustrates Lee's mastery of narrative compression by cinematically condensing much of the *Autobiography*'s eleventh chapter, "Saved," into a longer sequence that illustrates Malcolm's devotion to his prison education, his newfound passion for reading, and his growing acceptance that, as he states in the book, "the teachings of Mr. Muhammad stressed how history had been 'whitened'—when white men had written history books, the black man had simply been left out. Mr. Muhammad couldn't have said anything that would have struck me much harder."[70] Malcolm and Baines's interlude with the dictionary, in Lisa Kennedy's opinion, is "an example of Lee's capacity to capture in a single scene a psycho-socio-racial moment that would require pages of explication."[71] Lee, indeed, adeptly adapts all of the *Autobiography*'s prison chapters, dramatizing Malcolm's changing perspective by combining the *Autobiography*'s pseudonymous "Bimbi" (a fellow black inmate whom Malcolm meets at Charlestown State Prison in 1947 and whom he describes as "the first man I had ever seen command total respect . . . with his words"[72]) and Malcolm's siblings Reginald, Philbert, and Hilda (who helped convert him to Islam as practiced by Elijah Muhammad) into the composite character Baines, who guides Malcolm into greater knowledge of his heritage after recognizing the younger man's fierce intelligence, helping him overcome his drug habit, and preparing him for entry into NOI.

Malcolm X's dictionary sequence, much to Lee's credit, gains profound intellectual and emotional power by forcing viewers to consider how fundamental white supremacy is to America's national history, experience, and character. By depicting Malcolm's shocked realization that racial prejudice is encoded in the English language, Lee prepares the audience for Malcolm's later denunciations of how America's "whitewashed" language, politics, and history create a debilitating self-hatred that destabilizes African American identity and culture. The *Autobiography* discusses this theme in nearly every chapter, laying out Malcolm's case that African American progress, hobbled by the structural racism of American society (and Western culture more broadly conceived), faces appalling institutional constraints that individuals, by themselves, cannot overcome, thereby demanding the collective economic action that leads Elijah Muhammad and Malcolm, following Marcus Garvey's early-twentieth-century political program, to recommend strict separation between black and white communities. This black-nationalist political philosophy caused Malcolm to focus on the conditions of working-class and poor African Americans, whom he inspired in large numbers, while disparaging the "blue-eyed devils" who, in his estimation, passively accepted, when they were not actively aiding, America's oppressive political, economic, and cultural system.

Malcolm X highlights the idea of white supremacy's crippling power in the prison sequence before expanding this theme in the film's third act, when Malcolm rises to become NOI's top minister by ceaselessly confronting America's history of slavery and segregation in speeches, lectures, and media appearances that, expertly played by Denzel Washington, convey Malcolm's combative intelligence, charismatic passion, and raffish charm. Lee's movie, however, downplays the institutional and structural elements of Malcolm's social analysis, sidelining Malcolm's passionate interest in Africa's anticolonial movements and the tentative acceptance of socialism (as an alternative to capitalism's inequities) that fascinated Malcolm during his final. eighteen months of life, after he leaves NOI, goes on *hajj*, and begins rethinking many of his previous positions. The movie becomes a tale of redemption in which Malcolm casts off his beliefs in strict racial separation and the white man's inherent evil when, during his spiritual transformation in Mecca, Malcolm recognizes the common humanity of all people under Islam. This personal journey holds more interest for Lee than Malcolm's changing political trajectory, placing *Malcolm X* firmly within the conventions of the Hollywood biopic. Stressing Malcolm's personal enlightenment follows the *Autobiography*'s structure, but dilutes the revolutionary impact of Malcolm's political philosophy after he departs NOI. This choice seems to verify David Bradley's analysis in his illuminating essay "Malcolm's Mythmaking," which chronicles Bradley's efforts to adapt *The Autobiography of Malcolm X* for producer Marvin Worth and Warner Brothers before Lee joined the project (Bradley, in fact, was one of at least five screenwriters to work on *Malcolm X* during its twenty-five-year journey to multiplexes). Bradley argues that, because Malcolm's life does not easily fit Hollywood's preferred three-act screenplay structure and because Malcolm refused to adopt the turn-the-other-cheek, integrationist line of other civil-rights leaders, Hollywood studios "didn't keep firing writers because the scripts were wrong. They kept firing writers because the *story* was wrong."[73] Malcolm's life, in other words, exceeds the ability of traditional biopics—with their emphasis on exceptional individuals—to depict his work in the comprehensive detail necessary to dramatizing the radical political positions that made Malcolm a threat to American power structures throughout his adult career. Avoiding these complications, for viewers invested in radical politics, sells out Malcolm's legacy by misrepresenting his beliefs, underplaying his activist vision for social change, and reducing his importance as a national leader speaking uncomfortable truths about the fundamental problems ailing the American body politic. The movie, from this perspective, is a failure of vision that emphasizes Malcolm's legitimate status as an

American hero at the expense of his most revolutionary attitudes, thoughts, and arguments.

TELLING TALES

Lee's *Malcolm X*, while not politically timid, nonetheless softens Malcolm's most searing attacks on white supremacy, his most piercing calls for separatism, and his most radical recommendations for social progress, especially his embrace of pan-Africanism and proto-socialism after travelling in Africa and the Middle East during 1964, where he recognizes that reframing the American civil-rights struggle as an international human-rights liberation movement, along with fundamentally restructuring America's capitalist economy, is necessary to free black Americans from the oppression they suffer. Yet criticizing the film for overlooking this perspective assumes that *Malcolm X* must include these matters to be a successful depiction of its subject's life, which raises pressing questions about representation, iconography, and historical memory explored in notable scholarly essays about the movie's cultural significance, Malcolm and Alex Haley's construction of identity in *The Autobiography of Malcolm X,* and the implications of autobiographical narrative's historical utility. Malcolm Turvey's "Black Film Making in the USA: The Case of *Malcolm X*," for instance, defends Lee's movie by noting, in words similar to Jacquie Jones's *Cineaste* analysis, that the critical response to *Malcolm X,* "despite ranging from approbation to condemnation, has been depressingly uniform and univocal in the use of a single strategy or heuristic to interpret the film. 'How faithful to the *true* spirit of Malcolm is this film?' has been the standard question posed by critics and cultural commentators from positions both within and beyond the entire spectrum of institutions,"[74] leading Turvey to ask, "For beneath the insistence of this question, its continued and varied return in review after review and commentary after commentary, is there not a single and oppressive *demand* that *Malcolm X* be truthful, that it live up to expectations, that it please all those who need and desire Malcolm?"[75]

This restrictive standard of judgment, for Turvey, fosters false images of Malcolm X and Spike Lee as men beholden to no one but themselves, defining them as exceptional individuals who, finally, cannot fulfill the fantasies foisted upon them by competing groups invested in the success or failure of their social, political, and artistic projects. Turvey sketches the cultural and institutional parameters affecting Lee's work on *Malcolm X* as demanding that Lee become an impossible figure: the radical black artist capable of portraying the complete, unvarnished truth about African American life. "What is this desire that structures Lee's persona, enabling and constraining his actions?" Turvey asks, answering this question by rebuking its governing assumption: "It is the desire for the mythical figure of the radical black artist. It is a fantasy of pure 'otherness', of the authentic black film-maker who can depict the truth, who can speak for oppressed peoples and show the reality of their oppression, the *real-thing* itself."[76] This "culturally dominant fantasy," according to Turvey, "has powerful and far-reaching effects in terms of the identity it sets into place for black film-makers such as Lee, the type of films 'green-lighted' or deemed acceptable for black film-makers to make, and the way these films are critically received and interpreted."[77] Turvey's comments reflect his concern with how insisting that *Malcolm X* meet the contradictory expectations of audience members heavily invested in Malcolm's memory plays into false notions of black authenticity that unfairly target Lee as a bourgeois moviemaker held to standards that white directors evade, thereby "control[ling] *who* may be a 'black film-maker', and *what* black film-makers may produce."[78] This argument interrogates the complex interactions of industrial capital, racial privilege, and socioeconomic class that structure the cultural reception of African American filmmakers like Lee, who cannot live up to the many expectations of radical black artists that committed participants in the cultural conversation about *Malcolm X* set.

These legitimate anxieties do not insulate *Malcolm X* or Spike Lee from criticism, as Turvey notes near his essay's conclusion, but they remind critical viewers that, despite Lee's insistence that *Malcolm X* is his film (best illustrated when Lee writes in the companion volume's preface, "*Malcolm X* is my artistic vision. The film is my interpretation of the man. It's nobody else's"[79]), Lee's effort is but one element in the much broader institutional processes, cultural currents, and generic conventions that determine *Malcolm X*'s final form. Lee is certainly the driving force behind the movie's narrative, while his commitment to *Malcolm X* overcame challenges that kept the project in developmental turnaround for twenty-five years, but Lee, although crucial to the film's success, was not the sole participant in *Malcolm X*'s production. He, as David Bradley indicates in "Malcolm's Mythmaking," was one large cog in the gigantic industrial machine that made *Malcolm X* possible.[80]

Lee's decision to adapt *The Autobiography of Malcolm X* into a Hollywood biopic, moreover, renders his film as the heroic story of one man's struggle to surmount the daunting obstacles that a racist society sets in his path, which produces a powerful, fascinating, and consummate movie that respects more than interrogates the *Autobiography*'s narrative structure, emotional impact, and political effects. The core of *Malcolm X* is the *Autobiography,* as John Locke comments in his *Cineaste* essay "Adapting the Autobiography: The Transformation of Malcolm X," writing that Malcolm's book is "a story that draws from the breadth of twentieth century African American experience," but which, because it "contains elements that most moviegoers today would find antiquated or irrelevant," means that "Lee's intent to tell history is at odds with the needs of a mass market, and the film's transformation of Malcolm X to meet contemporary expectations has significant consequences for historical accuracy and dramatic impact"[81] that the movie cannot fully resolve, and, keeping in mind Turvey's admonition about the stultifying power of authenticity as a marker of black filmmaking success, that Lee is correct not to attempt. For other commentators, the restraints imposed upon Malcolm's story by the film's running time and chosen genre improve it, with Michael Eric Dyson arguing in his fine book *Making Malcolm: The Myth and Meaning of Malcolm X,* "The genre of *Malcolm X*—the epic—and the film's real-life subject impose historical limits, aesthetic constraints, and artistic conventions that work wonders for Lee's treatment of the complexities of race."[82] Even so, Dyson concedes that the movie, while "an often impressive, occasionally stunning achievement,"[83] faithfully follows the *Autobiography,* which chronicles "the lineaments of Malcolm's various emergences and conversions" in a text that "has been criticized for avoiding or distorting certain facts."[84] This last declaration considerably understates the matter, as anyone who has read the extensive scholarship about the *Autobiography,* especially the objections to its historical veracity raised by Bruce Perry's and Manning Marable's biographies, knows.

Although Locke's, Dyson's, Perry's, and Marable's comments remind attentive readers and viewers that autobiographies, by virtue of their status as narrative constructions, do not report the truth of an individual's life so much as the subject's perception of that life's truth, the *Autobiography*'s and *Malcolm X*'s tremendous artistry can tempt their audiences into forgetting this observation. The situation is made more complicated by *The Autobiography of Malcolm X*'s status as an "as told to" book that required Alex Haley's active involvement to complete. Haley's influence on this joint project is important to acknowledge even if he concludes his lengthy epilogue to the *Autobiography* by writing, "After signing the contract for this book, Malcolm X looked at me hard. 'A writer is what I want, not an interpreter.' I tried to be a dispassionate chronicler,"[85] indicating in roundabout fashion that his attempts were not always successful. Alex Gillespie, in his terrific essay "Autobiography and Identity: Malcolm X as Author and Hero," clarifies how the partnership between Malcolm and Haley helps Malcolm reconstitute his life by organizing the *Autobiography* around narrative templates that "do not contain specific facts or events; rather they are abstract plot structures which shape many specific stories,"[86] structures that help both Malcolm and his reader make sense of the man's complex, changing, and occasionally mystifying experience. Malcolm and Haley, Gillespie notes, select a template that "has variously been called a conversion narrative and a metamorphosis narrative. It is a classic format: a story of someone who has fallen, in a moral sense, and who 'sees the light.'"[87] Lee's *Malcolm X* employs a tripartite structure (that condenses Malcolm's life into the three-act screenplay format that David Bradley finds ill-suited to the task) by tracking Malcolm from his dissolute, hell-raising youth as "Detroit Red" through his harrowing prison years as "Satan" and into his redeemed maturity as Malcolm X, a moral exemplar for all Americans who finally adopts the name El-Hajj Malik El-Shabazz to signify his new identity as a fully autonomous person. The movie, indeed, follows this format so precisely that, per Gillespie, it becomes a classic tale of American perseverance, transformation, and triumph.

The *Autobiography*, as such, seems perfectly suited to the epic-length biopic that Lee fashions for its screen adaptation, with the resulting reduction of Malcolm's political radicalism mirroring what Thomas Doherty, in "Malcolm X: In Print, On Screen," points to as difficulties with the book's historical accuracy: "By the measure of autobiography, the most notoriously untrustworthy of genres, *The Autobiography of Malcolm X* is no less a work of hindsighted reconstruction, strategic omission, and outright fabrication than, say, *The Autobiography of Benjamin Franklin*."[88] Malcolm's *Autobiography*, for Doherty, is "at once a political tract, a religious conversion narrative, and an underground commentary on twentieth-century American culture [that] has entered the restricted canon of American literary classics," meaning that "Malcolm X's legacy lies in who he was and what he wrote, a presentation self crafted in literature"[89] that prompts Lee to organize his film as the redemption tale of a sinner whose eventual notoriety finds "Malcolm's life increasingly becom[ing] a self-conscious public performance."[90] Lee shows Malcolm authoring his public image as a process of continual self-enlightenment, -education, and -improvement, thereby obeying the biopic's most fundamental convention (and the *Autobiography*'s narrative pattern) to demonstrate the shrewd "reconceptualization of autobiography" that Alex Gillespie finds so significant to Malcolm's book, a reformulation that "situates the autobiography within the life of the individual, not as a reflection of that life, but as a reconstitutive moment in that life."[91] Malcolm, like all autobiographers, crafts and re-crafts his own experience throughout the book, but receives assistance from Haley and, later, from Lee, who includes three separate versions of Malcolm—degenerate hustler, repentant prisoner, and firebrand minister—in his movie to dramatize the constant evolution of Malcolm's identity. The true measure of Denzel Washington's superb performance is that he skillfully distinguishes these roles from one another yet demonstrates, with tremendous grace and nuance, how they are all part of the same personality.

David LaRocca finds Lee's fascination with Malcolm's transformations to be *Malcolm X*'s great achievement, noting in his perceptive essay "Rethinking the First Person: Autobiography, Authorship, and the Contested Self in *Malcolm X*" that Lee "proposes one of the most sympathetic aspects of X's personality and temperament: that he undergoes these changes [of identity and naming] reluctantly, almost involuntarily and accidentally. X does not shift frivolously from one identity to another, from one set of beliefs and activities to another; rather, X suffers—agonistically—each subsequent version of himself."[92] This insight implies that the film's approach to Malcolm's growth depicts no simple path of personal improvement, learning, and progress, but rather portrays a difficult series of advances and reversals that complicate Malcolm's evolving identity. LaRocca, indeed, credits Lee for "ably highlight[ing] one of the core contributions of X's life to a philosophical understanding of autobiography and, subsequently, to film biography: the ability and humility to fathom identity as indefinite and perpetually unfinished."[93]

As empowering as this accomplishment may be, particularly at expanding the conventions of the standard biopic, the fluidity that LaRocca praises in *Malcolm X*, while certainly in line with the *Autobiography*'s presentation of Malcolm's ever-changing identity, respects its literary source in a less salutary way by endorsing sexist, even regressive, notions of African American women that align with the masculine prerogatives of traditional American biographical pictures. Maurice E. Stevens, in "Subject to Countermemory: Disavowal and Black Manhood in Spike Lee's *Malcolm X*," sees this correspondence between book and film as the product of persistent conditions that constrain the social, political, and economic advancement of black American men. Writing that "while the *Autobiography* presented Malcolm's life in the frame of American exceptionalism and epic heroism because of the cultural barriers that barred black admittance to those categories," Stevens underscores how "Lee's *Malcolm X* reinscribes the figure of a 'shining' black masculinity in response to the institutionalized and systematic targeting of black men constituted as the embodiment of criminality and threat."[94] The film's patriarchal mindset, no less than the *Autobiography*'s, may be a regrettable response to these ongoing circumstances, but Lee misses a prime opportunity to examine Malcolm's sexism more critically than *Autobiography* does. This failure is a serious drawback to an otherwise excellent work of American cinema.

Anna Everett finds both this insufficiency and Lee's combative attitude toward dramatizing Malcolm X's life to be reasonable developments given Lee's own experiences as a black man who has thrived within America's racially inequitable society. Commenting on how, in the companion volume *By Any Means Necessary*, Lee praises Malcolm as a great, strong, courageous "Black man who did not back down from anybody, even toward his death,"[95] Everett writes in "'Spike, Don't Mess Malcolm Up': Courting Controversy and Control in *Malcolm X*," her incisive analysis of the film's production and reception, "Clearly, Lee was not insulated from the burden of blackness in American society and thus could cast himself in the same fearless mold of black masculinist pride, militancy, self-determination, and group uplift that Malcolm X espoused."[96] This comparison, so implicit in Lee's public sparring with Warner Brothers throughout *Malcolm X*'s production, becomes a structuring principle for the entire movie. Lee's on-screen presence as Malcolm's friend Shorty during the movie's first act, when "Detroit Red" becomes an accomplished hustler in Harlem and a daring burglar in Boston whose conked hair and romantic involvement with Sophia mark him as a self-hating black man unaware of the extent of his own racial confusion, serves to remind all viewers that Lee is just as insistent, assertive, and demanding as Malcolm, whose years as an NOI minister and, after his spiritual reformation in Mecca, as El-Hajj Malik El-Shabazz pursuing the project of black nationalism from a more inclusive perspective, are good analogues for Lee's persona during *Malcolm X*'s production. The similarities between both men also vindicate Lee's dogged determination in bringing the film to theaters by seeking the assistance of African American financial partners to help complete the movie. Lee unfortunately lessens the role of women in *Malcolm X* to shape its subject's life into a more comfortable biopic that, like Lee's own stand against Hollywood intransigence and bigotry, requires the figure and the legend of a man beholden to no one else, a man who carves his own path and who creates his own life out of the difficult circumstances that America forces upon him.

Lee's engagement with Malcolm X in his earlier films—whether seeing Nola Darling prepare a collage of famous African American leaders in her loft apartment that prominently features Malcolm in *She's Gotta Have It*, having Dap Dunlap advocate black-nationalist ideas and attitudes reminiscent of Malcolm in *School Daze*, or including Malcolm's notion that violence in self-defense is a mark of intelligence at *Do the Right Thing*'s conclusion—combines personal and political views that become inseparable from Lee's public persona. Lee adopts Malcolm's forthright determination to speak truth to power, making *Malcolm X* both a valentine to and memorial of the slain leader whose *Autobiography* Lee calls "the most important book I'll ever read" in *Sight and Sound*, the *New Yorker*, and an interview with film critic Roger Ebert soon after *Malcolm X*'s 1992 theatrical premiere.[97] Linking Lee to Malcolm X, indeed, finds its zenith in the 1999 republication of *The Autobiography of Malcolm X*, which prominently features on its cover, just below Alex Haley's "as told to" byline, a quotation by Lee: "The most important book I'll ever read. It changed the way I thought; it changed the way I acted. It has given me courage that I didn't know I had inside me. I'm one of hundreds of thousands whose life was changed for the better."[98] This honor, coming seven years after *Malcolm X*'s premiere, attests to Lee's public identification with his hero as well as the high regard in which the film is held by mainstream observers, including Ballantine Books.

Such recognition cannot obscure difficulties with *Malcolm X*'s problematic depiction of women or its subdued portrayal of Malcolm's political radicalism. Anna Everett fittingly judges Lee's effort: "While Lee's assertion that the 'film never got made' in more than two decades of attempts because 'it wasn't s'pose to be made until now' reflects his penchant for grandstanding public relations more than the actual facts of project *X*'s troubled production history, few would argue that Lee's *Malcolm X* is not an impressive achievement."[99] Lee's painstaking direction, Wynn Thomas's and Ruth Carter's scrupulous production and costume design, Ernest Dickerson's atmospheric cinematography, and, especially, Denzel Washington's overwhelming performance in the title role not only ensure that *Malcolm X* will endure as the primary cinematic adaptation of Malcolm's *Autobiography* but also as the entrance for many viewers into knowledge of one of twentieth-century America's most important social critics, leaders, and thinkers. Lee's film is no substitute for learning about the nuances of Malcolm's life, work, and political philosophy, but, by showing the human face behind the historical personage, it serves as a commanding introduction to the man's significance. *Malcolm X* remains essential viewing for anyone interested in Malcolm's life, Lee's career, and the turbulent decades of twentieth-century American history that it dramatizes with passion, wit, and intelligence. The movie's faults do not nullify its achievements, but they require thoughtful viewers, rather than taking Lee's interpretation of Malcolm X's life as gospel, to question received notions of propriety, authority, and history as insistently, as searchingly, and as honestly as Malcolm did throughout his adult life.

4

Black Magic Women

WOMAN'S WORK

The most persistent criticism of Spike Lee's films, even for the director's admirers, involves their intractable sexism. This charge appears so frequently in mainstream and scholarly evaluations of Lee's cinema that it seems unassailable, particularly when considering three movies that feature women in prominent roles: *Jungle Fever* (1991), *Girl 6* (1996), and *She Hate Me* (2004). This last film also invokes another common indictment of Lee's movies, namely that they traffic in rampant homophobia. Lee's masculine worldview, according to this argument, transforms his films into regrettable antifeminist and antigay narratives that so uncomfortably marginalize, sexualize, or objectify heterosexual women, gay men, and lesbian women that Lee's gender politics seem not only conventional but also regressive.

Previous chapters have addressed Lee's problematic representation of women, but *Jungle Fever, Girl 6,* and *She Hate Me* expose his complicated artistic rendering of female characters in special measure. Analyzing the feminist implications of these films, however, is impossible without acknowledging the work of bell hooks, the scholar who most consistently and most intelligently criticizes Lee's cinematic sexism. His earliest movies, indeed, have no better commentator than hooks, whose insightful essays about *She's Gotta Have It, School Daze, Do the Right Thing, Malcolm X,* and *Crooklyn* first appeared in publications as diverse as *Cineaste, Sight and Sound,* and *Z Magazine*. Although originally printed as film reviews, these articles' deep engagement with Lee's cinema yields fascinating insights about his entrenched antifeminism. Hooks, however, far from settling feminist scores in these pieces, instead laments Lee's chauvinism as the most disappointing drawback of this talented filmmaker's body of work. Declaring her admiration for Lee's cinematic gifts on many occasions, hooks commends him for constructing unusual narratives that counteract predominant Hollywood prejudices about African Americans. This accomplishment not only explains Lee's position as late-twentieth-century America's most famous black director but also helps make possible what hooks terms "counterhegemonic cinema," or movies that resist conventional depictions of black American life. Lee, hooks repeatedly argues, remains a significant figure for feminist scholars to evaluate even if his movies include sexist representations. That Lee so often fails to disrupt dominant Hollywood biases about women does not condemn him to cinematic irrelevance, but rather, in hooks's view, demonstrates just how pervasive Hollywood's restrictive gender stereotypes are. Lee, as captive to these widespread ideas as any other cultural artist working in late-twentieth- and early-twenty-first-century America, seems uninterested in forcefully shattering them, which prevents his movies from becoming full-fledged counter-hegemonic films. Lee instead produces mainstream fare that occasionally questions conservative views of black women, yet fails to deconstruct these depictions in convincing fashion.

As the preceding comments suggest, hooks is unafraid to criticize Lee's antifeminism in pitiless detail. She begins her now-famous 1993 *Cineaste* review "Male Heroes and Female Sex Objects: Sexism in Spike Lee's *Malcolm X*" with the declaration, "In all Spike Lee's films, he is at his creative best in scenes highlighting black males"[1] before demolishing Lee's cinematic chauvinism: "Like many females in Lee's audience, I have found his representation of women in general, and black women in particular, to be consistently stereotypical and one-dimensional."[2] Hooks suggests that Lee's move from independent filmmaking to studio-backed productions explains the director's desire "to acquire an audience not necessarily interested in challenging, unfamiliar representations," meaning that "no matter how daring his films, how transgressive their subject matter, to have a predictable success he provided viewers with stock images."[3] Calling sexism "the familiar construction that links his films to all the other Hollywood dramas folks see," hooks identifies the central weakness of Lee's otherwise unusual movie narratives: "Just when a viewer might possibly be alienated by the radical take on issues in a Spike Lee film, some basic sexist nonsense will appear on the screen to entertain, to provide comic relief, to comfort audiences by letting them know that the normal way of doing things is not being fully challenged."[4]

This passage's regret indicates how deeply hooks admires Lee, for her disillusionment is correspondingly intense. She places great stock in Lee's ability to disrupt traditional images of women, yet understands that even directors who defy Hollywood conventions may still forward distasteful, even poisonous, representations. Lee's early work, much to hooks's chagrin, embraces this paradox. Despite her criticisms of *She's Gotta Have It* (in the memorably titled article "'Whose Pussy is This?'"), hooks writes in "Male Heroes and Female Sex Objects" that, "ironically, Nola Darling in *She's Gotta Have It* remains one of Lee's most compelling representations of black womanhood. Though a failed portrait of a liberated woman, Darling is infinitely more complex than any of the women who follow her in Lee's work,"[5] which, according to hooks, refuses to deconstruct sexist Hollywood tropes. *She's*

Gotta Have It, hooks writes, "showed an awareness on Lee's part that there has indeed been a Women's Liberation movement that converged with the so-called 'sexual revolution,'" demonstrating that hooks does not unfairly criticize Lee when she declares, "This film shows that Lee is capable of thinking critically about representations of black women"[6] despite Nola's rape by Jamie Overstreet. Yet Lee's subsequent female characters, hooks claims, degenerate into stock sexism: "Just as Lee abandons Nola Darling, undermining the one representation of black womanhood that breaks new cinematic ground, from that moment on he apparently abandoned all desire to give viewing audiences new and different representations of black females."[7]

Lee, it seems, relegates women to subservient roles even when they are central characters. This pattern indicates his inability or his unwillingness to disrupt patriarchal views of women (especially black women) even when he contests them. The resulting contradiction leads Heather E. Harris and Kimberly R. Moffitt to coin the term "Spiked Lens," which they define as "a style of filmmaking that describes Lee's unique ability to create, in some ways, counter-hegemonic portrayals of African Americans, diametrically opposed to the Blaxploitation representations of the 1970s, which included quasi-empowered, overly aggressive (and at times, violent) 'superheroes' that only existed on screen."[8] Invoking blaxploitation differentiates Lee's movies from earlier films that, while empowering their African American protagonists in ways rarely seen in previous Hollywood movies, nevertheless restricted them to the impoverished urban spaces that, as Paula J. Massood's *Black City Cinema: African American Urban Experiences in Film* argues, produced "the wave of urban rebellions that shook the nation from 1965 through 1968" and that "acted as a momentary 'warp' in the surface of the nation's racial repressed."[9] For Harris and Moffitt, Lee's cinema diverges from this older model to include counter-hegemonic images that hooks fails to recognize.

Harris and Moffit also notice continuities between Lee's movies and their blaxploitation predecessors by conceptualizing the Spiked Lens "as an unflinchingly racialized, macho, and liberatory style of filmmaking that centers African American lifestyles and life choices. Thought- and dialogue-provoking, his messages are controversial, edgy, assertive, and innovative."[10] The machismo of Lee's movies may be less strident than Melvin Van Peebles's *Sweet Sweetback's Baadasssss Song* (1971), Gordon Parks's *Shaft* (1971), and Gordon Parks, Jr.'s *Super Fly* (1972), but it nonetheless shunts female characters to the narrative sidelines. The liberation from racial containment that the Spiked Lens promises, however, privileges black men over black women to affirm hooks's judgment of Lee's underlying sexism.

Harris and Moffitt, indeed, catalogue feminist objections to Lee's work from authors as diverse as hooks, Patricia Hill Collins, Jannette L. Dates, Wahneema Lubiano, Thomas Mascaro, and Mark McPhail to "agree with the aforementioned positions regarding [Lee's] patriarchal reinforcement and the resulting sexualized images of these women" even if Harris and

Moffitt "neither condone nor condemn Lee's works."[11] This nuanced evaluation identifies Lee's movies as significant contributions to American cinema even if they contain stereotypical female images. Lee's antifeminism,
therefore, is no negligible aspect of an otherwise sterling career that the
viewer can easily explain away. Lee himself claims in a 1990 *Essence* magazine interview titled "Mo' Better Spike" that he desires "to simply entertain and offer provocative storytelling"[12] when defending himself against
charges of sexism, yet the fact that his concerns about dismantling white-
supremacist images of African Americans do not often enough include his
female characters reduces his films' counter-hegemonic power.

Bell hooks remains Lee's most insistent critic in this regard. Her assertion
that his movies' antifeminism prevents them from fully challenging conventional American cinematic depictions of women is, while accurate, also unfair in that few independent films wholly contest such images (Julie Dash's
Daughters of the Dust is the exception that proves this rule), while Lee has
never claimed that abolishing sexism is his primary goal. Lee, indeed, addresses problems with his female characters in his autobiography, *That's My
Story and I'm Sticking to It;* in his production journals for *She's Gotta Have It,
Do the Right Thing,* and *Malcolm X;* and in numerous interviews, particularly
with David Breskin in *Rolling Stone* (reprinted in Breskin's 1997 book *Inner
Views: Filmmakers in Conversation*), Marlaine Glicksman in *Film Comment,*
and Elvis Mitchell in *Playboy.* Lee admits to Breskin that the most accurate
criticism of his (Lee's) films concerns their problematic female characters,
while the passage that best represents Lee's attitude about his movies' sexism
occurs in *By Any Means Necessary: The Trials and Tribulations of the Making
of "Malcolm X,"* the companion volume (co-written with Ralph Wiley) to
Lee's 1992 biopic. This book's third section chronicles Lee's observations
while shooting the movie. Early in this section's first entry, dated September
1991, Lee praises actor Angela Bassett's performance by saying, "Angela Bassett is doing a fantastic job of portraying Betty Shabazz. I mean fantastic"[13]
before briefly analyzing his cinematic women: "It matters to me, what people
have said in the past about my depictions of women in my films. The first
thing I think they have to understand is, I'm not a woman, so I can't see
women as women see women. But I can understand women saying there
should have been more or better-developed female characters in my films."[14]
This comment may demonstrate Lee's willingness to accept criticism of his
female characters, but it also essentializes them. Stating that he cannot see
women as they see themselves indicates a potentially troubling inability on
Lee's part to imagine his way into a woman's experience despite the fact that
he does so, with modest success, in *She's Gotta Have It.*

Lee, who couches this response as a frank admission of his personal limitations in a rhetorical move meant to demonstrate honest self-awareness, indulges a straw-man (or straw-person) argument. The critics of his cinematic
sexism, after all, do not accuse Lee of poorly representing women because, as

a man, he cannot fully understand (or empathize with) female lives. To do so would affirm the gender stereotypes that feminist scholars protest. Instead, the concerns that hooks and other writers express about Lee's sexism involve his films' repeated marginalization of even significant female characters. For scholars like hooks, this pattern recurs in almost every movie, sometimes to a greater extent than others, but remains so apparent that even Lee himself recognizes it. As such, examining how *Jungle Fever, Girl 6*, and *She Hate Me* portray straight and lesbian women will demonstrate Lee's maddening tendency to simultaneously liberate and constrict them. Each film's gender discourse, as a result, exerts a peculiar effect that, as Harris and Moffitt observe, is an unmistakable aspect of the Spiked Lens.

JUNGLE FEVER (1991)

Jungle Fever represents a departure for Lee by extensively addressing interracial romance, unlike the glancing treatment this issue receives in *Do the Right Thing* and *Mo' Better Blues*. Despite *Do the Right Thing* casting Mookie's girlfriend, Tina, as a Puerto-Rican woman (played by Rosie Perez), the film elliptically alludes to their different backgrounds by having Tina's mother, Carmen (Diva Osorio), dislike Mookie when he visits her daughter (during the scene in which Mookie rubs ice cubes over Tina's body). Carmen, however, distrusts Mookie because he is an absent father, not simply because he is African American. Although Lee, during *Do the Right Thing*'s early development, contemplated casting a black actress as Tina, he changed this detail after seeing Perez dance at the Los Angeles nightclub Funky Reggae during his March 1988 birthday party.

Lee's *Do the Right Thing* production journal, for instance, includes this passage in its March 26, 1988, entry: "Mookie's girlfriend Tina is one of the thousands of teenage Black girls who has a child, but is still a child herself. . . . I want an unknown young woman, maybe someone who's not an actress, to play Tina. I need a real live Ghetto Babe."[15] This final comment's chauvinism continues four days later, in the March 30th entry, when Lee effusively praises Perez: "I met this babe at my birthday party in L.A. at Funky Reggae. She was dancing atop a speaker, then she got on the dance floor and was killin'. I mean killin'. This babe can dance."[16] Making certain that Perez gets the production office's phone number, Lee is ecstatic when she calls, writing, "She's definitely what I'm looking for: a fine young ghetto babe. Rosie is Puerto Rican, but she looks Black. I know it's early, but I'm stuck on her for the role of Tina."[17] Lee's delight at discovering Perez, however, essentializes her appearance. She may be Puerto Rican by heritage, yet "looks Black" and, even more, matches the "Ghetto Babe" stereotype that Lee desires for the role. He does not judge Perez by her ability to play a young, harried, and overwhelmed mother, but rather by how well she fits his mental image of Tina. Although cinematic casting decisions frequently depend upon how closely a performer matches the director's view of the character, the racial dynamics of these passages suggest that Lee's willingness to alter his conceptualization of Tina does not commendably acknowledge his racial pluralism (or even the indisputable fact that interracial couples exist) so much as the racial conservatism that *Do the Right Thing* depicts, contests, and, in crucial scenes, affirms. Lee's comments reveal that Mookie (like his creator) finds Tina attractive because she looks black even if she is not African American.

Lee, however, demonstrates more maturity (or perhaps more public-relations awareness) when discussing his first meeting with Perez in *That's My Story and I'm Sticking to It*. He tells her to stop dancing on Funky Reggae's speaker, prompting a spirited reaction: "[S]he cursed me out. Now, you know how Rosie speaks—I had never heard a voice like *that* before. . . . That's where I started to get the idea of making Mookie's sometimes girlfriend Puerto Rican."[18] This anecdote indicates that Lee quickly adjusted the role for Perez, while the history of *Do the Right Thing*'s screenplay substantiates this notion. Lee's handwritten first draft, which he began on March 1, 1988 (before encountering Perez), introduces Tina as a young black woman when Mookie delivers pizza to her apartment: "Mookie rings the bell and a 'FINE' sister answers the door."[19] Tina's mother does not appear in this script, but the second draft, also dated March 1, 1988 (yet clearly revised after Lee's birthday party), inserts a short scene in which Carmen yells at Tina (in Spanish) long before Mookie arrives. When he brings pizza to Tina's apartment, the script reads, "Mookie rings the bell and a fine Puerto Rican sister answers the door."[20] Despite changing Tina from an African American to a Puerto Rican woman, neither *Do the Right Thing*'s screenplay nor the finished film ponders the tensions of interracial romance, perhaps because Mookie and Tina's liaison is one of many contested interracial relationships that *Do the Right Thing* chronicles. As with narcotics, Lee chooses not to examine this aspect of Bedford-Stuyvesant life in detail, knowing that future movies can do so.

Mo' Better Blues makes interracial romance a running joke by having Left Hand Lacey (Giancarlo Esposito), piano player for the Bleek Gilliam Quintet—the film's fictional jazz combo—romantically involved with a white Frenchwoman named Jeanne (Linda Hawkins). The band's other members and its manager, Giant (Spike Lee), make snide remarks about Jeanne, causing Lacey to accuse them, particularly Giant, of disliking her because she is Caucasian. This gag barely rises to the level of a leitmotif, much less a theme, despite Giant telling a story about how his mother once paddled his brother for hanging pinups of *Archie Comics'* Betty Cooper and Veronica Lodge on their bedroom walls. Moreover, neither *She's Gotta Have It* nor *School Daze* contemplate interracial dating, marriage, or sex, making *Jungle Fever* the first film in Lee's oeuvre to tackle this topic.

Lee's family experience with interracial romance informs his approach to *Jungle Fever*. His mother, Jacquelyn Shelton Lee, died of liver cancer in 1977, leading Lee to become upset when his father, Bill Lee, quickly started dating Susan Kaplan, whom the elder Lee eventually married. As co-author Kaleem Aftab recounts in *That's My Story and I'm Sticking to It,* Spike was livid that Bill had undertaken a new relationship so close to his mother's death, with Spike telling Aftab, "In retrospect, I blame my father. He could have stopped her from systematically kicking all of us out of the house, but he didn't. And one by one we got the boot."[21] Aftab even reveals that the lingering tension between Spike and Bill Lee, despite their collaboration on Spike's first four theatrical films, caused Spike to ask that Bill not be interviewed for Spike's autobiography.[22]

Such strong emotions frame *Jungle Fever*'s dual narrative about protagonist Flipper Purify's (Wesley Snipes's) problematic family life. Flipper, the sole African American architect at his high-priced Manhattan firm, indulges an extramarital affair with his Bensonhurst-born assistant, Angela "Angie" Tucci (Annabella Sciorra), and nearly destroys his marriage. This plotline intersects Flipper's attempts at reconciling his parents, the Good Reverend Doctor and Lucinda Purify (Ossie Davis and Ruby Dee), with his crack-addicted older brother, Gator (Samuel L. Jackson). Although Flipper remains *Jungle Fever*'s central character, the film features women in significant roles, while interracial sex becomes an important, but hardly exclusive, theme.

Jungle Fever, then, would seem to follow the pattern of Lee's previous movies by marginalizing its female characters. This conclusion, however, does not give due credit to either Angela Tucci or Drew Purify (Lonette McKee), Flipper's wife, who are memorable presences in a film that, true to Lee's earlier work, freely mixes genres, visual styles, and social commentary. Drew is a strong-willed, professional woman who not only works as a fashion buyer for Bloomingdale's but also promptly throws Flipper out of their Harlem brownstone when she learns of his infidelity. She rejects his overtures of returning home when Flipper arrives at Drew's work site with roses, excoriating his choice to bed a white woman by saying, "Don't you know white people hate black people 'cause they're not black? They can't relate."[23] The light-skinned Drew also demonstrates the internal tensions that African Americans face about their complexions when she tells Flipper that, growing up, "I told you how they called me high yellow, yellow bitch, white honky, honky white, white nigger, nigger white, octoroon, quadroon, half-breed, mongrel!" Drew, well played by McKee throughout *Jungle Fever,* remains resolute, although the pain caused by Flipper's affair raises anxieties, rooted in childhood, about her racial identity. Flipper's response illustrates colorism's complications when he says, "Did your white father hate your black mother? Color's got you fucked up, too." This exchange explores the personal and political tensions besetting Drew and Flipper's marriage to highlight how issues surrounding skin tone affect their choice of sexual partners. Drew, earlier in the scene, laments the fact that "I guess I just wasn't light enough" to keep Flipper from straying with a white woman before accusing Flipper of having "a complex about color. You've always had it. I never wanted to believe it until now. All the girls you've ever dated have been light-skinned girls." These comments incorporate a social perspective typical of Lee's films to transform a scene of domestic melodrama into a short, but effective, examination of African American marriage that resonates with wider concerns about American racism. Drew has no final answers, yet offers a social analysis that indicts the primary sexual mythology encompassing American interracial romance, namely that white women, long considered the epitome of American beauty, exert a fascination upon black men that transcends individual attraction.[24] Drew believes that Flipper desires a white woman to validate his status as a successful American black man, not knowing that Angie, a temporary worker with only a high-school education, occupies a lower socioeconomic status than either Drew or Flipper.

Drew, in other words, is neither a perfectly drawn, stereotypically mouthy black woman nor a weakly passive victim who mutely accepts her lot in life. She is an intelligent, tough, and loving person whose insecurities make her realistically vulnerable. Lee's screenplay portrays Drew more fully than the one-dimensional women that bell hooks criticizes, while McKee's textured performance is one of the movie's highlights. Even so, Drew, by *Jungle Fever*'s conclusion, allows Flipper, in a concluding sequence that mimics the film's opening, to make love to her. Unlike their passionate, playful, and loving sex in this first scene, so joyous that their daughter Ming (Veronica Timbers) smiles and laughs as she listens to them from her bedroom, Drew and Flipper's final lovemaking is troubling, with Drew crying during the act. She then tells Flipper that he is not yet welcome to return home: "You better go now. Just leave." Lee directs their sexual congress exactly as his screenplay describes it: "Drew and Flipper are making love like mad, but not like the beginning of the film where the loving was done with a great deal of enthusiasm and fun; this morning it's all about desperation."[25] Drew's tears make this despair evident, which may seem to reduce her power in the movie's last moments. She, however, refuses to forgive Flipper, meaning that Drew sleeps with him to see if their sexual intimacy will fulfill her in the same way that it once did. Her response suggests that it never will, which may signal the marriage's death. Drew, as such, concludes the film as a woman in distress. Her imperfections are startlingly genuine, largely thanks to McKee's excellent acting, meaning that Lee, in helping create Drew, counteracts his tendency to dismiss important female characters at crucial moments.

Angie Tucci, although much different from Drew Purify in education, outlook, and socioeconomic class, succeeds as one of Lee's intriguing cinematic women, although her attempt to breach Bensonhurst's social restrictions (by becoming involved with Flipper) fails. Angie does not impress Flipper during their introduction, claiming that being a temporary worker suits her preference for meeting new people rather than admitting the hard truth, namely that Angie's limited education restricts her job prospects. Lee, however, handles Angie with the same mixture of affection, exasperation, and sympathy as the working-class characters of *Do the Right Thing*, demonstrating that she is an intelligent and discerning woman despite her lack of formal education. Angie at first resembles Pino and Vito in Lee's earlier movie by living in Bensonhurst and working small jobs, recalling Lee's character analysis of both men (in *Do the Right Thing*'s production journal) as essentially unschooled men condemned to a life of low-wage employment.[26] Angie, however, regularly challenges Flipper's pronouncements about their relationship to demonstrate her awareness of the racial forces in play even when she does not understand them as acutely as Flipper. She is not the simple, stereotypical Italian American woman that Flipper expects upon first meeting her and, as *Jungle Fever* progresses, cannot accurately be described as uneducated. Thanks to Annabella Sciorra's spirited performance, Angie transcends the character type to which the film initially assigns her.

Angie, however, suffers the indignities associated with her family's racism. She lives with her father, Mike (Frank Vincent), and two brothers, Jimmy (Michael Imperioli) and Charlie (David Dundara), in Bensonhurst. Angie, assuming all household responsibilities after her unnamed mother's death, cooks all meals, washes all clothes, and cleans all rooms. She does not complain about fulfilling these tasks ("wifely duties," as the character Lou Carbone, played by Anthony Quinn, calls them), but tells Jimmy to prepare the family's meals when he thoughtlessly comments that he prefers his mother's cooking. Although her father Mike defends Angie, he is nonetheless proud that she follows her mother's path (by working all day before caring for the family at night) to illustrate how ingrained traditional female roles are in the Tucci household. Angie, however, alludes to these limitations when, irritated by her family's loutish behavior, she declares, "Shut up for ten minutes! What a fucking life."

Angie, like Drew, will not easily accept male disrespect and, in this early scene, appears more intelligent and resolute than her brothers, who first appear watching a New York Mets baseball game on television while speaking about the team's black players in casually racist terms. This bigotry, however, rebounds on Angie when, one night after spending time with her longtime neighborhood boyfriend (and Lou's son), Paulie Carbone (John Turturro), in the Carbone family candy story, her father severely beats her. Mike strikes Angie with his hands and belt for nearly two minutes, ranting about her temerity in dating a black man. He then disowns her, saying that he no longer has a daughter. Lee expertly directs this scene, with Mike unexpectedly hitting Angie just after she opens the house's front door. The explosion of movement, invective, and tumult that ensues is disturbingly authentic. Frank Vincent plays Mike as a crazed patriarch who cannot tolerate his daughter's romantic attachment to Flipper (Mike's first words, uttered immediately after striking Angie, are "A nigger! A nigger!"). Angie tries, but fails, to defend herself from her father's violence, which is as much emotional as physical.

Telling Angie that he wishes her mother were alive and she (Angie) were dead, Mike's response illustrates the toxic racism that he reserves for African American men. His brutality surprises Jimmy and Charlie, who, in making little effort to stop the assault, tacitly agree with their father's perspective. They do not protest Mike's declaration that Angie must leave the house over the sin of sleeping with a black man, thereby consigning Angie to temporary homelessness. *Jungle Fever* here illustrates a hard lesson for its viewers: Despite Angie's familial loyalty and dutiful domestic behavior, she, by violating the household's unwritten rules against interracial romance, becomes disposable.

This development reduces Angie's power while simultaneously underscoring how working-class women, despite their willingness to earn money, depend upon men for financial support. Angie eventually elects to live with Flipper in a studio apartment that he rents (commenting that it costs "an arm and a leg"), making the disparity in their relationship as clearly economic as racial. *Jungle Fever* reverses Hollywood conventions by making its black protagonist more financially secure than its primary white character, as Henry Louis Gates, Jr., notes in "*Jungle Fever*; or, Guess Who's Not Coming to Dinner?," his contribution to *Five for Five: The Films of Spike Lee:* "In *Jungle Fever*, Lee deftly establishes the economic foundation of racism, on which white Western xenophobia has constructed an entire metaphysics of black sexuality, by *reversing* our normal expectations of the distribution of class status, educational background, and financial stability among the film's black and white characters."[27] This development, however, is not a feminist victory since a male character being more successful than his female partner is hardly unusual. Angie's lack of social mobility undergirds her relationship with Flipper to reveal how *Jungle Fever* links race, class, and sex together more powerfully (and more directly) than Lee's previous films. Lee, indeed, sees Angie as trapped by circumstances more than Flipper during his *Inner Views* discussion with David Breskin, who compliments Lee for staging the parallel scenes of Flipper and Angie confessing their affair to their friends with chain-link fences in the background: "It's such a beautiful metaphor for the sense of being fenced in by your surroundings."[28] Lee agrees, but notes a significant difference: "I think that's true, but I think Angie is much more fenced in than Flipper is. She's trapped. She's trapped in that neighborhood, that environment of Bensonhurst. And Flipper is her one way out."[29]

This comment suggests that Lee sees Angie as a predatory woman who involves herself with Flipper to improve her financial situation. If true, it endorses another prevalent stereotype about women circulating in Hollywood movies: the wily gold digger. Lee's words, however, indicate that Angie's constricted living arrangements (trapped in Bensonhurst by an unloving family) influence her attraction to Flipper, making their relationship a complicated tangle of conflicting erotic, economic, and exploratory desires. Sciorra plays Angie as a woman unsure of herself once the affair begins, but open to the possibilities of love and commitment to Flipper (despite his marriage to Drew). Angie also violates her family's and community's norms by dating Flipper, which Richard A. Blake's *Street Smart: The New York of Lumet, Allen, Scorsese, and Lee* characterizes as a defiant act: "Angie takes advantage of the occasion to rebel against her suffocating home and neighborhood by breaking the ultimate taboo."[30] This disobedience fulfills Angie's wish not merely to escape but to transcend her working-class origins. Dating Flipper, in a subtle bit of parallelism, validates her status as a successful American woman.

Angie's limited knowledge of black culture, moreover, does not inhibit her concern or compassion for Flipper, perhaps best represented during the scene in which the lovers playfully box on the street, only to see NYPD Officers Long and Ponte (Rick Aiello and Miguel Sandoval)—the same cops who murdered Radio Raheem (Bill Nunn) in *Do the Right Thing*—arrive in their squad car, force Flipper against a wall, and hold a gun to his head. Angie protests by saying that Flipper is her boyfriend, but Flipper vociferously denies this fact. Long and Ponte release Flipper, saying that they had received reports of a woman being assaulted by a black man. Angie correctly identifies their response as an example of rank racism, but Flipper furiously repudiates her by asking, "You trying to get me killed?" Angie cannot stomach Long and Ponte's bigotry, but Flipper, despite his upscale profession and lifestyle, is all too familiar with both racial profiling and the consequences of violating the city's ultimate taboo. Angie's ignorance of the tense relationship between New York City cops and African American men leaves her helpless to understand her error in identifying Flipper as her boyfriend. She is appalled by the entire experience, which illustrates not only how institutional racism affects individual lives but also how naïve Angie's assumptions about New York City's racial landscape are. Sciorra smoothly moves from confusion and fear to anger and regret in this starkly lit scene, captured by Lee on handheld cameras to emphasize the visceral danger that the couple endures. Angie's believable responses demonstrate that she is not a cardboard personality, but rather a flawed and feeling woman whose imperfections enhance her importance to *Jungle Fever*'s narrative.

Angie, therefore, unlike Lee's disposable female characters, is not a sex object, a harpy, a nag, or an attachment. She, as a white working-class woman, represents new territory avoided by Lee's previous films, but that *Jungle Fever* incorporates into an unusual storyline that nonetheless consigns Angie to a conventional fate. She leaves Flipper when their relationship becomes too strained to continue, demonstrating her own will, but, having no money of her own, Angie must return to her father's house. The movie's final glimpse of Angie is a long shot of her walking up the steps to her front door, then tentatively entering when Mike opens it. This forlorn image suggests that she will return to her old life (and, as Blake puts it, her suffocating family) to toil in domestic obscurity. Lee's choice to afford Angie fewer options than Flipper may signal *Jungle Fever*'s underlying sexism by confining his female protagonist to her unenviable destiny, although it is a plausible outcome for a working-class woman with few options. The bitterness of Angie's experience, falling for Flipper only to discover that he does not return her love, would be stereotypical but for Angie's relatively well-drawn (and well-performed) personality. Angie, like Drew, signals a new maturity for Lee's cinematic women, but remains a satellite to *Jungle Fever*'s male protagonist.

The film also includes thinly developed female characters that conform to Lee's old pattern, including Lucinda Purify and, especially, Gator's crack-addicted girlfriend, Vivian (Halle Berry, in her inaugural feature-film appearance). Lucinda is a long-suffering preacher's wife whose role alternates between pleading with her family not to fight at the dinner table and trying to placate Gator's manic requests for money. Vivian, despite Berry's impressive transformation from glamorous *Vanity Fair* model into disreputable junkie (who, like Gator, seems to reek whenever on-screen), is little more than the "five-dollar crack ho" that Lee identifies in *That's My Story and I'm Sticking to It*,[31] a woman who offers to fellate Flipper for money while he walks Ming to school. The movie takes no interest in Lucinda's and Vivian's struggles, making them minor, one-note characters whose sole function is to service Flipper's story.

Jungle Fever, however, includes one remarkable scene that demonstrates Lee's commitment to widening his fictional representation of women. Referred to by Flipper's friend Cyrus (Spike Lee) as a "war council," Drew and four female friends, including Cyrus's wife Vera (Victoria Webb), discuss Flipper's infidelity in the context of interracial marriage, dating, and sex. The scene is an acting tour de force with all five actresses (in addition to Webb and Lonette McKee, Theresa Randle, Phyllis Yvonne Stickney, and Pamela Tyson round out the cast) so authentically playing this frank discussion that their dialogue seems improvised. Lee, indeed, tells Janice Mosier Richolson in their 1991 *Cineaste* interview that this sequence "was completely improvisational. We did between twenty and twenty-five takes. I find the more you talk the more honest you get,"[32] although *Jungle Fever*'s July 9, 1990, screenplay draft includes a four-page version of this scene that offers an outline for the filmed dialogue. Whether or not the conversation was scripted, the women reveal their divergent views about dating and marrying within their race with impressive, sometimes lacerating honesty. As Henry Louis Gates, Jr., comments in his essay, "This is a refreshingly open and revealing scene, the ultimate communal feminist moment in a major black film released to this time."[33] Lee's screenplay, indeed, includes stage directions that nicely summarize the scene as shot: "What we have here is a WAKE. A MOURNING for another SISTER who has been WRONGED. Drew, Vera and her three girlfriends, NILDA, INEZ and ANGELA sit in the living room, laughing, crying and discussing the state of THE BLACK MAN."[34]

Vera, thinking that Flipper was a perfect husband, takes his infidelity as proof that all men are dogs, but Drew affirms her belief that "there's good black men out there. . . . The problem is we're looking in the wrong places. . . . We're not lookin' at bus drivers or truck drivers or garbage men, and a lot of them are doing that. And we just won't give them the time of day, but they're good men." Angela (Pamela Tyson) comments upon the difficulty of finding mates who can handle educated women that make more money. She also, later in the scene, discusses her self-image, saying, "Do any of you know what it is like not being thought of as attractive? I was always the darkest one in my class. . . . All the guys ran after the light-skin girls with long, straight hair, and that left me out." This comment, along with the ensuing conversation, raises the same tensions over class, complexion, and hair that *School Daze*'s Wannabees and Jigaboos enact, but acknowledges them more directly, openly, and honestly than the earlier movie. As Gates notes, "The intraracial color-as-class tensions that Lee parodied in *School Daze* are in this scene rendered in full and beautiful detail. In this communal, feminist sharing of traditional racial wisdom, the tensions brought on by race and class and by color and hair texture are revealed as never before in the history of film."[35] The entire five-minute scene, far from descending into a shallow display of "girl power," crackles with wit. By making space for its participants to discuss their outlooks and disagreements, the War Council shows Lee's respect for his female characters despite Cyrus's militant name for this gathering, which implies that the women metaphorically attack men. The conversation, instead, is a refreshing example of Lee stretching the movie's free-form narrative to include female perspectives that might otherwise go unheard.

Jungle Fever, as such, is a limited success for its female characters. Prominently featured, they are nonetheless subordinate to Flipper Purify's story. Lee, however, gives more time, attention, and detail to their characterization, thereby eluding the egregious displays of sexism associated with his other films. The movie, although not a feminist exploration of women's lives, improves Lee's earlier efforts on this score to pave the way for a film that does so more successfully: *Girl 6*.

GIRL 6 (1996)

Girl 6 was the first of two Lee films released in 1996, the second being *Get on the Bus*. They bookend one another well, with *Girl 6* focusing on its female protagonist, a phone-sex operator and aspiring actress named Judy (Theresa Randle), while *Get on the Bus* tells the story of fifteen black men riding from South Central Los Angeles to Washington, D.C., to attend the Million Man March. These movies are also the first Spike Lee films in which Lee does not share screenplay credit: Suzan-Lori Parks writes *Girl 6* while Reggie Rock Bythewood writes *Get on the Bus*. *Girl 6* is a poetic and fanciful meditation upon the oppressive power of female objectification, whereas *Get on the Bus* takes a documentary approach to its male subjects. *Girl 6*'s most notable aspect, apart from Randle's splendid performance as the title character, is how sharply it diagnoses the nearly fatal power of images to undermine a woman's self-worth and sexual agency. The film, therefore, complements *She's Gotta Have It* by taking the heroine's sexuality as its prime subject, then manipulating the audience's expectations to expose Hollywood cinema's misguided (and frequently vile) representations of African American women.

Lee planned this outcome from the movie's inception, telling the titular host of PBS's *The Charlie Rose Show* (on its March 20, 1996, episode) that choosing a woman as *Girl 6*'s protagonist came about because "ten years has been long enough if you don't count *Crooklyn*,"[36] referring to the decade-long gap since *She's Gotta Have It*'s debut. Commenting that "the story really came from thinking about *She's Gotta Have It*," especially Nola Darling's sexual involvement with three lovers, Lee tells Rose, "Man, people thought that was cute and stuff like that, but that was before AIDS, and now ten years later, that kind of conduct or behavior, is dangerous. And ten years ago the phone sex business was not a multi-billion dollar industry, you see. So, [with] these two things, it's really a look at how things have changed in the past ten years."[37] Connecting these two ideas—the era of "safe sex" that occurred after Americans became better educated about the extent of the AIDS crisis and the rise of phone-sex as a profitable business—allows *Girl 6* to dramatize how psychologically uncertain Judy becomes by repeatedly fulfilling male sexual fantasies as a condition of her employment. The film suggests that this profession—in which Judy not only adopts the name "Lovely" when speaking with her clients but also agrees to her boss Lil's (Jenifer Lewis) suggestion that she pretend to be a white woman unless a caller requests otherwise—prevents Girl 6 (as she is known throughout the film, her given name only being spoken twice) from separating her professional and personal lives. Although treading on potentially stereotypical material, *Girl 6* is, in some ways, Lee's most feminist film by demonstrating the frightening and tragic consequences of reducing a woman's value to her sex appeal.

Bell hooks, long the sharpest critic of Lee's cinematic sexism, finds the movie a groundbreaking shift in the director's work. In "Good Girls Look the Other Way," hooks writes, "Contrary to what most viewers imagine before they see *Girl 6* this is not a film that exploits the objectification of women. This is a film that explores the eroticization of stardom, of attention. It is a long slow narrative about lack, about where the inability to feel pleasure can take one."[38] The praise does not end here, with hooks stating, "The longing of women and men in this film is not for sexual satisfaction but for undivided, unconditional attention. It is the desire to be seen, to not be erased or rendered invisible that fuels individual longings."[39] This comment appreciates the irony of *Girl 6*'s central premise. The film begins with the as-yet-unnamed protagonist auditioning for a movie role from Q.T., "the hottest director in Hollywood,"[40] a man played by Quentin Tarantino in what hooks calls "a masterfully satiric moment"[41] that acknowledges Tarantino's newfound fame and critical respectability (due to *Pulp Fiction*'s success). Q.T. tells Girl 6 that, since he intends to direct the greatest black romantic film ever made, he needs a lead actress who represents the "total package"[42]—the ideal African American woman—and he will know her when he sees her. Q.T. interrupts Girl 6 when she begins discussing herself, curtly telling her to disrobe so that he can evaluate her topless appearance. Girl 6, surprised because her agent has not mentioned that the role requires nudity, does so after Q.T. asks whether or not she wants the part. As hooks writes, "When she submits exposing her gorgeous full rounded breasts, shame overwhelms and she leaves."[43] This embarrassment leads Girl 6, after being fired by her agent and her acting coach, to take the job as a phone-sex operator so that she can continue to perform without having to appear naked on camera. Girl 6 thereby renders herself invisible to the male gaze despite her desire to be seen, on stage and on film, as a talented individual. Girl 6's clients cannot see her, but she nonetheless exposes herself to their sexual desires, becoming emotionally vulnerable as the movie continues.

Girl 6, as this synopsis implies, depicts the many ways that sexual objectification influences its protagonist's self-image, containing, as Karen D. Hoffman notes in her fine essay "Feminists and 'Freaks': *She's Gotta Have It* and *Girl 6*," "an exposé of the sources of the oppression of women."[44] Hoffman, better than any other writer, demonstrates how such subjugation depends upon men's ability to define, to command, and to control women, seeing Q.T.'s behavior in *Girl 6*'s opening scene as emblematic: "It is clear from the beginning that his gaze is what counts; it does not matter what Girl 6 says or does. What matters is how she looks, whether she 'oozes sexuality,' and whether she fits the ideal image that exists in his mind."[45] This comment recalls Lee's problematic casting of Rosie Perez as Tina in *Do the Right Thing* because she fits his image of the ideal "ghetto babe" who "looks Black."[46] *Girl 6,* indeed, may represent progress in Lee's fictional depiction of women, as Hoffman indicates: "Perhaps Lee means to call attention to his awareness of the fact that, as a director and author working in the industry, his films might be complicit in such objectification."[47] Noting that Lee interviewed female friends before writing *She's Gotta Have It*'s screenplay "in an attempt to accurately represent women's voices, particularly about their sexuality and sexual experiences," Hoffman notes that, "by the time of *Girl 6,* he may be more aware of the difficulties involved in taking those experiences out of their particular contexts. Moreover, he may be more aware that those experiences can reinforce rather than revolutionize problematic sex and gender stereotypes."[48] Bell hooks certainly agrees with this perspective, writing, "In many ways *Girl 6* shows that Spike Lee's artistic vision regarding the representation of female sexuality has expanded. His maturation as a filmmaker is evident, and with it his capacity to represent women characters in more complex ways. The film is not an orgy of pornographic sexism."[49]

While true, *Girl 6*, by referring to its protagonist by either her operator number or her "stage" name (Lovely, inspired by Pam Grier's character in *Foxy Brown*) rather than her given name (Judy), obscures her personal identity in favor of the roles that she plays at work. This choice risks reducing Judy to an object that merely gratifies her client's longing for companionship, titillation, and fantasy. Bell hooks claims that the "women working in the sex industry whose job it is to respond to those fantasies are never portrayed as victims" because "*Girl 6* lets audiences know that women working in this aspect of the sex industry, as in so many other areas, are doing it for the money. And that sometimes it can be pleasurable work like any other job any other worker does for the money, while at other times it is dehumanizing, degrading labor."[50] Although accurate, this analysis minimizes Girl 6's increasing inability to separate fantasy from reality, leading her to agree to meet a well-to-do client named Bob (Peter Berg), who, by repeatedly discussing his dying mother, forms a bond with Girl 6 that she takes too seriously in her search for authentic human connection. Girl 6 dresses up to meet Bob on Coney Island, but he never arrives. As hooks writes, "When a white male walks by not even noticing her, she calls out to him. He does not turn and look her way. Invisible within the realm of whiteness, Girl 6 is powerless to fulfill her fantasies."[51] This dispiriting erasure of Girl 6's power demonstrates that she is not the agent of her own actions so much as a woman relying upon the kindness of strangers to provide the warmth she seeks, but does not receive, from the actual men in her life, particularly her neighbor, Jimmy (Spike Lee), and her kleptomaniac ex-husband, known only as Shoplifter (Isaiah Washington, in a superb performance).

In truth, both Jimmy and Shoplifter offer Girl 6 emotional and sexual connection, but she refuses them (never, for instance, seeing Jimmy as a potential lover). This development signals *Girl 6*'s complicated depiction of its female protagonist. Judy, thanks to Randle's casting, is a beautiful woman who, in another film, would have no trouble finding sexual partners. During her audition with Q.T. at the movie's opening and with actor-director Ron Silver (playing himself) at its conclusion, Girl 6 chooses Nola Darling's first monologue from *She's Gotta Have It* ("The only reason I'm consenting to doing this is because I wish to clear my name") as her preferred piece, suggesting that she finds Nola's words liberating. Yet Nola maintains relationships with three lovers, actively enjoying sex with all of them, whereas Judy denies herself physical intimacy in favor of helping her phone-sex clients satisfy their own desires. Rather than making Girl 6 a simple sex object, the movie illustrates her sexuality as a deeper, more troubling aspect of her personality. Girl 6 refuses on-camera nudity, apart from the brief glimpse of her breasts visible during the Q.T. audition, which Roger Ebert, in his negative review, finds problematic: "Now if Lee is saying Tarantino is a cretin for making her do this, then logically he shouldn't let us see her breasts even if Tarantino can. But he does. What we have here is a scene about a woman being shamed by exposing herself, and the scene is handled so that she exposes herself. That puts Lee in the same boat with the lecher."[52] This argument, despite its merit, misses that Girl 6's distress, so evident when removing her blouse, demonstrates how Hollywood productions exploit female bodies (particularly the bodies of African American women) for crude sexual purposes. Randle skillfully plays Judy's shame, which bell hooks finds crucial to the film's satiric intent. The scene emphasizes Judy's discomfort in a moment far more unnerving than arousing, disrupting the male gaze so successfully that Q.T. angrily yells, "What the hell is going on here? What is happening?" when Judy walks out of the audition.

Even so, Girl 6's personality appears, at crucial moments, to be stunted, as Hoffman comments in "Feminists and 'Freaks'": "Despite the fact that she leads a life in which female characters play an important role, they do so as her bosses and coworkers, not as her personal friends and confidantes. Like Nola [Darling], Girl 6 gives no indication that she is actively cultivating deeper relationships with women or that she puts a premium on doing so."[53] Hoffman, who later notes that Girl 6, "because she is paid to pretend to be the various female characters her callers want her to be" is conscious "of the extent to which she is performing her gender"[54] more than Nola, underscores how arduously Girl 6 defines herself according to (rather than against) the expectations of men that she never meets (no matter how intimate their connection may feel). This development insinuates that *Girl 6*, far from disrupting female stereotypes, simply chronicles garden-variety sexism in a patriarchal narrative that constricts its protagonist's ability to live as an independent woman. She may not be a sexual object, but she is also not an emancipated person.

Critics such as Ebert and scholars such as Hoffman note the feminist tensions in *Girl 6*, perhaps explaining why it received such poor reviews upon its 1996 release. Even Lee's wife, Tonya Lewis Lee, finds the movie difficult to countenance, as her comments in *That's My Story and I'm Sticking to It* reveal. "I've always felt that *Girl 6* was Spike's way of rebelling against marriage and children," Lewis Lee says, revealing that she only discovered her husband was making the film when other people mentioned it: "And I always felt he had a guilty conscience about it: why not tell me about it?"[55] This analysis broadly agrees with Ebert's attitude, although suggesting that *Girl 6* is Lee's revolt against the enforced domesticity of marriage and parenthood implies that it endorses a married man's vulgar, sexist grief about lost freedom. Lewis Lee certifies this reading in her later comments: "I thought that the script was so poorly developed that I did not understand the main character, her motivation, her history. How did she get to that place? It was like, 'Dress up a lot of pretty sexy girls and make them talk dirty.'"[56] This criticism returns longtime viewers of Lee's films to a primary charge against them, namely that their female characters represent little more than male wish fulfillment. Girl 6's growing obsession with her work leads Tonya Lewis Lee to state that *Girl*

6's entire plot symbolizes "this secret place that men go—that when you have the Madonna wife and child at home, then you have to secretly go off and get your primitive, instinctual sexual gratification elsewhere."[57]

These assessments are tough denunciations of a movie whose protagonist works to define herself throughout the picture. Lewis Lee's observation that *Girl 6*'s viewers know little about Judy's background (beyond the fact that she is divorced) is true insofar as Judy does not discuss her parents, siblings, or past life in detail. Although she and her ex-husband refer to their shared history, little information is forthcoming. Judy, in Lewis Lee's estimation, is a thinly drawn character whose motivation requires more explanation. *Girl 6,* however, resists conventional explanations of Judy becoming obsessed with her phone-sex occupation. She never refers to difficult relationships with her parents; to a history of addiction; or to emotional, physical, or sexual abuse. She defies these expectations, forming herself as the film unfolds, although by *Girl 6*'s conclusion, Judy remains mysterious. She leaves New York City when another regular caller (played by Michael Imperioli), whose snuff fantasies escalate to potential violence, learns her home address before threatening to suffocate her. Arriving in Hollywood, Judy continues auditioning for films, refusing to disrobe for Ron Silver, but still defining herself through other female icons (including Dorothy Dandridge and Nola Darling, repeating the latter's opening monologue for Silver). These plot developments cause the movie to end with Girl 6 as a cypher for *Girl 6*'s viewer, with Karen D. Hoffman claiming, "it is not clear, even by the film's end, that Judy is a fully developed character. At best, she appears to be on her way to self-definition. And although this is important, it is not sufficient to constitute a model for liberation."[58]

Hoffman's evaluation, along with her comment that the snuff caller's threat "seems to suggest that women who are too sexually active or attractive will be punished by at least the threat of physical violence,"[59] poses a serious challenge to *Girl 6*'s feminist credentials. The movie, however, commendably illustrates the uncertainties besetting Girl 6's life, while her protean character—Girl 6 easily assumes roles for different callers without, at first, being consumed by them—suits her ambiguous, permeable, and ever-shifting identity. Girl 6's past, in other words, is of little interest to the movie because she takes so little interest in it herself. In the film's most satirical comment about identity formation, Girl 6 constructs her personality from mass-media models that *Girl 6* adroitly parodies in three terrifically funny scenes: Otto Preminger's 1954 film *Carmen Jones* (the famous adaptation of Georges Bizet's 1875 opera *Carmen* with an all-black cast that starred Dorothy Dandridge and Harry Belafonte), Jack Hill's aforementioned 1974 blaxploitation film *Foxy Brown,* and Norman Lear's now-classic 1975–1985 sitcom *The Jeffersons.* Girl 6 imagines herself in significant roles in all three instances, playing Carmen Jones, Foxy Brown, and, in the *Jeffersons* parody, a daughter whom her George Jefferson-like father (nicely played by Spike

Lee) protects from the calls of a male suitor by shooting the family tele-phone.[60]

These sequences hint that Girl 6 is, in fact, a case of arrested development. Her identity comprises bits of African American popular culture that block a more mature personality from evolving. As bell hooks observes in "Good Girls Look the Other Way," "Throughout the film, Lee suggests that indi-viduals who are psychically wounded are trapped in infantile states. Addiction to fantasies begins in childhood as a way the self is nurtured when there is no real nurturance, when life is without substance or meaning."[61] The film intimates that Judy's childhood was not terribly healthy or happy, but indi-cates this possibility indirectly rather than employing flashbacks to visualize it. These parodies not only prefigure Lee's most bracing attack against media representations of African American life (2000's feature-length satire *Bam-boozled*) but also demonstrate how toxic the sexist images of all three earlier texts are to Judy's personality. Even Foxy Brown, the ass-kicking heroine whom Judy imagines herself playing in *Girl 6*'s parody of Jack Hill's movie, asserts her power by destroying men, becoming, in hooks's judgment, "a pseudo male in drag, hence her ability to assert her sexual agency."[62] Employ-ing mass-media images as her primary models of womanhood is problematic for Girl 6 and for hooks, who notes, "Girl 6 can find no representations of liberatory sexuality. She must either be victim, vamp, or castrator. All of these roles still require that she shape her sexuality in response to the eroticism of the patriarchal phallic imaginary. For that imaginary controls the world of media images—of representations."[63]

This analysis perceptively unveils just how well *Girl 6* criticizes the image-making institutions of Hollywood film studios, television networks, and their financiers. Girl 6, although a victim of their representations of women, does not retire into victimhood, but instead embarks on an uncertain journey as a Hollywood actress who understands her value better at the film's conclusion than at its beginning. She refuses to undress during her audition with Ron Silver, then performs Nola Darling's opening confession with assured grace. Girl 6 leaves the audition and briefly pauses over Dorothy Dandridge's star on the Hollywood Walk of Fame, then crosses the street toward a movie the-ater whose marquee reads *Girl 6*. This reflexive moment signals Lee's status as an inside man who nonetheless maintains crucial creative independence from Hollywood studios. As hooks writes, "Up to a point he has played the game and made it, doing more feature films than any other black director to date. Yet he has refused to go all the way. *Girl 6* is his gesture of resistance."[64] This rebellion bears fruit, with Lee, according to hooks, offering "viewers the most diverse images of black female identity ever to be seen in a Hol-lywood film in *Girl 6*. Represented as mothers, newscasters, business execu-tives, phone sex operators, black women have center stage in this film."[65] The movie, as much satire as cri de coeur, casts Judy in multiple roles that she cannot resolve into a single identity. She is neither a victimized nor liberated woman by *Girl 6*'s conclusion, but instead a person searching for connection in an impersonal world over which she exercises tenuous power.

 Girl 6, therefore, qualifies as a feminist film even if the valuable objections of Roger Ebert and Tonya Lewis Lee deserve respectful attention. Karen D. Hoffman grants this conclusion despite her own misgivings, writing that the movie "provides a critique of oppressive institutions that is consistent with the goals of feminism."[66] She encourages like-minded people to watch *Girl 6* because "even though the film's title character ultimately does not represent a model of liberated female sexuality, this film helps reveal some of the social and cultural forces that inhibit Girl 6's emancipation, and feminists might, on closer examination, find much to admire in this film, which is one of Spike Lee's most underrated."[67] *Girl 6,* as these comments suggest, is an imperfect, yet fascinating exploration of female sexuality, agency, and identity that demonstrates Lee's growth as a cinematic artist. Mediocre reviews to the contrary, the movie remains a worthwhile contribution to Lee's filmography, as well as necessary viewing for anyone interested in how he depicts women. *Girl 6* also anticipates significant themes in the worst-reviewed movie of Lee's career, *She Hate Me.*

SHE HATE ME (2004)

She Hate Me, despite ambitiously fusing corporate satire with sex farce, provoked a backlash against Lee's portrayal of lesbian women that still haunts his reputation. Jasmine Nichole Cobb and John L. Jackson, in their excellent essay "They Hate Me: Spike Lee, Documentary Filmmaking, and Hollywood's 'Savage Slot,'" vividly recount the outrage that the film incited during its 2004 release:

> At a Harlem screening of the movie during its opening weekend, Jackson (co-author) sat in a Magic Johnson theater where one thirty-something black woman got up from her seat during the denouement . . . to vehemently scream at the film as she stormed out of the auditorium: "Motherfuck you, Spike Lee!" A good portion of the audience then erupted in an impromptu round of applause, as if to second her condemnation.[68]

This response emblematizes the critical and commercial drubbing that *She Hate Me* endured, with Kaleem Aftab, in *That's My Story and I'm Sticking to It,* stating that the movie had almost no box-office presence upon its July 2004 release, that "critics were unanimous in their derision" and that "lesbian groups were offended."[69] The first portion of this evaluation is true, with *She Hate Me* earning just under $370,000 against its estimated $8-million budget.[70] This enormous loss did not deter Lee from releasing his most financially successful film, *Inside Man,* in 2006, yet signifies that his movies are not blockbuster studio fare, but rather stories that appeal to smaller, niche audiences.

She Hate Me's controversial reception, however, demonstrates that not even sympathetic audiences uncritically support Lee's work. Even so, Aftab errs in claiming that critical derision was total. Roger Ebert, for one, proclaims the movie a more successful satire than *Bamboozled,* although his review identifies *She Hate Me* as a prime cinematic example of negative capability. The viewer, in other words, must feel comfortable within the film's many absurdities, improbabilities, and insensitivities to understand its effects, particularly its plotline of well-to-do lesbian women eagerly paying the protagonist, John Henry "Jack" Armstrong (Anthony Mackie), to impregnate them during acts of coitus so passionate that they experience sexual pleasure. "But to work without the safety net," Ebert writes, "to deliberately be offensive, to refuse to satisfy our generic expectations, to dangle the conventional formula in front of us and then yank it away, to explode the structure of the movie, to allow it to contain anger and sarcasm, impatience and wild, imprudent excess, to find room for both unapologetic, melodramatic romance *and* satire—well, that's audacious."[71] Ebert does not stop here, slyly appreciating Lee's lack of restraint: "To go where this film goes and still to have the nerve to end the way he does (with a reconciliation worthy of soap opera, and the black hero making a noble speech at a congressional hearing) is a form of daring beyond all reason."[72] *She Hate Me,* according to Ebert's argument, is a gonzo, go-for-broke satire that subverts all viewer expectations. This judgment is both an accurate and charitable reading of the rage that, according to Cobb and Jackson's article, attended the movie's release.

Ebert, who begins his analysis by acknowledging, "Spike Lee's *She Hate Me* will get some terrible reviews. Scorched earth reviews. Its logic, style, presumption and sexual politics will be ridiculed,"[73] later identifies the film's unwelcome presentation of African American men and lesbian women as integral to its political project: "My guess is that Lee is attacking African American male and gay/lesbian stereotypes not by conventionally preaching against them, but by boldly dramatizing them. . . . By getting mad at the movie, we arrive at the conclusions he intends. In a sense, he is sacrificing himself to get his message across."[74] This conclusion is not only generous when compared to the vitriolic response described by Cobb and Jackson but also credits Lee with enacting stereotypes in an attempt to confront, demystify, and disempower them. Having characters mouth platitudes about how terrible homophobia is would follow conventional Hollywood storytelling patterns that Lee, both here and throughout his career, refuses. *She Hate Me,* for Ebert, evokes anger at its antigay typecasting to demonstrate just how terrible these portrayals are.

Ebert, however, does not deny that *She Hate Me* traffics in lesbian stereotypes, particularly in its portrayal of Jack's ex-fiancée, Fatima Goodrich (Kerry Washington), and her partner, Alex Guerrero (Dania Ramirez). Fatima, as her surname indicates, becomes Jack's business agent when, after Jack loses his job as the highly paid vice president of the pharmaceutical company Progeia for whistleblowing the corporation's financial malfeasance to the Securities and Exchange Commission, she proposes that Jack impregnate her lesbian friends for $10,000 per conception. Fatima, in Jack's eyes, functions as his pimp, since he is not simply a sperm donor, but rather a man who sleeps with five or more lesbian woman each night, getting them pregnant every time he ejaculates while, in the film's most offensive move, bringing them to pleasurable, bed-shaking orgasms. Fatima and Alex, when Jack objects to this plan on the basis of the fact that they are, indeed, lesbians, respond by saying, "We're businesswomen."[75] Fatima later tells Jack that she does not consider herself either a lesbian or bisexual woman because she prefers not to restrict her identity to her sexuality, but, as the most well-developed woman in the movie, she remains a satellite to Jack's conflicting desires and needs in a film that, at least on its surface, represents a step back for Lee's portrayal of women.

Bernadette Barton's "Male Fantasies about Lesbian Desire: A Review of Spike Lee's Film *She Hate Me*" confirms this perspective by condemning "Spike Lee's cartoonish portrayal of lesbian relationships, desire, and reproduction."[76] Her perceptive essay, among the most insightful analyses of *She Hate Me* yet printed, is perhaps the film's harshest assessment to date. Barton denounces Fatima, Alex, and the other lesbian women as caricatures, going so far as to state that they "resembled no real life lesbian I have ever encountered. They were Spike Lee lesbians. Or perhaps better put, the lesbians in *She Hate Me* most accurately resemble the women in a girl-on-girl porno flick you might order from the adult selections during a boring hotel stay. *She Hate Me* is an under the covers masturbatory fantasy for heterosexual men."[77] This condemnation rebukes the film in the strongest possible terms, making, as Cobb and Jackson note in "They Hate Me," heterosexuality's primacy incontestable.[78] Barton's notion of "Spike Lee lesbians" also coheres with Heather E. Harris and Kimberly R. Moffitt's formulation of the "Spiked Lens" as a prism that distorts female characters even when attempting to liberate them from Hollywood stereotypes. Harris and Moffitt comment that, although Fatima and Alex become mothers to Jack's children, "they remain visible and attractive because they fulfill John's fantasy. He gets the women and children without the grief, and Fatima and Alex become questionable lesbians and honorary mothers instead of overbearing wives and mothers."[79] This last observation is hardly comforting in light of *She Hate Me*'s improbable conclusion: Fatima and Alex invite Jack into their family to live as the patriarch who will help raise their two children (both women having conceived during sexual congress with Jack). The film's final image—of Jack's father Geronimo (Jim Brown) chuckling at the absurdity of Jack, Fatima, Alex, and their children playing on the beach—is curiously appropriate. Lee seems to acknowledge, if not anticipate, the criticism *She Hate Me* will receive by having the family's true patriarch, its grandfather, not quite believe what he watches.

Lee defends *She Hate Me* in his engaging DVD audio commentary by claiming that he test-screened the film for lesbian audiences, finding that half supported and half derided the movie's portrayal of lesbian women.[80] Lee then repeats statements made in his audio commentaries for *School Daze*, *Do the Right Thing*, and *Get on the Bus* that viewers should not ascribe the homophobic views espoused by a film or its characters to Lee himself. Lee makes this claim most vociferously in his contentious 1995 interview with *The Advocate*'s Alan Frutkin, saying at one point, "This is the way these characters speak. Because I use the words *faggot* and *homo*, people try to pin me as fucking homophobic, and that's bullshit. If homosexuals don't think people call them 'faggots' and 'homos,' then they're stupid"[81] before modifying his tone, in response to more questions by Frutkin, by noting, "People have to understand that just because you have a character say a word, that is not necessarily the view of the director."[82] The interview concludes with Frutkin asking, "For the record, what do you think of homosexuality?," to which Lee evasively responds, "I think people are free to pursue whatever they want to."[83] Since *She Hate Me*'s characters, particularly Jack, do not employ homophobic slurs against Fatima, Alex, and the other lesbian characters, Lee's audio-commentary apologia fails to address claims that the film's portrayal of lesbian women is a heterosexual male fantasy.

In his long 2004 *Salon* interview with Rebecca Walker titled "Female Trouble," Lee tackles these charges: "What I like to say to people when they say, 'This is Spike's fantasy, or this is a male's fantasy,' is that it is, up to a point, but then it turns to a nightmare."[84] When Walker, who describes *She Hate Me* as "fascinating and entertaining" in the interview's introduction, asks, "At what point is that?," Lee replies, "When Jack starts to realize what he's doing. I mean, there's a ton of money in his hands and he throws it down in disgust. He is worn out. Mentally, physically, spiritually. He's thinking, if I never see another piece of you know what, I'd be happy."[85] Jack's experience as a nightmare, despite Walker's sympathy for Lee's response, suggests that Fatima, Alex, and the other mothers fulfill an old Hollywood stereotype: the predatory lesbian who drains her partner (in this case, a man whom she pays for sperm) of life and energy. Rather than repudiating *She Hate Me*'s antigay subtext, Lee's answer seems to confirm it.

Charges of homophobia have followed Lee as doggedly as accusations of sexism, which Walker addresses in her introduction: "As a bisexual woman, I had a few mixed feelings about the way lesbians are portrayed and many more about Jack's ambivalence about his role as a daddy donor, but ultimately think, again, Lee has pushed some of the hottest buttons in the culture and asked some critical questions about what it means to be a man in America today."[86] Yet this defense again spotlights how problematic *She Hate Me*'s depiction of lesbian women is. The crisis of Jack's masculinity depends upon his encounter with Barton's "Spike Lee lesbians," whom she defines as reinforcing "every popular salacious stereotype about lesbians: we are all sexy femme women who really want a hard dick to make us whole. In the absence of said hard dick, we will go to any hysterical lengths to achieve our compulsive sexual and maternal desires."[87] Fatima, indeed, begins her business venture by pairing Jack with conventionally sexy women, but continues with prospective mothers who do not fit this mold (who are, in popular parlance, more "butch" than Fatima, Alex, and the lesbian characters played by Monica Bellucci, Sarita Choudhury, and Bai Ling) to demonstrate Fatima's keen appreciation of Jack's personality. She, in other words, understands how appealing the fantasy of sleeping with attractive lesbians is for Jack, which allows Fatima, in Walker's words, to "hook him through his own susceptibility to [this] fantasy."[88] True as this idea may be, *She Hate Me*'s whimsical approach to lesbian parenting continues until its conclusion, with contented grandfather Geronimo chuckling at the newly formed nuclear family of Jack, Fatima, and Alex. Progressive as this configuration may seem (by indirectly arguing that American families exist on a continuum that cannot be confined to the traditional heterosexual model of the one-man, one-woman couple), it also denies the possibility of Fatima and Alex raising their children alone. *She Hate Me*'s denouement, in other words, reduces their independence despite ostensibly celebrating it.

Lee denies this subtext in a 2004 interview with About.com's *Hollywood Movies,* responding to the question "Are you saying it's important to have a male and female influence on a child?" with "No, I'm not saying that. I mean, there's been no scientific studies saying that children of same sex parents grow up to be any worse than any children with a mommy and a daddy at home."[89] Lee also endorses gay marriage in his 2012 *Vulture* interview with Will Leitch by responding to Leitch's question "There is a lot of talk these days about the parallels between gay marriage and civil rights. Do you think that's valid?" by saying, "All I can say is, I support gay marriage. They want to marry each other, I support it. That is their choice."[90] These laudable perspectives, however, do not alter *She Hate Me*'s questionable rendering of lesbian relationships, parenting, and sexual desire. The fact that Lee employed film director and *Village Voice* writer Tristan Taormino to review the film's screenplay and to put the heterosexual actresses playing lesbians through what Kerry Washington, in *That's My Story and I'm Sticking to It,* calls a two-week "lesbian boot camp"[91] does little to justify, or even explain away, these representations. Lee's similarly feeble observations in his 2004 interview with *The Advocate*'s Anne Stockwell about Taormino assuring him that no film will please all lesbian viewers, meaning that "the range of thoughts is all over the place. And [reactions are] really divided upon race. The women of color are much more—they can understand the ending. It's not that [women of color] want to be with the man, but they can understand it,"[92] cannot obscure how farfetched *She Hate Me*'s conclusion is. The movie, despite its excellent cinematography by Matthew Libatique, evocative score by Terence Blanchard, and good acting (particularly from Anthony Mackie, in his first leading-man performance, and Kerry Washington), remains a problematic depiction of lesbian women that makes Opal Gilstrap (Raye Dowell), the sole gay character in *She's Gotta Have It* who chases Nola Darling nearly as much as Nola's three male lovers, seem a model of enlightened cinematic lesbianism on Lee's part.

She Hate Me may not qualify as a rampantly homophobic film (Stockwell, in her *Advocate* article, praises the movie as "Lee's gayest story yet, and happily we're among the good guys"[93]), but its attempt at presenting complicated, conflicted, and realistic lesbian characters founders more often than it flourishes to inscribe the stereotypes that it hopes to disrupt. Deborah Elizabeth Whaley, in her fascinating essay "Spike Lee's Phantasmagoric Fantasy and the Black Female Sexual Imaginary in *She Hate Me*" (the most substantial scholarly article yet published about the film), bluntly states the matter after identifying Tristan Taormino as a "film director and feminist pornographer": "Spike Lee seems to suggest that some sort of 'boot camp' for the actors legitimizes the film. However . . . I see this film for what it is: a convoluted, male phatasmagoric fantasy, which reifies normative conceptions of sexuality, while purporting to represent the non-normative Black female sexual imaginary in a sympathetic way."[94] The movie, for Whaley, tricks the viewer into thinking that it will shatter homophobic formulations of traditional families, proper sexual roles, and lesbian desire, only to abandon this project by appointing Jack Armstrong as the triumphant patriarch who not only lives the heterosexual male fantasy of sleeping with beautiful lesbians but also convinces them to permit him to help raise their children. Whaley finds *She Hate Me* "similar to Lee's previous films, insofar as a main component of the film is to reveal the plight of a Black male protagonist and to present Black women as co-conspirators in Black male subjugation."[95] Jack, however, resists this subjugation by forming a nuclear family with Fatima and Alex (as equal partners) that nonetheless marginalizes them, both within the film's narrative and within their own relationship. *She Hate Me*'s conclusion, as this analysis implies, subjugates its two primary lesbian characters to Jack's strong desire to remain involved in his children's lives, contravening the reality that sperm donors cede all parental rights to their children upon receiving payment (and the agreement to this effect that Jack makes with all the lesbian mothers that he impregnates).

Such intriguing, provocative, and muddled gender dynamics lead Bernadette Barton to conclude, "This is not a progressive portrayal of women or lesbians. It's Orwellian doublespeak. By reversing institutional gender power so that women are represented as the ones buying and men providing the sexual services, Spike Lee simplifies feminism into a vengeful *fait accompli*, most certainly nothing we need to concern ourselves with anymore."[96] *She Hate Me*, as such, does not dilute Lee's reputation for sexism as much as

Jungle Fever or, certainly, *Girl 6*. His evolving perspectives and portrayals of women do not always advance as far as scholars like hooks, Barton, and Whaley would prefer, nor do they remain stagnant. Lee's filmography offers many different female characters and female characterizations that, for critical viewers, are inconsistent. They are progressive, regressive, enlightened, and reactionary, sometimes in the same film (with *She Hate Me* being the primary example of this complicated—or indecisive—stance).

Although labeling Lee a sexist and homophobic filmmaker is too simplistic given his stated awareness of these flaws, his movies—however fascinating—are, at best, challenging depictions of women, whether straight, lesbian, or bisexual. Lee remains an artist who endorses patriarchal attitudes despite occasional attempts to unsettle these assumptions, making his efforts to improve his portraits of women, especially black women, tenuous at best. Audiences should applaud Lee's ability to acknowledge and address his own failings in this area without falling prey to the notion that his willingness to do so absolves him of criticism. Lee's cinematic career testifies to his good will in wanting to improve his reputation as a sexist and homophobic filmmaker, while *Jungle Fever, Girl 6,* and *She Hate Me* attempt to accomplish this goal. They, however, are not stunning successes even if closer examination reveals Lee's alternately sophisticated and naïve approaches to expanding the complexity, realism, and believability of his on-screen women. The best Lee's committed viewers can hope is that he continues this struggle with the same openness that has characterized the first quarter century of his life as a socially conscious film artist.

5

Brooklyn's Finest

SIX OF ONE

In 2011, while preparing his eighteenth feature film, the self-financed *Red Hook Summer,* Spike Lee began referring to this movie as the sixth entry in his "Chronicles of Brooklyn" series (or, as Lee's December 17, 2011, Twitter post calls it, "Da Chronicles of Brooklyn"[1]). This loose hexalogy comprises, in order of production, *She's Gotta Have It* (1986), *Do the Right Thing* (1989), *Crooklyn* (1994), *Clockers* (1995), *He Got Game* (1998), and the aforementioned *Red Hook Summer* (2012). The connections among these films, apart from geographical setting, are not always apparent, with each entry inhabiting a different primary genre: sex comedy, slice-of-life tragicomedy, family melodrama, crime thriller, sports film, and coming-of-age tale. All six movies, however, manifest Lee's penchant for mixing genres, modes, and styles to resist simple classification. *She's Gotta Have It,* for instance, deconstructs sexual mythologies about middle-class African Americans even while reaffirming them. *Do the Right Thing,* for careful viewers, dramatizes intergenerational conflicts alongside racial tensions. *Crooklyn* rewrites that maudlin Hollywood staple, the fatal-illness picture, to demonstrate the emptiness of American ideas about upward social mobility. *Clockers* is Lee's first literary adaptation (of Richard Price's mammoth 1992 novel of the same title), *He Got Game* uses college basketball as the backdrop for its story of father-son estrangement, and *Red Hook Summer* explores the contradictions of religious faith. Such diversity emphasizes Lee's willingness to tackle multiple themes even if all six films qualify as works of social commentary.

These movies offer vivid portraiture of Brooklyn's African American residents, but the term *chronicle* suggests that they constitute a chronology of local experiences, conditions, and events. Lee's series does not fit this general definition in one significant respect: *Crooklyn*'s 1970s setting, unlike the other movies, resembles a period piece by taking place two decades before its production. *Crooklyn,* however, is not an historical drama so much as an affectionate, semi-autobiographical rendition of Lee's own family life. Even so, Lee's declaration that these six films form a singular unit implies that they share continuities of theme, approach, and style that, at first blush, may not be obvious.

This label, therefore, becomes critically useful even if the "Chronicles of Brooklyn" is also a marketing strategy: these six movies, after all, can now be packaged, sold, and celebrated as the definitive cinematic rendition of Brooklyn life by America's foremost black filmmaker. Lee's shrewd public-relations sense encourages this reading, for as Andrew deWaard argues in his provocative article "Joints and Jams: Spike Lee as Sellebrity Auteur," even directors who avoid full immersion in Hollywood's industrial practices nonetheless find themselves in a "strange new dimension" where "contemporary cinematic authorship is promoted and highlighted to an unhearlded degree,"[2] thereby exacerbating conflicts between art and commerce that have typified Hollywood moviemaking since its early twentieth-century inception.

This result, deWaard writes, fractures the venerable status of the filmic auteur that French critics (particularly André Bazin, Claude Chabrol, Jean-Luc Godard, and François Truffaut) took pains to build during the 1950s and 1960s. Hollywood studios reconfigure the auteur's movies as commercial objects around which they construct market-driven campaigns that subsume any individual film within sprawling public-relations rhetoric: "Rather than perceiving an auteur film as some sublime expression of individual genius, it is now regarded as a *site* for the interaction of biography, institutional context, social climate, and historical moment."[3] Lee, as a famously controversial director who courts and receives media attention for his opinions about political, cultural, and social issues that transcend (even when they implicate) his movies, fulfills these four criteria so well that, in deWaard's view, Lee provides "an exemplary case study for the sellebrity auteur, as he occupies a unique position within Hollywood with regard to economics and celebrity,"[4] meaning that the "Chronicles of Brooklyn" is not simply a consumer label that increases each film's commodity value but also a unifying concept that evokes previously unremarked connections among six otherwise divergent movies. Lee's "Chronicle" films, from this perspective, are not merely or solely examples of mass culture—works designed to make quick profits for cast, crew, and financiers in a cinematic marketplace that relegates artistic independence to the vagaries of commercial imperatives—but are instead aesthetically notable texts, as well as significant popular artworks, that transcend their commodity status.

Few serious observers can deny that Lee's cinematic career devotes substantial time, effort, and energy to recounting Brooklyn's cultural and social idiosyncrasies, although Ed Guerrero's assessment (in *Framing Blackness: The African American Image in Film*) that "the real adversary of Lee's creativity and eroding guerilla stance arises out of the subtle, co-opting currents and crossover pressures of the studio system"[5] reminds critical viewers that

Lee's status as an inside man—namely, his ability to secure studio funding and distribution to help produce his movies—invisibly and perhaps unconsciously pushes him toward more conventional plots, themes, characters, and viewpoints. Guerrero's analysis of Lee's career after *School Daze* identifies studio co-optation already at work: "Correspondingly, what is revealed in the ever-grander and slicker promenade of images in the trajectory of Lee's films is that, unlike [Michelangelo] Antonioni, Jim Jarmusch, or Charles Burnett, Lee is diligently struggling to learn the conventions and clichés of market cinema language, instead of struggling to change the dominant system by creating a visionary language of his own."[6] Guerrero counterposes Lee's more traditional visual sense with the visionary efforts of Antonioni, Jarmusch, and Burnett to imply that Lee hews closer to classical Hollywood style than his films—even with their many departures from, deformations of, and alterations to this approach—might suggest. Particularly when compared with the hallucinatory images that characterize Burnett's *Killer of Sheep* (1979) and Julie Dash's *Daughters of the Dust* (1991), *Do the Right Thing*'s visual style, to take only one example, may strike the viewer as conventional, even stodgy by contrast, but Guerrero underplays Lee's consistent disruption of the fluid mise-en-scène that classical Hollywood cinema indulges (and even mandates, in David Bordwell's view[7]).

Lee's Brooklyn movies, therefore, strike a precarious balance between classical Hollywood cinema, guerrilla moviemaking, and independent production. They take African American experiences as their primary thematic material, but do not adopt a single narrative stance, visual style, or cinematic genre. Each film, indeed, fuses competing storytelling, stylistic, and generic devices—sometimes jarringly—to produce a movie that develops in unexpected ways, making the "Chronicles of Brooklyn" less a coherent film series than a picaresque ramble through the borough's diversity. Lee did not attempt to unify these six movies during production, for even if they examine similar themes, characters, and issues, each film was produced under varying circumstances. The fourteen-year gap between *He Got Game* and *Red Hook Summer* may have given Lee time to consider the correspondences among his six Brooklyn films, but their similarities do not overpower their differences. Although the label "Chronicles of Brooklyn" suggests harmonies of purpose and approach that even casual viewers should notice, each movie deserves specific attention to understand its unique contribution to Lee's filmography. Previous chapters have examined *She's Gotta Have It* and *Do the Right Thing* in detail, so considering *Crooklyn, Clockers, He Got Game,* and *Red Hook Summer* in turn will reveal their importance to Lee's oeuvre.

CROOKLYN (1994)

Lee's seventh feature film fulfilled his desire to present a story smaller in scope and more intimate in tone than *Malcolm X* (1992), whose grueling, contentious, and controversial production worked Lee nearly to exhaustion. *Crooklyn* is a family affair not only in its semi-autobiographical portrait of Lee's upbringing as the child of a committed schoolteacher mother and shiftless musician father but also in its inception as the product of a screenplay initially written by Lee's siblings Joie (credited as Joie Susannah Lee) and Cinque Lee that the director revised before shooting began. *Crooklyn* also marks the only film in Lee's cinematic *corpus* to feature a young African American girl, Troy Carmichael (Zelda Harris), as its protagonist (*Red Hook Summer*'s Chazz Morningstar, played by Toni Lysaith, is an important but finally supporting character to Jules Brown's Flik Royale and Clarke Peters's Bishop Enoch Rouse in that story).

The movie's affectionate, yet exasperated rendition of 1970s Brooklyn, culminating with the death of family matriarch Carolyn Carmichael (Alfre Woodard) from cancer, is so uncommon that bell hooks, in "*Crooklyn:* The Denial of Death," writes that the film "superficially represents issues of death and dying in black life as though our survival matters, as though our living bodies count, while in the final analysis reaffirming the usual Hollywood message about black death," namely that it "is inevitable, meaningless, not worth much. That there is nothing to mourn."[8] Hooks, despite reservations about what she concludes is the film's antifeminist stance, credits *Crooklyn* for making Troy its viewpoint character: "Positively radical in this regard, *Crooklyn* invites audiences to look at black experience though Troy's eyes, to enter the spaces of her emotional universe, the intimate world of family and friends that ground her being and give her life meaning."[9] This focus, attentive viewers should note, is not entirely Spike Lee's doing. Joie Lee receives sole credit for *Crooklyn*'s story, testifying to the fact that the film began as Joie's attempt to fictionalize her own life's events. Kaleem Aftab, in Lee's autobiography *That's My Story and I'm Sticking to It,* reveals that the original script (co-written by Joie and Cinque Lee before they sold it to their brother's production company) featured an older, presumably teenaged girl as the protagonist, one who experimented with sex, but whom Spike Lee made younger in the final movie. Cinque tells Aftab that, although a good deal of initial screenplay's material was excised to obtain a PG-13 rating, "for me, what really made the film unique was that it was told from this young black girl's viewpoint."[10]

Although focusing *Crooklyn* on an African American girl's sexual coming-of-age would have produced a fascinating, yet still rare, film, Lee's choice to lower Troy's age reframes *Crooklyn* as a child's narrative that, at this point in Lee's career, was unprecedented. Although *Mo' Better Blues*' opening scene shows the young Bleek Gilliam (Zakee Howze) being called outside by friends, that movie does not linger on its childhood sequence, which, Krin Gabbard argues, "is a wish-fulfillment fantasy in which Spike Lee rewrites his own story."[11] Gabbard's judgment also applies to *Crooklyn,* although Lee's decision to focus on ten-year-old Troy for *Crooklyn*'s duration not only distinguishes this film from his earlier movies but also explains the Carmichael neighborhood's somewhat idealized depiction, filtered as it is through Troy's naïve perceptions and, presumably, the childhood memories that Spike, Joie, and Cinque Lee brought to the project. The gentle, tolerant, and multiracial environment that *Crooklyn* constructs sharply contrasts the far tenser urban spaces that Lee presents in *Do the Right Thing, Mo' Better Blues,* and *Jungle Fever,* all of which, if not racial tinderboxes, eventually reveal the strains of integration in their city-bound settings.

Reducing the original screenplay's sex and profanity to pursue a PG-13 rating also demonstrates Lee's willingness to make *Crooklyn*'s story about familial dysfunction into family entertainment. This choice endorses Ed Guerrero's conviction that Lee mimics conventional Hollywood strategies as much as he contests them, although as Mark D. Cunningham, in his splendid essay "Through the Looking Glass and Over the Rainbow: Exploring the Fairy Tale in Spike Lee's *Crooklyn*," notes, "*Crooklyn*'s presentation of Brooklyn's residents and streets in the 1970s takes on an almost mythical aura . . . because the narrative is drawn from the conventions of the classic fairy tale, particularly *Alice's Adventures in Wonderland* and *The Wizard of Oz.*"[12] These fairy-tale elements, however, do not elide the challenges facing the Carmichaels, especially Carolyn's status as the sole breadwinner for her jazz-composer husband Woody (Delroy Lindo), her four sons, and Troy. The family may inhabit, as Cunningham states, "this enchanted Brooklyn, but that ideality is disproved by the continual intrusion of the strains of financial problems and marital contention within their home."[13] Carolyn, indeed, frequently loses patience with her children and, especially, with Woody, who (like Bill Lee during Spike, Joie, and Cinque's upbringing) remains so dedicated to his artistic calling that he favors purist recitals (that only his family and scant devotees attend) over commercial music gigs offering better pay. Troy, despite these pressures, is a spitfire child who stands up to the boys in her family and her neighborhood by repudiating their insults with cutting remarks like the one she hurls when a rapscallion named Greg (Peewee Love) throws a cat onto one of Troy's female friends as they jump rope: "Shut up, Greg, with you and your welfare self! How many times have you been left back? You stupid-ass dummy!"[14]

Troy, in this and similar scenes, reproduces her mother's strength, determination, and independence. Growing up with four brothers may require the toughness of mind that Troy demonstrates throughout *Crooklyn,* but it does not fully account for Troy's fiery personality. Troy, like Carolyn, is more mature than the males around her, leading to irritation and frustration that she cannot keep to herself. This trait might seem to empower *Crooklyn*'s female characters, but Carolyn and Troy are forced by circumstances into becoming full-time caretakers for the wayward men and boys in their lives. *Crooklyn,* indeed, simultaneously splinters and consolidates its female protagonist's stereotypical roles, requiring Troy to nurture her family after

Carolyn's death forces Troy to act as the Carmichaels' primary caregiver. The film effects Troy's transition from girl to woman by sending her to stay with three Virginia relatives—Uncle Clem (Norman Matlock), Aunt Song (Frances Foster), and their adopted daughter Viola (Patriece Nelson)—who enjoy a conventionally suburban life so foreign to Troy's Brooklyn experience that Lee and his cinematographer, Arthur Jaffa, employ anamorphic lenses to distort the film's visual presentation of *Crooklyn*'s twenty-seven-minute Virginia sequence. The stretched images and elongated faces disorient the movie's viewer, placing the audience within Troy's discombobulated psyche to rupture *Crooklyn*'s fluid visual style even more forcefully than the dreams and nightmares that plague Troy throughout the movie. This anamorphic sequence so confused audiences that, according to *That's My Story and I'm Sticking to It,* movie theaters posted signs notifying viewers that Lee intended this distorted look.[15] Visiting Virginia also teaches Troy about her heritage as a descendent of the Great Migration by demonstrating the Southern roots that her immediate family seldom acknowledges. Lee's previous films touch on this issue: *School Daze* is set in Atlanta; *Do the Right Thing* includes the supporting characters of Da Mayor (Ossie Davis) and Mother Sister (Ruby Dee), whose Southern accents suggest that they migrated north long before the film's events begin; and *Jungle Fever* features the Good Reverend Doctor and Lucinda Purify (again played by Davis and Dee) as protagonist Flipper Purify's (Wesley Snipes) parents, who reproduce Southern mannerisms and expectations when confronting Flipper's extramarital, interracial affair with his Caucasian assistant, Angela Tucci (Annabella Sciorra). Troy may not fully comprehend the historical journey that she undertakes when visiting Virginia, but she comes to appreciate her cousin Viola (a pampered child who nevertheless rebels against her adoptive mother, Aunt Song) even if Troy wishes to go home after receiving letters from Carolyn that recount their Brooklyn neighborhood's major events.

Crooklyn's Virginia sequence offers perspective about Troy's home borough by taking her to a less-urban environment. This development, according to Paula J. Massood's *Black City Cinema: African American Urban Experiences in Film,* typifies Lee's "entire cinematic oeuvre, which, from almost its beginnings, has both acknowledged and explored the past in the context of the present—symbolized most often by references to particular character's and the city's [New York City's] southern roots."[16] Lee himself, in *That's My Story and I'm Sticking to It,* compares Troy's trip to Virginia to *Alice in Wonderland* to justify using anamorphic lenses to distort the film's cinematic images,[17] a description that Cunningham finds appropriate because "the moments of youthful dissidence and acclimation to new surroundings in this portion of the film bear more than a passing resemblance to [Lewis] Carroll's fantasy."[18] Cunningham, however, finds Troy's Virginia trip more "analogous to the journey Dorothy takes down the Yellow Brick Road in *The Wizard of Oz*"[19] by exposing the girl to unexpected experiences, emotions, and people. Aunt Song, in particular, dismisses Carolyn Carmichael's life choices as unbecoming for a proper woman to make: Aunt Song, unlike Troy's mother, does not work outside the home, does not discipline Viola by shouting at her, and does not approve of Troy's colorfully braided hair. Virginia, Troy soon learns, enforces suburban conformity on its residents, to which Aunt Song happily subscribes. Cunningham reads "this tension between the different spaces . . . as tensions between assimilation and cultural nationalism"[20] within African American communities, recognizing that Troy's Virginia sojourn prepares her for the motherhood that she assumes upon returning to New York, where Carolyn has been hospitalized with terminal cancer. This painful development, as anyone familiar with Lee's life can attest, is *Crooklyn*'s most autobiographical portion. Lee's mother, Jacquelyn Shelton Lee, died of liver cancer in 1977 while Spike was attending Morehouse College, leading him to dream repeatedly about he and his mother conversing.[21] *Crooklyn* reproduces these conversations when Troy dreams that the deceased Carolyn writes letters praising Troy's performance as the Carmichael family caretaker. In one of the film's funniest sequences, Troy, accompanied by Isaac Hayes's "Theme to *Shaft*," learns that neighborhood bully Snuffy (Spike Lee) has stolen money from her younger brother. Troy finds Snuffy sniffing glue on a neighborhood stoop and smacks him in the head with a stickball bat hard enough to draw blood. Troy, in this scene, becomes her family's fiercest protector by accepting the role that Carolyn once played.

This development, however, ends Troy's childhood. Sporting an Afro that signals her transition to womanhood, she tells her younger brother Joseph (Tse-Mach Washington) "I'm not Mommy" when he complains that Troy too roughly combs his hair, but the viewer is hard pressed to disagree with Cunningham that, for *Crooklyn*'s women, "the loss of childhood fantasy seems to be the price of adulthood."[22] Neither the film's boys nor men, however, incur this cost. Troy's forced maturity leads bell hooks to pronounce *Crooklyn* an antifeminist film that "completely valorizes and upholds sexist and misogynist thinking about gender roles. Order is restored in the Carmichael house when the dominating mother figure dies. The emergence of patriarchy is celebrated, marked by the subjugation of Troy,"[23] transforming *Crooklyn* into "an ahistorical narrative wherein there is no meaningful convergence of black liberation and feminist politics."[24] This perspective has many merits, even if hooks's contention that Carolyn Carmichael is an emasculating heroine—one who "has concrete reasons to be disappointed, annoyed, angry" but is portrayed "as vengeful, anti-pleasure, as dangerous and threatening, her moments of tenderness and sweetness" not being "enough to counter the negatives"[25]—overlooks just how good Alfre Woodard is in the part. *Crooklyn* sympathizes with Carolyn as much as it criticizes her, especially in scenes when her husband, Woody (played with shambling charm by Delroy Lindo), takes little notice of the problems that his refusal to seek gainful employment causes. Woody remains calm when Consolidated Edison cuts off the family brownstone's power; feeds his children ice cream despite Carolyn's preference for healthy eating; and generally subverts his wife's domestic authority by appearing as the patient, understanding, and level-headed parent to whom the children naturally gravitate. Woodard, however, inflects Carolyn's distress with wit, warmth, and wry humor to demonstrate that she recognizes Woody's ploys to win over their kids as the behavior of a man who has not fully grown up himself. Hooks accurately notes that Carolyn fulfills existing cinematic stereotypes about black matriarchs who give no quarter when challenged, but *Crooklyn* neither condemns Carolyn nor her breadwinner role. The movie instead dramatizes how Carolyn must shoulder the slack for her immature husband, who uses the excuse of pursuing art to justify his inaction. Although Troy's childlike perspective filters *Crooklyn*'s story, Lee regularly breaks its narrative progression with dreams, nightmares, canted angles, and the anamorphic Virginia sequence to depict Carolyn and Troy more positively than hooks claims. Woody, contrary to hooks's declaration that "he is the good guy. His irresponsibility and misuse of resources are given legitimacy by the suggestion that his is an artistic, non-practical mindset" that means "he cannot be held accountable,"[26] is a complicated figure whose anger at Carolyn's repeated, accurate criticisms of his indolence provokes domestic violence. *Crooklyn* neither forgives Woody nor censures Carolyn as much as hooks claims, counteracting the gender stereotypes that the film dramatizes. Carolyn's death, however, compels Troy to play a maternal role that she skeptically regards, thereby demonstrating that *Crooklyn* is not, in the end, a fable of female liberation.

Crooklyn also offers a rare representation of African American family life as politically liberated, causing hooks to herald this "property-owning, artistic, progressive black family" as "unique. The Carmichaels in no way represent the conventional black bourgeoisie. They are not obsessed with upward mobility, with the material trappings of success. Counter-cultural—a mixture of nationalist movement for racial uplift and a bohemian artistic subculture—they represent an alternative to the bourgeois norm."[27] Woody and Carolyn, despite their problems, encourage all five children to pursue their individual interests and independence, even allowing Troy and her brothers to ramble through the neighborhood with little supervision. This fact, in one of *Crooklyn*'s subtle touches, counters Carolyn's image as an abrasive, smothering parent. Carolyn also reverses traditional gender norms by assuming the dominant role that a more conventional movie would see Woody play. Troy likewise asserts herself rather than passively following the boys' lead. The fairy-tale elements that Cunningham identifies, when combined with *Crooklyn*'s alternately progressive and regressive tendencies, transform the film into a poignant family melodrama that casts Brooklyn as a complex-yet-genial place: the neighborhood is simultaneously happy, sad, nostalgic, and imperfect. *Crooklyn,* indeed, deserves a wider audience than it has received, making its inclusion in the "Chronicles of Brooklyn" an important act of retroactive recuperation by Lee. The movie, both heartfelt and observant, eschews maudlin sentimentality even when dealing with Carolyn Carmichael's death. As one of Lee's most underappreciated efforts, *Crooklyn* offers audiences an unconventional perspective about black Brooklyn life that Lee has never again attempted. For this reason alone, *Crooklyn* is a notable addition to its director's filmography.

CLOCKERS (1995)

Lee followed *Crooklyn* with *Clockers,* a movie diametrically opposed in tone, theme, and subject matter. Where *Crooklyn* is nostalgic, *Clockers* is spare. Where *Crooklyn* is affectionate, *Clockers* is unforgiving. Where *Crooklyn* is idyllic, *Clockers* is despondent. Adapting the film from Richard Price's 600-page novel (first published in 1992 to excellent reviews), Lee sets out to correct the nihilistic portrait of lower-class African American men that, in his opinion, a notable group of early 1990s films "variously described," according to Paula J. Massood's *Black City Cinema,* "as 'ghettocentric,' 'New Jack,' 'New Black Realism,' or hood films"[28] had romanticized. Lee, indeed, once described movies like Mario Van Peebles's *New Jack City* (1991), Matty Rich's *Straight Out of Brooklyn* (1991), John Singleton's *Boyz N the Hood* (1991), Ernest Dickerson's *Juice* (1992), and the Hughes Brothers' *Menace II Society* (1993) as the "black gangsta, hip-hop, shoot-'em-up genre,"[29] even commenting in a 1997 *Face* magazine interview with Jonathan Bernstein, "It was always our intention that if we succeeded with this film, that this might be the final nail in the coffin and African American filmmakers would try telling new stories."[30]

By this score, *Clockers* is a failure, as Lee recognizes in *That's My Story and I'm Sticking to It* by telling Aftab that he wished to challenge the "hip-hop gangsta films" that had followed John Singleton's *Boyz N the Hood* (1991) and the Hughes Brothers' *Menace II Society* (1993): "[I]n my naïveté I thought that this film could end that genre altogether. . . . I said, 'Let's do something to *stop* this stuff.'"[31] Whether Lee's goal was naïve, arrogant, or both, his movie's high quality did not stem the tide of hood films. *Clockers'* screenplay (revised by Lee from Richard Price's early drafts) nonetheless develops a deft psychological portrait of protagonist Ronald "Strike" Dunham that actor Mekhi Phifer, in his debut feature-film performance, transforms into a complicated, contradictory, and nuanced human being. Strike—a street-corner, low-level cocaine dealer known as a clocker ("so named," as Stephen Pizzello observes, "because the runner is on the street 'around the clock'"[32])—is no simple ruffian whose criminal activities mark him as a worthless social parasite, but instead a complex personality who understands that his profession will eventually kill him. The resulting stress produces an acute ulcer that Strike calms by drinking Moo Moo (the film's substitute for the novel's vanilla Yoo Hoo) and by building model train sets (a detail absent from Price's novel), but he cannot escape the pressures of his job supervising a team of clockers for Rodney Little (Delroy Lindo), the menacing drug lieutenant who controls the film's fictional Nelson Mandela Homes, a housing project filmed at the Gowanus Houses in Brooklyn's Boerum Hill.[33] Rodney indirectly suggests that Strike kill Darryl Adams (Steve White)—another clocker whom Rodney suspects of skimming from his operation's drug profits—to prevent Rodney's unseen superior, the drug lord Champ, from blaming Rodney for the losses. Strike, uncertain about committing murder, briefly tries to convince his older brother, Victor Dunham (Isaiah Washington), to kill Adams, but soon regrets doing so. Strike finds himself unable to shoot Adams in cold blood, but Adams is murdered anyway. Victor, a straight-laced family man working two low-wage jobs to feed his wife and children, confesses to homicide detectives Rocco Klein (Harvey Keitel) and Larry Mazilli (John Turturro) that he (Victor) killed Adams in self-defense. The film, told from Strike's perspective, chronicles Klein's relentless attempts to wheedle a confession out of Strike, whom Klein believes to be the true culprit. Klein, falling prey to both racial and social stereotypes, cannot accept that the hardworking Victor would commit murder because Strike—the impoverished and outwardly unrepentant clocker—seems a more appropriate suspect.

Lee's film, like Price's novel, challenges conventional thinking about the people who toil in inner-city drug economies, although the cinematic *Clockers* modifies significant aspects of its source material. Price sets *Clockers* is Dempsey, a fictional fusion of Newark and Jersey City, New Jersey, the two cities where Price researched the novel. Lee, by locating his film in Brooklyn, not only continues his fictional exploration of the borough's African American residents but also demonstrates the terrible consequences that the urban drug trade inflicts on black New York neighborhoods. *Clockers,* from this perspective, functions as Lee's cinematic response to observers like David Denby, who criticized *Do the Right Thing* for not including drug references in its depiction of Brooklyn life. Lee's four intervening films include drug subplots—*Mo' Better Blues* features marijuana use by some of its jazz-musician characters, *Jungle Fever* dramatizes the horrors of drug abuse by making protagonist Flipper Purify's brother Gator (Samuel L. Jackson) a heroin addict, *Malcolm X* openly portrays the title character's drug and alcohol addictions, and *Crooklyn* sees neighborhood glue sniffers (played by Spike Lee and N. Jeremi Duru) create mischief—that, however important, do not pervade their stories in the way that crack cocaine dominates *Clockers*. Lee, to his credit, dramatizes the moral compromises that drug dealing extracts from the clockers, their families, and their neighbors. Strike Dunham's work embarrasses his law-abiding mother, Gloria (Frances Foster), and infuriates a local woman named Iris Jeeter (Regina Taylor), who vocally confronts Strike after he becomes friendly with her son Tyrone (Peewee Love). Many project residents deplore the living conditions they must endure as a result of Strike's, Rodney's, and Champ's drug business, illustrating how the narcotics trade fractures urban communities.

Clockers also refuses to romanticize, glorify, or ennoble drug trafficking, although Strike's conflicted position within his neighborhood's social hierarchy humanizes his choices rather than making him unsympathetic. This dual project explains Lee' second major revision of Price's novel: telling the story exclusively from Strike's perspective. Price's *Clockers* alternates its chapters between Strike's and Klein's viewpoints to provide an exhaustive portrait of each man's psyche. This narrative approach achieves the depth, complexity, and delicacy of modernist novels like Virginia Woolf's *Mrs. Dalloway,* Henry James's *The Wings of a Dove,* and William Faulkner's *As I Lay Dying* by demonstrating how Klein and Strike remain captive to the social forces that surround and separate them (especially race and socioeconomic class). Keith M. Harris, in his superb essay "*Clockers* (Spike Lee, 1995): Adaptation in Black," notes that Price's novel is not only "ready-made" for the screen[34] but also "a throwback, of sorts, to literary naturalism. The emphasis on naturalism can be seen in the ways in which the lives of the characters are determined by their environment and in the special attention Price pays to the racial representations and stratifications of the crack epidemic."[35] Each *Clockers* chapter advances the novel's plot by allowing Strike, then Klein, to reflect upon his life in passages of searing intensity, bleak melancholy, and bitter disappointment. Price's bravura achievement, summarized by Jim Shepard's June 21, 1992, *New York Times* book review as the novel being "both clear-eyed and bighearted, able to illuminate and celebrate, in the midst of the most uncompromising circumstances imaginable, a cop's heroism and a small-time drug dealer's stubborn resilience, without overly sentimentalizing either,"[36] gives Lee and his production crew ample material to adapt.

Lee's cinematic narrative jettisons Rocco Klein's backstory and inner monologue to concentrate on Strike's untenable situation. Price—who shifted the screenplay's focus to Klein when Martin Scorsese, the film's original director, cast Robert De Niro as the downtrodden detective—was upset with Lee's alterations to the film after Scorsese and De Niro left the project to make 1995's *Casino.* Although Lee credits Price in *That's My Story and I'm Sticking to It* as a terrific screenwriter, Lee says that he told Scorsese and Price to find another director if they wished because he had no desire to make a movie about Rocco Klein, "a cop in a middle-aged crisis. That would have been just another cop story to me."[37] Lee's repudiation of Price's original screenplay draft as "just another cop story" illustrates the director's desire to make an unconventional, yet commercial film that shifts perspective from the white homicide detective—protagonist of countless American novels, movies, and television programs—to the black drug dealer, a character so frequently overlooked or demeaned by Hollywood productions that the hood film capitalized on this dismissal by glorifying the dealer's outlaw status. Paula J. Massood identifies how crucial Lee's choice to concentrate on Strike Dunham is: "This alteration expanded audience identification with (and thus sympathy for) a character traditionally lacking psychological development in most of the films focusing on similar protagonists."[38] Lee's Clockers, for Massood, does not "start from the presumption that such a decision [Strike's choice to clock] is made inevitably or comes naturally,"[39] but results from the restrictive economic opportunities available to inner-city African American boys and men. Price's novel certainly illustrates this unfortunate social truth, but Lee's adaptation, by making Strike the center of all attention, foregrounds it.

Lee arranges the film's mise-en-scène so that Strike occupies the center of numerous shots, angles, and setups, especially those moments when Strike sits on benches in the Nelson Mandela Homes' courtyard. Strike, in these scenes, seemingly makes the best of a bad situation, acting as lord of the projects until residents like Iris Jeeter accuse him of helping destroy his home and his people. Despite Strike's anger at Jeeter's outbursts, he becomes more introspective as Clockers unfolds, thanks to his blunt-yet-poetic dialogue and to Mekhi Phifer's subtle performance. Harvey Keitel capably suggests Rocco Klein's dogged weariness, but the movie's interest in Strike fulfills Lee's overriding goal: "I really wasn't interested in telling a cop's story. I was much more passionate about telling the story of this young African American kid who comes from a strong family, who's gone off the straight and narrow and has turned to a life of drugs."[40]

Lee also bookends Clockers with alternately shocking and soothing images to suggest that Strike, despite his difficulties, will not repeat the mistakes that Rodney Little's other employees make. The opening-credit sequence comprises still photos of restaged crime scenes that reveal the terrible violence of inner-city life. As Douglas McFarland's essay "The Symbolism of Blood in Clockers" argues, "Lee goes much further" than standard Hollywood fare by using "the opening credits rhetorically to shock, to repulse, perhaps even to shame the audience with graphic images of the self-destructive violence of African American urban culture. This staging of slain bodies in varying degrees of decay powerfully immerses the audience in blood."[41] This shaming sets the stage for Clockers' gritty cinematography, shot by Malik Hassan Sayeed with natural light during outdoor scenes and with overexposed illumination during interrogations, to submerge the viewer in Strike's rapidly changing, vertiginous experience.

Sam Pollard's editing enhances these effects by permitting Strike's conversations with Victor Dunham and Tyrone Jeeter to play languidly, with only minimal interruptions, while Strike's interactions with Rocco Klein whipsaw the viewer between each man, so frequently cutting from shot to shot that the audience loses track. The jangling anxiety of these interrogations provokes unwise responses by Strike that culminate when the boy Tyrone, whom Strike has befriended, shoots Errol Barnes (Thomas Jefferson Byrd), Rodney Little's most fearsome drug enforcer, with Strike's gun. This development, along with Rodney's belief (encouraged by Klein) that Strike has confessed details about Rodney's drug operation, so frighten Strike that he decides to leave town, particularly after his mother ensures that his brother Victor will serve prison time by confirming Victor's murder confession. Klein, indeed, drives Strike to Grand Central Station, where the younger man purchases an all-pass train ticket. *Clockers*, as Massood comments in *Black City Cinema*'s masterful final chapter (perhaps the best single essay published about Lee's eighth feature film), "concludes with aureate shots of Strike riding on a train, headed into the sunset."[42] Yet any suggestion that this ending documents a redemptive journey from grimy city streets to pastoral landscapes (in what initially seems a misplaced homage to the Western film's equation of empty spaces with moral cleanliness) founders on the fact that, as Douglas McFarland notes, "there is little of the pastoral in the arid southwestern landscape [Strike] surveys from his seat on the train. The tension between escape and expulsion remains unresolved at the end of the film."[43] Massood's argument emphasizes how Strike's fascination with trains "inserts the tropes of migration, mobility, and settlement in the narrative in order to suggest a dialogue between African American history and contemporary African American filmmaking,"[44] marking *Clockers* as a movie that, rather than demonizing its inner-city neighborhood and drug-dealer protagonist, embeds them in a rich tradition of black migration, settlement, and stagnation that, in Lee's coup de grâce, is neither unremittingly dystopian nor naïvely utopian. Strike may not escape Brooklyn by choice, but leaving behind his family avoids certain death at Rodney's hands and continual harassment by Klein. Strike, indeed, regards the forbidding desert beauty with enough wonder to suggest that his future, while far from certain, is also far from hopeless.

Clockers, as such, is a fascinating, troubling, and superbly acted story of inner-city life that never lapses into nihilistic despair despite the violence at its narrative's core. Lee depicts Brooklyn's lower-class spaces in untraditional ways that revise, even shatter, the strictures established by earlier hood films. For instance, "the plaza" of the Nelson Mandela Homes, in Massood's words, "differs from more conventional renderings of inner-city space. It is green, lush, and infused with a rich light that calls attention to the colors found in both the space's vegetation and the clothing worn by the clockers."[45] Lee does not faithfully adapt Richard Price's *Clockers*, even claiming in *That's My Story and I'm Sticking to It* that he has never truly adapted a novel to the screen (including 2002's *25th Hour*, whose screenplay was written by David Benioff, the author of its source novel).[46] *Clockers*, despite deviating from Price's book, is an excellent movie that captures the novel's texture, nuance, and mood. Richard Price's disagreements to the contrary,

Clockers remains, two decades after its theatrical release, one of the 1990s' best American films.

HE GOT GAME (1998)

He Got Game, Lee's third collaboration with Denzel Washington (and the first since 1992's *Malcolm X*) sees its star give a performance equal to his groundbreaking turn as the slain civil-rights leader. Washington, indeed, is so good in *He Got Game* that his work sometimes overshadows the film's effective, original, and unusual story of felon Jake Shuttlesworth trying to connect with his son, high-school basketball prodigy Jesus Shuttlesworth (Ray Allen). Jake, convicted of murdering his wife Martha (Lonette McKee) during a domestic dispute, receives a conditional, one-week prison pass in the hopes that he can convince Jesus (the nation's top-ranked high-school player)—named after Baltimore Bullets and New York Knicks guard Earl Monroe (known as "Black Jesus" during his professional career)—to sign with fictional Big State University, alma mater of the state's governor, in exchange for early release. This premise allows Lee, writing his first solo screenplay since 1991's *Jungle Fever*, to comment upon the National Collegiate Athletic Association's (NCAA's) treatment of so-called student athletes while examining the difficult relationship between an imprisoned father and his disaffected son. *He Got Game* also helps Lee pursue a longtime cinematic dream (making a sports movie that avoids the genre's clichés) while marking a significant departure: *He Got Game* is the first Spike Lee joint not scored by Bill Lee or Terence Blanchard. Lee instead employs the music of Aaron Copland to buttress *He Got Game*'s fractured portrait of the American Dream.

Lee, in *That's My Story and I'm Sticking to It*, declares that avoiding the come-from-behind, big-game finale that defines too many on-court dramas is his paramount goal.[47] Spotlighting basketball's less attractive elements, therefore, becomes Lee's method of making an unconventional, yet gripping movie about the underbelly of college sports: "What we were really trying to do was show the whole hypocrisy of the NCAA, how they really pimp what they call 'student athletes.' "[48] The fact that New York State's governor conspires with the Attica Correctional Facility's warden, Marcel Wyatt (Ned Beatty), to sign Jesus Shuttlesworth by promising his father's freedom highlights the corrupt collusion of collegiate sports and statewide politics.[49] Jesus, a spirited yet naïve young man who detests Jake, cannot forgive his father for abusing and murdering his mother. Jesus's memories of his father's brusque, sometimes violent training sessions on the basketball court intermingle with Jake's initially insincere attempts to renew their relationship in a cinematic narrative that probes how violence affects African American families even more intimately than *Clockers*.

This tragic theme intensifies the fact that Jesus is objectified by almost everyone in his life. Jesus's potential earning power as a star college and professional player causes many important relationships to change: his girl-friend, Lala Bonilla (Rosario Dawson); his high-school basketball coach, Mr. Cincotta (Arthur J. Nascarella); his Uncle Bubba (Bill Nunn) and Aunt Sally (Michele Shay); sports agents; famous college coaches (Temple's John Chaney, Arizona's Lute Olson, Kentucky's Rick Patino, Arkansas's Nolan Richardson, North Carolina's Dean Smith, Georgetown's John Thompson); and media personalities (including Dick Vitale) all encourage Jesus—sincerely played by Ray Allen (who, during the film's shoot, was in his inaugural seasons as a guard for the Milwaukee Bucks)—to earn as much money as possible. Lala and Coach Cincotta, in particular, reveal themselves as predators hoping to profit from Jesus's basketball talents by allying themselves with agents who promise the young man easy access to money and women, reinforcing just how untrustworthy even close associates can be. Jesus's growing disenchantment with the college-selection process feeds his suspicions of Jake, who eventually confesses that his intentions are not pure. The emotional violence that Jesus suffered as a child, due to Jake's tough parenting and domestic violence, redounds at the film's climax when Jake challenges Jesus to a one-on-one basketball game with simple, but significant stakes: If Jake wins, Jesus will sign with Big State University. If Jake loses, he will never bother Jesus again no matter how popular or wealthy the younger man becomes. This game—masterfully shot by cinematographer Malik Hassan Sayeed and crisply edited by Barry Alexander Brown—sees Jesus vent his anger on Jake, who loses the increasingly rough-and-tumble match. Besting his father does not fully resolve Jesus's emotional turbulence, yet Jesus nonetheless signs with Big State the day after Jake returns to prison. Jake, in one of *He Got Game*'s cruelest ironies, learns that the governor may not reduce his sentence because Jake failed to secure Jesus's signature on a letter of intent prepared by the governor's office.

He Got Game's concluding basketball match is significant, but the film does not end as exultantly as sports movies like *The Natural* (1984) and *Hoosiers* (1986).[50] Jesus's future may seem secure, but his relationship with Jake, even at the end, is far from perfect. This reality testifies to Krin Gabbard's point, in his fine essay "Spike Lee Meets Aaron Copland," that "*He Got Game* exposes the predicament of Jesus Shuttlesworth, who would seem to be among the most successful members of black youth culture," but who "is entering a cutthroat world of agents, coaches, and hangers-on. Any number of mishaps can quickly end his career, even before he arrives in the NBA," leading Gabbard to conclude, "for all its celebration of the game and its flamboyant personalities, *He Got Game* does not hold out much hope for Jesus Shuttlesworth."[51] Gabbard argues that Lee's decision to score the film with Copland's music "allows the music of a white composer to enhance the playfulness, grace, and masculinity of black youths on the basketball court."[52] These aspects, however, cannot overshadow the depressing realities that confront both Jesus and Jake Shuttlesworth, making *He Got Game* a movie that revises (and even reverses) sports-film conventions by acknowledging the seedy motives underlying college and professional basketball. "This is not so much a movie about sports as about capitalism," Roger Ebert observes in his May 1, 1998, *Chicago Sun-Times* review before proclaiming, "It's about the real stakes, which involve money more than final scores, and showmanship as much as athletics."[53] This analysis aptly describes the doubts that Jesus Shuttlesworth voices about his future throughout the movie. Despite Jake's and Lala's soothing words about Jesus's economic prospects, *He Got Game* is no rags-to-riches saga, but instead a film that contests the easy seductions of wealth and fame that basketball holds for talented players like Jesus.

The professional college-recruiting system that relentlessly pursues Jesus throughout the movie co-opts him more easily than his father's unlikely plan, indicating how difficult their relationship remains despite the tentative resolution they achieve by the movie's conclusion. Money trumps human connection, particularly within Jesus and Lala's deteriorating relationship. Lala, even more than Dakota Burns (Milla Jovovich)—the prostitute who lives next door to Jake in the low-rent motel where he stays during his week of freedom—dramatizes Lee's antifeminist tendencies by emerging as little more than a gold-digging parasite with so little faith in her own agency that she sees Jesus as her ticket to a better life. Rosario Dawson, in only her second film performance, invests Lala with ingenuous charm and disingenuous motives, but the character remains flat throughout *He Got Game*. Her money-grubbing ways also illustrate the film's contradictory political renunciation of sports capitalism. *He Got Game* criticizes how professional sports teams entice young black men with riches, fame, and sex when these players' talents make them attractive laborers (even if such teams have little regard for their players' intellectual or emotional development). The movie, at the same time, celebrates the aggressive athleticism that players like Jesus embody. Victoria E. Johnson summarizes this tendency in Lee's films by concluding her excellent article "Polyphony and Cultural Expression: Interpreting Musical Traditions in *Do the Right Thing*" with words that apply as much to *He Got Game* as to *Do the Right Thing*:

> Lee's 'politicized' voice is most conflicted—in its calls for immediate racial and economic representation, recognition, challenge, and change—as his films grant expression to voices that are typically marginalized in relation to the mainstream, only for those oppositions to be subsumed by larger commodification practices that recoup them for popular sale as black history and politics.[54]

The voice of Jesus Shuttlesworth—a young black man who remains marginalized until his athletic ability forces institutions that normally ignore him to take notice—is sometimes unreflective, but it eventually confronts his father's emotional and physical abuse to speak against the violence that Jesus

experienced as a child. *He Got Game* achieves remarkable intensity and intimacy in these scenes, with Ray Allen capably conveying Jesus's pent-up anger
and sadness, but thanks to the movie's opening-credits montage and courtside action, it also advertises basketball's energetic thrills, thereby inscribing
commodity practices into its cinematic narrative. The film cannot repudiate
basketball's significance to young African American men even if the sport's
profit-mongering ways overrun any concern for its players' emotional health.
Lee poignantly evokes this truth by inserting a direct-to-camera montage
(paralleling similar sequences in *She's Gotta Have It, School Daze,* and *Do the
Right Thing*) in which Jesus and four of his high-school teammates speak
about their fondness for basketball. Their pride masks the uglier truths that
await them if they become prey for teams more interested in their court skills
than their full humanity.

Jason Holt and Robert Pitter call *He Got Game*'s ambivalent evocation of
basketball's primacy in Jesus Shuttlesworth's life "the prostitution trap of elite
sport."[55] They develop the theme of commodification even more extensively
than Victoria Johnson by writing, in "The Prostitution Trap of Elite Sport in
He Got Game," "Commodified sport, in which a person exchanges his or her
abilities for money or other material gains, significantly alters . . . idealized notions of sport. The commodified sporting self is not so free; it is constrained
and objectified as physical capital through the rules of current socioeconomic
systems," meaning that "the elite athlete tends to be treated as a commodified body, as is the prostitute, and both are subject to a sense of alienation
from themselves."[56] Holt and Ritter's analysis not only demonstrates how
similar are Dakota's and Jesus's situations but also explains why Jesus feels so
trapped by the liberating future of financial security that his talent promises:
"Understanding the body as a commodity challenges the sense of self and
others as people, as subjects in their own right, because idealized notions
of self (as a free and creative being) are confronted with the undeniable fact
that people are often treated as objects to be bought, sold, manipulated, or
exploited."[57] All four possibilities pertain to Jesus's experiences in *He Got
Game,* leading him to refute Coach Cincotta's statement that "People really
do care about you" by saying, "People don't care about me. They care about
themselves. I mean, they're just tryin' to get over, tryin' to get a piece of
Jesus, that's all."[58] This recognition—that Jesus is an object for sale, manipu-
lation, and exploitation—resonates with the advice articulated by Big Time
Willie (Roger Guenveur Smith), the Coney Island mobster who functions as
Jesus's personal Greek chorus. Willie warns Jesus about the dangers of ciga-
rettes, alcohol, illegal drugs, and HIV-infected women before alluding to the
agents and lawyers who will descend upon him: "And I didn't even mention
the bloodsucking leeches. Oh yeah, the newfound family. Pygmy buzzards be
hovering over you, trying to get that loose change." Willie may trumpet his
business acumen by driving a nice car and wearing stylish clothes, but nonetheless rejects the all-consuming capitalism that threatens Jesus. The irony of

a gangster mouthing anticapitalist sentiments signifies the film's conflicted attitudes about Lee's best-known obsession outside filmmaking: basketball.

He Got Game, from its Coney Island setting to its observant rendering of father-son estrangement, improves with repeated viewings. The movie may dramatize the difficulties that a talented young black man faces on his way to maturity, but remains problematic, particularly considering its thinly developed female characters. Even so, *He Got Game's* overall complexity—particularly Lee's resonant dialogue and Denzel Washington's beautifully nuanced performance—demonstrates its writer-director's cinematic acuity. Lee presents the lives of the movie's black Brooklyn residents sympathetically, if unsentimentally, to produce an accomplished film that, like its lead performance, is too little known. Not only does Stanley Crouch, a sometimes acidic critic of Lee's work, pronounce *He Got Game* "a hell of a movie,"[59] but Edward Norton, the actor who plays Monty Brogan in Lee's contemplative 2002 film *25th Hour,* considers *He Got Game* "a stylistic masterpiece, such a great American film, and a deeply American film" that Norton labels "an epic poem. . . . You have this hero, moving on an almost Homeric journey through these moral sirens."[60] Lee's movie is not so much an epic poem as a cinematic tone poem that employs Aaron Copland's score to stress its American roots. Copland, as Krin Gabbard notes, might have been raised in Brooklyn, but was excluded from mainstream America due to his leftist politics, homosexuality, and Jewish background. These allegiances placed Copland outside traditional American society,[61] which eventually embraced him as a great—even quintessential—American artist. Since Spike Lee's career has followed a similar, if less stormy trajectory, Copland's work is an appropriate choice for *He Got Game.* The movie's commendable empathy makes it a welcome addition to the Chronicles of Brooklyn.

RED HOOK SUMMER (2012)

Red Hook Summer, Lee's eighteenth feature film (in twenty-six years), repeats so many aspects of *She's Gotta Have It's* production that the latter movie is an ideal bookend for the Chronicles of Brooklyn. Lee summarizes these similarities and differences in his August 9, 2012, *Ebony* magazine interview with Miles Marshall Lewis: "Technology has really been the biggest difference. We shot *She's Gotta Have It* in the summer of 1985: 12 days, two six-day weeks. Super 16 mm, $175,000. We shot *Red Hook Summer* in the summer of 2011: 18 days, three six-day weeks, digitally [with] the Sony F3 camera."[62] Lee financed both movies himself, raising *She's Gotta Have It's* budget by securing film-foundation grants, selling investment shares, and scrounging funds from family and friends. One measure of Lee's success in the intervening quarter century is the fact that he paid for *Red Hook Summer's* production himself. "I wrote the check," Lee states during his DVD audio commentary after thanking viewers for watching a movie that opened on only sixty-six American screens.[63] Chris Lee (no relation), in his January 26, 2012, *Daily Beast* article "Spike Lee Talks Hollywood Racism, New Film *Red Hook Summer*," states that the film "represents a return to Lee's days as an art-house auteur operating on a guerilla budget. The movie cost less than $1 million, relying heavily on labor by graduate students in New York University's Tisch School of the Arts."[64] As Lee's June 28, 2012, *Bloomberg Businessweek* interview with Diane Brady, "Spike Lee on Self-Financing *Red Hook Summer*," notes, "From the get-go, I knew it would be self-financed. I never went to the studios. . . . I couldn't get them to finance a sequel to *Inside Man*, my most successful film ever. If that wasn't a signal, I don't know what is. . . . With *Red Hook Summer*, we had 18 days of shooting. A third of my crew were [*sic*] my students at New York University—who got paid."[65]

These comments recall the conditions affecting *She's Gotta Have It* so closely that, apart from Lee's ability to pay for *Red Hook Summer* himself, their correspondences reveal a depressing story about twenty-first century black American cinema. Lee endorses this notion by telling Brady that he and *Red Hook Summer* co-screenwriter James McBride (with whom Lee first worked on the 2008 adaptation of McBride's 2002 novel *Miracle at St. Anna*), during their initial discussion about the movie's story, "were bemoaning the fact that there's a low point right now in African American cinema."[66] Despite Lee's progress as a filmmaker, cultural critic, and celebrity, black cinema is not thriving as much as Lee would hope, although he fails to mention Tyler Perry's success as a film and television writer, director, and producer. Lee faults major movie studios (at least in the twenty-first century's second decade) because they "would never let him make 'a multidimensional portrait of a young African American' "[67] as "Hollywood is really superhero land now."[68] Lee expands this final criticism in his August 14, 2012, *Vanity Fair* interview with Jason Guerrasio by saying, "And there's always going to be big-budget Hollywood films, and I like many of them; I grew up on many of them. But that type of film, that genre of film, is strangling the creativity out of Hollywood films, which are becoming dominated by special effects, again and again and again."[69] Lee sees *Red Hook Summer* as a profoundly different movie, on a much smaller and more intimate scale that defies the all-or-nothing logic dominating the studio system: "They want every film to be a tentpole. They aren't going to make a film if they don't feel there's a sequel in it. . . . The marketing departments sit on the green-light committees. And if the marketing department at a studio says, 'We can't sell it,' they aren't making that motherfucker. Before it was, 'We're making this film, and it's *your* job to sell it.' "[70]

Lee's assessments about *Red Hook Summer*'s prospects so resemble statements he made during *She's Gotta Have It*'s production that his progress as a moviemaker has not translated into African American cinema or television as a whole. Other black directors have experienced varying success in film and television production (including Lee's former cinematographer, Ernest Dickerson, along with Paris Barclay, Janice Cooke, Julie Dash, Carl Franklin, Antoine Fuqua, Anthony Hemingway, Kevin Hooks, Kasi Lemons, Darnell Martin, Michael Schultz, Millicent Shelton, John Singleton, and Mario Van Peebles), but Lee's enthusiasm about the resurgence of black cinema during the 1990s (helped in part by *She's Gotta Have It*'s success) has waned as he finds smaller projects about African American life harder to get produced by major studios and networks.

These provisos are important to remember when assessing *Red Hook Summer*'s impact, for Lee deliberately avoided studio involvement to ensure his creative control. Lee submitted the movie to 2012's Sundance Film Festival, where it became an official selection, found distribution through Variance Films, and grossed $338,803[71] in its limited theatrical run. *Red Hook Summer*'s financial failure does not indicate its aesthetic quality, for the movie presents Red Hook, Brooklyn in a much different light than Matty Rich's nihilistic debut film, 1991's *Straight Out of Brooklyn*. Whereas Rich's movie dramatizes the unremittingly tragic experiences of Dennis Brown (Larry Gilliard, Jr.) and his immediate family, *Red Hook Summer* combines religious fervor, teenage angst, alcoholism, and child molestation into a story that, while undoubtedly tragic in specific moments, does not submit to despair or depression. *Red Hook Summer,* like *She's Gotta Have It,* is a slice-of-life drama that attempts to show Brooklyn's black inhabitants as flawed, nuanced, and, for the most part, noble people. Its story of the middle-class, thirteen-year-old Atlanta resident Silas "Flik" Royale (Jules Brown) spending the summer with his maternal grandfather, the fire-and-brimstone Bishop Enoch Rouse (Clarke Peters), comprises vignettes of Flik learning about the neighborhood's people, daily routines, and cultural rhythms before revealing that Bishop Rouse is, in fact, Richard Benjamin Broadnax, a Baptist minister exiled from his Waycross, Georgia church fifteen years before *Red Hook Summer*'s events begin for molesting a boy named Blessing Rowe (Sincere Peters), who, now grown (and played as an adult by Colman Domingo), confronts Rouse while the bishop preaches to his congregation at Red Hook's Li'l Peace of Heaven Baptist Church. Flik despises his time in Red Hook until meeting Chazz Morningstar (Tony Lysaith)—the thirteen-year-old daughter of Sharon Morningstar (Heather Alicia Simms), a sister of the church who serves as Bishop Rouse's confidante—but leaves Red Hook at summer's end after Box (Nate Parker), the leader of the neighborhood's Blood street gang, beats Rouse for not revealing his past indiscretions to the community. The film does not offer easy conclusions or pat resolutions to the issues it dramatizes, aligning *Red Hook Summer* with *She's Gotta Have It* (and Lee's other Chronicles of Brooklyn entries) by avoiding the happy endings that, in Lee's opinion, characterize too many Hollywood movies.

Red Hook Summer mixes various characters, themes, and issues while combining different visual textures, saturations, and film stocks to produce a fragmented style. Lee, working with cinematographer Kerwin DeVonish and editor Hye Mee Na, melds Sony-F3-digital, Super-8-mm, and iPad-2 footage into a movie of varying tones and colors that reflects the narrative's picaresque movement from place to place, incident to incident, and subplot to subplot. The film, much like *She's Gotta Have It,* breaks classical Hollywood style at every opportunity. The notion of a fluid and continuous story that includes instantly recognizable characters, conflicts, and resolutions, along with one overarching theme, is foreign to *Red Hook Summer,* whose multiplicity of characters, issues, and storylines opens it to criticisms of being unfinished, disjointed, inelegant, and unsatisfying. The title of Betsy Sharkey's August 23, 2012, *Los Angeles Times* review ("Spike Lee's *Red Hook Summer* a Mess of Sinners, Saints"), for instance, indicates her dissatisfaction with the movie despite her fondness for many of its characters and cast members (particularly Clarke Peters's Bishop Rouse). She declares, "In truth, the film fizzles as much as it fumes. There is a kind of lassitude that sets in, even as it builds toward some kind of reckoning. It can be felt in the difficulty the filmmaker has knitting all the grievances together."[72] Roger Ebert's August 22, 2012, *Chicago Sun-Times* review treads similar ground: "Spike Lee's *Red Hook Summer* plays as if the director is making it up as he goes along. That's not an entirely bad thing, although some will be thrown off-balance by an abrupt plot development halfway through that appears entirely out of the blue and is so shocking that the movie never really recovers."[73] Ebert enjoys portions of the film, but faults the narrative's construction: "Here is Lee at his most spontaneous and sincere, but he could have used another screenplay draft, and perhaps a few more transitional scenes. . . . Some of his scenes are strong in a free-standing way. I'm not sure what they add up to."[74] Claudia Puig's August 23, 2012, *USA Today* evaluation is far blunter, saying that *Red Hook Summer* "has the pace of a long, languid August day—until about 90 minutes in. Then, this formless drama, anchored by the powerful performance of Clarke Peters, goes from vague and meandering to incendiary."[75]

Not all critics, however, emphasize unities of plot, theme, and character. Richard Brody's advance August 9, 2012, *New Yorker* review is both the most admiring mainstream piece yet written about *Red Hook Summer* and an essay that anticipates many charges that Sharkey, Ebert, and Puig (among others) make. *Red Hook Summer,* according to Brody, is "a rousing yet deeply reflective new movie, which is, in effect, a gospel musical that gets its narrative drive from the conflict between a young skeptic and an elderly preacher in a predominantly black neighborhood in Brooklyn."[76] Brody, not content with these plaudits, proclaims, "It's one hell of a tall order, and Lee rises thrillingly to his own audacious challenge. *Red Hook Summer* is a brave and accomplished film in which the filmmaker, true to his mission, looks back and ahead as well as around and, with a lurching plot and a teeming cast of characters, both embraces and criticizes a world that he loves and rues."[77]

Even more intriguing is Brody's assessment of how *Red Hook Summer*'s lurching, meandering storyline reflects Lee's long filmography: "From the very start of his career, Lee has been as much of a documentarist—a folklorist and chronicler—as a fictioneer, and his films convey his ardor to preserve the ephemeral and record the unspeakable. Among other things, he's a poet of urban spaces, of sunlight on brick."[78] These observations are as incisive as any scholarship about Lee's oeuvre, underscoring how Lee mixes and matches his movies' visual, aural, and narrative styles to achieve authenticities of place and person that defy classical Hollywood cinema. Brody's conclusions about *Red Hook Summer* also describe Lee's approach in *She's Gotta Have It* to offer observations connecting the Chronicles of Brooklyn's first and (so far) final entries. These movies may have been produced twenty-six years apart, but their parallels are too great to ignore.

The most obvious connection between *She's Gotta Have It* and *Red Hook Summer* is the presence of Nola Darling (as a central character in the former film and a minor presence in the latter). Tracy Camilla Johns returns to play Nola, referred to only as Mother Darling by *Red Hook Summer*'s characters and end credits, as a committed Jehovah's Witness who offers her church's *Watchtower* magazine for sale while evangelizing to the neighborhood's residents. Nola's life, as this thumbnail sketch indicates, has not fulfilled the promise suggested by *She's Gotta Have It*. No longer working as a layout artist, she has moved from her middle-class Bedford-Stuyvesant loft to the working-class Red Hook projects. Nola's personal life, as Bishop Rouse reveals to Flik, has also drastically changed, for her only son died of AIDS some years before the film begins. The movie makes no further mention of Nola's past, leaving unanswered questions about whether she ever married (she wears no wedding band) or what precipitated her spiritual conversion, although the movie suggests that Nola's personal loss drove her to religion. A flash of Nola's former passion occurs when Bishop Rouse introduces her to Flik: she takes the boy's chin in her hands while remarking how attractive he is. Rouse later approves of Nola's fortitude as she prays in the Red Hook Project's courtyard, explaining to Flik that Nola's commitment to her faith makes Red Hook a good place to live because its residents endure personal anguish by turning to God.

Red Hook Summer, by returning *Do the Right Thing*'s Mookie to the screen for the first time since Lee's 1989 masterpiece, then cements its status as a Chronicles of Brooklyn film. Mookie (who the end credits call "Mr. Mookie" in a role that Lee relishes) still works as a deliveryman for Sal's Famous Pizzeria, even continuing to wear the same shirt he did in the earlier movie. This revelation implies that either Sal or his sons have relocated the business to Red Hook after its destruction in *Do the Right Thing*.[79] Mookie has lost none of his fire, screaming "Hell to the no!" when Nola tries to hand him the *Watchtower* (paralleling an early *Do the Right Thing* scene), then telling Rouse, "I gotta get paid!" The fact that Mookie has achieved little career or financial independence in the twenty-three years since his first appearance indicates the limited economic opportunities in working- and lower-class Brooklyn neighborhoods, although no one, including Mookie, comments upon this fact. Mookie, indeed, seems content in his life, smiling during his brief appearances and, toward *Red Hook Summer*'s conclusion, walking down the street with a young boy (who may be his grandson). The news of Mookie's appearance generated such excitement before *Red Hook Summer*'s release that Lee, in his January 26, 2012 *Daily Beast* interview with Chris Lee, specifies that the film "is not a motherfuckin' sequel to *Do the Right Thing*."[80] Even so, *Red Hook Summer* recalls Lee's earlier Chronicles of Brooklyn movies by focusing on the daily lives of its primary characters. Box, for instance, reminds viewers of Strike Dunham in *Clockers,* just as the Red Hook Project's courtyard evokes memories of the Nelson Mandela Homes in Lee's 1995 film. The pressure that Bishop Rouse puts on Box to reform his drug-dealing ways even coheres with Rocco Klein's attempts to convince Strike Dunham to renounce his loyalty to Rodney Little's drug organization, although Rouse wishes to save Box's soul rather than extract a murder confession from him.

Red Hook Summer, despite these connections to its predecessors, develops a unique identity by setting much of its action inside the Li'l Peace of Heaven Church, then tackling the issue of clergymen who molest young children. *Jungle Fever,* identified by Lee's *Red Hook Summer* audio commentary as a partial Chronicles of Brooklyn film (because half of that movie was shot in Bensonhurst), may cast Ossie Davis as the Good Doctor Reverend Purify, the rigid preacher-father of protagonist Flipper Purify (Wesley Snipes) and his heroin-addict brother Gator (Samuel L. Jackson), but no previous Lee film devotes so much narrative attention to religion. *Red Hook Summer,* thanks to Clarke Peters's accomplished performance as Bishop Rouse, also illustrates the significance of churches in predominantly African American communities. This theme, according to Lee's audio commentary, reflects the childhood of co-screenwriter James McBride, who grew up as a regular churchgoer. McBride's parents also built the New Brown Memorial Church in Brooklyn that served as the filming location for Rouse's Li'l Peace of Heaven congregation.

Peters so magnificently plays the three sermons that Rouse delivers in the film—excoriating drugs, alcohol, television, lax moral standards, and political inaction, among other topics—that, as Lee states more than once during his audio commentary, "we were having church up in there." The crowd's call-and-response reactions to Rouse's sermons were not scripted, meaning, Lee says, that the actors "were feeling the spirit" during repeated takes. *Red Hook Summer* neither demonizes nor promotes Rouse's religious beliefs, but illustrates the power that they hold over his parishioners during the joyous gospel singing that accompanies Rouse's homilies. These scenes acknowledge the prominence of black churches in the twentieth-century freedom struggle even if Rouse's small congregation indicates a subsequent loss of religious fervor.

Red Hook Summer irrevocably changes when Blessing Rowe accuses Rouse of molestation, leaping over pews in an attempt to attack the bishop, whom Rowe calls a "poisonous bastard" responsible for destroying the younger man's faith. This turn of events transcends simple exposition when a troubling flashback reveals Rouse's seduction of Rowe: Rouse, sitting on a bed with the thirteen-year-old Rowe (Sincere Peters), tells the boy that God commends their love and encourages Rowe to read passages from the Song of Solomon. Rouse caresses the boy's head and unbuttons Rowe's shirt before pushing the boy down onto the bed (in a movement that resembles baptism), then bending down, out of frame, and leaning toward the young Rowe's crotch. The viewer instinctively looks away just before the boy screams, "Stop, stop, stop, stop, stop!" This scene, disturbing in its power and execution, provoked disagreement between Lee and James McBride, as Lee reveals in his *Vanity Fair* interview with Jason Guerrasio: "He [McBride] felt that audiences would not want to see that on-screen and I had a different opinion. I mean James had a point. It is ugly, so we had to find the right balance. But at the same time not punk out and skirt around it. That would have been fake. If you're going to bring something up and don't follow through, why bring it up? That was my thinking."[81] Lee, in his DVD audio commentary, identifies this scene as the toughest he has ever directed and that Peters has ever acted, which seems likely insofar as the scene offers an honest if guarded dramatization of child molestation within a religious setting. *Red Hook Summer,* however, is unconventional by depicting molestation within a Baptist, not Catholic, church. The film, moreover, includes a fascinating but potentially distressing development by punishing Bishop Rouse, but refusing to condemn him. Box comes into Li'l Peace of Heaven, enraged by Rouse's hypocrisy, and beats the bishop with a tambourine until blood streams from the older man's temple. Box then places the instrument over Rouse's head in a sick evocation of the Crucifixion's crown of thorns before ordering three fellow gang members to stomp Rouse. After this violence, the bishop walks home in physical pain and psychological distress intensified by the disgust that greets him when people on the street, particularly the church's Deacon Yancy (Stephen Henderson), see him.

Rouse, returning to his apartment, confesses his crime to Flik after telling the boy to record his words. Clarke Peters is terrific in this scene, which incorporates the flashback to Rouse's molestation of Blessing Rowe into the bishop's self-narrated autobiography. Still, the question of why Flik's mother, Colleen Royale (De'Adre Aziza), allows her son to spend the summer with a pedophile whom she has spurned for years (and whom Flik has never met) looms large over *Red Hook Summer*'s final thirty minutes. The film never provides a clear answer, although Lee's DVD audio commentary elucidates three interlocking possibilities: (1) The death of Flik's Marine father (and Colleen's husband) in Afghanistan has taken an emotional toll that demands solitude if she is to heal; (2) Flik, in response to this tragedy, has become a sullen teenager whose behavior is increasingly difficult to manage, demanding a father figure in his life; and (3) Bishop Rouse, having asked to see his grandson for many years, finally convinces his daughter to relent. This explanation raises other queries, particularly when Rouse, after finishing his video confession, claims that prayer and therapy have allowed him to overcome his "sickness." As Andre Seewood writes in his January 2, 2013, article "The Decline of Spike Lee: A Prisoner of the Middle Class," these questions include, "Did Flik's mother know of her Father's past? How could she not know of his past if he changed his name to hide it? Were there other young male victims?"[82] More to the point, the fact that Bishop Rouse gave Colleen the hush money that his Georgia church offered to ensure his departure to New York (and that enabled her to purchase the house that Flik calls home) makes it unlikely that Colleen is ignorant of her father's crimes. Seewood, suggesting that *Red Hook Summer* is partially based on "the 2010 scandal and allegations of sexual molestation in the Black church concerning Bishop Eddie Long and New Birth Missionary Baptist Church in Georgia,"[83] challenges Rouse's rehabilitation: "The idea that Bishop Enoch had renounced his pedophiliac ways long ago and was no longer attracted to or molesting young boys flies in the face of much of the information that we know about pedophiles who hide behind institutions that have consistent contact with their youthful prey."[84]

Lee and McBride's screenplay is uninterested in resolving these quandaries, but *Red Hook Summer* subtly questions the bishop's belief that his sickness has been healed. Box's physical punishment of Rouse becomes, in retrospect, the anger of a man who, if he was not abused by Rouse, saw someone close to him molested by the bishop. The loyalty of church organist (and neighborhood cabbie) T. K. Hazelton (Jonathan Batiste) to Rouse may result from his own victimization by the older man, while Li'l Peace of Heaven's declining membership reflects the wider community's suspicion of Rouse's actions to the point that the church's economic viability is threatened. The bishop does not defend himself when Box beats him, which, according to Lee's audio commentary, indicates the older man's deep guilt over his crime. This passivity, in other words, is perverse penance for the pain Rouse knows he has inflicted on the community, emphasizing one of *Red Hook Summer*'s fundamental ironies: the neighborhood's most fearsome street thug behaves more morally than its appointed clergyman.

Yet no one calls the police and Rouse shows no sign of submitting himself to the criminal-justice system. The morning after his confession, the bishop makes certain that Flik reaches his flight back to Atlanta on time. Sharon Morningstar stands in silent rebuke, glaring at Rouse as her daughter Chazz says goodbye to Flik, but the bishop escapes additional scrutiny. *Red Hook Summer,* indeed, concludes with a musical montage that pays tribute to the area's residents by interweaving footage of these people's daily lives with previously unseen images of Flik and Chazz's explorations of Red Hook's streets.

The final scene sees Lee writing the movie's title in chalk on a blackboard before calling "Cut," thereby denying the resolution that Betsey Sharkey and Roger Ebert implicitly desire: Rouse's arrest, trial, and imprisonment. This conclusion, so dissatisfying from the perspective of classical Hollywood cinema's preference for tidy endings that punish all criminals and vindicate all victims, frustrates the viewer's expectations. Blessing Rowe never reappears, Flik never recoils from his grandfather's admission, and Rouse never openly apologizes for his crime. *Red Hook Summer* may be painfully realistic by not legally punishing its pedophiliac reverend, but the film is even more subversive by humanizing its protagonist, thereby encouraging audience members to sympathize with him, thanks in no small measure to Clarke Peters's passionate performance.

This effect, as Lee's audio commentary confirms, is deliberate. Rather than portraying a monster, Lee wants to dramatize the life of a flawed, feeling man who is also a pedophile. *Red Hook Summer,* careful viewers should note, reserves this explosive revelation for its final act to avoid becoming a single-issue movie. This narrative structure risks trivializing pedophilia, but the film avoids maudlin melodrama and moralistic immaturity by acknowledging the pain that Rouse inflicts even while refusing final answers and absolutions.

This imperfect ending becomes, in its way, a suitable reflection of Rouse's uncertain life, just as *Red Hook Summer* is a fitting conclusion to the Chronicles of Brooklyn. The movie remains observant, large hearted, and cluttered. Lee's audio commentary promises more films like it even if he must finance them himself. Such movies, like the existing Chronicles of Brooklyn entries, will not please all viewers—or even most viewers—once they make it to the screen, but they will surely document Brooklyn's African American communities in ways that few other filmmakers have attempted. Spike Lee, in other words, cannot turn a blind eye to the borough's polyglot residents even if, from time to time, his field of vision remains limited. The Chronicles of Brooklyn, thanks to his efforts, constitutes a significant rejection of Hollywood simplifications about black Americans, a major artistic statement about urban America, and, happily, an important achievement in American cinema.

6

Documentary Evidence

OBSERVER EFFECTS

Although Spike Lee's official career as a documentary filmmaker began in 1997 with the theatrical release of *4 Little Girls,* careful viewers had long noted the documentary aspects of his earlier movies. The black-and-white photography, still images, and direct-to-camera address that begin *She's Gotta Have It* (1986), for instance, announce this film's debt to cinéma vérité; *School Daze*'s (1987) opening credits mix photographs, diagrams, and the spiritual song "I'm Building Me a Home" to chronicle the history of black America in just under four minutes; and *Do the Right Thing*'s (1989) authentic presentation of its characters' lives has received so much praise that uninitiated viewers may mistake this movie for a documentary. Beyond Lee's first three films, *Malcolm X* (1992) concludes with archival footage and still photographs of the actual Malcolm X (rather than actor Denzel Washington in costume) as Ossie Davis provides voiceover narration of the eulogy that Davis first spoke at Malcolm's 1965 funeral. *Crooklyn* (1994) is a thinly veiled depiction of Lee's family upbringing, lending many scenes a vérité feel, while *Clockers* (1995) so realistically tells its story of urban injustice that, like its source novel, the film occasionally dupes the viewer into believing that Lee set out to document actual people going about their daily lives.

Lee's career, in other words, exemplifies his desire to capture the conflicting truths of his characters' experience, underscoring not only his documentary impulses but also how deftly his feature films unsettle the distinction between fact and fiction. Lee's movies seem designed to spotlight the provisional, even arbitrary, division between documentary film's supposed objectivity and feature work's assumed freedom (from reality, from believability, and, especially, from factual truth). The terms themselves are problematic, with *documentary* suggesting a neutrality that does not restrict fictional cinematic stories to the prison house of factual accuracy, while *movie* (along with its synonyms, *moving picture* and *feature film*) presumes disinterest in faithfully representing the world, thereby allowing these productions to tell whatever stories their creators wish in whatever styles they can imagine. Jasmine Nichole Cobb and John L. Jackson perceptively question such binaries in "They Hate Me: Spike Lee, Documentary Filmmaking, and Hollywood's 'Savage Slot'" by observing, "one of the most common responses to Spike's filmic excesses is to portray him as a much-better (and clearer) documentarian than fictional filmmaker."[1] Cobb and Jackson find this judgment problematic because it ignores Lee's tremendous artistry—his stylized settings, colors, and dialogue; his multifocal narration; his ambiguous conclusions—in favor of the director's talent at recording different facets of American and African American life. Lee finds himself "reduced to a flat-footed (and transparent) practitioner, a sheer receptacle for 'the real,' and not a truly introspective theoretician and architect of alternative realities," Cobb and Jackson write, highlighting how unfair they find lauding Lee's documentaries at the expense of his feature films: "He becomes a mere chronicler of facts, an emptied cipher, and not a truly self-conscious auteur."[2]

This dissatisfying perspective leads Cobb and Jackson to write "They Hate Me" to challenge "the caricatured readings of Spike the cultural producer that constitute this impoverished reading of his work, a reading that polarizes racial realities along the lines of documentation versus fiction to perpetuate modernist notions about realism."[3] This polarity defines realism as the accurate, truthful recording of human life, behavior, and conflict that, unlike the fanciful possibilities and invented characters of fictional narratives, typifies documentary films more than even realistic fiction, which, despite creating plausible characters and believable happenings, deforms reality in a way that documentaries supposedly do not. Nola Darling and Flipper Purify, in other words, may seem realistic in their words, thoughts, and deeds, but they do not exist in the world as Tracy Camilla Johns and Wesley Snipes do.

This seemingly basic division, Cobb and Jackson note, carries tremendous implications for Lee's status as a documentarian: "Not only does such a divide"—between Lee's documentary and fictional films—"ignore the fact that his motion pictures are part of a larger, single-raced project that cuts across film genres; more importantly, we argue that it fetishizes the fiction/documentary divide in ways that ultimately misread the nature and significance of Spike's films and filmic philosophy."[4] Although Lee's cinematic career is far from the "single-raced project" that Cobb and Jackson identify, they productively note the inadequacies of judging Lee's documentaries as more accomplished than his fiction films. "They Hate Me," indeed, is the best scholarly article yet published about falsely dichotomizing Lee's movies into opposing camps: feature films whose excesses risk narrative incoherence versus superb documentaries whose restraint demonstrates just how good a fictional filmmaker Lee could be if he adopted classical Hollywood style (by telling easily identifiable stories with sympathetic characters, simple plots, clear resolutions, and unobtrusive camerawork).

Cobb and Jackson persuasively analyze how the narrative skills, stylistic flourishes, and thematic ambiguities that characterize Lee's movies also wend their way into his documentaries to erode the assumptions governing the documentary's formal principles, particularly the genre's reputation for presenting objective facts in journalistic fashion. Audiences, therefore, may too easily conclude that Lee inserts himself into his movies while effacing himself from the documentaries when, for Cobb and Jackson, he brings similar techniques to both forms: "His use of 'talking-heads' and archival footage lends Spike a clinical credibility and objectivity that seems to assume, just a bit too quickly, that Spike makes very few directorial decisions that unduly bear on the story presented to viewers."[5] This claim's falsity does not demolish the narrative invisibility that audiences often ascribe to documentary films, a trait that their creators rarely challenge and frequently abet. Desires for probity, honesty, and neutrality lead viewers to judge documentaries as more truthful (and, indeed, as more earnest) than fictional films, which, in this reading, primarily function as commercial entertainments offering pleasant, yet momentary diversions from the serious business of living, unlike documentaries, which supposedly educate audiences about important topics.

Cobb and Jackson recognize the subtle tensions between information and entertainment that the documentary's generic conventions epitomize: "We are seduced by the documentary form as a kind of hands-off approach to storytelling that simply allows the filmed subjects to 'speak for themselves.'"[6] This idea, that documentaries offer apparently direct access to truth by having their subjects offer personal reflections to expectant viewers, remains powerful despite the editorial decisions that all documentarians make, from selecting interviewees, posing questions, and assembling a coherent argument about the chosen topic. Lee's cinematic productions, however, exist on a continuum that sees his documentaries incorporate many of his movies' stylistic idiosyncrasies and thematic indeterminacies in a technique that, Cobb and Jackson observe, exhibits a type of "hypertheatricality, even as it overcommits to a form of hyper-urban (and racial realism). In many ways, Spike's films are productively schizophrenic texts: one part verite-esque homage to ultrarealism . . . and one part fanciful, cartoon-like allegory of racial loss and redemption."[7] Lee's work, these comments suggest, boldly crosses traditional boundaries between movies and documentaries in a pattern reminiscent of his signature aesthetic approach. Cobb and Jackson write, "part of what makes Spike's films demanding as texts is their supple short-circuiting of conventional borders between reality and fable, realism and antirealism, the proscenium artificialities of theatre and the indexical/iconic self-evidentialities of photochemical reproducibility."[8] Lee, from this viewpoint, deconstructs the dichotomies generally assumed to differentiate documentaries from movies: fact/fiction, reality/fantasy, truth/untruth, realism/antirealism, constraint/freedom, and simplicity/complexity. Even so, this conclusion overlooks how African American documentarians before Lee explore their topics in sometimes startlingly fresh ways. Phyllis R. Klotman and Janet K. Cutler argue in *Struggles for Representation: African American Documentary Film and Video* that a long tradition of activism informs documentaries about black life: "Many socially and politically committed film/videomakers view documentary as a tool with which to interrogate and reinvent history; their works fill gaps, correct errors, and expose distortions in order to provide counter-narratives of African American experience."[9] Lee inherits from the work of earlier black documentarians the creative freedom to integrate narrative cinema's techniques into his documentaries, with Stuart Heisler's *The Negro Soldier* (1944) and Henry Hampton's multipart PBS series *Eyes on the Prize* (1987 and 1990) being particularly important forerunners. Lee brings familiar intensity, focus, and passion to his documentaries, but he does not operate in a vacuum. Moreover, impulses to reinvent and to revise history, not merely to uncover it, exemplify Lee's documentaries.

These films fall into four categories: concert movies/musical profiles— *Pavarotti & Friends for the Children of Liberia* (1998), *Pavarotti & Friends: 99 for Guatemala and Kosovo* (1999), *The Original Kings of Comedy* (2000), *Passing Strange* (2010), and *Bad 25* (2012);[10] sports profiles—*Jim Brown: All-American* (2002) and *Kobe Doin' Work* (2009); one-man shows—*Freak* (1998), *A Huey P. Newton Story* (2001), and *Mike Tyson: Undisputed Truth* (2013); and significant historical/cultural examinations, particularly the films that most concern this chapter: *4 Little Girls* and *When the Levees Broke: A Requiem in Four Acts* (*If God Is Willing and Da Creek Don't Rise,* Lee's sequel to *When the Levees Broke,* follows its predecessor's stylistic approach so closely that it requires fewer comments). As with his feature films, these variegated productions demonstrate Lee's diverse interests and cinematic versatility. *4 Little Girls* and *When the Levees Broke,* however, are significant not simply because they interrogate major historical incidents (respectively, the September 15, 1963, bombing of Birmingham, Alabama's Sixteenth Street Baptist Church and the devastation wrought by Hurricane Katrina along America's Gulf Coast—especially New Orleans, Louisiana—in August 2005), but because they inventively collapse the divide between movies and documentaries, bringing tremendous intimacy to otherwise monumental events.

This approach laudably humanizes history, making the Civil Rights Movement and an overwhelming national catastrophe understandable by chronicling the emotional reactions, intellectual musings, and on-the-ground experiences of the people who endured them. Less interested in offering an overarching, bird's-eye perspective or big-picture objectivity, Lee's documentaries include the subjective impressions of many different individuals to interrogate, reinvent, and uncover the events they discuss. This project, indeed, questions the possibility, utility, and desirability of the documentary form's presumed neutrality. The emotional investment that viewers of *4 Little Girls* and *When the Levees Broke* make in each film's topics, issues, and interviewees demonstrates, exactly as Cobb and Jackson argue, how adroitly Lee transfers narrative techniques from his movies into documentaries unashamed to make social, economic, and political statements. Lee's success in this venture, however, results from his previous experimentation with documentary effects in his narrative films. The best example is *4 Little Girls*' immediate predecessor, *Get on the Bus* (1996), a movie that—seemingly conceived, written, and shot as a documentary—amounts to a dress rehearsal for Lee's later contributions to this genre. Functioning as a prologue to *4 Little Girls, Get on the Bus* assembles dramatic vignettes, multiple storylines, and political conflicts into a searching precursor of Lee's best documentaries.

MARCHING MEN

Get on the Bus, as Gabriella Beckles-Raymond notes, "remains the only feature-length depiction of the Million Man March, and despite being a fictional account, it provides us with a unique opportunity to explore the march as part of a social movement, a political event, and a commentary on the black community and race relations in America."[11] These remarks, appearing early in Beckles-Raymond's essay "We Can't Get Off the Bus: A Commentary on Spike Lee and Moral Motivation," describe a documentary as well as a narrative film. *Get on the Bus,* however, does not depict the march itself (held on October 16, 1995), but rather the interactions of fifteen African American men wishing to attend the event as they share a tour bus from South Central Los Angeles to Washington, D.C. Lee includes archival footage of the march itself on waiting-room television sets that the characters watch after Jeremiah Washington (Ossie Davis), the oldest man on the trip (and the "group's griot,"[12] in Beckles-Raymond's words), is rushed to a D.C. hospital after a heart attack. The movie's structure, developed by Lee and screenwriter Reggie Rock Bythewood, comprises vignettes (of the men discussing their lives, outlining their politics, and airing their conflicts) that recall Haskell Wexler's 1965 documentary *The Bus,* which chronicles black riders travelling from San Francisco, California, to Washington, D.C., to attend 1963's now-legendary March on Washington for Jobs and Freedom.

Wexler's film spends less time on the bus than Lee's movie, with Wexler choosing to follow the riders as they walk Washington's streets until they arrive at the National Mall. *Get on the Bus,* however, includes a surrogate for Wexler in the character of Xavier Moore (Hill Harper), a University of California-Los Angeles (UCLA) film student shooting a documentary of the trip for his senior thesis. Xavier, who calls himself Xavier X, operates the camera, asks the riders questions, and follows them throughout their travels, just as Wexler does in his documentary. Xavier, called "Spike Lee Junior"[13] at one point, also serves as Lee's proxy in moments that breach the walls between documentary and feature film despite the fact that, as Kaleem Aftab observes in *That's My Story and I'm Sticking to It,* Wexler's *The Bus* is "a film that Spike

Lee, surprisingly, hasn't seen."[14] Lee and Bythewood, by this account, do not model their movie on *The Bus*, yet the two projects' similarities demonstrate how well Lee absorbs documentary aesthetics into *Get on the Bus*, meaning that Wexler's film functions as an indirect precursor to Lee's movie.

Wexler also serves as a spiritual father to Lee's life as a documentarian. Moving from feature film to documentary with the same ease as Lee, Wexler's career as a cinematographer, screenwriter, director, and documentarian embodies the rapport between fact and fiction that talented filmmakers can achieve. Wexler's 1969 movie *Medium Cool*, for instance, tells the story of television-news cameraman John Cassellis (Robert Forster) as he navigates ethical quandaries affecting his professional life, mixing feature-film scenes of the movie's actors with documentary footage of Chicago's 1968 Democratic National Convention (particularly the civil unrest provoked by this event) to achieve the cinéma-vérité style that characterizes *Get on the Bus*. Indeed, as David Charpentier comments in his insightful "Truth is Fiction: Haskell Wexler, Part I," "His (Wexler's) work in *cinema vérité* brought a new style to Hollywood that attempted the wedding of documentary and feature. A new realism, a sense of *being there* was instilled into features. Enhanced by naturalist Method acting and existential narratives, Wexler's filmmaking style blurred the lines between truth and fiction."[15] This willingness to defy conventional boundaries, styles, and genres produces an authenticity that Charpentier associates with French New Wave cinema, although it just as forcefully implicates Italian Neorealism. Charpentier writes that Wexler belongs to "a group of *auteurs* that pushed the boundaries of cinematic form and content"[16] in a description that comfortably applies to Spike Lee. *Get on the Bus* inherits so many elements from Wexler's movies-cum-documentaries that Lee's film becomes their clear descendent despite Lee's failure to acknowledge Wexler's example.

Charpentier's analysis emphasizes realism, naturalism, and existentialism, three traits that *Get on the Bus* shares with *Medium Cool*. Lee and Bythewood, however, restrict three quarters of their film to the bus, meaning that, as S. Craig Watkins notes in "Reel Men: *Get on the Bus* and the Shifting Terrain of Black Masculinities," his superb analysis of the movie's production, "the specifications of the shoot were unlike any other Spike Lee Joint. *Get on the Bus* was his first road movie."[17] This genre virtually demands an episodic plot that glides from person to person (and place to place) while the narrative unfolds, thereby allying road pictures with cinéma vérité, as Dennis Hopper's 1969 motorcycle drama *Easy Rider*—one of the most famous and influential road movies ever made—demonstrates. Restricting most of the action to a single set also connects *Get on the Bus* to Alfred Hitchcock's *Lifeboat* (1944). Watkins, noting the parallels, highlights the demands of shooting a movie in such confinement: "In situations like these, the director has to come up with inventive ways of translating the story; thus, the use of camera movement and angles, sound, editing, and other technical details become [*sic*] even more crucial."[18]

Lee, like Wexler before him, ably rises to this challenge. He (Lee) accentuates *Get on the Bus*'s visuals with various cinematic techniques: incorporating Xavier's grainy documentary footage into filmed scenes, employing canted angles, using light and shadow in unconventional ways, choosing bold colors (ranging from the comforting ambers of South Central, Los Angeles, and the dusty reds of the Mojave Desert to the cool blues of nighttime Knoxville, Tennessee), and, in perhaps his most important decision, electing to film *Get on the Bus* on Super-16-mm stock (with the exception of Xavier's movie-within-a-movie camcorder footage). Watkins, ascribing this decision to the tight, eighteen-day shooting schedule imposed by *Get on the Bus*'s small, $2.4-million budget, notes its aesthetic effects: "The decision to go with Super-16 also gave the film a cinema vérité style that enhanced its power of realism. Although it is a fictional narrative, *Get on the Bus* has the look and texture of a documentary."[19] This judgment is incontestable by the movie's conclusion. Viewers unacquainted with *Get on the Bus*'s talented cast (including Richard Belzer, Andre Braugher, Thomas Jefferson Byrd, Charles S. Dutton, Albert Hall, Harry Lennix, Wendell Pierce, Roger Guenveur Smith, and Isaiah Washington) might mistake the film for a journalistic account of this group's trip to the Million Man March. Despite characters who begin as stock personages (the wise old man, the enthusiastic film student, the arrogant actor), the movie lives up to its vérité stylings. Roger Ebert agrees with this perspective in his admiring *Chicago-Sun Times* review: "What makes *Get on the Bus* extraordinary is the truth and feeling that go into its episodes. Spike Lee and his actors face one hard truth after another, in scenes of great power."[20] By examining what *San Francisco Examiner* film critic Barbara Shulgasser calls "the meaning of the march" and by trying "to offer every point of view a black man (and a Jewish man, and a few black women) could possibly have about race in America,"[21] *Get on the Bus* becomes a fascinating hybrid of road picture, character study, and civil-rights documentary that prepares Lee for *4 Little Girls* and *When the Levees Broke*.

HUMAN TARGETS

Lee's efforts in *4 Little Girls* make this documentary a watershed entry in his filmography. Home Box Office (HBO), the premium-cable network that funded it, was so impressed by Lee's final cut that *4 Little Girls* premiered in movie houses during July 1997 (to guarantee its entry in the 1998 Academy Awards) before appearing on cable television. Although *4 Little Girls* was nominated in the Oscars' 1998 "Best Documentary, Feature" category, it lost to Mark Jonathan Harris's *The Long Way Home* (1997), a film that explores the experiences of European Jews from World War II's conclusion to State of Israel's founding. Despite this setback, *4 Little Girls* won several other awards in 1998: the Broadcast Film Critics Association Award for Best Documentary; the Golden Satellite Award for Best Documentary Film; the

Image Award for Outstanding News, Talk, or Information Special; the National Educational Media Network's Gold Apple Award; and the Online Film Critics Society Award for Best Documentary.

Industry honors are no guarantee of any film's quality, but *4 Little Girls* deserves these plaudits. The documentary, Janet Maslin declares in her *New York Times* review (titled "Still Reeling from the Day Death Came to Birmingham"), "is Spike Lee's immensely dignified and moving reassessment of a terrorist crime."[22] The film achieves remarkable emotional intimacy by allowing its subjects, particularly the family members and close friends of bombing victims Addie Mae Collins, Denise McNair, Carole Robertson, and Cynthia Wesley, to recount their experiences in sometimes devastating detail. Christine Acham precisely pegs the resulting effect in her essay "We Shall Overcome: Preserving History and Memory in *4 Little Girls*" by writing, "*4 Little Girls* succeeds in shaking both black and white viewers out of their contemporary apathy to U.S. racial history. Lee moves the viewer between the personal history of the families of the victims and the more recognized, public, political history of Birmingham. Focusing on the individual puts a face on the atrocities of the civil-rights struggle."[23] Lee, indeed, carefully builds the bombing's historical context, devoting *4 Little Girls*' first half hour to outlining Birmingham's racial tensions through interviews with public officials, ordinary citizens, and the girls' acquaintances. Setting the city's racial terrorism in stark relief permits *4 Little Girls* to examine the lives of the bombing's four victims by mixing photographs, remembrances, and extended interviews with family members to pursue a technique that, in Acham's words, "creates a bridge between the personal and the political in black history."[24]

This connection is essential to recuperating the violence, terror, and vitriol that characterized the Civil Rights Movement for viewers who may have forgotten (or may never have known) the racial hatred that confronted Birmingham's African American residents. Lee himself speaks to this necessity in a July 13, 1997, article by *New York Daily News*' Denene Millner, saying that *4 Little Girls* addresses the disturbing ignorance of young black Americans about the Civil Rights Movement:

> African Americans are far too quick to want to forget. We don't want to remember it. It's always: 'Let's forget about slavery, Emmit [*sic*] Till, Rosa Parks, Medgar Evers. Why you wanna go back and bring that up—dredge up that stuff?' Consequently, we have a generation of black kids who think this is the way it always was—that we could always live where we wanted, eat where we wanted, have church where we wanted. We need to remember.[25]

Acham notes the same trend in "We Shall Overcome," observing that "some African American students in my classes, while enjoying the fruits of the civil-rights struggle, consider this ancient history and a topic that does not need to be addressed."[26] These judgments also apply to students of other racial and ethnic backgrounds, leading Acham, a professor of African and African American studies at the University of California-Davis, to realize that she cannot "assume that African American stories, no matter how significant, are passed down. Unfortunately, while from the days of slavery oral histories were a given part of the African American life, in this highly mediated world, these important traditions have fallen by the wayside."[27] Lee's film, therefore, constitutes a significant intervention in the dispiriting cultural and pedagogical amnesia that characterizes America's late-twentieth-century knowledge about its own racial past.

Lee, according to his *4 Little Girls* DVD audio commentary, several interviews, and his autobiography, wanted to make the film while still in graduate school. Lee was so affected by reading Howell Raines's July 24, 1983, *New York Times Magazine* investigative article "The Birmingham Bombing" that he wrote to Christopher McNair, the father of victim Denise McNair, to seek permission to make a film about Denise's death.[28] Receiving no reply, Lee kept the idea in mind, and, after establishing himself as a notable cinematic player, visited McNair and his wife Maxine while receiving an award in Birmingham.[29] Eventually convincing them to participate in the project, Lee secured funding from Sheila Nevins, president of HBO Documentary Films, before returning to Birmingham to perform research and conduct interviews for the film. Raines's article provides a loose template for *4 Little Girls'* opening thirty minutes, in which Lee chronicles the racial extremism that regularly confronted black residents of the city perversely nicknamed "Bombingham." Raines, for instance, notes in his exposé that "over the course of 15 years, about 50 dynamite bombs went off on 'Dynamite Hill,' a white residential section a couple of miles from my neighborhood where blacks were buying homes."[30] Distressing as this statistic is, Raines points out how local authorities implicitly sanctioned such tactics: "The police were never able to make any arrests, even though the home of Arthur D. Shores, the city's most prominent black attorney, was bombed so often that he used to stand guard on his front porch with a shotgun, and even though . . . Robert E. Chambliss"—the man convicted of masterminding the Sixteenth Street bombing in 1977—"went by the nickname of 'Dynamite Bob.'"[31]

Raines illustrates, in exhaustive detail, not only that "to understand the crime that took place two decades ago, it is necessary to reconstruct a picture of a city where racial terrorism was routine, a city with a police tradition of tolerance for the Klan"[32] but also that the legal injustice of not punishing the perpetrators until decades after the crime's commission resulted from "official bungling, most notably on the part of F.B.I. Director J. Edgar Hoover," who, Raines convincingly demonstrates, "was responsible for hamstringing the local, state and Federal investigators who were close to solving the murders shortly after they occurred."[33] Perhaps *4 Little Girls'* most notable accomplishments are skillfully examining these facts while, at the same time, subtly reconstructing Raines's moral outrage, best seen in his article's open-ing paragraph: "In the number of people killed at a single stroke, the bomb-ing was the most terrible incident of racial violence during the peak years of the Southern civil-rights movement. In the mindlessness of its evil, the 16th Street bombing was also the most heinous act of the era."[34] Lee does not make such statements himself, but allows the film's subjects (including Howell Raines, in one of the film's best interviews) to lead viewers to these conclusions. Lee, indeed, stays off camera for *4 Little Girls*' entire length, and, except for the few times his voice is briefly heard asking off-screen ques-tions or making off-screen comments, remains invisible. This talking-heads approach promotes the conclusion that *4 Little Girls* embraces the hands-off storytelling that Jasmine Nichole Cobb and John L. Jackson dispute in "They Hate Me," suggesting that Lee interferes less forcefully and less frequently in this film than in his fictional movies. This flawed perspective ignores just how cogently, expertly, and artfully Lee constructs *4 Little Girls* to convince its viewer that the Sixteenth Street Church bombing is, as Raines argues in his article and in Lee's documentary, a momentous event not just in the Civil Rights Movement, but in American history. The many decisions that Lee and his editor, Sam Pollard, make in structuring the film to parallel Birmingham's civic life with the bombing's victims' lives steer the audience through the event's horror into the conflicted feelings, dignified restraint, and philosophi-cal outlook that the girls' friends and family display throughout *4 Little Girls*.

Cobb and Jackson recognize how *4 Little Girls* seems different from Lee's fictional movies. Although viewers are "less bombarded by the visual markers that typify Spike films," they write, "he continues to guide the story presented, choosing to ask specific questions and to edit in particular re-sponses."[35] These divergences, Cobb and Jackson suggest, are illusory in-sofar as they characterize both Lee's documentaries and his fiction films, as the direct-to-camera moments in *She's Gotta Have It, School Daze, Do the Right Thing, Malcolm X, Clockers,* and even *25th Hour* reveal. Cobb and Jackson underscore the danger of assuming that Lee's documentaries, due to their generic conventions, achieve objectivity: "In assuming that Spike 'gets out of the way' in his documentaries, critics fail to consider how these offerings present stories from a narrative perspective that reiterates Spike's politics, even if a bit less explicitly (and, therefore, more persuasively)."[36] Lee himself nearly abolishes the lines between documentary and movie by noting, in *That's My Story and I'm Sticking to It*, how each genre reinforces the other despite their differences: "And my fiction films have helped me with my documentaries because the common denominator between the forms to me is still storytelling."[37]

His comments to the *San Francisco Chronicle*'s Ruthe Stein (during an October 7, 1997, interview) not only buttress this idea but also vindicate the notion that, in his documentaries, Lee purposefully stays in the back-ground: "My approach to each film is determined by the subject matter, and in this film there was no need for me to assert myself. I mean, this film is not about Spike Lee. The best treatment of the story would be to let the people who were there tell it. There is no way I can write dialogue that can describe the pain of a parent at losing a daughter at a young age."[38] Lee implies that the documentary's conventions—especially the audience's expectation that 4 Little Girls tells a true story—makes the active, even activist role he takes in previous films unnecessary. He focuses instead on creating empathy with Birmingham's black residents to illustrate just how perilous their lives were.

Lee, as Christine Acham notes, does not employ flashy camera movement in 4 Little Girls. The stylized cinematography of his earlier movies—including whip pans, jump cuts, canted angles, long dolly rolls, quick zooms, and hand-held tracking shots—gives way to stationary images of the interview subjects looking into the camera, directly at the viewer, or, at other moments, just off camera, at the unseen Lee as he poses questions that the viewer rarely hears. This confidential style, long part of both cinematic documentaries and television news programs, is, according to Acham, atypical for Lee. "Far from his better-known and dynamic cinematography," Acham writes, "in these scenes the camera remains static, and the image is often held for several seconds more than is comfortable to the viewer"[39] as the participants, recalling the pain of losing the four girls, sometimes weep on screen. Such passages, far from exploiting the victims' families, not only drive home the suffering that they endured to demonstrate their resilience, their bravery, and their full humanity, but also powerfully indict the racial violence, white supremacy, and police malfeasance that were daily aspects of African American life in Birmingham (and throughout the South) during the era of Jim Crow segregation.

Lingering on the emotional devastation of the bombing, however, caused Lee some trepidation. He says in "4 Little Girls: How It All Began," a behind-the-scenes feature on the 4 Little Girls DVD release, that "what was difficult on my part was to ask probing questions knowing that on several occasions it was going to make people break down on camera."[40] Ruthe Stein writes that Lee eventually dismissed these qualms by reasoning, "It was just a question of when you cut. I didn't want anyone onscreen crying for a great length of time."[41] This decision produces some of 4 Little Girls' richest sequences, creating, as Acham says, "a strong sense of empathy with the families, revealing the contemporary reality of those living with this historical tragedy."[42] These glimpses into the bombing's human cost also underscore the film's argumentative shrewdness. By piling individual comments, memories, and reflections atop one another, 4 Little Girls weaves subjective perspectives into an impressive emotional, psychological, and historical tapestry that reminds the viewer how crucial regular people were to nourishing the Civil Rights Movement. Their courage, 4 Little Girls suggests, was neither unusual nor ephemeral, but the product of sustained opposition to the hazards that

African American residents faced from segregation's legal, social, and cultural machinery. Focusing on the movement's unheralded contributors also aligns *4 Little Girls* with Henry Hampton's *Eyes on the Prize*. Although both documentaries include comments by icons such as Martin Luther King, Jr., they significantly recuperate the importance of the everyday people who gave the movement life.

Acham understands this approach's importance to teaching viewers easily forgotten truths about America's racial past: "Whereas the majority of public histories of the movement rely on the stories, testimony, or recollections of the better-known participants of the Civil Rights Movement, such as Rosa Parks or Andrew Young, the film allows these 'ordinary' citizens a voice in their history."[43] This point is relevant because, Acham argues, "The Civil Rights Movement was always a grassroots movement; over time, the concentration on figures such as Martin Luther King Jr. has diminished the power of the movement that came in the sheer numbers of black people who sustained it."[44] Lee's decision to feature his interviewees' individual viewpoints not only underscores the psychological realism that *4 Little Girls* achieves but also highlights the historical perspective made possible by allowing witnesses who have lived with the bombing's effects for nearly twenty-five years to unveil, without rancor or hatred, the details of African American life under Jim Crow segregation. The scene that perfectly embodies this fusion of the personal and the political comes when Christopher McNair describes the ugly reality of explaining racism to his daughter. While shopping at a downtown Birmingham store, Denise smelled onions cooking at a lunch counter and asked to eat a sandwich. McNair says, "That was the night that I made up my mind that I guess I had to tell her that she couldn't have that sandwich because she was black." His distress is evident: "Well, I want you to know that night couldn't have been any more painful than seeing her laying up there with a rock smashed in her head than to tell her that I couldn't buy her that sandwich down there because she was black. And I'm not sure if she ever understood that."[45] This revelation, in Acham's words, "brings home the reality of the situation to an audience who may have either become desensitized over time or may not have a true understanding of how dehumanizing or emasculating it was for a man not to have the power to give his child what she wanted."[46] McNair's bravery in revealing this extraordinarily painful memory is honored by Lee's choice to include it in *4 Little Girls* as a powerful, telling, and appalling example of racism's insidious effects. McNair's dignity, so characteristic of all the film's speakers, demonstrates just how emotionally and intellectually affecting the documentary form becomes in Lee's hands. The director does not sacrifice the narrative techniques or political passions of his earlier movies, but rather embroiders them into the documentary's generic conventions to produce a potent historical memoir.

This scene also highlights a crucial difference between *4 Little Girls* and films directed (or inspired) by the work of Ken Burns, perhaps America's foremost (and certainly best-known) documentarian. Lee eschews voiceover narration, allowing the film's many different voices, images, and details to accrue until *4 Little Girls*' arguments about the barbarity of racial terror, the banality of racial segregation, and the backwardness of racist stereotypes become clear. This inductive approach may shield Lee's perspective from obvious view, but his outlook nonetheless drives the film's narrative, which is insistently ethical in the way that Bill Nichols, in his book *Introduction to Documentary*, defines this term: "Ethics becomes a measure of the ways in which negotiations about the nature of the relationship between filmmaker and subject have consequences for subjects and viewers alike."[47] If, as Nichols suggests, ethical considerations influence what he calls a documentary's emotional realism (defined as "creating an appropriate emotional state in the viewer"[48]) and, especially, its psychological realism ("convey[ing] the inner states of characters or social actors in plausible and convincing ways"[49]), then *4 Little Girls* is a notable accomplishment for documentary ethics that interrogates, reinvents, and recuperates a terrible moment in American history. The film, much to Lee's credit, expands its viewer's intellectual knowledge and emotional sensitivity about the Sixteenth Street Church bombing's significance to the Civil Rights Movement. As such, *4 Little Girls* is not simply Lee's first feature-length documentary but also his best. It serves as an important antecedent to Lee's multipart explorations of Hurricane Katrina's aftermath (*When the Levees Broke: A Requiem in Four Acts* and *If God Is Willing and Da Creek Don't Rise*), but this lineage should not obscure just how finely Lee crafts *4 Little Girls*. The bulk of Lee's reputation as a documentarian may rest on the two later projects, especially *When the Levees Broke*, but the extraordinary contribution of *4 Little Girls* to burnishing his cinematic credentials cannot be denied or diminished because, as multiple viewings reveal, *4 Little Girls* is one of the twentieth century's finest American documentaries.

STORMY WEATHER

In the nine years that passed between *4 Little Girls* and *When the Levees Broke*, Lee directed six more documentaries, although only 2002's *Jim Brown: All-American* resembles *4 Little Girls* in any meaningful degree. This film, also produced for HBO, stitches together interviews with Jim Brown and notable people in his life to generate a fascinating biographical profile. Lee's other efforts are concert movies (*Pavarotti & Friends for the Children of Liberia*, *Pavarotti & Friends: 99 for Guatemala and Kosovo*, and *The Original Kings of Comedy*) or one-man shows (John Leguizamo's *Freak* and Roger Guenveur Smith's *A Huey P. Newton Story*) that, while intriguing, do not match the scale of *When the Levees Broke*, Lee's four-hour examination of Hurricane Katrina's devastating effect on the residents of the American Gulf Coast.

Lee originally pitched a two-hour documentary costing $1 million to HBO's Sheila Nevins, who, in an unprecedented step, doubled the running time and budget when the project's scope became clear. Lee interviewed more than one hundred people during nine separate trips to Louisiana and Mississippi, necessitating more money and screen time to render the complicated (and contradictory) feelings, thoughts, and speculations of coastal residents, first responders, local journalists, interested scholars (including Tulane history professor Douglas Brinkley, University of Pennsylvania religious-studies professor Michael Eric Dyson, and Tulane engineering professor Calvin Mackie), elected officials (including New Orleans Mayor C. Ray Nagin and Louisiana Governor Kathleen Babineaux Blanco), and concerned celebrities (including jazz artist Wynton Marsalis, actor Sean Penn, and singer Kanye West). Nevins, in "Spike Lee on Race, Politics and Broken Levees" (Reese Erlich's August 13, 2006, segment for National Public Radio's *All Things Considered*), says, "We're always willing to make a documentary as long as it has to be, but we've never made a four-hour documentary before. And we've never doubled the time."[50] She justifies this decision by invoking Marcel Ophüls's masterful four-hour film about occupied France's Vichy government, 1969's *The Sorrow and the Pity,* as a relevant comparison: "It seemed like [*When the Levees Broke*] needed to be longer and I guess I thought about the great documentaries of the past, like *The Sorrow and the Pity,* and I thought, 'You know, what the heck, this is Spike's *Sorrow and the Pity* and let's go for it.'"[51] Ophüls's documentary combines numerous interviews with participants on all sides of its topic to build a convincing portrait of time, place, and life during Nazi Germany's occupation of wartime France. The disastrous consequences of the Vichy government's collaborationist agenda are Ophüls's most pronounced themes, linking *The Sorrow and the Pity* to *When the Levees Broke.* Lee's film accomplishes a similar objective by indicting governmental officials at the local and state levels for their failure to evacuate New Orleans's most vulnerable residents when the city flooded after Hurricane Katrina's storm surge breached the levees responsible for protecting it, as well as the federal government's failure to offer enough assistance to Gulf Coast residents to help them rebuild their cities, communities, and lives in a timely manner.

When the Levees Broke, therefore, is a political documentary that witheringly criticizes governmental incompetence and bureaucratic intransigence. Lee, for instance, includes Ray Nagin's confirmation that National Hurricane Center Director Max Mayfield personally called the mayor on the evening of Saturday, August 27, 2005 (two days before Katrina's August 29 landfall) to recommend that Nagin issue a mandatory evacuation order for all New Orleans residents, which Nagin did the next day (on Sunday, August 28, 2005). The second hour-long episode (titled "Act II") also demolishes claims that the administration of President George W. Bush did not anticipate Katrina's ferocity by showing footage of Mayfield briefing Bush and his advisors about Katrina's destructive force. Lee, in perhaps his most political decision, directly counters the Bush Administration's vigorous assertions that no one could have predicted the possibility of breached levees. Mayfield, while updating Bush, Federal Emergency Management Agency (FEMA) Director Michael Brown, and other officials about the storm's intensity during an August 28, 2005, videoconference, says, "I don't think anyone can tell you with any confidence right now whether the levees will be topped or not, but that's obviously a very, very grave concern."[52] Commenting that the storm's surge might overwhelm New Orleans's flood-protection system, however, merely implies levee breaches, so Lee interviews experts, including mechanical-engineering professor Calvin Mackie and deputy director of Louisiana State University's Hurricane Center Ivor van Heerden, who blame poorly engineered levees, not Hurricane Katrina itself, for flooding New Orleans. These interviews—along with remarks by history professor Douglas Brinkley (author of *The Great Deluge: Hurricane Katrina, New Orleans, and the Mississippi Gulf Coast*, a massive but problematic history of the event[53]), Garland Robinette (local journalist and host of radio station WWL's *Think Tank* program), and numerous New Orleans residents—emphasize the point that the deluge was not a natural, but rather human-made, disaster.

Lee, therefore, sculpts *When the Levees Broke* to match his political outlook. The director tells Chuleenan Svetvilas, during an interview published in the article "Bamboozled on the Bayou: Spike Lee Profiles Katrina Survivors," that mixing accounts of the storm's everyday survivors with expert testimony permits these victims to "tell the world how this is unprecedented—that the United States government turned its back on half a million of its own citizens on U.S. soil."[54] Lee goes even further in the interview with Kaleen Aftab that concludes *That's My Story and I'm Sticking to It* by stating that working on *When the Levees Broke* forced him to recognize that "class is catching up to race as far as America goes," which suggests a chilling corollary: "If you are a poor person, black, white, Latino, whatever—this government and administration do not have your best interest at heart."[55] This analysis makes Lee's perspective clear: the government's response, particularly at the federal level, was not merely the product of arrogance and incompetence, but instead a glaring confirmation of American racial and economic discrimination. This dispiriting conclusion drives *When the Levees Broke*'s argument that the property destruction, economic turmoil, and lost life caused by the levee breaches were preventable, making the flooding of New Orleans a disaster of epic size, yet human provenance.

In "Spike Lee's Katrina *Requiem* Mixes Anger, Sorrow," Buck Wolf's August 18, 2006, *ABC News* story about the New Orleans premiere of *When the Levees Broke,* Lee calls the anemic official reaction to Katrina's destruction "a criminal act" before asking, "Was it a conspiracy it took five days for the United States government to get here? Was it a conspiracy it took President Bush 12 days to get here?," then answers his own query by saying, "These questions need to be asked"[56] to insinuate his opinion that the Bush administration ignored the plight of working-class and poor Gulf Coast residents.

When the Levees Broke reflects this perspective through harsh comments about federal politicians and bureaucrats in which interviewees castigate the performance of Bush, Vice President Richard Cheney, Secretary of Homeland Security Michael Chertoff, and Secretary of State Condoleezza Rice in the days after the storm's devastation. Early in the second episode ("Act II"), Tulane engineering professor Calvin Mackie rhetorically asks, "How could it be that in a country that's supposedly the richest country in the world, where the 82nd Airborne are prepared to be anywhere in the world in a day and a half, where we were in the region of Sri Lanka when the tsunami hit in less than two days, and here we are, day four, day five, and the federal government still had not made it to New Orleans?" Lee and editor Sam Pollard soon follow this hard-hitting (and unanswered) question with Douglas Brinkley noting that President Bush gave a speech in San Diego, California, on August 30, 2005 (the day after Katrina's landfall) that barely mentioned the storm or its effects before stating, "In the Bush Administration, I mean if you go through each one of them and say, 'Where were you when the Golden Hour came?' Dick Cheney, fly fishing; Karl Rove, nowhere around; you have Chertoff going to Atlanta on a disease-prevention kick. I mean, you see Condoleezza Rice shopping."

These segments offer disheartening responses to Terence Blanchard's comments near the first episode's ("Act I's") conclusion. Blanchard, the New Orleans native who composes *When the Levees Broke*'s fine musical score, muses, "You have to worry about a country that can look at a vast number of mistakes that this administration has made that has directly affected people's lives. You have to worry about a country that can look at all of that and still not see this guy (Bush) for who he is." Blanchard, aware of how radical his opinion may sound, continues by saying, "I know I'm going to get mail, I know I'm going to get ostracized, but you gotta say that because I'm worried about the country," then makes a salient observation: "When you look at an organization like FEMA that was passing the buck about, you know, how to just bring in normal stuff—water, man, water and food—how hard could that be? I still haven't heard any answers about that that convince me that it couldn't have been done differently." Blanchard's puzzlement and understated anger appear genuine, causing the critical viewer to recognize just how carefully Lee structures *When the Levees Broke* to lead to the inescapable conclusion that local, state, and federal authorities did not manifest enough concern or capability to minimize New Orleans's and the Gulf Coast's suffering. The film does not spare Mayor Nagin or Governor Blanco from well-earned criticism, but President Bush receives the most vituperative reproaches. Lee, however, leavens such comments with humor, best seen in the testimony of Robert Rocque, a resident of New Orleans's Lower Ninth Ward whom Lee interviews on a rubble-strewn street. Rocque, ecumenical in his criticism, says, "Ray Nagin, what, what happened? You dropped the ball. Then I would tell, say the same thing to the governor: 'Ms. Blanco, what were you thinking about? You know, what, what the hell was going on?' Then I would ask Bush, 'You out of touch and you don't have a clue.' You know, he's the type person that gives 'C' students all over the world a bad name." This approach—melding expert testimony, man-(and woman)-on-the-street interviews, and gallows humor—allows *When the Levees Broke* to make Lee's case without the director ever verbalizing his opinions onscreen.

Lee, therefore, transfers the narrative, stylistic, and thematic concerns of *4 Little Girls* to the expanded scope of *When the Levees Broke*. He avoids neutrality to argue, forcefully and persuasively, that the human tragedy of Katrina transcends statistics, scholarship, and committee reports, although *When the Levees Broke* cites all three sources to provide context for the alternately enraged, amused, and heartrending testimonies of its profiled survivors. The film, as such, does not separate emotion from intellect, but rather knits them into a resonant, multifocal portrait of a city in crisis. Lee's accomplishment in *When the Levees Broke* both defies and endorses David Denby's *New Yorker* appraisal. "Viewers seeking detailed information about the economy and the politics of New Orleans will have to go elsewhere,"[57] Denby writes in a passage that ignores how Lee melds witness statements with expert analysis (from Douglas Brinkley, Calvin Mackie, Wynton Marsalis, and Ivor van Heerden, among others) to offer a fragmented history of the Crescent City. Denby is closer to the mark when noting, "But anyone hoping to reclaim Katrina emotionally—to experience what the city went through in all its phases of loss, anger, and contempt—needs to see Lee's movie, which is surely the most magnificent and large-souled record of a great American tragedy ever put on film."[58] *When the Levees Broke,* indeed, emerges as an exemplary oral history of Hurricane Katrina's personal and political effects on Gulf Coast residents that rejects the documentary form's supposed objectivity. Assuming otherwise, Jasmine Nichole Cobb and John L. Jackson explain in "They Hate Me," unfairly reduces Lee's documentaries to mere reports of African American experience that offer little critical perspective or insight: "While he is thought to poorly fictionalize (i.e., analyze) blackness, Spike can be allowed to 'document' the sheer fact of blackness (ostensibly for other, more reasoned, minds to analyze)."[59] Cobb and Jackson have little patience for this line of argument because it minimizes Lee's many directorial and editorial interventions, which are inseparable from *When the Levees Broke*'s impact on its viewer. Lee, in other words, does not simply chronicle the angry responses of Katrina's victims, but instead anatomizes the disaster at least as well as other observers have.

Cobb and Jackson draw particular attention to the "documentary flourishes" that characterize *When the Levees Broke* but that Lee's critics miss, correctly pointing out that "his nonfiction films are also very self-consciously and heavy-handedly predicated on Spike's liberal use of fictional conceits—for instance, the stylized backdrops for interviews that feature the natural disaster as background to help construct an almost music video-like scene."[60]

Blanchard's mournful, jazz-infused score is another crucial element that undergirds the film's unsettling effect: pain and sorrow are predominant leitmotifs, both of the documentary's musical and visual iconography. Lee wants the audience to comprehend, not merely acknowledge, the scale of the tragedy that *When the Levees Broke* records. Such aesthetic and editorial choices, therefore, demonstrate why Denby is wrong to comment, "Lee has always possessed a gift for tirade, but this time he doesn't have to write anything; he has only to release the flow" after praising the work of Sam Pollard and the editorial team: "The movie is heroic in the delicacy of its craftsmanship."[61] This contradiction speaks to the problems that Cobb and Jackson identify in dismissing Lee's authorial choices. His visibility may recede in the documentaries, but Lee exerts the same control over *When the Levees Broke* as *Do the Right Thing, Malcolm X,* and *Bamboozled.*

Lee's editorial decisions also guarantee controversy by including the comments of Seventh and Lower Ninth Ward residents who claim that the city's government bombed the levees to preserve wealthier, mostly white areas (such as the French Quarter and the Garden District) at the expense of poorer, mostly African American neighborhoods. Thomas Doherty, in his *Journal of American History* review of *When the Levees Broke,* finds this aspect of Lee's film so troubling that he writes, "the downside of giving voice to the voiceless is the babble, blathering, ranting, and raving" of survivors who repeat unfounded rumors, or "express the word on the street," rather than maintaining "the balance between the emotional and the analytical, the passionate intensity of the victims on the ground and the need for big-picture orientation from above."[62] Lee, however, follows these conspiracy theories with testimony from Calvin Mackie, Douglas Brinkley, local political leader Henry "Junior" Rodriguez, and John M. Barry (author of *Rising Tide: The Great Mississippi Flood of 1927 and How It Changed America*) to offer necessary context that torpedoes the suspicions that the levees were bombed. Mackie says, "I don't believe that the levees were blown. I believe that my people heard explosions when the water gushed though a gaping hole. You know, you have a crack that go [*sic*] from being a crack to a gaping hole, you're going to hear some type of sound. The levees gave." Brinkley notes that similar unproven theories abounded in 1965 after Hurricane Betsy flooded New Orleans, including the Lower Ninth Ward, but that the region's long history of racial segregation and governmental indifference makes such popular beliefs understandable (even if they are unproven). Rodriguez, the president of St. Bernard Parish, says, "I don't think it was blown up, I'll be honest with you. I think what they heard was, it was a possibility they could have heard the snapping of the ropes that hold these barges, the, I almost have to believe they heard the barge hit that concrete wall." Barry offers further historical context by revealing that, after a 1927 flood devastated the entire region, the federal government intentionally dynamited a levee near New Orleans to spare the city from damage. This decision, Barry notes, was not racially motivated, since most of the one million residents (of St. Bernard and Plaquamines parishes) displaced by flood waters were white. This experience, however, has lingered in the memories of Gulf Coast inhabitants for so long that rumors of blown levees receive more weight than they should.

These four interviews make clear that *When the Levees Broke* lends little credence to conspiracy theories about bombed levees. Lee also interviews former New Orleans Mayor Marc Morial, who says that no evidence supports such notions despite their plausibility to longtime residents. Sheila Nevins, in her discussion with NPR's Reese Erlich, defends Lee's decision to include these mistaken accounts: "This may be Spike's film, but it's about their experiences. And you know, he's not reporting, he's not on camera, he doesn't have the responsibility to interpret for them. He only has the responsibility to present for them their disillusionment and maybe their slight inaccuracies."[63] Disillusionment is the sequence's overriding theme and unmistakable mood, with Brinkley and Mackie expressing regret that such beliefs remain convincing to so many people. Lee, despite Nevins's claim to the contrary, interprets the words of those witnesses who believe that the levees were bombed by juxtaposing their comments with expert testimony that, while disagreeing with their conclusions, does not dismiss their concerns. Editor Sam Pollard, during an August 22, 2006, online chat hosted by the *Washington Post,* mentions Lee's commitment to airing a diversity of voices from Katrina's survivors. "I think what Spike wanted to do was get across what the people in the community have been brought up with—this myth that the levees in previous hurricanes have been blown up," Pollard says in reply to a question about whether or not physical evidence (such as bomb fragments) exist. "The reality is," Pollard continues, "they were blown up in 1927 and that's on public record, but those who felt that there was an explosion in Hurricane Betsy of 1965 . . . that was never proven but people tend to still believe that and they carried that over to Hurricane Katrina."[64] Thomas Doherty's conclusion, therefore, is too harsh, for not even the survivors who claim that the levees were bombed babble, blather, rant, or rave. Instead, they recount their sincerely held beliefs for the viewer's consideration. *When the Levees Broke* gives them a hearing, but, in the end, refuses to sanction their mistaken impressions.[65]

This approach demonstrates Lee's cleverness as a documentarian. He allows viewers to determine their own conclusions, yet leads them to these judgments by skillfully arranging all the elements: the interviews, the on-screen images, the musical score, and the presented information. Lee's selectivity is equally important, for what he chooses not to include is just as significant as what he shows. *When the Levees Broke,* for instance, includes no interviews with Bush administration officials defending themselves. Lee, during media appearances conducted at the time of the documentary's 2006 broadcast and in his DVD audio commentary, says that these individuals refused to participate. He tells Gannett News Service reporter Ana Radelat (in her August 14, 2006, article "Spike Lee Showcases Heartbreak, Spirit of

New Orleans") that "nobody wanted to get on camera with me,"[66] saying that George W. Bush, Michael Chertoff, and Condoleezza Rice all declined interviews. Lee's reputation as a fierce critic of Bush's presidency may explain their hesitance, making *When the Levees Broke* a documentary unafraid of scathing political commentary guaranteed to rankle some viewers' sensibilities. Lee, although fair in his assessments of the local, state, and federal officials involved in Hurricane Katrina, most forcefully rebukes the federal authorities whom he believes abandoned New Orleans and the Gulf Coast in the days after the storm's landfall.

This censure continues in Lee's 2010 sequel, *If God Is Willing and Da Creek Don't Rise,* a sprawling, four-hour documentary that tracks the Gulf Coast's recovery efforts by revisiting many people first interviewed in *When the Levees Broke.* It also examines the ruinous 7.0 earthquake that struck Haiti on January 12, 2010, and explores the American federal government's response to April 20, 2010's *Deepwater Horizon* explosion, which released millions of barrels of crude oil into the Gulf of Mexico. This last event occupies most of *If God Is Willing*'s final hour, including numerous comments from Louisiana residents who roundly criticize President Barack Obama's handling of this situation. Although Lee is a vocal supporter of Obama's administration, many interviewees scorn the president's timidity concerning British Petroleum (BP)—the oil corporation most directly responsible for the explosion and resulting spill—and Transocean Ltd., the drilling contractor that leased the *Deepwater Horizon* oil rig to BP. Obama's failure to challenge BP's and Transocean's mismanagement more forcefully in the week after the massive explosion killed eleven oil-rig workers, along with Obama's contradictory stance about regulating offshore oil drilling, generates considerable disapproval.

Although Obama's response to the spill emerges as more involved and more competent than Bush's handling of Katrina, Lee configures the comments made during *If God Is Willing*'s final hour to reflect his perspective that Obama was not as effective as he should have been. During his September 2010 interview with *GQ* magazine's Mark Healy, Lee says, "The Gulf Coast states—Louisiana, Mississippi, Alabama—have historically been some of the poorest states, so they have very little political power, and Big Oil and Gas is [*sic*] coming in plundering. If this oil spill had reached the Hamptons, Martha's Vineyard, Cape Cod, that shit would have been fixed. It's this thing called environmental racism" before directly indicting Obama: "Before this catastrophe, our president was in favor of offshore drilling. And when this thing happened, he backtracked real quick. I don't know why Obama ever trusted these BP guys! They would lie to their mothers."[67] Lee does not stop here: "The thing we don't talk about is that eleven Americans lost their lives and it took seven weeks to invite their families to the White House. I'm not trying to bash my man, but that's a long time."[68] *If God Is Willing* includes these points, but adopts the same approach as *4 Little Girls* and *When the*

Levees Broke by having other people, rather than Lee, make arguments that he endorses, supervises, shapes, and constructs. It offers strong support for Cobb and Jackson's "They Hate Me" thesis that Lee authors his documentaries as vigorously as his movies, endorsing Cobb and Jackson's insight that "taken-for-granted realness dissolves despite the suggestion of objectivity based in documentary filmmaking."[69]

Lee's career as a documentarian, therefore, complements his career as a fiction filmmaker, extends his skills as a narrative storyteller, and supplements his status as a social commentator. Lee's documentaries freely violate the objectivity that some viewers assume characterize the genre, making these films into political statements rather than aloof, detached, and neutral analyses of important events. By doing so, Lee joins a cadre of documentarians who use the form not merely as an educational tool, but as an advocacy platform to refute conventional understandings of historical events, political policies, cultural practices, and social injustices. This tradition, which includes Henry Hampton, Werner Herzog, Lisa F. Jackson, Eugene Jarecki, Barbara Kopple, Michael Moore, Errol Morris, and Lourdes Portillo, gives Lee a podium from which to criticize his nation's historical and political excesses that, at first blush, may seem more respectable, more reserved, and more solemn than his fictional movies. These documentaries, however, are integral to the thematic, generic, and formal diversity that Lee has always pursued, existing on a cinematic continuum that reinforces his status as a politically involved filmmaker unafraid to instruct, to discomfit, and, when necessary, to infuriate his audiences. All Lee's documentaries are worthy efforts, but *4 Little Girls, When the Levees Broke: A Requiem in Four Acts,* and *If God Is Willing and Da Creek Don't Rise* are standout contributions that bear sustained, repeated, and critical viewing. They will not please everyone, which is hardly surprising given Lee's controversial reputation, but their acceptance as three of his best films highlights Lee's complicated reception by cinematic audiences. These three documentaries, indeed, epitomize Lee's protean interests, shifting persona, filmmaking talents, and personal biases as well as any other movies that he has directed. They are not hurried additions or unstudied afterthoughts to Lee's decades-long career, but rather aesthetic acts that reinvent American history as a tragedy of the commons, as a comedy of errors, and, especially, as the active creation of complicated, flawed, and feeling human beings.

Crime and Punishment

OPEN CASES

Spike Lee's enduring fascination with urban injustice, political inequality, and social commentary makes crime a significant concern of his movies. Lee, however, has not earned the reputation of genre filmmaker despite directing many projects that involve criminal acts, plots, and themes, perhaps because crime is never a Spike Lee joint's exclusive focus. Lee, indeed, prefers to examine the motives and consequences of criminality rather than romanticizing the violence that characterizes the gangster, heist, and serial-killer movies that Hollywood regularly releases, even staking an oppositional stance with his forays into crime cinema. Lee, for instance, hoped that his 1995 adaptation of Richard Price's *Clockers* would reduce, if not altogether end, the "black gangsta, hip-hop, shoot-'em-up genre"[1] that became popular after Mario Van Peebles's 1991 film *New Jack City*. Lee went so far as to tell *Face* magazine's Jonathan Bernstein, "It was always our intention that if we succeeded with this film, that this might be the final nail in the coffin and African American filmmakers would try telling new stories,"[2] but failed in his effort, even admitting this comment's naïveté in his autobiography, *That's My Story and I'm Sticking to It*.[3]

Lee's movies, however, are rarely immature ventures into crime despite criticisms to the contrary. His master's thesis film for New York University's Tisch School of the Arts, *Joe's Bed-Stuy Barbershop: We Cut Heads* (1983), tells the story of Zachariah "Zack" Homer (Monty Ross), who becomes manager of the titular barbershop when his partner, Joe Ballard (Horace Long), is killed by gangster Nicholas Lovejoy (Tommy Redmond Hicks) for skimming profits from the numbers racket that Lovejoy's gang, using the shop as a convenient front, runs in Brooklyn. Lovejoy, referred to as an "investor" in Ballard's shop, offers Zack the same "deal," but Zack wishes to run a legitimate business. Even so, he must decide whether or not to accept Lovejoy's proposal when profits dwindle. Lee describes this student production's genesis in *That's My Story*, saying, "Numbers-running has always been a key part of the African American community, so we wanted to do a semi-gangster film that takes place in a barbershop."[4] Lee sees the criminal aspects of *Joe's Bed-Study Barbershop* as culturally meaningful, even crucial, to black Brooklyn life, conceiving the movie as a "semi-gangster film" that uses crime as the backdrop for a narrative where the barbershop's customers converse, joke about, and discuss their daily lives. This depiction seems so authentic that author, filmmaker, and *Village Voice* columnist Nelson George, watching the movie on PBS, "saw a vision of black Brooklyn as sweet and salty as the one I know."[5]

Lee also addresses the inception of *Joe's Bed-Stuy Barbershop* in the interview with George (conducted on November 21, 1986) that opens *Spike Lee's Gotta Have It: Inside Guerrilla Filmmaking* (the companion publication to *She's Gotta Have It*), saying that setting a film about Lovejoy's numbers-running operation in a black barbershop not only allows him to use crime as a window into the communal aspects of African American life but also as a method of bringing black concerns and contexts to the gangster film, a genre that traditionally focuses on ethnic white characters by relegating African Americans to subsidiary roles (if they appear at all).[6] George, in his foreword to *Spike Lee's Gotta Have It,* finds pertinent connections between Lee's approach to black Brooklyn in *Joe's Bed-Stuy Barbershop* and Martin Scorsese's depiction of Italian American New Yorkers in his early movies due to the cinematic intimacy that both directors evoke in their respective ethnic enclaves.[7] Citing Scorsese's *Mean Streets* (1973) as a relevant precursor to *Joe's Bed-Stuy Barbershop*, George writes, "The Italian-American filmmaker lets us see more than we probably wanted to about Manhattan's Little Italy. Across the Manhattan Bridge, Lee makes one see and feel black Brooklyn with the same tenderness."[8] This affection, along with Lee's talent at capturing what George calls "the texture of life,"[9] informs critical viewers that crime, from the beginning of Lee's career, offers useful narrative, thematic, and generic models to examine the social, cultural, and economic dislocations of American politics.

Crime, therefore, serves as subtext in some Lee films, as subplot in others, and as significant in yet others. *She's Gotta Have It* only references wrongdoing when Greer Childs (John Canada Terrell) condescendingly suggests that Mars Blackmon (Spike Lee) is a low-class thug, *School Daze* obliquely considers the connection between crime and poverty when Dap Dunlap (Larry Fishburne) and his friends argue with working-class black men at a Kentucky Fried Chicken franchise near their Atlanta college campus, and *Do the Right Thing* concludes with an act of violence—the murder of Radio Raheem (Bill Nunn)—that provokes the destruction of Sal's Famous Pizzeria. *Mo' Better Blues* sees Lee's character of Giant, manager for the Bleek Gilliam Quintet jazz combo, accrue so many gambling debts that two loan sharks from whom he borrows money beat him nearly to death. *Jungle Fever* finds Flipper Purify (Wesley Snipes) dealing with the problems created by his brother Gator's

(Samuel L. Jackson) crack addiction, causing Flipper to search a hellish crack house for Gator before their father, the Good Reverend Doctor Purify (Ossie Davis), shoots Gator dead. Flipper's lover, Angela Tucci (Annabella Sciorra), is also attacked by her father, Mike (Frank Vincent), in a scene of remarkable domestic violence.

References to crime in Lee's filmography do not end here. *Malcolm X* devotes one third of its running time to Malcolm Little's criminal enterprises in Boston and Harlem, *Crooklyn* includes as minor characters two glue sniffers who are also petty thieves, and *Girl 6* sees its phone-sex-operator protagonist, Judy (Theresa Randle), threatened with physical harm by an unstable, irate caller (Michael Imperioli). In *Get on the Bus,* the character of Gary (Roger Guenveur Smith), a police officer, threatens to arrest Jamal (Gabriel Casseus), an orthodox Muslim, when Jamal recalls committing murder as a young member of the Bloods street gang. *He Got Game* tracks convicted murderer Jake Shuttlesworth (Denzel Washington) in his bid for early parole, *Bamboozled* concludes after television producer Pierre Delacroix (Damon Wayans) is accidentally shot by his assistant, Sloan Hopkins (Jada Pinkett-Smith), *25th Hour* chronicles the events of its drug-dealing protagonist Monty Brogan's (Edward Norton) final day before entering prison, and *She Hate Me* begins with protagonist Jack Armstrong (Anthony Mackie) blowing the whistle on corporate illegalities committed by his employer, the pharmaceutical corporation Progeia.

Other Lee films make crime and criminals their central subject. The documentary *4 Little Girls* dissects the causes and effects of an actual crime: the September 1963 bombing of Birmingham, Alabama's Sixteenth Street Baptist Church. *Clockers,* despite failing to prevent further hood films (or black gangster films, in Lee's words) from being produced, masterfully sketches the inner conflicts that Strike Dunham (Mekhi Phifer) endures while working as a low-level drug runner who discovers that his brother, Victor Dunham (Isaiah Washington), guns down a rival gang member. This movie's attention to Strike's circumscribed existence and his relentless interrogations by homicide detective Rocco Klein (Harvey Keitel) create a fascinating, if saturnine, atmosphere that surveys the social, cultural, and economic fabric of inner-city Brooklyn. Lee's four-hour documentary *When the Levees Broke: A Requiem in Four Acts* and its successor, *If God Is Willing and Da Creek Don't Rise,* chronicle the context, background, and history of Hurricane Katrina's and the *Deepwater Horizon* oil spill's effects on the residents of America's Gulf Coast. Lee, indeed, once labeled the bungled response of federal officials (particularly members of President George W. Bush's administration) to Hurricane Katrina's devastation as a "criminal act"[10] to demonstrate the severity of this disaster.

Lee also deals with crime and its consequences in notable television projects. He directed the pilot episode of Ian Biederman's series *Shark* (2006–2008), which tells the story of wealthy defense attorney Sebastian Stark (James Woods) becoming so disillusioned with his job that he joins the Los Angeles County District Attorney's office as chief of the newly created High Profile Crimes Unit. This episode, offered to Lee by producer Brian Grazer after Lee successfully directed Imagine Entertainment's 2006 heist film *Inside Man,* recalls Lee's work on *Sucker Free City* (2004), a telefilm financed and broadcast by the pay-cable network Showtime that Lee originally shot as the pilot for a television series about San Francisco street gangs. Although Showtime failed to approve this project for weekly production, *Sucker Free City* first brought Lee into contact with Anthony Mackie, whose performance so impressed Lee that he offered the actor the lead role in *She Hate Me.* Lee also directed the first and final episodes of the Nickelodeon Network's[11] *Miracle's Boys,* a 2005 six-part miniseries produced by Tonya Lewis Lee and based on Jacqueline Woodson's 2000 novel (of the same title), that dramatizes the lives of three orphaned brothers. The middle brother, Charlie (Sean Nelson), returns home from the Rahway Home for Boys, a juvenile correctional facility where he was incarcerated for armed robbery, not long before the series begins. One of *Miracle's Boys* major plotlines dramatizes Charlie's difficult adjustment to life as a teenage ex-convict.

Lee, as the foregoing summary reveals, is no stranger to crime stories. Good as many of them are, two projects in particular—1999's *Summer of Sam* and 2006's *Inside Man*—are exemplary films that use criminal acts as the launching point for incisive economic, cultural, and social commentary. *Summer of Sam* examines how the murders committed by David Berkowitz— the .44 Caliber Killer, also known as the Son of Sam—during the summer of 1977 affect the lives of Italian American residents in the Bronx's Throggs Neck and Country Club sections. Berkowitz's rampage, which kills six people and wounds seven more, exacerbates the parochial tendencies and nativist impulses of many neighborhood characters to the point that local mobster Luigi (Ben Gazzara) commands his associates to protect the neighborhood's residents by roughing up people who, because they live unconventional lives, are suspected of being the Son of Sam. Berkowitz (Michael Badalucco) is a minor character in this film, which focuses on the experiences of four protagonists: Vinny (John Leguizamo), a philandering hairdresser, his wife Dionna (Mira Sorvino), his friend Ritchie (Adrien Brody), and Ruby (Jennifer Esposito), a liberated local woman who becomes Ritchie's lover.

Ritchie's ambiguous sexuality, growing fascination with punk-rock music, and refusal to conform to neighborhood standards (of dress, speech, and behavior) lead other characters, including Vinny, to wonder whether or not he (Ritchie) is the Son of Sam. The film culminates with Ritchie being beaten by neighborhood toughs Joey T. (Michael Rispoli), Brian (Ken Garito), Anthony (Al Palagonia), and Woodstock (Saverio Guerra) just as the police arrest Berkowitz, the actual killer. *Summer of Sam,* however, exceeds this summary by depicting the Throggs Neck neighborhood as a microcosm not only of the Bronx but also of New York City during the summer of 1977. The many notable events that *Summer of Sam* weaves into its narrative produce a busy movie that, in addition to Berkowitz's shooting spree, includes the notoriously hot temperatures that afflicted the city, the blackout and consequent looting that occurred on July 13 and 14, 1977, the growing influence of punk-rock music on young white adults, the popularity of disco, the easy availability of narcotics, the underground subculture of pornography, and the sexual experimentation associated with clubs like Studio 54 and Plato's Retreat. *Summer of Sam*, in other words, employs the Son of Sam killings to provide narrative context for its almost sociological exploration of ethnic white New Yorkers at a moment of tremendous fear.

Just as *Summer of Sam* rewrites the serial-killer drama's conventions, *Inside Man* transforms the heist film into a complicated commentary about capitalism's immoral excesses. This movie sees Dalton Russell (Clive Owen) execute what he calls "the perfect bank robbery"[12] by taking hostages whom he forces to don masks and clothing identical to what Russell and his three accomplices wear. NYPD detective Keith Frazier (Denzel Washington) attempts to negotiate the hostages' freedom, but soon realizes that Russell does not intend to pursue a simple robbery. The bank's owner and chairman, Arthur Case (Christopher Plummer), hires influential Manhattan power broker Madeleine White (Jodie Foster) to retrieve the contents of a safe-deposit box that, if made public, would reveal Case's status as a war criminal who first became wealthy by collaborating with the Nazis to steal the life savings and possessions of Holocaust victims. White, securing permission from New York City's unnamed mayor (Peter Kybart) to interfere with Frazier's investigation, persuades the detective to allow her to talk with Russell, who tells her (as he tells the audience during the voiceover confession that ends *Inside Man*) that, apart from enriching himself, he wishes to expose Case's sordid past because "it's not worth much if you can't face yourself in the mirror. Respect is the ultimate currency." The police eventually storm the bank, arresting hostages and perpetrators alike, but cannot distinguish them from one another. Frazier, however, discovers while examining the bank's books that no record of safe-deposit box #392 exists. Upon opening it, Frazier finds a diamond ring that uncovers Case's collaborationist past. White again intervenes, asking the newly promoted Frazier to drop his investigation, but Frazier refuses. Case, when later confronted by White, admits that the box contained not only incriminating documents but also bags of diamonds that he stole from a Parisian Jewish friend whom Case later betrayed to the Nazis. The film concludes with Dalton Russell's monologue, which reveals that he hid behind a false wall built by his partners in the bank's supply room. Russell leaves this cubbyhole after one week, taking the documents and diamonds with him. Bumping into Frazier while exiting the bank, Russell slips a loose diamond into Frazier's pocket. The detective later interrupts Madeleine White's lunch with the mayor to urge her to contact the U.S. State Department to report Case's war crimes, and, in the movie's final scene, finds

Russell's diamond in his pocket. *Inside Man,* therefore, concludes with the master criminal getting away with his crime.

Inside Man, as this synopsis makes clear, revises the heist film's conventions to probe issues far more serious than whether or not Russell's caper will work, just as *Summer of Sam* modifies the serial-killer movie's parameters to examine ideas more complicated than whether or not law enforcement's manhunt for Berkowitz will succeed. Lee, in both films, deploys well-known cinematic genres to invigorate his penchant for social commentary despite not conceiving either film's initial screenplay. Co-writers Victor Colicchio and Michael Imperioli first approached Lee with their *Summer of Sam* screenplay (then titled *Anarchy in the Bronx*) at the 1996 premiere of *Girl 6,* while Imagine Entertainment purchased Russell Gewirtz's *Inside Man* screenplay (originally titled *The Inside Man*) in 2002 for Ron Howard to direct. Lee rewrote portions of *Summer of Sam*'s screenplay and made additions to *Inside Man*'s script to reflect New York City's diverse populace and the parochialism endemic to certain neighborhoods. Both movies, as such, employ crime to examine New York's economic, ethnic, and cultural tensions in some detail, becoming major additions to Lee's filmography.

NEW YORK STATE OF MIND

Summer of Sam continues Lee's portraiture of New York City experiences, neighborhoods, and residents, although R. Barton Palmer argues in his essay "Monsters and Moralism in *Summer of Sam*" that this movie marks "a significant departure from Lee's previous films in its focus on the cultural dynamics of an all-white community."[13] This claim acknowledges how the movie marginalizes African American characters in favor of Italian Americans, but ignores how *Do the Right Thing, Jungle Fever,* and *Summer of Sam* form a loose trilogy that examines Italian American concerns, characters, and communities. These frequently unflattering depictions draw criticism about their authenticity, best demonstrated by Andrew Sarris's caustic comment in his *New York Observer* review of *Summer of Sam:* "I hate to use the reverse racist card on the self-righteous Mr. Lee, but if an Italian-American director caricatured and defamed African-American characters in Bed-Stuy as Mr. Lee demonizes Italian-Americans here, we'd never hear the end of it."[14] Yet this perhaps predictable response does little to diminish *Summer of Sam*'s visual inventiveness, masterful editing, and narrative power. Cast members Ben Gazzara and Michael Badalucco defended the film to the *Guardian* newspaper soon after its release, with Gazzara saying, "This is an accurate portrayal of a certain class of Italian-Americans" and Badalucco commenting, "These kind of characters do exist."[15]

Although actors endorsing their latest project may be unsurprising, Kaleem Aftab, in *That's My Story and I'm Sticking to It,* calls media reports touting the film as the first Spike Lee joint without a predominantly black cast to be "one-dimensional pocketbooking"[16] of Lee's previous films that diminishes *Summer of Sam*'s connections to the director's earlier movies. *Do the Right Thing*, for instance, portrays Sal, Pino, and Vito as alternately tolerant and provincial residents of Bensonhurst who nonetheless work in Bedford-Stuyvesant, maintaining an outpost of what Sal calls "American Italians" in a place whose demographic shift toward African American, Asian, and Latino residents makes Sal and his sons minorities in a community where they were once members of the dominant ethnic and racial group. *Jungle Fever* demonstrates how Angela Tucci transcends her family's racist thinking, both by dating Flipper Purify and by recognizing Flipper's objections to biracial children as essentialist, even if she cannot finally escape Bensonhurst. Lee, moreover, does not exclude white characters from his films, so concerns about parochialism's dangers infuse *Summer of Sam* just as they do his previous movies.

Palmer comments that "reviewers and audiences saw *Sam* as ethnographic reportage" after noting that it "conveys, often vividly, something of the claustrophobic homeliness of an inward-looking metropolitan urban enclave."[17] Actor Delroy Lindo, conducting a 1999 Independent Film Channel interview with Lee, says, "This is an encyclopedia"[18] when discussing *Summer of Sam*'s numerous plots, characters, and events, while Lee himself, during a 1999 interview with *American Cinematographer*'s Stephen Pizzello, says that *Summer of Sam* "is not specifically an African American story, it's more of a story about New York as a whole. Most of my films have been set in New York, so I felt more at ease telling this particular story"[19] despite the fact that Lee at first intended only to produce the film.[20] Dan Flory establishes the clearest connections between *Summer of Sam* and Lee's earlier work in "Race and Black American *Film Noir: Summer of Sam* as Lynching Parable" to illustrate how the movie "offers a subtle and oblique form of racial analysis, for on the surface the narrative is not about race at all" by integrating film noir's fascination with urban criminality to underscore *Summer of Sam*'s "suspicion of difference through *noir* narrative, thereby transforming this Bronx tale into a parable for racial lynching."[21] Flory's perceptive essay understands how crime radiates throughout the film, but not for exploitative or sensationalist reasons. *Summer of Sam*'s scenes of "white neighborhood gangs roving the streets with baseball bats looking to beat up anyone who might not 'belong' there and individuals who look different being refused service at diners while police officials collude with vigilantism and mob hysteria" make, for Flory, "the allusions to the history of Black lynchings . . . striking."[22] The Son of Sam's murders, therefore, become a pretext for dramatizing the terror that ethnic white people (particularly men) felt during the summer of 1977. *Summer of Sam*, in Flory's view, allegorizes racial tensions by exposing the hazards of scapegoating those neighborhood residents who violate community norms. Ritchie, by looking, speaking, and acting differently after embracing punk attitudes and clothing, assumes the traditional position of a black man who endures insults, threats, and physical violence for challenging his neighbors' provincial attitudes. Ritchie's difference marks him as a foreign Other who must be expelled to preserve the neighborhood's stultifying, backward, and homogenous character.

Lewis R. Gordon's book *Bad Faith and Antiblack Racism* supports Flory's analysis by observing that, in racial lynching, "the victim is anonymous except insofar as he can be identified as a member of a hated *group*."[23] Ritchie's friends, including Vinny, frequently say that they do not know him despite having grown up together, thereby erasing Ritchie's identity in favor of group labels (Flory lists "cult member, punk rocker, degenerate," as well as "fag" and "freak"[24]). These terms distance Ritchie from his lifelong acquaintances in a process that recapitulates the cultural workings of white supremacy. Flory, taking cues from Gordon, finds that "the *racial* dimension of this human diminution reveals itself through the ways in which the power relations of such symbolic persecutions mimic those of white privilege. The anonymous outsider moves into the subject position of being Black, while the enraged mob as an instrument of retribution becomes empowered as white."[25] Flory reveals how *Summer of Sam* symbolically "races" Ritchie as a black man in a film that includes few African American characters, although John Jeffries, the television reporter played by Spike Lee, includes black voices in a live segment he conducts in Bedford-Stuyvesant irreverently titled "A Darker Perspective." Jeffries asks several black Brooklyn residents for their thoughts about the Son of Sam killings, prompting a woman named Cassandra Buchanan (Susan Batson) to respond, "I thank God that it is a *white* man that kills all of those *white* people, because if it were a *black* man who kills all of those *white* people, there would be the biggest race riot right here in New York City."[26] This comment suggests that the racial animosity percolating within the city might well explode into mob hysteria, while Buchanan's fear that white New Yorkers would violently persecute black New Yorkers if the Son of Sam were an African American killer recalls the lynchings and other forms of racial violence that black communities endured in earlier decades. Flory finds Jeffries's "A Darker Perspective"—added by Lee to the film's original screenplay—to be further evidence of *Summer of Sam*'s symbolic racism: "Such commentary by Black New York City residents enlists them as a Greek chorus whose remarks illuminate the panic and paranoia felt by whites in the city, who perhaps for the first time begin to acquire a sense of the fear and stress that is inextricably linked to the normal lives of persons of color in America."[27] The latent, palpable, and unmistakable threat of violence that undergirds the film "further alludes," Flory states, "to historical Black sentiments regarding lynching and everyday life."[28] The fact that Lee added all scenes with John Jeffries to Victor Colicchio and Michael Imperioli's screenplay buttresses this point,[29] as well as Flory's larger argument that Lee's choice to focus on Caucasian protagonists in *Summer of Sam* does not, as some viewers might suspect, renounce or dilute his fictional exploration of New York City's racial complexities.

R. Barton Palmer, however, considers Flory's perspective difficult to countenance, primarily because, "from the beginning, *Sam* was a personal project" for Lee, who "was enthusiastic about the script and devoted considerable time and energy to its modification and improvement."[30] More to the point, Palmer finds it "hard to imagine that if the never-reticent Lee were eager to make a film about lynching he would have chosen to approach it in such an oblique and indirect fashion that soft-pedals its horrific, shameful nature,"[31] noting that Lee holds little back when presenting extralegal violence against African American characters in *Malcolm X* and that "within the context of Lee's career at this point, it certainly would have been understandable if he had taken on the lynching of blacks, which was then a prominent topic of discussion in American culture as a collection of 'memorial' postcards and photographs of lynchings was making the rounds of American museums,"[32] eventually to be published as the book *Without Sanctuary: Lynching Photography in America*.[33] Palmer, in other words, sees efforts by Flory and other scholars to discover racial subtexts in *Summer of Sam* as ham-fisted attempts to label Lee as little more than a black filmmaker whose movies must deal with African American characters, communities, and issues even when their surface narratives do not reference or concern black themes. Lee seems to agree with this perspective in *That's My Story and I'm Sticking to It* when he tells Kaleem Aftab that white journalists have asked him "'How do you direct white actors?' 'Very carefully. . . .' I mean, it is crazy."[34]

Lee's discomfort with pigeonholing himself as an African American rather than American director reflects his creative independence, as well as the tendencies of both Hollywood studios and film observers (whether reviewers, critics, or scholars) to essentialize his work as naturally dramatizing black lives. Lee refuses to confine his movies to African American settings, symbols, and themes (at least after *She's Gotta Have It* and *School Daze*), meaning that their predominantly black casts should not provoke reductive judgments about Lee's limited subject matter if similar assessments are not applied to white directors (such as Steven Spielberg), whose predominantly white casts are rarely thought to constrain their cinematic range (especially considering that Spielberg's decision to direct the 1985 film adaptation of Alice Walker's 1982 novel *The Color Purple* was lauded as an example of Hollywood's enlightened, behind-the-scenes colorblindness). Barry Alexander Brown, the editor of *Summer of Sam* and many other Spike Lee joints, notes the hypocrisy of ignoring Lee's multiracial casts when Caucasian directors typically include few or no non-white characters in their movies, telling Kaleem Aftab in *That's My Story and I'm Sticking to It* that 299 of the 300 films Hollywood releases each year feature white protagonists: "Do you ever turn to one of the 299 other directors and say, 'When are you going to put a black person in? When are you going to put an Asian in? Why aren't you doing that?'"[35] Such comments interrogate the unthinking white essentialism (if not white supremacy) that typifies American film culture, particularly the unstated presumption that white characters, communities, and concerns are the ordinary, even obvious, subjects of American movies. Black cinema, from this perspective, is an outlier. If Lee is this cinema's foremost proponent, then his venture into "broader" territory with *Summer of Sam* becomes notable for its unusual focus on white rather than black characters. Palmer wishes to reverse this presumption by emphasizing its basic unfairness, its logical inconsistency, and its regressive politics.

These objections are intelligent, important, and insistent when dealing with Lee's cinematic diversity (whether of cast, genre, or narrative and visual style). Yet such observations neither weaken nor deny Dan Flory's argument about how *Summer of Sam* indirectly encodes lynching into its complex story about Italian American protagonists. Palmer thinks that "the kind of reading that Flory proposes offers a simplistic account of Lee's engagement with the film's social materials" because *Summer of Sam*, "with some subtlety . . . actually shows that evil cannot be located only in the would-be perpetrators of extralegal violence and in the psychopath who is their unintentional inspiration."[36] Lee's social commentary in *Summer of Sam* avoids blaming any single group or individual (including David Berkowitz) for the cultural instability that the film evokes, meaning that, as Palmer writes, "these breakdowns in sanity, emotional restraint, humaneness, and respect for the social order are revealed not as deviations but as symptomatic, even exemplary."[37] Palmer, however, errs when claiming, "It is the *decline* of the social order itself in an era of rapidly changing values that is the film's main subject: the disordering that manifests itself in the lives of individual characters as well as in the widespread looting and unrest occasioned by the July blackout."[38] *Summer of Sam*, contrary to Palmer's declaration, does not track the deterioration of social harmony so much as it illustrates how the hysteria overtaking New York City results from the festering racial, cultural, ethnic, and economic tensions that have always existed, but that have also gone unacknowledged for so long that residents—whether in Brooklyn, the Bronx, or Manhattan—convince themselves that they inhabit a peaceful metropolis when, in fact, the opposite is true. Social order, in *Summer of Sam*, becomes a civilizational veneer that Berkowitz's rampage quickly destroys. Palmer writes, "In *Sam*, the political filmmaker par excellence shows himself to be a moralist as well,"[39] but Lee does not condemn his characters for their drug use, sexual license, or, in Ritchie's case, alternative beliefs. The movie instead suggests that the long-held parochial and patriarchal attitudes of characters like Vinny, Luigi, and Joey T. are unable to weather the evolving social mosaic that *Summer of Sam* so deftly displays. Rather than railing against what, from a moralistic vantage point, are behavioral excesses, *Summer of Sam* criticizes provincial thinking.

Berkowitz's crimes, therefore, provide the backdrop for Lee to dissect the psychology of urban terror in *Summer of Sam*. Palmer properly states that Berkowitz "is never located precisely within the social space the film constructs"[40] but instead operates as a man driven insane by inner compulsions that he externalizes as Harvey the Dog, who (voiced by John Turturro) commands Berkowitz to kill. Palmer, however, erroneously claims that *Summer of Sam* "does not treat the murders and their aftermath from a sociopolitical perspective."[41] The movie may not see its characters discuss the larger reasons for scapegoating Ritchie and other unconventional Bronx residents, but it offers an impressive cross-section of their lives to imply that ethnic, geographical, and economic insularity produces the vigilantism perpetuated by Berkowitz, the mobster Luigi, and the police detectives who, early in *Summer of Sam,* enlist Luigi's assistance in finding the killer. This institutional corruption not only underscores the halting and rarely seen official investigation into Berkowitz's murders but also authorizes Luigi to pursue the rough justice that Joey T. and his gang impose on the neighborhood's residents, even drawing Vinny into their machinations to identify Ritchie as the true murderer. Palmer justifies his conclusion by citing Lee's comment to *All Movie Guide*'s Prairie Miller that "this film is not about David Berkowitz. It's not about Son of Sam. This film is about his evil energy that affected eight million New Yorkers,"[42] yet ignores Lee's later statements in the same interview, especially his response to the question "What is the movie suggesting about human anxiety against outsiders?": "I think that anybody, if you have that village mentality and somebody comes in as an outsider or is deemed strange, you're going to get treated like that."[43] This mentality results from complex, intersecting social factors that *Summer of Sam,* thanks to its literate screenplay and excellent cast, tracks for more than two hours.

The film, therefore, depicts Berkowitz's crime spree as merely one aspect of a lurid summer that reveals New York City's many conflicts, tensions, and flashpoints. Lee directs an unsparing portrait of urban insecurity that largely succeeds in its aims to disconcert the audience's preconceptions about the summer of 1977. *Summer of Sam,* neither a thriller nor a whodunit, is a crime film that twists generic conventions to produce an engrossing movie. The punishments meted out by *Summer of Sam*'s characters may do nothing to stop David Berkowitz's shooting spree, but they accentuate the cultural ennui that pervades the characters' lives, neighborhood, and city. Injustice remains, reminding viewers that, by refusing the comforting conclusion for which they may yearn, Lee's outlook remains more ambiguous and more sophisticated than the easy seductions of standard crime cinema. He accomplishes the same goal seven years later, in the project that, to date, is the most financially successful movie of Lee's career: *Inside Man.*

BANK SHOTS

Inside Man's impressive $185-million box-office performance[44] demonstrates that Lee, while capable of blockbuster success, neither chases nor values it as his primary artistic achievement. Some observers, however, comment that Universal Pictures obscured Lee's participation in the movie to increase

Inside Man's profitability. Vince Leo's favorable *Qwipster* review, for instance, concludes by saying, "The trailers and ads for *Inside Man* make little or no mention of Lee's involvement, probably because at this point in his career, you are either a Lee fan or you have learned to ignore his ambitious but sometimes overbearing output."[45] David A. Gerstner, in his fine essay "De Profundis: A Love Letter from the Inside Man," expands this idea by writing, "*Inside Man* buried the risk of low ticket sales by, well, burying the director's name and, for the most part, his face. From the studio's perspective, marginalizing Lee's presence and involvement served well their bottom line. Certainly Lee's association with a project is a blessing and a curse, since a sharp division cuts audiences' response to his films."[46] This assessment is accurate given how, as Leo notes, *Inside Man*'s trailer downplays Lee's connection by advertising the movie more on the strength of its superstar actors (particularly Denzel Washington) rather than its director, whose credit appears near the spot's end, rather than foregrounding Lee's presence as trailers for *Do the Right Thing, Malcolm X, Girl 6*, and *Get on the Bus* do.

Gerstner finds this decision reasonable given Lee's contentious reputation: "Selling *Inside Man* more as a star vehicle (Denzel Washington, Clive Owens [*sic*], Jodie Foster) makes institutional sense given the uneasy if not vituperative response to the mere mention of Lee's name."[47] Gerstner sees this development as part of Hollywood studios' move to strip recognizable directors of their auteur status (or the "filmmaker-as-artist"[48] mystique that Gerstner's article interrogates) to avoid controversial receptions by hostile audiences whose disagreements with a director's social, political, or religious stances may decrease a movie's financial performance. Gerstner writes that, despite the ongoing corporatization of Hollywood studios that undergirds this process, one major factor in the "de-auteuring phenomenon" is that "auteurs associated with urban subject matter, over-intellectualized or contemplative narrative style, personal scandal, or political interests viewed as discomfiting to 'mainstream audiences' are among those de-auteured."[49] That Lee fulfills most, if not all, these criteria suggests to Gerstner that emphasizing Lee's contribution to *Inside Man* might depress ticket sales. Highlighting the movie's cast and its heist-film genre, therefore, became Universal Pictures's principal marketing strategy for *Inside Man*.

Lee, indeed, was not producer Brian Grazer's first choice to direct the movie. As Kaleem Aftab's afterword to *That's My Story and I'm Sticking to It* reveals, Imagine Entertainment reportedly paid Russell Gewirtz more than $1 million for a script that Ron Howard was to helm. Although Howard intended Russell Crowe to star in the film, Aftab reveals that Lee took the reins after Howard and Crowe chose to make *Cinderella Man* (2005), deciding "the time was right for him to work with a famed Hollywood studio producer."[50] This statement spotlights Lee's general independence from studio politics, signaling how he gladly takes money from powerful Hollywood institutions (including Universal Pictures and Imagine Entertainment) to finance and distribute his movies, but disclaims their creative interference with his work. Lee's filmography reveals that he has produced all his movies, many by himself, to maintain the artistic freedom that he so zealously guards. Lee's interest in *Inside Man,* according to "The Man Inside . . .," his 2006 interview with the website *Total Film,* came primarily from reading first-time screenwriter Gewirtz's script. Grazer brought different directors onto the project after Howard departed to make *Cinderella Man,* but none, according to Lee, was suitable: "Other directors came in, rewrote the script and messed it up and someone slipped me a copy. I had a meeting with Brian about another project and before I got up to leave the meeting I said, 'By the way, I've read the script for *Inside Man,* I'd like to direct it.' He didn't even know I was aware of the script, so that's how the project came to be."[51]

This history suggests that Grazer did not initially consider Lee capable of overseeing the movie despite Lee's long and diverse career, perhaps because Lee's most profitable film (or "biggest hit," in Hollywood parlance) was *Malcolm X,* which grossed $48 million in 1992,[52] more than ten years before, while Lee's more recent, smaller-scale films (especially *Girl 6, Get on the Bus,* and *Bamboozled*), with their modest returns, were not the massive money-makers that defined Hollywood moviemaking during the 1990s and 2000s. Lee's reputation as a vocal critic of Hollywood's racial tokenism, exclusionism, and ignorance probably did him no favors, either, especially considering the image of loudmouthed rabble-rouser willing to infuriate both studio executives and movie audiences that Lee has earned in the decades since *She's Gotta Have It*'s release. Lee's cinematic dexterity may also have kept him off lists of bankable, big-budget directors due to the perception that he makes movies for smaller markets, not mainstream viewers. Despite tackling a variety of genres, styles, and projects, Lee has nonetheless been pigeonholed by studios, critics, and some scholars as a black director of independent fare who appeals to a narrow, primarily African American audience that cannot sustain the enormous profits that blockbuster filmmaking demands.

Grazer's decision to hire Lee as *Inside Man*'s director, however, produces a singular movie, both within Lee's oeuvre and within its nominal genre, the heist film. Vince Leo finds *Inside Man* to be an eminently enjoyable picture that Lee transforms from standard crime thriller into intellectual game: "In truth, this is easily his most accessible work, and like Woody Allen's *Match Point,* the *auteur* finds a way to take an average film and make it something special, weaving a complex, albeit messy, tapestry of many interesting ideas, enough to make this one of the more thoughtful mainstream crime dramas to come out in recent memory."[53] David A. Gerstner takes a dimmer view, not of the movie's cinematic quality, for "what makes *Inside Man* a pleasurable text, in part, is the locating of Lee-*isms* observed by the savvy viewer,"[54] but of the conformist political, cultural, and artistic climate surrounding the movie's production that required Lee to mask his identity in order to make a commercially and critically praised blockbuster, just as protagonist Dalton

Russell hides his face to correct the historical crime at the narrative's center: "The 'how' of *Inside Man* discloses the very process of de-auteuring at work in contemporary Hollywood, if not culture itself. *Inside Man* makes explicit the environment of ideological containment operating during a more conservative era (one that Hollywood finds itself pandering to and in which the director must insist on his or her directorial signature)."[55] Gerstner's essay implicates studio politics as much as governmental censorship to argue that *Inside Man*'s narrative stages the conditions of its own construction—revealing the film's covert theatricality, so to speak—by showcasing Dalton Russell's firm command of the bank heist's elements in exposing the nasty, objectionable, and criminal basis of Arthur Case's Manhattan Trust Bank, just as Lee controls each aspect of the movie's production to confound its viewer's comprehension of Russell's plan until the final sequence, when Detective Frazier realizes that Russell's perfect bank robbery in fact *restores* truth about Case's historical perfidy (and his bank's tainted wealth) rather than suppressing this knowledge from public scrutiny. Russell performs a reverse robbery of sorts, carrying out a Robin Hood scenario that steals ill-gotten gains from a rich man to attain a noble end. Russell, indeed, hopes to empower people lower down the socioeconomic ladder from Case by revealing the atrocities at the heart of American finance. Even so, *Inside Man* is no mere exercise in depicting wealthy and powerful people as rapacious parasites, for Case is a cultured, intelligent, and outwardly humble man that Christopher Plummer plays with grandfatherly sympathy. The movie, in a measure of its thematic sophistication, may conclude with Frazier, Russell, and Madeleine White aware of Case's appalling past, but only suggests (rather than guaranteeing) that the man will be punished.

This ambitious plot transforms *Inside Man*, according to R. Colin Tait's essay "Class and Allegory in Spike Lee's *Inside Man*," into a film that "is more acutely political than many of [Lee's] other works."[56] Tait's article masterfully traces how Lee includes intertextual references to Sidney Lumet's *Dog Day Afternoon* (1975) and John McTiernan's *Die Hard* (1988) to acknowledge significant American predecessors of *Inside Man*'s robbery/ heist/hostage synthesis, yet demonstrates that Akira Kurosawa's *Rashomon* (1950) may be *Inside Man*'s most crucial forerunner. Only by imaginatively reconstructing Russell's complex robbery, replete with false executions and staged performances, can Detective Frazier and the audience recognize the audacious elegance of Russell's plan: "At the same time, the film (and Lee) plays with the relativity of the situation in a manner which resembles . . . *Rashomon*, a film which parcels out perception and knowledge throughout the plot, ultimately leaving the spectator in a state of existential confusion."[57] Such bewilderment parallels Frazier's inability to comprehend Russell's plot as it unfolds, demonstrating just how significantly *Inside Man* revises the heist-film convention of the dogged detective winning the cat-and-mouse game he plays against the duplicitous thief by working out the criminal's plan in just enough time to capture the wrongdoer. The good guys, in Lee's film, do not triumph by prosecuting the bad guys, but rather by unwittingly allying themselves after the robbery's conclusion in the cause of revealing Arthur Case's villainy.

That Frazier pursues Case's disgraceful history out of dissatisfaction with the robbery's unresolved conclusion also subverts the standard heist-film ploy of presenting the cop and criminal as morally equivalent personalities who find themselves on different sides of the law. Frazier, suspected of stealing money from a crime scene, endures an internal-affairs investigation throughout the film that ultimately clears him of misconduct charges. Frazier, in other words, is neither the unethical rogue cop so prevalent in the crime novels, crime films, and television police dramas preceding *Inside Man*'s 2006 release nor an attractive antihero who, despite his flaws, holds the viewer in his thrall. This expectation, critical viewers will note, resulted in no small measure from Denzel Washington's Oscar-winning performance as corrupt detective Alonzo Harris in Antoine Fuqua's *Training Day* (2001). Casting Washington as *Inside Man*'s police protagonist is a shrewd intertextual reference that leads viewers familiar with *Training Day* to infer that Frazier will reveal himself as part of Russell's gang, becoming the "inside man" of the film's title who works as a mole within the police department. Yet Lee and Gewirtz restore the tarnished detective to his role as moral arbiter by having him fervently question Case in the man's ritzy office about his ignoble past. Frazier's success in publicly unmasking Case's crime is far from assured as the movie concludes, meaning that *Inside Man* only mirrors Frazier and Russell—cop and criminal—at the end, where both men pursue the honorable goal of righting the wrong of Case's immorally acquired fortune.

R. Colin Tait recognizes the competing ethical principles at play within *Inside Man*'s narrative, as well as how they push Frazier and Russell out of their traditional roles as hero and villain by raising the spectre of Nazism to provide a disgraceful (and disgraced) target for their mutual derision: "In other words, an inherently moral system of values is counterposed against the reprehensible actions of Case, who becomes the film's central villain through his association with Nazism."[58] The Nazis, Tait implies, are perhaps the most conventional cinematic villains of all, but by bonding Frazier and Russell together, Case's connection with Adolf Hitler's fascist regime sabotages the trite protagonist-versus-antagonist plot beloved by Hollywood blockbusters. Tait sees "Frazier's sense of self-worth, which has made him immune to blackmail and has linked him to Dalton" as wholly significant to *Inside Man*'s generic departures from heist-film conventions because Russell's "statement that 'respect is the ultimate currency' must be measured by presenting an alternate value system within the film. In this sense, Dalton and Frazier are 'good guys' in addition to being the good guys."[59] *Inside Man,* as such, does not offer a simplistic good-versus-bad-guy plot even if Frazier, Russell, and

White consider Case's wealth an obscenity founded upon the Holocaust's inherent evil.

Case's protestations that he has spent his entire career overcoming this noxious past receives no sanction or sympathy, indicating that *Inside Man*'s political leanings, far from merely rebuking Case's monstrous ambition, instead criticize globalized financial capitalism as irredeemably debased. Case's wealth emanates from historical circumstances so calamitous that this fortune symbolizes the moral, cultural, and, in White's carefully maintained distance from Case during their final conversation, physical contamination that Dalton Russell pillories throughout the film. Although one of Russell's partners suggests that he (Russell) will "smell like shit" after spending one week in the false room that allows their plan to succeed, Russell appears reasonably fresh upon leaving this hiding place with the documents and diamonds that incriminate Case's war crimes. Russell, dressed in jeans, shirt, and Yankees baseball cap, is clean compared to the immaculately tailored Case, who, unlike Russell the working-class everyman, looks every inch the patrician plutocrat. Lee also links Case to the Republican Party and to international conservative politics by including photos of Case with former president George H. W. Bush, former first lady Barbara Bush, and former British prime minister Margaret Thatcher on credenzas behind Case's desk, in plain view for Frazier and the movie's viewers to see.

Inside Man's political messages, therefore, range from the subtle to the blatant in a blockbuster heist film that implicates historical genocide as the basis of corporate capitalism. Tait, like most of the movie's reviewers, notes that Russell erases his hostages' diverse identities by forcing them to wear the same uniform as the robbers, but connects this theme to *Inside Man*'s larger discourse about political and financial malfeasance, particularly once the police storm the bank, arrest everyone in sight, and methodically question them. "What occurs as the hostages are stripped of their identity and subsequently stripped of their rights in the horrifying arrest scene," Tait writes, "is akin to the systematic processing of Holocaust victims, slaves of the Middle Passage, or prisoners of Camp X-Ray. This scene and their subsequent interrogation at the hands of Frazier speaks [*sic*] to present and past systemic dehumanization of presumed guilty parties."[60] Russell initiates and Frazier continues this diminishment, which at least helps expose Case's treachery, but the film's ends-justifies-the-means outcome reaffirms the conservative ideology that *Inside Man* ostensibly criticizes to illustrate how Russell and Frazier mirror certain aspects of Case's personality. They are not fascist partisans, to be sure, but they cannot separate themselves from the historical animosities that set the entire plot into motion.

Lee, indeed, underscores the hostages' multiplicity by focusing on their quirky personalities in the movie's extended opening sequence and in affecting close-ups—cut into the main storyline to fragment the narrative's chronology—during their responses to interrogation. Lee added certain characters to Gewirtz's original screenplay, noting in his DVD audio commentary that Vikram Walia (Waris Alhuwalia), the Sikh security guard who denounces the police's assumption that his turban makes him a Muslim terrorist, appears in the movie to demonstrate that post-9/11 New York's ethnic, racial, religious, and socioeconomic diversity is far from utopian, but instead represents a fractious coalition of people who uneasily share the same urban space.[61] Such observations enhance the main plot's fascination with the long-term effects of historical crimes like the Holocaust, thereby fulfilling Tait's conclusion that, because "it is still possible to assert that at the heart of all these issues the institutionalization of trade and globalization has always been founded on one form of atrocity or another"[62] and "because *Inside Man* presents its political message within what is ultimately a generic film form, it results in a meaningful film by both popular and political standards."[63] Lee and his collaborators, to their credit, rewrite the heist film to produce an intelligent blockbuster of uncommon depth.

Inside Man's success belies its improbabilities thanks to Lee's assured direction, Wynn Thomas's stylish sets, Terence Blanchard's accomplished score (particularly the opening sequence's inclusion of A. R. Rahman and Sampooran Singh Kalra's song "Chaiyya Chaiyya" to underscore New York City's human diversity), and the cast's top-notch performances, especially by lesser-known actors playing hostages and bank robbers. Russell's complicated plan, requiring clockwork precision, seems to anticipate every possible challenge and coincidence, while the most commonly cited implausibility involves Case's age. As Roger Ebert writes in his mixed review, "Christopher Plummer, as the bank president, doesn't look in his 90s. Giving him a mustache, a walking stick and some wrinkles doesn't do it. Yet we have to believe that in mid-World War II he was old enough to have risen high enough to do something important enough"[64] to call upon Madeleine White's services. Plummer's superb acting, however, overcomes this deficiency to make Case a gentlemanly villain who rationalizes his immoral pursuit of wealth as the means by which he accomplishes a lifetime of unspecified good deeds. Plummer plays a criminal who does not believe he is a criminal, skillfully embodying *Inside Man*'s warning about the dangers that occur when false equivalency masquerades as principled morality.

Lee, as with *Summer of Sam,* renovates crime cinema's hackneyed and encrusted conventions to produce a movie that stays true to his social, cultural, and political outlook. *Inside Man,* as Tait writes in his "brief survey of critical reactions to the film," fooled almost no one "into thinking that this was a typical heist film, and all considered the film as being consistent with Spike Lee's continued output."[65] Similar sentiments apply to *Summer of Sam,* making both movies prime examples of Lee's talent at fashioning generic material into cinema that belongs to him (and no one else). Crime becomes an arena for Lee to reconstruct, observe, and criticize the social issues that most concern him: class, race, ethnicity, and the depredations of unfettered capitalism. The penalties for wrongdoing that *Summer of Sam* and *Inside Man* portray are frequently unfair, leaving perpetrators—such as Arthur Case in *Inside Man* and the men who assault Ritchie in *Summer of Sam*—partially or fully unpunished. Lee, protesting crime cinema's largest clichés, offers no spotless resolutions that satisfy conventional preferences for ascendant truth and triumphant justice. Lee's vision is more complicated, ambiguous, and difficult than these straightforward alternatives, making his crime movies, despite their imperfections and excesses, accomplished contributions to genre filmmaking.

Facing Back, Facing Black

FUN AND GAMES

Spike Lee's career includes so many different roles, films, and styles that tallying them reveals his cinematic dexterity. Lee is a writer, director, producer, and actor whose movies fall into numerous categories: independent comedy, campus musical, urban slice-of-life drama, biographical epic, crime thriller, road movie, heist film, war picture, and revenge story are among the diverse genres that he has tackled during three decades of filmmaking. Lee, who generally works on modestly budgeted movies, sometimes ventures into television projects and big-budget Hollywood blockbusters when not shooting commercials, running his own production company, or teaching graduate courses at Harvard and New York Universities. Lee, as even a brief survey of his films attests, is a dramatist, a comedian, and a documentarian, but with *Bamboozled* (2000) he becomes a master satirist.

Although Lee's previous movies include satirical elements, *Bamboozled* remains unique by declaring its satirical intentions during the opening frame and never backing away from them. Far from the angry, shallow, and tedious film that some critics have accused Lee of producing, *Bamboozled* confirms his talent for exposing, exploding, and reconfiguring racial stereotypes into a story so uncomfortable that Armond White, in his scathing assessment "Post-Art Minstrelsy," writes that Lee "can just harangue and upbraid his viewers, whose defensive reactions seem as real to them as considered, legitimate responses to a work of art. They're simply responding to unresolved social issues; demagoguery."[1] This shortsighted reaction nonetheless maps the critical terrain that *Bamboozled* traverses by dramatizing the quest of protagonist Pierre Delacroix (Damon Wayans), the sole African American writer for the Continental Network Service (CNS) television network, whose disenchantment with his job leads Delacroix (known as "Dela" to friends and colleagues) to stage the most offensive weekly series he can imagine—a parade of crude racist stereotypes titled *Mantan: The*

New Millennium Minstrel Show—hoping that his boss, Thomas Dunwitty (Michael Rapaport), will exercise the severance clause in Dela's contract and fire him for creating such a repellant program. The fact that Dela refuses to quit in protest over Dunwitty's and CNS's racial insensitivities, preferring to maintain the upscale life that working for CNS provides even after leaving his duties, marks Dela as a politically confused member of the black bourgeoisie whose attachment to money, prestige, and cultural prominence outweighs his commitment to collective action and personal integrity.

That this compromised character begins *Bamboozled* by defining satire for the audience ("A literary work in which human vice or folly is ridiculed or attacked scornfully," Dela tells the viewer in a direct-to-camera address during the film's opening moments, as well as "Irony, derision, or caustic wit used to attack or expose folly, vice, or stupidity"[2]) signals how Lee not only understands but also anticipates the criticism that he and *Bamboozled* receive. Lee addresses this point in "Thinking about the Power of Images," his long and insightful 2001 interview with *Cineaste* magazine's Gary Crowdus and Dan Georgakas, when he says, "it amazes me how intelligent critics are with a lot of filmmakers, but when it comes to my work, there's a total misrepresentation."[3] He cites Liza Schwarzbaum's *Entertainment Weekly* analysis of *Summer of Sam* and Stephen Hunter's *Washington Post* assessment of *Bamboozled* as prime examples of reviews that "are not talking about the films but about the critic's perceptions of me,"[4] which Lee finds disingenuous because such appraisals evade *Bamboozled*'s withering attack on the embedded racial stereotypes of Hollywood cinema and television: "I've read so many reviews of *Bamboozled* that talk about everything except what the film is about. They do not want to deal with the historical debasement of a people through film and television."[5]

This response not only reveals Lee's complicated relationship with certain film critics but also indicts their skewed priorities. Lee does not whine about mistreatment in a thin-skinned display of bruised ego, elsewhere remarking, "I'm not saying I'm above criticism. I can take it,"[6] yet rightfully brands criticism that concentrates attention upon him, not the movie under review, as unproductive, unfocused, and unmindful. Lee's willingness to court media attention and controversy, however, makes such commentary unavoidable, particularly for a filmmaker who criticizes Hollywood's industrial system of production even while participating in it. Charges of hypocrisy are inevitable, but they miss the subtleties of Lee's project to broaden American cinema's portrayal of black life, which necessarily implicates the diverse peoples who form the nation's populace. Lee's statement to Crowdus and Georgakas that he grows frustrated with "reading movie reviews that include references to me being courtside at Knicks games"[7] underscores how *Bamboozled,* apart from confronting media racism, also meditates upon the black bourgeoisie's contested position within American society, a theme that Hunter's review (titled "Soul-Defying Success") raises in a passage that praises *Bamboozled* by stating, "what the movie lacks in clarity, it makes up for in honesty, toughness, relentlessness and passion" before noting what Hunter assumes drives the film's biting satire: "This is not a sunshine movie for summer viewers. It is the reflection of a black American who has made it in the white world yet has found himself assailed by members of his own race as well as by many of other races, a man who is materially comfortable and presumably feels guilty as hell about that."[8] Hunter, driving this point home, concludes that Lee "wants two things that happen to be mutually exclusive: to have a revolution and to keep his courtside seats at the Garden for Knicks games"[9] in the sentence that provokes Lee's disdain, who rejects such smug psychoanalysis as a shallow evaluation of *Bamboozled*'s narrative, symbolic, and thematic complications. Hunter, however, productively suggests that the movie, among many other concerns, interrogates America's class system as much as its racial tensions, a theme that stalks the narrative from beginning to end.

Bamboozled's complexities, in other words, defy the facile evaluations of some film reviewers to inspire a rich vein of scholarship that credits the movie's strengths while acknowledging its weaknesses. *Cineaste,* indeed, published "Race, Media and Money: A Critical Symposium on Spike Lee's *Bamboozled,*" a collection of five essays and Crowdus and Georgakas's "Thinking about the Power of Images" interview with Lee, in its January 2001 issue because *Bamboozled,* in the words of editor Cynthia Lucia, "asks us to ponder [the] interplay of self-deception and self-awareness, not only on the part of his characters, but also on the part of an entire American culture and its media establishment."[10] The fact that *Cineaste*'s symposium includes divergent readings of *Bamboozled,* ranging from Armond White's blistering "Post-Art Minstrelsy" to Saul Landau's admiring "Spike Lee's Revolutionary Broadside," illustrates the film's overall power. *Bamboozled* moves viewers, especially critics and scholars, to such passion that they cannot resist analyzing, sometimes at length, its assemblage of racial stereotypes, its denunciation of American entertainment, and its delight at skewering the Hollywood power players that motivate the movie's satire. *Bamboozled,* indeed, is so fruitful a narrative that Landau concludes his essay by writing, "But Lee has done in one film more to enlighten audiences on race, class, history and entertainment than Hollywood has done in a century,"[11] an assessment that White disputes in the first lines of "Post-Art Minstrelsy": "Money talks—even when Spike Lee has nothing to say. That's why academics and journalists pay attention to the noise of *Bamboozled* while continually ignoring more urgent and sincere topics addressed by filmmakers who lack Lee's industry backing."[12] These polarized responses speak to *Bamboozled*'s intricacies, which demand attentive scholarship that probes the film's intellectual indeterminacies and emotional ambiguities. *Bamboozled,* despite White's rejection, is too fascinating a movie to dismiss out of hand.

Lee's film, however, challenges its audience's expectations of satire. Despite Dela's opening definition, viewers anticipating a cinematic comedy that prompts laughter every few moments will find *Bamboozled* a disappointing experience, particularly compared to earlier films starring Damon Wayans such as *Blankman* (1994) and *Major Payne* (1995). *Bamboozled*, although funny in spots, forces audience members to question their willingness to laugh at comical African American characters who, in Lee's view, owe large (but hidden) debts to blackface minstrelsy's stock roles, coarse stereotypes, and childish antics. Selecting Wayans as *Bamboozled*'s protagonist, especially after the man's success as a cast member of his brother Keenan's variety show *In Living Color* (1990–1994), implies a style of fractious, racial, and no-holds-barred comedy that the film parodies as minstrelsy's problematic descendent. Although *Bamboozled*'s show-within-a-show *Mantan* does not directly impugn *In Living Color*, instead targeting programs such as *The Amos 'n Andy Show* (1951–1953) and *Good Times* (1974–1979), Lee indicates the powerful pull that minstrelsy exercises even on latter-day African American writers, producers, and performers by hiring Wayans to play a part that repudiates some of the actor's earlier roles (despite the clear affection for Wayans that Lee expresses during interviews, behind-the-scenes documentaries, and his audio-commentary for the film's DVD release).

Bamboozled, as such, is not the laugh riot that viewers might expect, desire, or easily appreciate. W.J.T. Mitchell, in his perceptive essay "Living Color: Race, Stereotype, and Animation in Spike Lee's *Bamboozled*," summarizes the charges made against the movie by Armond White, Roger Ebert, and James Berardinelli by noting, "A final defense against the film would, I suppose, be on the grounds of aesthetics and the pleasure principle, that it is such a relentlessly negative and grotesque spectacle no one could possibly enjoy it, just as no one could possibly laugh or take any pleasure in a prime-time TV revival of blackface minstrelsy."[13] *Bamboozled* does not amuse its viewers by placing them at ease, but rather by confronting them with objectionable images that demand thought, reflection, and, in the movie's most abject moments, soul searching. These responses may not figure into debased notions of entertainment as mindless pleasure, but neither Lee nor *Bamboozled* care. They instead recuperate the toughness of traditional satire by mercilessly examining the power of images to reproduce themselves, throughout time and through numerous media, to construct, in Saul Landau's terms, a broadside that spares no one—neither the characters inside *Bamboozled*'s narrative, the movie's creators, nor the audience's members—from criticism. Lee challenges the foundations of American entertainment by showing how racist and classist assumptions so pervade the act of watching film and television that no one, including Lee, can escape them. This dispiriting notion explains *Bamboozled*'s contested critical reception upon its 2000 release, as well as its growing reputation in the years since this first appearance. *Bamboozled*, in perhaps the best testament to its quality, repays repeated screenings to become a significant movie not just for Lee, but for twenty-first-century American cinema.

CRITICAL INTERVENTIONS

Lee's reputation as a rabble-rouser, troublemaker, and provocateur unites negative commentaries about *Bamboozled*'s effectiveness. Armond White, longtime detractor of Lee's work, spends inordinate space in "Post-Art Minstrelsy" damning critical fascination with Lee, which comes at the expense of better artists (better, at least, in White's opinion). "While his films are shallow and incoherent, it's Lee's individual standing as a black director who broke through to the white Hollywood mainstream—and has remained there for almost two decades—that means more to people than the actual catalog of ideas in his films," White writes, claiming that "Lee merely fills liberal Hollywood's quota. The fly in the buttermilk is not the same as a fly in the ointment."[14] These curious lines refuse to examine the doubtful liberalism of Hollywood studios and executives, whose market conservatism has provoked Lee's repeated battles over financing his projects. White assigns Lee the role of racial token making his way through the condescending world of Hollywood's limousine liberals, who care little for honest cinematic examinations of African American lives despite their protestations to the contrary. Lee's movies, "always so rhetorical and sloganeering,"[15] allow these false liberals, in White's telling, to salve their racial guilt by embracing a moviemaker whose questionable talent nonetheless generates a high public profile that squelches genuinely revolutionary cinematic artists: "The irony of Lee's aggrandizement is that other, more serious black filmmakers remain on the periphery, and Hollywood's racial discourse remains unenlightened. Lee usurps what little space media and scholars devote to the movies' racial politics."[16] White considers Charles Burnett's movies—especially *The Glass Shield* (1995) and the remarkable *Killer of Sheep* (1979), along with Burnett's fine television films *Nightjohn* (1996) and *The Wedding* (1998)—"better and more pertinent"[17] than anything Lee has directed before extolling Wayne Wang's *Smoke* (1995), James Toback's *Black and White* (1999), and David Gordon Green's *George Washington* (2000) as "smaller but superior films" that, "instead of furthering the racist pretense that a black filmmaker like Lee has substantive things to say about race," deserve greater attention because "it would be refreshing to explore the expressions of those white filmmakers who are equally implicated in this All-American social dilemma and bring sense to it."[18]

White offers little evidence for his conclusions, betraying his occupation as contrarian film reviewer, but condenses into a few paragraphs the difficulties that many other critics have with *Bamboozled*. Phil Chidester and Jamel Santa Cruze Bell characterize these unflattering opinions as mistaken in "'Say the Right Thing': Spike Lee, *Bamboozled*, and the Future of Satire in a Postmodern

World," their fascinating essay about the movie's postmodern implications, by writing, "That Lee's complex work has been broadly misunderstood as a contemporary form of the classical satire—and, in light of such a misunderstanding, that the film is clearly doing much more than simply following the expected form and plot structure of a classical satire—is evidenced in the critical and popular response to the film."[19] Chidester and Bell note that film reviewers contend that *Bamboozled* "is at once too complex and too obvious,"[20] that it "has been panned for both its obviousness and its subtlety,"[21] and that some writers think the movie "lacks the refined focus of its forebears in the genre."[22] These misperceptions are perhaps willful distortions of *Bamboozled*'s venomous demolition of American media's endemic racism (as seems the case with Armond White's incoherent "Post-Art Minstrelsy" analysis) or unexamined responses to a film that so energetically deconstructs the racial biases underlying much of American culture that they form a bulwark against comprehending the movie's numerous themes and subplots (as seems the case with Roger Ebert's perplexed *Chicago Sun-Times* review).

Chidester and Bell attribute this critical myopia to miscomprehending how Lee produces a postmodern satire that simultaneously adheres to classical satire's goal of harshly ridiculing "the behaviors and ideals of an existing power structure"[23] while fragmenting coherent images into a confusing mass of signifiers "by actively embracing postmodernism's fascination with the image as image."[24] They assert that *Bamboozled*'s frequently negative and sometimes hostile reception "says less about the quality of *Bamboozled* as a filmic text than about the critics' own misunderstanding of the exigencies and constraints into which the work was introduced," referring to Lee's decision to shoot the movie on digital video in order to maximize its small (by Hollywood standards) $10-million budget, "and about their failure to recognize the ways in which *Bamboozled* at once embraces and transforms aspects of the classical satire in order to preserve some measure of the satire's rhetorical power as a form of expression in postmodern times."[25] This final declaration concerns Lee's habit of including images and sequences in *Bamboozled* tangentially connected to the film's master narrative about Delacroix's commitment to *Mantan: The New Millennium Minstrel Show,* including shots of racist collectibles (such as the "Jolly Nigger Bank") and amusing commercial parodies (of malt liquor and Tommy Hilfiger apparel), that enmesh the viewer in the cultural prejudices that *Bamboozled* decries. Forcing the audience to watch not just *Bamboozled,* but also *Mantan,* not only makes viewers complicit in the bigotry that the film targets but also, for Chidester and Bell, fully expresses "the true satirical power of Lee's filmic images."[26] *Bamboozled,* in this reading, is far more erudite than its initial critical reception suggests, for the movie's blunt and brutal surface narrative masks the thematic sophistication that Lee engineers by presenting a new minstrel show to twenty-first-century viewers.

Bamboozled, in other words, is far better than the "sledgehammer satire"[27] that James Berardinelli proclaims in his problematic review, which nevertheless summarizes the critical dismay that Lee's film aroused upon its theatrical release. Berardinelli does not simply charge Lee with sloganeering, but with pontificating in the worst possible way: by boring his audience. "If I wanted to endure a two hour sermon," Berardinelli writes, "I would go to church on Sunday morning, not make my way to a movie theater. Spike Lee's latest film, *Bamboozled,* is a 135-minute rant against racist images of blacks in popular culture and the complacency with which the public accepts them."[28] Berardinelli comes close to deploring what he sees as Lee's pedantic and overbroad approach: "According to Lee, white America is all too happy to see the black man put down—as long as it occurs in a socially acceptable, non-threatening manner, such as on television. And, while those ideas have merit, Lee's heavy-handed approach turns *Bamboozled* into a tedious and overlong polemic."[29] These faults grow from Lee's refusal to trust his audience's intelligence, evinced by Dela's opening definition of satire, which demonstrates for Berardinelli that "making a good satire is a more difficult task than adhering to the definition. *Bamboozled* is neither humorous nor subversively clever. It is too obvious to engage the intellect or stimulate discussion."[30] The wealth of commentary, debate, and scholarship about *Bamboozled* neuters this last criticism, although Berardinelli's mistaken assumptions do not lie in his inability to predict the movie's academic reputation, but rather in obtuse declarations such as, "The only ones likely to be challenged by anything presented here are the painfully naïve or sheltered—and they're unlikely to see the film in the first place."[31] This comment insults the intelligence of the film's audience despite Berardinelli's earlier declaration that Lee commits the same sin (by presuming that viewers understand the history of blackface minstrelsy and Hollywood's exclusionary practices as well as Lee). Berardinelli also overlooks the character of Myrna Goldfarb (Dina Pearlman), the Caucasian media consultant whose Yale University degree in African American studies causes Dunwitty to hire her to manage the outrage that *Mantan* initially provokes. Goldfarb outlines the "*Mantan* Manifesto," a litany of methods to counter criticisms of the program's racism (including her final point, "If they can't take a joke, you know what, 'F' 'em!") that, like Berardinelli's declaration, infantilizes audience members when not actively dismissing them.

Berardinelli also claims that *Bamboozled* is not satire: "Subjecting everyone else to a soap box oratory masquerading as a satire is an act of ego worthy of Oliver Stone."[32] This *ad hominem* attack, beyond illustrating the truth of Lee's statement to Gary Crowdus and Dan Georgakas about critics reviewing him rather than the movie, emblematizes the approach taken by commentators who dislike *Bamboozled,* whether Berardinelli, Armond White, or even Roger Ebert, who, in his negative review, writes, "I think Spike Lee misjudged his material and audience in the same way Whoopi

Goldberg did, and for the same reason: He doesn't find a successful way to express his feelings, angers and satirical points."[33] Ebert refers to Ted Danson's infamous blackface performance at a 1993 Friar's Club roast of his then-girlfriend Goldberg that generated significant controversy. Danson later claimed that Goldberg herself conceived and wrote the skit, at which, Ebert writes, "The audience sat in stunned silence. I was there, and I could feel the tension and discomfort in the room."[34] Ebert's point is that white people no longer find blackface funny, but he exclusively blames individuals (Lee and Goldberg) rather than the Hollywood institutions that *Bamboozled* mocks for perpetuating the racist images, ideas, and practices of which blackface is the symptom, not the cause. Ebert, like many *Bamboozled* detractors, is simply wrong to declare, "Blacks in blackface eating watermelon and playing characters named Eat 'n Sleep [*sic*], Rufus and Aunt Jemima fail as satire and simply become—well, what they seem to be. Crude racist caricatures," just as he misjudges *Bamboozled*'s project of shattering stereotypical images from the inside by writing, "Blackface is over the top in the same way—people's feelings run too strongly and deeply for any satirical use to be effective. The power of the racist image tramples over the material and asserts only itself."[35] *Bamboozled* provokes intense emotions to compel its viewers into considering the power that these racist images hold over audiences amused by what Lee calls "coonery and buffoonery,"[36] the stereotypical portrayals of African American behavior that haunt twenty-first-century cinema and television by entertaining audiences of all backgrounds. *Bamboozled*, particularly in *Mantan: The New Millennium Minstrel Show*, exaggerates racist imagery to underline and undermine bigoted representations by rehearsing them in unpleasant, even distressing, sequences.

Ebert's review charges Lee with hypocrisy, albeit more mildly than Armond White's "Post-Art Minstrelsy," for daring to show *Mantan* in the first place: "That's the danger with satire: To ridicule something, you have to show it, and if what you're attacking is a potent enough image, the image retains its negative power no matter what you want to say about it."[37] This impoverished formulation of satire, however, implies that *Bamboozled* should have remained content to ridicule American cinema and television's racial prejudice. Yet, as Christiane Bohnert suggests in her fine essay "Early Modern Complex Satire and the Satiric Novel: Genre and Cultural Transposition," effective satire juxtaposes images and events that, by countering (if not contradicting) their surface meanings, make the audience aware of the gap between a text's presentation and the contrary implications derived from that presentation.[38] *Bamboozled* fulfills this project so well that the movie is sometimes tough to watch, not because it is poorly crafted, but rather the reverse. Lee and his collaborators so successfully stage *Mantan* that *Bamboozled*'s viewers cannot avoid an expertly constructed minstrel show. Its negative power rebounds upon the film's audience, performers, and makers, offering no escape from the spectacle of minstrelsy's terrible images.

Bamboozled, by accomplishing these goals, becomes quintessential satire. Its power to disturb viewers lies precisely in its evocation, reconfiguration, and devastation of Hollywood cinema and television's foundational racism. Presenting these media forms as inherently racist, indeed, confirms *Bamboozled*'s satirical legitimacy, at least as described by Brian A. Connery and Kirk Combe in "Theorizing Satire: A Retrospective and Introduction," their astute preface to the scholarly anthology *Theorizing Satire: Essays in Literary Criticism.* Connery and Combe write, "Reading satire is doubly perilous, for satirists specialize in demolition projects. The one thing we know about satire is that it promises to tell us what we do not want to know—what we may, in fact, resist knowing. One is apt to find one's former consciousness uninhabitable when the work of the satirist is done."[39] This passage nicely describes the experience of watching *Bamboozled,* for viewers cannot passively regard American film and television's underlying bigotry after enduring the movie's searing attack on media racism. *Bamboozled* prompts its audience to watch these media productions far more critically, to evaluate their potentially prejudicial representations of black behaviors, and to consider how excluding or marginalizing African American characters—or assigning them token roles—extends American entertainment's objectionable history of minstrelsy. *Bamboozled,* indeed, demands such intellectual reflection. The movie argues that merely including black characters in commercial media cannot ensure honest, capacious, or nuanced portrayals, but, indeed, all too often becomes an exercise in racial, ethnic, and cultural tokenism masquerading as inclusiveness, pluralism, and diversity. Hollywood, according to *Bamboozled,* perpetuates racial conservatism disguised as progressivism. The movie enrages, perplexes, and discomfits viewers by attacking the fundamental pleasure they take from cinema and television. *Bamboozled* not only challenges the satisfaction that audiences derive from the act of watching movies but also questions the validity of mass-media entertainment by inducing guilt in spectators for enjoying black characters whose buffoonery emanates from minstrelsy. Lee's film, in perhaps its greatest affront to easy viewing, strikes unsympathetic audience members as a text that destroys its own artistic foundation, with its director emerging as little more than a cinematic killjoy. Negative assessments of *Bamboozled* imply that viewers should be allowed to forget American entertainment's racial complexities and simply enjoy what they watch without worrying about how their preferences have been formed by the long, sorry, and contested tradition of blackface minstrelsy.

This notion explicitly motivates James Berardinelli's review, but *Bamboozled,* true to Lee's satiric purpose, repudiates faith in simple, enjoyable, uncomplicated entertainment. Connery and Combe, in a passage that predates yet perfectly describes *Bamboozled,* write, "satire is a form that desire rejects. . . . Most often, the interior of satire is messy, cluttered, and smelly as well. The taste and discrimination of satirists are questionable, and their references stink. In spite of this, they appear proud of their work and thus compound their offense."[40] The number of reviews, commentaries, and academic essays noting how *Bamboozled* risks narrative incoherence by including more characters, themes, incidents, and ideas than necessary qualifies the film not simply as messy and cluttered but as muddled, even chaotic. Berardinelli and White impugn *Bamboozled* for what they consider its impure, unentertaining, and inartistic desires, for its poor taste in subject matter, and especially for staging a minstrel show, while its box-office losses (making between $2.2 and $2.5 million against a $10-million budget)[41] suggest that audiences rejected *Bamboozled* for similar reasons. Lee's extensive press appearances, moreover, allowed him to discuss the film's ideas at length and with insight, but certainly compounded his offenses against the genial cinematic entertainment that Berardinelli extols.

Bamboozled, therefore, is also quintessential Lee. Its uncompromising stand, abrasive approach, and bellicose intelligence are hallmarks of Lee's career, while its deconstruction of racist imagery marks an even more sophisticated development in his thinking about American history, politics, and culture. Stanley Crouch, the critic whose review of *Do the Right Thing* declared Lee an Afro-fascist, reverses course in "The Making of *Bamboozled*," a behind-the-scenes documentary included on the movie's DVD release, by referring to the film and its director as generously understanding "the prison of stereotypes,"[42] an apt summary of how *Bamboozled*'s racist imagery confines each character and viewer in ways that they scarcely realize. Crouch's approval does not indicate, as Armond White argues in "Post-Art Minstrelsy," that "Lee's hectoring has joined Crouch's conservative view, ridiculing and lambasting the wayward actions of pop-culture magpies, rappers, actors, liberal-activists"[43] so much as Lee's broadened perspective understands that no one involved with American film and television, either as creator or consumer, escapes the prison of racial stereotypes unscathed. Gary Crowdus, in his editorial preface to *Cineaste*'s 2001 critical symposium about *Bamboozled*, articulates this insight as the central "new and disturbing" question that the movie asks its viewers: "Does deep-seated racism within the mainstream entertainment industry and in mainstream American culture at large deem it impossible for African Americans to achieve success in that industry without degrees of complicity in extending the very stereotypes and prejudices their positions would enable them to combat?"[44] *Bamboozled* dares to answer "yes," but does not argue that American media entertainment's debt to blackface minstrelsy so sullies the movie's characters, creators, and viewers that they can neither prevent nor reject the prejudice that minstrelsy evokes (and that *Bamboozled*, through *Mantan: The New Millennium Minstrel Show*, records). *Bamboozled*, instead, refuses harmonious visual style, coherent narrative, and steady character development to reflect the "militant disunity"[45] that Connery and Combe find so indispensable to classical satire, a discord that predisposes satire "towards open-endedness, irresolution, and thus chaos."[46] A better description of *Bamboozled*'s overall effect is difficult to imagine, but examining how the movie treats socioeconomic class in relation to minstrelsy demonstrates just how carefully Lee constructs a film that may at first appear to tackle too many characters, stories, and issues, but that defies its harshest critics' charges of narrative and thematic sloppiness to emerge as a necessary satire for twenty-first-century American cinema.

MINCING WORDS

Bamboozled's willingness to display demeaning images of black Americans by repeatedly staging sketches from *Mantan: The New Millennium Minstrel Show* revives the tradition of blackface minstrelsy that, by the time of the movie's 2000 release, had receded from public memory. As Jada Pinkett-Smith, the actress who plays Sloan Hopkins (Delacroix's administrative assistant, onetime lover, and the person most forcefully opposed to *Mantan* at the movie's outset), says in Sam Pollard's documentary "The Making of *Bamboozled*," "I knew minstrel shows existed, but it never dawned on me, like, what it really was"[47] in words that undoubtedly parallel the response of many *Bamboozled* viewers. American cultural amnesia about minstrelsy, resulting from the shame inspired by this institution's offensive past, ensures that the moviegoing public has little (or no) knowledge of minstrelsy's complex history. Lee, in "Thinking about the Power of Images," credits Mark Daniels and Melvin Van Peebles's 1998 documentary *Classified X* as one inspiration for *Bamboozled* due to that film's "history of black images in the cinema. I was amazed by the imagery, so I contacted the film's researcher, Judy Aley, since she'd done a lot of the work already, and she was able to get us a lot of this material," which allowed Lee, his cast, and his crew to school themselves in minstrel traditions that not even Lee knew: "None of us had seen this material. For example, I had never seen Bugs Bunny in blackface!"[48] *Bamboozled,* therefore, strives to make its audience aware of minstrelsy's significance as a primary forerunner of American mass-media entertainment. The film does not stop here, either, but razes American cinema and television's minstrel heritage with bitter satire that turns malicious after *Mantan* becomes a ratings hit. Lee's movie, Dan Flory argues in "*Bamboozled:* Philosophy through Blackface," wishes "to get people to *think* about their own reactions to many examples of mass art and the degree to which they may be complicit with stereotypes and presumptions that owe their existence and vitality to blackface minstrelsy. In this sense, Lee's aim is overtly didactic, which isn't necessarily a bad thing."[49] *Bamboozled* hopes not only to entertain but also to shock its viewers into realizing how deeply (and invisibly) minstrelsy influences their perceptions of black Americans, thereby shaking audience members out of their historical ignorance. They may resist the film's lessons, but, as Connery and Combe observe, some viewers will come away from *Bamboozled* with different attitudes about cinema and television's influence in fashioning prominent images of African Americans—perhaps even with a different consciousness about these matters—thanks to Lee's satirical demolition job.

Bamboozled, as such, minces no words about Hollywood's racist practices, but Dela, in the film's most heartbreaking turn, does. As CNS's only African American writer (and, based on repeated shots of the network's corporate boardrooms and hallways, one of its only African American employees), Dela adopts stilted manners of posture, walking, and speech that mark him as a team player who wishes to fit into a white-dominated workplace that defines "blackness" as little more than a suitable subject for its cultural productions (Dunwitty, for instance, demands funny television programs with black characters who appeal to the broadest possible audience), not as an appropriate topic for office culture or gossip. The corporation's idea of blackness, *Bamboozled* quickly demonstrates, depends upon rank stereotypes, as Dunwitty's protestation during his first creative brainstorming session with Dela—"Brother man, I'm blacker than you! I'm keepin' it real. I'm 'bout it, 'bout it. I got the roll. You're just frontin', tryin' to be white"—indicates. The ironies do not end here, for Dunwitty asks Dela to create a sitcom "blacker" than *The Cosby Show,* which, despite being "revolutionary," represents a genre—stories of black middle-class people and families—that Dunwitty finds "too clean" and "too antiseptic," not realizing (or not caring) that this statement invokes the tried-and-true racist dichotomy of seeing white experience as pure, wholesome, and boring, but black experience as dirty, exciting, natural, and, therefore, genuine. Dunwitty even defends himself against charges of racism by brazenly using the term *nigger,* saying that his marriage to an African American woman and his two biracial children support his claim to be more sincerely black than Dela.

This stunted view of black authenticity provokes Dela's ire, leading him to conceive *Mantan,* at least in part, as a vicious satire of Dunwitty's ignorant musings. Dunwitty, as his name implies, dimwittedly overlooks how broad, multifarious, and varied black American lives are, refusing to believe that primetime dramas about middle-class black characters will entertain network audiences. Dunwitty demands sitcoms with recognizably "black" (meaning stereotypical) characters, insulting Dela's work by saying, "The material you've been writing for me, it's too white-bread. It's white people with black faces," despite earlier praising Dela as the "most creative person I've got on staff. I mean, you're hip, you know what's happening. I've got a bunch of pasty-ass white boys and girls writing for me, you know what I mean?" These convictions do not stop Dunwitty from hiring an all-white writing staff for *Mantan* or from revising Dela's pilot-episode script to increase the audience's identification with its minstrel characters, in the process making *The New Millennium Minstrel Show* even coarser (and, therefore, less satirical) than Dela intends. Dunwitty's bracing historical amnesia endorses minstrelsy's worst excesses not only by requiring *Mantan*'s black performers to wear blackface but also by encouraging the studio audience, after the show becomes a cultural phenomenon, to wear blackface at *Mantan*'s live tapings. Dunwitty even dons blackface in a late scene, as if to justify that he is, indeed, blacker than Dela.

Gregory Laski, in his fine essay "Falling Back into History: The Uncanny Trauma of Blackface Minstrelsy in Spike Lee's *Bamboozled*," recognizes how retrograde these developments are, noting that Dunwitty, Dela, and Sloan's "conception of the presumed distance between their present position and the past betrays a severe misreading of how far the nation has (not) progressed beyond the nineteenth-century world from which the minstrel show derives."[50] Their mistaken belief that American viewers have transcended the racial fetters that produced minstrelsy (and that, in Stanley Crouch's terms, help construct "the prison of stereotypes" that *Mantan* represents) leads Laski to cite Eric Lott's insight, in his important book *Love and Theft: Blackface Minstrelsy and the American Working Class*, that if minstrelsy springs from what Lott calls "the quite explicit 'borrowing' of black cultural materials for white dissemination, a borrowing that ultimately depended on the material relations of slavery,"[51] as it certainly does, "then," according to Laski, "the popularity of blackface on the stage in the nineteenth century and on the screen in the twentieth century (and beyond) was one of the basic means by which the ideology of white supremacy was maintained in the post-slavery era."[52] This disheartening statement raises the question of whether *Bamboozled* disrupts this pernicious ideology through satire, reaffirms it by allowing *Mantan*'s sketches to be unabashedly entertaining (thanks in large part to the tremendous talents of Savion Glover and Tommy Davidson playing, respectively, the minstrel stage characters Mantan and Sleep'n Eat despite the toll that blackface performance takes on their offstage alter egos, Manray and Womack), or mediates these two possibilities by resurrecting minstrelsy's most racist caricatures but evading this action's serious moral consequences. Roger Ebert and Armond White find the film dissatisfying, even distasteful, for not honestly dealing with the implications of marching such negative African American images onscreen, while Ray Black, in his thoughtful article "Satire's Cruelest Cut: Exorcising Blackness in Spike Lee's *Bamboozled*," comments that understanding Dela's narrative is crucial because his story mediates every other character, subplot, and theme, "all of which occur under the shadow of the destructive legacy of blackface minstrelsy that Lee's film shows underlies contemporary society. Blurred and buried beneath these interwoven themes is the story of Delacroix and his relationship to his ethnicity [and] to his black heritage."[53] Black persuasively argues that Dela erases his racial origins—indeed, attempts to exorcise blackness completely from his life—so that Dela may succeed as a professional worker in white-dominated Hollywood. Dela's false accent is only one sign of this erasure, for, as Sloan points out, Pierre Delacroix is an assumed name, with Dela believing that his birth name—Peerless Dothan— might diminish his opportunities for acceptance and advancement in CNS's corporate bureaucracy. Adopting a French moniker, pretentious diction, and formal body language not only distances Dela from his familial background as the son of itinerant comedian Junebug (Paul Mooney) but also fulfills Dela's stereotypical vision of how a Harvard-educated, successful black man should behave.

Bamboozled, therefore, portrays Dela as a minstrel figure, one who adopts a (metaphorical) whiteface mask in the mistaken hope that his CNS colleagues and superiors will respect him. He becomes the cracked-mirror counterpart to Dunwitty, whose affectations of blackness transform him into what Margo Jefferson, during a November 2000 New York University panel discussion about *Bamboozled,* calls "a minstrelized performance of whiteness."[54] Dela's whiteface personality, especially his pompous speech (and repeated references to himself and other African Americans as "Negroes") also minstrelizes whiteness, albeit from the opposite perspective, of a black man performing the role of a stereotypically uptight white man, down to shaving his head before work and using awkwardly precise hand gestures that Damon Wayans mines for subtle (but telling) comedy during his scenes with Dunwitty. Rachael Ziady Delue sees Dela's thick white shaving cream as one of *Bamboozled*'s most powerful masks in her essay "Envisioning Race in Spike Lee's *Bamboozled,*" writing, "The careful scraping off of shaving cream after its application may be read as a figure for the unacknowledged and unseen existence of a white mask to rival that of blackness (the mask is there, but it has been rendered invisible), what Ralph Ellison characterized as a counterfeit identity passing tragically for truth."[55] Dela, in this reading, effaces his racial identity by masquerading as a white corporate flunky who regards blackness as divergence from the naturalized norm of whiteness. As Delue argues, "Whiteness's visibility is made such by virtue of our witnessing its removal from view and its subsequent sublimation or secretion in Delacroix's affected speech and in the giddy, desperate top-o-the-morning-to-you greetings he dispenses to his coworkers at CNS," exaggerated mannerisms that "register as anything but natural and their jarring and bizarre effects work to make us see whiteness as something unnatural, abnormal, and odd."[56]

Delue identifies how *Bamboozled* minstrelizes Dela's workplace demeanor to illustrate his racial self-hatred, which runs so deep that he continually parodies stereotypical white behavior. Lee and Wayans, in "The Making of *Bamboozled,*" confirm that these affectations come from an unnamed black television writer whom Wayans met not long before shooting the movie,[57] a man whose mannerisms helped Wayans develop Delacroix into a telling parody of upper-crust affectation that, as Michael Sragow observes in "Black Like Spike" (Sragow's October 26, 2000, *Salon* interview with Lee), "seems to have stylized himself into a parody of white cultivation."[58]

MONEY TALKS

This idea also underscores the class dynamics and tensions that *Bamboozled* chronicles by dramatizing the different socioeconomic positions of the up-scale Dela, his working-class father Junebug, and the initially homeless street performers Manray and Womack. Dela's large Manhattan clocktower condo-minium signifies his economic success (as Manray says, Dela has "made it"), causing Dela to repudiate all association with middle-, working-, and lower-class black people. Dela, early in the movie, condescendingly tells Manray and Womack that he might write a new script with roles for them while they hustle money by dancing outside CNS's corporate office, but only hires them to help fulfill his scheme of producing *Mantan* to get fired by the network, thereby retaining his lavish lifestyle rather than quitting CNS in protest. Lee deliberately juxtaposes the movie's opening scene of Dela moving through his well-appointed condo (while defining satire for *Bamboozled*'s audience) with the first sight of Manray and Womack sleeping in a crumbling, con-demned, and ugly apartment building (that shelters many other homeless people) to emphasize their different material circumstances. Dela instructs Sloan to buy Manray and Womack new clothing, shoes, and basic household items before their successful audition with Dunwitty, who becomes so en-thused by Manray's inimitable tap-dancing skills and Dela's racist concept for *Mantan: The New Millennium Minstrel Show* that he greenlights the pro-gram's production on the spot. Dela promises both performers fame and wealth if they agree to play Mantan and Sleep'n Eat, essentially encouraging them to sell out their racial pride for the riches that starring in a hit television program will generate. *Bamboozled* here parodies the clichéd rags-to-riches story so beloved by Hollywood studios by showing how newfound success intoxicates Dela, Manray, Womack, and even Sloan once *Mantan* becomes a certified cultural blockbuster that draws attention from all quarters, whether praise from audiences, critics, and award ceremonies or condemnation from protesters led by Johnnie Cochran and Al Sharpton (playing themselves).

This storyline recalls Elia Kazan's *A Face in the Crowd* (1957), Mel Brooks's *The Producers* (1967), and Sidney Lumet's *Network* (1976), three films that Lee acknowledges as notable influences on *Bamboozled*,[59] by depicting the se-ductive thrills of overnight success, the financial rewards of media stardom, and the exhilarating power of cultural influence. Dela, who chafes against CNS's and Dunwitty's corporate bigotries early in *Bamboozled* (even imagining himself punching Dunwitty in the face for saying the word *nigger*), comes to embrace *Mantan*'s success by defending the program in newspaper, radio, and television interviews, where he recites provisos from Myrna Goldfarb's "*Mantan* Mani-festo" when not claiming that the show's critics try to censor his artistic output (when, in fact, they do nothing of the kind). Dela quells Womack's uneasiness about portraying Sleep'n Eat by increasing his salary in a bid to salve doubts about embodying uncouth racist stereotypes. This subplot also demonstrates that Manray and Womack are not noble lower-class heroes who maintain their dignity in the face of financial temptation. In an earlier scene, both men examine portfolios of racist billboards, memorabilia, and articles that Sloan assembles while researching minstrelsy, but Womack cannot believe what he sees, saying, "Whoa, wait—wait a minute. Hey, we're gonna need a little more money for this." Manray, by contrast, harbors few concerns about playing a minstrel character as long as his involvement with *Mantan* permits him to make a good living by tap dancing. *Bamboozled* may appear to encourage reading Manray and Womack as sellouts who sign away their personal integrity for easy money, but the film's audition and hiring scenes highlight the inequitable power relationships between CNS's corporate players and these impoverished creative artists. Dunwitty, the executive who approves *Mantan*'s production, controls the resources necessary to mount the program, while Dela, *Mantan*'s showrunner, exercises hiring-and-firing authority over Manray and Womack, who find their careers at the mercy of people primarily interested in exploiting their talents—particularly Manray's gifted dancing—for financial gain. Even so, both men enjoy the attention, affection, and adulation they receive once *Mantan* becomes a hit, to say nothing of the money that allows Manray to buy an upscale Manhattan condo. *Bamboozled,* through these two characters, illustrates how quickly corporate wealth co-opts lower-class workers into supporting its profit-making enterprises.

Opposed to Dela and Dunwitty's corporate ethos, as well as Manray and Womack's willingness to play along, is Dela's estranged father, Junebug, a comedian who works in African American clubs with names like Mama's Sugar Shak, confining himself, as Ray Black notes, to "the tradition of the 'chitling circuit,' black support of uniquely black humor, an authentic marker of an aspect of black culture that fostered and nurtured Richard Pryor, who is a touchstone for many contemporary comedians black, white and other."[60] This authenticity counters every aspect of Dela's constructed image—the whiteface mask that erases his blackness—to make Lee's shrewd casting an important consideration. Paul Mooney, who co-wrote some of Pryor's best material (including 1976's *Bicentennial Nigger,* 1977's short-lived *The Richard Pryor Show,* and 1982's *Live on the Sunset Strip*), is the perfect actor to play Junebug, a man at peace with his career performing in "another little nigger club" who takes comfort in his relationship with a much younger, "pretty woman" named Dot (Sarah Jones) while remaining thankful for remaining "above ground" and "ahead of the game." Junebug sees through Dela's corporate façade, repudiating his son by asking, "Nigger, where the fuck did you get that accent?" while wearing a bright orange jacket and hat that not only lampoon Dela's back leather ensemble but also recall, in Ray Black's words, "Pryor's 1979 comedy act, immortalized in the film *Live in Concert.*"[61] Although *Bamboozled*'s screenplay includes a short routine that introduces Junebug, Lee allows Mooney to improvise his character's on-stage lines, meaning that he films Mooney performing his actual comedy act to differentiate Junebug's approach to creative life from Dela, who appears, despite his greater money and fame, poorer by comparison.

Lee, in his *Salon* interview with Michael Sragow, certifies this disparity by saying, "well, to me, Paul Mooney is really playing himself. . . . He's a great talent who could've maybe had a much bigger career, but just wouldn't play along. He wouldn't play the Hollywood game. And that's who Junebug was."[62] Junebug, in other words, is not a working-class hero so much as a man whose example demonstrates Dela's inability to see his drunken, imperfect father as successful. Dela, after leaving Junebug passed out in his dressing room, confesses in voiceover that his father is the reason he (Dela) went into show business, but that Junebug "was a broken man. He had been a strong man, with conviction, integrity, principles, and look where it had gotten him. I had to ask myself did I want to end up where he was? Hell emphatically no." Yet equating career success with material wealth and cultural influence finally kills both Dela and Manray, both of whom die as a result of their connection to *Mantan*. Manray, whose partnership ends when Womack quits the show because he can no longer stomach the disgust of playing Sleep'n Eat, becomes increasingly disturbed by the studio audience's racist behavior. Its members, regardless of racial or ethnic background, wear blackface to the tapings and proudly declare "I'm a nigger!" at the behest of *Mantan*'s emcee and warm-up act, Honeycutt (Thomas Jefferson Byrd), an African American man who sings the song "Niggers Is a Beautiful Thing" while costumed as a blackface Uncle Sam (wearing, for good measure, a ridiculous American-flag suit). Manray, in his final appearance on *Mantan*, chooses to take the stage as himself (meaning without makeup or costume), dancing beautifully for a stunned audience that cannot process his rejection of blackface minstrelsy or the racial hatred it implies. Dunwitty promptly fires Manray, throwing him out of the studio, but Manray's actions validate Womack's analysis of *Mantan* as "the same bullshit, just done over." Manray, however, is immediately captured by a self-styled revolutionary rap group named the Mau Maus, led by Sloan's brother Julius Hopkins (Mos Def), who refers to himself as "Big Blak Afrika." The Mau Maus, enraged by *Mantan*'s revival of minstrelsy, air Manray's real-time murder over Internet video, which all television networks (including CNS) broadcast to reach the widest possible audience. The Mau Maus shoot at Manray's feet, making him tap dance for his life, before discharging their weapons into his chest. In the even more violent scene that follows, the Mau Maus are gunned down by the police outside the abandoned factory where they have just murdered Manray.

This bloodshed causes Sloan, who was romantically involved with Manray, to visit Dela's apartment. Overcome by grief, Sloan forces Dela at gunpoint to watch a videocassette of racist clips from Hollywood film and television, compiled while she researched minstrelsy for *Mantan,* so that Dela (now wearing blackface both to express and mask his shame) understands his creation's enormous destructive lineage and power. Sloan shoots Dela in the stomach, perhaps accidentally, but he forgives her anger as justified, then wipes Sloan's fingerprints off the gun as his dying voiceover, in an homage to Billy Wilder's *Sunset Boulevard* (1950), reveals Dela's understanding that this outcome is proper recompense for unleashing *Mantan* on America: "As I bled to death, as my very life oozed out of me, all I could think of was something the great Negro James Baldwin had written: 'People pay for what they do, and still more for what they have allowed themselves to become, and they pay for it very simply by the lives they lead.'" Dela then recalls Junebug's parting advice ("Always keep 'em laughing") before the camera cuts to a disturbing close-up of Manray, dressed in his blackface costume, smiling so broadly that this overstated image reminds the viewer just how exaggerated, regrettable, and appalling are the minstrel stereotypes that *Mantan* and *Bamboozled* present. Sloan's three-and-a-half-minute montage of racist clips, indeed, brings the narrative's satire full circle by permitting Dela's physical demise to complete the spiritual death that creating, developing, and defending *Mantan* precipitate.

Baldwin's quote, from his 1972 book *No Name in the Street,* applies the vocabulary of commerce, money, and banking (debt, liability, and payment) to help describe, in explicitly socioeconomic terms, Dela's crime in foisting *Mantan* upon the viewing public. *Bamboozled*'s concluding violence—with Dela, Manray, and the Mau Maus all shot to death, but the white corporate executives responsible for *Mantan* still alive—certifies what Dan Flory, among many other observers, calls the movie's "tonal shift in mid-narrative from biting comic satire to melodramatic seriousness."[63] Some critics (including Roger Ebert and Armond White) find this transition unpersuasive, with Saul Landau usefully summarizing this line of argument by writing, "Lee uses the Mau Maus to fashion the film's ending. They become his *deus ex machina*—as if he didn't know how to end the film without a violent scene, or had become tired after two hours of unrelenting drama about race, class, history, and sexual relations."[64] Yet sparing Dunwitty and his CNS superiors at the expense of black creative artists (including the Mau Maus, who, although confused in their political sympathies and revolutionary impulses, still write, perform, and record hip-hop songs) highlights the long-term exploitation of African American talent by white Americans that stretches back to nineteenth-century minstrelsy. The true perpetrators of *Mantan*'s abysmal racism, namely the purveyors who ensure that it reaches millions of American homes and who profit from its crass marketing, remain untouched while the people most directly affected by the program's existence are killed (Dela and Manray), marginalized (Sloan, whom Dela fires for dating Manray), or driven to murder (the Mau Maus and, potentially, Sloan). The fact that the Mau Maus kill Manray just after he refuses to appear in blackface or perform the demeaning sketches scripted for him underscores how little they understand the nature of institutional capital. They lash out at the person whom they consider *Mantan*'s primary beneficiary, but fail to attack, reform, or even criticize the system that produces it.

(BLACK)FACING THE MUSIC

Bamboozled indulges such criticism through its ferocious, even cruel, satire. The film's "scattershot approach,"[65] as Armond White phrases it, does not forgive Manray, Dela, or Sloan, who all profit by association with *Mantan* despite their misgivings. Even Womack, who survives the movie's brutal events with some dignity, participates in the enterprise long enough to accumulate sufficient funds to leave behind his life as a homeless street performer squatting in condemned buildings just to survive. *Bamboozled* may seem to condemn indiscriminately these characters for partaking in *Mantan*'s commercial success, but Lee, in his interviews with *Salon* and *Cineaste,* refers to the decision to exact violence upon Dela, Manray, and the Mau Maus as a way "to pay the piper,"[66] invoking the language of debt and repayment to ensure that the film examines the question, "What are the consequences going to be for the choices that people have made connected with this show?"[67] Dunwitty and CNS's executives escaping retribution stresses the systemic injustice that *Bamboozled* chronicles, transforming the film, in Michael Sragow's inventive phrase, into "an industrial-strength satire"[68] that upends all sense of fairness, equanimity, or narrative tidiness. The movie's African American characters suffer the indignities that Hollywood foists upon them, failing in their quest to challenge mass media's profit-driven system yet generating tremendous financial gains for the institutional gatekeepers who control their employment. *Bamboozled,* by presenting its story this way, forces viewers to question the white privilege so heavily lampooned by Dunwitty's down-with-black-culture character, yet generates a double bind that implicates black creative artists, including Lee, in Hollywood's all-consuming commercial system. Lee affirms his contested position in Hollywood's rigid hierarchy to *Cineaste*'s Gary Crowdus and Dean Georgakas, saying, "I do think there is some way to operate within the system. That's something I've been able to do, even though I'm on the fringes of it. *Bamboozled,* believe it or not, was made through a Hollywood studio."[69] Although this statement suggests that Delacroix functions, in some measure, as a fictional stand-in for Lee, it more properly demonstrates how Lee, despite his celebrity and wealth, cannot become fully independent of Hollywood backing even when making a satirical film that eviscerates the industry's long tradition of creating, endorsing, and spreading racist images. *Bamboozled*'s final montage, therefore, becomes crucial to demonstrating how Lee's dependence upon New Line Cinema to distribute the film does not compromise his message. This concluding sequence exhibits what Lee, during his DVD audio commentary, calls the remarkable hatred that American culture has historically felt toward African Americans.[70] The montage functions as a living museum piece that educates *Bamboozled*'s viewer about the crudity with which black Americans have been represented onscreen to suggest the troubling, yet unavoidable, conclusion that no one, at least no one familiar with Hollywood cinema and television, can avoid their pervasive, shaping influences.

Rachael Ziady Delue expresses this quandary as fundamental to *Bamboozled*'s fascination with spectacle, vision, and seeing: "Because we cannot stop looking, Lee seems to be saying, because the world already appears to us as if a museum, everything on display, we (*all* of us) cannot dismantle the connection between identity and visibility, perceived essence and envisioning, at least not without great difficulty or a radical (perhaps impossible) reorientation of our perceptual sets."[71] The film, as such, depends upon an essential paradox: "Lee's movie-museum shows us the double-bind of vision: seeing is the problem and the solution at one and the same time."[72] Lee corroborates this analysis by concluding his *Cineaste* interview with the wish that *Bamboozled*'s audience will "think about the power of images, not just in terms of race, but how imagery is used and what sort of social impact it has—how it influences how we talk, how we think, how we view one another" not merely as an exercise in lamenting American mass media's regrettable past, but to understand "how film and television have historically, from the birth of both mediums, produced and perpetuated distorted images. Film and television started out that way, and here we are, at the dawn of a new century, and a lot of that madness is still with us today."[73]

Bamboozled succeeds in this project, as the impressive commentary, debate, and scholarship about it confirms. Critical viewers cannot watch Hollywood productions, no matter how progressive, the same way after encountering Lee's eccentric, uncomfortable, and unsparing film. *Bamboozled* is a masterful satire that, although indebted to *A Face in the Crowd, The Producers,* and *Network,* deconstructs with unsettling intensity mass media's power to create false images. Yet the movie benefits its audience in another way, by reviving the tradition of blackface minstrelsy to demonstrate that, no matter how terrible its racism, this form of entertainment's working-class roots also allowed supremely talented black performers, including Bill "Bojangles" Robinson, Hattie McDaniel, Mantan Moreland, and Bert Williams, to become creative artists who subverted Hollywood stereotypes even when consigned to subservient roles.

Bamboozled's final montage helps accomplish this end, as do repeated shots of Manray and Womack applying blackface, sometimes in tears, before taking the stage to display superb comic timing and talent in *Mantan: The New Millennium Minstrel Show.* As Lee reveals in several interviews, in "The Making of *Bamboozled,*" and in his DVD audio commentary, this process was difficult for Savion Glover and Tommy Davidson, although it also gave them renewed appreciation for what earlier generations of African American performers had to endure. Lee tells Crowdus and Georgakas, "The reality of black people putting this stuff on their face was devastating for Tommy Davidson and Savion Glover. It took away part of their soul, it took away part of their manhood, and it made us think of Bert Williams. Tommy and Savion did it for a couple of weeks, but Williams had to do that his entire career."[74] *Bamboozled* provokes the stark but complex realization that nineteenth- and twentieth-century African American stage, radio, film, and television performers often had no choice but to accept demeaning roles if they wished to work as creative artists, yet performed so well that their accomplishments cannot be denied. They paved the way for later entertainers, including Davidson, Glover, Pinkett-Smith, and Wayans, as well as Lee, who acknowledges that making *Bamboozled* opened his eyes to the merits of actors, dancers, and singers whom he had previously dismissed due to their connections (and seeming capitulation) to minstrelsy. Lee comments to Crowdus and Georgakas, "What was really beneficial for me in doing the research for *Bamboozled* was gaining a greater understanding of that generation of Negro performers," confessing to judging people such as Bert Williams, Mantan Moreland, and even Lincoln Perry (whose most famous character, Stepin Fetchit, is now synonymous with racist African American stereotypes) much too harshly: "In the past I've said such ignorant things about these people—that they were Uncle Toms and Mammies—but saying that without a full understanding that that was the only choice they had. As Hattie McDaniel said, "It's better to play a maid than to be a maid.'"[75] Lee does not end here, however, mentioning that *Bamboozled* increased his consciousness about the connections between Hollywood's past and present: "While this film gave me a greater understanding of what they [earlier generations of black artists] had to go through, at the same time it's made me much more critical of the roles that African American entertainers or athletes choose to play today."[76]

Bamboozled's fragmented narrative and final montage so skillfully impress these notions on viewers that the film qualifies as superb satire. It also demonstrates how the historical success of blackface minstrelsy (in usurping African American culture to entertain white audiences who enjoy its racist depictions) influences everyday perceptions of black people regardless of the viewer's racial and ethnic background. Lee is his own shrewdest critic in this regard, telling Crowdus and Georgakas, "Culture should be appreciated by everybody, but for me there is a distinction between *appreciation* of a culture and *appropriation* of a culture. People like Dunwitty are dangerous because they appropriate black culture and put a spin on it as if they are the originators of it. There's a big difference."[77] This difference becomes the narrative, thematic, and symbolic playground for *Bamboozled*'s assault on mass-media racism. Lee comprehends how America's culture industry continually reproduces itself by mixing, melding, and combining disparate influences to produce problematic, yet fascinating, texts that disseminate distorted images and mistaken assumptions about the people they portray.

This fact, however, is not reason for despair because counter-images and portrayals are possible, which Lee provides in *Bamboozled,* confirming how correct Saul Landau is to state that the movie offers more enlightenment about the influence of blackface minstrelsy in two hours than the viewer can profitably expect.

Bamboozled, in sum, is an effective, harrowing, and clever film: remarkably funny in certain spots, needlessly unsophisticated in others (particularly its depiction of women), difficult to endure, and, once seen, unforgettable. It demonstrates Lee's intelligent grasp of Hollywood's industrial power, as well as the many ways that cinema and television promulgate stereotypical images of black Americans. *Bamboozled,* thanks to these elements, is mandatory viewing for all students of American mass media, as well as for anyone who wishes to understand how minstrelsy, far from going bankrupt, remains part of American mass entertainment. This message may be depressing, but *Bamboozled* transmutes it into inspired satire that demolishes unthinking ignorance about the relationship between minstrelsy, black culture, and white privilege. Lee's movie, therefore, earns praise that it does not always receive, but certainly deserves.

All Night Long

CITY LIGHTS

Spike Lee's fascination with New York City so palpably enlivens his films and public comments that referring to him as a "New York icon," whether in mainstream or scholarly venues, has become a cliché. Lee's affection for Brooklyn is so famous, thanks chiefly to the Chronicles of Brooklyn movies, that he will forever be associated with this borough, while, in all likelihood, Brooklyn will forever be associated with Spike Lee. His passionate support of the New York Knicks is so expansive that Lee devotes his memoir *Best Seat in the House* to describing in impressive detail his love and knowledge of basketball, while Lee's courtside presence at Madison Square Garden (during Knicks games) remains so frequent that he seems to have taken up residence there. Lee's contributions to the city's arts scene, educational institutions, charitable organizations, and cultural life are so prominent that he, along with eight other honorees, received Mayor Michael Bloomberg's "Made in NY" Award on June 10, 2013.[1] Lee's cinematic rendering of New York City is so powerful that film scholar Richard A. Blake nominates him as one of four exemplary New York directors in the book *Street Smart: The New York of Lumet, Allen, Scorsese, and Lee.*

Although Lee's dedication to New York City is unquestionable, his willingness to criticize his hometown's drawbacks is clear even to casual viewers of his feature films, documentaries, and television projects. Lee refuses to portray the city in the always-idyllic manner of a naïve booster, but neither does he depict it as the nightmarish maelstrom of urban chaos, criminality, and violence that films like *Assault on Precinct 13* (1976), *Escape from New York* (1981), and *Fort Apache, The Bronx* (1981) do. Lee's willingness to examine the city's ethnic, racial, and socioeconomic tensions with a mature, almost diagnostic, and occasionally unforgiving eye demonstrates his commitment to telling forthright stories that, by avoiding saintly/sinful dichotomies, embrace New York City's textures, nuances, and ambiguities. Lee, as his cinematic career attests, can be a harsh critic of New York's social inequities, economic disparities, political insensitivities, and endemic racism, yet his fondness for the city is evident in every film.

Lee's decision to direct *25th Hour*, his 2002 adaptation of David Benioff's 2000 debut novel *The 25th Hour*, continues his complicated cinematic love affair with New York. The film tells the story of Montgomery "Monty" Brogan (Edward Norton), a midlevel drug dealer sentenced to seven years in prison, during his final twenty-four hours before reporting to the federal correctional institute in Otisville, New York. Monty walks through New York City with his dog Doyle, visiting sites from his childhood and eating dinner with his father, James Brogan (Brian Cox), in the man's Irish pub before accompanying his girlfriend, Naturelle Riviera (Rosario Dawson), and two boyhood friends, Wall Street stockbroker Francis "Frank" Slaughtery (Barry Pepper) and high-school English teacher Jacob Elinsky (Philip Seymour Hoffman), to the VelVet nightclub to enjoy one final evening together. The movie's autumnal plot wistfully meditates on friendship, loyalty, betrayal, and self-destruction by paralleling Monty's imminent incarceration with the trauma experienced by the city's residents after the ordeal of September 11, 2001. Scripted by Benioff from his own novel, *25th Hour* is a faithful cinematic rendition that nonetheless bears Lee's imprint. The movie's melancholy tone, assisted by Lee's assured direction, the cast's inspired performances, and Terence Blanchard's poignant score, haunts viewers with a sense of futile inevitability about both its protagonist's and its setting's fate, a feeling that reflects the deep wounds, uncertain futures, and unenviable lives of characters moving through a city still recovering from the shock and sadness of 9/11. Lee transforms Benioff's excellent novel, written and published before the attack, into a movie of stylistic grace whose wide-ranging empathy becomes more powerful as it unfolds. *25th Hour* is a bravura performance by a director so fully in control of his creative talents that the film qualifies as one of the best American movies of the twenty-first-century's inaugural decade.

Even so, *25th Hour* has not inspired the fevered scholarly commentary of other Spike Lee joints, and certainly nothing equivalent to the critical firestorm that greeted his previous feature film, *Bamboozled*. This relative dearth of attention leads Paula J. Massood to exclude *25th Hour* from *The Spike Lee Reader*, the academic anthology that Massood edited for Temple University Press in 2008 and that remains essential reading for anyone interested in Lee's contributions to American cinema. As Massood writes in her introduction, "Films were selected for the collection because of their place in Lee's oeuvre and the critical coverage they may or may not have received," leading her to include *25th Hour* among movies that "are arguably 'minor' films according to this criterion."[2] This statement's qualifiers—*arguably* and the quotation marks around *minor*—particularly apply to *25th Hour*, which may be a less-popular academic topic than *Do the Right Thing*, *Malcolm X*, and *Bamboozled*, but remains a significant accomplishment for Lee, his cast, and his production crew. The movie is even more impressive considering that its modest, $15-million budget[3] required (according to Lee's DVD audio commentary) all actors and most crewmembers—especially star Edward Norton—to accept one-tenth of their normal salaries to participate in *25th Hour*'s production.[4] Despite positive reviews, the movie was seen by fewer people than Lee hoped, due primarily to the scheduling of *25th Hour*'s theatrical release. Touchstone Pictures, the Walt Disney Company subsidiary that funded and distributed the film, opened it in five New York City theaters during December 2002 as part of a marketing strategy that was intended, according to Lee's autobiography, *That's My Story and I'm Sticking to It,* "to qualify [*25th Hour*] for the Oscars" by opening between Martin Scorsese's *Gangs of New York* and Peter Jackson's *The Lord of the Rings: The Two Towers.*[5] This plan backfired, with the film garnering no Oscar nominations (although Terence Blanchard's score received a Golden Globe nomination), while its correspondingly modest box-office success ($13 million in domestic and nearly $11 million in foreign ticket sales[6]) speaks to *25th Hour*'s limited commercial appeal. The movie's aesthetic fineness, however, once again proves that such measurements are poor gauges of any film's quality. Lee is familiar with this phenomenon, with his most challenging movies receiving scant attention by general audiences or Hollywood award organizations (*Clockers, Get on the Bus,* and *Summer of Sam* are notable examples), while *25th Hour*'s status as the first American feature film set in New York City that directly acknowledges 9/11 also distinguishes it, in the words of Mark Kermode's *New Statesman* review "A Talent to Offend," as "either bravely symbolic or mildly opportunistic."[7]

Charges of opportunism have followed Lee since *She's Gotta Have It*'s 1986 release, but Kermode's statement surmises a dichotomy between artistic aspiration and commercial exploitation that *25th Hour* neither embodies nor endorses. This tired film-reviewer's trope presumes that cinematic depictions of national traumas are crass attempts to trade on the public's morbid fascination with large-scale death and destruction, yet generally reserves its opprobrium for movies that chronicle recent domestic events rather than historical traumas (especially incidents occurring during World War II, with the Holocaust first and foremost among them) or American military actions abroad, as the critical praise bestowed upon Terrence Malick's *The Thin Red Line* (1998), Steven Spielberg's *Schindler's List* (1998), Ridley Scott's *Black Hawk Down* (2001), and Kathryn Bigelow's *Zero Dark Thirty* (2012)—to take only four movies released within ten years of *25th Hour*— illustrates. Lee consistently describes the decision to incorporate 9/11 into *25th Hour* as a matter of historical and artistic accuracy, telling Kaleem Aftab in *That's My Story* that, by making the film in New York City so close to the events of 9/11, "in being responsible filmmakers we had to reflect that in the film," leading Lee to decide that "New York City became even more of a character in the film, even though it was a wounded New York

City with people trying to cope with their own particular lives."[8] Lee goes further in his January 16, 2003, interview with *Cinema Gotham,* saying, "I just knew that we were going to do this film, that we were going to be shooting after September 11th. I just thought it would be criminal on my part to not include it. So, I didn't think of it as such a big decision," revealing that the largest issue confronting him "was how to implement September 11th into the film. We did not want to appear like it was appended or anything like that. It had to feel organic, like it was there from the beginning. And I think that we were successful in doing that."[9] Lee's earlier, December 2002 interview with *Blackfilm*'s Wilson Morales affirms this approach: "That was a much bigger and harder decision because I didn't want to offend anyone and we still knew there was a way to deal with it in a tasteful way but not run away from what happened."[10]

These comments reflect more thoughtful intentions than Frank Kermode credits Lee for having, as do Lee's remarks in his April 2003 interview with *Sight and Sound* magazine's Leslie Felperin: "We didn't want it to seem stuck on—it had to be seamless, but at the same time respectful of the people who got murdered, of the loved ones who got left behind. So we decided to use the music, locations, dialogue and visual references to recreate this mood of post-9/11 New York City and America."[11] Lee also links 9/11 to his sense of global identity in "The Quintessential New Yorker and Global Citizen," his 2003 interview for *Cineaste* magazine, telling Paula J. Massood, "I felt compelled to [include 9/11] because I'm a New Yorker; I'm an American; I'm a world citizen"[12] in words far less provincial than so many public responses to the tragedy. Even if critics and scholars discount Lee's statements as predictable apologias for making 9/11 into cinematic fodder fifteen months after the event, *25th Hour* nonetheless examines the wounds that 9/11 inflicts on New York City in microcosm by dramatizing the restless melancholia that afflicts its central characters. Lee's film does not depict the attack itself or sloganeer about its origins, but relies upon sober imagery to express the sadness, loss, and regret affecting Monty, Naturelle, Frank, and Jacob. Indeed, *25th Hour*'s opening-credits sequence features a montage of the Tribute in Light, the two columns of searchlights that annually memorialize the Ground Zero site, in a sequence that, as *Cinema Gotham*'s introduction to its 2003 interview with Lee states, "has the sorrowful feel befitting such an austere monument."[13] Accompanied by Blanchard's somber score, the credits set the tone for a movie that thoughtfully deals with 9/11's aftermath by incorporating the event into *25th Hour*'s visual palette more than its dialogue. The characters, apart from a few stray references, do not discuss 9/11. Lee instead uses visual markers (of the Tribute in Light, of Ground Zero's reconstruction, and of firefighter tributes inside James Brogan's pub) to create spaces of mourning, remembrance, and hope that Monty's final day, with its sense of oncoming defeat, contests despite his best efforts to remain upbeat by spending the evening with friends at the popular nightclub VelVet. The film, therefore, uses 9/11 as the backdrop to its story about loss, punishment, and victimhood to illustrate the difficulty of accepting the consequences of actions that are not wholly understandable. Lee's incorporation of 9/11 is far more restrained, sophisticated, and dignified than the resoundingly jingoistic causes that employed the tragedy as justification (the American invasions of Afghanistan in 2001 and Iraq in 2003 chief among them), or, as Ivan Cañadas writes in his perceptive essay "Spike Lee's 'Uniquely American [Di]vision': Race and Class in *25th Hour*," "Lee's possible opportunism seems rather trivial alongside the ritualized, political exploitation and appropriation of 9/11 over the last few years."[14] *25th Hour*, like Lee's best work, refuses definitive answers to the questions raised by its narrative, but attempts to illuminate the difficulties, contradictions, and doubts that define early twenty-first-century urban American life.

RAGE AGAINST THE SCENE

Among *25th Hour*'s most notable aspects are its careful cinematography, lighting, and casting. Lee and cinematographer Rodrigo Prieto use various lenses and film stocks to capture New York City's visual majesty, employ naturalistic lighting in outdoor scenes to depict the changing hours of the movie's single-day timeframe, and choose bold primary colors (particularly blues and reds) to symbolize the characters' intense moods and emotional states during their sojourn inside VelVet. Lee, as in *Summer of Sam*, directs a cast of predominantly Caucasian actors, although this choice evinces Lee's fidelity to Benioff's source novel, which includes only one major non-white character—Naturelle Rosario (renamed Naturelle Riviera in the movie, Benioff reveals in his DVD audio commentary, to avoid confusion with Rosario Dawson's given name[15])—in a story that, Cañadas argues, examines white privilege in ways that earlier Lee films only suggest.

These three elements—cinematography, lighting, and casting—ensure that *25th Hour* is an accomplished movie that becomes, per Cañadas, a companion piece to one of Lee's most underappreciated films: *Clockers*. Both projects, adapted from novels concerning the drug trade written by white novelists, find Lee probing, insistently and intelligently, the racial problems and paradoxes associated with contemporary urban America, although the films diverge in important ways. Whereas Lee revised early drafts of Richard Price's *Clockers* script to shift the narrative's focus from white homicide detective Rocco Klein (Harvey Keitel) to black drug dealer Strike Dunham (Mekhi Phifer), taking a co-screenwriting credit in the process, he did not alter Benioff's early draft of *25th Hour*'s script as extensively, did not shift the story's focus from the novel's chief protagonist (because Benioff's novel, although alternating among internal monologues from all four major characters, concentrates on Monty Brogan by filtering Naturelle, Frank's, and Jacob's experiences through their relationships with Monty), and did not take a writing credit despite working closely with Benioff to make changes. Lee, during his 2002 *Blackfilm* interview, replies to Wilson Morales's question "How involved was the novelist with the film?" by saying, "David Benioff wrote a great script and then I took it over"[16] to illustrate his respect for the first-time screenwriter, but also Lee's desire to craft the film to his own preferences.

Lee praises Benioff in many venues, particularly his DVD audio commentary and *That's My Story and I'm Sticking to It,* yet this admiration should not obscure Lee's contributions to *25th Hour*'s script. Benioff, indeed, says in *That's My Story* that Lee wished to revise the early screenplay (one draft of which, dated April 30, 2001, still bears the title *The 25th Hour*[17]) to be more faithful to the novel in matters of plot despite small differences in character names (for instance, Barry Pepper's character, Frank Slaughtery, is known as Frank Slattery in Benioff's novel and his first-draft script, while Philip Seymour Hoffman's Jacob Elinsky spells his name *Jakob* Elinsky in these two documents). Confessing his anxiety upon first meeting Lee, Benioff tells Kaleem Aftab that the director, unlike everyone else he had met about the film adaptation, was thoroughly familiar with the book: "The pages were all dog-eared and sections were underlined. A lot of what he was saying was, 'I really liked your book and I don't understand why you weren't more faithful to it in the script.'"[18] Lee, for instance, wondered why Benioff cut "a long cursing monologue to a mirror by Monty"[19] that appears in Chapter Twelve of the novel, a monologue that finds Monty, while sitting on a toilet seat (rather than facing a mirror) in a small restaurant bathroom, react when he notices, "Someone has written *Fuck you* in silver marker above the roll of toilet paper. Sure, he thinks. And fuck you too. Fuck everyone."[20]

Monty then mentally defames every racial and ethnic group in New York City, along with the police, the urban poor, local sports teams, homosexuals, his father, his girlfriend, his friends, and anyone else who comes to mind ("Fuck this city and everyone in it. The panhandlers . . . the turbaned Sikhs and unwashed Pakistanis . . . the Chelsea faggots . . . the Korean grocers . . . the white-robed Nigerians . . . the Russians in Brighton Beach . . . the black-hatted Hasidim . . . the Wall Street brokers . . . the Puerto Ricans . . . the Bensonhurst Italians . . . the uptown brothers"[21]) in a fury that indiscriminately razes everything in its path, including the city itself, until belatedly settling upon himself as the source of his problems: "Fuck this city and everyone in it . . . let the Arabs bomb it all to rubble; let the waters rise and submerge the whole rat-crazed place; let an earthquake tumble the tall buildings; let the fires reign uncontested; let it burn, let it burn, let it burn. And fuck you, Montgomery Brogan, you blew it."[22] Monty's reference to Arabs bombing the city holds particular resonance for anyone reading the novel after 9/11, so Lee and Benioff's choice to eliminate this line from Monty's cinematic diatribe speaks to their sensitive rendering of the changes that befell New Yorkers in the attack's immediate aftermath.

Monty's inner rage, so brazen that it leaves no one unscathed before condemning the city to destruction, is evident in the movie's parallel sequence, set in the bathroom of James Brogan's pub after he (James) laments that Monty could have lived a better life working as a fireman, a lawyer, or a doctor. Monty, irritated but not wishing to argue, enters the bathroom to collect himself, but sees the words "Fuck You!" written in permanent silver ink on the mirror. Lee stages the novel's internal monologue as a five-minute exchange between Monty and the mirror, allowing Edward Norton ample time for a virtuoso performance that sees Monty's reflection unburden his anger, aggression, and contempt in explicitly racist and sexist terms, while Monty himself, not saying a word, bows his head in sadness, exasperation, and regret not only for wasting his life (and receiving a seven-year prison sentence in consequence) but also for thinking these heinous thoughts at all. Monty's film tirade, recalling *Do the Right Thing*'s racial-slur montage, hurls vitriolic abuse at every conceivable group, yet despite their similarities, these sequences accomplish different narrative and thematic goals. *Do the Right Thing*'s montage shows five different individuals insulting specific groups (Italians, African Americans, Koreans, Latinos, and, via Mayor Ed Koch, Jews) to reflect the ironic diversity of New York City's racial and ethnic prejudice. The speakers may not share cultural, economic, or political backgrounds, but their suspicion of outsiders unites them in mutual antipathy, distrust, and invective to demonstrate New York's tenuous social compact, which reverses admiring proclamations of the city's diversity into appalling examples of bellicose bigotry. Naïve pronouncements about New York's laudable and cosmopolitan populace, in other words, cannot long survive *Do the Right Thing*'s slur montage. This sequence exposes the city's legendary openness and embrace of difference as comfortable myths that obscure the much-harsher reality of racial and ethnic tension. Monty's mirror rant in *25th Hour*, by contrast, sees a single person vent his rage at significant groups and individuals who have angered, annoyed, vexed, or wronged him, thereby expressing Monty's dawning realization that these exasperations conceal his unwillingness to take responsibility for choosing an occupation (drug dealing) that exposes him to tremendous legal risk. The New York people, neighborhoods, and institutions that Monty insults become proxies for foibles and flaws that result from his skill at thriving in an illicit business that confers many material rewards. Monty's insensitivity to the misfortunes of other people and the ease with which he inhabits an outwardly respectable, upper-middle-class life permit him to ignore the socioeconomic difficulties, political restrictions, and racial/ethnic bigotries faced by everyday citizens who follow rules and laws that Monty so casually flouts. He, therefore, uses the film's mirror montage to abuse everyone from "the panhandlers, grubbing for money, and smiling at me behind my back" and the "squeegee men dirtying up the clean windshield of my car" (who, Monty's reflection shouts, should "get a fucking job!"[23]) to "the Sikhs and the Pakistanis bombing down the avenues in decrepit cabs, curry steaming out their pores, stinking up my day" (men who are also, Monty screams, "terrorists in fucking training") and "the uptown brothers" that Monty hates because "they never pass the ball, they don't want to play defense, they take five steps on every lay-up to the hoop, and then they want to turn around and blame everything on the white man," leading Monty's mirror image to hurl the racist bromide, "Slavery ended 137 ago. Move the fuck on!"

Lee and editor Barry Alexander Brown insert short scenes—sometimes two- or three-second snippets—of the people whom Monty condemns into the mirror montage to provide an extraordinary visual tour of New York City's residents, neighborhoods, and urban sights. Rodrigo Prieto shoots these cutaways on different film stock, overexposing the light in several, to achieve the grainy appearance of displaced memories and thoughts surfacing after long repression. Illustrating Monty's rant with these images provides necessary visual counterpoint to his hateful words, but also hollows them out by demonstrating New York's living diversity, which is as attractive as Monty's speech is ugly. Lee and Brown employ the techniques of cross-cutting and flashcutting to satirize Monty's tirade while it unfolds, turning Norton's splendid acting back on itself until the final moment, when the despondent Monty, having watched his reflection expel the bile and rage inside him, turns on his mirror image: "No. No, fuck you, Montgomery Brogan. You had it all and you threw it away, you dumb fuck!" Blanchard's jazzy, trumpet-infused score also rises to jubilant highs during this sequence, which, as it progresses, features fewer shots of Monty as images of New York's people and places accelerate until the final moment, when Monty, through his reflection's final reprimand, takes responsibility for his fate. The city and its residents emerge triumphant from Monty's diatribe, demonstrating their resilience, their variety, and their quotidian dignity. Lee carefully controls the cinematography, lighting, editing, and music of Monty's outburst to challenge its fundamental assumptions about, harsh judgments of, and outsized fury at the people who make New York a fascinating yet frustrating place to live. No single sequence in *25th Hour* better expresses Lee's multifaceted love for New York City than Monty's rant, which may seem contradictory, but demonstrates Lee's talent for mixing conflicting tensions, styles, and themes into seamless visual poetry. Lee, the mirror montage makes clear, astutely demanded that Benioff, despite the novelist's hesitance, include this sequence in the film's screenplay as a necessary illustration of Monty's psychological ambivalence. Benioff says in *That's My Story* that, although he was unsure how this montage could be shot, Lee told him, "Why don't you let me worry about that? You just write it."[24]

Benioff also disputes notions that Monty's mirror montage lionizes New Yorkers or their city. In "Doyle's Law: An Interview with David Benioff," he tells *Cineaste*'s Paula J. Massood, "There's a passion there. That's not to say that there's not anger there, as well. I've heard the scene cast as a love letter to New York. There's some truth to it, but that kind of whitewashes it a little bit too. It's a love letter and a hate letter. For any New Yorker there are times when you adore your city, and there are times when you can't stand it. There's a lot of hostility."[25] The filmed sequence reflects this ambivalence, as well as hostility, to make the mirror montage less a valentine to New York than a tone poem that celebrates the city by paradoxically denigrating it. Benioff alludes to this possibility during his interview with Massood, saying, "It's not really a valentine, though the interesting thing is that when I first wrote the novel, all the chapters had titles and the title for that chapter was 'Monty's Valentine.'"[26] The ambiguity of Benioff's comments indicates just how fractured, contrary, and confused Monty's feelings are at this point in *25th Hour*, following an argument with his father that raises what is clearly a familiar lament from James Brogan: that Monty, so attractive and intelligent, has wasted his potential pursuing the drug trade. James does not accuse Monty of outright failure, but instead blames himself for accepting loans from his son to keep the struggling pub in business. James, a former firefighter whose descent into alcoholism after his wife's death prompted Monty to begin selling drugs, nearly martyrs himself during the dinner conversation, although Brian Cox's fine performance underplays this aspect of James's character. Cox never raises his voice or speaks in an angry tone, but the extent of James's regret is evident, causing Monty to rebuke his father for raising the subject before exiting to the restroom. Monty, unable to avoid the difficult emotions provoked by this disagreement, unloads them during the mirror montage. Edward Norton, in a short but insightful 2003 interview with *Sight and Sound*'s Demetrios Matheou, credits Lee with this sequence's effective staging: "Monty is essentially having a dialogue with himself, and this is where working with Spike Lee kicks in—he takes a very literary moment and turns it into a dynamic piece of visual cinema."[27]

The complicated relationship between man and metropolis sketched by *25th Hour*'s mirror montage also includes an historical resonance that Ivan Cañadas detects. Noting in "Spike Lee's 'Uniquely American [Di]vision'" that, "in its attention to detail, and its very comprehensiveness, this tirade amounts to a figurative *beating of the bounds,* the traditional Anglo-Saxon custom whereby young boys were taken to the limits of local communal land to be reminded—often through ritualized violence—of what belonged to the village and what to outsiders," Cañadas recognizes how psychologically cleansing Monty's vitriol is, both for himself and for *25th Hour*'s viewer: "For, alongside the pain and rage felt by Lee's protagonist, there is clearly a deep attachment, if not love, for the place, an attachment that motivates his outburst."[28] The boundaries between Monty and his fellow citizens briefly collapse, then reassert themselves when Monty tries, but fails, to rub the handwritten words "Fuck You!" off his father's mirror. Monty, Cañadas implies, recognizes that the physical and financial freedoms that he has taken for granted will soon belong to the people who inhabit New York City's neighborhoods and boroughs, but not to himself. Monty, once he enters prison, will become an outsider, not the consummate insider he has been, which the movie's repeated references (mostly by Frank Slaughtery) to Monty "going away" reinforce.

The mirror montage's sociological subtext is notable for excoriating so many different people, but its political barbs are equally intriguing. Monty derides Wall Street brokers as "self-styled masters of the universe—Michael Douglas, Gordon Gekko-wannabe motherfuckers, figuring out new ways to rob hardworking people blind" before directly impugning the rapacious profit-mongering of fraudulent corporations and the politicians who support them: "Send those Enron assholes to jail for fucking life! You think Bush and Cheney didn't know about that shit? Give me a fucking break! Tyco! ImClone! Adelphia! WorldCom!" This litany of failed multinational corporations and firms, whose financial misfeasance provoked outrage not long before *25th Hour* began production, is a cri de coeur that indicts President George W. Bush and Vice President Richard Cheney as willing co-conspirators in what, at the time, were the largest fiscal failures since the 1980s' savings-and-loan crisis. Monty here vents against political collusion with multinational capital, which produces, according to him, corruption that rises to the highest levels of power.

Considering Lee's harsh criticisms of Bush and Cheney's performance in office, Monty seemingly voices the director's domestic political opinions, but the rant then turns to international menaces by mentioning 9/11 in one of *25th Hour*'s only verbal references to this tragedy. After denouncing black men, corrupt cops, pedophile priests, the Catholic Church, and even Jesus Christ, Monty's reflection yells, "Fuck Osama bin Laden, Al-Qaeda, and backward-ass, cave-dwelling, fundamentalist assholes everywhere. On the names of innocent thousands murdered, I pray you spend the rest of eternity with your seventy-two whores roasting in a jet-fueled fire in hell. You towel-headed camel jockeys can kiss my royal Irish ass!" The final line's invective pits Monty's ethnicity against bin Laden's Middle Eastern heritage to express, in the mirror montage's angriest moment, the anti-Arab and anti-Muslim racism so prevalent in the weeks, months, and years after 9/11. Monty's statement displays the abject pain and suffering provoked by bin Laden's attack on New York that, combined with stock footage of bin Laden, resembles a primal scream against the death and destruction inflicted upon New York City that manages to overlook Al-Qaeda's political motives in perpetrating 9/11. Monty is in no mood to examine the event's deeper implications, paralleling his refusal to interrogate his own motivations due to the pain that his forthcoming incarceration inflicts upon friends and family. Monty's reference to 9/11 enhances the terrible emptiness confronting him by setting it within the larger context of New York City mourning its dead.

This juxtaposition makes New York City the epicenter of *25th Hour*'s consideration of how traumatic loss affects individuals and communities. Patricia

O'Neill discusses these twin themes in her essay "Where Globalization and Localization Meet: Spike Lee's *The 25th Hour*" by linking Monty's diatribe to its predecessor, *Do the Right Thing*'s racial-slur montage. "The idea of the monologue," O'Neill writes, "comes from Benioff's book but here it gets added ammunition from its allusion to 9/11 and its aftermath and to a similar sequence in *Do the Right Thing*," a correspondence that "shows how the individual's immediate sense of anger over social and economic inequality contributes to a general pattern of racist stereotypes that perpetuate social divisions among people who otherwise share the same frustrations with the city's political economy."[29] These anxieties reveal the city's tenuous communal ties despite the expressions of civic pride, resilience, and unity that followed 9/11. Monty does not lament New York's social and economic inequality until his arrest and conviction demonstrate how his own behavior participates in (and, indeed, profits from) such inequities. Monty's involvement with Brighton Beach gangsters, for instance, offers financial rewards that insulate him from the Wall Street depredations that he decries, but that deleteriously affect many other New Yorkers. Monty's frustrations, per O'Neill, do not surface until the loss of his own freedom forces Monty to realize how strongly his vulnerabilities connect him to his fellow citizens, whom Monty upbraids during the mirror montage, but who, thanks to the cutaway scenes that Lee stages, become mirror images of himself. Monty's overdue acknowledgment of his own culpability, coming at the montage's conclusion, fortifies *25th Hour*'s collapse of political and personal concerns into a narrative that intimately connects them.

The movie, like so many Lee productions before it, is a vehicle for social criticism that does not stop here. *25th Hour*'s discourse about race, class, and justice remains a substantial (if subdued) aspect of its story buttressed by visual flourishes that Lee employs to startling effect. Three scenes (overlooking Ground Zero, inside the VelVet nightclub, and during a fantasy sequence concocted by James Brogan) are notable examples of cinematic storytelling that support and extend *25th Hour*'s political subtext. Their prominence also reveals the extent to which the movie exists in conversation with *Clockers,* a pairing that not only informs *25th Hour*'s approach to its protagonist's economic, social, and cultural position but also defines its status as one of Lee's finest films.

RED, WHITE, BLACK, AND BLUE

Monty Brogan is a son of white privilege, although David Benioff's novel rarely explores this idea. Lee's film adaptation may not foreground this theme as audiences might expect from the director of *Do the Right Thing* and *Malcolm X,* but Lee's casting choices and visual cues create an intertextual bridge with *Clockers* that invites attentive viewers to ponder the differences between Monty and New York City's minority residents. *25th Hour,* as such, covertly implicates issues of race, class, and justice—certainly far less visibly than *Bamboozled*—to suggest that white privilege, being invisible to its beneficiaries, perpetuates the social inequities that Monty's mirror montage so memorably identifies.

Lee achieves this goal by employing what Ivan Cañadas calls a race-reversal technique similar to Joyce Carol Oates's 1995 one-act play *Negative*, which dramatizes the meeting of two young women—one: naïve and white, the other: patronizing and black—during their first day of college. Oates writes in the play's staging notes, "in this encounter, racial stereotypes are reversed, as in a photograph negative."[30] This topsy-turvy situation, intellectually stimulating in the abstract, nonetheless risks reinforcing prejudicial assumptions that African Americans routinely indulge in reverse discrimination, particularly against white people, to cement the claims of political reactionaries in the years following Barry Goldwater's landmark 1964 presidential defeat that anti-black racism has not simply receded, but virtually disappeared from American civic life (claims that achieved unprecedented popularity after Barack Obama's 2008 presidential victory). This blinkered perspective argues that further discussions of racism impede realizing a colorblind, race-neutral society that places all Americans on equal social, political, and economic footing. Similar difficulties attend Desmond Nakano's intriguing, but problematic 1995 film *White Man's Burden,* whose alternate-world premise poses black people as America's dominant socioeconomic and political group, a privileged majority free to ignore the white Americans who struggle to overcome setbacks emanating from their historically disenfranchised, minority position. The settings of Oates's and Nakano's fictions are rich in possibilities for examining racial prejudice from unorthodox perspectives, yet both texts cast their black characters in roles that confirm long-held racist stereotypes about African Americans as provincial, limited, and narrow-minded people who are more bigoted than the white-supremacist society that excludes them. Since charges of reverse discrimination ignore the historical contexts, details, and extent of anti-black racism, such allegations must be carefully sifted and interrogated in ways that Oates and Nakano's race-reversal scenarios evade. The complicated social, cultural, political, and economic effects of American racism, to say nothing of the causes, disappear in well-intentioned narratives that, by posing African Americans as the true oppressors, erase the historical wrongs perpetrated against them.

25th Hour does not follow this path. Cañadas writes that Oates's *Negative* "was clearly intended to appeal to a mainstream, predominantly white audience, by exposing the workings of prejudice all the better for that reversal; it is also a curiously Socratic technique, which requires the audience to reach their own conclusions."[31] Lee's film, Cañadas implies, may similarly target white viewers, but quickly upends standard American racial assumptions by reversing the power relationships presented in *Clockers:* rather than a black drug dealer pursued by white detectives, *25th Hour* finds Monty investigated, interrogated, and arrested by black DEA agents. This alteration to Benioff's novel stamps the movie as Lee's artistic creation, with the director changing *The 25th Hour*'s details to suit his purposes. Benioff's novel depicts Monty's arrest as happening when "four men, all white, none much older than Monty,"[32] present a warrant to search his apartment. The lead agent, Brzowski, seats himself on Monty's sofa, then makes a show of finding it uncomfortably lumpy before unzipping the center cushion to find "a package the size of a bottle of wine. . . . Brzowski raised his eyebrows in feigned shock while the other agents oohed and clucked," telling Monty, in a line that recurs later in the novel, "Mr. Brogan, I do believe you're fucked."[33] This behavior alerts Monty to his betrayal by a confidante who knows where he hides his stash. Benioff's novel never returns to Agent Brzowski, who serves little purpose beyond participating in this flashback to Monty's arrest, which occurs soon after Naturelle's introduction to the story and hints that she may be less trustworthy than she seems.

Benioff's first-draft screenplay retains Brzowski, but Lee's *25th Hour* expands the agent's role. In the film, he becomes Agent Amos Flood, played by talented character actor Isiah Whitlock Jr., "a Lee stalwart," Cañadas writes, "whose trademark is his broad Southern pronunciation of the word 'shit' as a tri-syllabic: 'sheeeeeeeeyit!'"[34] This change from the novel is no minor adjustment, for Flood's presence in two flashbacks—Monty's arrest and his subsequent interrogation—highlights the movie's deeper consideration of white privilege. Flood, accompanied by another black agent named Cunningham (Michael Genet), sits on Monty's sofa while joking with Cunningham. The scene unfolds just as it does in Benioff's novel until the final moment, when Flood, discovering packages of cash and heroin in the cushions, playfully says, "Sheeeeeeeyit! Mr. Brogan, I do believe you're fucked." Whitlock's jovial delivery of this Southern black colloquialism underscores the moment's seriousness, while the actor's performance, along with Genet's, offers welcome respite from the gloom afflicting Monty (even though this flashback, in a significant irony, chronicles the genesis of Monty's legal troubles).

This scene's racial dynamics slyly allude to the Great Migration, the twentieth-century journey of African Americans from the rural South to the industrialized North that Paula J. Massood so sagely analyzes in *Black City Cinema: African American Urban Experiences in Film*, a reference not lost on Cañadas: "In contrast to the white—implicitly middle-class—character, these black characters, therefore, stand symbolically for the historically provincial Southern blacks, later marginalized as the black community of the Northern, inner-city ghettos."[35] The race reversal of *25th Hour*'s premise, with a white criminal apprehended by black law-enforcement officials, permits Lee, in Cañadas's view, to rewrite *Clockers* by "[a]ppropriating these stereotypes for the purpose of an inversion of popular culture stereotypes about crime—particularly drug-related crime—and class and race."[36] Lee's concern with social injustice manifests itself when *25th Hour*, like *Clockers*, considers New York State's problematic Rockefeller drug laws, but from a different angle. Monty's whiteness permits a new approach to these statutes that the earlier movie, with its black protagonist, cannot sustain. Lee, indeed, inserts Monty's interrogation by Flood and Cunningham—a new scene absent from Benioff's novel—to criticize how the drug laws' sentencing guidelines unfairly affect white and black offenders. This discourse is a deliberate consequence of casting Whitlock and Genet in roles that the novel reserves for white men, with Monty's interrogation crucially enhancing the film's racial subtext, particularly when Flood and Cunningham suggest that seven years in prison will be too difficult for a bourgeois white man like Monty to endure. "In this respect," Cañadas comments, "Lee's own commentary [track] includes a key observation concerning the scene in which the D.E.A. officers taunt Monty about the Rockefeller Laws—the mandatory sentencing provision for drug dealing enacted in 1973 by then-New York Governor Nelson Rockefeller—that 'historically' these laws had primarily affected the black community."[37] This unfortunate truth, documented in studies like Marc Mauer's *The Changing Racial Dynamics of the War on Drugs* and Human Rights Watch's *Cruel and Unusual: Disproportionate Sentences for New York Drug Offenders,* leads Flood and Cunningham to use it against Monty by suggesting that his minority status in prison will make him vulnerable to sexual predation. The agents try to manipulate Monty's racial fears (or what they presume to be his racial fears) of hardened black criminals to extract a confession from him in a scene that, for Cañadas, emphasizes Monty's white identity "when the same officers taunt him with the consequences of incarceration for someone like him—namely sexual victimization in the tough, minority-dominated prison environment."[38] Monty takes his forthcoming sexual humiliation for granted, even goading Frank Slaughtery, late in the film, into pummeling his (Monty's) face in an effort to "make me ugly" so that Monty will be less attractive when he arrives at the Otisville penitentiary. Monty, in other words, shares Flood's suspicion that prison is an environment where his whiteness will, rather than protecting him, for the first time expose him to danger.

This outcome contrasts *Clockers'* conclusion, which sees Strike Dunham escape New York City at Rocco Klein's insistence. Rather than going to prison, Strike boards a train that takes him to the American West's open landscapes, allowing that movie's black protagonist to escape New York State's fearsome drug laws and penal system for an uncertain, yet unconstrained future. Cheerful as this outcome may seem, particularly compared to Monty's fate in *25th Hour,* Cañadas recognizes how differing racial subtexts affect *Clockers'* and *25th Hour's* reception. "The question is whether a mainstream audience will feel more sympathy if the dealer is a clean-cut representative of the white majority—just a 'normal,' *white* young man who has made a mistake for which he is going to be cruelly punished," Cañadas writes, observing that "the film's implicit indictment of modern society is that Lee had already told this tale before, in *Clockers*, which failed to garner the attention that *25th Hour* managed."[39] Lee's choice to underscore Monty's whiteness by having African American agents arrest him, in this context, demonstrates not only the inequities of New York's Rockefeller laws but also the unfairness of Hollywood's representational practices and the extent of white privilege. Monty's crimes do not prevent *25th Hour*'s characters and viewers from commiserating with him, whereas a black character in the same position might elicit less sympathy.

Indeed, *25th Hour*'s premise illustrates Monty's favored status by placing him on "step-back," which Kaleem Aftab, in *That's My Story and I'm Sticking to It,* defines as the jail time given to a "nonviolent offender not judged to be a risk to public safety between sentencing and serving the jail sentence to put his affairs in order."[40] Monty's freedom is partially secured by James Brogan pledging his pub as collateral, as Benioff's novel explains: "Mr. Brogan's bar is his bond to the court, his guarantee that Monty will not run away. Since June, Monty has been free because of the bar: free before trial, during trial, after conviction, after sentencing. Mr. Brogan has owned the bar for thirty years, but sometimes he wishes Monty would run."[41] Lee omits this clarification from the film, telling Aftab that he did not want to take too much time explaining that "just because you are arrested you can still walk around, especially if you are kind of privileged too: father is a fireman, not like he was some guy in Harlem or Bed-Stuy,"[42] but the implication remains. Careful viewers can infer the dispensation that Monty receives from the criminal-justice system, making Lee's restraint an even more telling creative decision. *25th Hour* does not explicitly moralize about the drug war's racial inequities, but the protection afforded by Monty's white privilege (at least before he enters prison) is evident to anyone who looks.

Lee visualizes the movie's discourse about race, class, and justice in three significant sequences. The first occurs when Jacob Elinsky visits Frank Slaughtery's expensive, high-rise condominium abutting Ground Zero. Jacob and Frank discuss Monty's future while sitting in a window overlooking the site. This five-minute shot never cuts to different angles, requiring the audience to watch Frank and Jacob talk about Monty's fate while, far below them, trucks, bulldozers, and men work to clean up the destruction's rubble. Linking Monty's incarceration to 9/11 is *25th Hour*'s most direct correlation between personal and communal forms of injustice, underscored by a disagreement between Frank and Jacob. Whereas Jacob confesses his anxiety about seeing Monty later that night, not knowing how to react or what to say, Frank outlines three choices, all of which involve "going away," meaning that they will irretrievably alter Monty's life and relationships. Monty, according to Frank, can become a fugitive from justice, can commit suicide, or can go to prison for seven years, all of which mean that "he's gone. You'll never see him again." Frank, however, does not stop here, saying that Monty's jail sentence is justified because Monty profited off other peoples' misery for several years.

This discussion, taking place above the pit at Ground Zero, recontextualizes the site's meaning by asserting, then disrupting the connection between the injustice done to New York City and to Monty. Frank repudiates the idea that Monty has been unfairly treated, instead placing the blame for his incarceration squarely upon Monty. This development suggests that the city's experience after 9/11 may not be the suffering of fully blameless victims despite the commonly held feeling that the tragedy was senseless and unprovoked. Patricia O'Neill sees this scene as a prime example of how *25th Hour* represents America as the wounded victim of its own militarism and participation in global events. "Although it was not Benioff's intention to see the story of Montgomery Brogan as an allegory for the United States and the consequences of its role in globalization," O'Neill writes in "Where Globalization and Localization Meet," "Lee's visual emphasis on a post 9/11 cityscape and the self-accusations and conflicts between the characters give the movie a confessional tone, a sense of at least potential awareness of how 'bad luck' might also be interpreted as bad choices."[43] Lee does not hammer home this possibility, but staging Frank and Jacob's conversation about Monty's future above Ground Zero allows competing notions of justice to underline a scene whose characters continue to mourn the death and destruction before their eyes.

Lee, in other words, does not claim that New York deserved the attack, but rather pairs Ground Zero with Monty's incarceration to demonstrate how irrevocably diminished they have become. O'Neill insightfully appraises the scene's overall intent: "As we look over their shoulders into the lighted pit where once stood the tallest buildings in NY's cityscape, Frank's sarcasm and Jake's naïvete are both overwhelmed by a sense of dread that life will never be the same, not only for Monty, but for anyone."[44] Lee's camera, indeed, dollies to Frank's window after he and Jacob finish talking to include a startling view of what O'Neill calls "the scene of ruin. The haunting score of Terence Blanchard, which mixes Irish and Arabic elements, and the lingering shots of slow moving trucks and bulldozers pay tribute to the devastation. In the nighttime work of the clean-up crews, we are also given a sobering look at how the work of the city never stops."[45] The screen for the first time cuts to closer views of this clean-up effort to offer, in O'Neill's words, "a documentary moment without any specific suggestion for how we should interpret it,"[46] although the dismay provoked by the scene's conclusion leaves the audience feeling unsettled.

This final image also puts Frank's earlier cavalier attitude about the site's potential danger into relief. Jacob, amazed by the devastation's scale, tells Frank that, according to the *New York Times*, "the air's bad down here." Frank, who reads the *New York Post*, says that the Environmental Protection Agency claims the air is fine, leading Jacob to ask if Frank intends to move. "Fuck that, man," Frank says. "As much good money as I pay for this place? Hell no. Tell you what, bin Laden can drop another one right next door.

I ain't moving." The reference to bin Laden adapts Monty's "let the Arabs bomb it all the rubble" line from Benioff's novel into a statement of defiance that proclaims Frank's (and New York's) resolute determination to carry on despite the tragedy inflicted upon them. Monty, in a telling irony, must demonstrate such persistence to survive prison, but Frank's dialogue, delivered by Barry Pepper with offhanded bravado, reveals Frank's insecurity about his city and his friend. Frank compensates for this weakness with braggadocio that cannot hide his fear or his uncertainty about the future, thereby illustrating the psychic and civic fractures produced by 9/11.

Lee contrasts the visual restraint of Frank and Jacob's conversation with bold primary colors when they, Monty, and Naturelle arrive at Club Vel-Vet for a going-away party arranged by the gangsters who employ Monty. Lee bathes Monty and his friends in cerulean blue when they arrive at the club's entrance, where Monty, encountering a bouncer named Khari (Patrice O'Neal), tells the larger man that the thought of going to prison makes him nervous. Khari, one of the few black characters to speak in the movie, advises Monty, "Don't lose your temper until it's time to lose your temper" before hugging him. The blue's beautiful, calming effect cannot eliminate Monty's disquiet, making this juxtaposition all the more jarring. Lee repeats this visual motif inside the club when Monty, just before going for his final meeting with his boss, Uncle Nickolai (Levani Uchaneishvili), discusses his regrets, fears, and future with Frank in a room overlooking VelVet's dance floor. While Naturelle dances amidst the crowd, Monty tells Frank that he intended to bring all his "loot" to Frank (for investment in stocks) six months before being arrested, but that his greed kept him dealing drugs. Frank objects to this line of thinking, but Monty says he may not survive prison because "there's a thousand guys up there who are harder than me." Frank disagrees, but Monty sketches his expectations of prison life:

> Up there, I'm a skinny white boy with no friends. Those guys are gonna use me up and end me. . . . I'm going in a room with two hundred other guys, Frank. So picture this: first night, lights out, guards are moving out of the space, looking back over their shoulders, laughing at me: "You are miles from home." Door closes, boom: I'm on the floor. I got some big guy's knee in my back. I can give it a little go, but there will be too many of 'em. Someone takes a pipe out from under a mattress, starts beating me in the face. Not to hurt me, just to knock all my teeth out so I can give him head all night and they don't have to worry about me biting.

Monty's fear of domination transforms the cool blue light enveloping the scene from a symbol of relaxed security to one of sexual perversion. The titillating shots of female bodies dancing together recede as Monty's vision of prison rape turns appropriately blue, with its off-color references to fellatio disturbing Frank, who reacts by looking away and shaking his head. Edward Norton delivers this monologue in a matter-of-fact, no-nonsense tone that bolsters the assumption running throughout Lee's film and Benioff's novel that, as Mark T. Conard writes in his essay "Aristotle and MacIntyre on Justice in *25th Hour*," "Monty will be easy prey for the hardened cons in prison, such that the seven-year sentence will mean the end of his life as he knows it."[47] Conard also notes, "The plot is somewhat oddly driven by Monty's fear of prison rape. It's what he dreads and what everyone believes will break him,"[48] although the implicit racialization of Monty's anxiety remains significant. No character need explicitly state that black prisoners will prey on Monty because he and his friends assume that the disproportionately high number of incarcerated African Americans leaves little doubt that Monty will become a target.

Monty's reference to being a "skinny white boy" brings this racial subtext to the surface, making *25th Hour* as much about race as previous Lee films despite the dearth of minority characters. America's inequitable prison system, indeed, becomes Lee's proxy for the movie's racial discourse. Derik Smith summarizes this concept in his insightful essay "True Terror: The Haunting of Spike Lee's *25th Hour*" by writing that Lee's adaptation of Benioff's novel "suggests that, despite programs of gentrification, suburbanization and incarceration which have virtually inoculated the affluent white body against racial hazard, America remains deeply troubled by its dark bogeymen" thanks to "a specific post-9/11 historical context that was—among other things—animated by rhetoric of American interracial solidarity marshaled against a cave-hidden threat from abroad."[49] This temporary unity, Smith recognizes, never erased American society's racial disparities: "Lee's film carefully hollows out this rhetoric by demonstrating that for the American imagination, even in the post-9/11 moment, the most potent menace lurks at home—in a sepulchral prison system that efficiently disappears black male bodies from civil society and social discourse, while intensifying the terror they produce in the national psyche."[50] This fear manifests itself in Monty's doubts about the future, which conveniently help him avoid thinking about his culpability. Taking for granted that he will become the sexual plaything of African American men allows Monty to evade full responsibility for his fate. This defeatist attitude surrenders active control to make Monty the victim of a cruel system in which black men hold more power than he does. The specter of black male sexual aggression, indeed, plagues Monty throughout *25th Hour*.

Lee's final commentary about white privilege appears in the expertly staged fantasy sequence that finishes the film. Monty, hoping to eliminate his good looks before entering prison, provokes Frank into pummeling his (Monty's) face into a bloody, bruised mask just before departing for Otisville. Mr. Brogan volunteers to drive his wounded son, but after getting on the road, James tells Monty that he will head west if Monty wishes it. *25th Hour* again alters Benioff's novel, which concludes with Monty's imagined vision of escape, by having Mr. Brogan narrate a dream sequence where the onscreen images match his words. For Benioff, the scene is a private conjuring that Monty's mind unveils as his father drives through the snow: "But for the space of a mile, as the old car wheezes and hacks through the slush, as the tire chains chant *deh-deh-leh-deh-deh, deh-deh-leh-deh-deh,* Monty closes his eyes and unleashes the temptation, lets it run free in his mind. He has thought these thoughts a thousand times, but they've never been so pure as now, when a left turn westward can make them reality."[51] For Lee, *25th Hour*'s concluding four-minute fantasy sequence is an outstanding fusion of acting, editing, cinematography, and music anchored by Brian Cox's pensive voiceover narration. Lee and Rodrigo Prieto overexpose all shots to give them a bright, shimmering intensity that emphasizes their oneiric status and that reminds careful viewers of *Clockers'* interrogation scenes. As Mr. Brogan tells Monty to get a job that pays in cash, the audience watches images of Monty becoming a bartender in a small Texas town. Naturelle arrives after a few years to live with Monty, quickly becoming pregnant, all while Mr. Brogan tells Monty to give his new family "what they need." The sequence cuts to a shot of the aged Monty and Naturelle standing in front of a white house with their two grown children, each child's spouse, and two small grandchildren, all dressed in clean white clothing and shoes.

This preponderance of white gleams in the overexposed light to suggest an even more dreamlike state, but equally significant is that Monty is the only white person in sight. Both his biracial children (a son and a daughter) have married Latino partners, producing lovely brown granddaughters. Lee here accentuates Monty's privilege through costuming, cinematography, and color scheme by bathing the screen in white to depict Monty's racially mixed fantasy family as a beautiful sight. Mr. Brogan advises Monty to one day tell his relatives about his past as the sequence cuts to an interior shot of the family sitting inside the house as Monty begins confessing the truth. Mr. Brogan's words highlight the wistful, aching regret that the entire sequence evokes: "You gather your whole family together and tell them the truth: who you are, where you come from. You tell them the whole story. And then you ask them if they know how lucky they are to be there. It all came so close to never happening." This comforting, lovely vision has lingered onscreen so long that the viewer nearly jumps when the movie, cutting to Mr. Brogan's vehicle driving along the highway to Otisville, restores its earlier, lusher color palette. *25th Hour*'s final words—Mr. Brogan's voiceover lament "This life came so close to never happening"—match the last sentence of Benioff's novel, but Cox's resigned delivery brings tremendous poignancy to the moment. The screen cuts again to Monty's bruised face as he sleeps in the passenger seat. Since Monty's face healed in the dream's first minute, the viewer now realizes that the previous sequence was a fantasy that provides Monty badly needed refuge.

Although some viewers interpret this ending as ambiguous, the geography of the final shot, with Mr. Brogan's car bypassing the George Washington

Bridge and heading north toward Otisville, implies that he does not drive west or make his son a fugitive. Lee and Benioff both insist that Monty goes to prison, with Benioff's audio-commentary track revealing that he never intended the novel to conclude ambivalently because, to his mind, its final pages clearly mark themselves as fantasy. Lee, by all accounts, was determined that *25th Hour* end with Monty heading to jail, even telling Paula J. Massood during their 2003 *Cineaste* interview that he and Edward Norton, not wanting to glamorize Monty's character, elected for a decisive conclusion: "Number one, in the novel the ending is very ambiguous about whether he goes to prison or not. We did not want to have that type of ending. We wanted him to be going to the slammer, the hoosegow."[52] Lee's audio commentary makes the same point, while Edward Norton tells Kaleem Aftab in *That's My Story,* "Spike was immediately definitive on that: he said that there is no reason to make this movie if he does not go to jail in the end."[53]

The fact that *25th Hour* closes with Monty passively asleep supports the idea that he goes to prison rather than resisting his fate, an ending much different from Strike Dunham's wide-awake wonder at seeing the American West's beautiful landscapes as *Clockers* concludes. Strike, by escaping New York law, fulfills Mr. Brogan's dream, but the image of the dozing Monty stripped of his future depicts Monty more sympathetically than Strike. Both movies conduct dialogues about drugs, race, and justice that, by acknowledging the inequities afflicting America's criminal-justice system, become powerful cinematic dramas. *25th Hour,* as Ivan Cañadas implies, skillfully bookends the racial tensions, dynamics, and subtexts of *Clockers* to illustrate retroactively just how good the earlier film is. Each movie complements the other, leaving the viewer to appreciate how politically complicated, narratively ambitious, and emotionally resonant they are. *25th Hour,* therefore, is a bravely restrained masterwork whose stylistic flourishes make it, along with *Clockers,* one of the best films of Lee's long career.

10

A Good Man Goes to War

FAITH, FLAGS, AND FATHERS

Spike Lee, not content to rest on the critical and commercial laurels he received from 2006's *Inside Man,* took a new and (to outside observers) unexpected direction with his next feature film, 2008's *Miracle at St. Anna.* This adaptation of James McBride's 2002 novel (of the same title) tells the story of four African American soldiers of the segregated 92nd Infantry Division caught behind Nazi lines in 1944 Tuscany after a disastrous German attack on the Serchio River kills everyone else in their squad. These men (colloquially known as buffalo soldiers, "so named," according to McBride's book, "by the Native Americans who saw the first black cavalry as having hair akin to that of their beloved buffalo"[1] in reference to the nineteenth century's six all-black U.S. Army regiments) cross into occupied Italian territory during the battle's tumult and find a traumatized eight-year-old boy named Angelo Torancelli (Matteo Sciabordi) wandering near a blasted farmhouse who quickly bonds with Private First Class Sam Train (Omar Benson Miller), a large infantryman whom Angelo (referred to as "the Boy" for most of the film) calls the "Chocolate Giant." The soldiers, led by Second Staff Sergeant Aubrey Stamps (Derek Luke), eventually take refuge in the small Italian village of Colognora, whose residents cautiously accept the men as protectors from the Nazi troops who, retreating from Allied forces, stalk the surrounding countryside.

Stamps and his men, in perhaps the film's primary irony, must wait for their superior officer, Captain Nokes (Walton Goggins), to bring reinforcements to Colognora, thereby depending upon the man most responsible for their plight to save them. Nokes, a racist Southerner who despises the "nigra soldiers"[2] under his command, mistakenly orders American artillery battlements to fire on the buffalo soldiers' position along the Serchio River (rather than on the Nazi forces) because he refuses to believe that the 92nd Division troops could have advanced so close to the German lines. Stamps and his men endure anxious days in Colognora, but come to enjoy the spirit and generosity of the poor villagers, who, having little food, feel abandoned by the American and British forces liberating Italy from the Nazis. Nokes orders Stamps, Train, and their two other comrades—Corporal Hector Negron (Laz Alonso), the company's radio operator and unofficial translator, and Sergeant Bishop Cummings (Michael Ealy), a charismatic preacher, gambler, and womanizer—to capture a German prisoner of war from the retreating Nazi troops, who, bedraggled and starving, are deserting the German war effort in large numbers. Nokes, under orders from his superior officer, Colonel Jack Driscoll (D. B. Sweeney), must confirm the veracity of a blurry, high-altitude reconnaissance photograph that seems to show thousands of Nazi troops massing in the mountains near Colognora.

When a small band of Italian partisans—local resistance fighters conducting guerrilla raids against Nazi targets—arrives in Colognora with a captured German deserter named Hans Brundt (Jan Pohl), Stamps sees an opportunity to fulfill Nokes's demand. Brundt, who seems as troubled as the boy Angelo, flees the Nazi massacre of 560 villagers in Sant'Anna di Stazzema (anglicized as St. Anna di Stazzema in both McBride's novel and Lee's film) on August 12, 1944. For refusing to participate in this bloodshed and, indeed, trying to save young Stazzema villagers (including Angelo), Brundt is branded a traitor to the Nazi cause and hunted by his own troops. Although neither the partisans nor the buffalo soldiers initially know about the massacre, they eventually realize that Angelo's mental infirmities (the boy, listless and apparently feebleminded, talks to his imaginary friend "Arturo" throughout the film) are in fact responses to witnessing his family and friends—especially his older brother, Arturo (Leonardo Borzonasca)—gunned down by Nazi troops at Stazzema. Brundt attempts to help Angelo and Arturo escape this fate, but Arturo is shot dead as the boys flee their German captors, leaving Angelo orphaned, alone, and traumatized in the Tuscan hills. This revelation comes not long before Nokes and a detachment of 92nd Division buffalo soldiers reach Colognora, only to be attacked by Nazi troops advancing through the mountains. The ensuing battle kills everyone save Angelo and Hector Negron, who receives a Purple Heart for his bravery, returns to New York City, marries, and finds employment as a Harlem postal worker. Negron's later life, indeed, frames the movie's World War II narrative, with the elderly Hector's experiences beginning and ending *Miracle at St. Anna*.

This extensive synopsis, however, offers little justice to the story's emotional nuances, political complexities, and spiritual strivings. The differences among the four buffalo-soldier protagonists form the narrative's spine, while the film treats villagers such as the fascist Ludovico Salducci (Omero Antonutti) and his daughter Renata (Valentina Cervi), a passionate woman embarrassed by her father's political beliefs, as sympathetic characters. *Miracle at St. Anna* also sees the leader of the partisan band, Peppi Grotta (Pierfrancesco Favino), and his second-in-command, Rodolfo Tringali (Sergio

Albelli), command scenes that powerfully sketch their complicated relationship. Peppi, known to the villagers and the Nazi troops as "the Great Butterfly" for his ruthless tactics in fighting the Germans, slowly recognizes that Rodolfo is a Nazi informer, which indirectly provokes both the Stazzema massacre and the movie's climactic battle in Colognora's streets. *Miracle at St. Anna,* in a departure from McBride's novel, does not confine itself to Allied characters, either, but extends its portrait of war's insanity across enemy lines to include Nazi soldiers who, rather than being simplistic black-hatted villains, reveal themselves as thoughtful men troubled by the violence that surrounds them. Apart from Brundt's moral horror at the Stazzema massacre, the most important German character is Captain Eichholz (Christian Berkel), the commander of the Nazi forces near Colognora, who expresses disgust at his German superiors for demanding that his troops continue fighting without adequate food or supplies.

Miracle at St. Anna, therefore, is no rousing combat film that indiscriminately applauds American participation in World War II even if it honors the sacrifices of the 92nd Division soldiers whose story Lee and McBride wish to give wider prominence. The film, like its source novel, avoids the jingoistic heroism of earlier movies in the genre, particularly those starring John Wayne, such as 1949's *The Sands of Iwo Jima* and 1962's *The Longest Day.* The elderly Negron watches the latter film in *Miracle at St. Anna*'s opening scene, muttering "Pilgrim, we fought for this country too" as Wayne's character, Lieutenant Colonel Benjamin Vandervoort, reacts in horror at seeing the corpses of American paratroopers hanging from telephone poles. Negron's line explicitly rebukes Hollywood's long history of erasing African American soldiers from cinematic renditions of the war effort, although *Miracle at St. Anna* follows *The Longest Day* in one significant respect by having all characters speak their native language, with non-English dialogue subtitled onscreen. Even so, Negron's withering contempt for Wayne's iconic performance alerts viewers to the fact that they will encounter an atypical, unconventional, and sometimes strange war picture.

Miracle at St. Anna, as Negron's frame story demonstrates, does not begin as a World War II tale, but rather as a murder mystery set in 1983 Harlem, meaning that audiences unfamiliar with McBride's novel and the film's advance press (including its one-sheet poster) might not realize that they are watching a war movie at all. Negron, working at the Harlem Post Office the next day, sees the aged Rodolfo standing before him, asking to purchase a twenty-cent stamp. Rodolfo, the viewer learns much later in the film, escapes from 1944 Colognora moments after slitting Hans Brundt's throat and attempting to kill Negron. This act of betrayal goes unpunished for thirty-nine years, until Rodolfo improbably encounters Negron at the post office. Hector, with contempt of his face, pulls a German Luger pistol from his desk and shoots Rodolfo dead. This murder's consequences bookend the movie's story in a narrative device that recalls Steven Spielberg's *Saving Private Ryan*

(1998), a film that *Miracle at St. Anna* consistently revisits, reconsiders, and revises. Both movies, by employing frame stories that see elderly World War II veterans remember their time in combat, provoke extended flashbacks recounting the experiences of a small band of soldiers that survives the war's horrors by taking refuge with local villagers and by learning about one another's civilian lives before engaging a final battle that kills all but one man. Other parallels include combat scenes of appalling visceral power that do not flinch from showing just how terrible close-quarters fighting is, fine musical scores that swing from delicate melodies to stentorian marches, and location shooting that emphasizes authentic cinematic re-creations of the conditions facing actual combat troops.

The similarities shared by *Miracle at St. Anna* and *Saving Private Ryan*, however, should not conceal their differences. Spielberg's film reverses the standard war-film plot of a single man sacrificing his life to save an entire squad by assigning Captain John Miller (Tom Hanks) and his crew of seven soldiers to save one man, Private First Class James Francis Ryan (Matt Damon), after his three brothers, all servicemen, die in battle. *Miracle at St. Anna*, by contrast, sees Aubrey Stamps's four-man squad save the boy Angelo's life, but as an act of unexpected mercy by Sam Train that his fellow soldiers do not at first support. The boy's presence, however, redeems the buffalo soldiers' humanity to the point that the self-centered Bishop Cummings sacrifices his life during the battle of Colognora to protect Angelo from Nazi fire. *Saving Private Ryan*'s opening combat scene recounts in grisly detail the U.S. Army's June 6, 1944, landings on Normandy Beach in wrenchingly realistic, yet undeniably heroic, terms that underscore Miller's bravery, while *Miracle at St. Anna*'s opening battle scene along the Serchio River demonstrates the tragic ineptitude of the U.S. Army's policy of allowing white Southerners to command segregated troops. Captain Nokes's foolish refusal to believe the reality of Stamps's call for artillery fire emanates from his (Nokes's) pathological unwillingness to credit black infantrymen's competence: Nokes cannot accept that they are smart, committed, or brave enough to advance as far toward enemy lines as they do. *Miracle at St. Anna*, in other words, adopts a grimmer, more pessimistic, and less noble view of the American military's effectiveness than *Saving Private Ryan* to illustrate just how unfair, intemperate, and bigoted its official policy of segregation was (a reality that Spielberg's movie never acknowledges or even mentions).

Saving Private Ryan's final sequence also undercuts the film's vaunted status as a realistic, convention-shattering war picture by endorsing one of the genre's largest clichés: the hopeless battle whose doomed American soldiers demonstrate their patriotism by sacrificing themselves in the name of freedom, becoming in the process heroes worthy of the veneration that they receive as members of what Tom Brokaw has famously dubbed "the Greatest Generation" fighting what Stephen E. Ambrose, without irony, calls "the Good Fight" and Studs Terkel, with more pause, calls "the Good War."[3] *Miracle at St. Anna,* although concluding with a climactic battle that sees

American soldiers gunned down while trying to save Colognora's villagers, demonstrates that the servicemen's noble sacrifice comes amid shocking carnage that amounts to a second massacre of innocent civilians by Nazi troops. Although the sequence nicely illustrates Stamps's, Train's, Bishop's, and Negron's individual courage, honor, and fidelity, it refuses to celebrate this confrontation or the larger war effort as glorious battles against oppression, but rather sees them as upsetting displays of human butchery that leave no one unscathed. The fact that Hector Negron goes back to New York City to live in obscurity rather than being celebrated as a hero speaks to the unfair treatment that black soldiers received during and after World War II, returning to America as second-class citizens living in a segregated nation. These realities, which *Miracle at St. Anna* sketches in both its frame story and during its long flashback to 1944 Tuscany, distinguish Lee's film from Spielberg's more triumphant rendering of the war's effects. Lee, in other words, rejects uncritically portraying World War II as a good war, much less the Good War, even if his film records many acts of kindness.

Perhaps the most noteworthy distinction between *Miracle at St. Anna* and *Saving Private Ryan* is their public reception. Spielberg's movie was released to rapturous praise by film reviewers, extraordinary box-office returns (grossing more than $480 million against its $70-million production budget[4]), and numerous industry awards (including five Academy Awards, two BAFTA Awards, and two Golden Globe Awards[5]). *Miracle at St. Anna* fell far short of these honors in every instance. Lee's movie received mixed reviews (some quite punishing in their assessments, although nothing on par with the critical scorn heaped upon *She Hate Me*), was remarkably unprofitable (grossing just $9 million against its $45-million production budget[6]), and won no awards (being nominated for six Black Reel Awards and three Image Awards, but losing them all[7]). Film reviewers, indeed, dissected *Miracle at St. Anna*'s flaws almost as extensively as they ignored *Saving Private Ryan*'s drawbacks. David Sterritt usefully summarizes the movie's initial critical reception in his book *Spike Lee's America* as collecting "unfavorable reviews from critics who focused on its cinematic quality, and somewhat better ones from critics who gave more weight to its good intentions, historical significance, and intermittent moments of effective filmmaking."[8]

This final assessment, at base, recalls the oldest challenge to Lee's skills as a cinematic storyteller: that he violates the principles of classical Hollywood style by structuring his films as fragmented narratives stuffed with unlikeable characters, multiple themes, and ambitious symbols that do not produce a coherent movie. The most common observation by *Miracle at St. Anna*'s critics is that the film wanders through its story, tackling too many subplots and too many characters for audiences to understand. Roger Ebert begins his review with words that reflect the critical consensus that *Miracle at St. Anna* is, in some ways, a missed opportunity. The movie, Ebert writes, "contains scenes of brilliance, interrupted by scenes that meander. There is too much, too many characters, too many subplots. But there is so much here that is powerful that it should be seen no matter its imperfections."[9] Wesley Morris, writing in the *Boston Globe*, dislikes the film's neither-here-nor-there plotting, which leads to generic confusion, meaning that *Miracle at St. Anna* "is a Hollywood war picture that, at some variously inopportune moments, is also a bunch of other things—a police procedural, a docudrama, a courtroom drama, a nighttime soap (in broad, fraught daylight), and a small-Italian-village fable. It's *Of Mice and Men, Saving Private Ryan,* a Roberto Benigni-less Benigni movie, and occasionally Spike Lee."[10] Mick LaSalle, in the *San Francisco Chronicle,* agrees that *Miracle at St. Anna,* despite including powerful individual scenes that function as vignettes rather than a cohesive narrative, falters by mixing Angelo's story with the movie's commendable desire to recoup the buffalo soldiers' heroism. "Lee's problem is not merely that there are two movies here, but that these two strains are in conflict and undermine each other," LaSalle writes. "On the one hand, the film pulls in the direction of fable as seen through the eyes of the little boy, promising a mix of horror, magic and miracles, similar to *Pan's Labyrinth.* On the other, Lee does his best to make a realistic epic about the experience of black soldiers, a kind of African American *Saving Private Ryan.*"[11]

LaSalle's comparison of Lee's and Spielberg's movies, by assuming that the buffalo soldiers' experience recapitulates that of the white characters who populate *Saving Private Ryan,* is misguided. Although LaSalle briefly acknowledges this notion's impropriety, writing in a later passage, "when the staff sergeant [Aubrey Stamps] observes that he feels more at home and accepted in Italy than in his own country, Lee begins to make a case for a realistic movie about the black GIs' experience,"[12] LaSalle mostly ignores the history of segregation that *Miracle at St. Anna,* like its source novel, dramatizes, interrogates, and repudiates. *Miracle at St. Anna,* however, revises *Saving Private Ryan*'s approach to World War II (and to World War II movies) through three principal strategies that recall films associated with the cinematic movement of Italian Neorealism: (1) embracing a meandering plot that allows disparate characters, ideas, and themes to exist on the same screen and in the same story without resolving themselves into tidy conclusions; (2) employing the relationship between Sam Train and the boy Angelo to invert the paternalistic treatment of the buffalo soldiers by their white superiors; and (3) emphasizing religious imagery to illustrate how faith both succeeds and fails at redeeming men traumatized by war. These aspects of *Miracle at St. Anna* make it a challenging, problematic, and worthwhile adaptation of McBride's mystical novel that, while not wholly successful, is stronger than *Saving Private Ryan, The Longest Day,* and many so-called enduring films of its genre.

WAR STORY?

The question of classification, however, haunts *Miracle at St. Anna.* Both Lee and McBride dispute pigeonholing the film and the novel as war narratives.

Lee, during a 2008 interview with *FLOWInsiders'* Kam Williams, notes that the movie's religious concerns transcend many traditional war-picture conventions. Responding to Williams's question "Would you say *Miracle at St. Anna* is more than just a war movie?," Lee replies, "This film is definitely more than just a war film. Of all the movies I've done, this one, by far, has more discussions of religion, faith and hope. That reflects James McBride's novel which is all about hope, faith, prayer, belief and God."[13] Despite previous Lee films (especially *Jungle Fever*) including religious characters, moments, and themes, the director correctly evaluates the range of *Miracle at St. Anna*'s spiritual scope, which only Lee and McBride's later cinematic collaboration, 2012's *Red Hook Summer,* surpasses. McBride, in a *BookBrowse* interview devoted to his novel, also sees *Miracle at St. Anna* as more than a war narrative, saying, "The war simply serves as a backdrop for the human drama that takes place in the relationships among these four Negro soldiers, the six-year-old boy, a group of Italian partisans, and the Italian villagers," allowing him to create a detailed portrait of people and place that, in McBride's opinion, too rarely appears in fictional renderings of World War II: "Italy was a fascinating place during that time. The Italians suffered terribly during the war. The ramifications of those years still reverberate throughout the country today."[14] These resonances inform his novel and Lee's film by grounding both texts in geographical, historical, and cultural details that might otherwise have been lost. *Miracle at St. Anna,* in its print and cinematic forms, is neither a history text nor a documentary, but uses factual details to weave a story that combines bracingly realistic and unabashedly fanciful scenes into a strange narrative that considers the war from odd angles.

McBride's extensive research for the novel (and, consequently, the film adaptation) involved interviewing many surviving 92nd Division soldiers and Italian partisans to underscore that *Miracle at St. Anna,* despite his protestations, is a novel primarily about World War II. He tells *BookBrowse,* "I read roughly 25 books about the war in Italy. I interviewed dozens of 92nd Division vets from all across the country," but did not stop here: "I even traveled to Italy with some of them when they went back for a reunion. I studied Italian at the New School in Manhattan and then spent about eight months in Italy, including a five-month stint with my entire family."[15] This experience allowed McBride a unique opportunity to enhance his appreciation for *Miracle at St. Anna*'s historical context: "While there I interviewed just about anyone I could find including civilians who had survived the war, survivors of massacres, former soldiers, fascists, and partisans including the sons and daughters of men and women who had died during the war and wanted to tell their parents' stories."[16] These tales support the novel's narrative, which moves from terrifying combat scenes involving the buffalo soldiers and the Italian partisans through Train and Angelo's winsome relationship to the tension besetting Peppi's partisan squad (thanks to Rodolfo's secret life as a Nazi informant). McBride also describes *Miracle at St. Anna*'s genesis in the novel's acknowledgments section, revealing, "This book began many years ago, when I was a boy of about nine, sitting in the crowded living room of my stepfather's brownstone in Fort Greene, Brooklyn" listening to his stepfather's brothers and friends "flinging tall tales across the room like bullets."[17] These memories lead McBride to analyze, with insight and honesty, *Miracle at St. Anna*'s approach to World War II: "I am thankful to these survivors of the so-called Good War, the veterans of the 92nd Infantry Division who fought in Italy, the Italians who fought with them, and the Germans who fought against them—they were victims all."[18]

McBride refuses to depict the war as a crude contest of good versus evil that casts the Americans (along with their Italian allies) as upright heroes and the Germans as remorseless villains, suggesting that all participants are, in some measure, political pawns in a struggle that they neither fully understand nor unconditionally support. His reference to the "so-called Good War" indicates a more complicated view of World War II that the novel captures, while defining the Nazi soldiers who opposed the American and Italian fighters as victims announces McBride's concern for the human costs of enduring combat. He seeks not to demonize these men, but to dramatize the terrible conditions facing German troops who were undernourished, undersupplied, and underequipped by Berlin's central planners. This compassion extends to Lee's film adaptation, as McBride discusses in "The Making of a King," his foreword to *Miracle at St. Anna: The Motion Picture—A Spike Lee Joint,* a companion publication that includes generous on-set photographs, Lee's notes about the movie's three-month shoot, and McBride's screenplay. McBride credits Lee with supervising the script's writing process to enhance its authenticity: "He added real historical figures like Mildred 'Axis Sally' Gillars [Alexandra Maria Lara], the German equivalent of Tokyo Rose, who taunted the Buffalo soldiers even as they fought and died in battle, broadcasting to them that the enemy was not in front, but rather behind them in the form of their racist commanders."[19] Equally significant for McBride is Lee's commitment to broadening the story's sympathy for all its characters, especially the Nazi troops that American war films traditionally depict as mindless killers: "He added Captain Eichholz and Colonel Pflüger to give dimension to the German perspective in the film, determined that the Germans would not be portrayed as the one-dimensional, stereotypical goose-stepping Nazis so often seen in American war movies, but rather as starving, exhausted men trapped in the lost cause of a war many of them despised."[20] McBride's novel alludes to these matters, but Lee's film commendably clarifies them by illustrating Eichholz's hatred of what he considers his craven, incompetent, and uncaring superiors, as well as Hans Brundt's disgust at the Stazzema massacre.

Lee's impulse to dramatize the German perspective has precedent in *The Longest Day,* which includes scenes focusing on Nazi officers and troops before, during, and after the Normandy invasion. *Miracle at St. Anna,* however, goes further when malnourished German soldiers object to Axis

Sally's droning voice, pity certain Italian villagers whom they encounter, and even desert the Nazi lines. These scenes, absent from McBride's novel, remain unusual for an American World War II film set in Europe. *Saving Private Ryan,* for example, includes no comparable elements save one sequence involving Czech conscripts in the Nazi Army shot to death by Captain Miller's squad while trying to surrender. Spielberg's earlier film *Schindler's List* (1993) includes Nazi roles, but, apart from S.S. Captain Amon Goeth (Ralph Fiennes), commandant of the Kraków-Plaszów concentration camp (and the film's only significant Nazi character), German soldiers receive little dialogue. Goeth, despite Fiennes's good performance, appears more as a homicidal psychotic than a flesh-and-blood human being, making *Schindler's List* less effective than its many industry honors suggest. Lee's additions to *Miracle at St. Anna,* therefore, enlarge the film's scope and humanitarian concerns to transform it into a war movie that, while rooted in its primary genre, is unafraid to reexamine, rewrite, and expand this category's conventions. Lee's deliberate intervention in the tried-and-true tropes of a venerable Hollywood genre qualifies *Miracle at St. Anna* as a notable hybrid of traditional and eccentric movie storytelling that, unsurprisingly, characterizes its director's entire cinematic career.

A.O. Scott's "Hollywood War, Revised Edition," his incisive *New York Times* review of *Miracle at St. Anna,* recognizes this development as typical of Lee's moviemaking approach. "Like the French director Rachid Bouchareb, whose *Days of Glory* followed Arab soldiers fighting for France against the Nazis," Scott notes, "Mr. Lee sticks to the sturdy conventions of the infantry movie, adapting old-fashioned techniques to an unfamiliar, neglected story. And the cinematic traditionalism of *Miracle at St. Anna* is perhaps its most satisfying trait."[21] This conventional approach, however, cloaks Lee's political project in revisiting the World War II film, which Scott properly gauges as central to its narrative effect: "At its best, this is a platoon picture, and if it's not exactly like the ones Hollywood made in the late '50s and early '60s, that's part of Mr. Lee's argument: it's the movie someone should have had the guts or the vision to make back then. Better late than never."[22] Focusing on four black army soldiers in a major American theatrical film, in other words, is long overdue even if African American combat troopers were previously dramatized in Charles Haid's *Buffalo Soldiers* (1997), a fine but little-seen television movie produced for Turner Network Television that features an excellent central performance by Danny Glover as the leader of the all-black Calvary Troop H, assigned to capture an Apache warrior in the days after the Civil War, and Robert Markowitz's *The Tuskegee Airmen* (1995), an effective television film produced for Home Box Office that features good performances by Laurence Fishburne, Andre Braugher, and Cuba Gooding Jr. as the first all-black squadron of U.S. Army Air Corps pilots.

Miracle at St. Anna, as such, breaks ground for American feature films by depicting the experience of African American combat soldiers in World War II, and stood alone until Anthony Hemingway's *Red Tails* arrived on multi-plex screens in 2012. This big-screen retelling of the Tuskegee Airmen story (budgeted at $58 million, produced by George Lucas, and starring Cuba Gooding Jr.), like *Miracle at St. Anna,* takes place in 1944 Italy, shows the unfair racial segregation confronting its protagonists, and received similarly mixed reviews. *Red Tails,* however, depicts its central characters' nobility so solemnly that it resembles the old-fashioned war movies that *Miracle at St. Anna,* despite its moments of earnest traditionalism, resists in key sequences. Lee's film, while never dismissing the heroism or dignity of Stamps, Train, Bishop, and Negron, shows them as imperfect men who squabble among themselves about Angelo's presence, tactical decisions, local women, and their attitudes toward fighting for a nation that oppresses them. The charac-ters discuss their lives, opinions, and attitudes in scenes that A. O. Scott finds "corny and didactic,"[23] but that, in his view, further strengthen *Miracle at St. Anna*'s debt to previous World War II films. "Every now and then, the action slows down to make time for a speech or a carefully staged argument about racial injustice," Scott comments. "But if you're tempted to roll your eyes, recall that such speeches—on the subjects of liberty and democracy and the mortal threat to those ideals posed by Hitler and his army—have always been a staple of all but the most hardboiled and cynical World War II movies."[24]

This accurate appraisal of earlier war pictures, however, ignores key facts about *Miracle at St. Anna,* which not only regards Hitler as an equal menace to his own troops as to their Allied opponents but also contemplates the ideas of liberty and democracy from a more jaded perspective than many previous World War II films. Bishop's cynical regard for army life, Stamps's confession that he feels more at home in Italy than in America, and a crucial flashback to the squad's racist treatment by a café owner in Alexandra, Louisiana, dur-ing their training at Camp Polk ensure that *Miracle at St. Anna* manifests a world-weariness about America's racial dynamics that earlier war films ut-terly avoid. Scott, to his credit, identifies the essential point of including such sequences in *Miracle at St. Anna* when he writes, "as in *Days of Glory,* the high-minded talk and theme-announcing scenes illuminate a thorny and crucial paradox, namely that the countries fighting against totalitarian race-hatred had some serious race problems of their own."[25] This contradiction not only drives *Miracle at St. Anna*'s patchwork plot but also demonstrates how classifying the film as a war story is perfectly appropriate even if Lee and McBride prefer other descriptions. *Miracle at St. Anna*'s traditionalism, in other words, neither negates nor contradicts its revisionist tendencies, which, when closely examined, reveal a complex film that explores familiar Lee ter-ritory in unfamiliar ways.

OLD AND NEW

Miracle at St. Anna's greatest challenge to first-time audiences is its mean-dering storyline, which ambles from scene to scene and sequence to sequence without the clear narrative markers that classical Hollywood style demands. This approach is no surprise to longtime viewers of Lee's films, who are accustomed to his preference for plots that string together incidents, characters, and themes into loosely connected vignettes telling multiple stories that compete with one another for attention. Some plotlines advance to firm conclusions, some loop back on themselves, and, in what strikes audiences who value clear endings as Lee's most maddening tendency, some subplots never clearly resolve. Joe Morgenstern speaks for these people in his *Wall Street Journal* review of *Miracle at St. Anna* by writing, "Yet [Lee's] storytelling this time is fragmented to the point of incoherence,"[26] referring to the movie's numerous flashbacks (occurring, thanks to the frame story about Hector Negron shooting Rodolfo, inside the extended flashback that constitutes *Miracle at St. Anna*'s main narrative). The film fuses stark combat narrative with the father-and-son dynamic of Train's relationship with Angelo, plentiful religious symbols, and the details of daily life in Colognora as its residents, struggling to survive the Nazi occupation of Italy, deal with disruptions caused by the buffalo soldiers' arrival. Scenes of American and Nazi commanders facing the difficulties of their respective tactical positions mingle with gentle sequences of Train interacting with Angelo and of the villagers dancing at a community feast, interspersed with yet more scenes of the partisans conducting guerrilla raids against Nazi troops, Hans Brundt's capture and interrogation, disagreements among Stamps and Bishop over Renata, and, in the film's most disturbing sequence, the Nazi massacre at Stazzema.

This mixture, for Morgenstern, Mick LaSalle, and even defenders like Roger Ebert and A.O. Scott, is simply too unwieldy to produce a gripping cinematic experience. They all suggest that *Miracle at St. Anna*, with more disciplined editing, could become a formidable film, but imply that Lee refuses to shape the movie's story into a more lucid and intelligible form. Morgenstern, indeed, condenses the objections of several reviewers (and, according to the "Reviews and Ratings" section of *Miracle at St. Anna*'s Internet Movie Database entry,[27] just as many viewers) by writing, "The irony of the production as a whole is that an impassioned filmmaker with a strong tale to tell has managed to lose track of it. Instead of staying close to the troops and their travails, the film wanders through wartime Tuscany like an addled tourist, mesmerized by village life and eager for miracles."[28] *Miracle at St. Anna*, for these observers, is a self-indulgent exercise in sentiment that, in LaSalle's words, is also "an awful mess."[29] The movie cannot overcome the burdens imposed by Lee's slapdash vision, causing the *Washington Post*'s Ann Hornaday to condemn *Miracle at St. Anna* as an "overwrought, overproduced, overbusy and overlong" epic that "finally suffers from the worst filmmaking sin of all: the failure of trust, in the story and the audience. And no miracle can overcome that."[30]

Such harsh appraisals are fully justified from the perspective of classical Hollywood style. *Miracle at St. Anna*, at first blush, is a difficult movie to follow, thanks to inconsistent pacing, ever-changing narrative tones (running the gamut from tenderness to brutality), and characters as symbolic as they are realistic. The film, for Hornaday, risks boring viewers who prefer more traditional war pictures, who find its tangled storyline off-putting, and who may be forgiven for criticizing its diffuse plotting. These reactions do not reflect unsophisticated cinematic sensibilities, either, but rather preferences for a straightforward narrative style that decades of Hollywood filmmaking have inculcated in audiences, but that *Miracle at St. Anna* cannot (and seems determined not to) satisfy.

Lee, indeed, structures his movie after the similarly scattered narrative of McBride's novel. More significant, however, is how Lee patterns *Miracle at St. Anna* after key films associated with Italian Neorealism, including Roberto Rossellini's *Rome, Open City* (1945) and Vittorio De Sica's *Bicycle Thieves* (1948). Lee extols their influence in "Deeds Not Words," his introduction to the movie's companion volume, by writing, "I truly believe the fathers of Italian neo-realism willed this film to fruition."[31] Lee lists the neo-realist movies that, in his view, make *Miracle at St. Anna* possible. "Let's all give thanks and praises," Lee writes, "to Vittorrio De Sica (*Shoeshine*, 1946; *The Bicycle Thief*, 1948; *Miracle in Milan*, 1951); Roberto Rossellini (*Rome, Open City*, 1945; *Paisan*, 1946; *Germany Year Zero*, 1948); and Luchino Visconti (*Ossessione*, 1943; *The Earth Trembles*, 1948; *Bellissima*, 1951) for their blessings and inspiration," which, in Lee's bold estimation, "allowed a miracle birth to occur from the intertwining of Italian and African American cinemas."[32] Readers might expect a filmmaker discussing his own movie in a book dedicated to its production to lavish fulsome praise on his cinematic forbears (as a smart commercial strategy intended to increase ticket and book sales, if nothing else), but Lee's indebtedness to his predecessors shrewdly positions *Miracle at St. Anna* as heir to movies that may now be regarded as classics, but that, in their own day, drew mixed notices. As Mark Shiel comments in *Italian Neorealism: Rebuilding the Cinematic City*, "neorealist films were not generally commercially and critically successful although, when they were, they were often high-profile in their success and in the public and critical controversies they provoked."[33] These words aptly describe *Miracle at St. Anna*'s contested reception, its controversial depiction of the Stazzema massacre, and Lee's public spat with director Clint Eastwood that preceded *Miracle at St. Anna*'s theatrical release. These elements, alongside *Miracle at St. Anna*'s penchant for blending stark realism with fable-like fantasy, mark Lee's movie as a descendent of Italian Neorealism that never wholly indulges neorealist conventions.

Lee and McBride, by including American characters as protagonists, violate one salient feature of neorealism, namely its desire to record the quotidian difficulties of Italian life during and after fascism. Millicent Marcus, in her fine book *Italian Film in the Light of Neorealism*, insightfully appraises the movement's underlying impulses and unifying themes: "As the cinematic offspring of the Resistance (*Open City*, for example, was originally intended to commemorate the anti-Fascist underground of Rome), neorealism became the repository of partisan hopes for social justice in the postwar Italian state. Its means were at once epistemological, moral, and political."[34] Marcus quotes Vittorio De Sica's comments about his movie *Shoeshine* when noting, "The neorealist resolve 'to plant the camera in the midst of real life, in the midst of all that struck our astonished eyes' enabled filmmakers and their audiences to see an Italy that Mussolini had concealed for two full decades."[35] *Miracle at St. Anna*, despite focusing on American characters, reflects this commitment's complications. The buffalo soldiers begin empathizing with the villagers' plight after arriving in Colognora, at first ignoring Nokes's order to capture a Nazi soldier in favor of assisting, however meagerly, their benefactors. Train's concern for Angelo, particularly his fierce devotion to the boy's safety, tells in microcosm the movie's larger story of the American squad's deepening sense of obligation to the people who house them. Stamps expresses this sentiment best when he tells Negron that he (Stamps) hopes to stay in Italy after the war because "Somethin' wrong here. Getting to love Italy. I ain't a nigger here. I'm just me." His affection for Colognora's inhabitants develops from their willingness to recognize his full humanity, or, as Stamps puts it, "these Italians catching holy hell, but they ain't studying about how to keep a Negro down." Stamps articulates the other buffalo soldiers' feelings, although Train, Negron, and Bishop rarely say so. Their actions and reactions—sharing food, offering solace, pledging protection, and, in the case of Bishop and Renata, having sex—validate Stamps's faith in both the villagers and his own squad as *Miracle at St. Anna* unfolds. Stamps may regard fighting for the American Army as a matter of pride that will help lead his nation along the path of racial progress, but he cannot ignore his life's segregated reality, saying in the same speech, "I ain't never felt so free in my life. It makes me feel ashamed to feel more free in a foreign country than I do my own. All my tomorrows was based on America gettin' better. What if it doesn't?" This bleak possibility occurs while Stamps, his men, and the villagers dance with one another in Colognora's church, drawing together *Miracle at St. Anna*'s concerns for social justice, political progress, and religious faith in a setting so reminiscent of neorealist films that Lee's fluency with these movies becomes evident.

Angelo's presence is another crucial aspect of *Miracle at St. Anna*'s neorealist homage. Lee highlights this fact in the companion volume, writing, "A key characteristic of the great Italian neo-realism films is a child being a main character. James McBride's novel had this even though, at the time, he had not seen any of the classics like *Rome, Open City,* and *Bicycle Thief.*"[36] McBride's unfamiliarity notwithstanding, both his novel and his screenplay underscore Angelo's symbolic capacity to redeem the buffalo soldiers' bitter experiences in combat despite the boy's war trauma. Witnessing the Stazzema massacre shatters Angelo's memories, which, according to McBride's novel, "were like tiny single slivers of glass blowing through a wind tunnel with a giant fan at one end and him at the other, the slivers jarring and jumbling about, slicing through the air past him, dangerous and deadly when they hit, even more dangerous when they missed, for more often than not they were lost in the roar and din and shrill yelling of fleeing villagers."[37] This vivid description, coming early in the book, enables McBride's readers to understand Angelo's odd behavior, particularly his tendency to address his imaginary friend Arturo (who, in fact, is the boy's vision of his dead brother), but viewers of Lee's movie, receiving no such exposition, must ponder Angelo's strange actions without warning, introduction, or preparation. The resulting confusion alienates some audiences, but the affecting presentation of Angelo's mental disturbance, aided by first-time actor Matteo Sciabordi's lovely performance, is yet another reminder of *Miracle at St. Anna*'s neorealist character.

The film's production design, cinematography, and location shooting contribute to its neorealist resonances. Mark Shiel defines Italian Neorealism's "distinctive visual style" as "typified by a preference for location filming, the use of nonprofessional actors, the avoidance of ornamental *mise-en-scène*, a preference for natural light, a freely-moving documentary style of photography, a non-interventionist approach to film directing, and," most notably, "an avoidance of complex editing and other post-production processes likely to focus attention on the contrivance of the film image."[38] Shiel quickly points out that "not all neorealist films employed *all* of these strategies, especially in the 1950s when neorealism became increasingly concerned with subjective experience," asserting that "most of these strategies are evident in all neorealist films."[39] *Miracle at St. Anna*, shot on location in Tuscany with untrained and inexperienced performers (such as Sciabordi) alongside more seasoned actors, fulfills some, but not all, of these criteria to become a neorealist hybrid. Cinematographer Matthew Libatique, for instance, uses natural light, even in nighttime scenes, while his cameras, particularly during battle sequences, adopt the vérité whips, pans, and zooms of documentary filmmaking. Barry Alexander Brown, by contrast, edits certain sequences, especially the buffalo soldiers' disastrous battles at the Serchio River and inside Colognora, with hard cuts, jump cuts, and occasional stutter cuts to underline combat's chaotic terror. This aesthetic decision in fact enhances *Miracle at St. Anna*'s realism by presenting wartime fighting as a difficult and disorienting experience, thereby reminding critical viewers that even the most faithful neorealist film is an artistic representation (or interpretation) of events, or, as Millicent Marcus argues, "the mimetic accuracy of a work can never stand alone as the measure of realism, since no representation can give an unmediated rendering of objective reality."[40] *Miracle at St. Anna*, like its source novel, fits this description by freely merging historical fact, fabulist fantasy, and religious symbols into a sometimes perplexing war story.

The thorny issue of defining realism—having confounded philosophers, novelists, literary scholars, and film theorists as diverse as Aristotle, Søren Kierkegaard, Emile Zola, Erich Auerbach, and André Bazin—leads Marcus to the "inescapable conclusion . . . that all realism is predicated on illusions—illusions that, however, find their ultimate justification in their service to a higher truth: the revelation of the world order in a way that would otherwise escape our unaided notice."[41] *Miracle at St. Anna,* from this perspective, illuminates the difficult lives of African American soldiers under army segregation, the suffering of Italian villagers under fascism, and the redemption of Angelo thanks to Sam Train's compassion. It is neither a realistic movie nor a neorealist film, but rather a text that straddles multiple tones, styles, and genres to chart new territory for American World War II movies.

BATTLE LINES

Miracle at St. Anna may amalgamate many prior influences into its intriguing, if difficult, narrative, but, in the best neorealist tradition, the movie remains notable for the disputes that its production provoked. The best-known controversy involves Lee's public melee with film director, producer, and actor Clint Eastwood over the absence of black soldiers from Eastwood's 2006 World War II duology, *Flags of Our Fathers* and *Letters from Iwo Jima.* Lee, while promoting *Miracle at St. Anna* at a May 2008 Cannes International Film Festival press conference, faulted Eastwood for suppressing African American troopers from his films, which chronicle the Battle of Iwo Jima—along with its emotional, political, and cultural fallout—from American and Japanese perspectives. Paul Lewis, writing in the *Guardian* newspaper, quotes Lee as telling the Cannes audience, "Clint Eastwood made two films about Iwo Jima that ran for more than four hours total, and there was not one Negro actor on the screen. If you reporters had any balls you'd ask him why. There's no way I know why he did that. . . . But I know it was pointed out to him and that he could have changed it. It's not like he didn't know."[42] *Guardian* newspaper reporter Jeff Dawson, in a June 5, 2008, interview with Eastwood, details the director's response: "Eastwood has no time for Lee's gripes. 'He was complaining when I did *Bird* [Eastwood's 1988 film starring Forest Whitaker as jazz legend Charlie Parker]. Why would a white guy be doing that? I was the only guy who made it, that's why. He could have gone ahead and made it. Instead he was making something else.'"[43]

This defense, however, ignores Lee's point about Eastwood extending Hollywood's long tradition of producing World War II films that downplay or eliminate the participation of African American troops. Dawson raises this matter with Eastwood, writing, "As for *Flags of Our Fathers,* he [Eastwood] says, yes, there was a small detachment of black troops on Iwo Jima as a part of a munitions company, 'but they didn't raise the flag. The story is *Flags of Our Fathers,* the famous flag-raising picture, and they didn't do that. If I go ahead and put an African American actor in there, people'd go, "This guy's lost his mind." I mean, it's not accurate.'"[44] This response is true insofar as *Flags of Our Fathers* focuses on the six men who raised the flag, but Eastwood still sidesteps the fact that black soldiers were crucial to the U.S. Marine Corps' ability to land on Iwo Jima. As documented by Kam Williams in "Miracle of St. Spike: Spike Lee—The *Miracle at St. Anna* Interview," New York University faculty member Yvonne Latty not only published the book *We Were There: Voices of African American Veterans, from World War II to the War in Iraq* in 2004 but also sent a copy to Eastwood before he began filming *Flags of Our Fathers* to urge the director "to include black soldiers in the film since somewhere between 700 and 900 African Americans had fought on Iwo Jima."[45] Latty, moreover, rejects Eastwood's defense of *Flag of Our Fathers'* historical accuracy in Alex Altman's "Were African-Americans at Iwo Jima?," a June 9, 2008, *Time* magazine article devoted to the controversy. Altman writes, "Eastwood is also correct that black soldiers represented a small fraction of the total force deployed on the island,"[46] but Latty finds fault with this characterization because Eastwood stages the Marines' difficult landing on Iwo Jima, where they face tremendous Japanese fire. "Black soldiers 'had the most dangerous job,'" Latty tells Altman, pointing out an overlooked truth: "If you were going to show the soldiers' landing, you'd need to show [African Americans] on the beach."[47] This comment leads Altman to observe, "In *Flags of Our Fathers*, which shows the landing in significant detail, African Americans appear only in fleeting cutaway shots and in a photograph during the film's closing credits."[48]

Altman also notes important facts about black troopers' contributions to the Battle of Iwo Jima, writing, "Those soldiers were restricted from frontline combat duty, but they played integral noncombat roles. Under enemy fire, they piloted amphibious truck units during perilous shore landings, unloaded and shuttled ammunition to the front lines, helped bury the dead, and weathered Japanese onslaughts on their positions even after the island had been declared secure."[49] Altman also mentions that Christopher Paul Moore, the author of *Fighting for America: Black Soldiers—The Unsung Heroes of World War II*, despite admiring Eastwood's films, nonetheless explains that "'thousands' more [black soldiers] helped fashion the airstrips from which U.S. B-29 aircrafts could launch and return from air assaults on Tokyo, about 760 miles northwest. Hosting that air base, Moore says, was Iwo Jima's primary strategic importance."[50]

These historical nuances, however, do not prevent Eastwood, in his *Guardian* interview with Jeff Dawson, from saying, in reference to Lee, that "a guy like him should shut his face,"[51] prompting Lee to defend himself by both praising and condemning Eastwood in a June 6, 2008, interview with *ABC News*'s Sheila Marikar. Lee says, "First of all, the man is not my father and we're not on a plantation either. He's a great director. He makes his films, I make my films. The thing about it though, I didn't personally attack him. And a comment like 'a guy like that should shut his face'—come on Clint, come on. He sounds like an angry old man right there."[52] Lee rebuffs Eastwood's claims of historical accuracy by saying, "If he wishes, I could assemble African American men who fought at Iwo Jima and I'd like him to tell these guys that what they did was insignificant and they did not exist"[53] to rebuke Eastwood's implication that the black soldiers' small detachment was unimportant to the Iwo Jima landing. Lee then declares, "I'm not making this up. I know history. I'm a student of history. And I know the history of Hollywood and its omission of the one million African American men and women who contributed to World War II."[54] This perspective, more measured in its criticism of Eastwood and its indictment of Hollywood's racial blindness about World War II, leads Lee to state, "Not everything was John Wayne, baby" before reminding Marikar, "I never said he should show one of the other guys holding up the flag as black. I said that African Americans played a significant part in Iwo Jima. For him to insinuate that I'm rewriting history and have one of the four guys with the flag be black . . . no one said that."[55] Yet Lee misrepresents both *Flags of Our Fathers* and *Letters of Iwo Jima* by saying, "It's just that there's not one black in either film. And because I know my history, that's why I made that observation."[56] As Alex Altman observes in his *Time* magazine article, closely watching both movies reveals that African American soldiers appear during the Iwo Jima battle, but only in brief shots that, in truth, are easily missed upon first viewing. Lee's mistaken description of *Flags of Our Fathers* and *Letters from Iwo Jima*, therefore, may be slight, but his reasonable argument would be more compelling if he acknowledged that Eastwood's movies include African American soldiers, but minimize their participation in the Iwo Jima landing.

This public feud, beyond its heat-of-the-moment passion, indicates how important context and detail are to cinematic representations that memorialize and dramatize historical events. Both Eastwood and Lee voice intriguing perspectives, but Lee is on firmer historical footing by bringing greater context (and fewer insults) to his analysis. David Sterritt perceptively discusses Lee's and Eastwood's competing claims in *Spike Lee's America*, writing that "what we find in this disagreement are complementary critiques of America's hypocrisy with respect to war. Lee mounts a counteroffensive against the culture industry's elision of African American heroism and patriotism, while Eastwood makes a similar move on behalf of Japanese sacrifice, suffering, and death in *Letters from Iwo Jima*" before underscoring how Eastwood "attacks the culture industry's readiness to lie, mislead, and propagandize in *Flags of Our Fathers*."[57] This impulse, indeed, is central to both of Eastwood's movies, making them valuable contributions to American World War II films, yet by downplaying the presence and significance of African American soldiers to the Marines' bloody battle on Iwo Jima, Eastwood earns the criticisms that Lee and Yvonne Latty offer. Eastwood's choice to focus on the six men who raised the flag (rather than other aspects of the Iwo Jima battle) in *Flags of*

Our Fathers, of course, follows the story told in James Bradley and Ron Powers's book (of the same title) that Eastwood adapts for his film, while Eastwood's desire to dramatize the harsh conditions endured by Japanese soldiers in *Letters from Iwo Jima* helps demystify the shallow patriotism and jingoistic nativism of many Hollywood World War II movies. Perhaps the largest irony of the Eastwood-Lee debate is that *Miracle at St. Anna* pursues similar goals by piercing the propaganda of older, all-white war movies to show World War II from the perspectives of people too frequently overlooked by those films.

More intriguing for this discussion is Lee's response to charges of historical inaccuracy made against *Miracle at St. Anna* by Italian war veterans from the National Association of Italian Partisans (ANPI) who, after the film's September 30, 2008, premiere in Florence, Italy, criticized its depiction of Rodolfo's collaboration with the Nazis, "contradicting," according to the *Telegraph* newspaper's Nick Pisa, "Italian versions of the massacre, which record it as an unprovoked war crime."[58] Pisa, in his September 30, 2008, article "Spike Lee's *Miracle at St. Anna* Denounced by Italian War Veterans as 'Insulting,'" quotes ANPI vice president Giovanni Cipollini as saying, "We had asked for a meeting with Spike Lee several times to discuss the inaccuracies and said we were willing to talk but we never heard back. His film is made up of half-truths which have nothing to do with what really happened—and to add insult to injury we have not even been invited to the premier."[59] James McBride, misidentified by Pisa as a World War II combat veteran, apologizes when asked about ANPI's claims by saying, "I am sorry if I have offended the partisans. I am a historical writer and just wanted to give life to the victims. As a black American I have utmost respect for the partisans but I wanted to show that in war everything is possible. I want to stress that the book is fiction. I write historical novels not books on history."[60] This response differentiates between historical fiction and scholarly history, but seems a weak defense of a movie previously mired in controversy (of Lee's own making) about the necessity of historical accuracy in World War II films.

As recounted by Pisa, an unrepentant Lee countered McBride's regret at a separate Florence press screening:

> "I am not apologising for anything," [Lee] said, warning Italians that there was clearly "a lot about your history you have yet to come to grips with." After receiving [an] honorary citizenship award from Sant'Anna mayor Michele Silicani, Lee said: "I have no doubts that the partisans were great but they were not universally loved by the civilian population. There are no heroes or villains in my film, the majority of Nazis were brutal killers but some were better than others and the same goes for the partisans. It was a complicated time and there are many different ways of interpreting history and before I made the film I spoke to many survivors and got their blessing."[61]

This justification rehearses Lee's concern with acknowledging the nuances of complex historical incidents (even when they are unsavory), while assessing *Miracle at St. Anna* as a story that refuses to condone unsophisticated good-and-evil depictions. Both positions have merit, but whether or not Lee received the approval of some survivors, he represents *Miracle at St. Anna* in this interview (and in the movie's companion volume) as a film that, while adapted from a fictional source, depends upon significant historical research for its effect. Imagining Rodolfo as a potential Nazi collaborator, indeed, is elemental to the story told by McBride's novel and Lee's film, helping generate the entire narrative by giving Hector Negron ample motivation to shoot Rodolfo dead after encountering him in 1983 Harlem. Negron repays Rodolfo's betrayal to achieve some small measure of justice for the historical crime that the Nazis perpetrate at Stazzema in a scenario that configures *Miracle at St. Anna*'s as a story that allows such unlikely coincidences to occur.

Yet Lee's statement places him in the same position as Clint Eastwood during their earlier debate about *Flags of Our Fathers*' accuracy, arguing the right to interpret history within a fictional context. This irony does not reveal blatant hypocrisy on Lee's part since the Stazzema massacre's precise details (unlike the presence of African American soldiers at Iwo Jima) have been disputed by scholars. Still, Lee's argument does not entirely satisfy the charges made against the film (and, by extension, McBride's novel) by ANPI no matter how effective *Miracle at St. Anna*'s fictional re-creation of the massacre may be. This sequence is not simply heartbreaking to consider, but appalling to watch: Nazi soldiers execute the village priest before shooting, bayonetting, and mutilating nearly one hundred people rounded into Stazzema's town square. The Nazis plunge their blades into pregnant women's bellies and, in a horrifying moment near the conclusion, stab to death a crying infant who survives their onslaught. Lee's honesty in staging this butchery as appropriately sickening does not negate the fact that Rodolfo, a fictional creation of McBride's, inadvertently provokes the episode by telling his Nazi conspirators that Peppi "the Great Butterfly" Grotta will visit Stazzema, thereby giving them an opportunity to capture a partisan hero. When Peppi fails to arrive, the Nazis punish the entire village, leading Hans Brundt to help the boy Angelo flee the violence. These events propel *Miracle at St. Anna*'s plot to illustrate just how terrible, chaotic, and uncertain the Nazi occupation of Italy was, but they revise (or, in ANPI's view, manipulate) the historical record to envision a plausible scenario about the massacre's origin that nonetheless weakens the partisan cause and reputation. Peppi's grief and shame while recounting this story to one of Colognora's elders, beautifully played by Pierfrancesco Favino, demonstrates that Rodolfo's betrayal is, indeed, an individual act unconnected to the partisan agenda, but Lee, rather than making this point at the press screening, too harshly dismisses ANPI's concern about *Miracle at St. Anna*'s historical truthfulness.

This hullabaloo, however, demonstrates that *Miracle at St. Anna* stands as an exemplary summary of Lee's cinematic career. The movie tackles historical, racial, and cultural tensions in a film that violates classical Hollywood filmmaking principles without apology or lament to tell an unconventional story that, by mixing genres, tones, and styles, divides audiences about its quality. *Miracle at St. Anna* frequently succeeds on the terms that Lee sets for it, but cannot placate viewers searching for more traditional fare because its imperfections prevent a unified story from emerging. While not as incoherent as Joe Morgenstern and other prominent film critics charge, *Miracle at St. Anna* is a demanding, even grueling movie to watch that remains a worthwhile contribution to American war pictures. The film, like its director, courts controversy and splits audiences by posing intellectual, moral, and emotional challenges guaranteed to upset some viewers. *Miracle at St. Anna* may never be as popular as other entries in Lee's filmography, but the movie remains a significant aesthetic and political statement that, despite its narrative inadequacies, compels its audience to question long-held assumptions about the virtues of America's participation in World War II. *Miracle at St. Anna,* therefore, is not only quintessential Lee but also a better film than its public reception suggests.

Conclusion
Spike's Place

On September 17, 2013, the Dorothy and Lillian Gish Prize Trust, an organization established by film and theatre actress Lillian Gish's estate upon her 1993 death, announced Spike Lee as the recipient of the 20th Annual Dorothy and Lillian Gish Prize. First given to architect Frank Gehry in 1994, the Trust annually bestows this award upon a person who, according to Gish's will, has "made an outstanding contribution to the beauty of the world and to mankind's enjoyment and understanding of life."[1] This heady praise, along with the award's $300,000 honorarium, legitimates Lee's artistic pursuits while capping the cinematic career of a man who has never won an Academy or Golden Globe Award despite writing, directing, producing, and acting in films for more than twenty-five years.

Receiving the Gish Prize, which Lee accepted at a ceremony held at New York City's Museum of Modern Art on October 30, 2013, presents notable ironies for the director. Lee, in the public statement included in the Prize's official press release, says, "Would you believe, two of the most important films that impacted me while I was studying at NYU starred Miss Lillian Gish. Those films were D. W. Griffith's *The Birth of a Nation* and Charles Laughton's *The Night of the Hunter*."[2] *The Birth of a Nation*, of course, is the movie whose depiction of savage African Americans and noble Ku Klux Klansmen in the days after the American Civil War so enraged Lee that he constructed 1980's *The Answer*, his first short film as a student in New York University's (NYU's) Tisch School of the Arts graduate-film program, as an explicit response to *The Birth of a Nation*'s bigoted narrative. *The Answer* tells the story of a black filmmaker hired to write and direct a $50-million, major-studio remake of Griffith's 1915 movie that, according to Kaleem Aftab in *That's My Story and I'm Sticking to It*, became Lee's way of excoriating the racism of Griffith's original while also saying "'fuck you' to the NYU faculty for celebrating it."[3] *The Answer* shows its moviemaker protagonist unable to finish his high-profile project, after which the Klan burns a cross on his front lawn and, in what Lee's longtime friend and collaborator Ernest Dickerson, in

John Colapinto's "Outside Man: Spike Lee's Unending Struggle" (Colapinto's revealing September 22, 2008, *New Yorker* profile of Lee), calls "a really powerful image," the movie concludes with its hero turning on his attackers: "Low angle, shooting up the stairs—as the guy is going downstairs, knife in hand, to do battle. It fades out. It was an amazing film."[4]

Lee, who discusses *The Answer*'s controversial reception in both *That's My Story* and his October 2013 appearance on musician Pharrell Williams's YouTube Reserve Channel program *ARTST TLK,* tells Aftab that, when NYU's film-school faculty members screened and graded all first-year students' movies, choosing whom to keep and whom to dismiss from the program based on each film's accomplishment, they might have preferred not to bring him back due to *The Answer*'s incendiary approach, but that a prior bureaucratic decision to offer Lee a job as a graduate teaching assistant saved him. "I had worked the whole first year in the equipment room and I was a hard worker," Lee says. "So they *wanted* to kick me out, but they couldn't."[5] This story, or legend[6] (as he calls it in *That's My Story*), demonstrates Lee's awareness of his own reputation, for, as Colapinto notes in "Outside Man," although *The Answer* incensed some faculty members, others saw it as an overwrought film that nonetheless indicated Lee's creative potential. Colapinto writes, "But talent was not an issue with *The Answer*" before quoting retired NYU film professor Roberta Hodes as saying, "'I just think it offended everyone. I felt offended, too, I'm ashamed to say.' (She added, 'I don't think he was very much liked. He was very fresh—as we used to say in the olden days—and very aggressive.')"[7] Hodes expresses sentiments repeated so frequently during Lee's long career (as both a rabblerousing filmmaker and a contentious public figure) that they form a near-mantra that many observers would agree accurately assesses his strengths and weaknesses as a cinematic storyteller. Even so, Colapinto points out that both Lee and *The Answer* had defenders, including Eleanor Hamerow, the former chair of the Tisch School's graduate-film program, who "said that the problem was not the film's content but, rather, its overweening ambition," for which Hamerow offers this explanation: "In first year, we're trying to teach them the basics, and certainly the idea was to execute exercises, make small films, but within limits. . . . He was trying to solve a problem overnight—the social problem with the blacks and the whites. He undertook to fix the great filmmaker who made that movie, D. W. Griffith. He was going to teach him a lesson,"[8] which indicates that Lee, despite his artistic promise, was not yet a good moviemaker. "Hamerow," according to Colapinto, "says that she was among those faculty members who voted to keep Lee in the program, so that he could 'go on and learn more.'"[9]

Lee completed his education, winning a 1983 Student Academy Award for his thesis film *Joe's Bed-Stuy Barbershop: We Cut Heads* as if to rebuke the uncertain faith that some professors demonstrated in his early abilities. That Lee became an NYU graduate-film faculty member in 1997 and artistic director of the entire program in 2002 is an irony underscored by receiving the Gish Prize, especially in light of the controversy caused by Lee's filmic response to what may be Lillian Gish's most famous screen appearance in *The Birth of a Nation*. Her presence in *The Night of the Hunter* (1955) also intersects Lee's career at perhaps its most important moment, since the love-and-hate speech that Bill Nunn's Radio Raheem gives in *Do the Right Thing* (1989) is a direct homage to the "little story of right hand-left hand, the story of good and evil"[10] that Robert Mitchum's nefarious character, serial killer and false preacher Harry Powell, narrates in Charles Laughton's now-classic film adaptation of Davis Grubb's 1953 novel. Lee's life and career, indeed, seem to achieve perfect closure by receiving the Gish Prize.

Lee, as this book demonstrates many times, repudiates such finality as the type of false resolution beloved by Hollywood studios but mostly avoided by his movies, meaning that, to the dismay of certain viewers, his films sometimes have no firm closure at all. Lee's life, no less than his art, refuses such clear resolutions, for despite accepting the Gish Prize, Lee shows no signs of retiring from moviemaking or from public controversy anytime soon. *Mike Tyson: Undisputed Truth,* Lee's filmed record of the one-man show that Lee first directed for the Broadway stage and that stars the former heavyweight champion as himself, premiered on Home Box Office on November 16, 2013; *Oldboy,* Lee's American adaptation of Park Chan-wook's crackerjack 2003 revenge film *Oldeuboi,* opened to mixed reviews and low box-office returns on November 27, 2013; *Da Sweet Blood of Jesus,* the film funded entirely by Kickstarter donations, premiered on June 22, 2014, at the 18th American Black Film Festival in New York City; and, perhaps most promisingly, Lee has agreed to adapt his debut feature film, *She's Gotta Have It*, into a half-hour series for premium-cable network Showtime that he will write, produce, and direct. This prolificacy even created fresh headlines for Lee when graphic artist Juan Luis Garcia, on November 27, 2013, published an open letter titled "Dear Spike Lee" on his (Garcia's) professional website claiming that the advertising agency that Lee hired to design *Oldboy*'s one-sheet posters stole Garcia's layouts after Garcia declined their "insultingly low offer."[11] Lee, never one to shirk what he considers attacks on his integrity, responded on his official Twitter page by writing, on November 28, 2013, "I Never Heard Of This Guy Juan Luis Garcia, If He Has A Beef It's Not With Me. I Did Not Hire Him, Do Not Know Him. Cheap Trick Writing To Me. YO"[12] and by posting, on his official Instagram page (also on November 28, 2013) this reply to a commenter who urges Lee to pay Garcia for his efforts: "Why Should I Pay Someone Who I Never Met Nor Had Any Contact With Ever? He Never Made Any Deal With Me. Why Don't You Pay Me For Your Stupid Text On Thanksgiving Day?"[13]

The ensuing reaction, at least on Twitter and websites covering this story, overwhelmingly assumed that Lee mistreated Garcia by not taking up the cause of a fellow artist exploited by a powerful corporation. Accusations of class snobbery, noblesse oblige, and racism pervaded these responses to indict Lee's purported personal and institutional hypocrisy. Lee's detractors presumed that, as a wealthy celebrity who famously fought his way into the creative limelight from total obscurity, Lee's bourgeois attitudes were on full display by dismissing Garcia's assertions when, in their view, Lee should have confronted the moneyed interests that, by helping fund *Oldboy,* successfully compromised Lee's principles. In this telling, Lee is a false revolutionary who preaches the abstract virtues of fighting power but quails when presented with the opportunity to do so.

This public dispute, however, is a perfect microcosm of Lee's career as an American artist. That, within the space of one month, he could be vilified as an unconscionable hustler using his prominence to avoid responsibility for cheating another person out of honorably earned profits and commended, in the words of the Gish Prize's 2013 selection-committee chairperson Darren Walker, "for his brilliance and unwavering courage in using film to challenge conventional thinking, and for the passion for justice that he feels deep in his soul"[14] sketches, as tellingly as any other example from Lee's professional life, the divisive responses that Lee's personality and work evoke. This study, as such, documents that Lee is an artist whom audiences have never universally embraced, while acknowledging that his checkered reputation interferes with his cinematic achievements as much as it promotes them.

Gary Younge, in a December 1, 2013, *Guardian* article titled "Spike Lee on *Oldboy,* America's Violent History and the Fine Art of Mouthing Off," insightfully assesses Lee: "Braggadocious, brazen, playful, cocky and combative, the one adjective that doesn't fit him, even as a difficult interviewee, is the one with which he is most commonly associated: angry."[15] These words usefully describe Lee's persona, reputation, and career to underscore how he desires public validation despite his carefully cultivated aura of fierce independence. Lee, according to Younge, may not appear to care what other people think of him, but, in the end, he is "a slight man with thin skin" who has nevertheless produced "an impressive body of work not just because of its quantity but its quality . . . and its range."[16] Lee's oeuvre, Younge confidently predicts, assures him a place in film history. The contradictions that Younge elucidates—Lee is thin-skinned but resolute, overbearing but shy, disputatious but thoughtful, accomplished but insecure—reflect the personal and professional complexities of one of the great cultural artists to emerge from late-twentieth-century America. These nuances, no less than Lee's formidable intelligence, mark him as a master craftsman whose films are essential viewing for people interested in how black cinema is, finally, a necessary but insufficient category to classify how Lee's movies, along with the work of his fellow African American filmmakers, speak to the American experience as entertainingly, as incisively, and as powerfully as any other art.

Spike Lee, therefore, augments his viewer's appreciation of the tremendous diversity of both African American and American cinema, as well as the astonishing capacity of film to depict black, white, and other American communities with wit, insight, and vigor. Lee's films will never satisfy all audiences, but their visual, narrative, and thematic accomplishments—as well as their drawbacks—ensure that they will continue to provoke interested viewers. Lee's cinema is a combative, fascinating, maddening, and revelatory gift to American popular art that, like the man who makes it, insists that audiences face the intricacies of American history with honesty, with courage, and, best of all, with the saving grace of humor. Lee's movies, despite their rancorous reputation, leave viewers with a generosity of understanding that enlivens their sympathies, enhances their intellects, and enriches their lives. Spike Lee, as such, is an American social critic, cultural observer, and cinematic artist of the first order. His work, in the best testament to Lee's talent, will survive long after its creator exits the public stage.

Notes

INTRODUCTION: "STILL A MOTHERFUCKER"— SPIKE LEE IN THE TWENTY-FIRST CENTURY

1. Spike Lee as told to Kaleem Aftab, *Spike Lee: That's My Story and I'm Sticking to It* (New York: W.W. Norton & Company, 2006), 354.

   Although Lee is not technically credited as an author, his name's prominence on the book's cover and title page, along with the as-told-to designation (mimicking *The Autobiography of Malcolm X* as told to Alex Haley), gives him equal billing with Kaleem Aftab, who nonetheless receives sole credit as the book's author in future references.

2. Ibid.

3. Ibid., 7.

4. Spike Lee, interview by Nelson George, *Spike Lee's Gotta Have It: Inside Guerrilla Filmmaking* (New York: Fireside, 1987), 20.

5. The title *Da Blood of Jesus* is visible on several images of the film's production slate that Lee has posted to his official Instagram page (http://instagram.com/sheltonjlee). See Tambay A. Obenson's *Shadow and Act* article "What Can the Title of Spike Lee's Kickstarter-Funded Joint Tell Us about the Film's Plot?" (http://blogs.indiewire.com/shadowandact/what-can-the-title-of-spike-lees-kickstarter-funded-joint-tell-us-about-the-films-plot) for more information about this image and the movie itself.

   Lee, in a November 19, 2013, *Slashfilm* interview with Germain Lussier promoting *Oldboy*'s theatrical release, says that his Kickstarter movie's title is now *The Sweet Blood of Jesus*, that he shot it in sixteen days in October 2013, and that he hopes to take the project to the 2014 Cannes International Film Festival. See Lussier's "Spike Lee Talks *Oldboy*, *The Sweet Blood of Jesus* and (Obviously) the New York Knicks" (http://www.slashfilm.com/film-interview-spike-lee-talks-oldboy-the-sweet-blood-of-jesus-and-obviously-the-new-york-knicks/).

   Lee's Instagram page, however, consistently refers to the movie's title as either *Da Sweet Blood of Jesus* or *Da Blood of Jesus*.

6. Lee raised $1,418,910 from 6,421 Kickstarter backers during a one-month period from July 22 to August 21, 2013 (http://www.kickstarter.com/projects/

spikelee/the-newest-hottest-spike-lee-joint) for a project that, at that point, he only referred to as "the Newest Hottest Spike Lee Joint."

7. Lee's *Squawk on the Street* appearance can be found on CNBC's official website (http://www.cnbc.com/id/100928889), while his *Street Smart* interview is available on YouTube (http://www.youtube.com/watch?v=t38bi5dAxZY&feature=youtu.be).

8. Spike Lee, response to Simon Hobbs, *Squawk on the Street* (CNBC, July 31, 2013), http://www.cnbc.com/id/100928889.

9. Box Office Mojo (http://www.boxofficemojo.com/movies/?id=insideman.htm) reports *Inside Man*'s final worldwide gross as $184,376,254 (split between domestic ticket sales of $88,513,495 and foreign sales of $95,862,759) against its $45-million budget, while the Internet Movie Database (IMDb) (http://www.imdb.com/title/tt0454848/business?ref_=tt_ql_dt_4) reports the film's domestic gross ticket sales as $88,504,640 against its estimated $45-million budget.

The long-rumored *Inside Man* sequel has been cancelled, with Lee commenting in several 2010 and 2011 interviews that this project has fallen apart.

10. Barbara Grizzuti Harrison, "Spike Lee Hates Your Cracker Ass," *Esquire,* October 1992, http://www.esquire.com/features/spike-lee-1092.

11. Ibid.

12. Aftab, *That's My Story,* 210.

13. Spike Lee, interview by James Verniere, "Doing the Job," *Sight and Sound* 3, no. 2 (February 1993): 10.

This article is also available in *Spike Lee: Interviews,* ed. Cynthia Fuchs, Conversations with Filmmakers Series (Jackson: University Press of Mississippi, 2002), 79–85.

14. Spike Lee, interview by John Colapinto, "Outside Man: Spike Lee's Unending Struggle," *New Yorker,* September 22, 2008, 55.

Readers who consult Colapinto's original profile—published in the *New Yorker*'s September 22, 2008, issue—or its reproduction at the *New Yorker*'s digital archive (http://archives.newyorker.com/?i=2008–09–22#folio=052) will see the subtitle "Spike Lee's Unending Struggle." Readers who consult the *New Yorker*'s general website (http://www.newyorker.com/reporting/2008/09/22/080922fa_fact_colapinto?currentPage=all) will see a different subtitle, "Spike Lee's Celluloid Struggles."

15. Ernest Dickerson, interview by Colapinto, "Outside Man: Spike Lee's Unending Struggle," 55–56.

16. Lee, interview by George, *Spike Lee's Gotta Have It,* 52.

17. Spike Lee, interview by David Breskin, *Inner Views: Filmmakers in Conversation,* Expanded ed. (New York: Da Capo Press, 1997), 156.

18. Spike Lee, interview by Elvis Mitchell, "Spike Lee: The *Playboy* Interview," in *Spike Lee: Interviews,* ed. Cynthia Fuchs, Conversations with Filmmakers Series (Jackson: University Press of Mississippi, 2002), 61.

Mitchell's interview first appeared in *Playboy* (July 1991): 51–68.

19. John R. Howard, *Faces in the Mirror: Oscar Micheaux and Spike Lee* (Lady Lake, FL: Fireside Publications, 2009), 27.

20. Lee, interview by Mitchell, "*Playboy* Interview," 43.

21. Ibid.

22. Aftab, *That's My Story,* 14.
23. Ibid., 15.
24. Spike Lee, *Spike Lee's Gotta Have It: Inside Guerrilla Filmmaking* (New York: Fireside, 1987), 17.
25. Aftab, *That's My Story,* 22–27.
26. Ibid., 30–34.
27. Mitchell, "*Playboy* Interview," 36.
28. Paula J. Massood, "We've Gotta Have It—Spike Lee, African American Film, and Cinema Studies," in *The Spike Lee Reader,* ed. Paula J. Massood (Philadelphia: Temple University Press, 2008), xxiv.
29. Ibid.
30. Ibid.
31. Ibid., xv.
32. Ibid.
33. Amiri Baraka, "Spike Lee at the Movies," in *Black American Cinema,* ed. Manthia Diawara (New York: Routledge, 1993), 146.
34. Ibid., 147.
35. Aftab, *That's My Story,* 182.
36. Jerold J. Abrams, "Transcendence and Sublimity in Spike Lee's Signature Shot," in *The Philosophy of Spike Lee,* ed. Mark Conard (Lexington: The University Press of Kentucky, 2011), 187.
37. John Belton, *American Cinema/American Culture* (New York: McGraw-Hill, 1994), 348.
38. David Bordwell, Janet Staiger, and Kristin Thompson, *The Classical Hollywood Cinema: Film Style & Mode of Production to 1960* (New York: Columbia University Press, 1985), 3.
39. Ibid.
40. Ibid., 3–4.
41. Belton, *American Cinema/American Culture,* 26–27.
42. Lee's IMDb entry is available at http://www.imdb.com/name/nm0000490/. His IMDb "Message Boards" page is available at http://www.imdb.com/name/nm0000490/board/?ref_=nm_bd_sm.
43. Lee, interview by George, *Spike Lee's Gotta Have It,* 36.
44. Aftab, *That's My Story,* 377.
45. Ibid.
46. Ibid.
47. Breskin, *Inner Views,* 149.
48. Ibid., 181.
49. Lee, interview by Breskin, *Inner Views,* 181.
50. Ibid.
51. Ibid.
52. Ibid.
53. Ibid., 185.
54. Ibid. The emphasis is Breskin's.
55. Spike Lee, interview by Henry Louis Gates Jr., "Final Cut," *Transition* 52 (1991): 198.
56. Ibid.

CHAPTER ONE: MEN AT WORK

1. Spike Lee, *Spike Lee's Gotta Have It: Inside Guerrilla Filmmaking* (New York: Fireside/Simon & Schuster, 1987).

   Although Lee is hardly the first independent filmmaker to employ the term "guerrilla filmmaking" to describe the low-budget, run-and-gun, fast-paced shooting schedule that characterized *She's Gotta Have It*'s production, he assigns this concept central prominence by choosing it as the subtitle of his movie's companion volume. The term's military resonances, suggesting an insurgent army conducting unauthorized operations, cohere with Lee's production diary, which occasionally likens making *She's Gotta Have It* to small-scale warfare.

2. Readers interested in an early theoretical examination of classical Hollywood style should consult André Bazin's influential essay "The Evolution of the Language of Cinema," in *What Is Cinema?*, Volume 1, trans. Hugh Gray (1967; Berkeley: University of California Press, 2005), 23–40.

3. *She's Gotta Have It,* written by Spike Lee, directed by Spike Lee, released by Island Pictures, 1986, 85 min. All future quotations, summaries, and paraphrases refer to Metro Goldwyn Mayer's DVD version of Lee's film.

4. Lee, *Spike Lee's Gotta Have It,* 279.

5. Ibid., 73.

6. Ibid., 83.

7. Todd Gitlin, *Inside Prime Time* (1983; Berkeley and Los Angeles: University of California Press, 2000), 273.

8. Desson Howe, "*School Daze,*" *Washington Post,* February 12, 1988, http://www .washingtonpost.com/wp-srv/style/longterm/movies/videos/schooldaze howe.htm.

9. Rita Kempley, "*School Daze,*" *Washington Post,* February 12, 1988, http://www .washingtonpost.com/wp-srv/style/longterm/movies/videos/schooldaze.htm.

10. Ibid.

11. W.E.B. Du Bois, *The Souls of Black Folk,* ed. Henry Louis Gates Jr. and Terri Hume Oliver (1903; New York: W.W. Norton, 1999), 11.

12. Apart from Desson Howe's and Rita Kempley's dismissive *Washington Post* pieces, David Breskin, in his introduction to *Inner Views: Filmmakers in Conversation,* Expanded ed. (New York: Da Capo Press, 1997), finds *School Daze* to be both ambitious and uneven (149), while Roger Ebert, in his favorable *Chicago Sun-Times* review (published on February 12, 1988), comments that the film's "revolutionary approach is found in a daffy story about undergraduates at an all-black university. The movie is basically a comedy, with some serious scenes that don't always quite seem to fit."

   This "fit," however, presumes the narrative cohesion that characterizes classical Hollywood style, but that *School Daze* challenges from its opening frames. Owen Gleiberman, reviewing John Singleton's *Poetic Justice* in *Entertainment Weekly*'s July 23, 1993, edition, understands *School Daze* even more poorly by calling Singleton's second feature film "a dawdling mishmash of themes and moods" before damning *School Daze* with faint praise: "If [*Poetic Justice*] were simply too ambitious for its own good, one could applaud its intentions and pronounce it a passionate misfire, like Spike Lee's *School Daze* or Martin Scorsese's *New*

York, New York. Poetic Justice, however, manages to be both inept *and* obnoxious." This assessment, however, is startlingly clumsy, for *School Daze* does not resemble *Poetic Justice* apart from being the second movie written and directed by a talented African American filmmaker whose first effort was so well received that his name became synonymous with black American cinema.

Ebert's review is available at http://www.rogerebert.com/reviews/school-daze-1988. Gleiberman's review is available at http://www.ew.com/ew/article/0,307326,00.html.

13. Breskin's preface to his *Inner Views* interview with Lee notes that *She's Gotta Have It* received numerous admiring press notices (149), Nelson George's interview with Lee in *Spike Lee's Gotta Have It* mentions that the film became a cause célèbre (49), and Terry McMillan's essay "Thoughts on *She's Gotta Have It,*" in *Five for Five: The Films of Spike Lee* (New York: Stewart, Tabori & Chang, 1991), recounts the excitement that she and other filmgoers experienced while standing in line to see the movie at Manhattan's Cinema Studio after hearing positive buzz. McMillan, however, admits, "I had refused to read any reviews, especially those in *The New York Times, Time* magazine, and *Newsweek* magazine" because "I don't trust white critics' judgment of most things that deal with black life, particularly when a black person is the creator" (21).

D.J.R. Bruckner's favorable August 8, 1986, *New York Times* review, however, might have assuaged McMillan's fears despite noting problems with *She's Gotta Have It:* "In fact, the story is so good that I regret the film is sometimes technically messy and some of Mr. Lee's directing experiments ill-conceived." Despite these drawbacks, Bruckner writes that the film's "characters will interest everyone. Stripped of some of the distractions of this presentation, their story has a touch of the classic" that "would be more enjoyable in a more polished film, but it has a power that is not dissipated by this one's weaknesses."

Bruckner's review is available at http://movies.nytimes.com/movie/review?res=9A0DEFDF143CF93BA3575BC0A960948260.

14. Gladstone L. Yearwood, *Black Film as a Signifying Practice: Cinema, Narration and the African American Aesthetic Tradition* (Trenton, NJ: Africa World Press, 2000), 142.

15. Ibid.

16. Ibid.

17. bell hooks, " 'Whose Pussy Is This?': A Feminist Comment," in *Reel to Real: Race, Class and Sex at the Movies* (1996; New York: Routledge, 2009), 291–92.

This essay also appears in hooks's earlier collection *Talking Back: Thinking Feminist, Thinking Black* (Boston: South End Press, 1989), 134–41 and in Paula J. Massood's invaluable scholarly anthology *The Spike Lee Reader* (Philadelphia: Temple University Press, 2008), 1–9.

18. Ibid., 292.

19. Ibid., 294.

20. Ibid.

21. Ibid., 302.

22. Laura Mulvey, "Visual Pleasure and Narrative Cinema," in *Film Theory and Criticism: Introductory Readings,* ed. Leo Braudy and Marshall Cohen, 6th ed. (New York: Oxford University Press, 2004), 842.

Mulvey's influential essay first appeared in the autumn 1975 issue of the film journal *Screen* and remains available in Mulvey's *Visual and Other Pleasures*, 2nd ed. (New York: Palgrave Macmillan, 2009), 14–28.

23. McMillan, "Thoughts on *She's Gotta Have It*," 24.

24. Ibid., 26. The emphasis is McMillan's.

25. Ibid., 27.

26. Ibid., 29.

27. Ibid.

28. Lee's *Spike Lee's Gotta Have It* production journal and Chapter 3 of *Spike Lee: That's My Story and I'm Sticking to It*, written in collaboration with Kaleem Aftab (New York: W.W. Norton & Company, 2006), exhaustively address the financial difficulties that Lee faced while making *She's Gotta Have It*. Lee's diary reveals, on June 13, 1985, that the cast and crew largely worked on deferment, taking no upfront money before beginning the twelve-day shoot (207).

29. *Spike Lee's Gotta Have It*'s October 22, 1985, production-journal entry specifies the tense situation with DuArt, although Lee's friend Nelson George gives him $1,000 to pay for the movie's negative. Despite these financial pressures, Island Pictures eventually agrees to distribute the film, which, according to *That's My Story*, makes $8 million in domestic box-office receipts (61).

30. Lee, *Spike Lee's Gotta Have It*, 132.

31. Ibid., 137 and 140.

32. Ibid., 140.

33. Ibid., 142.

34. Ibid., 234–35.

35. Ibid., 70.

36. Ibid., 79.

37. Ibid., 81.

38. Ibid., 68.

39. Ibid., 74.

40. Ibid., 69.

41. Ibid., 75–76.

42. Ibid., 66.

43. Ibid., 67.

44. Ibid., 71.

45. Richard A. Blake, *Street Smart: The New York of Lumet, Allen, Scorsese, and Lee* (Lexington: University Press of Kentucky, 2005), 224.

46. Heather E. Harris and Kimberly R. Moffitt, "A Critical Exploration of African American Women through the 'Spiked Lens,'" in *Fight the Power!: The Spike Lee Reader*, ed. Janice D. Hamlet and Robin R. Means Coleman (New York: Peter Lang Publishing, Inc., 2009), 313.

    To read bell hooks's analysis of Hollywood's sexual dichotomy, consult "Male Heroes and Female Sex Objects: Sexism in Spike Lee's *Malcolm X*," *Cineaste* 19, no. 4 (1993): 13–15.

47. Ed Guerrero, *Framing Blackness: The African American Image in Film* (Philadelphia: Temple University Press, 1993), 140.

48. Michele Wallace, "Spike Lee and Black Women," in *The Spike Lee Reader*, ed. Paula J. Massood (Philadelphia: Temple University Press, 2008), 24–25.

Wallace's essay first appeared, and remains available, in Wallace's *Invisibility Blues: From Pop to Theory* (New York: Verso, 1990), 100–106.

49. Lee's production journal explicitly makes this point in its November 24, 1984, entry by comparing *She's Gotta Have It* to Akira Kurosawa's *Rashomon* (1950): "Every witness has his or her own version, his or her own view of Nola Darling. A lot of views are contradictory but Nola herself is a contradiction" (85).

50. Harris and Moffitt, "African American Women through the 'Spiked Lens,'" 309.

51. Spike Lee, DVD audio commentary, *School Daze,* written by Spike Lee, directed by Spike Lee, released by Columbia Pictures, 121 min., 1988.

52. McMillan, "Thoughts on *She's Gotta Have It,*" 25.

53. Lee, *Spike Lee's Gotta Have It,* 150. Lee also notes during his interview with Nelson George (at the beginning of *Spike Lee's Gotta Have It*) that, during the movie's sex scenes, Nola only lights candles for Jamie Overstreet (41).

54. This four-minute, fifteen-second scene is also *She's Gotta Have It*'s largest stylistic disruption of the film's narrative. Shot in color, it affectionately recalls Victor Fleming's 1939 cinematic adaptation of L. Frank Baum's *The Wizard of Oz* by dropping a color sequence into the middle of a black-and-white movie. If any doubts remain about Lee's willingness to draw the viewer's attention to *She's Gotta Have It*'s status as a filmic construction, Nola's birthday sequence allays them.

55. hooks, "'Whose Pussy Is This?,'" 297.

56. Ibid., 299.

57. Ibid., 298.

58. Wallace, "Spike Lee and Black Women," 25.

59. Harris and Moffitt, "African American Women through the 'Spiked Lens,'" 306.
    Harris and Moffitt cite Patricia Hill Collins's *Black Feminist Thought: Knowledge, Consciousness, and the Politics of Empowerment* (Boston: Unwin Hyman, 1990) as the source of this passage's reference to Nola as a jezebel.

60. Lee, *Spike Lee's Gotta Have It,* 349.

61. Spike Lee, *That's My Story and I'm Sticking to It,* as told to Kaleem Aftab (New York: W.W. Norton & Company, 2006), 63.

62. Guerrero, *Framing Blackness,* 142.

63. Ibid.

64. Ibid.

65. Ibid., 141.

66. Stanley Crouch, in *That's My Story and I'm Sticking to It,* finds Nola uninspiring, boring, and shallow, meaning that she is not worth the fascination that Mars, Greer, and Jamie display (57–58).
    Donald Bogle, in the fourth edition of *Toms, Coons, Mulattoes, Mammies, and Bucks: An Interpretive History of Blacks in American Film* (New York: Continuum, 2001), feels that black women may one day view Nola without affection: "While free-spirited and unfettered by traditional assumptions about a woman's place, Nola is also a bit of a pretty blank, who serves as a backdrop for the story of the men" (299). Terry McMillan, in "Thoughts on *She's Gotta Have It,*" makes this point with rhetorical questions: "What was it these men really saw in Nola? Was her stuff really that good? Did they realize that they were making fools of themselves? Did they know they were acting foolish?" (29).

67. McMillan, "Thoughts on *She's Gotta Have It*," 25.

68. Lee, *Spike Lee's Gotta Have It*, 69.

69. Ibid., 73.

70. Ibid., 124.

71. Spike Lee with Lisa Jones, *Uplift the Race: The Construction of "School Daze"* (New York: Fireside, 1988), 70.

72. Lee, *That's My Story*, 72–73.

73. Ibid., 72.

74. Ibid.

75. Donald Bogle, *Toms, Coons, Mulattoes, Mammies, and Bucks: An Interpretive History of Blacks in American Films*, 4th ed. (2010; New York: Continuum, 2001), 300.

76. Roger Ebert, "*School Daze*," *Chicago Sun-Times*, February 12, 1988, http://www.rogerebert.com/reviews/school-daze-1988.

77. Ibid.

78. Lee with Jones, *Uplift the Race*, 185.

79. Aftab, *That's My Story*, 75.

80. Lee with Jones, *Uplift the Race*, 60.

81. Ronald Jemal Stephens, "The Aesthetics of *Nommo* in the Films of Spike Lee," in *Fight the Power!: The Spike Lee Reader*, ed. Janet D. Hamlet and Robin R. Means Coleman (New York: Peter Lang Publishing, Inc., 2009), 9.

82. Lee with Jones, *Uplift the Race*, 62.

83. Wallace, "Spike Lee and Black Women," 26.

84. Ibid.

85. Ibid.

86. Blake, *Street Smart*, 231.

87. Ibid.

88. Wahneema Lubiano, "But Compared to What?: Reading Realism, Representation, and Essentialism in *School Daze*, *Do the Right Thing*, and the Spike Lee Discourse," in *The Spike Lee Reader*, ed. Paula J. Massood (Philadelphia: Temple University Press, 2008), 45.

    Lubiano's essay first appeared in *Black American Literature Forum* 25, no. 2 (summer 1991): 253–82.

89. Ibid., 37.

90. Ibid., 38–39.

91. See Raymond Williams, *Keywords: A Vocabulary of Culture and Society* (New York: Oxford University Press, 1976); Suzette Elgin, *Native Tongue* (New York: Daw Books, 1984); Kobena Mercer, "Diaspora Culture and the Dialogic Imagination: The Aesthetics of Black Independent Film in Britain," in *Black Frames: Critical Perspectives in Black Independent Cinema*, ed. Mbye B. Cham and Claire Andrade-Watkins (Cambridge: MIT Press, 1988), 50–61; and Coco Fusco, "An Interview with Black Audio Film Collective: John Akomfrah, Reece Auguiste, Lina Gopaul and Avril Johnson," in *Young, British, and Black: The Work of Sankofa and Black Audio Film Collective* (Buffalo, NY: Hallwalls/Contemporary Art Center, 1988), 41–60, for additional information about each author's perspectives on realism and authenticity as cinematic criteria.

92. Lubiano, "But Compared to What?," 50.

93. Toni Cade Bambara, "Programming with *School Daze*," in *Five for Five: The Films of Spike Lee* (New York: Stewart, Tabori & Chang, 1991), 47.

Bambara's essay also appears in *The Spike Lee Reader*, ed. Paula J. Massood (Philadelphia: Temple University Press, 2008), 10–22.

94. Ibid., 48.

95. Ibid.

96. *School Daze*, written by Spike Lee, directed by Spike Lee, released by Columbia Pictures, 1988, 121 min. All quotations, summaries, and paraphrases refer to Columbia's DVD version of Lee's film.

97. S. Craig Watkins, *Representing: Hip Hop Culture and the Production of Black Cinema* (Chicago: University of Chicago Press, 1998), 142.

98. Ibid., 140.

99. Ibid., 143. The emphasis is Watkins's.

100. Ibid., 145.

101. Ibid., 145–46.

102. Breskin, *Inner Views*, 176.

103. Lee with Jones, *Uplift the Race*, 316.

104. Ebert, "*School Daze*," http://www.rogerebert.com/reviews/school-daze-1988.

105. Bambara, "Programming with *School Daze*," 52–53.

106. Ibid., 53.

107. Ibid.

108. Spike Lee, "Five for Five," in *Five for Five: The Films of Spike Lee* (New York: Stewart, Tabori & Chang, 1991), 13–14.

109. Ibid., 14.

CHAPTER TWO: THE RIGHT STUFF

1. The American Film Institute (AFI) most recently updated its "100 Years . . . 100 Movies" list (http://www.afi.com/100years/movies10.aspx) in 2007. *Do the Right Thing* ranks as the ninety-sixth movie (between Peter Bogdanovich's *The Last Picture Show* and Ridley Scott's *Blade Runner*) out of one hundred entries.

2. The British Film Institute (BFI) also conducts a *Sight and Sound* Director's Poll that ranks *Do the Right Thing* as the 132nd best movie out of 250 international entries. The five directors who voted for Spike Lee's third feature film are Wanuri Kahiu, Asif Kapadia, Khalo Matabane, Steve McQueen, and Akin Omotoso. *Do the Right Thing*'s BFI entry is available at http://explore.bfi.org.uk/sightandsoundpolls/2012/film/4ce2b794e6dfb.

3. David Sterritt, "*Do the Right Thing* (1989)," in *The A List: The National Society of Film Critics' 100 Essential Films*, ed. Jay Carr (New York: Da Capo Press, 2002), 91–94.

4. Peter M. Nichols, ed., *The "New York Times" Guide to the Best 1,000 Movies Ever Made*, Updated and Revised ed. (New York: St. Martin's Press, 2004).
   This list also appears at http://www.nytimes.com/ref/movies/1000best.html.

5. The National Film Registry's complete list of preserved films is available at http://www.loc.gov/film/registry_titles.php.

6. W.J.T. Mitchell, "The Violence of Public Art: *Do the Right Thing*," in *Spike Lee's "Do the Right Thing,"* ed. Mark A. Reid, Cambridge Film Handbooks Series (Cambridge: Cambridge University Press, 1997), 125n2.

Mitchell's essay first appeared in the scholarly journal *Critical Inquiry* 16, no. 4 (1990): 880–99.

7. David Denby, "He's Gotta Have It," *New York Magazine,* June 26, 1989, 54.

Denby's review is available at http://books.google.com/books?id=VucCAA AAMBAJ&pg=PA53&lpg=PA53&dq=david+denby+do+the+right+thing&sour ce=bl&ots=5dtdRpSxWp&sig=SgWkW59EN2TpPT6vLeWXCyntL-k&hl=en& sa=X&ei=aky7UOXgHMyuigLOqIHIAw&ved=0CC0Q6AEwAA#v=onepage& q=david%20denby%20do%20the%20right%20thing&f=false.

8. Lee's full-page letter, titled "Say It Ain't So, Joe," appears on page 6 of *New York Magazine*'s July 17, 1989, edition to challenge Denby's parochialism and Joe Klein's bigotry as expressed in Klein's article "Spiked?" (published on pages 14 and 15 of the same June 26, 1989, issue as Denby's *Do the Right Thing* review).

Lee also addresses *Do the Right Thing*'s initial critical reception in his long *Rolling Stone* interview with David Breskin, reprinted in *Inner Views: Filmmak- ers in Conversation,* Expanded ed. (New York: Da Capo Press, 1997), especially pages 170–73; in his 1989 *Film Comment* interview with Marlaine Glicksman, reprinted in *Spike Lee: Interviews* (Jackson: University Press of Mississippi, 2002), 13–24; in Chapter 5 of *That's My Story and I'm Sticking to It,* written in collabo- ration with Kaleem Aftab (New York: W.W. Norton & Company, 2006), espe- cially pages 121–24; and in Logan Hill's retrospective April 7, 2008 *New York Magazine* article "How I Made It: Spike Lee on *Do the Right Thing,*" http:// nymag.com/anniversary/40th/culture/45772/.

9. Denby, "He's Gotta Have It," 53.

10. Ibid., 54.

11. Joe Klein, "Spiked?," *New York Magazine,* June 26, 1989, 14.

Klein's article is available at http://books.google.com/books?id=VucCA AAAMBAJ&pg=PA14&lpg=PA14&dq=joe+klein+spiked?&source=bl&ots=5 dtdSoXxQp&sig=KYyRjtlrXucYMBR5UhmuiIGb-DQ&hl=en&sa=X&ei=Rr- 8UIzcCcXbiwKaqYHQDg&ved=0CDkQ6AEwAg#v=onepage&q=joe%20 klein%20spiked%3F&f=false.

12. Ibid.

13. Ibid.

14. Ibid., 15.

15. Ibid. The emphasis is Klein's.

16. Spike Lee, "Say It Ain't So, Joe," *New York Magazine,* July 17, 1989, 6.

Lee's letter is available at http://books.google.com/books?id=8ecCAAAAM BAJ&pg=PA6&dq=spike+lee+do+say+it+ain%27t+so+joe&hl=en&sa=X&ei=gs W8UOacG8eeiQLhrYDIAg&ved=0CC8Q6AEwAA#v=onepage&q=spike%20 lee%20do%20say%20it%20ain%27t%20so%20joe&f=false.

17. Ibid.

18. Stanley Crouch, "Do the Race Thing: Spike Lee's Afro-Fascist Chic," *Village Voice,* June 20, 1989, 74.

19. Amiri Baraka, "Spike Lee at the Movies," in *Black American Cinema,* ed. Man- thia Diawara (New York: Routledge, 1993), 146–47.

20. Terrence Rafferty, "Open and Shut," *New Yorker,* July 24, 1989, 81.

Rafferty's review is available for *New Yorker* subscribers at http://archives.new yorker.com/?i=1989–07–24#folio=078.

21. Murray Kempton, "The Pizza Is Burning!," *New York Review of Books,* September 28, 1989, 37.
    Kempton's article is available for *NYRB* subscribers at http://www.nybooks .com/articles/archives/1989/sep/28/the-pizza-is-burning/?pagination=false.
22. Mitchell, "The Violence of Public Art," 125n1.
23. Toni Cade Bambara, "Programming with *School Daze,*" in *Five for Five: The Films of Spike Lee* (New York: Stewart, Tabori & Chang, 1991), 50.
24. Roger Ebert, "*Do the Right Thing,*" *Chicago Sun-Times,* June 30, 1989, http://www.rogerebert.com/reviews/do-the-right-thing-1989.
25. Roger Ebert, "*Do the Right Thing,*" *Chicago Sun-Times,* May 27, 2001, http://www.rogerebert.com/reviews/great-movie-do-the-right-thing-1989.
26. Norman K. Denzin, "Spike's Place," in *Fight the Power!: The Spike Lee Reader,* ed. Janice D. Hamlet and Robin R. Means Coleman (New York: Peter Lang Publishing, Inc., 2009), 109.
    Denzin lists nine major academic articles or book chapters devoted to *Do the Right Thing,* but many more exist (including several articles published in *Fight the Power!,* a collection that takes its title from the Public Enemy song that begins *Do the Right Thing* and that serves as Radio Raheem's musical anthem).
27. Ibid., 110.
28. hooks first published "Counter-Hegemonic Art" in *Z Magazine*'s 1989 issue, but reprinted this essay in her excellent 1990 book *Yearning: Race, Gender, and Cultural Politics* (Boston: South End Press, 1990), 173–84.
    Lubiano first published "But Compared to What?" in *Black American Literature Forum*'s summer 1991 issue, but reprinted this essay in Paula J. Massood's *The Spike Lee Reader* (Philadelphia: Temple University Press, 2008), 30–57.
29. bell hooks, "Counter-Hegemonic Art: *Do the Right Thing,*" *Yearning: Race, Gender, and Cultural Politics* (Boston: South End Press, 1990), 175.
30. Ibid., 183.
31. Spike Lee with Lisa Jones, *Do the Right Thing: A Spike Lee Joint* (New York: Fireside, 1989), 30.
32. Paul Krugman, in his November 19, 2007, *New York Times* editorial "Republicans and Race" (http://www.nytimes.com/2007/11/19/opinion/19krugman .html), states, "Reagan repeatedly told the bogus story of the Cadillac-driving welfare queen—a gross exaggeration of a minor case of welfare fraud. He never mentioned the woman's race, but he didn't have to."
    A February 9, 1976, newspaper article titled "Reagan's Stories Don't Always Check Out" (http://news.google.com/newspapers?nid=1310&dat=19760209 &id=Y9ZVAAAAIBAJ&sjid=K-ADAAAAIBAJ&pg=4138,2275149), written by John Fialka and published in the Eugene, Oregon *Register-Guard,* quotes James Piper, the Illinois Assistant State's Attorney who prosecuted Linda Taylor for welfare fraud, as saying, "You have to go with what you can prove" to explain why, contrary to Reagan's claim that Taylor used eighty aliases to bilk Illinois out of $150,000, she was charged with inventing four aliases to steal $8,000. Comparable newspaper and magazine articles disputing Reagan's statements about Taylor's larceny appeared throughout his 1976 and 1980 presidential campaigns.
    Josh Levin, in his December 19, 2013, *Slate* investigative article "The Welfare Queen" (http://www.slate.com/articles/news_and_politics/history/

2013/12/linda_taylor_welfare_queen_ronald_reagan_made_her_a_notorious_
american_villain.html), demonstrates that Reagan's, Krugman's, and Fialka's depictions of Taylor were all inaccurate in some regard:

> When I set out in search of Linda Taylor, I hoped to find the real story of the
> woman who played such an outsize role in American politics—who she was,
> where she came from, and what her life was like before and after she became
> the national symbol of unearned prosperity. What I found was a woman who
> destroyed lives, someone far more depraved than even Ronald Reagan could
> have imagined. In the 1970s alone, Taylor was investigated for homicide, kid-
> napping, and baby trafficking. The detective who tried desperately to put her
> away believes she's responsible for one of Chicago's most legendary crimes,
> one that remains unsolved to this day. Welfare fraud was likely the least of the
> welfare queen's offenses.

Levin's piece demonstrates that, while Taylor was indeed a criminal who served
time in prison after being convicted in 1977 of defrauding Chicago's welfare
system, this offense was merely one of numerous other crimes that she allegedly
committed. Levin reports that Illinois ASA James Piper became head of a special
welfare-fraud unit that, in its first year, indicted 241 people and led to increased
perceptions around the nation that welfare swindles constituted a major problem.
Even so, Levin notes, "The rising level of prosecutions didn't correspond to an
increase in benefit levels either," explaining that "monthly welfare benefits (that
is, payments via Aid to Families With Dependent Children and, after President
Bill Clinton's 1996 welfare reform legislation, Temporary Assistance for Needy
Families) began a long, steady decline in real dollars around the time of Taylor's
trial, one that's continued to the present day."

Levin's investigation condemns Taylor, but refuses to exonerate Reagan's
race-baiting campaign tactics. As Levin writes early in his article, "Linda Taylor,
the haughty thief who drove her Cadillac to the public aid office, was the embodiment of a pernicious stereotype. With her story, Reagan marked millions
of America's poorest people as potential scoundrels and fostered the belief that
welfare fraud was a nationwide epidemic that needed to be stamped out" before
noting, "This image of grand and rampant welfare fraud allowed Reagan to sell
voters on his cuts to public assistance spending. The 'welfare queen' became a
convenient villain, a woman everyone could hate. She was a lazy black con artist, unashamed of cadging the money that honest folks worked so hard to earn."

Other texts to consult about racialized representations of America's welfare
system include Thomas Byrne and Mary D. Edsall's *Chain Reaction: The Impact
of Race, Rights, and Taxes on American Politics* (New York: W.W. Norton &
Company, 1992); Martin Gilen's *Why Americans Hate Welfare: Race, Media, and
the Politics of Antipoverty Policy* (Chicago: University of Chicago Press, 2000);
Franklin D. Gilliam Jr.'s "The 'Welfare Queen' Experiment: How Viewers React
to Images of African American Women on Welfare," *Nieman Reports* 53, no. 2
(1999); Kenneth J. Neubeck and Noel A. Cazenave's *Welfare Racism: Playing
the Race Card against America's Poor* (New York: Routledge, 2001); and Mark

Robert Rank's *One Nation, Underprivileged: Why American Poverty Affects Us All* (New York: Oxford University Press, 2005).

33. Herman Gray, *Watching Race: Television and the Struggle for Blackness* (Minneapolis: University of Minnesota Press, 1995), 17.

This book's second chapter, "Reaganism and the Sign of Blackness," is among the finest analyses of Reagan's use of racial rhetoric ever written.

34. Ibid.

35. Lee with Jones, *Do the Right Thing: A Spike Lee Joint*, 63.

36. Wahneema Lubiano, "But Compared to What?: Reading Realism, Representation, and Essentialism in *School Daze, Do the Right Thing*, and the Spike Lee Discourse," in *The Spike Lee Reader*, ed. Paula J. Massood (Philadelphia: Temple University Press, 2008), 41.

37. Ibid.

38. *Do the Right Thing*, written by Spike Lee, directed by Spike Lee, released by Universal Pictures, 1989, 120 min. All future quotations, summaries, and paraphrases refer to Universal's Blu-ray version of Lee's film.

39. Lubiano, "But Compared to What?," 41.

40. Ibid., 46.

41. Ibid.

42. Ibid., 47.

43. Ibid.

44. Ibid., 49.

45. Lee with Jones, *Do the Right Thing: A Spike Lee Joint*, 40.

46. Aftab, *That's My Story*, 96.

47. Ibid.

For other accounts of the Howard Beach incident, consult Dwayne Mack's entry on BlackPast.org (http://www.blackpast.org/aah/howard-beach-incident-1986), Charles J. Hynes and Bob Drury's *Incident at Howard Beach: The Case for Murder*, 25th Anniversary ed. (1990; Bloomington, IN: iUniverse, 2011), Alphonso Pinkney's *Lest We Forget: White Hate Crimes: Howard Beach and Other Racial Atrocities* (Chicago: Third World Press, 1994), and the *New York Times* online archive (particularly articles written by Joseph Fried and Robert McFadden).

48. Lee with Jones, *Do the Right Thing: A Spike Lee Joint*, 40.

49. *That's My Story and I'm Sticking to It* summarizes the difficult relationship between New York City's police force and African American residents on pages 96 and 97 by describing incidents involving Yvonne Smallwood, Eleanor Bumpers, Edmund Perry, and Michael Stewart.

Smallwood was beaten by a male police officer while she sat in a car that he was ticketing on December 3, 1987, and died on December 9, 1987. Perry was shot on June 12, 1985, by Officer Lee Van Houten, who claimed to have been in a fight with Perry. Van Houten was exonerated by both an internal NYPD investigation and a grand jury when as many as twenty-three witnesses confirmed Van Houten's claim that Perry and another assailant tried to mug Van Houten in Morningside Park, although the circumstances are still debated in New York City.

Michael Stewart was arrested by eleven police officers, but subsequently choked to death while in custody, although the evidence of this incident was, according to official NYPD files, lost. The chokehold applied to Stewart by a New York City transit officer using a nightstick (on September 15, 1983) inspired Radio Raheem's death in *Do the Right Thing*.

Lee even has the block's disgusted residents scream Stewart's and Bumpers's names after police officers haul away Raheem's corpse, just before they attack Sal's Famous Pizzeria.

50. Lee with Jones, *Do the Right Thing: A Spike Lee Joint*, 47–48.
51. Ibid., 48.
52. Ibid., 240.
53. Ed Guerrero, *Framing Blackness: The African American Image in Film* (Philadelphia: Temple University Press, 1993), 146.
54. Ibid., 147–48.
55. Ibid., 148.
56. Ibid., 149.
57. Ibid.
58. Paula J. Massood, *Black City Cinema: African American Urban Experiences in Film* (Philadelphia: Temple University Press, 2003), 131.
59. Ibid.
60. Ibid.
61. Douglas S. Kellner, "Aesthetics, Ethics, and Politics in the Films of Spike Lee," in *Spike Lee's "Do the Right Thing,"* ed. Mark A. Reid, Cambridge Film Handbooks Series (Cambridge: Cambridge University Press, 1997), 75.
62. Ibid.
63. Ibid., 76.
64. Ibid., 90.
65. Ibid., 89.
66. Ibid., 93.
67. S. Craig Watkins, *Representing: Hip Hop Culture and the Production of Black Cinema* (Chicago: University of Chicago Press, 1998), 157.
68. Ibid.
69. Ibid., 162.
70. Ibid.
71. Ibid., 163.
72. Lee with Jones, *Do the Right Thing: A Spike Lee Joint*, 250.
73. Ibid., 138.
74. Nelson George, "*Do the Right Thing*: Film and Fury," in *Five for Five: The Films of Spike Lee* (New York: Stewart, Tabori & Chang, 1991), 79.
75. Consult the following texts for additional perspectives on the melting-pot metaphor: Roger Daniels, *Guarding the Golden Door: American Immigration Policy and Immigrants since 1882* (New York: Hill and Wang, 2004); Lawrence H. Fuchs, *The American Kaleidoscope: Race, Ethnicity, and the Civic Culture* (Middletown, CT: Wesleyan University Press, 1990); David A. Hollinger, "Amalgamation and Hypodescent: The Question of Ethnoracial Mixture in the History of the United States," *American Historical Review* 108, no. 5 (2003): 1363–90; Tamar Jacoby, ed., *Reinventing the Melting Pot: The New Immigrants and What It Means to Be American* (New York: Basic Books, 2004); and Aristide R. Zolberg, *A Nation by Design: Immigration Policy in the Fashioning of America* (Cambridge: Harvard University Press, 2009).

76. Lee with Jones, *Do the Right Thing: A Spike Lee Joint,* 186.
77. Marlaine Glicksman, "Spike Lee's Bed-Stuy BBQ," in *Spike Lee: Interviews,* ed. Cynthia Fuchs, Conversations with Filmmakers Series (Jackson: University Press of Mississippi, 2002), 18.

 Glicksman's interview first appeared in *Film Comment* 25 (July/August 1989): 12–16.
78. Lee with Jones, *Do the Right Thing: A Spike Lee Joint,* 45.
79. George, "*Do the Right Thing:* Film and Fury," 79.
80. Dan Flory, "Spike Lee and the Sympathetic Racist," *Journal of Aesthetic and Art Criticism* 64, no. 1 (2006), 67.
81. Ibid., 68.
82. Ibid.
83. Ibid.
84. Danny Aiello, interviewed in *Making "Do the Right Thing,"* directed by St. Clair Bourne, 40 Acres & A Mule Filmworks and Chamba Organization, 1989, 58 min.

 This documentary, filmed during the 1988 production of Lee's third movie, is available on Universal Studios's Blu-ray version of *Do the Right Thing.*
85. Flory, "Spike Lee and the Sympathetic Racist," 71.
86. Ibid.
87. Ibid., 74.
88. Lee with Jones, *Do the Right Thing: A Spike Lee Joint,* 54.
89. Massood, *Black City Cinema,* 143.
90. Spike Lee and Jason Matloff, *Spike Lee: Do the Right Thing,* ed. Steve Crist (New York: AMMO Books, 2010), 351.

 Sal's comments occur on page 172 of Lee's handwritten, first-draft script.
91. Lee and Matloff, *Do the Right Thing,* 352.
92. Michael Silberstein, "The Dialectic of King and X in *Do the Right Thing,*" in *The Philosophy of Spike Lee,* ed. Mark Conard (Lexington: The University Press of Kentucky, 2011), 140.
93. King's Nobel Lecture, "The Quest for Peace and Justice" (http://www.nobelprize.org/nobel_prizes/peace/laureates/1964/king-lecture.html) features a slightly different version of this quotation:

> Violence as a way of achieving racial justice is both impractical and immoral. I am not unmindful of the fact that violence often brings about momentary results. Nations have frequently won their independence in battle. But in spite of temporary victories, violence never brings permanent peace. It solves no social problem: it merely creates new and more complicated ones. Violence is impractical because it is a descending spiral ending in destruction for all. It is immoral because it seeks to humiliate the opponent rather than win his understanding: it seeks to annihilate rather than convert.

 The version that appears at *Do the Right Thing*'s conclusion appears in many books of King's writings and speeches, particularly *The Words of Martin Luther King, Jr.* (New York: Newmarket Press, 1984), 73.
94. Malcolm X, "Communication and Reality," in *Malcolm X: The Man and His Times,* ed. John Henrik Clarke (1969; New York: Collier Books, 1990), 313.
95. James H. Cone, *Martin and Malcolm and America: A Dream or a Nightmare* (1991; New York: Orbis Books, 2001), 246.

96. Spike Lee, interview by David Breskin, *Inner Views: Filmmakers in Conversation,* Expanded ed. (New York: Da Capo Press, 1997), 173.

CHAPTER THREE: DANCING WITH DENZEL

1. Library of Congress, National Film Preservation Board, "Frequently Asked Questions about the National Film Registry," Updated May 21, 2014, http://www.loc.gov/film/faq.html.
2. Malcolm X's FBI file (http://vault.fbi.gov/malcolm-little-malcolm-x) is available at the Federal Bureau of Investigation's website, on its "FBI Records: The Vault" page, collected into seventy-two different digital packages divided into two groups: "HQ Files" and "New York Files."
3. Ossie Davis, quoted in "Foreword" by Attallah Shabazz, *The Autobiography of Malcolm X,* by Malcolm X with the assistance of Alex Haley (1965; New York: Ballantine Books, 1999), xii.
4. Attallah Shabazz, Foreword to *The Autobiography of Malcolm X,* by Malcolm X with the assistance of Alex Haley (1965; New York: Ballantine Books, 1999), ix.
5. S. Craig Watkins, *Representing: Hip Hop Culture and the Production of Black Cinema* (Chicago: University of Chicago Press, 1998), 125.
6. Spike Lee with Ralph Wiley, *By Any Means Necessary: The Trials and Tribulations of the Making of "Malcolm X" (While Ten Million Motherfuckers Are Fucking with You!)* (New York: Hyperion, 1992), 21.
7. Ibid., 21–22.
8. Aftab, *That's My Story,* 184
9. Watkins, *Representing,* 125.
10. See Amiri Baraka's "Spike Lee at the Movies," in *Black American Cinema,* ed. Manthia Diawara (New York: Routledge, 1993): 145–53; Clayborne Carson's *"Malcolm X,"* in *Past Imperfect: History According to the Movies,* ed. Mark C. Carnes (1995; New York: Agincourt Press, 1996), 278–83; and Manning Marable's "Malcolm as Messiah: Cultural Myth vs. Historical Reality in *Malcolm X,"* *Cineaste* 19, no. 4 (1993): 7–9, for their concerns about Lee commercializing Malcolm X's memory.
11. Spike Lee with Lisa Jones, *Mo' Better Blues: A Spike Lee Joint* (New York: Fireside, 1990), 102.
12. Ibid., 39.
13. Ibid.
14. Aftab, *That's My Story,* 132.
15. Ibid.
16. *Mo' Better Blues,* directed by Spike Lee, written by Spike Lee, released by Universal Pictures, 1990, 130 min. All future quotations, summaries, and paraphrases refer to Touchstone Pictures's DVD version of Lee's film.
17. bell hooks, "Male Heroes and Female Sex Objects: Sexism in Spike Lee's *Malcolm X,"* *Cineaste* 19, no. 4 (March 1993): 14.
    This essay also appears in *Feminisms: An Anthology of Literary Theory and Criticism,* Rev. ed., ed. Robyn R. Warhol and Diane Price Herndl (New Brunswick, NJ: Rutgers University Press, 1997), 555–58.
18. Ibid.

19. *Malcolm X,* written by Arnold Perl and Spike Lee, directed by Spike Lee, released by Warner Bros. Pictures, 1992, 202 min. All future quotations, summaries, and paraphrases refer to Warner Bros.'s Blu-ray version of Lee's film.

Although Lee revised a screenplay that James Baldwin and Arnold Perl prepared in the late 1960s and early 1970s, Paula Baldwin Whaley, Baldwin's sister and the executor of his estate, successfully petitioned the Writers Guild of America to have Baldwin's name removed from *Malcolm X*'s opening credits. *By Any Means Necessary,* however, lists Baldwin as the script's first author in its reproduction of the film's fourth-draft screenplay (see page 169). Lee also credited Baldwin's work in many press interviews at the time of *Malcolm X*'s release.

20. Malcolm X with the assistance of Alex Haley, *The Autobiography of Malcolm X* (1965; New York: Ballantine Books, 1999), 4.

21. Ibid., 21.

22. Jeffrey B. Leak, "Malcolm X and Black Masculinity in Process," in *The Cambridge Companion to Malcolm X,* ed. Robert E. Terrill (Cambridge: Cambridge University Press, 2010), 56.

See Als's "Philosopher or Dog?," in *Malcolm X: In Our Own Image,* ed. Joe Wood (New York: Palgrave Macmillan, 1992), 86–100 for his full article, which can be also be accessed at *BOMB* magazine's website (http://bombsite.com/issues/41/articles/1585).

23. Leak, "Malcolm X and Black Masculinity in Process," 56.

24. Ibid., 57.

25. Ibid.

26. Malcolm X with Haley, *Autobiography,* 160.

27. Ibid., 34.

28. Ibid., 41.

29. hooks, "Male Heroes and Female Sex Objects," 15.

30. Ibid.

31. Ibid.

32. Thomas Doherty, "Malcolm X: In Print, On Screen," *Biography* 23, no. 1 (winter 2000): 36.

33. hooks, "Male Heroes and Female Sex Objects," 15.

34. Sheila Radford-Hill, "Womanizing Malcolm X," in *The Cambridge Companion to Malcolm X,* ed. Robert E. Terrill (Cambridge: Cambridge University Press, 2010), 67.

35. Myrlie Evers-Williams, Foreword to *Betty Shabazz, Surviving Malcolm X,* by Russell J. Rickford (Naperville, IL: Sourcebooks, 2003), ix.

36. Ibid., x.

37. Ibid., x–xi.

38. Ibid., xi.

39. Radford-Hill, "Womanizing Malcolm X," 67.

40. Malcolm X with Haley, *Autobiography,* 237.

41. Ibid.

42. Ibid.

43. Ibid.

44. Ibid.

45. Radford-Hill, "Womanizing Malcolm X," 67.

46. Ibid., 68.
47. Ibid.
48. Ibid.
49. See David Birmingham's *The Decolonization of Africa* (1995; London: Rout-ledge, 2003); Frederick Cooper's *Africa since 1940: The Past of the Present,* New Approaches to African History Series (Cambridge: Cambridge University Press, 2002); Cooper's *Decolonization and African Society: The Labor Question in French and British Africa* (Cambridge: Cambridge University Press, 1996); and Basil Richardson's *The Black Man's Burden: Africa and the Curse of the Nation-State* (New York: Three Rivers Press, 1992) for further information about African liberation movements, decolonization efforts, and independence.
50. Malcolm X, "The Role of Women," in *By Any Means Necessary,* ed. George Breit-man (1970; New York: Pathfinder Press, 2010), 214.
51. Ibid., 214–15.
52. Radford-Hill, "Womanizing Malcolm X," 69.
53. Ibid., 65.
    Both Bruce Perry's *Malcolm: The Life of the Man Who Changed Black America* (1991; Barrytown, NY: Station Hill Press, 1992) and Manning Marable's *Malcolm X: A Life of Reinvention* (New York: Viking, 2011), although exceptionally controversial biographies of Malcolm's life, document the many women with whom he worked and sought counsel during his final years as a revolutionary activist working to reframe the American civil-rights debate as a global human rights struggle.
54. hooks, "Male Heroes and Female Sex Objects," 15.
55. Spike Lee, interview by Henry Louis Gates Jr., in "Generation X: A Conversation with Spike Lee and Henry Louis Gates," *Transition* 56 (1992): 178.
56. Ibid.
57. Page 180 of *That's My Story* states that Worth bought the *Autobiography*'s rights in 1968, while Bernard Weinraub's November 23, 1992, *New York Times* article "A Movie Producer Remembers the Human Side of Malcolm X" (http://www.nytimes.com/1992/11/23/movies/a-movie-producer-remembers-the-human-side-of-malcolm-x.html?src=pm) pegs the date as 1967.
58. Lee with Wiley, *By Any Means Necessary,* 166.
59. Aftab, *That's My Story,* 187.
    See pages 21–32 of Lee and Wiley's *By Any Means Necessary* for Lee's exten-sive comments about *Malcolm X*'s budget troubles.
60. Aftab, *That's My Story,* 209.
61. David Leeming, *James Baldwin: A Biography* (New York: Penguin, 1994), 300.
62. Brian Norman, "Reading a 'Closet Screenplay': Hollywood, James Baldwin's Malcolms and the Threat of Historical Irrelevance," *African American Review* 39, no. 1–2 (2005): 104.
    Norman quotes page 297 of David Leeming's *James Baldwin: A Biography* when referencing the studio's consideration of a darkened-up Charlton Heston for the role of Malcolm X.
63. Ibid., 105.
64. Brian Norman, "Bringing Malcolm X to Hollywood," in *The Cambridge Com-panion to Malcolm X,* ed. Robert E. Terrill (Cambridge: Cambridge University Press, 2010), 39.

65. Ibid., 40.
66. See Amiri Baraka's "Spike Lee at the Movies," in *Black American Cinema*, ed. Manthia Diawara (New York: Routledge, 1993), 145–53; Gerald Horne's "'Myth' and the Making of *Malcolm X*," *American Historical Review* 98, no. 2 (April 1993): 440–50; William Lyne's "No Accident: From Black Power to Black Box Office," *African American Review* 34, no. 1 (2000): 39–59; and Nell Irvin Painter's "Malcolm X across the Genres," *American Historical Review* 98, no. 2 (April 1993): 432–39 for their complete arguments about how *Malcolm X* underplays Malcolm's radical politics, especially after his break with the Nation of Islam.
67. Jacquie Jones, "Spike Lee Presents *Malcolm X:* The New Black Nationalism," *Cineaste* 19, no. 4 (1993): 10.
68. Ibid.
69. Ibid.
70. Malcolm X with Haley, *Autobiography*, 177.
71. Lisa Kennedy, "Is *Malcolm X* the Right Thing?," *Sight and Sound* 3, no. 2 (February 1993): 9.
    Kennedy paraphrases comments made by Lee's frequent collaborator Lisa Jones in this analysis.
72. Malcolm X with Haley, *Autobiography*, 157.
73. David Bradley, "Malcolm's Mythmaking," *Transition* 56 (1992): 25. The emphasis is Bradley's.
74. Malcolm Turvey, "Black Film Making in the USA: The Case of *Malcolm X*," *Wasafiri* 9, no. 18 (1993): 53.
75. Ibid., 54.
76. Ibid. The emphasis is Turvey's.
77. Ibid.
78. Ibid., 56. The emphasis is Turvey's.
79. Lee with Wiley, *By Any Means Necessary*, xiv.
80. Bradley, "Malcolm's Mythmaking," 33.
81. John Locke, "Adapting the Autobiography: The Transformation of Malcolm X," *Cineaste* 19, no. 4 (1993): 5.
82. Michael Eric Dyson, *Making Malcolm: The Myth and Meaning of Malcolm X* (New York: Oxford University Press, 1995), 133.
83. Ibid., 132.
84. Ibid., 134.
85. Alex Haley, Epilogue to *The Autobiography of Malcolm X*, by Malcolm X with the assistance of Haley (1965; New York: Ballantine Books, 1999), 463.
86. Alex Gillespie, "Autobiography and Identity: Malcolm X as Author and Hero," in *The Cambridge Companion to Malcolm X*, ed. Robert E. Terrill (Cambridge: Cambridge University Press, 2010), 27.
87. Ibid.
88. Doherty, "Malcolm X: In Print, On Screen," 31.
89. Ibid., 30.
90. Ibid., 34.
91. Gillespie, "Malcolm X as Author and Hero," 35.
92. David LaRocca, "Rethinking the First Person: Autobiography, Authorship, and the Contested Self in *Malcolm X*," in *The Philosophy of Spike Lee*, ed. Mark Conard (Lexington: The University Press of Kentucky, 2011), 232.

93. Ibid., 232–33.
94. Maurice E. Stevens, "Subject to Countermemory: Disavowal and Black Manhood in Spike Lee's *Malcolm X*," in *Fight the Power!: The Spike Lee Reader,* ed. Janice D. Hamlet and Robin R. Means Coleman (New York: Peter Lang Publishing, Inc., 2009), 338.
95. Lee with Wiley, *By Any Means Necessary,* 3.
96. Anna Everett, "'Spike, Don't Mess Malcolm Up': Courting Controversy and Control in *Malcolm X*," in *The Spike Lee Reader,* ed. Paula J. Massood (Philadelphia: Temple University Press, 2008), 95.
97. See James Verniere, "Doing the Job," *Sight and Sound* (February 1993): 10; John Colapinto, "Outside Man: Spike Lee's Unending Struggle," *New Yorker,* September 22, 2008, 52–63; and Roger Ebert, "The Moment of Truth Arrives for *Malcolm*," *Chicago Sun-Times,* November 5, 1992, http://www.rogerebert .com/rogers-journal/the-moment-of-truth-arrives-for-malcolm for Lee's quotes about *The Autobiography of Malcolm X* being the most important book he has ever read.

   Verniere's interview is also available in *Spike Lee: Interviews,* ed. Cynthia Fuchs, Conversations with Filmmakers Series (Jackson: University Press of Mississippi, 2002), 79–85. Lee's quote about the *Autobiography*'s importance appears on page 79 of this version.

   Colapinto's profile is also available on the *New Yorker*'s official website at http://www.newyorker.com/reporting/2008/09/22/080922fa_fact_ colapinto?currentPage=all.
98. Spike Lee, quoted on cover, *The Autobiography of Malcolm X* by Malcolm X with the assistance of Alex Haley (1965; New York: Ballantine Books, 1999), n.p.
99. Everett, "'Spike, Don't Mess Malcolm Up,'" 97.

   Everett quotes Lee's belief that Malcolm X was produced at the correct moment from page 9 of *By Any Means Necessary: The Trials and Tribulations of the Making of "Malcolm X."*

CHAPTER FOUR: BLACK MAGIC WOMEN

1. bell hooks, "Male Heroes and Female Sex Objects: Sexism in Spike Lee's *Malcolm X*," *Cineaste* 19, no. 4 (March 1993): 13.

   This essay also appears in *Feminisms: An Anthology of Literary Theory and Criticism,* Rev. ed., ed. Robyn R. Warhol and Diane Price Herndl (New Brunswick, NJ: Rutgers University Press, 1997), 555–58.
2. Ibid.
3. Ibid., 14.
4. Ibid.
5. Ibid., 13.
6. Ibid.
7. Ibid., 14.
8. Heather E. Harris and Kimberly R. Moffitt, "A Critical Exploration of African American Women through the 'Spiked Lens,'" in *Fight the Power!: The Spike Lee Reader,* ed. Janice D. Hamlet and Robin R. Means Coleman (New York: Peter Lang Publishing, Inc., 2009), 304.
9. Massood, *Black City Cinema,* 83.

10. Harris and Moffitt, "Spiked Lens," 304.
11. Ibid., 306.
12. Ibid., 303.

Harris and Moffitt, indeed, summarize Lee's position as fully stated in "Mo' Better Spike." See Jill Nelson, "Mo' Better Spike," *Essence,* August 1990, 54–56.

13. Spike Lee with Ralph Wiley, *By Any Means Necessary: The Trials and Tribulations of the Making of "Malcolm X" (While Ten Million Motherfuckers Are Fucking with You!)* (New York: Hyperion, 1992), 92.
14. Ibid.
15. Spike Lee with Lisa Jones, *Do the Right Thing: A Spike Lee Joint* (New York: Fireside, 1989), 73.
16. Ibid., 74.
17. Ibid., 75.
18. Spike Lee as told to Kaleem Aftab, *Spike Lee,* 105. The emphasis is Aftab's.
19. Spike Lee and Jason Matloff, *Spike Lee: Do the Right Thing,* ed. Steve Crist (New York: AMMO Books, 2010), 304.

This stage direction appears on page 125 of Lee's handwritten, first-draft script.

20. Spike Lee, *Do the Right Thing,* second-draft screenplay, March 1, 1988, http://www.awesomefilm.com/script/dotherightthing.txt.
21. Aftab, *That's My Story,* 20.
22. Ibid.
23. *Jungle Fever,* written by Spike Lee, directed by Spike Lee, released by Universal Pictures, 1991, 132 min. All future quotations, summaries, and paraphrases refer to Universal's DVD version of Lee's film.
24. Lee repeatedly made this point in interviews and other press appearances during *Jungle Fever*'s theatrical release. He most fully addresses America's race-based sexual mythology in two 1991 interviews, with *Cineaste*'s Janice Mosier Richolson ("He's Gotta Have It: An Interview with Spike Lee") and *Playboy*'s Elvis Mitchell ("Spike Lee: The *Playboy* Interview"), both included in Cynthia Fuchs's *Spike Lee: Interviews* (Jackson: University Press of Mississippi, 2002). See pages 25–34 for "He's Gotta Have It" and pages 35–64 for "The *Playboy* Interview."

Lee's explanation of Flipper's and Angie's motivations for pursuing their relationship, given to Richolson, is worth quoting in full:

> I think what we're trying to do with this film is to show sexual myths. What's important about this film is that the characters Flipper and Angie, played by Wesley Snipes and Annabella Sciorra, are not drawn to each other by love but by sexual myths. When you're a black person in this country, you're constantly bombarded with the myth of the white woman as the epitome of beauty—again and again and again—in TV, movies, magazines. It's blonde hair, fair skin, blue eyes, thin nose. If you're black, you never see yourself portrayed in that way—you don't fit that image, you're not beautiful. So we cut away our noses to get a thinner nose . . . we'll cut away our lips . . . wear blue and green contact lenses. Why do we do that? Because that's what's pounded into us constantly. Annabella Sciorra's character bought into the myth that the black male is a stud, a sexual superman with a penis that's two feet long. So those are the two sexual myths that bring these two people together. (28)

This analysis, however shrewd, ignores the deepening connection between the two characters as the film unfolds. Their fascination may begin with these myths, but is not confined to them, although race remains a factor throughout Flipper and Angie's relationship.

Richolson's interview first appeared in *Cineaste* 18, no. 4 (1991): 12–14, while Mitchell's interview first appeared in *Playboy* (July 1991): 51–68.

25. Spike Lee, *Jungle Fever,* second-draft screenplay, July 9, 1990, 124.

This script is not publicly available but can be purchased from www.scriptcity .com.

26. Lee with Jones, *Do the Right Thing: A Spike Lee Joint,* 47–48.

27. Henry Louis Gates Jr., "*Jungle Fever,* or, Guess Who's Not Coming to Dinner?," in *Five for Five: The Films of Spike Lee* (New York: Stewart, Tabori & Chang, 1991), 164. The emphasis is Gates's.

28. Breskin, *Inner Views,* 194.

29. Ibid.

30. Richard A. Blake, *Street Smart: The New York of Lumet, Allen, Scorsese, and Lee* (Lexington: University Press of Kentucky, 2005), 250.

31. Aftab, *That's My Story,* 160.

32. Janice Mosier Richolson, "He's Gotta Have It: An Interview with Spike Lee," in *Spike Lee: Interviews,* ed. Cynthia Fuchs, Conversations with Filmmakers Series (Jackson: University Press of Mississippi, 2002), 29.

33. Gates, "Guess Who's Not Coming to Dinner?," 167.

Gates's final comment, while true, was short lived. Julie Dash's *Daughters of the Dust,* which includes numerous communal feminist moments, was released six months after *Jungle Fever.*

34. Lee, *Jungle Fever* screenplay, 48.

35. Gates, "Guess Who's Not Coming to Dinner?," 168.

36. Charlie Rose, "Interview with Spike Lee: 1996," in *Spike Lee: Interviews,* ed. Cynthia Fuchs, Conversations with Filmmakers Series (Jackson: University Press of Mississippi, 2002), 117.

37. Ibid.

38. bell hooks, "Good Girls Look the Other Way," in *Reel to Real: Race, Class and Sex at the Movies* (1996; New York: Routledge, 2009), 13.

39. Ibid., 13–14.

40. Girl 6's agent, Murray (John Turturro), gives Tarantino this title in the film. Both hooks's "Good Girls Look the Other Way" (on pages 15–16) and Lee's *That's My Story and I'm Sticking to It* (on page 256) employ the same phrase to describe the character.

41. hooks, "Good Girls Look the Other Way," 15.

42. *Girl 6,* written by Suzan-Lori Parks, directed by Spike Lee, released by Fox Searchlight Pictures, 1996, 108 min. All future quotations, summaries, and paraphrases refer to Fox Searchlight and Anchor Bay Entertainment's DVD version of Lee's film.

43. hooks, "Good Girls Look the Other Way," 16.

44. Karen D. Hoffman, "Feminists and 'Freaks': *She's Gotta Have It* and *Girl 6,*" in *The Philosophy of Spike Lee,* ed. Mark Conard (Lexington: The University Press of Kentucky, 2011), 117.

45. Ibid.

46. Lee with Jones, *Do the Right Thing: A Spike Lee Joint,* 73 and 75.
47. Hoffman, "Feminists and 'Freaks,'" 117.
48. Ibid.
49. hooks, "Good Girls Look the Other Way," 15.
50. Ibid.
51. Ibid., 19.
52. Roger Ebert, "*Girl 6,*" *Chicago Sun-Times,* March 22, 1996, http://www.rog erebert.com/reviews/girl-6-1996
53. Hoffman, "Feminists and 'Freaks,'" 114.
54. Ibid.
55. Aftab, *That's My Story,* 263.
56. Ibid., 264.
57. Ibid.
58. Hoffman, "Feminists and 'Freaks,'" 115.
59. Ibid.
60. The father destroying the telephone, in another significant irony, signals what Girl 6 must do to develop her personality: renounce her phone-sex job before it devours her.
61. hooks, "Good Girls Look the Other Way," 19.
62. Ibid., 17.
63. Ibid.
64. Ibid., 23.
65. Ibid.
66. Hoffman, "Feminists and 'Freaks,'" 118.
67. Ibid.
68. Jasmine Nichole Cobb and John L. Jackson, "They Hate Me: Spike Lee, Documentary Filmmaking, and Hollywood's 'Savage Slot,'" in *Fight the Power!: The Spike Lee Reader,* ed. Janice D. Hamlet and Robin R. Means Coleman (New York: Peter Lang Publishing, Inc., 2009), 251–52.
69. Aftab, *That's My Story,* 374–75.
70. The Internet Movie Database (IMDb) (http://www.imdb.com/title/tt0384 533/business?ref_=tt_ql_dt_4) calculates *She Hate Me*'s final gross as $365,134, while Box Office Mojo (http://www.boxofficemojo.com/search/?q=she%20 hate%20me) lists the film's box-office receipts as $366,037. IMDb pegs *She Hate Me*'s budget as "$8 million (estimated)."
71. Roger Ebert, "*She Hate Me,*" *Chicago Sun-Times,* August 6, 2004, http://www .rogerebert.com/reviews/she-hate-me-2004. The emphasis is Ebert's.
72. Ibid.
73. Ibid.
74. Ibid.
75. *She Hate Me,* written by Michael Genet & Spike Lee, story by Michael Genet, directed by Spike Lee, released by Sony Pictures Classics, 2004, 138 min. All future quotations, summaries, and paraphrases refer to Sony Pictures's DVD version of Lee's film.
76. Bernadette Barton, "Male Fantasies about Lesbian Desire: A Review of Spike Lee's Film *She Hate Me,*" *Sexuality and Culture* 9, no. 3 (2005): 77.
77. Ibid., 79.
78. Cobb and Jackson, "They Hate Me," 251.

79. Harris and Moffitt, "Spiked Lens," 317.
80. Spike Lee, DVD audio commentary, *She Hate Me*, directed by Spike Lee, written by Michael Genet & Spike Lee, story by Michael Genet, released by Sony Pictures Classics, 138 min., 2004.
81. Alan Frutkin, "Spike Speaks," in *Spike Lee: Interviews*, ed. Cynthia Fuchs, Conversations with Filmmakers Series (Jackson: University Press of Mississippi, 2002), 113.
    Frutkin's interview first appeared in the October 31, 1995, issue of *The Advocate*, 49–50.
82. Ibid., 114.
83. Ibid., 115.
84. Rebecca Walker, "Female Trouble," *Salon*, August 19, 2004, http://www.salon.com/2004/08/19/lee_11/.
85. Ibid.
86. Ibid.
87. Barton, "Male Fantasies about Lesbian Desire," 77.
88. Walker, "Female Trouble," http://www.salon.com/2004/08/19/lee_11/.
89. "Spike Lee Discusses *She Hate Me*," About.com *Hollywood Movies*, n.d., http://movies.about.com/library/weekly/aaspikelee072804a.htm.
90. Will Leitch, "Spike Lee Talks Obama, the End of Mookie's Brooklyn, and the Hollywood Color Line," *Vulture*, July 8, 2012, http://www.vulture.com/2012/07/spike-lee-on-reality-tv-minstrelsy-and-hollywood.html.
91. Aftab, *That's My Story*, 373.
92. Anne Stockwell, "He Don't Hate Me," *The Advocate*, August, 17, 2004, 68.
    This article is available at http://books.google.com/books?id=CWUEAAAA MBAJ&pg=PA66&lpg=PA66&dq=spikelee+homophobic&source=bl&ots=5 uTFmlw7Zi&sig=fhVA1uNiMYK30Uvppsz3XGDf0hk&hl=en&sa=X&ei=rfI-UaPaEIT28wTblIHQAw&ved=0CDsQ6AEwAw#v=onepage&q=spike%20 lee%20homophobic&f=false.
93. Ibid., 66.
94. Deborah Elizabeth Whaley, "Spike Lee's Phantasmagoric Fantasy and the Black Female Sexual Imaginary in *She Hate Me*," *Poroi* 7, no. 2 (2011): 3.
95. Ibid., 2.
96. Barton, "Male Fantasies about Lesbian Desire," 79.

CHAPTER FIVE: BROOKLYN'S FINEST

1. Spike Lee, Twitter feed, December 17, 2011, https://twitter.com/SpikeLee/status/148016969281585153.
2. Andrew deWaard, "Joints and Jams: Spike Lee as Sellebrity Auteur," in *Fight the Power!: The Spike Lee Reader*, ed. Janice D. Hamlet and Robin R. Means Coleman (New York: Peter Lang Publishing, Inc., 2009), 345.
3. Ibid., 348. The emphasis is deWaard's.
4. Ibid., 346.
    DeWaard defines *sellebrity auteur* as "a paradoxical concept that signals the complexities and contradictions of contemporary commercial cinematic authorship" (345). For deWaard, this term "highlights, on the one hand, the cultural-economic factors in a film's creation and the struggle between art and

commerce that this process involves; on the other, it . . . [looks] at the auteur's brand identity and celebrity cachet as they are exploited both by the auteur in order to get a film made and by the studio in its marketing system" (345–46).

5. Ed Guerrero, *Framing Blackness: The African American Image in Film* (Philadelphia: Temple University Press, 1993), 147.

6. Ibid., 148.

7. David Bordwell, Janet Staiger, and Kristin Thompson, *The Classical Hollywood Cinema: Film Style & Mode of Production to 1960* (New York: Columbia University Press, 1985), 3.

   See especially the book's first seven chapters (pages 3–84) for Bordwell's extensive analysis of how classical Hollywood style came to seem the best, clearest, and most natural way to tell cinematic stories.

8. bell hooks, "*Crooklyn:* The Denial of Death," in *Reel to Real: Race, Class and Sex at the Movies* (1996; New York: Routledge, 2009), 45.

   Hooks first published this review in *Sight and Sound*'s August 1994 issue. See bell hooks, "Sorrowful Black Death Is Not a Hot Ticket," *Sight and Sound* 4, no. 8 (August 1994): 10–14.

9. Ibid.

10. Aftab, *That's My Story*, 225.

11. Krin Gabbard, "Spike Lee Meets Aaron Copland," in *The Spike Lee Reader*, ed. Paula J. Massood (Philadelphia: Temple University Press, 2008), 189.

    Gabbard first published this article in his book *Black Magic: White Hollywood and African American Culture* (New Brunswick, NJ: Rutgers University Press, 2004), 251–74.

12. Mark D. Cunningham, "Through the Looking Glass and Over the Rainbow: Exploring the Fairy Tale in Spike Lee's *Crooklyn*," in *The Spike Lee Reader*, ed. Paula J. Massood (Philadelphia: Temple University Press, 2008), 115–16.

13. Ibid., 117.

14. *Crooklyn;* screenplay by Spike Lee, Joie Susannah Lee, and Cinque Lee; story by Joie Susannah Lee; directed by Spike Lee; released by Universal Pictures, 1994, 115 min. All future quotations, summaries, and paraphrases refer to Universal's DVD version of Lee's film.

15. Aftab, *That's My Story*, 233.

16. Massood, *Black City Cinema*, 192.

17. Aftab, *That's My Story*, 233.

18. Cunningham, "Through the Looking Glass," 120–21.

19. Ibid., 121.

20. Ibid., 123.

21. Aftab, *That's My Story*, 15.

22. Cunningham, "Through the Looking Glass," 126.

23. hooks, "*Crooklyn:* The Denial of Death," 56.

24. Ibid., 57.

25. Ibid., 52.

26. Ibid., 51–52.

27. Ibid., 47.

28. Massood, *Black City Cinema*, 145.

    Massood culls these terms from Ed Guerrero's *Framing Blackness*, 182; Jacquie Jones, "The New Ghetto Aesthetic," *Wide Angle* 13, no. 3–4 (1991): 33;

and Manthia Diawara, "Black American Cinema: The New Realism," in *Black American Cinema,* ed. Manthia Diawara (New York: Routledge, 1993), 24.

29. David Bradley, "Spike Lee's Inferno, the Drug Underworld," *New York Times,* September 10, 1995, http://partners.nytimes.com/library/film/091095lee-clockers-essay.html.

    Lee first uses this term in Stephen Schaefer's "Spike Makes *Clockers* Timely," *New York Post,* August 25, 1995, 47.

30. Jonathan Bernstein, "Spike Lee," *Face* (December 1997): 202.

    Paula J. Massood also cites this quotation on page 189 of *Black City Cinema.*

31. Aftab, *That's My Story,* 239. The emphasis is Aftab's.

32. Stephen Pizzello, "Between 'Rock' and a Hard Place," in *Spike Lee: Interviews,* ed. Cynthia Fuchs, Conversations with Filmmakers Series (Jackson: University Press of Mississippi, 2002), 99. Pizzello's article first appeared in *American Cinematographer* 76, no. 9 (September 1995): 36–46.

    Lee's autobiography, *That's My Story and I'm Sticking to It,* defines a clocker as "the lowest of the low in the hierarchy of drug dealers, out on the streets peddling narcotics to passersby: they can always be found, 24/7, doing their rounds like clockwork" (237).

33. Massood, *Black City Cinema,* 191.

34. Keith M. Harris, "*Clockers* (Spike Lee, 1995): Adaptation in Black," in *The Spike Lee Reader,* ed. Paula J. Massood (Philadelphia: Temple University Press, 2008), 128.

35. Ibid., 129.

36. Jim Shepard, "Sympathy for the Dealer," *New York Times,* June 21, 1992, http://www.nytimes.com/books/98/06/07/specials/price-clockers.html.

37. Aftab, *That's My Story,* 239.

38. Massood, *Black City Cinema,* 190.

39. Ibid.

40. Bernstein, "Spike Lee," 202.

    Massood cites this quotation on page 252 of *Black City Cinema* (see Note 28, Chapter 6).

41. Douglas McFarland, "The Symbolism of Blood in *Clockers,*" in *The Philosophy of Spike Lee,* ed. Mark Conard (Lexington: The University Press of Kentucky, 2011), 3.

42. Massood, *Black City Cinema,* 204.

43. McFarland, "Blood in *Clockers,*" 12.

44. Massood, *Black City Cinema,* 189.

45. Ibid., 196.

46. Aftab, *That's My Story,* 238.

47. Ibid., 293.

48. Ibid.

49. While *He Got Game* never mentions the governor's name or state, the film's Brooklyn setting suggests that Lee targets then-New York governor George Pataki for criticism. Although Lee declares in *That's My Story and I'm Sticking to It* that he hates sports movies that create fake teams and uniforms (293), he nonetheless invents Big State University as the unidentified governor's alma mater rather than referring to an actual New York college or university.

50. Lee, in *Best Seat in the House: A Basketball Memoir* (written with Ralph Wiley) (New York: Crown Publishers, 1997), harshly criticizes come-from-behind sports movies, particularly David Anspaugh's *Hoosiers* (1986), for whitewashing the significant contributions of African American players, particularly in basketball:

> At the time, the NBA was becoming rife with black players, while Georgetown had been establishing a dominating presence in the fabric of the college game, so what do you do? You fill a nostalgic need with a fantasy, turn back the clock to a much simpler time, a time . . . when "nigras knew" their place. It helps if the story is good. This one was taken from real life. Indiana high school basketball in the 1950s, when a state championship was won by a tiny small-town lily-white high school. They had to do it as a period piece because it's not going to happen in contemporary life unless the state is Utah, Wyoming, or Montana. So reconstitute history as mythology. *Chariots of Fire* was similar in intention and effect. They are usually warmly embraced, these pictures about how wonderful and fine it was when, basically, niggers weren't around. (149)

Lee, however, favorably evaluates Gene Hackman's starring performance in *Hoosiers:* "Even with all the baggage, Gene Hackman was great in this. He usually is, come to think of it" (149).
51. Gabbard, "Spike Lee Meets Aaron Copland," 185.
52. Ibid., 178.
53. Roger Ebert, "*He Got Game,*" *Chicago Sun-Times,* May 1, 1998, http://www.rogerebert.com/reviews/he-got-game-1998.
54. Victoria E. Johnson, "Polyphony and Cultural Expression: Interpreting Musical Traditions in *Do the Right Thing,*" in *Spike Lee's "Do the Right Thing,"* ed. Mark A. Reid, Cambridge Film Handbooks Series (Cambridge: Cambridge University Press, 1997), 70.
55. Jason Holt and Robert Pitter, "The Prostitution Trap of Elite Sport in *He Got Game,*" in *The Philosophy of Spike Lee,* ed. Mark Conard (Lexington: The University Press of Kentucky, 2011), 15.
56. Ibid., 17.
57. Ibid.
58. *He Got Game,* written by Spike Lee, directed by Spike Lee, released by Touchstone Pictures, 1998, 136 min. All future quotations, summaries, and paraphrases refer to Touchstone's DVD version of Lee's film.
59. Aftab, *That's My Story,* 305.
60. Ibid., 306.
61. Gabbard, "Spike Lee Meets Aaron Copland," 179–81.
62. Miles Marshall Lewis, "Spike Lee Talks *Red Hook Summer,*" *Ebony,* August 9, 2012, http://www.ebony.com/entertainment-culture/interview-spike-lee-523#axzz2MEvdaZvz.
63. Spike Lee, DVD audio commentary, *Red Hook Summer,* directed by Spike Lee, written by Spike Lee & James McBride, released by Variance Films, Image Entertainment, and One Media, 121 min., 2012. All future quotations, summaries, and paraphrases refer to this commentary track.

The film's official website (http://www.redhooksummer.com/sundance .html) lists the sixty-six movie theatres that screened *Red Hook Summer* during summer and early fall 2012.

64. Chris Lee, "Spike Lee Talks Hollywood Racism, New Film *Red Hook Summer*," *Daily Beast*, January 26, 2012, http://www.thedailybeast.com/articles/ 2012/01/26/spike-lee-talks-hollywood-racism-new-film-red-hook-summer .html.

Lee states in this article that he told co-screenwriter and co-producer James McBride, "We just gotta write a script and make this film. We're gonna make it! We'll do it under the SAG Low Budget Agreement." Chris Lee then says to Spike, "So that means under $1 million," to which Spike Lee replies, "Yeah." Although the Screen Actor's Guild Low Budget Agreement specifies that any film made under its aegis cannot exceed a $2.5 million budget, Spike Lee has consistently indicated that *Red Hook Summer* cost less than $1 million.

65. Diane Brady, "Spike Lee on Self-Financing *Red Hook Summer*," *Bloomberg Businessweek*, June 28, 2012, http://www.businessweek.com/articles/2012-06-28/ spike-lee-on-self-financing-red-hook-summer.

66. Ibid.

67. Chris Lee, "Spike Lee Talks," http://www.thedailybeast.com/articles/2012/01/ 26/spike-lee-talks-hollywood-racism-new-film-red-hook-summer.html.

68. Diane Brady, "Self-Financing," http://www.businessweek.com/articles/2012- 06-28/spike-lee-on-self-financing-red-hook-summer.

69. Jason Guerrasio, "Q&A: Spike Lee on the Child-Abuse Scene in *Red Hook Summer*, His Michael Jackson Documentary, and Why He's Not Nervous for Mike Tyson on Broadway," *Vanity Fair*, August 14, 2012, http://www.vanityfair .com/online/oscars/2012/08/spike-lee-on-red-hook-summer-michael-jackson-documentary-mike-tyson-broadway.

70. Ibid.

71. Both the Internet Movie Database (http://www.imdb.com/title/tt1989593/ business?ref_=tt_dt_bus) and Box Office Mojo (http://www.boxofficemojo .com/search/?q=red%20hook%20summer) list *Red Hook Summer*'s box-office receipts as $338,803. Box Office Mojo calculates this total based on the film's performance in forty-one theatres, but the film's official website lists sixty-six screens.

72. Betsy Sharkey, "Spike Lee's *Red Hook Summer* a Mess of Sinners, Saints," *Los Angeles Times*, August 23, 2012, http://articles.latimes.com/2012/aug/23/enter tainment/la-et-mn-red-hook-summer-review-20120824.

73. Roger Ebert, "*Red Hook Summer*," *Chicago Sun-Times*, August 22, 2012, http:// www.rogerebert.com/reviews/red-hook-summer-2012.

74. Ibid.

75. Claudia Puig, "Spike Lee's *Red Hook Summer* Never Takes Shape," *USA Today*, August 23, 2012, http://usatoday30.usatoday.com/life/movies/revie ws/story/2012–08–24/red-hook-summer-clarke-peters-jules-brown/572 59804/1.

76. Richard Brody, "Spike Lee's *Red Hook Summer*," *New Yorker*, August 9, 2012, http://www.newyorker.com/online/blogs/movies/2012/08/red-hook-summer-the-image-of-the-spirit.html.

77. Ibid.

78. Ibid.
79. Locating Sal's Famous Pizzeria in Red Hook may seem to contradict the appearance of Sal's pizza at the Manhattan bank that drives the plot of Lee's 2006 heist movie *Inside Man*. Sal's pizza boxes are visible for only a moment when the food demanded by chief bank robber Dalton Russell (Clive Owen) arrives. Since Lower Manhattan sits across the East River from Red Hook, *Inside Man* suggests that someone on the hostage negotiating team, perhaps lead detective Keith Frazier (Denzel Washington), is a fan of Sal's Famous Pizzeria. Another possibility is that Sal's has been successful enough to open another location in Lower Manhattan.
80. Chris Lee, "Spike Lee Talks," http://www.thedailybeast.com/articles/2012/01/26/spike-lee-talks-hollywood-racism-new-film-red-hook-summer.html.
81. Guerrasio, "Q&A: Spike Lee on the Child-Abuse Scene in *Red Hook Summer*," http://www.vanityfair.com/online/oscars/2012/08/spike-lee-on-red-hook-summer-michael-jackson-documentary-mike-tyson-broadway.
82. Andre Seewood, "The Decline of Spike Lee: A Prisoner of the Middle Class," *Shadow and Act: On Cinema of the African Diaspora*, January 2, 2013, http://blogs.indiewire.com/shadowandact/the-decline-of-spike-lee-a-prisoner-of-the-middle-class.
83. Ibid.
84. Ibid.

CHAPTER SIX: DOCUMENTARY EVIDENCE

1. Jasmine Nichole Cobb and John L. Jackson, "They Hate Me: Spike Lee, Documentary Filmmaking, and Hollywood's 'Savage Slot,'" in *Fight the Power!: The Spike Lee Reader*, ed. Janice D. Hamlet and Robin R. Means Coleman (New York: Peter Lang Publishing, Inc., 2009), 253.
2. Ibid., 255.
3. Ibid.
4. Ibid.
5. Ibid., 263.
6. Ibid.
7. Ibid., 260.
    Cobb and Jackson flesh out these possibilities with relevant examples from Lee's films. Regarding ultrarealism, they invoke *Jungle Fever* and *Malcolm X*, writing how Lee's viewers become adept at "almost feeling the closed-fisted blows of racist Italian fathers, experiencing the crack-induced highs of drug-addicted siblings, witnessing the tiniest details of a racial leader's brutal assassination" (260). Regarding cartoonish allegory, they invoke the stylized cinematographic and acting techniques seen in many Lee films: "oversaturated color-palettes, characters deploying grand demonstrative gestures/gesticulations, and a camera's implausible movements though time and space" (260).
8. Ibid.
9. Phyllis R. Klotman and Janet K. Cutler, *Struggles for Representation: African American Documentary Film and Video* (Bloomington: Indiana University Press, 1999), xvii.

10. *Pavarotti & Friends for the Children of Liberia* and *Passing Strange* were first broadcast as episodes of PBS's long-running *Great Performances* television series (the former on December 2, 1998, the latter on January 13, 2010). *Freak* premiered on the premium-cable network Home Box Office (HBO) on October 10, 1998; *A Huey P. Newton Story* premiered on the premium-cable network Starz on June 18, 2001; and *Bad 25* premiered on American Broadcasting Corporation (ABC) television on November 22, 2012.

11. Gabriella Beckles-Raymond, "We Can't Get Off the Bus: A Commentary on Spike Lee and Moral Motivation," in *The Philosophy of Spike Lee,* ed. Mark Conard (Lexington: The University Press of Kentucky, 2011), 40.

12. Ibid., 43.

13. *Get on the Bus,* written by Reggie Rock Bythewood, directed by Spike Lee, released by Columbia Pictures, 1996, 120 min. All future quotations, summaries, and paraphrases refer to Sony Pictures's DVD version of Lee's film.

14. Aftab, *That's My Story,* 275.

    Aftab further blurs the boundaries between Wexler's documentary and *Get on the Bus* by mistakenly listing the title of Wexler's film as *On the Bus.*

15. David Charpentier, "Truth is Fiction: Haskell Wexler, Part I," *Popmatters,* November 17, 2011, http://www.popmatters.com/pm/column/150751-truth-is-fiction-the-work-of-haskell-wexler-part-1/. The emphasis is Charpentier's.

16. Ibid.

17. S. Craig Watkins, "Reel Men: *Get on the Bus* and the Shifting Terrain of Black Masculinities," in *The Spike Lee Reader,* ed. Paula J. Massood (Philadelphia: Temple University Press, 2008), 147.

18. Ibid.

    Watkins fails to mention Hitchcock's 1948 film *Rope,* another movie that occurs in a single setting (namely, the New York City apartment of John Dall's character, Brandon Shaw).

19. Ibid., 149.

20. Roger Ebert, "*Get on the Bus,*" *Chicago-Sun Times,* October 18, 1996, http://www.rogerebert.com/reviews/get-on-the-bus-1996.

21. Barbara Shulgasser, "*Get on the Bus,*" *San Francisco Examiner,* October 16, 1996, http://www.sfgate.com/style/article/Get-on-the-Bus-3119246.php.

    Shulgasser, commenting that *Get on the Bus* is in some ways an old-fashioned movie, notes its generic and narrative debts to Preston Sturges's 1941 film *Sullivan's Travels,* Delbert Mann's 1958 movie *Separate Tables,* and Stanley Kramer's 1965 cinematic adaptation of Katherine Anne Porter's novel *Ship of Fools.* She does not mention Edmund Goulding's 1932 adaptation of Vicki Baum's novel *Grand Hotel,* but could (and perhaps should) have.

22. Janet Maslin, "Still Reeling from the Day Death Came to Birmingham," *New York Times,* July 9, 1997, http://www.nytimes.com/movie/review?res=9500E ED71439F93AA35754C0A961958260.

23. Christine Acham, "We Shall Overcome: Preserving History and Memory in *4 Little Girls,*" in *The Spike Lee Reader,* ed. Paula J. Massood (Philadelphia: Temple University Press, 2008), 162.

24. Ibid., 163.

25. Denene Millner, "A New Documentary Finally Puts a Face on the Racial Terrorism That Claimed the Lives of Four Little Girls," *New York Daily News*

Sunday Edition, July 13, 1997, http://www.nydailynews.com/new-documentary-finally-puts-face-racial-terrorism-claimed-lives-girls-article-1.774093.

26. Acham, "We Shall Overcome," 160.

27. Ibid.

28. Aftab, *That's My Story*, 282.

29. Spike Lee, DVD audio commentary, *4 Little Girls*, directed by Spike Lee, released by Home Box Office, 102 min., 1997. All future references pertain to this audio commentary.

30. Howell Raines, "The Birmingham Bombing," *New York Times Magazine*, July 24, 1983, http://www.nytimes.com/1983/07/24/magazine/the-birmingham-bombing.html?pagewanted=1.

31. Ibid.

32. Ibid.

33. Ibid.

34. Ibid.

35. Cobb and Jackson, "They Hate Me," 264.

36. Ibid.

37. Aftab, *That's My Story*, 283.

38. Ruthe Stein, "Lee Explores Lingering Grief from Killing of '4 Girls,'" *San Francisco Chronicle*, October 7, 1997, http://www.sfgate.com/entertainment/article/Lee-Explores-Lingering-Grief-From-Killing-of-4-2826129.php.

39. Acham, "We Shall Overcome," 167.

40. Spike Lee, interviewed in "*4 Little Girls*: How It All Began," *4 Little Girls*, directed by Spike Lee, released by Home Box Office, 14 min., 1997.

41. Stein, "Lee Explores Lingering Grief," http://www.sfgate.com/entertainment/article/Lee-Explores-Lingering-Grief-From-Killing-of-4-2826129.php.

42. Acham, "We Shall Overcome," 167.

43. Ibid., 166.

44. Ibid.

45. Christopher McNair, interview by Spike Lee, *4 Little Girls*, directed by Spike Lee, released by Home Box Office, 102 min., 1997.

46. Acham, "We Shall Overcome," 165.

47. Bill Nichols, *Introduction to Documentary*, 2nd ed. (Bloomington: Indiana University Press, 2010), 52.

48. Ibid., 134.

49. Ibid.

50. Sheila Nevins, interview by Reese Erlich, "Spike Lee on Race, Politics and Broken Levees," *All Things Considered*, National Public Radio, 7 min., August 13, 2006, http://www.npr.org/templates/story/story.php?storyId=5641453.

51. Ibid.

52. *When the Levees Broke: A Requiem in Four Acts*, directed by Spike Lee, released by Home Box Office, 255 min., 2006. All future quotations, summaries, and paraphrases refer to HBO's DVD version of Lee's film.

Mayfield's comments first came to light when the Associated Press, on March 1, 2006, released footage of the August 28, 2005, video conference. Numerous articles during the subsequent days and weeks reported Mayfield's warning. See CNN's March 2, 2006, article "Transcripts, Tape Show Bush, Brown Warned on Katrina" (http://www.cnn.com/2006/POLITICS/03/02/fema.tapes/) for additional information and NBC News's March 2, 2006, *Nightly News* segment "Early Warning" (http://www.youtube.com/watch?v=1mSsPR-CXCA), along with *When the Levees Broke* and many other online videos, for the footage itself.

53. Brinkley's *The Great Deluge* received criticism upon its 2006 publication for staking a partisan claim in New Orleans's 2006 mayoral election. Brinkley harshly criticizes Ray Nagin's record in office while praising Nagin's unsuccessful challenger, then-lieutenant governor of Louisiana Mitch Landrieu, in passages that both Nagin's campaign and various book reviewers identified as heavily depending upon Landrieu's self-serving claims.

Allen Barra's *Salon* review, "In Too Deep" (http://www.salon.com/2006/06/27/brinkley/), comments that Brinkley rushed the book to publication only nine months after Katrina's landfall "to stamp [himself] as the 'official' historian of Katrina and give him proprietary rights over other writers as the go-to guy for comment on future developments on the Gulf Coast," while University of Tennessee-Chattanooga historian Wilfred M. McClay writes in "A Flood of Words on Katrina" (http://www.nysun.com/arts/flood-of-words-on-katrina/32704/), his harsh *New York Sun* review, "One can be excused for wondering from the outset whether enough time has passed for anything of this epic scale to be written about these tragic and infuriating events—or whether Mr. Brinkley is the man for the job" because Brinkley's scholarly reputation is suspect: "I cannot think of a historian or public intellectual who has managed to make himself so prominent in American public life without having put forward a single memorable idea, a single original analysis, or a single lapidary phrase—let alone without publishing a book that has had any discernable [*sic*] impact."

Brinkley, who concludes *The Great Deluge*'s Author's Note by writing, "My hope is that this history, fast out of the gates, may serve as an opening effort in Katrina scholarship, with hundreds of other popular books and scholarly articles following suit" (xxv), defended the book's arguments and sources in several media interviews, including Peter Whoriskey's May 19, 2006, *Washington Post* article "New Orleans in a Tempest over *Deluge*" (http://www.washingtonpost.com/wp-dyn/content/article/2006/05/18/AR2006051802284.html).

Nagin won the 2006 mayoral election, but, facing term limits, could not run again in 2010. Landrieu was elected as New Orleans's mayor on February 6, 2010, and assumed office on May 3, 2010.

54. Chuleenan Svetvilas, "Bamboozled on the Bayou: Spike Lee Profiles Katrina Survivors," *Documentary.org*, August 2006, http://www.documentary.org/content/bamboozled-bayou-spike-lee-profiles-katrina-survivors.

Lee makes similar statements in other interviews about *When the Levees Broke and If God Is Willing and Da Creek Don't Rise*.

55. Aftab, *That's My Story*, 393.

56. Buck Wolf, "Spike Lee's Katrina *Requiem* Mixes Anger, Sorrow," *ABC News,* August 18, 2006, http://abcnews.go.com/Entertainment/story?id=2330610&page=1.

57. David Denby, "Disasters," *New Yorker,* September 4, 2006, 139.

A digital copy of Denby's review is available at http://www.newyorker.com/archive/2006/09/04/060904crci_cinema.

58. Ibid.

59. Cobb and Jackson, "They Hate Me," 265–66. The emphasis is Cobb and Jackson's.

60. Ibid., 265.

61. Denby, "Disasters," 139.

62. Thomas Doherty, "*When the Levees Broke: A Requiem in Four Acts*," *Journal of American History* 93, no. 3 (2006): 999.

63. Nevins, interview by Erlich, "Spike Lee on Race, Politics and Broken Levees," http://www.npr.org/templates/story/story.php?storyId=5641453.

64. Sam Pollard, "*When the Levees Broke*" online chat, *Washington Post,* August 22, 2006, http://www.washingtonpost.com/wp-dyn/content/discussion/2006/08/21/DI2006082101122.html.

65. Lee, in media appearances after Hurricane Katrina, said that, given America's history of racial exclusion and discrimination, a person may reasonably believe that New Orleans's levees were bombed despite never explicitly claiming that they were. Lee, for instance, gets into a heated discussion with Tucker Carlson during an October 21, 2005, panel discussion on HBO's *Real Time with Bill Maher,* after Maher comments that, although he does not believe that the federal government blew the levees, he understands that the nation's racial history makes this idea plausible. "Exactly," Lee replies. "It's not far-fetched. And also I would like to say it's not necessarily blow it up. But the residents of that ward, they believe it. There was a Hurricane Betsy in '65, they felt the same happened where a choice had to be made, one neighborhood got to save one neighborhood and flood another 'hood, flood another neighborhood."

The discussion among Lee, Maher, Carlson, and ABC/NPR correspondent Michel Martin covers many viewpoints about this issue, with Carlson saying that Lee feeds the residents' paranoia by accepting claims with no factual basis. A partial, although accurate transcript of this *Real Time* episode is available in Brent Baker's October 24, 2005 *NewsBusters* article "Spike Lee: 'Not Far-fetched' to Say New Orleans Levees Deliberately Destroyed" (http://newsbusters.org/node/2441), while partial video of the conversation is available in the YouTube video "When the Levees Break—Bombing of the Lower Ninth Ward 6/8" (http://www.you tube.com/watch?v=9DDaqWv9wdg).

66. Ana Radelat, "Spike Lee Showcases Heartbreak, Spirit of New Orleans," *USA Today,* August 14, 2006, http://usatoday30.usatoday.com/life/television/news/2006-08-14-spike-lee_x.htm.

67. Mark Healy, "Spike Lee Is Still Doing the Right Thing," *GQ,* September 2010, http://www.gq.com/news-politics/big-issues/201009/spike-lee-new-orleans-katrina-bp-oil-obama-da-creek-dont-rise.

68. Ibid.

69. Cobb and Jackson, "They Hate Me," 267.

CHAPTER SEVEN: CRIME AND PUNISHMENT

1. David Bradley, "Spike Lee's Inferno, the Drug Underworld," *New York Times,* September 10, 1995, http://partners.nytimes.com/library/film/091095lee-clockers-essay.html.

Lee first uses this term in Stephen Schaefer's "Spike Makes *Clockers* Timely," *New York Post,* August 25, 1995, 47.

2. Jonathan Bernstein, "Spike Lee," *Face* (December 1997): 202.

Paula J. Massood also cites this quotation on page 189 of *Black City Cinema: African American Urban Experiences in Film* (Philadelphia: Temple University Press, 2003).

3. Lee, discussing his intentions about *Clockers* with co-author Kaleem Aftab, confesses his naïveté in thinking that the movie could end the genre of urban black gangster films (239).

4. Aftab, *That's My Story,* 25.

5. Nelson George, "He's Gotta Have It," Foreword to *Spike Lee's Gotta Have It: Inside Guerilla Filmmaking,* by Spike Lee (New York: Fireside, 1987), 12.

6. Spike Lee, interview by Nelson George, "The Interview: Spike Lee with Nelson George, November 21, 1986," *Spike Lee's Gotta Have It: Inside Guerilla Filmmaking,* by Spike Lee (New York: Fireside, 1987), 34.

7. George, "He's Gotta Have It," 12. The emphasis is George's.

8. Ibid.

9. Ibid., 13.

10. Buck Wolf, "Spike Lee's Katrina *Requiem* Mixes Anger, Sorrow," *ABC News,* August 18, 2006, http://abcnews.go.com/Entertainment/story?id=2330610&page=1.

11. *Miracle's Boys* premiered on The N, one of Nickelodeon's networks, over three nights: February 18, 19, and 20, 2005. The N shared channel space with Nickelodeon's Noggin Network until 2007, when The N became its own channel. Nickelodeon changed The N's name to TeenNick in 2009.

12. *Inside Man,* written by Russell Gewirtz, directed by Spike Lee, released by Universal Pictures, 2006, 129 min. All future quotations, summaries, and paraphrases refer to Universal Pictures's Blu-ray version of Lee's film.

13. R. Barton Palmer, "Monsters and Moralism in *Summer of Sam,*" in *The Philosophy of Spike Lee,* ed. Mark Conard (Lexington: The University Press of Kentucky, 2011), 55.

14. Andrew Sarris, "*Summer of Sam* Bursts with Trying to Be Important," *New York Observer,* July 12, 1999, http://observer.com/1999/07/summer-of-sam-bursts-with-trying-to-be-important/.

Palmer, in "Monsters and Moralism in *Summer of Sam,*" accuses Sarris of whining by making this statement (70).

15. "Cast Hit Back at Smear of *Sam,*" *The Guardian,* July 3, 1999, http://www.theguardian.com/film/1999/jul/03/news.

16. Aftab, *That's My Story,* 319.

17. Palmer, "Monsters and Moralism," 58.

18. Spike Lee, interview by Delroy Lindo, "Delroy Lindo on Spike Lee," in *Spike Lee: Interviews,* ed. Cynthia Fuchs, Conversations with Filmmakers Series (Jackson: University Press of Mississippi, 2002), 176.

19. Spike Lee, interview by Stephen Pizzello, "Spike Lee's Seventies Flashback," in *Spike Lee: Interviews,* ed. Cynthia Fuchs, Conversations with Filmmakers Series (Jackson: University Press of Mississippi, 2002), 158.

Pizzello's article first appeared in *American Cinematographer* 80, no. 6 (June 1999): 50–52.

20. Lindo's and Pizzello's interviews chronicle *Summer of Sam*'s genesis, including Lee's initial plan to produce rather than direct the film. Chapter 14 of *That's My Story and I'm Sticking to It* offers an in-depth production history of *Summer of Sam*, including Lee's decision to helm the movie after his fruitless search for directors who could visualize Victor Colicchio and Michael Imperioli's ambitious script.

21. Dan Flory, "Race and Black American *Film Noir: Summer of Sam* as Lynching Parable," in *The Spike Lee Reader*, ed. Paula J. Massood (Philadelphia: Temple University Press, 2008), 203.

22. Ibid.

23. Lewis R. Gordon, *Bad Faith and Antiblack Racism* (Amherst, NY: Humanity Books, 1995), 114–15. The emphasis is Gordon's.

24. Flory, "*Summer of Sam* as Lynching Parable," 203 and 206. The first three terms appear on page 206, while the final two appear on page 203.

25. Ibid, 206. The emphasis is Flory's.

26. *Summer of Sam*, written by Michael Imperioli & Victor Colicchio and Spike Lee; directed by Spike Lee; released by Buena Vista Pictures, 1999, 142 min. All future quotations, summaries, and paraphrases refer to Touchstone Pictures's DVD version of Lee's film.

27. Flory, "*Summer of Sam* as Lynching Parable," 205.

28. Ibid.

29. One version of *Summer of Sam*'s screenplay, dated October 31, 1997, includes many news reports and newscasters, but no scenes with John Jeffries or black Brooklyn residents. Lee mentions in several interviews, as well as in *That's My Story and I'm Sticking to It,* that his major contribution to the shooting script involved integrating aspects of New York City life that the original draft ignored. In "Spike Lee's Seventies Flashback," Lee tells *American Cinematographer*'s Stephen Pizzello, "It was a great script as it was, but I felt that we needed to incorporate more of New York City instead of just setting the story in this one Italian neighborhood in the Bronx" (156).

30. Palmer, "Monsters and Moralism," 63.

31. Ibid.

32. Ibid.

33. James Allen, Hilton Als, John Lewis, and Leon F. Litwack, *Without Sanctuary: Lynching Photography in America* (Santa Fe: Twin Palms Publishers, 2000). Lewis's official title, "Congressman John Lewis," appears on the book's title page.

34. Aftab, *That's My Story*, 319.

35. Ibid.

36. Palmer, "Monsters and Moralism," 63–64.

37. Ibid., 64.

38. Ibid. The emphasis is mine.

39. Ibid.

40. Ibid.

41. Ibid.

42. Spike Lee, interview by Prairie Miller, "*Summer of Sam:* An Interview with Spike Lee," in *Spike Lee: Interviews,* ed. Cynthia Fuchs, Conversations with Filmmakers Series (Jackson: University Press of Mississippi, 2002), 179.

    Miller's interview first appeared in the 1999 edition of *All Movie Guide*.

43. Ibid., 180.

44. Box Office Mojo (http://www.boxofficemojo.com/movies/?id=insideman.htm) lists *Inside Man*'s final gross as $184,376,254, split between domestic ticket sales of $88,513,495 and foreign sales of $95,862,759. The Internet Movie Database (IMDb) (http://www.imdb.com/title/tt0454848/business?ref_=tt_ql_dt_4) lists the film's domestic gross as $88,504,640. Despite these minor differences, *Inside Man* remains the most profitable film ever directed by Lee.

45. Vince Leo, "*Inside Man* (2006)," *Qwipster,* n.d., http://qwipster.net/inside man.htm.

46. David A. Gerstner, "De Profundis: A Love Letter from the Inside Man," in *The Spike Lee Reader,* ed. Paula J. Massood (Philadelphia: Temple University Press, 2008), 244.

47. Ibid., 245.

48. Ibid., 243.

49. Ibid., 244.

50. Aftab, *That's My Story,* 387.

51. "The Man Inside . . .," *Total Film,* March 24, 2006, http://www.totalfilm.com/features/the-man-inside.

52. Box Office Mojo (http://www.boxofficemojo.com/movies/?id=malcolmx.htm) lists *Malcolm X*'s final gross as $48,169,910, while IMDb (http://www.imdb.com/title/tt0104797/business?ref_=tt_ql_dt_4) lists the amount as $48,140,491.

53. Leo, "*Inside Man* (2006)," http://qwipster.net/insideman.htm.

54. Gerstner, "De Profundis," 245. The emphasis is Gerstner's.

55. Ibid.

56. R. Colin Tait, "Class and Allegory in Spike Lee's *Inside Man*," in *Fight the Power!: The Spike Lee Reader,* ed. Janice D. Hamlet and Robin R. Means Coleman (New York: Peter Lang Publishing, Inc., 2009), 43.

57. Ibid., 54.

58. Ibid., 53.

59. Ibid.

60. Ibid., 54.

61. Spike Lee, DVD audio commentary, *Inside Man,* directed by Spike Lee, written by Russell Gewirtz, released by Universal Pictures, 129 min, 2006.

62. Tait, "Class and Allegory in Spike Lee's *Inside Man*," 55.

63. Ibid., 57.

64. Roger Ebert, "*Inside Man*," *Chicago Sun-Times,* March 23, 2006, http://www.rogerebert.com/reviews/inside-man-2006.

65. Tait, "Class and Allegory in Spike Lee's *Inside Man*," 56.

CHAPTER EIGHT: FACING BACK, FACING BLACK

1. Armond White, "Post-Art Minstrelsy," *Cineaste* 26, no. 2 (2001): 13.

2. *Bamboozled,* written by Spike Lee, directed by Spike Lee, released by New Line Cinema, 2000, 135 min. All future quotations, summaries, and paraphrases refer to New Line Cinema's DVD version of Lee's film.

3. Gary Crowdus and Dan Georgakas, "Thinking about the Power of Images: An Interview with Spike Lee," *Cineaste* 26, no. 2 (2001): 7.

This interview is also available in *Spike Lee: Interviews,* ed. Cynthia Fuchs, Conversations with Filmmakers Series (Jackson: University Press of Mississippi, 2002), 202–17.

4. Ibid.

Schwarzbaum's July 9, 1999, review of *Summer of Sam* is available at http://www.ew.com/ew/article/0,272327,00.html while Hunter's October 20, 2000, review of *Bamboozled* is available at http://www.washingtonpost.com/wp-srv/entertainment/movies/reviews/bamboozledhunter.htm.

5. Crowdus and Georgakas, "Thinking about the Power of Images," 7.

6. Ibid.

7. Ibid.

8. Stephen Hunter, "*Bamboozled:* Soul-Defying Success," *Washington Post,* October 20, 2000, http://www.washingtonpost.com/wp-srv/entertainment/movies/reviews/bamboozledhunter.htm.

9. Ibid.

10. Cynthia Lucia, "Race, Media and Money: A Critical Symposium on Spike Lee's *Bamboozled,*" *Cineaste* 26, no. 2 (2001): 10.

11. Saul Landau, "Spike Lee's Revolutionary Broadside," *Cineaste* 26, no. 2 (2001): 12.

12. White, "Post-Art Minstrelsy," 12.

13. W.J.T. Mitchell, "Living Color: Race, Stereotype, and Animation in Spike Lee's *Bamboozled,*" in *What Do Pictures Want?: The Lives and Loves of Images* (Chicago: University of Chicago Press, 2005), 306.

14. White, "Post-Art Minstrelsy," 13.

15. Ibid.

16. Ibid.

17. Ibid.

18. Ibid., 14.

19. Phil Chidester and Jamel Santa Cruze Bell, "'Say the Right Thing': Spike Lee, *Bamboozled,* and the Future of Satire in a Postmodern World," in *Fight the Power!: The Spike Lee Reader,* ed. Janice D. Hamlet and Robin R. Means Coleman (New York: Peter Lang Publishing, Inc., 2009), 207.

20. Ibid., 204.

Chidester and Bell refer to Jeffrey M. Anderson's *Combustible Celluloid* review of *Bamboozled* (http://www.combustiblecelluloid.com/bambooz.shtml) and Ray Black's scholarly essay "Satire's Cruelest Cut: Exorcising Blackness in Spike Lee's *Bamboozled*" when making these comments. See *The Black Scholar,* 33 no. 1 (2003): 19–24 for Black's article.

21. Ibid., 207.

Chidester and Bell refer to Roger Ebert's *Chicago Sun-Times* review of *Bamboozled* (http://www.rogerebert.com/reviews/bamboozled-2000) and *Haro Movie Reviews*' online assessment of Lee's film (http://www.haro-online.com/movies/bamboozled.html).

22. Ibid., 204.

23. Ibid., 206.

24. Ibid., 207.

25. Ibid.

   The Internet Movie Database (IMDb) estimates *Bamboozled*'s budget as $10 million (http://www.imdb.com/title/tt0215545/business?ref_=tt_ql_dt_4). Lee, in an interview with *The Harvard Crimson*, says that the film "cost just under $10 million." See Rebecca Cantu, "About Face: An Interview with Spike Lee," *The Harvard Crimson*, October 20, 2000, http://www.thecrimson.com/article/2000/10/20/about-face-an-interview-with-spike/.

26. Chidester and Bell, "'Say the Right Thing,'" 208.

27. James Berardinelli, "*Bamboozled*," *Reelviews*, October 2000, http://www.reelviews.net/movies/b/bamboozled.html.

28. Ibid.

29. Ibid.

30. Ibid.

31. Ibid.

32. Ibid.

33. Roger Ebert, "*Bamboozled*," *Chicago Sun-Times*, October 6, 2000, http://www.rogerebert.com/reviews/bamboozled-2000.

34. Ibid.

35. Ibid.

36. Lee has used these terms in many venues, but most famously during a May 2009 interview with host Ed Gordon on *Our World with Black Enterprise*, in which Lee discusses black film and television, including Tyler Perry's work. Lee's comments, by situating *Bamboozled* as a relevant reference point for the recent history of black cinema and television, are worth quoting at length:

   > Each artist should be allowed to pursue their artistic endeavor, but I still think there—a lot of stuff that's on today is coonery and buffoonery. And I know it's making a lot of money and breaking records, but we could do better. That's just my opinion. I mean, I am a huge basketball fan, and when I watch the games on TNT, I see these two ads for these two shows [Tyler Perry's *Meet the Browns* and *House of Payne*], and I am scratching my head. You know, we got a black president, you know. Are we going back to Mantan Moreland and Sleep'n Eat?
   >
   > I mean, we've had this discussion back and forth because when John Singleton, you know, people came out to see *Boyz N the Hood*. When he did *Rosewood*, nobody showed up. So a lot of this is on us. A lot of this is on us, you know. You vote with your pocketbook, your wallet. You vote with your time sitting in front of the idiot box, and the man [Perry] has a huge audience. Tyler's very smart. . . . But at the same time, for me, the imagery is, is, is troubling.

   The YouTube video "Spike Lee on Tyler Perry's Movies Shows! Its Coonery Buffoonery" (http://www.youtube.com/watch?v=Ciwhh3fB6vE) includes these comments.

37. Ebert, "*Bamboozled*," http://www.rogerebert.com/reviews/bamboozled-2000.

38. Christiane Bohnert, "Early Modern Complex Satire and the Satiric Novel: Genre and Cultural Transposition," in *Theorizing Satire: Essays in Literary Criticism*,

ed. Brian A. Connery and Kirk Combe (New York: St. Martin's Press, 1995), 151–72.

39. Brian A. Connery and Kirk Combe, "Theorizing Satire: A Retrospective and Introduction," in *Theorizing Satire: Essays in Literary Criticism,* ed. Brian A. Connery and Kirk Combe (New York: St. Martin's Press, 1995), 1.

40. Ibid.

41. Box Office Mojo (http://www.boxofficemojo.com/movies/?id=bamboozled.htm) lists *Bamboozled*'s final worldwide gross as $2,463,650, while the Internet Movie Database (http://www.imdb.com/title/tt0215545/business?ref_=tt_ql_dt_4) lists the final figure as $2,185,266.

42. Stanley Crouch, interviewed in "The Making of *Bamboozled,*" directed by Sam Pollard, released by New Line Home Video, 2001, 53 min.

43. White, "Post-Art Minstrelsy," 13.

44. Gary Crowdus, "Editorial," *Cineaste* 26, no. 2 (2001): 1.

45. Connery and Combe, "Theorizing Satire," 6.

46. Ibid., 5.

47. Jada Pinkett-Smith, interviewed in "The Making of *Bamboozled,*" directed by Sam Pollard, released by New Line Home Video, 2001, 53 min.

48. Crowdus and Georgakas, "Thinking about the Power of Images," 4.

49. Dan Flory, "*Bamboozled:* Philosophy through Blackface," in *The Philosophy of Spike Lee,* ed. Mark Conard (Lexington: The University Press of Kentucky, 2011), 165. The emphasis is Flory's.

50. Gregory Laski, "Falling Back into History: The Uncanny Trauma of Blackface Minstrelsy in Spike Lee's *Bamboozled,*" *Callaloo* 33, no. 4 (2010): 1097.

51. Eric Lott, *Love and Theft: Blackface Minstrelsy and the American Working Class* (1993; New York: Oxford University Press, 1995), 3.

52. Laski, "Falling Back into History," 1097.

53. Ray Black, "Satire's Cruelest Cut: Exorcising Blackness in Spike Lee's *Bamboozled,*" *The Black Scholar* 33, no. 1 (2003): 20.

54. Margo Jefferson, panel participant, "Minding the Messenger: A Symposium on *Bamboozled*" (with Stanley Crouch, Eric Lott, Clyde Taylor, and Michele Wallace), *Black Renaissance/Renaissance Noire* 3 (2001): 12.

55. Rachael Ziady Delue, "Envisioning Race in Spike Lee's *Bamboozled,*" in *Fight the Power!: The Spike Lee Reader,* ed. Janice D. Hamlet and Robin R. Means Coleman (New York: Peter Lang Publishing, Inc., 2009), 75.

56. Ibid.

57. See comments by Lee and Wayans in Sam Pollard's "The Making of *Bamboozled*" (available on *Bamboozled*'s DVD release), as well as Lee's response to Michael Sragow's question "Was there a real-life model for Delacroix" during their October 26, 2000, *Salon* interview "Black Like Spike" (http://www.salon.com/2000/10/26/spike_lee_2/).

    Sragow's interview is also available in *Spike Lee: Interviews,* ed. Cynthia Fuchs, Conversations with Filmmakers Series (Jackson: University Press of Mississippi, 2002), 189–98.

58. Michael Sragow, "Black Like Spike," in *Spike Lee: Interviews,* ed. Cynthia Fuchs, Conversations with Filmmakers Series (Jackson: University Press of Mississippi, 2002), 193.

59. Lee credits *A Face in the Crowd, The Producers,* and *Network* as influences in many venues, both print and electronic. See his interviews with *Salon*'s Michael Sragow and *Cineaste*'s Gary Crowder and Dean Georgakas (both reprinted in Cynthia Fuch's *Spike Lee: Interviews*), as well as Sam Pollard's documentary "The Making of *Bamboozled*," for additional information.

60. Black, "Satire's Cruelest Cut," 22.

61. Ibid.

62. Sragow, "Black Like Spike," 191.

63. Flory, "*Bamboozled:* Philosophy through Blackface," 174.

64. Landau, "Spike Lee's Revolutionary Broadside," 12.

65. White, "Post-Art Minstrelsy," 13.

66. Sragow, "Black Like Spike," 192.
    Lee also uses this expression on page 8 of Crowdus and Georgakas's "Thinking about the Power of Images."

67. Ibid.

68. Ibid., 193.

69. Crowdus and Georgakas, "Thinking about the Power of Images," 7.

70. Spike Lee, DVD audio commentary, *Bamboozled,* directed by Spike Lee, written by Spike Lee, released by New Line Cinema, 2000, 135 min.

71. Delue, "Envisioning Race in Spike Lee's *Bamboozled*," 83. The emphasis is Delue's.

72. Ibid., 84.

73. Crowdus and Georgakas, "Thinking about the Power of Images," 9.

74. Ibid., 6.

75. Ibid., 5–6.

76. Ibid., 6.

77. Ibid., 5. The emphasis is Crowdus and Georgakas's.

CHAPTER NINE: ALL NIGHT LONG

1. "Alan Cumming, Spike Lee Honored at 'Made in NY' Awards," *CBS New York,* June 10, 2013, http://newyork.cbslocal.com/2013/06/10/alan-cumming-spike-lee-honored-at-made-in-ny-awards/#photo-1.

2. Paula J. Massood, "We've Gotta Have It—Spike Lee, African American Film, and Cinema Studies," in *The Spike Lee Reader,* ed. Paula J. Massood (Philadelphia: Temple University Press, 2008), xx.

3. Although some sources disagree as to whether *25th Hour* cost $5 million or $15 million, with Box Office Mojo (http://www.boxofficemojo.com/movies/?id=25thhour.htm) listing the smaller figure and the Internet Movie Database (http://www.imdb.com/title/tt0307901/business?ref_=tt_ql_dt_4) listing the larger, Lee's autobiography, *That's My Story and I'm Sticking to It,* and his February 3, 2003, interview with *SeeingBlack*'s Esther Iverem (http://www.seeingblack.com/2003/x020403/spike_lee.shtml) definitively peg the budget as $15 million.

4. Spike Lee, DVD audio commentary, *25th Hour,* directed by Spike Lee, written by David Benioff from his novel *The 25th Hour,* released by Touchstone Pictures, 2002, 135 min.

The website Celebnetworth lists Norton's *25th Hour* salary as $500,000, a steep cut from his previous two films, *Death to Smoochy* (2002) and *Red Dragon* (2002), for which Norton was paid $8 million each (for a total of $16 million).

5. Aftab, *That's My Story*, 360.
6. Box Office Mojo (http://www.boxofficemojo.com/movies/?id=25thhour.htm) lists *25th Hour*'s domestic ticket sales as $13,084,595 and foreign ticket sales as $10,843,908, for a total worldwide gross of $23,928,503.
7. Mark Kermode, "A Talent to Offend," *New Statesman*, April 21, 2003, https://www.newstatesman.com/node/145271.
8. Aftab, *That's My Story*, 355.
9. Spike Lee, interview in "Finest *Hour:* The Spike Lee Interview," *Cinema Gotham*, January 16, 2003, http://www.dvdtalk.com/cinemagotham/archives/001006.html.
10. Spike Lee, interview by Wilson Morales, "*25th Hour:* An Interview with Spike Lee," *Blackfilm*, December 2002, http://www.blackfilm.com/20021220/features/spikelee.shtml.
11. Spike Lee, interview by Leslie Felperin, "Interview: Spike Lee," *Sight and Sound* 13, no. 4 (April 2003): 15.
12. Spike Lee, interview by Paula J. Massood, "The Quintessential New Yorker and Global Citizen: An Interview with Spike Lee," *Cineaste* 28, no. 3 (summer 2003): 5.
13. Lee, interview in "Finest *Hour,*" January 16, 2003, http://www.dvdtalk.com/cinemagotham/archives/001006.html.
14. Ivan Cañadas, "Spike Lee's 'Uniquely American [Di]vision': Race and Class in *25th Hour,*" *Bright Lights Film Journal*, 63 (February 2009), http://brightlightsfilm.com/63/63spikelee.php#5begin.
15. David Benioff, DVD audio commentary, *25th Hour,* directed by Spike Lee, written by David Benioff from his novel *The 25th Hour,* released by Touchstone Pictures, 2002, 135 min.
    Benioff's audio commentary is a different track, recorded separately from Lee's, on Touchstone's DVD release.
16. Lee, interview by, Morales, "*25th Hour:* An Interview with Spike Lee," http://www.blackfilm.com/20021220/features/spikelee.shtml.
17. This script, with many typos and copyediting errors, is available in two formats: the *Internet Movie Script Database* (*IMSDb*) has an .html version at http://www.imsdb.com/scripts/25th-Hour.html, while *DailyScript* offers a .pdf version at www.dailyscript.com/scripts/25thhour_all.pdf.
18. Aftab, *That's My Story*, 350.
19. Ibid.
20. David Benioff, *The 25th Hour* (2000; New York: Plume, 2002), 111. The emphasis is Benioff's.
21. Ibid., 111–12.
22. Ibid., 112–13.
23. *25th Hour,* directed by Spike Lee, written by David Benioff from his novel *The 25th Hour,* released by Touchstone Pictures, 2002, 135 min. All future quotations, summaries, and paraphrases refer to Touchstone Pictures's DVD version of Lee's film.

24. Aftab, *That's My Story,* 350–51.
25. David Benioff, interview by Paula J. Massood, "Doyle's Law: An Interview with David Benioff," *Cineaste* 28, no. 3 (summer 2003): 9.
26. Ibid.
27. Edward Norton, interview by Demetrios Matheou, "Interview: Edward Norton," *Sight and Sound* 13, no. 4 (April 2003): 12.
28. Cañadas, "Spike Lee's 'Uniquely American [Di]vision,'" http://brightlights film.com/63/63spikelee.php#5begin. The emphasis is Cañadas's.
29. Patricia O'Neill, "Where Globalization and Localization Meet: Spike Lee's *The 25th Hour,*" *CineAction* 64 (August 2004): 23.
    Despite O'Neill's provocative argument, her essay consistently ascribes the novel's title (*The 25th Hour*) to Lee's film, which removes the definite article (*25th Hour*).
30. Joyce Carol Oates, "*Negative,*" in *Dr. Magic: Six One Act Plays* (New York: Samuel French Inc., 2004): 58.
    Negative, according to its headnote in *Dr. Magic,* was first performed at the Philadelphia Festival Theatre for New Plays in Philadelphia, Pennsylvania in 1995.
31. Cañadas, "Spike Lee's 'Uniquely American [Di]vision,'" http://brightlights film.com/63/63spikelee.php#5begin.
32. Benioff, *The 25th Hour,* 41.
33. Ibid., 42.
34. Cañadas, "Spike Lee's 'Uniquely American [Di]vision,'" http://brightlights film.com/63/63spikelee.php#5begin.
35. Ibid.
36. Ibid.
37. Ibid.
38. Ibid.
39. Ibid. The emphasis is Cañadas's.
40. Aftab, *That's My Story,* 349.
41. Benioff, *The 25th Hour,* 64.
42. Aftab, *That's My Story,* 349.
43. O'Neill, "Where Globalization and Localization Meet," 3.
44. Ibid.
45. Ibid.
46. Ibid.
47. Mark T. Conard, "Aristotle and MacIntyre on Justice in *25th Hour,*" in *The Philosophy of Spike Lee,* ed. Mark Conard (Lexington: The University Press of Kentucky, 2011), 26.
48. Ibid., 37n1.
49. Derik Smith, "True Terror: The Haunting of Spike Lee's *25th Hour,*" *African American Review* 45, no. 1–2 (2012): 2.
50. Ibid.
51. Benioff, *The 25th Hour,* 208.
52. Lee, interview by Massood, "Quintessential New Yorker," 6.
53. Aftab, *That's My Story,* 359.

CHAPTER TEN: A GOOD MAN GOES TO WAR

1. James McBride, *Miracle at St. Anna,* Movie tie-in ed. (2002; New York: Riverhead Books, 2008), 37.

2. *Miracle at St. Anna*, directed by Spike Lee, screenplay by James McBride from his novel *Miracle at St. Anna*, released by Touchstone Pictures, 2008, 160 min. All future quotations, summaries, and paraphrases refer to Touchstone Pictures's Blu-ray version of Lee's film.

3. Brokaw's book *The Greatest Generation* (New York: Random House, 2004), first published in 1998 (the same year that *Saving Private Ryan* was released in theatres), has become the standard text in discussions about the heroism of the American men and women raised during the Great Depression who participated in the war effort (often because they were drafted, not because they volunteered). Ambrose's book *The Good Fight: How World War II Was Won* (New York: Atheneum Books for Young Readers, 2001), written for child and adolescent readers, unabashedly celebrates the American military effort during World War II, while Terkel's *"The Good War": An Oral History of World War II* (New York: The New Press, 1984), as the quotation marks around its title indicate, complicates the mythmaking that Brokaw and Ambrose indulge by including firsthand accounts of American soldiers who question several aspects of their service.

4. Box Office Mojo (http://www.boxofficemojo.com/movies/?id=savingprivate ryan.htm) lists *Saving Private Ryan*'s final worldwide gross as $481,840,909 ($216,540,909 in domestic and $265,300,000 in foreign ticket sales) against its $70-million budget, while the Internet Movie Database (IMDb) (http:// www.imdb.com/title/tt0120815/business?ref_=tt_ql_dt_4) also lists the film's domestic gross as $216,540,909. Based on these figures, *Saving Private Ryan* was the most commercially successful American film of 1998.

5. IMDb's awards page for *Saving Private Ryan* (http://www.imdb.com/title/ tt0120815/awards?ref_=tt_ql_4) includes a comprehensive list of the film's award nominations and outcomes.

6. Box Office Mojo (http://www.boxofficemojo.com/movies/?id=miracleatstanna. htm) lists *Miracle at St. Anna*'s final worldwide gross as $9,323,833 ($7,919,117 in domestic and $1,404,716 in foreign ticket sales) against its $45-million budget, while IMDb (http://www.imdb.com/title/tt1046997/business?ref_=tt_ ql_dt_4) lists the film's domestic gross as $7,916,887. Based on these figures, *Miracle at St. Anna* was among the worst-performing American films of 2008.

7. IMDb's awards page for *Miracle at St. Anna* (http://www.imdb.com/title/ tt1046997/awards?ref_=tt_ql_4) includes a comprehensive list of the film's award nominations and outcomes.

8. David Sterritt, *Spike Lee's America*, America through the Lens Series (Cambridge, England: Polity Press, 2013), 187.

9. Roger Ebert, *"Miracle at St. Anna,"* *Chicago Sun-Times*, September 25, 2008, http://www.rogerebert.com/reviews/miracle-at-st-anna-2008.

10. Wesley Morris, "War without Much Fight," *Boston Globe*, September 26, 2008, http://www.boston.com/ae/movies/articles/2008/09/26/war_without_ much_fight/?page=full.

11. Mick LaSalle, "Movie Review: *Miracle at St. Anna*," *San Francisco Chronicle*, September 26, 2008, http://www.sfgate.com/movies/article/Movie-Review-Miracle-at-St-Anna-3192960.php.

12. Ibid.

13. Spike Lee, interview by Kam Williams, "Miracle of St. Spike: Spike Lee—The *Miracle at St. Anna* Interview," *FLOWInsider*, September 2008, http://www .flowinsiders.com/our2cents/style18.asp.

14. James McBride, interviewed in "A Conversation with James McBride, Author of *Miracle at St. Anna,*" *BookBrowse.com,* n.d., http://www.bookbrowse.com/ author_interviews/full/index.cfm/author_number/271/james-mcbride.
15. Ibid.
16. Ibid.
17. McBride, *Miracle at St. Anna,* 301.
18. Ibid., 302–303.
19. James McBride, "The Making of a King: A Foreword," in *Miracle at St. Anna: The Motion Picture—A Spike Lee Joint* (New York: Rizzoli International Publications, 2008), 5.
20. Ibid., 5–6.
21. A. O. Scott, "Hollywood War, Revised Edition," *New York Times,* September 25, 2008, http://movies.nytimes.com/2008/09/26/movies/26mira.html?_r=0.
22. Ibid.
23. Ibid.
24. Ibid.
25. Ibid.
26. Joe Morgenstern, "In *St. Anna,* Lee Fumbles Epic of War, Racism," *Wall Street Journal,* September 26, 2008, http://online.wsj.com/article/SB122238 344981876805.html.
27. See IMDb's *Miracle at St. Anna* "Reviews and Ratings" section (http://www .imdb.com/title/tt1046997/reviews?ref_=tt_ql_op_3) for further information.
28. Morgenstern, "Lee Fumbles Epic of War," http://online.wsj.com/article/ SB122238344981876805.html.
29. LaSalle, *Miracle at St. Anna,* http://www.sfgate.com/movies/article/Movie-Review-Miracle-at-St-Anna-3192960.php.
30. Ann Hornaday, *Miracle at St. Anna, Washington Post,* September 26, 2008, http://www.washingtonpost.com/gog/movies/miracle-at-st.-anna,1146328/ critic-review.html#reviewNum1.
31. Spike Lee, "Deeds Not Words: An Introduction," in *Miracle at St. Anna: The Motion Picture—A Spike Lee Joint* (New York: Rizzoli International Publications, 2008), 13.
32. Ibid.
33. Mark Shiel, *Italian Neorealism: Rebuilding the Cinematic City,* Short Cuts Series (New York: Wallflower, 2006), 5.
34. Millicent Marcus, *Italian Film in the Light of Neorealism* (Princeton: Princeton University Press, 1986), xiv.
35. Ibid.
36. Lee, *Miracle at St. Anna: The Motion Picture—A Spike Lee Joint,* 55.
37. McBride, *Miracle at St. Anna,* 14.
38. Shiel, *Italian Neorealism,* 1–2.
39. Ibid., 2. The emphasis is Shiel's.
40. Marcus, *Italian Film in the Light of Neorealism,* 5.
41. Ibid., 6.
42. Paul Lewis, "Spike Lee Gets in Clint Eastwood's Line of Fire," *Guardian,* June 5, 2008, http://www.theguardian.com/film/2008/jun/06/usa.race.
43. Jeff Dawson, "Dirty Harry Comes Clean," *Guardian,* June 5, 2008, http:// www.theguardian.com/film/2008/jun/06/1.

44. Ibid.
45. Williams, "Miracle of St. Spike: Spike Lee—The *Miracle at St. Anna* Interview," http://www.flowinsiders.com/our2cents/style18.asp.
46. Alex Altman, "Were African Americans at Iwo Jima?," *Time*, June 9, 2008, http://content.time.com/time/nation/article/0,8599,1812972,00.html.
47. Ibid.
48. Ibid.
49. Ibid.
50. Ibid.
51. Dawson, "Dirty Harry Comes Clean," http://www.theguardian.com/film/2008/jun/06/1.
52. Sheila Marikar, "Spike Strikes Back: Clint's 'An Angry Old Man,'" *ABCNews.com*, June 6, 2008, http://abcnews.go.com/Entertainment/story?id=5015524&page=1.
53. Ibid.
54. Ibid.
55. Ibid.
56. Ibid.
57. Sterritt, *Spike Lee's America*, 186.
58. Nick Pisa, "Spike Lee's *Miracle at St. Anna* Denounced by Italian War Veterans as 'Insulting,'" *Telegraph*, September 30, 2008, http://www.telegraph.co.uk/news/worldnews/europe/italy/3112154/Spike-Lees-Miracle-at-St-Anna-denounced-by-Italian-war-veterans-as-insulting.html.
59. Ibid.
60. Ibid.
61. Ibid.

CONCLUSION: SPIKE'S PLACE

1. "About the Prize," The 20th Annual Dorothy and Lillian Gish Prize, http://www.gishprize.com/about.htm.
2. "Director, Producer, Writer, Actor, and Master Teacher Spike Lee to Receive the 20th Annual Dorothy and Lillian Gish Prize," The 20th Annual Dorothy and Lillian Gish Prize, September 18, 2013, http://www.gishprize.com/press.htm.
3. Aftab, *That's My Story*, 23.
4. John Colapinto, "Outside Man: Spike Lee's Unending Struggle," *New Yorker*, September 22, 2008, 57.
    Readers who consult the print version of Colapinto's original profile, published in the *New Yorker*'s September 22, 2008, issue, or its reproduction at the *New Yorker*'s online archive (http://archives.newyorker.com/?i=2008–09–22#folio=052) will see the subtitle "Spike Lee's Unending Struggle." Readers who consult the *New Yorker*'s general website (http://www.newyorker.com/reporting/2008/09/22/080922fa_fact_colapinto?currentPage=all) will see a different subtitle: "Spike Lee's Celluloid Struggles."
5. Aftab, *That's My Story*, 23. The emphasis is Aftab's.
    Lee's appearance on Williams's *ARTST TLK* is available in two segments: Part 1, "Spike Lee and Pharrell Williams on Anthems and Artists" (http://www

.youtube.com/watch?v=p8RCqI9zSgU), first posted on October 8, 2013, and Part 2, "Spike Lee and Pharrell Williams on Hard Work and Opportunity" (http://www.youtube.com/watch?annotation_id=annotation_3642158243 &feature=iv&list=SPU4DWjN4gSDE-03Fm9NO-nRBQYCUgPYO6&src_vid=p8RCqI9zSgU&v=_aHpxr4Cw6o), first posted on October 10, 2013.

6. Ibid.

7. Colapinto, "Outside Man," 57.

8. Ibid.

9. Ibid.

10. *The Night of the Hunter*, directed by Charles Laughton, screenplay by James Agee from the novel *The Night of the Hunter* by Davis Grubb, released by United Artists, 1955, 93 min.

11. Trey Taylor, "Did Spike Lee Rip Off Juan Luis Garcia?," *Dazed Digital*, November 30, 2013, http://www.dazeddigital.com/artsandculture/article/18027/1/did-spike-lee-rip-off-juan-luis-garcia.

    Garcia's website no longer displays his open letter (http://juanluisgarcia .com/dear-spike-lee/). *Reddit*'s *r/MOVIES* page includes a November 28, 2013, post titled "Buddy's Friend Is Sending This Open Letter to Director Spike Lee, Hopefully with Enough Awareness This Can Reach Him for a Response" with a transcript of Garcia's full letter at http://www.reddit.com/r/movies/comments/1rjp44/buddys_friend_is_sending_this_open_letter_to/.

    Richard Feloni's November 27, 2013, *Business Insider* article "Spike Lee Accused of Stealing *Oldboy* Movie Poster from an Unpaid Designer" (http://www.busines sinsider.com/juan-luis-garcias-email-to-spike-lee-2013-11) features a detailed discussion of this issue.

12. Spike Lee, Twitter, November 28, 2013, https://twitter.com/SpikeLee/status/406084275969085440.

13. Taylor, "Did Spike Lee Rip Off Juan Luis Garcia?," http://www.dazeddigital .com/artsandculture/article/18027/1/did-spike-lee-rip-off-juan-luis-garcia.

14. "Lee to Receive Dorothy and Lillian Gish Prize," September 18, 2013, http://www.gishprize.com/press.htm.

15. Gary Younge, "Spike Lee on *Oldboy*, America's Violent History and the Fine Art of Mouthing Off," *Guardian*, December 1, 2013, http://www.theguardian .com/film/2013/dec/01/spike-lee-oldboy-interview-director.

16. Ibid.

Bibliography

Abrams, Jerold J. "Transcendence and Sublimity in Spike Lee's Signature Shot." In Conard, *Philosophy of Spike Lee*, 187–99.

Acham, Christine. "We Shall Overcome: Preserving History and Memory in *4 Little Girls.*" In Massood, *Spike Lee Reader*, 159–74.

Aiello, Danny. Interview by St. Clair Bourne. *Making "Do the Right Thing."* Directed by St. Clair Bourne. 40 Acres & A Mule Filmworks and Chamba Organization, 1989. 58 min.

"Alan Cumming, Spike Lee Honored at 'Made in NY' Awards." *CBS New York,* June 10, 2013, http://newyork.cbslocal.com/2013/06/10/alan-cumming-spike-lee-ho nored-at-made-in-ny-awards/#photo-1.

Allen, James, Hilton Als, John Lewis, and Leon F. Litwack. *Without Sanctuary: Lynching Photography in America.* Santa Fe: Twin Palms Publishers, 2000.

Als, Hilton. "Philosopher or Dog?" In *Malcolm X: In Our Own Image,* edited by Joe Wood, 86–100. New York: Palgrave Macmillan, 1992.

Altman, Alex. "Were African-Americans at Iwo Jima?" *Time,* June 9, 2008, http://content.time.com/time/nation/article/0,8599,1812972,00.html.

Ambrose, Stephen E. *The Good Fight: How World War II Was Won.* New York: Atheneum Books for Young Readers, 2001.

Anderson, Jeffrey M. "Off-Color Television." *Combustible Celluloid,* n.d., http://www.combustiblecelluloid.com/bambooz.shtml.

Baker, Brent. "Spike Lee: 'Not Far-fetched' to Say New Orleans Levees Deliberately Destroyed." *NewsBusters,* October 24, 2005, http://newsbusters.org/node/2441.

Baldwin, James. *The Devil Finds Work.* 1976. New York: Vintage, 2011.

Baldwin, James. *No Name in the Street.* 1972. New York: Vintage, 2007.

Baldwin, James. *One Day, When I Was Lost: A Scenario Based on Alex Haley's "The Autobiography of Malcolm X."* New York: Laurel, 1972.

Bambara, Toni Cade. "Programming with *School Daze.*" In *Five for Five,* 47–55.

Bambara, Toni Cade. "Programming with *School Daze.*" In Massood, *Spike Lee Reader,* 10–22.

Baraka, Amiri. "Spike Lee at the Movies." In Diawara, *Black American Cinema,* 145–53.

Baraka, Amiri. *Tales of the Out and Gone*. New York: Akashic Books, 2007.

Barra, Allen. "In Too Deep." *Salon*, June 27, 2006, http://www.salon.com/2006/06/27/brinkley/.

Barry, John M. *Rising Tide: The Great Mississippi Flood of 1927 and How It Changed America*. 1997. New York: Touchstone, 1998.

Barton, Bernadette. "Male Fantasies about Lesbian Desire: A Review of Spike Lee's Film *She Hate Me*." *Sexuality and Culture* 9, no. 3 (2005): 77–80.

Baum, L. Frank. *The Wizard of Oz*. 1900. New York: Puffin Books, 2008.

Baum, Vicki. *Menschenim Hotel (Grand Hotel)*. 1929. Cologne, Germany: Kiepenheuer & Witsch, 2007.

Bazin, André. "The Evolution of the Language of Cinema." In *What Is Cinema?*. Vol. 1, 23–40. 1967. Translated by Hugh Gray. Berkeley: University of California Press, 2005.

Beckles-Raymond, Gabriella. "We Can't Get Off the Bus: A Commentary on Spike Lee and Moral Motivation." In Conard, *Philosophy of Spike Lee*, 40–53.

Belton, John. *American Cinema/American Culture*. New York: McGraw-Hill, 1994.

Benioff, David. *The 25th Hour*. 2000. New York: Plume, 2002.

Berardinelli, James. "*Bamboozled*." *Reelviews*, October 2000, http://www.reelviews.net/movies/b/bamboozled.html.

Bernstein, Jonathan. "Spike Lee." *Face* (December 1997): 202–04.

Birmingham, David. *The Decolonization of Africa*. 1995. London: Routledge, 2003.

Black, Ray. "Satire's Cruelest Cut: Exorcising Blackness in Spike Lee's *Bamboozled*." *The Black Scholar* 33, no. 1 (2003): 19–24.

Blake, Richard A. *Street Smart: The New York of Lumet, Allen, Scorsese, and Lee*. Lexington: University Press of Kentucky, 2005.

Bogle, Donald. *Toms, Coons, Mulattoes, Mammies, & Bucks: An Interpretive History of Blacks in American Films*. 4th ed. New York: Continuum, 2001.

Bohnert, Christiane. "Early Modern Complex Satire and the Satiric Novel: Genre and Cultural Transposition." In *Theorizing Satire: Essays in Literary Criticism*, ed. Brian A. Connery and Kirk Combe, 151–72. New York: St. Martin's Press, 1995.

Bordwell David, Janet Staiger, and Kristin Thompson. *The Classical Hollywood Cinema: Film Style & Mode of Production to 1960*. New York: Columbia University Press, 1985.

Bradley, David. "Malcolm's Mythmaking." *Transition* 56 (1992): 20–46.

Bradley, David. "Spike Lee's Inferno, the Drug Underworld." *New York Times*, September 10, 1995. http://partners.nytimes.com/library/film/091095lee-clockers-essay.html.

Bradley, James with Ron Powers. *Flags of Our Fathers*. New York: Bantam Books, 2000.

Brady, Diane. "Spike Lee on Self-Financing *Red Hook Summer*." *Bloomberg Businessweek*, June 28, 2012. http://www.businessweek.com/articles/2012-06-28/spike-lee-on-self-financing-red-hook-summer.

Braudy, Leo, and Marshall Cohen. *Film Theory and Criticism: Introductory Readings*. 5th ed. New York: Oxford University Press, 1999.

Breskin, David. *Inner Views: Filmmakers in Conversation*. Expanded ed. New York: Da Capo Press, 1997.

Brinkley, Douglas. *The Great Deluge: Hurricane Katrina, New Orleans, and the Mississippi Gulf Coast*. 2006. New York: Harper Perennial, 2007.

Brody, Richard. "Spike Lee's *Red Hook Summer.*" *New Yorker,* August 9, 2012. http://www.newyorker.com/online/blogs/movies/2012/08/red-hook-summer-the-image-of-the-spirit.html.

Brokaw, Tom. *The Greatest Generation.* 1998. New York: Random House, 2004.

Bruckner, D.J.R. "*She's Gotta Have It* (1986)." *New York Times,* August 8, 1986. http://www.nytimes.com/movie/review?res=9A0DEFDF143CF93BA3575BC0A960948260

"Buddy's Friend Is Sending This Open Letter to Director Spike Lee, Hopefully with Enough Awareness This Can Reach Him for a Response." *r/MOVIES. Reddit,* November 28, 2013. http://www.reddit.com/r/movies/comments/1rjp44/buddys_friend_is_sending_this_open_letter_to/.

Byrne, Thomas, and Mary D. Edsall. *Chain Reaction: The Impact of Race, Rights, and Taxes on American Politics.* New York: W.W. Norton & Company, 1992.

Cañadas, Ivan. "Spike Lee's 'Uniquely American [Di]vision': Race and Class in *25th Hour.*" *Bright Lights Film Journal* 63 (February 2009). http://brightlightsfilm.com/63/63spikelee.php#5begin.

Cantu, Rebecca. "About Face: An Interview with Spike Lee." *The Harvard Crimson,* October 20, 2000. http://www.thecrimson.com/article/2000/10/20/about-face-an-interview-with-spike/.

Carroll, Lewis. *Alice's Adventures in Wonderland & Through the Looking-Glass.* 1865 and 1871. New York: Bantam Classics, 2006.

Carson, Clayborne. "Malcolm X." In *Past Imperfect: History According to the Movies,* edited by Mark C. Carnes, 278–83. 1995. New York: Agincourt Press, 1996.

Carson, Clayborne. *Malcolm X: The FBI File,* edited by David Graf. New York: Carroll & Graf, 1991.

"Cast Hit Back at Smear of *Sam.*" *Guardian,* July 3, 1999. http://www.theguardian.com/film/1999/jul/03/news.

Charpentier, David. "Truth is Fiction: Haskell Wexler, Part I." *Popmatters,* November 17, 2011. http://www.popmatters.com/pm/column/150751-truth-is-fiction-the-work-of-haskell-wexler-part-1/.

Chidester, Phil, and Jamel Santa Cruze Bell. "'Say the Right Thing': Spike Lee, *Bamboozled,* and the Future of Satire in the Postmodern World." In Hamlet and Coleman, *Fight the Power,* 203–22.

Clarke, John Henrik, ed. *Malcolm X: The Man and His Times.* 1969. New York: Collier Books, 1990.

Cobb, Jasmine Nichole, and John L. Jackson. "They Hate Me: Spike Lee, Documentary Filmmaking, and Hollywood's 'Savage Slot.'" In Hamlet and Coleman, *Fight the Power,* 251–69.

Colapinto, John. "Outside Man: Spike Lee's Unending Struggle." *New Yorker,* September 22, 2008, 52–63. http://www.newyorker.com/reporting/2008/09/22/080922fa_fact_colapinto?currentPage=all.

Colicchio, Victor, & Michael Imperioli. *Summer of Sam.* Screenplay. October 31, 1997.

Collins, Patricia Hill. *Black Feminist Thought: Knowledge, Consciousness, and the Politics of Empowerment.* Boston: Unwin Hyman, 1990.

Collins, Rodnell P. with A. Peter Bailey. *Seventh Child: A Family Memoir of Malcolm X.* New York: Citadel, 2000.

Conard, Mark T. "Aristotle and MacIntyre on Justice in *25th Hour.*" In Conard, *Philosophy of Spike Lee,* 26–39.

Conard, Mark T., ed. *The Philosophy of Spike Lee*. Lexington: University Press of Kentucky, 2011.

Cone, James H. *Martin and Malcolm and America: A Dream or a Nightmare*. 1991. New York: Orbis Books, 2001.

Connery, Brian A., and Kirk Combe. "Theorizing Satire: A Retrospective and Introduction." In *Theorizing Satire: Essays in Literary Criticism*, 1–15. New York: St. Martin's Press, 1995.

Connery, Brian A., and Kirk Combe, eds. *Theorizing Satire: Essays in Literary Criticism*. New York: St. Martin's Press, 1995.

"Conversation with James McBride, Author of *Miracle at St. Anna*, A." *BookBrowse*, n.d., http://www.bookbrowse.com/author_interviews/full/index.cfm/author_number/271/james-mcbride.

Cooper, Frederick. *Africa since 1940: The Past of the Present*. New Approaches to African History Series. Cambridge: Cambridge University Press, 2002.

Cooper, Frederick. *Decolonization and African Society: The Labor Question in French and British Africa*. Cambridge: Cambridge University Press, 1996.

Crouch, Stanley. "Do the Race Thing: Spike Lee's Afro-Fascist Chic." *Village Voice*, June 20, 1989, 73–76.

Crowdus, Gary. "Editorial." *Cineaste* 26, no. 2 (2001): 1.

Crowdus, Gary, and Dan Georgakas. "Thinking about the Power of Images: An Interview with Spike Lee." *Cineaste* 26, no. 2 (2001): 4–9.

Crowdus, Gary, and Dan Georgakas. "Thinking about the Power of Images: An Interview with Spike Lee." In Fuchs, *Spike Lee: Interviews*, 202–17.

Cruel and Unusual: Disproportionate Sentences for New York's Drug Offenders. Human Rights Watch Violations in the United States 9, no. 2 (March 1997). http://www.hrw.org/reports/1997/usny/.

Cunningham, Mark D. "Through the Looking Glass and Over the Rainbow: Exploring the Fairy Tale in Spike Lee's *Crooklyn*." In Massood, *Spike Lee Reader*, 115–27.

Daniels, Roger. *Guarding the Golden Door: American Immigration Policy and Immigrants since 1882*. New York: Hill and Wang, 2004.

Dawson, Jeff. "Dirty Harry Comes Clean." *Guardian*, June 5, 2008. http://www.theguardian.com/film/2008/jun/06/1.

Delue, Rachael Ziady. "Envisioning Race in Spike Lee's *Bamboozled*." In Hamlet and Coleman, *Fight the Power*, 61–88.

Denby, David. "Disasters." *New Yorker*, September 4, 2006, 139–41.

Denby, David. "He's Gotta Have It." *New York Magazine*, June 26, 1989, 53–54. http://books.google.com/books?id=VucCAAAAMBAJ&pg=PA53&lpg=PA53&dq=da vid+denby+do+the+right+thing&source=bl&ots=5dtdRpSxWp&sig=SgWkW59EN2Tp PT6vLeWXCyntL- k&hl=en&sa=X&ei=aky7UOXgHM yuigLOqIHIAw&ved=0CC0Q6AEwAA#v=onepag e&q=david%20denby%20do%20the%20right%20thing&f=false.

Denzin, Norman K. "Spike's Place." In Hamlet and Coleman, *Fight the Power*, 103–25.

deWaard, Andrew. "Joints and Jams: Spike Lee as Sellebrity Auteur." In Hamlet and Coleman, *Fight the Power*, 345–61.

Diawara, Manthia, ed. *Black American Cinema*. New York: Routledge, 1993.

Diawara, Manthia. "Black American Cinema: The New Realism." In Diawara, *Black American Cinema*, 3–25.

"Director, Producer, Writer, Actor, and Master Teacher Spike Lee to Receive the 20th Annual Dorothy and Lillian Gish Prize." *The 20th Annual Dorothy and Lillian Gish Prize,* September 18, 2013. http://www.gishprize.com/press.htm.

Doherty, Thomas. "Malcolm X: In Print, On Screen." *Biography* 23, no. 1 (winter 2000): 29–48.

Doherty, Thomas. "*When the Levees Broke: A Requiem in Four Acts.*" *Journal of American History* 93, no. 3 (2006): 997–99.

Du Bois, W.E.B. *The Souls of Black Folk,* edited by Henry Louis Gates Jr. and Terri Hume Oliver. 1903. New York: W.W. Norton & Company, 1999.

Dyson, Michael Eric. *Making Malcolm: The Myth and Meaning of Malcolm X.* New York: Oxford University Press, 1995.

Ebert, Roger. "*Bamboozled.*" *Chicago Sun-Times,* October 6, 2000. http://www.rogerebert.com/reviews/bamboozled-2000.

Ebert, Roger. "*Do the Right Thing.*" *Chicago Sun-Times,* June 30, 1989. http://www.rogerebert.com/reviews/do-the-right-thing-1989.

Ebert, Roger. "*Do the Right Thing.*" *Chicago Sun-Times,* May 27, 2001. http://www.rogerebert.com/reviews/great-movie-do-the-right-thing-1989.

Ebert, Roger. "*Get on the Bus.*" *Chicago Sun-Times,* October 18, 1996. http://www.rogerebert.com/reviews/get-on-the-bus-1996.

Ebert, Roger. "*Girl 6.*" *Chicago Sun-Times,* March 22, 1996. http://www.rogerebert.com/reviews/girl-6-1996.

Ebert, Roger. "*He Got Game.*" *Chicago Sun-Times,* May 1, 1998. http://www.rogerebert.com/reviews/he-got-game-1998.

Ebert, Roger. "*Inside Man.*" *Chicago Sun-Times,* March 23, 2006. http://www.rogerebert.com/reviews/inside-man-2006.

Ebert, Roger. "*Miracle at St. Anna.*" *Chicago Sun-Times,* September 25, 2008. http://www.rogerebert.com/reviews/miracle-at-st-anna-2008.

Ebert, Roger. "Moment of Truth Arrives for *Malcolm,* The." *Chicago Sun-Times,* November 5, 1992. http://www.rogerebert.com/rogers-journal/the-moment-of-truth-arrives-for-malcolm.

Ebert, Roger. "*Red Hook Summer.*" *Chicago Sun-Times,* August 22, 2012. http://www.rogerebert.com/reviews/red-hook-summer-2012.

Ebert, Roger. "*School Daze.*" *Chicago Sun-Times,* February 12, 1988. http://www.rogerebert.com/reviews/school-daze-1988.

Ebert, Roger. "*She Hate Me.*" *Chicago Sun-Times,* August 6, 2004. http://www.rogerebert.com/reviews/she-hate-me-2004.

Elgin, Suzette. *Native Tongue.* New York: Daw Books, 1984.

Ellison, Ralph. *Invisible Man.* 1947. New York: Vintage, 1989.

Erlich, Reese. "Spike Lee on Race, Politics and Broken Levees." In *All Things Considered* video, 6:55. National Public Radio. August 13, 2006. http://www.npr.org/templates/story/story.php?storyId=5641453.

Everett, Anna. "'Spike, Don't Mess Malcolm Up': Courting Controversy and Control in *Malcolm X.*" In Massood, *Spike Lee Reader,* 91–114.

Evers-Williams, Myrlie. Foreword to *Betty Shabazz, Surviving Malcolm X,* by Russell J. Rickford, ix–xii. Naperville, IL: Sourcebooks, 2003.

Fanon, Frantz. *Black Skin, White Masks.* Foreword by Kwame Anthony Appiah, translated by Richard Philcox. 1952. Reprint, New York: Grove Press, 2008.

Faulkner, William. *As I Lay Dying.* 1930. New York: Vintage, 1990.

Feloni, Richard. "Spike Lee Accused of Stealing *Oldboy* Movie Poster from an Unpaid Designer." *Business Insider,* November 27, 2013. http://www.businessinsider .com/juan-luis-garcias-email-to-spike-lee-2013-11.

Felperin, Leslie. "Interview: Spike Lee." *Sight and Sound* 13, no. 4 (April 2003): 15.

Fialka, John. "Reagan's Stories Don't Always Check Out." *The Register-Guard,* February 9, 1976. http://news.google.com/newspapers?nid=1310&dat=197602 09&id=Y9ZVAAAAIBAJ&sjid=K-ADAAAAIBAJ&pg=4138,2275149.

"Finest *Hour:* The Spike Lee Interview." *Cinema Gotham,* January 16, 2003, http:// www.dvdtalk.com/cinemagotham/archives/001006.html.

Five for Five: The Films of Spike Lee. New York: Stewart, Tabori & Chang, 1991.

Flory, Dan. "*Bamboozled:* Philosophy through Blackface." In Conard, *Philosophy of Spike Lee,* 64–83.

Flory, Dan. "Race and Black American *Film Noir: Summer of Sam* as Lynching Parable." In Massood, *Spike Lee Reader,* 196–211.

Flory, Dan. "Spike Lee and the Sympathetic Racist." *Journal of Aesthetics and Art Criticism* 64, no. 1 (2006): 67–79.

Frutkin, Alan. "Spike Speaks." *The Advocate,* October 31, 1995, 49–50.

Frutkin, Alan. "Spike Speaks." In Fuchs, *Spike Lee: Interviews,* 112–15.

Fuchs, Cynthia, ed. *Spike Lee: Interviews.* Jackson: University Press of Mississippi, 2002.

Fuchs, Lawrence H. *The American Kaleidoscope: Race, Ethnicity, and the Civic Culture.* Middletown, CT: Wesleyan University Press, 1990.

Fusco, Coco. "An Interview with Black Audio Film Collective: John Akomfrah, Reece Auguiste, Lina Gopaul and Avril Johnson." In *Young, British, and Black: The Work of Sankofa and Black Audio Film Collective,* 41–60. Buffalo, NY: Hallwalls/Contemporary Art Center, 1988.

Gabbard, Krin. "Spike Lee Meets Aaron Copland." In Massood, *Spike Lee Reader,* 175–95.

Gates, Henry Louis, Jr. "Final Cut." *Transition* 52 (1991): 176–204.

Gates, Henry Louis, Jr. "Generation X: A Conversation with Spike Lee and Henry Louis Gates." *Transition* 56 (1992): 176–90.

Gates, Henry Louis, Jr. "*Jungle Fever,* or, Guess Who's Not Coming to Dinner?" In *Five for Five,* 163–69.

George, Nelson. "*Do the Right Thing:* Film and Fury." In *Five for Five,* 77–81.

George, Nelson. "He's Gotta Have It." In *Spike Lee's Gotta Have It: Inside Guerrilla Filmmaking,* by Spike Lee. New York: Fireside/Simon & Schuster, 1987.

George, Nelson. "The Interview: Spike Lee with Nelson George, November 21, 1986." In *Spike Lee's Gotta Have It: Inside Guerrilla Filmmaking,* by Spike Lee. New York: Fireside/Simon & Schuster, 1987.

Gerstner, David A. "De Profundis: A Love Letter from the Inside Man." In Massood, *Spike Lee Reader,* 243–54.

Gewirtz, Russell. *Inside Man, The.* Screenplay. January 17, 2005.

Gilens, Martin. *Why Americans Hate Welfare: Race, Media, and the Politics of Antipoverty Policy.* Chicago: University of Chicago Press, 2000.

Gillespie, Alex. "Autobiography and Identity: Malcolm X as Author and Hero." In Terrill, *Cambridge Companion,* 26–38.

Gilliam, Franklin D., Jr. "The 'Welfare Queen' Experiment: How Viewers React to Images of African-American Women on Welfare." *Nieman Reports* 53, no. 2 (1999). http://www.nieman.harvard.edu/reportsitem.aspx?id=102223.

Gitlin, Todd. *Inside Prime Time*. 1983. Berkeley and Los Angeles: University of California Press, 2000.

Gleiberman, Owen. "*Poetic Justice* (1993)." *Entertainment Weekly,* July 23, 1993. http://www.ew.com/ew/article/0,307326,00.html.

Glicksman, Marlaine. "Spike Lee's Bed-Stuy BBQ." In Fuchs, *Spike Lee: Interviews,* 13–24.

Gordon, Lewis R. *Bad Faith and Antiblack Racism*. Amherst, NY: Humanity Books, 1995.

Gray, Herman. *Watching Race: Television and the Struggle for Blackness*. Minneapolis: University of Minnesota Press, 1995.

Grubb, Davis. *The Night of the Hunter*. 1953. New York: Black Mask, 2008.

Guerrasio, Jason. "Q&A: Spike Lee on the Child-Abuse Scene in *Red Hook Summer,* His Michael Jackson Documentary, and Why He's Not Nervous for Mike Tyson on Broadway." *Vanity Fair,* August 14, 2012. http://www.vanityfair.com/online/oscars/2012/08/spike-lee-on-red-hook-summer-michael-jackson-documentary-mike-tyson-broadway.

Guerrero, Ed. *Framing Blackness: The African American Image in Film*. Philadelphia: Temple University Press, 1993.

Hamlet, Janice D., and Robin R. Means Coleman, eds. *Fight the Power!: The Spike Lee Reader*. New York: Peter Lang Publishing, 2009.

Haro Movie Reviews. "*Bamboozled*." n.d. http://www.haro-online.com/movies/bamboozled.html.

Harris, Heather E., and Kimberly R. Moffitt. "A Critical Exploration of African American Women through the 'Spiked Lens.'" In Hamlet and Coleman, *Fight the Power,* 303–20.

Harris, Keith M. "*Clockers* (Spike Lee 1995): Adaptation in Black." In Massood, *Spike Lee Reader,* 128–41.

Harrison, Barbara Grizzuti. "Spike Lee Hates Your Cracker Ass." *Esquire,* October 1992. http://www.esquire.com/features/spike-lee-1092.

Healy, Mark. "Spike Lee Is Still Doing the Right Thing." *GQ Magazine,* September 2010. http://www.gq.com/news-politics/big-issues/201009/spike-lee-new-orleans-katrina-bp-oil-obama-da-creek-dont-rise.

Hill, Logan. "How I Made It: Spike Lee on *Do the Right Thing*." *New York Magazine,* April 7, 2008. http://nymag.com/anniversary/40th/culture/45772/.

Hoffman, Karen D. "Feminists and 'Freaks': *She's Gotta Have It* and *Girl 6*." In Conard, *Philosophy of Spike Lee,* 106–22.

Hollinger, David A. "Amalgamation and Hypodescent: The Question of Ethnoracial Mixture in the History of the United States." *American Historical Review* 108, no. 5 (2003): 1363–90.

Holt, Jason, and Robert Pitter. "The Prostitution Trap of Elite Sport in *He Got Game*." In Conard, *Philosophy of Spike Lee,* 15–25.

hooks, bell. "Counter-Hegemonic Art: *Do the Right Thing*." In hooks, *Yearning: Race, Gender, and Cultural Politics,* 173–84.

hooks, bell. "*Crooklyn*: The Denial of Death." In hooks, *Reel to Real,* 43–58.

hooks, bell. "Good Girls Look the Other Way." In hooks, *Reel to Real,* 13–25.

hooks, bell. "Male Heroes and Female Sex Objects: Sexism in Spike Lee's *Malcolm X*." *Cineaste* 19, no. 4 (1993): 13–15.

hooks, bell. "Male Heroes and Female Sex Objects: Sexism in Spike Lee's *Malcolm X*." In *Feminisms: An Anthology of Literary Theory and Criticism,* Rev. ed., edited by Robyn R. Warhol and Diane Price Herndl, 555–58. New Brunswick, NJ: Rutgers University Press, 1997.

hooks, bell. *Reel to Real: Race, Class and Sex at the Movies.* 1996. Reprint, New York: Routledge, 2009.

hooks, bell. *Talking Back: Thinking Feminist, Thinking Black.* Boston: South End Press, (1989–2009).

hooks, bell. "'Whose Pussy Is This': A Feminist Comment." In hooks, *Reel to Real,* 291–302.

hooks, bell. *Yearning: Race, Gender, and Cultural Politics.* Boston: South End Press, 1990.

Hornaday, Ann. "*Miracle at St. Anna.*" *Washington Post,* September 26, 2008. http://www.washingtonpost.com/gog/movies/miracle-at-st.-anna,1146328/critic-review.html#reviewNum1.

Horne, Gerald. "'Myth' and the Making of *Malcolm X.*" *American Historical Review* 98, no. 2 (April 1993): 440–50.

Howard, John R. *Faces in the Mirror: Oscar Micheaux and Spike Lee.* Lady Lake, FL: Fireside Publications, 2009.

Howe, Desson. "*School Daze.*" *Washington Post,* February 12, 1988. http://www.washingtonpost.com/wp-srv/style/longterm/movies/videos/schooldaze howe.htm.

Human Rights Watch. *Cruel and Unusual: Disproportionate Sentences for New York Drug Offenders. Human Rights Violations in the United States* 9, no. 2 (March 1997). http://www.hrw.org/reports/1997/usny/.

Hunter, Stephen. "*Bamboozled:* Soul-Defying Success." *Washington Post,* October 20, 2000. http://www.washingtonpost.com/wp-srv/entertainment/movies/reviews/bamboozledhunter.htm.

Hynes, Charles J., and Bob Drury. *Incident at Howard Beach: The Case for Murder.* 25th Anniversary ed. 1990. Bloomington, IN: iUniverse, 2011.

Iverem, Esther. "Spike Lee to Black Audiences: Grow Up." *SeeingBlack.com,* February 3, 2003. http://www.seeingblack.com/2003/x020403/spike_lee.shtml.

Jacoby, Tamar, ed. *Reinventing the Melting Pot: The New Immigrants and What It Means to Be American.* New York: Basic Books, 2004.

James, Henry. *The Wings of the Dove.* 1902. New York: Penguin, 2008.

Johnson, Victoria E. "Polyphony and Cultural Expression: Interpreting Musical Traditions in *Do the Right Thing.*" In Reid, *Do the Right Thing,* 50–72.

Jones, Jacquie. "New Ghetto Aesthetic, The." *Wide Angle* 13, no. 3–4 (1991): 32–44.

Jones, Jacquie. "Spike Lee Presents *Malcolm X:* The New Black Nationalism." *Cineaste* 19, no. 4 (1993): 9–11.

Kellner, Douglas. "Aesthetics, Ethics, and Politics in the Films of Spike Lee." In Reid, *Do the Right Thing,* 73–106.

Kempley, Rita. "*School Daze.*" *Washington Post,* February 12, 1988. http://www.washingtonpost.com/wp-srv/style/longterm/movies/videos/schooldaze.htm.

Kempton, Murray. "The Pizza is Burning!" *New York Review of Books,* September 28, 1989, 36–38.

Kermode, Mark. "A Talent to Offend." *New Statesman,* April 21, 2003. http://www.newstatesman.com/node/145271.

King, Martin Luther, Jr. "The Quest for Peace and Justice." *Nobel Peace Prize Lecture.* Oslo, Norway, December 11, 1964. http://www.nobelprize.org/nobel_prizes/peace/laureates/1964/king-lecture.html.

King, Martin Luther, Jr. *The Words of Martin Luther King, Jr.* New York: Newmarket Press, 1984.

Klein, Joe. "Spiked?" *New York Magazine,* June 26, 1989, 14–15. http://books.google.com/books?id=VucCAAAAMBAJ&pg=PA14&lpg=PA14&dq=joe+klein+spiked?&source=bl&ots=5dtdSoXxQp&sig=KYyRjtlrXucYMBR5UhmuiIGb-DQ&hl=en&sa=X&ei=Rr-8UIzcCcXbiwKaqYHQDg&ved=0CDkQ6AEwAg#v=onepage&q=joe%20klein%20spiked%3F&f=false.

Klotman, Phyllis R., and Janet K. Cutler. *Struggles for Representation: African American Documentary Film and Video.* Bloomington: Indiana University Press, 1999.

Krugman, Paul. "Republicans and Race." *New York Times,* November 19, 2007. http://www.nytimes.com/2007/11/19/opinion/19krugman.html.

Landau, Saul. "Spike Lee's Revolutionary Broadside." *Cineaste* 26, no. 2 (2001): 11–12.

LaRocca, David. "Rethinking the First Person: Autobiography, Authorship, and the Contested Self in *Malcolm X*." In Conard, *Philosophy of Spike Lee,* 215–41.

LaSalle, Mick. "Movie Review: *Miracle at St. Anna*." *San Francisco Chronicle,* September 26, 2008. http://www.sfgate.com/movies/article/Movie-Review-Miracle-at-St-Anna-3192960.php.

Laski, Gregory. "Falling Back into History: The Uncanny Trauma of Blackface Minstrelsy in Spike Lee's *Bamboozled*." *Callaloo* 33, no. 4 (2010): 1093–15.

Latty, Yvonne. *We Were There: Voices of African American Veterans, from World War II to the War in Iraq.* New York: HarperCollins, 2004.

Leak, Jeffrey B. "Malcolm X and Black Masculinity in Process." In Terrill, *Cambridge Companion,* 51–62.

Lee, Chris. "Spike Lee Talks Hollywood Racism, New Film *Red Hook Summer*." *Daily Beast,* January 26, 2012. http://www.thedailybeast.com/articles/2012/01/26/spike-lee-talks-hollywood-racism-new-film-red-hook-summer.html.

Lee, Spike. *Best Seat in the House: A Basketball Memoir.* With Ralph Wiley. New York: Crown Publishers, 1997.

Lee, Spike. *By Any Means Necessary: The Trials and Tribulations of the Making of "Malcolm X."* With Ralph Wiley. New York: Hyperion, 1992.

Lee, Spike. "Deeds Not Words: An Introduction." In *Miracle at St. Anna: The Motion Picture—A Spike Lee Joint,* 9–13. New York: Rizzoli International Publications, 2008.

Lee, Spike. *Do the Right Thing.* Second Draft Screenplay. March 1, 1988. http://www.awesomefilm.com/script/dotherightthing.txt.

Lee, Spike. *Do the Right Thing: A Spike Lee Joint.* With Lisa Jones. New York: Simon & Schuster, Fireside, 1989.

Lee, Spike. "Five for Five." In *Five for Five,* 11–17.

Lee, Spike. *Jungle Fever.* Second Draft Screenplay. July 9, 1990.

Lee, Spike. *Mo' Better Blues: A Spike Lee Joint.* With Lisa Jones. New York: Simon & Schuster, Fireside, 1990.

Lee, Spike. "Say It Ain't So, Joe." *New York Magazine,* July 17, 1989, 6. http://
    books.google.com/books?id=8ecCAAAAMBAJ&pg=PA6&lpg=PA6&dq=spi
    ke+lee+say+it+aint+so+joe&source=bl&ots=KovQy6A1de&sig=jMy5Gcsmyn
    NvzDchG8oG6conbmI&hl=en&sa=X&ei=qeSkU4KwLYSRyAS0pYKIAQ&
    ved=0CB8Q6AEwAA#v=onepage&q=spike%20lee%20say%20it%20aint%20
    so%20joe&f=false.
Lee, Spike. *Spike Lee: That's My Story and I'm Sticking to It.* As Told to Kaleem Aftab.
    New York: W.W. Norton & Company, 2006.
Lee, Spike. *Spike Lee's Gotta Have It: Inside Guerrilla Filmmaking.* New York: Fire-
    side/Simon & Schuster, 1987.
Lee, Spike. *Twitter.* December 17, 2011. https://twitter.com/SpikeLee/status/
    148016969281585153.
Lee, Spike. *Twitter.* November 28, 2013. https://twitter.com/SpikeLee/status/
    406084275969085440.
Lee, Spike. *Uplift the Race: The Construction of "School Daze."* With Lisa Jones. New
    York: Simon & Schuster, Fireside, 1988.
Lee, Spike, and Jason Matloff. *Spike Lee: Do the Right Thing,* edited by Steve Crist.
    New York: AMMO Books, 2010.
Leeming, David. *James Baldwin: A Biography.* New York: Penguin, 1994.
Leitch, Will. "Spike Lee Talks Obama, the End of Mookie's Brooklyn, and the Holly-
    wood Color Line." *Vulture,* July 8, 2012. http://www.vulture.com/2012/07/
    spike-lee-on-reality-tv-minstrelsy-and-hollywood.html.
Leo, Vince. "*Inside Man* (2006)." *Qwipster,* http://qwipster.net/insideman.htm.
Lewis, Miles Marshall. "Spike Lee Talks *Red Hook Summer.*" *Ebony,* August 9,
    2012.   http://www.ebony.com/entertainment-culture/interview-spike-lee-
    523#axzz2MEvdaZvz.
Lewis, Paul. "Spike Lee Gets in Clint Eastwood's Line of Fire." *Guardian,* June 5,
    2008. http://www.theguardian.com/film/2008/jun/06/usa.race.
Lindo, Delroy. "Delroy Lindo on Spike Lee." In Fuchs, *Spike Lee: Interviews,* 161–77.
Locke, John. "Adapting the Autobiography: The Transformation of Malcolm X."
    Cineaste 19, no. 4 (1993): 5–7.
Lott, Eric. *Love and Theft: Blackface Minstrelsy and the American Working Class.*
    1993. New York: Oxford University Press, 1995.
Lubiano, Wahneema. "But Compared to What?: Reading Realism, Representa-
    tion, and Essentialism in *School Daze, Do the Right Thing,* and the Spike Lee
    Discourse." *Black American Literature Forum* 25, no. 2 (Summer 1991):
    253–82.
Lubiano, Wahneema. "But Compared to What?: Reading Realism, Representation,
    and Essentialism in *School Daze, Do the Right Thing,* and the Spike Lee Dis-
    course." In Massood, *Spike Lee Reader,* 30–57.
Lucia, Cynthia. "Race, Media and Money: A Critical Symposium on Spike Lee's *Bam-
    boozled.*" *Cineaste* 26, no. 2 (2001): 10–11.
Lyne, William. "No Accident: From Black Power to Black Box Office." *African
    American Review* 34, no. 1 (2000): 39–59.
Mack, Dwayne. "Howard Beach Incident (1986)." *BlackPast.org.* http://www
    .blackpast.org/?q=aah/howard-beach-incident-1986.
"Man Inside . . ., The." *Total Film,* March 24, 2006. http://www.totalfilm.com/
    features/the-man-inside.

Marable, Manning. "Malcolm as Messiah: Cultural Myth vs. Historical Reality in *Malcolm X.*" *Cineaste* 19, no. 4 (1993): 7–9.

Marable, Manning. *Malcolm X: A Life of Reinvention.* New York: Viking, 2011.

Marcus, Millicent. *Italian Film in the Light of Neorealism.* Princeton: Princeton University Press, 1986.

Marikar, Sheila. "Spike Strikes Back: Clint's 'An Angry Old Man.'" *ABCNews.com,* June 6, 2008. http://abcnews.go.com/Entertainment/story?id=5015524&page=1.

Maslin, Janet. "Still Reeling from the Day Death Came to Birmingham." *New York Times,* July 9, 1997. http://movies.nytimes.com/movie/review?res=9500EED71439F93AA35754C0A961958260.

Massood, Paula J. *Black City Cinema: African American Urban Experiences in Film.* Philadelphia: Temple University Press, 2003.

Massood, Paula J. "Doyle's Law: An Interview with David Benioff." *Cineaste* 28, no. 3 (Summer 2003): 8–10.

Massood, Paula J. "Quintessential New Yorker and Global Citizen, The: An Interview with Spike Lee." *Cineaste* 28, no. 3 (Summer 2003): 4–6.

Massood, Paula J., ed. *Spike Lee Reader, The.* Philadelphia: Temple University Press, 2008.

Massood, Paula J. "We've Gotta Have It—Spike Lee, African American Film, and Cinema Studies." In Massood, *Spike Lee Reader,* xv–xxviii.

Matheou, Demetrios. "Interview: Edward Norton." *Sight and Sound* 13, no. 4 (April 2003): 12.

Mauer, Marc. *The Changing Racial Dynamics of the War on Drugs.* Washington, DC: The Sentencing Project, 2009.

McBride, James. "The Making of a King: A Foreword." In *Miracle at St. Anna: The Motion Picture—A Spike Lee Joint,* 4–6. New York: Rizzoli International Publications, 2008.

McBride, James. *Miracle at St. Anna.* New York: Riverhead Books, 2002.

McClay, Wilfred M. "A Flood of Words on Katrina." *New York Sun,* May 15, 2006. http://www.nysun.com/arts/flood-of-words-on-katrina/32704/.

McFarland, Douglas. "The Symbolism of Blood in *Clockers.*" In Conard, *Philosophy of Spike Lee,* 3–14.

McMillan, Terry. "Thoughts on *She's Gotta Have It.*" In *Five for Five,* 19–29.

McNair, Christopher. Interview by Spike Lee. *4 Little Girls.* Directed by Spike Lee. Home Box Office. 102 min. 1997.

Mercer, Kobena. "Diaspora Culture and the Dialogic Imagination: The Aesthetics of Black Independent Film in Britain." In *BlackFrames: Critical Perspectives in Black Independent Cinema,* edited by Mbye B. Cham and Claire Andrade-Watkins, 50–61. Cambridge: MIT Press, 1988.

Miller, Prairie. "*Summer of Sam:* An Interview with Spike Lee." In Fuchs, *Spike Lee: Interviews,* 178–83.

Millner, Denene. "A New Documentary Finally Puts a Face on the Racial Terrorism that Claimed the Lives of Four Little Girls." *New York Daily News Sunday Edition,* July 13, 1997., http://www.nydailynews.com/new-documentary-finally-puts-face-racial-terrorism-claimed-lives-girls-article-1.774093.

Miracle at St. Anna: The Motion Picture—A Spike Lee Joint. New York: Rizzoli International Publications, 2008.

Mitchell, Elvis. "Spike Lee: The *Playboy* Interview." In Fuchs, *Spike Lee: Interviews*, 35–64.

Mitchell, Elvis. "Spike Lee: The *Playboy* Interview." *Playboy* (July 1991): 51–68.

Mitchell, W.J.T. "Living Color: Race, Stereotype, and Animation in Spike Lee's *Bamboozled*." In *What Do Pictures Want?: The Lives and Loves of Images*, 294–308. Chicago: University of Chicago Press, 2005.

Mitchell, W.J.T. "The Violence of Public Art: *Do the Right Thing*." In Reid, *Do the Right Thing*, 107–28.

Moore, Christopher Paul. *Fighting for America: Black Soldiers—The Unsung Heroes of World War II*. New York: One World, 2005.

Morales, Wilson. "*25th Hour:* An Interview with Spike Lee." *Blackfilm.com*, December 2002. http://www.blackfilm.com/20021220/features/spikelee.shtml.

Morgenstern, Joe. "In *St. Anna*, Lee Fumbles Epic of War, Racism." *Wall Street Journal*, September 26, 2008. http://online.wsj.com/article/SB122238344981876805.html.

Morris, Wesley. "War without Much Fight." *Boston Globe*, September 26, 2008. http://www.boston.com/ae/movies/articles/2008/09/26/war_without_much_fight/?page=full.

Morrison, Toni. *Beloved*. 1987. New York: Vintage, 2004.

Mulvey, Laura. *Visual and Other Pleasures*. 2nd ed. New York: Palgrave Macmillan, 2009.

Mulvey, Laura. "Visual Pleasure and Narrative Cinema." In Braudy and Cohen, *Film Theory and Criticism*, 833–44.

Nelson, Jill. "Mo' Better Spike." *Essence*, August 1990, 54–57.

Neubeck, Kenneth J., and Noel A. Cazenave. *Welfare Racism: Playing the Race Card against America's Poor*. New York: Routledge, 2001.

Nevins, Sheila. Interview by Reese Erlich. "Spike Lee on Race, Politics and Broken Levees." In *All Things Considered*. National Public Radio. 7 min. August 13, 2006. http://www.npr.org/templates/story/story.php?storyId=5641453.

Nichols, Bill. *Introduction to Documentary*. 2nd ed. Bloomington: Indiana University Press, 2010.

Nichols, Peter M., ed. *The "New York Times" Guide to the Best 1,000 Movies Ever Made*. Updated and Revised ed. New York: St. Martin's Press, 2004.

Norman, Brian. "Bringing Malcolm X to Hollywood." In Terrill, *Cambridge Companion*, 39–50.

Norman, Brian. "Reading a 'Closet Screenplay': Hollywood, James Baldwin's Malcolms and the Threat of Historical Irrelevance." *African American Review* 39, no. 1–2 (2005): 103–18.

Oates, Joyce Carol. "*Negative*." In *Dr. Magic: Six One Act Plays*, 58–74. New York: Samuel French Inc., 2004.

O'Neill, Patricia. "Where Globalization and Localization Meet: Spike Lee's *The 25th Hour*." *CineAction* 64 (August 2004): 22–27.

Painter, Nell Irvin. "Malcolm X across the Genres." *American Historical Review* 98, no. 2 (April 1993): 432–39.

Palmer, R. Barton. "Monsters and Moralism in *Summer of Sam*." In Conard, *Philosophy of Spike Lee*, 54–71.

Perry, Bruce. *Malcolm: The Life of the Man Who Changed Black America*. 1991. Barrytown, NY: Station Hill Press, 1992.

Pinkney, Alphonso. *Lest We Forget: White Hate Crimes: Howard Beach and Other Racial Atrocities.* Chicago: Third World Press, 1994.

Pisa, Nick. "Spike Lee's *Miracle at St. Anna* Denounced by Italian War Veterans as 'Insulting.'" *Telegraph,* September 30, 2008. http://www.telegraph.co.uk/news/worldnews/europe/italy/3112154/Spike-Lees-Miracle-at-St-Anna-denounced-by-Italian-war-veterans-as-insulting.html.

Pizzello, Stephen. "Between 'Rock' and a Hard Place." In Fuchs, *Spike Lee: Interviews,* 99–111.

Pizzello, Stephen. "Spike Lee's Seventies Flashback." In Fuchs, *Spike Lee: Interviews,* 155–60.

Pollard, Sam. "*When the Levees Broke.*" *Washington Post,* August 22, 2006. http://www.washingtonpost.com/wp-dyn/content/discussion/2006/08/21/DI2006082101122.html.

Porter, Katherine Anne. *Ship of Fools.* 1962. New York: Back Bay Books, 2000.

Price, Richard. *Clockers.* Boston: Houghton Mifflin, 1992.

Puig, Claudia. "Spike Lee's *Red Hook Summer* Never Takes Shape." *USA Today,* August 23, 2012. http://usatoday30.usatoday.com/life/movies/reviews/story/2012-08-24/red-hook-summer-clarke-peters-jules-brown/57259804/1.

Radelat, Ana. "Spike Lee Showcases Heartbreak, Spirit of New Orleans." *USA Today,* August 14, 2006. http://usatoday30.usatoday.com/life/television/news/2006-08-14-spike-lee_x.htm.

Radford-Hill, Sheila. "Womanizing Malcolm X." In Terrill, *Cambridge Companion,* 63–77.

Rafferty, Terrence. "Open and Shut." *New Yorker,* July 24, 1989, 78–81.

Raines, Howell. "The Birmingham Bombing." *New York Times Magazine,* July 24, 1983. http://www.nytimes.com/1983/07/24/magazine/the-birmingham-bombing.html?pagewanted=1.

Rank, Mark Robert. *One Nation, Underprivileged: Why American Poverty Affects Us All.* New York: Oxford University Press, 2005.

Reid, Mark. A., ed. *Spike Lee's "Do the Right Thing."* Cambridge Film Handbooks Series. Cambridge: Cambridge University Press, 1997.

Richardson, Basil. *The Black Man's Burden: Africa and the Curse of the Nation-State.* New York: Three Rivers Press, 1992.

Richolson, Janice Mosier. "He's Gotta Have It: An Interview with Spike Lee." *Cineaste* 18, no. 4 (1991): 12–14.

Richolson, Janice Mosier. "He's Gotta Have It: An Interview with Spike Lee." In Fuchs, *Spike Lee: Interviews,* 25–34.

Rickford, Russell J. *Betty Shabazz, Surviving Malcolm X.* Naperville, IL: Sourcebooks, 2003.

Rose, Charlie. "Interview with Spike Lee: 1996." In Fuchs, *Spike Lee: Interviews,* 116–26.

Sarris, Andrew. "*Summer of Sam* Bursts with Trying to Be Important." *New York Observer,* July 12, 1999. http://observer.com/1999/07/summer-of-sam-bursts-with-trying-to-be-important/.

Schaefer, Stephen. "Spike Makes *Clockers* Timely." *New York Post,* August 25, 1995, 46–47.

Schwarzbaum, Lisa. "*Summer of Sam* (1999)." *Entertainment Weekly,* July 9, 1999. http://www.ew.com/ew/article/0,272327,00.html.

Scott, A.O. "Hollywood War, Revised Edition." *New York Times,* September 25, 2008. http://movies.nytimes.com/2008/09/26/movies/26mira.html?_r=0.

Seewood, Andre. "The Decline of Spike Lee: A Prisoner of the Middle Class." *Shadow and Act: On Cinema of the African Diaspora,* January 2, 2013. http://blogs.indiewire .com/shadowandact/the-decline-of-spike-lee-a-prisoner-of-the-middle-class.

Shabazz, Attallah. Foreword to *The Autobiography of Malcolm X,* by Malcolm X with the assistance of Alex Haley, ix–xxiv. 1965. New York: Ballantine Books, 1999.

Shabazz, Ilyasah. *Growing Up X: A Memoir by the Daughter of Malcolm X.* With Kim McLarin. 2002. New York: One World Books, 2003.

Sharkey, Betsy. "Spike Lee's *Red Hook Summer* a Mess of Sinners, Saints." *Los Angeles Times,* August 23, 2012. http://articles.latimes.com/2012/aug/23/enter tainment/la-et-mn-red-hook-summer-review-20120824.

Shepard, Jim. "Sympathy for the Dealer." *New York Times,* June 21, 1992. http:// www.nytimes.com/books/98/06/07/specials/price-clockers.html.

Shiel, Mark. *Italian Neorealism: Rebuilding the Cinematic City.* Short Cuts Series. New York: Wallflower, 2006.

Shulgasser, Barbara. "*Get on the Bus.*" *San Francisco Examiner,* October 16, 1996. http://www.sfgate.com/style/article/Get-on-the-Bus-3119246.php.

Silberstein, Michael. "The Dialectic of King and X in *Do the Right Thing.*" In Conard, *Philosophy of Spike Lee,* 123–43.

Smith, Derik. "True Terror: The Haunting of Spike Lee's *25th Hour.*" *African American Review* 45, no. 1–2 (2012): 1–16.

"Spike Lee Discusses *She Hate Me.*" About.com *Hollywood Movies,* n.d., http://movies .about.com/library/weekly/aaspikelee072804a.htm.

Sragow, Michael. "Black Like Spike." *Salon,* October 26, 2000. http://www.salon .com/2000/10/26/spike_lee_2/.

Sragow, Michael. "Black Like Spike." In Fuchs, *Spike Lee: Interviews,* 189–98.

Stein, Ruthe. "Lee Explores Lingering Grief from Killing of '4 Girls.'" *San Francisco Chronicle,* October 7, 1997. http://www.sfgate.com/entertainment/article/ Lee-Explores-Lingering-Grief-From-Killing-of-4-2826129.php.

Stephens, Ronald Jemal. "The Aesthetics of *Nommo* in the Films of Spike Lee." In Hamlet and Coleman, *Fight the Power,* 3–21.

Sterritt, David. "*Do the Right Thing* (1989)." In *The A List: The National Society of Film Critics' 100 Essential Films,* edited by Jay Carr, 91–94. New York: Da Capo Press, 2002.

Sterritt, David. *Spike Lee's America.* America through the Lens Series. Cambridge, England: Polity Press, 2013.

Stevens, Maurice E. "Subject to Countermemory: Disavowal and Black Manhood in Spike Lee's *Malcolm X.*" In Hamlet and Coleman, *Fight the Power,* 321–41.

Stockwell, Anne. "He Don't Hate Me." *The Advocate,* August, 17, 2004, 66–73.

Svetvilas, Chuleenan. "Bamboozled on the Bayou: Spike Lee Profiles Katrina Survivors." *Documentary,* August 2006. http://www.documentary.org/content/ bamboozled-bayou-spike-lee-profiles-katrina-survivors.

Tait, R. Colin. "Class and Allegory in Spike Lee's *Inside Man.*" In Hamlet and Coleman, *Fight the Power,* 41–60.

Taylor, Trey. "Did Spike Lee Rip Off Juan Luis Garcia?" *Dazed Digital,* November 30, 2013. http://www.dazeddigital.com/artsandculture/article/18027/1/did-spi ke-lee-rip-off-juan-luis-garcia.

Terkel, Studs. "*The Good War*": *An Oral History of World War II*. New York: The New Press, 1984.

Terrill, Robert E., ed. *The Cambridge Companion to Malcolm X*. Cambridge: Cambridge University Press, 2010.

Toomer, Jean. *Cane*. 1923. New York: Liveright/W.W. Norton & Company, 2011.

"Transcripts, Tape Show Bush, Brown Warned on Katrina." *CNN.com*, March 2, 2006. http://www.cnn.com/2006/POLITICS/03/02/fema.tapes/.

Tsuchiya, Garon, and Nobuaki Minegishi. *Orūdo Bōi (Old Boy)*. Tokyo: Futabasha, 1996–1998.

Turvey, Malcolm. "Black Film Making in the USA: The Case of *Malcolm X*." *Wasafiri* 9, no. 18 (1993): 53–56.

Verniere, James. "Doing the Job." *Sight and Sound* 3 (February 1993): 10–11.

Verniere, James. "Doing the Job." In Fuchs, *Spike Lee: Interviews*, 79–85.

Walker, Alice. *The Color Purple*. New York: Harcourt Brace Jovanovich, 1982.

Walker, Rebecca. "Female Trouble." *Salon*, August 19, 2004. http://www.salon.com/2004/08/19/lee_11/.

Wallace, Michele. *Invisibility Blues: From Pop to Theory*. New York: Verso, 1990.

Wallace, Michele. "Spike Lee and Black Women." In Massood, *Spike Lee Reader*, 23–29.

Washington, Booker T. *Up from Slavery*. 1901. New York: Signet Classics, 2010.

Watkins, S. Craig. "Reel Men: *Get on the Bus* and the Shifting Terrain of Black Masculinities." In Massood, *Spike Lee Reader*, 142–58.

Watkins, S. Craig. *Representing: Hip Hop Culture and the Production of Black Cinema*. Chicago: University of Chicago Press, 1998.

Weinraub, Bernard. "A Movie Producer Remembers the Human Side of Malcolm X." *New York Times*, November 23, 1992. http://www.nytimes.com/1992/11/23/movies/a-movie-producer-remembers-the-human-side-of-malcolm-x.html?src=pm.

Whaley, Deborah Elizabeth. "Spike Lee's Phantasmagoric Fantasy and the Black Female Sexual Imaginary in *She Hate Me*." *Poroi* 7, no. 2 (2011): 1–34.

White, Armond. "Post-Art Minstrelsy." *Cineaste* 26, no. 2 (2001): 12–14.

Whoriskey, Peter. "New Orleans in a Tempest over *Deluge*." *Washington Post*, May 19, 2006. http://www.washingtonpost.com/wp-dyn/content/article/2006/05/18/AR2006051802284.html.

Williams, Kam. "Miracle of St. Spike: Spike Lee—*The Miracle at St. Anna* Interview." *FLOWInsider*, September 2008. http://www.flowinsiders.com/our2cents/style18.asp.

Williams, Raymond. *Keywords: A Vocabulary of Culture and Society*. New York: Oxford University Press, 1976.

Wolf, Buck. "Spike Lee's Katrina *Requiem* Mixes Anger, Sorrow." *ABC News*, August 18, 2006. http://abcnews.go.com/Entertainment/story?id=2330610&page=1.

Woodson, Jacqueline. *Miracle's Boys*. New York: G. P. Putnam's Sons, 2000.

Woolf, Virginia. *Mrs. Dalloway*. 1925. Oxford: Oxford University Press, 2000.

Wright, Richard. *Native Son*. 1940. New York: HarperPerennial, 1998.

X, Malcolm. *The Autobiography of Malcolm X*. As Told to Alex Haley. 1965. New York: Ballantine Books, 1999.

X, Malcolm. *By Any Means Necessary*, edited by George Breitman. 1970. New York: Pathfinder, 1992.

X, Malcolm. "Communication and Reality." In Clarke, *Malcolm X: The Man and His Times*, 307–21.

X, Malcolm. "The Role of Women." In *By Any Means Necessary*, edited by George Breitman, 214–15. 1970. New York: Pathfinder, 1992.

Yearwood, Gladstone L. *Black Film as a Signifying Practice: Cinema, Narration and the African American Aesthetic Tradition*. Trenton, NJ: Africa World Press, 2000.

Younge, Gary. "Spike Lee on *Oldboy*, America's Violent History and the Fine Art of Mouthing Off." *Guardian*, December 1, 2013. http://www.theguardian.com/film/2013/dec/01/spike-lee-oldboy-interview-director.

Zolberg, Aristide R. *A Nation by Design: Immigration Policy in the Fashioning of America*. Cambridge: Harvard University Press, 2009.

Filmography

All entries follow the Writers Guild of America's official system for determining credits. An ampersand (&) joins the names of writers who worked together, as a team, on a screenplay or teleplay, while the word *and* joins the names of writers who worked independently on the same script, with the names listed in succession (meaning that the final writer to work on the script is the final writer credited in the entry). For example, the screenplay for *Summer of Sam* (1999) is credited as "Screenplay by Victor Colicchio & Michael Imperioli and Spike Lee," indicating that Colicchio & Imperioli wrote a draft of *Summer of Sam*'s screenplay together, as a team, only to have Spike Lee revise this draft after they completed their duties. Since Lee was the final person to work on *Summer of Sam*'s screenplay, he is the final person credited.

FEATURE FILMS, DOCUMENTARIES, AND TELEVISION PROGRAMS DIRECTED BY SPIKE LEE

Answer, The. Directed by Spike Lee. Screenplay by Spike Lee. 20 min. New York University's Tisch School of the Arts, 1980.

Bad 25. Directed by Spike Lee. 131 min. ABC Television and 40 Acres & A Mule Filmworks, 2012.

Bamboozled. Directed by Spike Lee. Screenplay by Spike Lee. 135 min. New Line Cinema and 40 Acres & A Mule Filmworks, 2000.

Clockers. Directed by Spike Lee. Screenplay by Richard Price and Spike Lee, from the novel *Clockers* by Richard Price. 128 min. Universal Pictures and 40 Acres & A Mule Filmworks, 1995.

Crooklyn. Directed by Spike Lee. Screenplay by Joie Susannah Lee & Cinqué Lee and Spike Lee. Story by Joie Susannah Lee. 115 min. Universal Pictures and 40 Acres & A Mule Filmworks, 1994.

Da Brick. Directed by Spike Lee. Screenplay by John Ridley. 115 min. HBO Entertainment, 2011.

Da Sweet Blood of Jesus. Directed by Spike Lee. Screenplay by Spike Lee. 40 Acres & A Mule Filmworks, 2014.

Do the Right Thing. Directed by Spike Lee. Screenplay by Spike Lee. 120 min. Universal Pictures and 40 Acres & A Mule Filmworks, 1989.

4 Little Girls. Directed by Spike Lee. 102 min. HBO Documentary Films and 40 Acres & A Mule Filmworks, 1997.

Freak. Directed by Spike Lee. Screenplay by David Bar Katz & John Leguizamo. 89 min. HBO Films and Lower East Side Films, 1998.

Get on the Bus. Directed by Spike Lee. Screenplay by Reggie Rock Bythewood. 120 min. Columbia Pictures, 15 Black Men, and 40 Acres & A Mule Filmworks, 1996.

Girl 6. Directed by Spike Lee. Screenplay by Suzan-Lori Parks. 108 min. Fox Searchlight Pictures and 40 Acres & A Mule Filmworks, 1996.

He Got Game. Directed by Spike Lee. Screenplay by Spike Lee. 136 min. Touchstone Pictures and 40 Acres & A Mule Filmworks, 1998.

Huey P. Newton Story, A. Directed by Spike Lee. Screenplay by Roger Guenveur Smith. 86 min. Starz! Encore Entertainment, Luna Ray Films, and 40 Acres & A Mule Filmworks, 2001.

If God is Willing and Da Creek Don't Rise. Directed by Spike Lee. 4 episodes. 240 min. HBO Documentary Films and 40 Acres & A Mule Filmworks, 2010.

Inside Man. Directed by Spike Lee. Screenplay by Russel Gewirtz. 129 min. Universal Pictures, Imagine Entertainment, and 40 Acres & A Mule Filmworks, 2006.

Jim Brown: All-American. Directed by Spike Lee. 140 min. HBO Sports and 40 Acres & A Mule Filmworks, 2002.

Joe's Bed-Stuy Barbershop: We Cut Heads. Directed by Spike Lee. Screenplay by Spike Lee. 60 min. New York University's Tisch School of the Arts, 1983.

Jungle Fever. Directed by Spike Lee. Screenplay by Spike Lee. 132 min. Universal Pictures and 40 Acres & A Mule Filmworks, 1991.

Kobe Doin' Work. Directed by Spike Lee. 84 min. ESPN Films and 40 Acres & A Mule Filmworks, 2009.

Last Hustle in Brooklyn. Directed by Spike Lee. 40 min. New York University's Tisch School of the Arts, 1977.

Malcolm X. Directed by Spike Lee. Screenplay by Arnold Perl and Spike Lee, from *The Autobiography of Malcolm X* by Malcolm X as told to Alex Haley. 202 min. Warner Bros. Pictures and 40 Acres & A Mule Filmworks, 1992.

Mike Tyson: Undisputed Truth. Directed by Spike Lee. Screenplay by Kiki Tyson. 90 min. HBO Films, 2013.

Miracle at St. Anna. Directed by Spike Lee. Screenplay by James McBride, from the novel *Miracle at St. Anna* by James McBride. 160 min. Touchstone Pictures, Rai Cinema, and 40 Acres & A Mule Filmworks, 2008.

Miracle's Boys. 6 episodes. Based on the novel *Miracle's Boys* by Jacqueline Woodson. MTV Entertainment and Nickelodeon, 2005.

Mo' Better Blues. Directed by Spike Lee. Screenplay by Spike Lee. 130 min. Universal Pictures and 40 Acres & A Mule Filmworks, 1990.

Oldboy. Directed by Spike Lee. Screenplay by Mark Protosevich, based on the film *Oldeuboi* by Park Chan-wook and the manga *Orūdo Bōi* by Garon Tsuchiya and Nobuaki Minegishi. 104 min. Film District and 40 Acres & A Mule Filmworks, 2013.

Original Kings of Comedy, The. Directed by Spike Lee. Screenplay by Cedric the Entertainer, Steve Harvey, D. L. Hughley, and Bernie Mac. 115 min. MTV Films, Latham Entertainment, and 40 Acres & A Mule Filmworks, 2000.

Passing Strange. Directed by Spike Lee. Written by Stew. *Great Performances*. 135 min. Apple Core Holdings, The Shubert Organization, and 40 Acres & A Mule Filmworks, 2010.

Pavarotti & Friends: 99 for Guatemala and Kosovo. Directed by Spike Lee. 100 min. Pavarotti International, 1999.

Pavarotti & Friends for the Children of Liberia. Directed by Spike Lee. *Great Performances*. 106 min. Public Broadcasting Service, British Broadcasting Corporation, and Radiotelevisione Italiane, 1998.

Red Hook Summer. Directed by Spike Lee. Screenplay by James McBride & Spike Lee. 121 min. Variance Films and 40 Acres & A Mule Filmworks, 2012.

Sarah. Directed by Spike Lee. Screenplay by Spike Lee. 20 min. New York University's Tisch School of the Arts, 1981.

School Daze. Directed by Spike Lee. Screenplay by Spike Lee. 121 min. Columbia Pictures and 40 Acres & A Mule Filmworks, 1988.

She Hate Me. Directed by Spike Lee. Screenplay by Michael Genet & Spike Lee. Story by Michael Genet. 138 min. Sony Pictures Classics and 40 Acres & A Mule Filmworks, 2004.

She's Gotta Have It. Directed by Spike Lee. Screenplay by Spike Lee. 85 min. Island Pictures and 40 Acres & A Mule Filmworks, 1986.

Sucker Free City. Directed by Spike Lee. Screenplay by Alex Tse. 113 min. Showtime Network and 40 Acres & A Mule Filmworks, 2004.

Summer of Sam. Directed by Spike Lee. Screenplay by Victor Colicchio & Michael Imperioli and Spike Lee. 142 min. Buena Vista Pictures and 40 Acres & A Mule Filmworks, 1999.

25th Hour. Directed by Spike Lee. Screenplay by David Benioff, from the novel *The 25th Hour* by David Benioff. 135 min. Buena Vista Pictures, 25th Hour Productions, and 40 Acres & A Mule Filmworks, 2002.

When the Levees Broke: A Requiem in Four Acts. Directed by Spike Lee. 4 episodes. 255 min. HBO Documentary Films and 40 Acres & A Mule Filmworks, 2006.

FILMS, DOCUMENTARIES, AND TELEVISION PROGRAMS BY OTHER DIRECTORS

American Cinema: One Hundred Years of Filmmaking. Directed by Alain Klarer. 10 episodes. PBS Television, 1995.

Amos 'n Andy Show, The. Created by Charles J. Correll and Freeman F. Gosden. CBS Television, 1951–1953.

Andha Naal. Directed by Sundaram Balachander. Screenplay by Javar Seetharaman. Story by Sundaram Balachander. 130 min. AVM Productions, 1954.

Animal House. Directed by John Landis. Screenplay by Harold Ramis, Douglas Kenney, & Chris Miller. 109 min. Universal Pictures, Oregon Film Factory, and Stage III Productions, 1978.

Assault on Precinct 13. Directed by John Carpenter. Screenplay by John Carpenter. 91 min. Overseas Film Group and the C K K Corporation, 1976.

Back to School. Directed by Alan Metter. Screenplay by Steven Kampmann & Will Porter and Peter Torokvei & Harold Ramis. Story by Rodney Dangerfield, Greg Fields, & Dennis Snee. 96 min. Orion Pictures and Paper Clip Productions, 1986.

Bellissima. Directed by Luchino Visconti. Screenplay by Luchino Visconti, Suso Cecchi D'Amico, & Franceso Rosi. Story by Cesare Zavattini. 108 min. CEI-Incom, 1951.

Betrayal, The. Directed by Oscar Micheaux. Screenplay by Oscar Micheaux, based on the novel *The Wind from Nowhere* by Oscar Micheaux. 183 min. Astor Picture Corporation, 1948.

Bicycle Thieves (*Ladri di Biciclette*). Directed by Vittorio De Sica. Screenplay by Cesare Zavattini, Suso D'Amico, Vittorio De Sica, Oreste Biancoli, Adolfo Franci, & Gerardo Guerrieri, from the novel *Ladri di Biciclette* by Luigi Bartolini. 93 min. Produzioni de Sica, 1948.

Bird. Directed by Clint Eastwood. Screenplay by Joel Oliansky. 161 min. Warner Bros. Pictures and The Malpaso Company, 1988.

Birth of a Nation, The. Directed by D. W. Griffith. Screenplay by D. W. Griffith & Frank E. Woods, based on the novel *The Clasman: An Historical Romance of the Ku Klux Klan* by Thomas Dixon, Jr. 133 min. David W. Griffith Corp. and Epoch Producing Corporation, 1915.

Black and White. Directed by James Toback. Screenplay by James Toback. 98 min. Sony Pictures and Bigel/Mailer Films, 1999.

Black Hawk Down. Directed by Ridley Scott. Screenplay by Ken Nolan, from the book *Black Hawk Down* by Mark Bowden. 144 min. Revolution Studios, Scott Free Productions, and Jerry Bruckheimer Films, 2001.

Blade Runner. Directed by Ridley Scott. Screenplay by Hampton Fancher and David Peoples, from the novel *Do Androids Dream of Electric Sheep?* by Philip K. Dick. 117 min. Warner Bros. Pictures, 1982.

Blankman. Directed by Mike Binder. Screenplay by Damon Wayans & J. F. Lawton. Story by Damon Wayans. 92 min. Columbia Pictures and Wife 'N Kids Productions, 1994.

Bonfire of the Vanities, The. Directed by Brian De Palma. Screenplay by Michael Cristofer, from the novel *The Bonfire of the Vanities* by Tom Wolfe. 125 min. Warner Bros. Pictures, 1990.

Boyz N the Hood. Directed by John Singleton. Screenplay by John Singleton. 112 min. Columbia Pictures, 1991.

Buffalo Soldiers. Directed by Charles Haid. Screenplay by Frank Military and Susan Rhinehart. Story by Jonathan Klein & Frank Military. 100 min. Turner Network Television, Turner Pictures, and Citadel Enterprise Productions, 1997.

Bus, The. Directed by Haskell Wexler. Screenplay by Haskell Wexler. 62 min. Institute for Cinema Studies, 1965.

Carmen Jones. Directed by Otto Preminger. Screenplay by Harry Kleiner, from the opera *Carmen* by Georges Bizet, based on the novella *Carmen* by Prosper Mérimée. 105 min. Twentieth Century Fox and Carlyle Productions, 1954.

Casino. Directed by Martin Scorsese. Screenplay by Martin Scorsese & Nicholas Pileggi, from the book *Casino: Love and Honor in Las Vegas* by Nicholas Pileggi. 178 min. Universal Pictures, 1995.

Chariots of Fire. Directed by Hugh Hudson. Screenplay by Colin Welland. 124 min. Twentieth Century Fox, Allied Stars, and Enigma Productions, 1981.

Cinderella Man. Directed by Ron Howard. Screenplay by Cliff Hollingsworth and Akiva Goldsman. Story by Cliff Hollingsworth. 144 min. Universal Pictures, Miramax Films, and Imagine Entertainment, 2005.

Classified X. Directed by Mark Daniels. Screenplay by Melvin Van Peebles. 53 min. Channel 4 Television Corporation and Ecoutez Voir, 1998.

Color Purple, The. Directed by Steven Spielberg. Screenplay by Menno Meyjes, from the novel *The Color Purple* by Alice Walker. 154 min. Warner Bros. Pictures, the Guber-Peters Company, and Amblin Entertainment, 1985.

Cosby Show, The. Created by Bill Cosby, Michael Leeson, & Ed. Weinberger. NBC Television and Carsey-Werner Company, 1984–1992.

Daughters of the Dust. Directed by Julie Dash. Screenplay by Julie Dash. 112 min. American Playhouse, Geechee Girls, and WMG Film, 1991.

Days of Glory (Indigènes). Directed by Rachid Bouchareb. Screenplay by Rachid Bouchareb & Olivier Bourelle. 120 min. Tessalit Productions, 2006.

Dead End. Directed by William Wyler. Screenplay by Lillian Hellman, based on the stage play *Dead End* by Sidney Kingsley. 93 min. United Artists and the Samuel Goldwyn Company, 1937.

Death to Smoochy. Directed by Danny DeVito. Screenplay by Adam Resnick. 109 min. Warner Bros. Pictures, 2002.

Diary of a Mad Black Woman. Directed by Darren Grant. Screenplay by Tyler Perry, based on the stage play *Diary of a Mad Black Woman* by Tyler Perry. 116 min. Lionsgate Films and the Tyler Perry Company, 2005.

Die Hard. Directed by John McTiernan. Screenplay by Jeb Stuart and Steven E. de Souza, based on the novel *Nothing Lasts Forever* by Roderick Thorp. 131 min. Twentieth Century Fox and Silver Pictures, 1988.

Dog Day Afternoon. Directed by Sidney Lumet. Screenplay by Frank Pierson, from the article "The Boys in the Bank" by P. F. Kluge and Thomas Moore. 125 min. Warner Bros. Pictures, 1975.

Earth Trembles, The (La Terra Trema). Directed by Luchino Visconti. Screenplay by Luchino Visconti & Antonio Pietrangeli, from the novel *I Malavoglia* by Giovanni Verga. 160 min. Universalia Film, 1948.

Easy Rider. Directed by Dennis Hopper. Screenplay by Peter Fonda, Dennis Hopper, & Terry Southern. 95 min. Raybert Productions and Columbia Pictures, 1969.

Escape from New York. Directed by John Carpenter. Screenplay by John Carpenter & Nick Castle. 99 min. AVCO Embassy Pictures, 1981.

Eyes on the Prize. Produced by Henry Hampton. 14 episodes. 360 min. Blackside and Public Broadcasting Service, 1987 and 1990.

Face in the Crowd, A. Directed by Elia Kazan. Screenplay by Budd Schulberg. 126 min. Warner Bros. Pictures and Newtown Productions, 1957.

Fall of the Roman Empire, The. Directed by Anthony Mann. Screenplay by Ben Barzman, Basilio Franchina, & Philip Yordan. 188 min. Paramount Pictures and Samuel Bronston Productions, 1964.

Flags of Our Fathers. Directed by Clint Eastwood. Screenplay by William Broyles, Jr. and Paul Haggis, from the book *Flags of Our Fathers* by James Bradley with Ron Powers. 132 min. Warner Bros. Pictures, DreamWorks SKG, Amblin Entertainment, and Malpaso Productions, 2006.

Fort Apache, The Bronx. Directed by Daniel Petrie. Screenplay by Heywood Gould, suggested by the experiences of Thomas Mulhearn and Pete Tessitore. 125 min. Twentieth Century Fox and Time-Life Television Productions, 1981.

Foxy Brown. Directed by Jack Hill. Screenplay by Jack Hill. 94 min. American International Pictures, 1974.

Gangs of New York. Directed by Martin Scorsese. Screenplay by Jay Cocks and Steve Zaillian and Kenneth Lonergan. Story by Jay Cocks. 167 min. Miramax Films and Alberto Grimaldi Productions, 2002.

George Washington. Directed by David Gordon Green. Screenplay by David Gordon Green. 89 min. Blue Moon Productions, Downhome Entertainment, and Muskat Filmed Properties, 2000.

Germany Year Zero (*Germania Anno Zero*). Directed by Roberto Rossellini. Screenplay by Roberto Rossellini, Carlo Lizzani, Max Colpet, & Sergio Amidei. 78 min. G.D.B. Film, Tevere Film, SAFDI, and Union Générale Cinématographique, 1948.

Glass Shield, The. Directed by Charles Burnett. Screenplay by John Eddie Johnson & Ned Welsh and Charles Burnett. 109 min. Miramax Films, 1995.

Gold Diggers of 1935. Directed by Busby Berkeley. Screenplay by Peter Milne and Manuel Seff. Story by Robert Lord & Peter Milne. 95 min. Warner Bros. Pictures and First National Pictures, 1935.

Good Times. Created by Mike Evans & Eric Monte. Developed by Norman Lear. CBS Television and Lear/Tandem Productions, 1974–1979.

Grand Hotel. Directed by Edmund Goulding. Screenplay by William A. Drake and Béla Balazs, adaptation by William A. Drake, from the novel *Menschen im Hotel* by Vicki Baum. 112 min. Metro-Goldwyn-Mayer, 1932.

Great Performances. Created by Marion J. Caffrey, Daniel Ezralow, & Josh Groban. Public Broadcasting Service, 1970-present.

Hate That Hate Produced, The. Narrated by Mike Wallace. Produced by Mike Wallace & Louis Lomax. 5 episodes. *News Beat.* WNTA Television, July 13–17, 1959.

Heaven's Gate. Directed by Michael Cimino. Screenplay by Michael Cimino. 219 min. United Artists and Partisan Productions, 1980.

Homesteader, The. Directed by Oscar Micheaux. Screenplay by Oscar Micheaux, based on the novel *The Conquest: The Story of a Negro Pioneer* by Oscar Micheaux. 75 min. Micheaux Film and Micheux Book & Film Company, 1919.

Hoosiers. Directed by David Anspaugh. Screenplay by Angelo Pizzo. 114 min. Orion Pictures, 1986.

House of Payne. Created by Tyler Perry. TBS Television and the Tyler Perry Company, 2006–2012.

House Party. Directed by Reginald Hudlin. Screenplay by Reginald Hudlin. 100 min. New Line Cinema, the Hudlin Brothers, and the Jackson/McHenry Company, 1990.

Hunger Games, The. Directed by Gary Ross. Screenplay by Gary Ross & Suzanne Collins and Billy Ray, based on the novel *The Hunger Games* by Suzanne Collins. 142 min. Lionsgate Films, 2012.

In Living Color. Created by Keenan Ivory Wayans. Twentieth Century Fox Television and Ivory Way Productions, 1990–1994.

Ishtar. Directed by Elaine May. Screenplay by Elaine May. 107 min. Columbia Pictures and Delphi V Productions, 1987.

Jeffersons, The. Created by Don Nicholl, Michael Ross, & Bernie West. Developed by Norman Lear. CBS Television, 1975–1985.

JFK. Directed by Oliver Stone. Screenplay by Oliver Stone & Zachary Sklar, from the books *On the Trail of the Assassins* by Jim Garrison and *Crossfire: The Plot That Killed Kennedy* by Jim Marrs. 189 min. Warner Bros. Pictures and Ixtlan, 1991.

Juice. Directed by Ernest R. Dickerson. Screenplay by Ernest R. Dickerson & Gerard Brown. Story by Ernest R. Dickerson. 95 min. Island World, 1992.

Jules et Jim. Directed by François Truffaut. Screenplay by François Truffaut & Jean Gruault, from the novel *Jules et Jim* by Henri-Pierre Roché. 105 min. Les Films du Carrosse and Sédif Productions, 1962.

Killer of Sheep. Directed by Charles Burnett. Screenplay by Charles Burnett. 83 min. Milestone Films, 1979.

Kuhle Wampe, oder: Wem gehört die Welt? (Kuhle Wempe, or Who Owns the World?). Directed by Slatan Dudow. Screenplay by Bertholt Brecht & Ernst Ottwald. 71 min. Praesens-Film, 1932.

Lady Sings the Blues. Directed by Sidney J. Furie. Screenplay by Terence McCloy and Chris Clark & Suzanne de Passe, from the book *Lady Sings the Blues* by Billie Holiday with William Dufty. 144 min. Paramount Pictures, Jobete Productions, and Motown Productions, 1972.

Last Picture Show, The. Directed by Peter Bogdanovich. Screenplay by Larry McMurtry and Peter Bogdanovich, from the novel *The Last Picture Show* by Larry McMurtry. 118 min. Columbia Pictures and BBS Productions, 1971.

Lawrence of Arabia. Directed by David Lean. Screenplay by Robert Bolt and Michael Wilson, based on the writings of T.E. Lawrence. 216 min. Columbia Pictures, 1962.

Letters from Iwo Jima. Directed by Clint Eastwood. Screenplay by Iris Yamashita. Story by Iris Yamashita & Paul Haggis, from the book *Picture Letters from the Commander in Chief* by Tadamichi Kuribayashi. 141 min. Warner Bros. Pictures, DreamWorks SKG, Amblin Entertainment, and Malpaso Productions, 2006.

Lifeboat. Directed by Alfred Hitchcock. Screenplay by Jo Swerling. Story by John Steinbeck. 97 min. Twentieth Century Fox, 1944.

Longest Day, The. Directed by Ken Annakin, Andrew Marton, and Bernhard Wicki. Screenplay by Cornelius Ryan and Romain Gary, James Jones, David Pursall, & Jack Seddon, from the book *The Longest Day* by Cornelius Ryan. 178 min. Twentieth Century Fox, 1962.

Long Way Home, The. Directed by Mark Jonathan Harris. Screenplay by Mark Jonathan Harris. 120 min. Moriah Films and the Simon Wiesenthal Center, 1997.

Lord of the Rings, The: The Two Towers. Directed by Peter Jackson. Screenplay by Fran Walsh, Philippa Boyens, Stephen Sinclair, & Peter Jackson, from the novel *The Lord of The Rings: The Two Towers* by J.R.R. Tolkien. 179 min. New Line Cinema and Wing Nut Films, 2002.

Madea's Family Reunion. Directed by Tyler Perry. Screenplay by Tyler Perry, based on the stage play *Madea's Family Reunion* by Tyler Perry. 107 min. Lionsgate Films, Reuben Cannon Productions, and Tyler Perry Studios, 2006.

Major Payne. Directed by Nick Castle. Screenplay by Dean Lorey & Damon Wayans and Gary Rosen. Story by Joe Connelly & Bob Mosher, from the screenplay *The Private War of Major Benson* by William Roberts & Richard Alan Simmons. 95 min. Universal Pictures and Wife 'N Kids Productions, 1995.

Making "Do the Right Thing." Directed by St. Clair Bourne. 58 min. 40 Acres & A Mule Filmworks and Chamba Organization, 1989.

Making of "Bamboozled," The. Directed by Sam Pollard. 53 min. 40 Acres & A Mule Filmworks and New Line Home Video, 2001.

Man Called Adam, A. Directed by Leo Penn. Screenplay by Lester Pine & Tina Pine. 99 min. Embassy Pictures and Trace-Mark Productions, 1966.

Man of Steel. Directed by Zack Snyder. Screenplay by David S. Goyer. Story by David S. Goyer & Christopher Nolan, based on *Superman* created by Jerry Siegel & Joe Shuster. 143 min. Warner Bros., Legendary Pictures, and Syncopy, 2013.

Match Point. Directed by Woody Allen. Screenplay by Woody Allen. 124 min. BBC Films, Jada Productions, and Kudu Films, 2005.

Mean Streets. Directed by Martin Scorsese. Screenplay by Martin Scorsese & Mardik Martin. Story by Martin Scorsese. 112 min. Warner Bros. Pictures and Taplin-Perry-Scorsese Productions, 1973.

Medium Cool. Directed by Haskell Wexler. Screenplay by Haskell Wexler. 111 min. Paramount Pictures and H&J Productions, 1969.

Meet the Browns. Created by Tyler Perry. TBS Television and Tyler Perry Studios, 2009–2011.

Menace II Society. Directed by Albert Hughes & Allen Hughes. Screenplay by Tyger Williams. Story by Albert Hughes, Allen Hughes, & Tyger Williams. 97 min. New Line Cinema, 1993.

Midnight Cowboy. Directed by John Schlesinger. Screenplay by Waldo Salt, based on the novel *Midnight Cowboy* by James Leo Herlihy. 113 min. United Artists, 1969.

Miracle in Milan (Miracolo a Milano). Directed by Vittorio De Sica. Screenplay by Cesare Zavattini, Vittorio De Sica, Suso Cecchi D'Amico, Mario Chiari, & Adolfo Franci, from the novel *Totò il Buono* by Cesare Zavattini. 100 min. Produzioni De Sica and Ente Nazionale Industrie Cinematografiche, 1951.

Natural, The. Directed by Barry Levinson. Screenplay by Robert Towne and Phil Dusenberry, from the novel *The Natural* by Bernard Malamud. 134 min. Tri-Star Pictures, 1984.

Negro Soldier, The. Directed by Stuart Heisler. Written by Carlton Moss. 43 min. United States War Department, 1944.

Network. Directed by Sidney Lumet. Screenplay by Paddy Chayefsky. 121 min. Metro-Goldwyn-Mayer and United Artists, 1976.

New Jack City. Directed by Mario Van Peebles. Screenplay by Thomas Lee Wright and Barry Michael Cooper. Story by Thomas Lee Wright. 97 min. Warner Bros. Pictures and Jacmac Films, 1991.

New York, New York. Directed by Martin Scorsese. Screenplay by Earl Mac Rauch and Mardik Martin. Story by Earl Mac Rauch. 155 min. United Artists and Chartoff-Winkler Productions, 1977.

Nightjohn. Directed by Charles Burnett. Screenplay by Bill Cain, from the novel *Nightjohn* by Gary Paulsen. 92 min. Disney Channel and Hallmark Entertainment, 1996.

Night of the Hunter, The. Directed by Charles Laughton. Screenplay by James Agee, from the novel *The Night of the Hunter* by Davis Grubbs. 93 min. United Artists and Paul Gregory Productions, 1955.

Nothing But Trouble. Directed by Dan Aykroyd. Screenplay by Dan Aykroyd. Story
by Peter Aykroyd. 94 min. Warner Bros. Pictures and Applied Action, 1991.

Obsession (Ossessione). Directed by Luchino Visconti. Screenplay by Luchino Visconti,
Mario Alicata, Giuseppe De Santis, & Gianni Puccini, from the novel *The Post-
man Always Rings Twice* by James M. Cain. 140 min. Industrie Cinematografiche Italiane, 1943.

Of Mice and Men. Directed by Lewis Milestone. Screenplay by Eugene Solow, from
the novella *Of Mice and Men* by John Steinbeck. 106 min. United Artists and
Hal Roach Studios, 1939.

Oldboy (Oldeuboi). Directed by Park Chan-wook. Screenplay by Park Chan-wook,
Hwang Jo-yoon, & Im Joon-hyeong, based on the manga *Orūdo Bōi* by Garon
Tsuchiya and Nobuaki Minegishi. 120 min. Tartan Films, Egg Films, and Show
East, 2003.

On the Waterfront. Directed by Elia Kazan. Screenplay by Budd Schulberg, based on
the *New York Sun*'s "Crime on the Waterfront" articles by Malcolm Johnson.
108 min. Columbia Pictures and Horizon Pictures, 1954.

Paisan (Paisà). Directed by Roberto Rossellini. Screenplay by Sergio Amidei, Federico Fellini, Roberto Rossellini, & Rod Geiger. Story by Sergio Amidei, Klaus
Mann, Federico Fellini, Marcello Pagliero, & Alfred Hayes. 120 min. Organiz-
zazione Film Internazionali, 1946.

Pan's Labyrinth (El Laberinto del Fauno). Directed by Guillermo del Toro. Screenplay by Guillermo del Toro. 118 min. Warner Bros. Pictures, Estudios Picasso,
Tequila Gang, and Esperanto Filmoj, 2006.

Paris Blues. Directed by Martin Ritt. Screenplay by Jack Sher & Irene Kemp and Wal-
ter Bernstein, adaptation by Lulla Adler, from the novel *Paris Blues* by Harold
Flender. 98 min. United Artists and Pennebaker Productions, 1961.

Poetic Justice. Directed by John Singleton. Screenplay by John Singleton. 109 min.
Columbia Pictures and New Deal Productions, 1993.

Producers, The. Directed by Mel Brooks. Screenplay by Mel Brooks. 88 min. Embassy
Pictures and Springtime Productions, 1967.

Pulp Fiction. Directed by Quentin Tarantino. Screenplay by Quentin Tarantino. Story
by Quentin Tarantino & Roger Avary. 154 min. Miramax Films, A Band Apart,
and Jersey Films, 1994.

Rashomon. Directed by Akira Kurosawa. Screenplay by Akira Kurosawa & Shinobu
Hashimoto, from the short stories "Rashomon" and "In a Grove" by Ryuno-
suke Akutagawa. 88 min. Daiei Motion Picture Company, 1950.

Real Time with Bill Maher. Created by Bill Maher. HBO Television, Bill Maher Productions, and Brad Grey Television, 2003–present.

Red Dragon. Directed by Brett Ratner. Screenplay by Ted Tally, from the novel *Red
Dragon* by Thomas Harris. 124 min. Universal Pictures and Dino De Laurentiis
Company, 2002.

Red Tails. Directed by Anthony Hemingway. Screenplay by John Ridley & Aaron Mc-
Gruder. Story by John Ridley, from the book *Red Tails, Black Wings: The Men
of America's Black Air Force* by John B. Holway. 125 min. Twentieth Century
Fox, Lucasfilm Ltd., and Partnership Pictures, 2012.

Revenge of the Nerds. Directed by Jeff Kanew. Screenplay by Steve Zacharias & Jeff
Buhai. Story by Tim Metcalfe & Miguel Tejada-Flores and Steve Zacharias &

Jeff Buhai. 90 min. Twentieth Century Fox and Interscope Communications, 1984.

Richard Pryor: Live in Concert. Directed by Jeff Margolis. Screenplay by Richard Pryor & Paul Mooney. 78 min. SEE Theater Network and Elkins Entertainment, 1979.

Richard Pryor Show, The. Created by Richard Pryor. NBC Television and Burt Sugarman Productions, 1977.

Rome, Open City (Roma, Città Aperta). Directed by Roberto Rossellini. Screenplay by Sergio Amidei and Roberto Rossellini & Federico Fellini. Story by Sergio Amidei and Alberto Consiglio & Roberto Rossellini. 100 min. Minerva Film and Excelsa Film, 1945.

Rope. Directed by Alfred Hitchcock. Screenplay by Arthur Laurents, adapted by Hume Cronyn, from the stage play *Rope* by Patrick Hamilton. 80 min. Warner Bros. Pictures and Transatlantic Pictures, 1948.

Rosewood. Directed by John Singleton. Screenplay by Gregory Poirier. 140 min. Warner Bros. Pictures and Peters Entertainment, 1997.

'Round Midnight. Directed by Bertrand Tavernier. Screenplay by David Rayfiel and Bertrand Tavernier. 133 min. Warner Bros. Pictures and Little Bear, 1986.

Sands of Iwo Jima, The. Directed by Allan Dwan. Screenplay by Harry Brown & James Edward Grant. Story by Harry Brown. 100 min. Republic Pictures, 1949.

Saving Private Ryan. Directed by Steven Spielberg. Screenplay by Robert Rodat. 169 min. Paramount Pictures, Amblin Entertainment, and DreamWorks SKG, 1998.

Schindler's List. Directed by Steven Spielberg. Screenplay by Steve Zaillian, from the novel *Schindler's List* by Thomas Keneally. 195 min. Universal Pictures and Amblin Entertainment, 2002.

Separate Tables. Directed by Delbert Mann. Screenplay by Terence Rattigan and John Gay, from the stage play *Separate Tables* by Terence Rattigan. 100 min. United Artists, 1958.

Shaft. Directed by Gordon Parks. Screenplay by Ernest Tidyman and John D. F. Black, from the novel *Shaft* by Ernest Tidyman. 100 min. Metro-Goldwyn-Mayer and Shaft Productions Ltd., 1971.

Shark. Created by Ian Biederman. CBS Television, Twentieth Century Fox Television, and Imagine Television, 2006–2008.

Ship of Fools. Directed by Stanley Kramer. Screenplay by Abby Mann, from the novel *Ship of Fools* by Katherine Anne Porter. 149 min. Columbia Pictures and Stanley Kramer Productions, 1965.

Shoeshine (Sciuscià). Directed by Vittorio De Sica. Screenplay by Sergio Amidei, Adolfo Franci, Cesare G. Viola, & Cesare Zavattini. 93 min. Societa Cooperativa Alfa Cinematografica, 1946.

Singin' in the Rain. Directed by Stanley Donen & Gene Kelly. Screenplay by Adolph Green and Betty Comden. 103 min. Metro-Goldwyn-Mayer, Loew's, and RKO-Pathe Studios, 1952.

Smoke. Directed by Wayne Wang. Screenplay by Paul Auster. 112 min. Miramax Films, 1995.

Sorrow and the Pity, The (Le Chagrin et La Pitié). Directed by Marcel Ophüls. Screenplay by André Harris & Marcel Ophüls. 251 min. Télévision Recontre, 1969.

Squawk on the Street. CNBC Television, 2005-Present.

St. Louis Blues. Directed by Allen Reisner. Screenplay by Ted Sherdeman and Robert Smith. 105 min. Paramount Pictures, 1958.

Straight Out of Brooklyn. Directed by Matty Rich. Screenplay by Matty Rich. 91 min. The Samuel Goldwyn Company and American Playhouse, 1991.

Stranger Than Paradise. Directed by Jim Jarmusch. Screenplay by Jim Jarmusch. 89 min. The Samuel Goldwyn Company and Cinesthesia Productions, 1984.

Straw Dogs. Directed by Sam Peckinpah. Screenplay by David Zelag Goodman and Sam Peckinpah, from the novel *The Siege of Trencher's Farm* by Gordon M. Williams. 118 min. Amerbroco Films, Talent Associates Films, and Cinerama Releasing Corporation, 1971.

Street Smart. Bloomberg Television, 2011–present.

Sullivan's Travels. Directed by Preston Sturges. Screenplay by Preston Sturges. 90 min. Paramount Pictures, 1941.

Sunset Boulevard. Directed by Billy Wilder. Screenplay by Charles Brackett, Billy Wilder, & D. M. Marshman, Jr. 110 min. Paramount Pictures, 1950.

Super Fly. Directed by Gordon Parks, Jr. Screenplay by Phillip Fenty. 93 min. Warner Bros. Pictures, Sig Shore Productions, and Superfly Ltd., 1972.

Sweet Sweetback's Baadasssss Song. Directed by Melvin Van Peebles. Screenplay by Melvin Van Peebles. 97 min. Cinemation Industries, 1971.

Thin Red Line, The. Directed by Terrence Malick. Screenplay by Terrence Malick, from the novel *The Thin Red Line* by James Jones. 170 min. Fox 2000 Pictures and Phoenix Pictures, 1998.

Training Day. Directed by Antoine Fuqua. Screenplay by David Ayer. 122 min. Warner Bros. Pictures and Village Roadshow Pictures, 2001.

Tuskegee Airmen, The. Directed by Robert Markowitz. Screenplay by Paris Qualles, Trey Ellis, and Ron Hutchinson. Story by Robert Williams & T. S. Cook. 106 min. HBO Television and Price Entertainment, 1995.

Wedding, The. Directed by Charles Burnett. Screenplay by Lisa Jones, from the novel *The Wedding* by Dorothy West. 180 min. ABC Television and Harpo Productions, 1998.

West Side Story. Directed by Robert Wise & Jerome Robbins. Screenplay by Ernest Lehman, from the Broadway musical by Jerome Robbins & Arthur Laurents and the play *Romeo and Juliet* by William Shakespeare. 152 min. United Artists and Beta Productions, 1961.

White Man's Burden. Directed by Desmond Nakano. Screenplay by Desmond Nakano. 89 min. A Band Apart, Home Box Office Films, and Rysher Entertainment, 1995.

Wire, The. Created by David Simon. HBO Television and Blown Deadline Productions, 2002–2008.

Wizard of Oz, The. Directed by Victor Fleming. Screenplay by Noel Langley & Florence Ryerson and Edgar Allan Woolf, adaptation by Noel Langley, from the novel *The Wizard of Oz* by L. Frank Baum. 101 min. Metro-Goldwyn-Mayer and Loew's, 1939.

Woman in Question, The (Five Angles on Murder). Directed by Anthony Asquith. Screenplay by John Cresswell. 88 min. Javelin Films and Vic Films Productions, 1950.

Zero Dark Thirty. Directed by Kathryn Bigelow. Screenplay by Mark Boal. 157 min. Columbia Pictures and Annapurna Pictures, 2012.

INTERNET VIDEOS

"Spike Lee and Pharrell Williams on Anthems and Artists." *ARTST TLK.* Uploaded October 8, 2013. http://www.youtube.com/watch?v=p8RCqI9zSgU.

"Spike Lee and Pharrell Williams on Hard Work and Opportunity." *ARTST TLK.* Uploaded October 10, 2013. http://www.youtube.com/watch?annotation_id=annotation_3642158243&feature=iv&list= SPU4DWjN4gSDE-03Fm9NO-nRBQY CUgPYO6&src_vid= p8RCqI9zSgU&v=_aHpxr4Cw6o.

"Spike Lee on Tyler Perry's Movies Shows! Its Coonery Buffoonery." YouTube video. Uploaded December 29, 2009. http://www.youtube.com/watch?v=Ci whh3fB6vE.

"Video Shows Bush Got Explicit Katrina Warning." YouTube Video. Uploaded October 4, 2011. http://www.youtube.com/watch?v=1mSsPR-CXCA.

"When the Levees Break—Bombing of the Lower Ninth Ward 6/8." YouTube video. Uploaded December 29, 2007. http://www.youtube.com/watch?v=9D DaqWv9wdg.

ALBUMS, MUSICAL PRODUCTIONS, OPERAS, RADIO PROGRAMS, AND SONGS

Bicentennial Nigger. Written by Richard Pryor & Paul Mooney. Recorded in February and July 1976. 41 min. Warner Bros. Records, 1976.

Carmen. Composed by Georges Bizet. Libretto by Henri Meilhac & Ludovic Halévy, from the novella *Carmen* by Prosper Mérimée. First performed on March 3, 1875 in Paris, France.

"Chaiyya Chaiyya." Written by A. R. Rahman and Gulzar (Sampooran Singh Kalra). From the film *Dil Se,* directed by Mani Ratnam, 1998.

"I'm Building Me a Home." Traditional spiritual.

Richard Pryor: Live on the Sunset Strip. Written by Richard Pryor & Paul Mooney. Recorded in December 1981 and January 1982. 60 min. Warner Bros. Records, 1982.

Think Tank with Garland Robinette. WWL FM 105.3 New Orleans. http://www.wwl.com/pages/11169697.php?

Index

Please note: All mentions of "Lee" refer to Spike Lee unless otherwise noted.

About the Author

Jason P. Vest, PhD, is associate professor of English at the University of Guam. His published works include ABC-CLIO's *Future Imperfect: Philip K. Dick at the Movies* (2007) and *The Wire, Deadwood, Homicide, and NYPD Blue: Violence Is Power* (2010), as well as Scarecrow Press's *The Postmodern Humanism of Philip K. Dick* (2009).